SIXTH EDITION

COLLABORATION, CONSULTATION, AND TEAMWORK FOR STUDENTS WITH SPECIAL NEEDS

PEGGY DETTMER

Kansas State University

LINDA P. THURSTON

Kansas State University

ANN KNACKENDOFFEL

Kansas State University

NORMA J. DYCK

Kansas State University

Columbus, Ohio
Upper Saddle River, New Jersey

Library of Congress Cataloging-in-Publication Data

Collaboration, consultation, and teamwork for students with special needs / Peggy Dettmer . . .[et al.].—6th ed.

    p. cm.

  Rev. ed. of: Consultation, collaboration, and teamwork for students with special needs. 5th ed. c2005.

  Earlier eds. entered under: Dettmer, Peggy.

  Includes bibliographical references and index.

  ISBN-13: 978-0-205-60837-9 (pbk.)

  ISBN-10: 0-205-60837-X (pbk.)

  1. Children with disabilities—Education—United States. 2. Special education—United States. 3. Educational consultants—United States. 4. Teaching teams—United States. I. Dettmer, Peggy. II. Dettmer, Peggy. Consultation, collaboration, and teamwork for students with special needs.

  LC4031.D47 2009

  371.90973—dc22

                                2008015435

Vice President and Executive Publisher: *Jeffery W. Johnston*
Senior Editor: *Ann Davis*
Director of Marketing: *Quinn Perkson*
Editorial Assistant: *Penny Burleson*
Marketing Manager: *Krista Clark*
Production Editor: *Mary Beth Finch*
Editorial Production Service: *Omegatype Typography, Inc.*
Composition Buyer: *Linda Cox*
Manufacturing Buyer: *Megan Cochran*
Electronic Composition: *Omegatype Typography, Inc.*
Cover Administrator: *Linda Knowles*

This book was set in Times by Omegatype Typography, Inc. It was printed and bound by Hamilton Printing. The cover was printed by Phoenix Color Corp.

Pearson Education Ltd.
Pearson Education Singapore Pte. Ltd.
Pearson Education Canada, Ltd.
Pearson Education—Japan

Pearson Education Australia Pty. Limited
Pearson Education North Asia Ltd.
Pearson Educación de Mexico, S.A. de C.V.
Pearson Education Malaysia Pte. Ltd.

Merrill
is an imprint of

www.pearsonhighered.com

10 9 8 7 6 5
ISBN 13: 978-0-205-60837-9
ISBN 10: 0-205-60837-X

CONTENTS

CHAPTER TWO

Differences in Perspectives and Preferences among Co-Educators   36

CHAPTER THREE

Foundations and Frameworks for Consultation, Collaboration, and Teamwork   72

**PART II   PROCESSES FOR WORKING TOGETHER
AS CO-EDUCATORS   107**

CHAPTER FOUR

**Communication Processes in Collaborative School Consultation
and Co-Teaching   109**

CHAPTER FIVE

Problem-Solving Strategies for Collaborative Consultation and Teamwork   142

CHAPTER SIX

Management and Evaluation of Collaborative School Consultation   179

CHAPTER NINE
Working Together for Students from Diverse Populations   305

PART IV SYNTHESIS FOR WORKING TOGETHER AS CO-EDUCATORS 331

CHAPTER TWELVE

Leadership, Professional Development, and Positive Ripple Effects of Collaborative Consultation and Teamwork   399

As educators we aspire to have our students become knowledgeable, caring, and self-fulfilled individuals in an increasingly complex and interconnected world. To achieve these aims it is vital that we connect and interact to build solid relationships as co-educators. This includes general education teachers, special education teachers, families of students, school and special education administrators, early childhood education teachers, school psychologists, school counselors, related services and support personnel, professional development and curriculum personnel, and community leaders.

Collaboration, consultation, and teamwork are vital elements in educating students successfully. When these processes are applied with skill and optimism, they have the potential to create positive ripple effects throughout schools and education agencies for all students and particularly those with special needs.

Students of the twenty-first century will soon be adults living and working in a sea of information and opportunity. They must exercise sound judgment and strong ethical principles. Their fields of work and production will demand much more of them than basic knowledge and dependable work habits. They will need skills in problem solving, communicating and collaborating with others, thinking critically and creatively, recognizing the needs of others, speaking and listening and writing effectively, knowing how to learn new things, using technology effectively, and assessing their work for accountability.

Education assigns myriad responsibilities to educators and many of these call for working with colleagues as co-educators. But not all are comfortable working with others in collaborative environments. Professional preparation programs in the past did not stress the development of interpersonal skills among colleagues. Even now many preservice teachers do not have sufficient opportunity in their teacher preparation programs to practice collaborating, consulting, co-teaching, and networking.

This book is a vehicle for developing these skills, which are necessary for educators in today's interactive world. It is designed to be a bridge between *theories* of interrelationships in the school context and *practices* of the processes and content that can facilitate working together for students' needs.

The twelve chapters are divided among four parts: Contexts, Processes, Content, and Synthesis. The theme of each part is symbolized by a geometric figure that is identical for all parts but with differentiated shadings. Part I, Contexts, is depicted as a square. Part II, Processes, is represented as a circle within the square. Part III, Content, is designated by a triangle within the circle. Part IV, Synthesis, concludes with the final three chapters and is shown as a circle surrounding the square, circle, and triangle.

Each chapter in the book begins with Focus Questions and Key Terms. Chapter Scenarios set the stage. We recommend that persons using this book with a group read each of the scenarios aloud, having readers contribute their parts in conversational tone and style. In this way the situations will seem relevant and facilitative rather than artificial and contrived. A few Applications appear in chapters; there are purposefully more in Chapter 2. These brief exercises promote reflection and, where apropos, stimulate group discussion or activity. Tables and Figures provide organization, visual representations, and practical checklists. Tips are concise suggestions for using major concepts. Chapter Review sections match the introductory question sections for summary of main points. A section of To Do and Think About activities allows for further reflection and practice. Additional Readings and Resources sections suggest material for extended exploration of some chapter topics.

The positive results from collaboration among schools, families, and communities who work together as co-educators can spread far and wide to create powerful multiplier effects well beyond school campuses. Furthermore, when students observe educators functioning as collaborative partners on their behalf and for their welfare, they assimilate useful skills and ethical principles for application in their own adult lives and careers.

ACKNOWLEDGMENTS

Revisions of books for professional study are needed from time to time, and this is particularly relevant in fields such as special education. Frequent changes in legislation, new research findings, outcomes of professional development programs, action research by teachers, heightened involvement of parents in educational matters, expanded goals of funding agencies, increased public attention toward education, and concerned communities all coalesce to dictate periodic reassessment of educational issues.

Revisions retain what has proven to be valuable, eliminate what has not been so useful or is no longer relevant, report recent research findings, reexamine earlier material for new insight, and offer new ideas. The five previous editions of this book were dedicated in turn as follows:

- First Edition: *Graduate students* who would be working collegially with other educators, their students, and students' families
- Second Edition: *Practicing educators* who were being called on to collaborate with colleagues in new ways
- Third Edition: *Educators for the future* who inherit not only unsolved problems but also the progress made by their predecessors
- Fourth Edition: Those in *the array of agencies* who have become increasingly important in providing the span of services so vital to students with very special needs
- Fifth Edition: *Children and adolescents* so capably served by all the factions of caring and dedicated people over the years

And now this sixth edition is dedicated to *preservice teachers* who are completing their teacher preparation programs and anticipating their first roles as professional educators. It seems fitting to underscore the importance of preparing preservice teachers for their first months on the job in schools where they will be interacting as co-educators with experienced teachers. Novice teachers will consult and collaborate with veteran teachers as professional equals. Before too long they will be the leaders who shape the future of schools and mold the skills of the students in those schools.

We extend appreciation to all those individuals who contributed to this revision with their thinking, writing, research, and practices in working together as educators. In a collaborative process it is not easy to tell where the contribution of one appears, another interfaces, and yet another goes on from there. This demonstrates once again the complexity and the beauty of working together to achieve lofty goals. The shared perceptions and suggestions of teaching colleagues, students and their families, reviewers, and the publisher's editorial staff have been an important part of the process and the product. That is what collaboration and teamwork are all about.

We also express our gratitude to the sixth edition's reviewers: Debra J. Johnson, Prairie View A&M University; Robbie Ludy, Buena Vista University; Jo Ellyn Peterson, Bluffton University; and Barrie Jo Price, The University of Alabama. These reviewers were among the best we have had in our many years of work in the education profession. Their critiques were especially insightful and helpful. Hearty thanks also go to the leadership provided by our editor Virginia Lanigan and her assistant Matthew Buchholz at Allyn and Bacon.

Once again we recognize posthumously the wisdom and wit of Jane More Loeb as shown in her pen-and-ink drawings. Jane influenced many children and adults in her lifetime as she taught students with learning disabilities, behavioral disorders, and advanced abilities. She developed differentiated curriculum for these diverse groups and, along with being a loving wife and mother, pursued her special interests in photography and art.

Our aim for this book, as it was for the earlier editions, is to cultivate affinities and skills for interacting productively with all educators in schools, homes, and communities. We envision it as a means of helping transform learning environments into settings in which education is special for *every* student and *all* educators are successful and fulfilled in their complex, demanding roles.

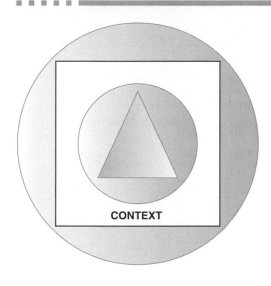

CONTEXT

CONTEXTS FOR WORKING TOGETHER AS CO-EDUCATORS

Part I, indicated by the square, will frame the contexts for collaboration, consultation, and teamwork in twenty-first-century schools. The three chapters focus on:

- purpose, definitions, key elements in working together, benefits of collaborative school consultation, collaborative competencies needed by co-educators, and ethical climates for working collaboratively
- professional perspectives and personal preferences that affect collaborative activity and working as teams
- history, legislative mandates, theory, research, traditional models, and newer models for collaborative school consultation and co-teaching

CHAPTER ONE

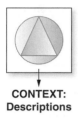

CONTEXT:
Descriptions

Working Together in Collaboration, Consultation, and Co-Teaching

Why do teachers choose education as a career? Some of us over the course of many years have posed that question to experienced teachers, graduate students in education, and undergraduate students in teacher preparation programs. Their responses have been like this:

> "I want to make a difference in children's lives."
> "I want to do my part to make the world better."
> "I want to help kids reach their potential."

Some teachers, especially those at the secondary level, also mention having a fondness for their curricular areas and a desire to share their enthusiasm for content in those areas with students. But other probable incentives such as respect from the public, desire to emulate a favorite teacher, plentiful job opportunities, steady salary, or even the anticipation of an extended summer vacation are farther down on teachers' lists of priorities for wanting to be an educator.

Goals to mold younger generations and make the world into a better place are lofty ones indeed. Such goals have tended in the past to be predicated on expectations of being in "my classroom," with "my students," using "the teaching ideas I have been assembling and now can put into practice." But these goals no longer fit neatly into the environment of twenty-first-century schools and classrooms. Teachers are being called on to work in more collegial ways by consulting and collaborating and often teaching as partners with their colleagues, for "*our* students" in "*our inclusive* classrooms," with "*our* shared plans and ideas."

FOCUSING QUESTIONS

1. What factors influence educators to become collaborative, collegial professionals rather than teachers in more isolated and autonomous roles?
2. How are collaboration, consultation, and team activities such as co-teaching defined?

3. What perspectives on collaboration, consultation, and teamwork are appropriate within contemporary educational contexts?

4. What four key elements are necessary for strong collaborative school environments?

5. What benefits can be expected from collaborative school consultation, and what competencies are needed for educators to be effective collaborators and team members?

6. What ethical principles should guide the collaborative, consultative, and team-oriented processes in schools?

KEY TERMS

asynchronous	consultant	role clarification
client	consultation	role delineation
co-educator	consultee	role parity
collaboration	consulting teacher	synchronous
collaborative ethic	co-teaching	teamwork
collaborative school consultation	exceptional learning needs (ELN)	
collaborator	preservice teacher	

SCENARIO 1.A*

The setting is the faculty room of a typical high school where four faculty members are sharing school news and airing their concerns.

English Teacher: I'm getting another special education student next week—with rather severe learning disabilities this time. I guess this is more fallout from the IDEA legislation, or inclusion, or whatever. Anyway, I'll have this student in my composition and literature classes, along with a student with behavior disorders I'm coping with, and state assessments, and our district curriculum standards committee, and on and on.

Math Teacher: (chuckling) Must be because you're doing such a great job. (serious tone) But I know what you mean. Our special ed teachers don't seem to be taking these kids out of our classes like they did when I first started teaching. But that was before we'd ever heard the words "inclusion" or "collaboration" or "co-teaching."

Music Teacher: And before legislators and national committees had come up with things like Goals 2000 and No Child Left Behind.

English Teacher: Well, they say a "consulting teacher" is coming to our next departmental meeting to talk about our roles in helping these students with their special needs. I understand we're going to be asked to collaborate—whatever that involves—along with all the other things we do, of course. We may even be encouraged to co-teach with other teachers.

Physical Education Teacher/Coach: Hmmm, don't those two words cancel each other out? "Consult" and "collaborate," that is. I believe you English teachers call that an oxymoron.

Music Teacher: I guess I'd be inclined to consult a tax accountant for some expert advice and think of collaboration as when everyone works together to accomplish some common goals they've agreed on. As for co-teaching, I can tell you what a difficult process that is when you have a group of independent thinkers and free spirits who like to do things their own way and want to be the star!

English Teacher: Well, frankly I'm not interested in word games right now. I'm more concerned about finding out where the time is going to come from to do one more thing. My schedule is packed, and my few minutes of free time don't jibe with anyone else's except for this brief lunch period. And I want to know who will have the bottom-line responsibility for which students, and when, and where. And how!

Math Teacher: Right. I've had some concerns about including all students in my instruction and testing, not to mention the NCLB-required testing. I think we need more help to do all of this and I hope we get it.

*We recommend that persons using this book with a group read each of the scenarios aloud, having readers contribute their parts in conversational tone and style. In this way the situations will seem relevant and facilitative rather than artificial and contrived.

TEACHER AUTONOMY IN THE PAST

In the past, teachers worked alone in their classrooms for the most part. They marked attendance forms, took lunch counts, completed other daily procedures, and then closed their classroom doors to begin instruction of the required content. They tried to handle each learning situation with minimal outside help. Asking for assistance would have been tantamount to showing insecurity or demonstrating incompetence. After all, hardy and capable teachers in the past had managed eight grades in one-room schoolhouses without help, hadn't they?

In more recent times schools have become multidimensional centers of activity and very social places. But the individual teacher with myriad responsibilities and goals for personal as well as professional accomplishment can still feel stranded in a crowded setting devoid of adult interactions and professional stimulation. Paradoxically, teachers are just next door or down the hall from other adults, yet somewhat insulated from each other during the school day. They tend to go about their responsibilities autonomously without much meaningful adult interaction. This can make teaching a lonely occupation in a very public place. (See Figure 1.1.)

As one example, at the secondary level Inger (1993) notes that academic and vocational teachers are expected to work together and make connections between their

FIGURE 1.1   "I feel so alone!"

school-based subjects and the world of work. But the insularity of some subjects and departmental boundaries are barriers for meaningful collaboration where, even if teachers would want to collaborate and co-teach, there is limited opportunity. Nevertheless, they have mutual expectations for students that include development of good work habits, punctuality, ability to follow directions, and most importantly, capacities for complex reasoning and problem solving. These shared goals are grounds for collaborating with each other even though they may be located far from the main buildings along the perimeters of sprawling campuses (Inger, 1993).

Many teachers, particularly those who are just beginning their careers, have been reluctant to discuss their concerns or ask for assistance from support personnel lest their confidence and competency be called into question. This absence of dialogue with peers has been consistently recognized as contributing to teachers' feelings of isolation and even inhibiting their inclination to modify classroom practices (Johnson & Pugach, 1996). In the meantime, resource teachers, related services personnel, and support personnel have waited in the wings until called on for assistance with a student's escalating learning or behavioral problems. Too often these potential co-educators are involved only after situations reach crisis level, rather than when they could have a more participatory and helpful role in problem identification and early intervention.

So as teachers' lists of responsibilities grow and the time available for instructing their class as an intact group becomes shorter, the burden of trying to meet the needs of all students becomes heavier. Chunking of the typical school day can further insulate teachers from sources of ideas beyond their own background of experiences. Here again, this is particularly evident at the high school level where teachers might have up to five classes and several different preparations daily while interacting with more than 100-plus students during the course of the day and sometimes the evening.

Adding to the complexity of the school day with its myriad curricular *and* extracurricular activities is the growing awareness by perceptive teachers that *every* student has special needs requiring special attention. Furthermore every student has unique abilities and talents. The task of developing the potential of all students and preparing them for future careers, more education, and responsibilities as citizens can be overwhelming. That "little red schoolhouse" concept of having one teacher serve a wide range of student needs and abilities and attend to the expanding curricular demands of the twenty-first century just will not do.

WHY WORK TOGETHER AND NOT AUTONOMOUSLY?

Today, in our increasingly interdependent and specialized world, it is unlikely that any one person possesses enough knowledge and ability in any field of endeavor to handle every circumstance. So it is reasonable and prudent to consult, collaborate, and team up, working in partnerships with others to achieve common goals. Consultation and collaboration are routine in fields as varied as medicine, law, industry, fashion, sports, construction, scientific research, journalism, decorating, finance—the list is endless. Some consultants even have their own consultants! Teamwork is emphasized frequently in a wide range of work settings from professions to trades to government to community affairs. In fields that encourage networking with others who have similar yet helpfully different perspectives, the results have been dramatic. Sharing of expertise stimulates productivity and growth as colleagues collaborate and provide consultation for peers in their areas of special abilities.

Teaching is a multidimensional activity. An educator's role has never been easy and it is becoming more challenging each year. School personnel are bombarded with more and more responsibilities, and the legislatures and general public are raising expectations for student achievement and measurable yearly progress. Cosmetic alteration of existing programs and practices will not be enough to address such complex issues and multiple concerns. Responsibilities for instruction, management of the learning environment, assessment of student achievement, professional development activity, and communication with a broad range of school personnel and families have escalated and expanded well beyond the one-room schoolhouse or isolated classroom where the teacher was be-all and end-all for students.

■ ■ ■ ■ ■

APPLICATION 1.1
IDENTIFYING TEACHER RESPONSIBILITIES

What does a teacher do in the course of a day, a week, a school year? With short phrases list all the specific responsibilities you can think of that a teacher typically performs during the course of a school year. Draw upon recollections of your student days, college coursework, student teaching, and any teaching experiences that you have had. Remember to include, along with instruction and curriculum preparation, responsibilities for things such as assessment, classroom management, extracurricular and supervisory duties, maintenance responsibilities, and professional development and involvement. Expect to come up with dozens and dozens.

If you collaborate with other teachers in various grade levels, content areas, and specialized roles to do this activity, your combined lists could become a colorful and impressive collection of teaching responsibilities. The process itself will be an example of collaborative consultation, with each person adding information from his or her own perspectives and experiences.

DEFINING CONSULTATION, COLLABORATION, AND CO-TEACHING

Practical definitions of collaboration, consultation, and team teaching for school settings must be general enough to apply to a wide range of school structures and circumstances, yet flexible enough for adapting to many types of schools and communities. Defining is difficult due to the challenges of drawing meaningful boundaries and the risks of being too limiting or too broad (John-Steiner, Weber, & Minnis, 1998). *Webster's Third New International Dictionary* (1976), *Webster's New Collegiate Dictionary* (1998), and *World Book Dictionary* (2003) provide several shades of meaning and a number of synonyms for terms relevant to schools and education. The words and synonyms complement each other to form a conceptual foundation for collaboration, consultation, and teamwork in educational environments.

The issue of definitions or descriptions requires careful attention to semantics because meanings can vary from user to user and from context to context. People who say, "Oh, it's just semantics; don't bother," fail to recognize the importance of appropriate word selection for verbal or written communication (or signs for signed communication). Consider the foreign diplomat in a press conference who is striving to communicate complex ideas and delicate nuances of meanings that are critical to matters on the world stage. It is possible that much potential for achieving international understanding is eroded in the translation process, especially in face-to-face, here-and-now discourse. Discussing abstract concepts such as respect, effort, expectations, and fairness with others is oftentimes a land mine that can blow up the best intentions to communicate. Consider concrete words also, such as *chair*. That word might signal time-out to a misbehaving toddler, or a place for a tired teacher to sit. A dentist may see a chair as a special piece of equipment for work, while to a college professor it might mean a coveted position, or to a convicted murderer it might portend imminent death (Sondel, 1958).

> Words make the trip through the nervous system of a human being before they can be referred outward to the real thing—chair, or whatever it is. Don't assume that everyone responds to your words in precisely the same way you do. Make the context in which you use the words clear, and do this through the use of words that refer to specific things. (Sondel, 1958, p. 55)

Perusing synonyms for a particular word can give a sense of the shades of meaning available for diverse settings. Definitions that will be helpful here are

collaborate: To labor together or work jointly in cooperative interaction to attain a shared goal.

collaborative ethic in schools: An educational philosophy encompassing a shared spirit and interdependence practices among co-educators who are working together in the best interests of students and schools.

teamwork, teaming: Joint action in which persons participate cooperatively; also, joining forces or efforts so that each individual contributes a clearly defined portion of the effort and subordinates personal prominence to the effectiveness of the whole.

consult: To advise or seek advice, confer, confab, huddle, parley, counsel, discuss, deliberate, consider, examine, refer to, communicate in order to decide or plan something, take counsel, seek an opinion as a guide to one's own judgment, request information or facts from, talk over a situation or subject with someone.

consultation: Advisement, counsel, conference, or formal deliberation to provide direct services to students or work with co-educators to serve students' special needs.

consulting: Deliberating together, asking for information or opinion, conferring.

consultant: One who gives professional advice or renders professional services in a field of special knowledge and training, or more simply, one who consults with another.

client: Individual, group, agency, or other entity receiving consulting services to enhance abilities for learning (knowing the material) and for doing (applying the learning) in school and beyond. In some instances *target* is used as a synonym. The client is often, but not always, the student.

consultee: As traditionally described in social science literature, a mediator between a consultant and client (Tharp, 1975); one who confers with the consultant to gather and exchange information and advice and then applies it for the client's needs. The consultee is often, but by no means always, the general education or classroom teacher.

co-educator: An educator who collaborates, consults, teams with, co-teaches, or networks with other educator(s) to address students' needs for learning and doing. May be a school educator, a home educator (parent or other family member), or a community resource person.

co-teaching: Two or more teachers planning and implementing instruction, and monitoring and assessing student achievement, typically in an inclusive classroom setting.

network: A system of connections among individuals or groups having similar interests who interact to accomplish shared goals.

Drawing from the words just defined, the following descriptions frame major concepts presented in this book.

The concept of collaborative school consultation and teamwork denotes an interactive process whereby school personnel in general education and special education, related services and support personnel, families of students, and the students themselves are working together and sharing their diversity of knowledge and expertise to define needs, plan, implement, assess, and follow up on ways of helping students develop to their fullest.

Co-educators are persons who collaborate, consult, and work in teams to provide appropriate learning experiences for students' diverse needs. Co-educators can be school-based such as teachers and related services or support personnel, home-based such as family members or caregivers of students, and community-based in support roles.

In Scenario 1.A earlier, the targeted client is the new student who has a learning disability. The learning disabilities consultant in this case will serve that student indirectly for the most part by collaborating with the classroom English teacher who will be consultee and provider of direct services to the student. Some direct service may be given to the student by the learning disabilities consultant, but for the most part, direct service comes to the student from the classroom teacher. Those in the consultant role do not hold claim to all the expertise. Competent consultants also listen and learn. They sometimes help consultees discover what they already know. They help them recognize their own talents and trust their own skills. Johnson and Donaldson (2007) present collaboration as a way of overcoming the triple-threat norms of autonomy, egalitarianism, and deference to authority that have long characterized schools.

Sheridan (1992) characterizes consultation as a form of collaboration. Consultation helps consultees develop skills to solve current problems and generalize those skills to other problems. Consultation is interactive and requires the active participation of the consultee, not an imposition of the relationship. Sheridan calls for consultants to engage in self-reflection and self-evaluation about the impact they will have on the interactive process of consultation. Co-teaching and other team interactions would be examples of collaboration.

A collaborative consultation relationship is characterized by mutual trust and behaviors that facilitate joint exploration of ways to help students. Effective collaborative school consultation and teamwork result in having co-educators who are more capable and have more confidence in their abilities than they did when teaching in autonomous contexts.

WHY COLLABORATION IS SO IMPORTANT FOR EDUCATORS

The word *collaborate* has come a long way from days when it was often construed to mean working in collusion with the enemy. In recent years it has popped up everywhere with a much different meaning. Greer (1989) describes goals for collaboration as sharing resources, fostering and improving institutional cooperation, creating linkages and partnerships, building trust, encouraging accountability, and taking other positive actions for the benefit of students. But Greer also expresses concern that goals can become institutionalized rather than put students' needs first. So the primary question must be, "Collaborate for whom?" Collaborative efforts are meaningful only when they help educators function in ways that promote student learning (Brownell, Adams, Sindelar, Waldron, & Vanhover, 2006).

A vital area of need is that of students with exceptional learning needs (ELN). In categorizing exceptionality, one would like to say, "Labels are for jelly jars, not children." But special education services and goals for Individualized Education Plans (IEPs) are based on definitions of the disability or disabilities. Lists may vary among federal, state, and local agencies, but typical terms include autism, behavioral disorder, communicative disability, cultural and linguistic diversity, deafness or being hard of hearing, developmental disability or mental retardation, dual sensory impairment, emotional disturbance, learning disability, multiple disabilities, physical disability, traumatic brain injury, and visual impairment or blindness. More than half of states in the United States also include gifted and talented as a part of special education because of the students' exceptional learning needs.

In comparison and contrast with practices in business, industry, and numerous other professions, collaboration on a regular basis in school settings tends to be more occasional and happenstance than frequent and planned. Available and congruent time blocks are necessary for productive interaction with colleagues, but these opportunities are few in the course of a busy school day. Then, too, practical structures for working together and training for these less familiar roles have been minimal. It follows that careful assessment of collaborative outcomes has been the exception, rather than the rule. However, the growing complexities of teaching and escalating demands for student achievement and accountability of schools underscore the strong need for working together in many dimensions. Furthermore, the twenty-first century has brought major differences in ways educators can communicate with colleagues as well as with students. Schools are connected electronically with multiple opportunities for collaborating and networking. These opportunities, which undoubtedly will increase in number and function in the decades to come, include:

- Computer-mediated communication, such as instant messaging and text messaging, hypertext, distance learning, Internet forums, bulletin boards, chat rooms, videoconferencing, e-mail, webcasts, podcasts, web logs, wikis, and more
- Technology devices for assistance with special needs in classrooms
- Virtual education

Technology has revolutionized the processes of collaboration and consultation among educational colleagues. School personnel who collaborate must communicate often and coordinate plans. With help from modern technology, communication can take place asynchronously, that is, intermittently without the requirement of a "common clock" for transmission between sender and receiver.

The autonomous teacher in that little red, eight-grade schoolhouse would have been amazed at the kinds and wonders of technological assistance. Information can be retrieved on just about any topic the teacher or student wants. Data can be analyzed and stored efficiently. Students are motivated by the newest methods of social computing and connecting with each other.

A note of caution is in order when highlighting the effects of technology on interactions. Do these tools make us more communicative or less so? More accessible or more isolated? More efficient or less? These questions bear analysis and careful study by educators who want to be effective communicators and successful collaborators and are exploring ways that technology can help them. The best approach is probably to accept the benefits of technology after setting stringent guidelines for use—for example, limiting the times one checks e-mail each day, taking care to make text messages and other electronic mail convey tone and substance so they are not likely to be misinterpreted, foregoing electronic connections when person-to-person interactions are almost as convenient and could be much more effective, monitoring personal attitudes toward technology so we are using it to help and not to intentionally remove ourselves from the fray of human experiences.

A later chapter will describe a number of technological assists that are available. These tools free up time and facilitate ways in which co-educators can locate pertinent information for dealing with topics and issues. They improve teacher efficiency with routine tasks so more time is available for collaborative activities, and importantly, for more direct services to students. Furthermore, technology can improve achievement and feelings of self-esteem for many students with disabilities. Technology tools are powerful motivators for students who have experienced failure and frustration in school. Many electronic communication devices allow students to speak and add their voices to those of their classmates.

Most preservice students today are quite comfortable with technology and many absorb much of their information in electronic contact using asynchronous communication that happens at any time they wish, not just at set intervals. Their book learning and teacher instruction have been enhanced by multifarious opportunities for interconnections with agencies, travel experiences, community involvement, parent partnerships, and mentorships. As one university professor put it, "My students are always connected and always on."

Veteran teachers who completed their teacher preparation programs years ago are less advantaged in the use of technology. But they are learning to learn and to be prepared for their students' high-level skills through self-study, tutorials, professional development activities, and social networking via electronic communication. Sometimes they are disposed to become mentees in technology with students as their mentors. The entire process of planning for use of technology in teaching and learning extends across all disciplines with many opportunities for professional collaboration.

■ ■ ■ ■ ■

APPLICATION 1.2
CATEGORIZING TEACHER RESPONSIBILITIES

Sort the list of teacher responsibilities you compiled in Application 1.1 into categories of tasks—for example, instructional, curricular, managerial, evaluative, supportive, and professional growth–related. Then decide which tasks might be carried out most productively and enjoyably in collaborative contexts. As an example, if the responsibility for ordering books and supplies is classified as managerial, teams of teachers might collaborate to pool their library allocations and make decisions about materials that could be shared or used for team teaching. Then mark with an asterisk (*) others with collaborative potential. Add some that may have been overlooked such as "organizing cross-grade tutors and study-buddies," or "involving families in preparing a notebook of potential community resources."

Motivation for Working Together

Teachers may wish for more small-group meetings that are focused on mutual interests and more grade-level meetings that address common concerns. They may want more opportunities to observe other teachers and other schools. They may seek richer professional development experiences. But that does not mean they are keen on engaging in collaboration and consultation activities. Some even comment candidly that they did not choose teaching as a career to work all that much with adults. Others feel that teaming up with co-teachers or consulting teachers will be perceived as a flag calling attention to their weaker areas or a no-confidence vote in their abilities. They could argue as well that too little time is available for the careful planning and concentrated effort that productive interaction requires. Opportunities may be rare and hard to arrange for meaningful observation of educators in other school settings. One more aspect that troubles special education teachers is the possibility that collaboration may siphon off time available for direct services to students.

When teachers do have time and opportunity to interact with colleagues for learning new ideas and revitalizing their professional enthusiasm, it is likely to be during professional development sessions. Unfortunately, these activities are often too highly structured and short-lived to allow for productive interaction. Many are scheduled at the end of a hectic day, when teachers are tired and want to reflect a bit on their teaching day, set the stage for the next day, and then turn their attention toward home or community activities. Now and again teachers are visited in their classrooms by other teachers, supervisors, administrators, student teachers, and sometimes parents. However, these occasions tend to trigger feelings of anxiety and defensiveness more than support and collegiality. Some school systems do promote co-teaching as a way of allowing teachers to support each other and broaden their teaching repertoires. But well-intentioned efforts to co-teach can result in turn-teaching—"You teach this part of the lesson and then take a break or make the copies we need for next hour, while I handle the part coming up."

Professionals cannot be coerced into being collegial (Wildman & Niles, 1987). Teachers who are accustomed to being in charge and making virtually all the day-to-day decisions in their classrooms cannot be ordered to just go out and collaborate with each other or co-teach to any significant degree. Along with incentive and time, they need structure, practice, encouragement, and positive feedback about their effectiveness in order to perform these sophisticated and demanding functions successfully.

In laboring together, collaborators do not compromise and cooperate so much as they confer and concur. Compromise often means giving up some part of, or conceding, something, and cooperation may dilute interaction so that it does not fully benefit the student. Collaboration, on the other hand, involves talking and planning, contributing, adding to, and coming to agreement so all can benefit.

DuFour (2004) finds that educators may equate collaboration with congeniality and camaraderie, but a professional learning community must have the right structures to build a culture of collaboration. He asserts that collaborative teachers must not ask what they are expected to teach, but rather how they will know each of their students has learned. Team members should make public such educational matters as goals, strategies, materials, and outcomes, and everyone in the school should belong to a team that focuses on student learning.

Reports from school districts throughout the United States identify collaboration as a key variable in the successful implementation of inclusive education (Villa & Thousand, 2003, p. 22). In collaboration, differentiated tasks can be allocated among individuals having various skills to contribute. Sometimes collaboration means recognizing differences and finding ways to accommodate those differences. The collaborative process is enriched by diversity among collaborators—diversity of experience, perspectives, values, skills, and interests. Individual differences of adults who consult and collaborate are rich ingredients for successful collaborations. The great need to recognize adult differences and use them constructively in collaborative enterprises will be the focus of Chapter 2.

The concept of team teaching is receiving increased attention among school professionals. Teamwork as co-educators means working for the good of the whole—where individual preferences are subtended or set aside for the larger cause. Many heads and hearts are better than one, and the pooled experiences, talents, knowledge, and ideas of a group are even better than the sum of the individual parts. Various forms for team teaching exist, with many different terms used to describe the process, such as team teaching, co-teaching (discussed further in Chapter 7), cooperative teaching, and collaborative teaching (Welch, 1998). Welch and Sheridan (1995) suggest that team-taught instruction can be micro-level staff development when each teacher models instruction for the other. Commercial companies offer activities, games, puzzles, and outdoor gaming equipment for team building. They purport to develop rapport and team spirit by energizing members to work together harmoniously. Some seem glitzy and merely playful, but others have potential for building awareness and trust through cohesion-building activities. Professional development consultants should observe in schools and query school personnel to determine if such techniques would be a turn-on or a turn-off for that group. Simple, straightforward collaborative structures, with explanation of benefits they provide for helping students with their special needs, may be most time efficient and acceptable to busy teachers.

Distinguishing among Consultation, Collaboration, and Working in Teams

All three processes—collaboration, consultation, and teamwork as they occur in the school context—involve interaction among school personnel, families and students, and community in working together to achieve common goals. However, subtle distinctions can be made.

In school consultation, the consultant contributes specialized expertise toward an educational problem, and the consultee delivers direct service utilizing that expertise. Consultants and consultees begin to collaborate when they assume equal ownership of the problem and solutions. Collaboration is a way of working in which power struggles *and* ineffectual politeness are regarded as detrimental to team goals. Friend and Cook (1992) stress that collaborative consultation must be voluntary, with one professional assisting another to address a problem concerning a third party. They further emphasize that successful consultants use different styles of interaction under different circumstances within different situations.

Collaborating as a teaching team fuels group spirit, develops process skills that help teachers interact in more productive ways, and fosters a more intellectual atmosphere (Maeroff, 1993). One of the best examples of working together is a musical ensemble. Whether one is accompanying, performing with a small group, or playing with an orchestra, band, or choir, it is the united effort that creates the musical experience. Musicians of many instruments are not brought together to play the same note. Doing so would make the music only louder, not richer and more harmonious. In similar fashion, co-teachers work in concert, not usually in perfect unison, to create an effective learning experience for all students in the class. Consultation, collaboration, and teaming up to co-teach or partner in learning activities will create many opportunities to engage in a strengths-type interaction so that each person is learning from and building on the strengths of the others.

What Collaborative Consultation *Is*

As illustrated by Pugach and Johnson (2002), collaboration is a way of being, not a set of isolated actions. The collaborative process reframes how educators interact in school contexts, including special education teachers with regular education teachers, public schools with institutions of higher education, and agencies with schools and families.

Welch (1998) deconstructs the term *collaboration* and comes up with a unique concept of working together for mutual benefit. It is different from cooperation in which all come to agreement but perhaps not all are benefiting. He contends that schools tend to be more cooperative than collaborative, explaining it as parallel but sometimes uneasy coexistence of general and special education. He further notes that coordination is more characteristic of interagency involvement such as in the Individualized Family Service Plan (IFSP) than of school-managed IEP. Welch faults the IEP process as often involving little or no collaboration during development and implementation; it tends to be drafted before a meeting using a generalized template, then quickly reviewed and hastily approved by the team, thus "essentially negating the 'I' in the IEP process" (Welch, 1998, p. 128.). One way to improve the process would be for the classroom teacher, who is required by IDEA 2004 to participate, to participate very actively rather than as a relatively passive observer.

Wesley and Buysse (2006) distinguish consultation as operating on two planes simultaneously; that is, consulting co-educators manage consultation components while concentrating on interpersonal aspects of trusting relationships with consultees. These early childhood special educators propose that critical elements in the consultative process are having the best research findings available, using family and professional wisdom, and drawing on family and professional values. The collaborating consultant must first do no harm and then deliver services that are academically and ethically sound (Wesley & Buysse, 2006).

When educators—special education teachers, classroom teachers, school administrators, related services and support personnel, as well as families and community agencies—are consulting and collaborating as members of an educational team, what specific kinds of things are they doing? A summary list typically includes engaging in one or more of these:

- Discussing students' needs and ways of addressing those needs
- Listening to colleagues' concerns about a teaching situation
- Identifying learning and behavior problems
- Assisting families in transition periods—from early childhood education programs to kindergarten, from elementary to middle school, from middle school to high school, and from high school to work or postsecondary education
- Planning for students' needs in the school setting
- Recommending classroom alternatives as first interventions for students with special learning and behavior needs
- Serving as a medium for student referrals
- Demonstrating instructional techniques to help with special needs or abilities
- Providing direct assistance to colleagues in learning and behavioral needs of students
- Leading or participating in professional development activities
- Designing and implementing individual education programs
- Sharing resources, instructional materials, and teaching ideas
- Utilizing technology for efficient and productive interactions among students as well as among co-educators
- Participating in co-teaching or demonstration teaching
- Engaging in observation, assessment, and evaluation activities
- Serving on curriculum committees, textbook committees, extracurricular activities committees, and school advisory councils
- Following through and following up on educational issues and concerns with co-educators, students and their families, and communities
- Networking with other educational professionals and other agencies who can be resources for students' needs

And these are just some of the activities that educators engage in when they are collaborating.

What Collaborative Consultation Is *Not*

School consultation is *not* therapy, counseling, or supervision. West and Idol (1987) and Morsink, Thomas, and Correa (1991) have distinguished consultation as being focused on issues, contrasting with counseling that is focused on individuals. The focus must be on educational concerns relevant to the welfare of the client and not on problems of consultees. Conoley and Conoley (1982) caution that the consultant must collaborate for issues and needs of the client, typically the student, and not on the consultee who tends to be the teacher.

Consulting specialists have to work diligently to shed the "expert" image held by many teachers toward consultants or specialists (Pugach & Johnson, 1989). So it is important for classroom teachers to be recognized as having expertise and resourcefulness to contribute. Collaborative consultation can emanate from any role pertinent to the case if the participants are well-informed. As a professional in the medical field commented, patients collaborate with their doctors because they are so well informed about their own conditions. This approach could be applied legitimately and productively to collaborative school consultation. No consultant is the be-all, end-all expert. Any co-educator can play a consultant role when circumstances dictate.

Collaboration among professional colleagues is *not* talk or discussion for its own sake. Furthermore, collaboration during co-teaching must not be hierarchical or judgmental, but voluntary and entered into with parity among the teaching partners.

It is very important that collaborative services *not* be used as a money-saving strategy in inclusive settings to eliminate or reduce the number of school personnel. Then, too, consultative and collaborative structures that provide indirect service must not be substituted in cases for which there is a strong need for direct services. School administrators and members of local school boards must plan carefully to avoid setting up hierarchical climates and unintentionally encouraging inappropriate consultative practices.

Collaborative school consultation and co-teaching cannot be forced on educators. As stated earlier, the process *must* be voluntary. There will be times when teachers relish having some autonomy in their work. Also, having quality think time is important for busy, multitasking educators. For example, individual brainstorming is an important process, not a frill. To elaborate, the benefits of individual brainstorming as occasional precursor to group brainstorming will be discussed in Chapter 5.

Another important consideration is to protect the rights of teachers to have some ideas that are theirs alone. Most teachers are willing, even eager, to share ideas and lend help to colleagues; however, they should not be asked to give up their specialties any more than chefs should be expected to relinquish their most prized recipes. Such altruistic behavior would result in giving up practices that are individually special and personally satisfying. That is not the purpose of collaboration, nor should it be a presumed condition of co-teaching. Instead, collaborators should help and encourage colleagues to develop their skills and personal strengths to come up with their own teaching specialties.

ROLE RESPONSIBILITIES IN COLLABORATIVE ENDEAVORS

When contemplating collaborative and consultative roles, educators often express their concerns by asking questions such as these:

- Who am I in this role?
- How do I carry out the responsibilities of this role?

- How will I know whether I am succeeding?
- How can I prepare for the role?

First, it is essential that central administrators and policy makers such as school boards explain the importance of consultative, collaborative, and co-teaching roles. Then building-level administrators must reiterate the value of these practices to the school, staff, and students. Parity, voluntary participation, and collegial interdependence must be emphasized. A key factor for success is allocating sufficient time and suitable places for interactions to take place.

Teachers will need encouragement to share enthusiastically the responsibilities for all students in collaborative environments. Related services personnel and support personnel will need to be integrated into a collaborative context. Families must receive information about the purposes and benefits of collaborative roles and partnered teaching. They will need to be assured that these services are right for their child. Students should be an integral part of the planning process and have opportunities to participate as young collaborators intensely involved in their own educational process. Ultimately, the community should support the establishment of a collaborative climate and anticipate its potential benefits for all.

SCENARIO 1.B

Now consider another event. This one takes place in the same school district a short time after Scenario 1.A described at the beginning of this chapter. Four special education teachers are talking in the district's main conference room before their special education director arrives for a planning meeting.

Secondary Learning Disabilities Teacher: I understand we're here to decide how we're going to inform staff and parents about the consultation and collaboration and perhaps co-teaching practices we'll be implementing soon. But first, I think we'd better figure out just what it is we *will* be doing in these roles.

Behavioral Disorders Teacher: Definitely. I have a really basic question that I've been thinking about a lot. What am I going to do the first week, even the first day, as a consulting teacher? I understand a few people on our staff have had some training in collaboration and consulting in former positions, but this is new to the rest of us.

Gifted Education Teacher: I agree. I've been thinking about all those different teaching styles and methods of doing things that will surface as we work closely together. Teachers won't all like or want the same things for their classrooms and their students.

Elementary Learning Disabilities Teacher: And remember, we are supposed to say, "*Our* students." Yes, I doubt this is something we can become experts about very quickly. From what little I've had a chance to read about collaborative processes, the key to success is using good communication skills and problem-solving techniques.

Gifted Education Teacher: Yes, and at the same time we have to take into account the wide array of resources it will take to provide the materials and methods each student needs. I'm a bit apprehensive about it all, but I'm willing to try it.

Behavioral Disorders Teacher: I guess I am, too. I've been thinking for some time now that our current methods of dealing with learning and behavior problems are not as effective and efficient as they should be. And I realize really bright kids are being kept on hold in the classroom much of the time. Besides, changing the way we do things can be energizing, you know. I think we have to be optimistic about the possible benefits for both students *and* teachers.

Secondary Learning Disabilities Teacher: Well, I for one happen to feel a sense of urgency because my first experience of consulting and collaborating is coming up soon. I'll be doing some observation and perhaps co-teaching with an English teacher at the high school next week. We'll be organizing a plan for working with a new student with severe learning disabilities who's enrolling in that school. That's why I'd like to talk it over and arrive at some consensus about collaborative consultation and also about co-teaching.

Elementary Learning Disabilities Teacher: I'll be interested both professionally and personally in how you get along with that. As I think you all know, I have a son at the high school who has learning disabilities with severe attention-deficit and behavioral disorders. It's been a struggle for him *and* the teachers in many of his high school classes. In my family we are concerned about his eventual transition either to getting more education or going to the job market. From what I've read and heard about resource consultation and interagency networking, I'm very interested in having more collaborative efforts in our schools.

Interchangeable Roles and Responsibilities

Educators are becoming more and more aware that collaborating to achieve a common goal often produces more beneficial results than do isolated efforts by an individual. The whole of the combined efforts is greater than the sum of its parts (Slavin, 1988). This describes the well-known homily that two heads are better than one, and several heads are better yet. The collaborative consultation process channels each individual's strengths and talents toward serving a client's needs.

Any person who consults in one situation may be a consultee or even a client in another. In each of these instances, consultant and consultee would share responsibility for working out a plan to help the client. As examples, a special education teacher might be a consultant for one situation and a consultee in another. The student is typically a client (as target of the intervention), but in some cases could be a consultee or even a consultant. Consultation might be initiated by a social worker, a special reading teacher, or a general classroom teacher. Consultation in which several educators collaborate could also be requested by a parent or a school counselor. The combinations of "people roles" that might participate in school collaboration and consultation to help students and teachers are virtually limitless. In Figure 1.2, depending on the circumstance, each collaborator could be a consultant, a consultee, or a client. Although roles and responsibilities may vary among individuals and across situations, if there is understanding about the nature of the role and appreciation for its possibilities, a collaborative and facilitative spirit can prevail.

Special education teacher	Student with learning disability
General classroom teacher	Student with behavioral disorder
School psychologist	Preschool student
School counselor	Student with mental retardation
Reading specialist	Student with high aptitude
Building administrator	Student with attention deficit disorder
Gifted program facilitator	Student with physical disabilities
School nurse	Parent of student with disability(ies)
Media specialist	Parent of student with advanced aptitude
Assistive technology specialist	Community-based mentor
Resource room teacher	Student with autism or Asperger's syndrome
School cafeteria staff	Pediatrician
School bus driver	University professor in special education
School custodian	Speech and language pathologist
Special education director	University professor in general education
Early childhood teacher	Probation officer
Curriculum specialist	Head Start personnel
Professional development staff	State Department of Education staff
Health care specialist/School nurse	Textbook publishers

FIGURE 1.2   Potential Collaborators as Consultants, Consultees, or Clients

INITIATING COLLABORATIVE ACTIVITIES

School improvement issues and legislative mandates may have convinced educators that the concept of collaborative school consultation is a promising method for helping students with special needs. But conversion of concepts to practice is not so simple. Questions in Scenario 1.B earlier that were voiced in the school district conference room by four special educators raised practical concerns and hinted at even more issues:

- Where do I begin as a collaborating school consultant?
- What do I do the first day on the job? And the first week?
- Let me see a sample schedule for the first week. And the first month as well.
- Where am I to be headed by the end of the year?

Other questions and concerns that are likely to surface sooner or later include:

- Will I have opportunity to work with students? That is why I chose teaching as a career.
- Where's my room? Will I have office space and supplies?
- Will I have a space for group work with students?
- Will I be welcomed and regarded as an important part of the teaching staff?
- If I need some special preparation for this role, how do I get that?
- How will I be evaluated in this role, and by whom?
- As a collaborating consultant who helps consultees meet special needs, will I be working myself out of a job?

Novice teachers may be thinking:

- Will participating in collaboration and consultation make me appear less competent?
- How much of my classroom time with students will be needed to provide this service to kids and how do I go about allocating that time?
- Don't I need to work out a plan for my classroom and get experience with that before I collaborate and certainly before I co-teach?
- When in the world will I find time and space to interact like this with other teachers anyway?

Participants in consultation and collaboration must voice their concerns and work through their feelings of insecurity as they sort out the dynamics of their new roles. School administrators have the responsibility of initiating open, candid expressions of concerns and encouraging intensive discussions about issues before they escalate into problems.

KEY ELEMENTS IN SUCCESSFUL COLLABORATION

Four essential elements of consultation, collaboration, and teamwork processes are pictured in the clocklike Figure 1.3:

1. Preparation for the roles
2. Delineation of roles
3. Framework for structuring the roles
4. Evaluation of outcomes

Within the four categories, twelve key areas are to be addressed. Each will be introduced and previewed, with references made to the subsequent chapters in which they will be developed more fully.

The sequence of the twelve elements is very important. Note that the recommended starting point for collaborative school consultation is shown at about the 6:30 position in

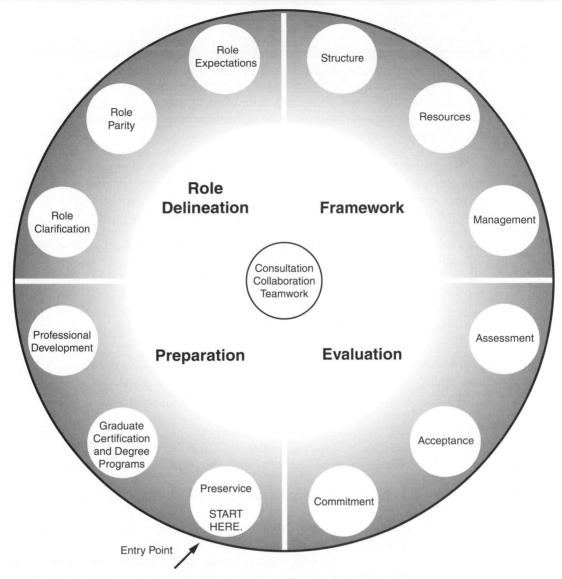

FIGURE 1.3   Key Elements for Working Together Effectively

Figure 1.3. Educators who intend to collaborate must resist the temptation to begin "too late in the day"—for example, at "11:30." with role expectations. Neither should they begin with a call for commitment to the process, shown at "5:30," or development of a structure for interactions, shown at "12:30." The place to begin for best results is at the early-in-the-day preparation position, and then proceed clockwise through the other elements.

Preparation

Educators in every role—administrators, teachers, support staff, and instructors of preservice teachers—will want to prepare mindfully for co-educator participation. Preparation for this should take place at the preservice level before novice teachers step into that first classroom and attend their first faculty meeting or IEP conference. Preparation and practice should continue at the graduate level with more advanced coursework, and then at the professional development level for experienced personnel who want to expand their skills and move into leadership roles.

A collaborative school climate can be developed through well-planned professional growth experiences, careful coaching, and constructive feedback in process areas such as communication, problem finding, and problem solving for example, and in content areas such as co-teaching models. In sum, preparation programs for developing skills of collaboration, consultation, and co-teaching are fundamental for three populations:

1. Preservice students who need orientation and practice in simulated roles as consultees and future consultants
2. Graduate students in advanced degree programs who will be collaborating and co-teaching, and also assisting others as co-educators
3. Veteran teachers who want to be collaborators, co-teachers, mentors, advocates, and school leaders in their school contexts

Preservice Preparation.   New teachers have many pressures that can curb their enthusiasm in those first years of teaching. This is the time when temptation to leave the profession is high. Novice teachers may be very stressed emotionally, physically, and socially. Babinski and Rogers (1998) reported that the two most frequently discussed problems of novice teachers were dealing with the special needs of children such as behavioral problems, learning disabilities, and attention deficits, and working with other adults such as parents, administrators, mentors, teaching assistants, and other teachers. Understandably, new teachers often fear being judged as incapable and failing if they ask for suggestions or outright assistance.

Novice teachers can benefit greatly by observing more experienced colleagues and participating in consultations, by working as part of teaching teams, and by collaborating with a wide range of school personnel. They will need knowledge about resources and strategies for sharing them, practice in interactive situations such as IEP conferences and parent conferences, and experience in showing accountability for their expenditures of time and energy in collaboration with co-educators. A particularly important area of preparation for novice teachers while they are still forming their teaching philosophies and strategies is that of relating to families of students and working with them as valued co-educators (Kerns, 1992).

Two decades ago, Phillips, Allred, Brulle, and Shank (1990) recommended that teacher preparation programs provide introductory education courses in which general and special education preservice teachers participate jointly in practicum experiences that serve a diverse range of children's needs. But this plan requires concerted effort by college and university personnel, many of whom are not prepared themselves to engage in collaboration and consultation functions, let alone to facilitate development of these behaviors in their students. But perhaps it is time to revisit the concept.

Some veteran educators may be nervous about having novice teachers engage in consultation practices before they have had teaching experiences in the real world. Nevertheless, the seeds of awareness can and should be planted early to bear fruit later in important ways. After all, for most new teachers there is not much time to acquire experience between the last day of a teacher education program and the first day of stepping into a bustling school environment and their own inclusive classroom. Preservice teachers will be a major topic in Chapter 10.

Mentoring of preservice and novice teachers in a collaborative atmosphere will benefit mentees and help the students of those mentees. Mentorships can build confidence in the mentee and generate a sense of professional satisfaction in the mentor as well. This type of professional partnership will be addressed in more detail in Chapter 12.

Preparation in Graduate Certification and Degree Programs.   Special education teachers who consult and collaborate with general education colleagues need to understand the scope and sequence of grade-level curriculum content. Kauffman (1994) stresses that they also must have particular expertise in instructional and behavioral techniques for students with disabilities or their input will have little significant import. Universities have far to go to meet these all-encompassing needs.

A source for delineating standards pertaining to collaboration among special educators, families, other educators, related service providers, and community agency personnel is the *NCATE/CEC Program Standards, Programs for the Preparation of Special Education Teachers* (2002). (These standards have been posted online at www.cec.sped.org/ps/perf_based_stds/knowledge_standards.html.)

One of the standards (*Standard 10: Collaboration*) in this document calls for special educators to collaborate with co-educators to ensure that exceptional learning needs (ELN) of students are addressed in schools. The standard refers to special educators as resources for their colleagues in understanding the laws and policies of special education and in facilitating transitions of students across many learning settings and contexts.

Some states require development of consultation skills for teacher certification. Inclusion of this training in standards for accreditation of teacher education programs is one way to encourage more emphasis on ensuring the presence of collaborative teachers and school environments. School administrators would be wise to recruit those who welcome opportunities to work collaboratively with their colleagues.

Every teacher preparation program for collaborative consultation and co-teaching would be unique. However, a basic program should include:

- Ensuring preparation of experienced teachers and preservice teachers, along with school administrators and related services personnel, for working together collegially and productively
- Delineating co-educator roles
- Gaining understanding of frameworks and skills that help educators fulfill those roles
- Evaluating effectiveness of collaborations and co-teaching activities

Graduate and undergraduate degree programs need to provide experiences that extend beyond a "mentioning" mode of superficial exposure to professional interaction.

Course syllabi should include not only the conventional learning strategies of lecture, reading, and discussion but also a strong focus on practical experiences and interactions. Small-group activities, simulations and role plays, interviewing, videotaped consultation practice, reaction and reflection papers, resource searches, practice with tools and strategies of technology, and assessment of outcomes will help educators to be more comfortable and capable in interactive school roles.

Preparation through Professional Development. Friend and Cook (1990) have stressed for a number of years that teachers are being set up to fail when they enter the profession having content expertise and skills in methods but not competencies for working effectively with colleagues. But the lack of preparation for consultation is compounded by absence of empirical studies that could justify such training. However, school improvement movements have begun to stimulate efforts toward accountability such as that reported some two decades ago by Rule, Fodor-Davis, Morgan, Salzberg, and Chen (1990). In their study Rule and colleagues identified the need for administrative support, technical assistance, and follow-up assistance along with professional development. Through inservice and other professional development activities, consultation and collaboration programs can be tailored to each school context. More recent studies have reported the impact of several newly developed models and these will be described in Chapter 3. Professional development techniques will be a major focus in Chapter 12.

Role Delineation

As indicated previously, a school role such as counselor, general classroom teacher, learning disabilities specialist, speech pathologist, or facilitator for gifted education programs does not automatically determine a specific consultative role. Rather, the consultative role emanates from the situation. For example, it might be that of a parent in providing information to the school administrator, or a learning disabilities teacher who helps the coach assess a student athlete's learning problem, or a mentor who gives the gifted program facilitator suggestions for materials to use with a student for enrichment and acceleration.

The consultee collaborates with the consultant to provide direct service to the client. The client is the one with the identified need or problem. This total concept reflects the contemporary approach to special services whereby student *needs,* not student labels, determine the service and delivery method, and an array of services are targeted and made available to address those needs.

Role Clarification. The first requirement of role delineation is to clarify the role as consultative *and* collaborative. Until educators become comfortable with that concept, ambiguous feelings may persist. Teachers and school staff may wonder why there are consulting teachers or what these people are supposed to be doing. Classroom teachers may blame their own heavy responsibilities on the seemingly lighter caseloads of consulting teachers. One high school English teacher told a newly appointed consulting teacher, "If you were back in your classroom teaching five hours of English instead of 'facilitating' for a few high-ability students part of the time, my own student numbers wouldn't be so high." Paradoxically, consulting teachers often have excessively demanding workloads when travel time among schools, conferencing with teachers and students and perhaps parents, preparing IEPs, and constructing or locating special curriculum and materials are taken into account. If their workload is too great, the effectiveness of their services will be diminished severely because little time and energy will remain for the coordination and communication activities that are integral to consultation success.

Seamless, well-coordinated instructional plans for students with special needs require keen awareness of role responsibilities and service possibilities among all who are involved. A classroom teacher and a reading specialist may have information to share in addressing a struggling reader's strengths and deficits, yet they may know relatively little about each other's curriculum, educational priorities, or expectations for the student. They must coordinate their efforts, or those efforts may be counterproductive. In one unfortunate case, a reading specialist was instructing a fifth-grader with reading problems to slow down and read more deliberately, while the learning disabilities specialist was encouraging him to read much more rapidly and was in the process of referring him to the gifted program facilitator. The student, a pleasant and cooperative child, was trying valiantly to please both teachers simultaneously before the situation came to light in the course of that referral process. Nevertheless, classroom teachers who have functioned autonomously for years may question how a process of collaborating with special education personnel or other classroom teachers can help their students. It is a fair and thoughtful question that deserves and will receive careful treatment throughout this book.

Teachers may doubt the ability of a consulting teacher or co-teacher to fit into their classroom structure, especially if that other person is young and inexperienced. As one classroom teacher put it when asked about involving the special education consulting teacher, "I'd never ask *her* for help. What does she know about managing a full classroom of students whose needs are all over the chart? She's never dealt with more than five or six at a time, and she's not yet been responsible for a regular classroom for an entire school year." Collaborative school consultation calls for people to relinquish traditional roles in order to share what they have learned and practiced. But many educators are not prepared for such flexibility and changes in school structure.

Role Parity.   Along with role ambiguity and misunderstanding, special education teachers who travel back and forth among several schools may feel an absence of role parity in that they do not belong exclusively to any one school or faculty. They may feel minimally important to students and the educational system, cut off from general classroom teachers because of differing responsibilities, and isolated from special education colleagues because of distance and schedules.

As an obvious example of nonparity, when consulting teachers are absent, substitutes are not often provided for them. In fact, on occasion they may be taken away from their own assignments to *be* the substitute for absent classroom teachers or to perform other tasks that come up suddenly. Consulting teachers have been asked to guide visitors on a school tour, monitor school events, and perform secretarial tasks. These feelings are accentuated by the misconception that they have no ownership in student welfare and development. Some who travel extensively, usually in their own cars or vans, from school to school have been dubbed "windshield" personnel.

General education teachers have their own complaints about lack of parity in collaborative enterprises. Oftentimes they are noticeably absent from lists of resource personnel for helping students with needs, so much so that some special education teachers have noticed the oversight and have asked why no one questioned them about what *they* had learned from the classroom teachers (Pugach & Johnson, 1989). They felt that not having been trained as specialists suggested that they were less able than the "experts" to consult with and assist. Meanwhile, as classroom teachers they are not going to wait with open arms for the specialists to come and save them. School life will proceed even in the absence of a consulting teacher or co-teacher. School bells will ring, classroom doors will open, and the school day will go on. All of this could foster a message of diminished parity among general education, special education, and related services and support personnel. Teachers who feel like second-class colleagues, not accepted or appreciated as a vital part of the staff, may develop defenses that erode their enthusiasm and effectiveness.

Role confusion and inequality may also fuel stress that leads to professional burnout. So continuous, specific recognition and reinforcement of consulting and collaborating teacher contributions toward student success are important for credibility and success of the role and professional morale of school personnel.

Role Expectations.   Sometimes colleagues have unreasonable expectations for partnerships or team involvement. They may be anticipating instant success and miraculous student progress in a very short while. When positive results with students are slow in forthcoming, attitudes may range from guarded skepticism to open disapproval of collaborative efforts. But they may simply be expecting too much too soon. A co-teacher or a special services consultant cannot provide an instant panacea for every student's difficulties. Furthermore, teachers sometimes neglect to monitor and record results carefully, so gradual day-to-day progress is not noticed. This is much like not seeing a child for some months and then thinking, "My, how she has grown." Then, too, consultees might pressure consultants unfairly by expecting them to "fix" the student, and then if this does not happen rather soon, impatiently dismiss consultation and collaboration as a waste of precious time.

As noted earlier, some consulting teachers expect to work only with students, not adults, and prefer it that way. "I was trained to work with kids, and that's what I enjoy," confessed one consulting teacher when assigned to an indirect service role. This preference presents a difficult situation for both consultee and collaborator. A team approach or co-teaching format may be awkward for the staunchly autonomous teacher at first. Unrealistic and unreasonable expectations must be set aside in the early planning stages of school collaboration practices. Co-educators should set reasonable goals for themselves and not try to do too much too soon. Another point to be considered is that sometimes the most difficult part of a collaborative consultation experience is stepping aside once the consultee experiences some success with students.

Collaborating consultants may wonder occasionally that "If I consult effectively, I may be working myself out of a job." However, that is highly unlikely. The more successful the consultation services are, the more teachers and administrators are apt to value them for both their immediate contribution and their long-range positive ripple effects. As one example, students missed in initial referrals often are noted and subsequently helped as a result of the interaction among classroom teachers and consulting teachers. One astute classroom teacher commented after using a checklist that she and the gifted program consulting teacher had drawn up, "I won't be recommending Chuck for special education testing yet, but I am definitely thinking differently about his many strengths now."

Involvement of as many co-educators as possible through needs assessments, interviews, professional development activities, and both formal and informal communications, will do much to alleviate inappropriate expectations for consulting and partnership roles. If collaborators can engage in successful teamwork with the more receptive and cooperative colleagues in their schools, it will generate confidence in the approach.

Framework

A framework for school consultation, collaboration, and co-teaching calls for structures that provide adequate blocks of time, management of schedules, suitable facilities in which to meet, and organization of details so that the interactive processes are carried out as conveniently and nonintrusively as possible. These conditions are deceptively simple to describe but much more difficult to put into operation.

Structure.   It is one thing to design a hypothetical method of consultation, but quite another to plan multiple methods for application in different situations, and then even more challenging to select and put into motion the right method for each situation. This is easier, of course, if preceded by thoughtful role clarification, genuine role parity, and appropriate role expectations.

Those who collaborate will want to generate a number of methods for consultation and collaboration in a variety of grade levels, subject areas, special needs categories, and school, community, and family contexts. The consultation structure should fit the context of the system. Traditional models and newer models for a variety of school contexts have been developed and put into practice. But school personnel should collaborate to design their own collaborative consultation and co-teaching systems to custom fit their school needs. Taking a survey of teachers to ask how they would use collaborative activities would be a good way to begin. Studying and observing co-teaching and collaborative and consultative structures in other school systems also can be helpful.

Resources.   Time is the ultimate nonrenewable resource. One of the most overwhelming and frustrating obstacles to collaborative activity is lack of time for it. The time needed for interfacing with colleagues and the scheduling of time blocks that fit into schedules of everyone involved are major deterrents to successful interactions. Sometimes willing teachers use their own planning time for consultation, but that is not an ideal way to instill positive attitudes toward a collaborative approach. The typical school day is simply not designed for incorporating collaboration time into the schedule without much careful planning. Even if a schedule for meeting and following up could be arranged, it may be next to impossible to find significant blocks of compatible time for all potential participants. Working out such a plan is often like working a complex puzzle; it is one of the most formidable tasks of those who want to collaborate, particularly those who have direct teaching responsibilities at specific times. Thus it is up to administrators to acknowledge the need for this quality time and to assume strong leadership in enabling it to happen. When administrators lend their authority to this endeavor, school personnel are more likely to find ways of getting together and to use that time productively. Unfortunately, when consulting teachers initiate consultation and collaboration, it is very likely that these activities come out of their own time—that is, before school, after school, during lunch hours, perhaps even on weekends. Even so, this *temporary* accommodation should be replaced as soon as possible with a more formal structure for allocation of time during the school day. This is not only for their well-being, but to emphasize that consultation and collaboration are not simply add-on services to be carried out by a zealous, dedicated, almost superhuman few.

As time is made available for working together, facilities must be accessible in which to conduct the consultation. These areas should be pleasant, quiet, convenient, and relatively private for free exchange of confidences. Such places are often at a premium in a bustling school community.

Management.   As everyone knows, school districts struggle to find money for ever-increasing educational needs. So there is a risk of letting fiscal issues, rather than factors that focus specifically on student needs, dictate the service delivery method. One such factor is the teacher caseload issue and it must be addressed carefully. Large caseloads may seem to save money in the short run, but not in the long run if student performance declines or if there is much attrition from the teaching profession. If a collaborating teacher's caseload is too great, direct service will be inadequate, possibilities for indirect services will be diminished, acceptance of the approach falters, and the program risks rejection.

Recommended caseload numbers vary depending on school context, travel time required, grade levels, exceptionalities and special needs served, and structure(s) of the interaction method. The numbers must be kept manageable to fulfill the intent and promise of consultation and collaboration. Part of the solution lies in documenting carefully all team activities *and* also making note of what should have happened but did not because of time constraints. Consultants must negotiate with their administrators for reasonable caseload assignments and blocks of time to communicate.

Although time is at a premium for busy educators, recent trends in computer technology and other electronic media are improving their situations. Teachers who work in partnerships with colleagues must be very organized and efficient. in recent years tedious, time-consuming tasks such as developing IEPs, preparing reports, collecting and recording academic and behavioral data, and communicating with families and support staff, have been made easier by technological advances. Software templates, e-mail, electronic calendars, and a variety of organizational tools give teachers more time. Tools and vehicles such as these also have allowed teachers to be more connected in networks that enhance collegiality and teamwork.

Technology has revolutionized the processes of collaboration and consultation among educational colleagues. School personnel who collaborate must communicate often and must coordinate plans and practices. With help from modern means of technology, communication can take place asynchronously rather than waiting for congruent schedules and compatible locations. Information can be retrieved on just about any topic teachers or students would want or need, and data can be analyzed and stored efficiently. Furthermore, technology can improve achievement and self-esteem of many students with disabilities and serve as a powerful motivator for students who have experienced failure and frustration in school.

Evaluation and Support

The fourth of the key elements in school consultation, collaboration, and co-teaching involves evaluation and support. Co-educators must document the effectiveness of consultation and collaboration in order to ensure continued support for this kind of educational service and avoid the tendency to overlook small, consistent gains. School personnel are understandably skeptical of indirect services if they do not prove their mettle. Co-educators may be involved initially because they are told to, or because they have been talked into giving it a try, or even because they are intrigued with the possibilities or just want to be collegial. But their interest will wane if the processes become a hassle and a burden, especially if positive results are not forthcoming and convincing.

Assessment.   Assessment is essential for providing evaluative data to measure outcomes of collaborative school consultation and co-teaching. School personnel will be more accepting if success is demonstrated with carefully collected, valid data. Unfortunately, evaluations of collaboration and consultation processes have been minimal and often not well planned and conducted. A few procedures such as rating scales of judgments that represent a variety of skills and activities, and survey estimates of engaged time for the required activities, have been used. Administrators, advisory council members, and policymakers should study carefully the procedures that have been tried and use their skills to design helpful and practical assessment techniques that fit their school contexts. In keeping with the philosophy of collaboration, personnel from diverse roles should design the evaluation tools and procedures cooperatively.

Not only should processes and content be evaluated, but the context of the school setting should be as well. For example, a consultant may have excellent communication skills and a wealth of content with which to consult and collaborate, but if the existing school context provides no time and space for interaction, positive results will be slim to none. Consultants will want to evaluate every stage of the collaborative processes to keep focusing on the right goals. (Evaluation will be addressed in more detail in Chapter 6.)

Assessment and evaluation should include a variety of data-collection methods to provide the kinds of information needed by target groups. Consultation and collaboration practices must not be judged inadequate for the wrong reasons or erroneous assumptions. If time has not been allocated for the interactions, if school personnel have not had preparation and encouragement, and if administrator support is lacking, those elements should be targeted for improvement before the collaborative process itself is faulted.

Acceptance.   Participation in collaborative programs must be a *willing* decision and ensure parity for all who are involved in order for the programs to be accepted. Administrator acceptance and encouragement will help in this regard to a great extent. By using techniques such as publicizing the successes and promoting the benefits of consultations and teamwork that have taken place, schools may get the collaboration bandwagon rolling with even the most reluctant persons on board. Most important, however, is involving people right from the start in needs assessments, planning efforts, evaluations, professional development activities, follow-up activities, and more and more personal contacts. This helps to instill ownership and even arouse a little curiosity, not to mention a left-out feeling if not yet on board. Techniques and incentives for promoting acceptance of consultation, collaboration, and teamwork through professional development and advocacy efforts will be discussed in Chapter 12.

Commitment. Consultation calls for redirection and change in old ways of doing things. Collaboration requires energy and practice. Co-teaching necessitates sharing ownership and taking risks. These realities make involvement by school personnel more difficult and maintenance of their commitment more challenging. In the minds of many educators, consultation has been associated with exclusionary special education programs and assistance in mainstreamed classes. So if teachers miss the opportunity for collaborative consultation service and come to resent having more responsibility for teaching special education students, they may blame collaborative school consultation and collaborative consultants for the situation.

Special education teachers and support personnel need a well-designed plan and a spirited collegial vision that will intrigue and enthuse them about joining in partnerships. Most of all, they need enthusiastic administrator support and sincere encouragement. (This issue will be discussed in more depth in Chapter 12.) Those who would consult, collaborate, and co-teach must recognize and build on every opportunity for dedicated participation by all.

COMPETENCIES OF EFFECTIVE COLLABORATORS, CONSULTANTS, AND TEAM PARTICIPANTS

Consultation, collaboration, and co-teaching competencies emanate from a foundation of understanding school contexts, demonstrating process skills, and delivering helpful content and resources. Guided by principles of caring and sharing, co-educators work together voluntarily and with parity as a team. Collaborative school consultants prepare themselves through teacher education programs and professional development activities for working together. When they collaborate and co-teach, they model the interactive skills their students will need for the future in their own lives.

Collaborative consultants support students, families, their schools, and the community while advocating for schools and students at every opportunity. What role could be better suited to the aspirations of would-be teachers as described in the opening lines of this chapter?

Competencies for teaching and collaborating will be addressed in each chapter as they emanate from the topics and are amplified in Applications and To Do activities. In Chapter 12, the characteristics will be summarized and a competencies checklist will be provided as a tool for assessment. Some readers may want to look ahead at the checklist (see Figure 12.8 on page 426). Others may wish to wait. Still others might find it interesting and beneficial to work as a group in creating their own checklists now or later for collaborative, consultative, and co-teaching skills.

BENEFITS FROM COLLABORATIVE
SCHOOL CONSULTATION

School environments that promote collaborative consultation tend to involve all school personnel in the teaching and learning processes. Information is shared and knowledge levels about student characteristics and needs, and strategies for meeting those needs, are broadened. Importantly, many of the strategies are helpful with other students who have similar but less severe needs. A number of specific benefits of school consultation and collaboration can be anticipated.

First, there is much-needed support and assistance for students in the inclusive classroom. Consulting special education teachers help classroom teachers develop repertoires of materials and instructional strategies. Many find this more efficient than racing from one student to another in a resource room as all work on individual assignments. As one learning disabilities teacher succinctly put it, "In my resource room, by the time I get to the last student, I find that the first student is stuck and has made no progress. So I frantically run through the whole cycle again. Tennis shoes are a must for my job!" Consulting teachers also find ways to help classroom teachers become confident and successful with special needs students. At times they can assume an instructional role in the classroom, which frees the classroom teacher to study student progress, set up arrangements for special projects, or work intensively with a small group of students. When general classroom and special education teachers collaborate, each has ownership and involvement in serving special needs.

Collaborative efforts to serve students in heterogeneous settings help minimize stigmatizing effects of labels such as "delayed," "having disabilities," "exceptional," or even "gifted." They also can reduce referrals to remedial programs. In a study of special education in an inclusionary middle school, Knowles (1997) found that collaboration and teamwork decreased special education referrals and grade-level retention of students. Fewer referrals for special education services means reduced expenditures for costly and time-consuming psychological assessments and special education interventions. Educators can focus more time and energy on teaching and facilitating, and less on testing and measuring. In addition, a ripple effect extends services to students by encouraging modifications and alternatives for their special needs.

A successful consultation process becomes a supportive tool that teachers increasingly value and use. As inclusive school systems become more prevalent, collaborative consultation will become even more critical for school program success. Consultation services contribute to the total school program as a bridge between the parallel systems of special education and general education (Greenburg, 1987) and are an effective way of alleviating confusion over goals and relationships of general and special education (Will, 1984).

Administrators can benefit from eased pressure and planning loads when classroom teachers are efficient in working with a wide range of student needs. Principals find it stimulating to visit and observe in classrooms as team participants, collaborating on ways of helping every student succeed in the school and reinforcing teacher successes with all of their students. This is for many administrators a welcome change from the typical classroom visitations they make for purposes of teacher evaluation.

Another important and frequently overlooked benefit is the maintenance of continuity in learning programs as students progress through their K–12 school experiences. This, too, is a savings in time, energy, and resources of the educational staff and often the parents as well. Transition periods in the student's school life will be discussed in Chapter 11.

A collaborative consultation approach is a natural system for nurturing harmonious staff interactions. Teachers who have become isolated or autonomous in their teaching styles and instructional outlook often discover that working with other adults for common goals is quite stimulating. Sharing ideas can add to creativity, open-endedness, and flexibility in developing educational programs for students with special needs. In addition, more emphasis and coordination can be given to cross-school and long-range planning, with an increased use of outside resources for student needs.

Collaborative consultants are catalysts for professional development. They can identify areas in which faculty need awareness and information sessions, and coordinate workshops to help all school personnel learn specific educational techniques (McKenzie, Egner, Knight, Perelman, Schneider, & Garvin, 1970). Just as removal of the catalyst stops a chemical process, so can the absence of collaborative consulting teachers curtail individualization of curriculum and differentiation of strategies for special needs (Bietau, 1994).

Parents or caregivers of the exceptional student often become extremely frustrated with the labeling, fragmented curriculum, and isolation from peers endured by their children. So they respond enthusiastically when they learn that several educators are functioning as a team for the student. Their attitudes toward school improve and they are more likely to become more involved in planning and carrying through with the interventions (Idol, 1988), more eager to share their ideas, and more helpful in monitoring their child's learning. They are particularly supportive when consulting services allow students in special education programs to remain in their neighborhood schools and to receive more assistance from interagency sources for their child's special needs.

■ ■ ■ ■ ■

APPLICATION 1.3
COLLABORATION THROUGHOUT THE GLOBAL COMMUNITY

The word *collaboration* is showing up more and more in newscasts, speeches, documentaries, sports reviews, entertainment and media discussions, political panels, printed material, organizational reports, web logs, casual conversations, science breakthroughs, community meetings, and many other arenas of our daily lives. Listen and watch for uses of the word. Tally on a piece of paper each time you see or hear the word and note in what context it appeared. If making a tally is not convenient, then just make a mental note, "There it is. I did hear or see *collaborate* mentioned today." Then consolidate your findings with those of others who are doing it and discuss when, where, and how the word was used.

ETHICS FOR WORKING TOGETHER
AS CO-EDUCATORS

A collaborative ethic is a set of values or principles that supports collegial styles of interaction among coequal individuals engaging voluntarily in making decisions or solving problems (Friend & Cook, 1990; Phillips & McCullough, 1990; Welch, Sheridan, Fuhriman,

Hart, Connell, & Stoddart, 1992). Specific ethics for collaboration and consultation describe a system of values and principles by which beliefs and actions about working together can be judged right or wrong, good or bad, just or unjust, in order to guide practices and inspire excellence.

Educators might ask why there is need for studying ethical principles and practices when their lofty professional aims and aspirations are already built on principled attitudes and behaviors. A better way to address the issue would be to determine, as models for the leaders of tomorrow, how educators can by their own actions and shared beliefs, convey to students the critical need for ethics in *every* field of endeavor. They can begin by modeling ethical principles in every facet of their roles, including interrelationships and teamwork with professional colleagues. These skills will be keys to success in virtually any work role that students may have in the future.

Each chapter of this book will conclude with a look at ethical considerations pertaining to the chapter's content. Conclusions can be drawn from each chapter about the ways in which consultants, collaborators, and co-teachers should conduct their responsibilities ethically within an ethical climate, and all will be summarized in Chapter 12.

Collaborators should work to create environments in which an ethic of care (Noddings, 1992) dominates professional interactions conducted for the purpose of educating children and youth (Pugach & Johnson, 1995). They must strive also to maintain personal integrity, even under pressure from others in their group, by standing firm as a model and monitoring potential violations of ethical principles by others.

Ethical collaborators respect the worth and potential of every individual. They acknowledge that every child is a minority of one with unique backgrounds, situations, abilities, and needs. They strive to serve special needs and abilities with diligence and perseverance, not because it is legislated but because it is the right thing to do. They acknowledge without rancor that some educators may not be keen on collaborating or co-teaching, but they continue to encourage participation by colleagues when it is of likely benefit for students. Special needs of students are the focus of most collaborative interactions. In addressing those special needs, it is important to keep in mind that consultants have complex roles with responsibilities that include the protection of privacy and caretaking of confidential material.

TIPS FOR WORKING TOGETHER IN SCHOOLS

1. Value and find ways to demonstrate beyond token lip service the worth of consultation, collaboration, and teamwork as tools for planning and coordinating instruction.
2. Do not wait to be approached for opportunities to consult, collaborate, and co-teach.
3. Try not to press for personally favored solutions to school needs, co-educator needs, or student needs. Strive instead for collaborative efforts to solve problems together, even if it means giving up some of your own agenda.
4. Refrain from assuming that colleagues are waiting around to be "saved."
5. Do not share problems or concerns with classroom teachers unless they can have significant input or you have a suggestion for them that might help.
6. Ask for help when you are facing a problem, because it has a humanizing, rapport-building effect.

7. Interact with every co-educator in the building(s) regularly.

8. Learn all you can about methods of consulting, collaborating, co-teaching, and engaging in other kinds of collegial teamwork, determining what worked and what didn't work that would be applicable to your environment.

9. Leave the door open, both figuratively and literally, for future partnerships and collaborations.

10. Encourage each member of a collaborative group to share knowledge and perceptions about an issue, in order to establish a solid framework in which to discuss the issue.

CHAPTER REVIEW

1. Educators of the twenty-first century can no longer be expected to work effectively in isolated environments and autonomous roles. Every child is "a minority of one" with special needs and abilities. A wide array of services and school personnel, working in collaboration, is needed to prepare all students for their future careers, continuing education, and responsibilities of citizenship.

2. Collaborative consultation and team activities such as co-teaching in school contexts describes interaction in which school personnel, families, and community agencies collaborate as a team within the school context to identify learning and behavioral needs, and to plan, implement, and evaluate educational programs that serve those needs. The collaborative school consultant is a facilitator of effective communication, cooperation, and coordination who works with co-educators in a team effort to serve the special learning and behavioral needs of students.

3. Collaborative consultation is a way of working together to identify the special needs of students; plan as a team for goal setting, curriculum, and assessment that will meet those needs in an inclusive setting; and interact with other school personnel, communities, and families for the welfare of students, schools, and communities.

4. Key elements in school consultation and collaboration are preparation for the consultative and collaborative roles at preservice, graduate, and experienced-teacher levels; role delineation with role clarity, parity, and appropriate expectations; a framework of structure, resources, and management; and evaluation and support through assessment, commitment, and acceptance. A consultant, consultee (or mediator), and client (or target) in one school-related situation may function in either of the other two roles under different circumstances. Several questions reflect the practical concerns of consultants and consulting teachers: What do I do? How do I begin? What is my schedule for a day/week/year? How will I know I am succeeding? How can I prepare for this kind of role?

5. Many benefits accrue from successful collaborative consultation and co-teaching. These include much-needed support and assistance for students with disabilities within in the inclusive classroom. Collaboration and teamwork can decrease special education referrals and grade-level retention of students, meaning reduced costs. Ripple effects bring about modifications and alternatives for students' special needs. Collaborative consultants are catalysts for professional development and can help ease burdens of building administrators. Parents respond enthusiastically when they learn that several educators are functioning as a team for the student. Competencies needed to bring about these benefits include context skills of understanding the role, working in parity and collegiality with others, and adhering to ethical principles; process skills of communication, organization, and management; and content skills for co-teaching and co-facilitating, addressing special needs of students in collaboration with resource and support personnel, and continuing to grow professionally.

6. Educators must convey to students the critical need for ethics in every field of endeavor. In their very visible teaching roles they can model ethical principles for students. In their interactions with professional colleagues they can model personal integrity and doing the right things in ways that demonstrate the collaborative ethics their students will need to be successful in virtually every work role of their future.

TO DO AND THINK ABOUT

1. Using material in this chapter, a dictionary, interviews, recollections from teaching experiences, discussion with colleagues or classmates, and any other pertinent references, develop a paragraph or two about collaborative consultation and co-teaching activities among co-educators to reflect your thoughts at this time.

2. Interview three school professionals (elementary, middle school, and high school levels if possible) and two parents to find out their views of consultation services, collaborative activities, and co-teaching in schools. If they ask, "What do you mean by collaboration, and consultation, and co-teaching?" you can approach this in one of two ways—giving them descriptions, perhaps based on those you developed in #1 above, or encouraging them to define the concepts in their own way. Compare the interview results, and draw inferences from your findings. Note any indication of willingness to collaborate or a glimmer of budding interest in consultation, and consider how these positive signs might be followed up productively.

3. Develop a chart for identifying obstacles that may appear in executing the four key elements of collaboration and consultation, namely, preparation, role delineation, framework, and evaluation, and add a section for proposing ways of sidestepping or overcoming those obstacles.

4. Before looking at the competencies checklist provided in Chapter 12, make a list of competencies you think are important for collaborative school consultants who will be working with other educators in groups or in pairs as co-teachers. If possible, compare your list with those done by others and exchange ideas.

5. In groups, discuss the topic of collaborative ethics by generating key words—for example, principles, values, fairness, communicating, caring. Record the words on chart paper or chalkboard so all can see them. Next, with these pooled words as catalysts, formulate a description of a collaborative ethical climate for educators that would work for your school context. Then talk about why ethical principles are so important in school-based education. Finally, generate ideas for ways in which ethical behaviors can be encouraged and modeled by co-educators in educational environments.

ADDITIONAL READINGS AND RESOURCES

Journal for Educational and Psychological Consultation. All issues have theory-based and research-based articles on the use of collaboration and consultation in teaching, psychology, counseling, and other education-based professions.

Thomas, C. C., Correa, V. I., & Morsink, C. V. (2001). *Interactive teaming: Enhancing programs for students with special needs* (3rd ed.). Upper Saddle River, NJ: Prentice Hall.
Unit I on context and foundations for interactive teaming.

Welch, M. (1998.) The IDEA of collaboration in special education: An introspective examination of paradigms and promise. *Journal of Educational and Psychological Consultation, 9*(2), 119–142.

Williams, J. M., & Martin, S. M. (2001). Implementing the Individuals with Disabilities Education Act of 1997: The consultant's role. *Journal of Educational and Psychological Consultation, 12*(1), 59–81.

Yocum, D. J., & Cossairt, A. (1996). Consultation courses offered in special education teacher training programs: A national survey. *Journal of Educational and Psychological Consultation, 7*(3), 251–258.

CHAPTER TWO

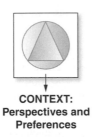

CONTEXT:
Perspectives and
Preferences

Differences in Perspectives and Preferences among Co-Educators

A patchwork quilt is made up of many colors, textures, shapes, and sizes. Each piece contributes something unique to the whole. Some of the pieces may seem to clash, but if every piece were the same, the quilt would be drab and dull. When put together they form a collage[1] in which each contributes to the beauty of the whole.

In much the same way, schools are a patchwork of attitudes, personalities, values, interests, and skills that blend to form a human collage. Each person within the school environment is different and contributes special qualities to enrich the whole. People may differ markedly and even take serious issue with one another on occasion because of their differences. But the wonderful array of individuals who come together in schools each day creates a montage[2] of unlimited opportunity for working together as teachers and learners.

Educators are attuned to studying individual differences of *students* as they plan for learning needs, but too often they overlook the individual differences among *adults* with whom they work. Why is this so important? The synergism created by adult differences, if recognized, respected, and used in constructive ways, will help educators to be better instructors and students to be better learners.

FOCUSING QUESTIONS

1. What professional and personal variables are factors in differentiating perspectives and preferences among educators?

2. How do major differences in professional perspectives and personal preferences affect interactions among co-educators within school contexts?

3. How do educational taxonomies in cognitive, affective, sensorimotor, and social domains guide instruction and learning?

[1]Collection or assemblage of diverse things grouped together and considered as a whole.

[2]Composite of diverse elements that forms a continuous representation of an area.

4. In what ways can differences among adults be recognized and used constructively to more fully address all students' learning needs?

5. How is the value of teaching teams maximized by co-educator differences in professional perspective and personal preference?

6. What are important ethical considerations regarding the recognition and constructive use of individual differences among co-educators?

KEY TERMS

assessment (domain-referenced, norm-referenced)

individual differences

instructional objectives

learning theory (cognitive, behavioral, social)

No Child *Held* Behind (NC*H*B)

No Child Left Behind (NCLB)

onedownsmanship

persona

personality

scores (raw, derived)

sensorimotor

synergism

taxonomy of the affective domain

taxonomy of the cognitive domain

taxonomy of the sensorimotor domain

taxonomy of the social domain

tests (mastery, differentiating)

thinking and doing processes

transfer (low-road, high-road)

variability

SCENARIO 2.A

Comments by various educators in hallways and gathering areas at various times during the school day:

"I'm eager to try that teaching strategy in our school. Why don't other people on the faculty want to give it a chance? It's been working so well in other schools."

"Here we go again. Another change that will probably spin us around for our latest ride on the school improvement merry-go-round."

"Why are some people so negative toward new ideas before they even try them out or at least wait and see what happens when other people use them?"

"We seem to see eye to eye on everything important in our department. What a great group of colleagues."

"Seems like we do the same old thing, and people fall into line like sheep. So I say, why not strike out for new ground? Let's take some risks and do something innovative for a change."

"Another meeting on 'school improvement' issues. They drag on and on, and we have nothing to show for all the time it wasted."

"I like the direction our school is heading to try out some co-teaching classrooms."

"Seems like we just get settled into some new method and it's going pretty well, when we're being prepared to jump to something entirely different."

"My first parent-teacher conference and things went so well! I'm glad my mentoring teacher and I sat down and went over everything that could go wrong. Because of that, nothing did!"

"I just can't figure out where that kid's family is coming from."

"What a disorganized fiasco that conference was! Not enough time even to figure out the main points, much less bring anything back to use."

"Wasn't that a great conference? With what I brought back to use, I'm off to a good start now and I'm really looking forward to this school year."

INDIVIDUAL DIFFERENCES AMONG ADULTS IN EDUCATIONAL ENVIRONMENTS

Much of the seemingly random variation within the patchwork quilt of human attitudes and behaviors is actually quite orderly and consistent because it is based on the way people prefer to use their perception and judgment (Keirsey & Bates, 1984; Lawrence, 1993). If one person views the world and reacts to it in ways unlike another, it is because that person processes information differently. Different viewpoints contribute diverse insights that help broaden the understanding of issues and problems. With expanded perspectives on educational philosophy and variations in personality among co-educators, greater opportunities exist for productive planning and problem solving.

It would be easy and convenient, but unfortunately somewhat myopic, to endorse only one way of doing something—one's own—while wondering why everyone else is not clever enough and agreeable enough to concur and fall into step. But a situation that is interpreted one way by one educator might be perceived in quite a different way by another. In the school setting this reality is an asset for students and help for teachers; however, if such factors are to be used fully, educators must recognize them as assets and capitalize on them. (See Figure 2.1.)

People in all walks of life bring perspectives and preferences to their work. A *perspective* is a mental view of facts and ideas, and seeing the relevant data in meaningful relationships. Perspectives are philosophical in nature—such as reasons for choosing one's profession, one's work ethics, views on what one's role is and what it should be, opinions about how the work should be done, outlook on the value of the work, and much more.

A *preference* is a selection or choice to which one gives priority. Preferences emanate from one's personality and persona (the public role a person assumes or is perceived to assume). Preferences indicate what a person likes better and holds higher than other things. An example would be a preference for making decisions based on facts *or* based on possibilities. Another would be liking to function in a planned and orderly way *or* preferring a flexible and spontaneous way, and yet another is being very aware of others' feelings and wishes when working in groups *or* being more analytical and impersonal toward the task.

People sometimes set aside their own perspectives and preferences for the good of the group. Teachers may do so to foster unanimity or to focus on the general interests of students, schools, or communities. Examples of deferring to other perspectives and preferences can surface in matters of grading systems, or posting of class rules, or adapting tests for stu-

FIGURE 2.1   Sharing Perspectives and Preferences

dents with learning disabilities. But then individuals typically use their own preferred ways of setting up their classroom, or teaching a favorite unit, or deciding to use portfolios, or providing feedback on student work.

Which should be addressed first in studying variables that can affect collaborative consultation and working in teams—professional perspectives or personal preferences? The proverbial chicken decided that it came before the proverbial egg because "chicken" was listed first in the dictionary. But the decision here to begin with professional perspectives is based on the assumption that much teaching philosophy comes from teacher education programs and preservice educators may defer personal preferences while they are learning from others and completing their programs to obtain teacher accreditation. Veteran teachers have a vital role in helping novice teachers develop their philosophical orientations and begin to manage their personal preferences in very professional ways. This is even relevant for college and university instructors of subject-based courses that students of education complete early in their teacher education programs.

A note of caution pertaining to perspectives and preferences is that this kind of information typically is obtained and shared by self-report. So there is always the possibility that such information is more self-serving than candid. But when this caution is kept in mind and the information is solicited in a professional manner as a helpful and positive activity, it need not be a major hindrance to studying perspectives and preferences.

RECOGNIZING DIFFERENCES
IN PROFESSIONAL PERSPECTIVES

In analyzing the problem-solving capacities of groups engaged in various team endeavors, Page (2007) finds that cognitive diversity is at least as important as intelligence in dealing with complex, multidimensional issues. Page further notes that those with different types of disciplinary training bring different tools and diverse understandings to the task. Conoley (1994) states,

> It requires courage to detail differences from the accepted ways of seeing, knowing, and doing. . . . If I say I am interested in learning about the world, but wish to do so in a way that puts a focus on connections, I hope that can be understood as another way. If you say you are interested in learning about the world, but wish to do so in a way that puts a focus on isolated events, I hope that can be understood as just another way. There are many ways to a truth with many faces. (p. 49)

In Chapter 1, a challenge was issued to think of and record 100 or more responsibilities that school personnel perform in their roles of duty. Any lists that were compiled most likely included tasks as varied as making lesson plans, helping individual students, attending staff meetings, conferencing with parents, ordering supplies, and much, much more. What if the challenge were to compile a list of ways in which teachers and all other school personnel can *differ* as they go about these tasks? A place to begin is to consider the plethora of variables that might set educators apart from each other.

■ ■ ■ ■ ■ ▬▬▬▬▬▬▬▬▬▬▬▬▬

APPLICATION 2.1*
IDENTIFYING CO-EDUCATOR DIFFERENCES

Think of important variables that codify differences among co-educators regarding their professional perspectives on teaching and learning and their personal preferences for ways of thinking and methods of doing—for example, years of teaching experience, areas for which certified, age, size of school, rural or urban or suburban or consolidated, and so forth.

Obvious categories in the professional realm would be grade level(s) and curricular areas. In the personal realm one difference could be the dichotomy of introversion or extroversion, or preferring to seek early closure when problem solving over examining more and more possibilities. As suggested in Chapter 1, if this application is done in collaboration with teachers from other grade levels, content areas, school sizes, and so forth, the list that is generated will be even richer.

*This chapter has more application activities than the remaining chapters do. The purpose is to provide an informal means of discovering and discussing differences that matter when educators consult, collaborate, and co-teach. If the applications are not used as group exercises, individuals will still want to read through them to arrive at deeper understanding of the chapter's themes.

General Education and Special Education

The list of differentiating variables in professional perspectives and preferences generated for Application 2.1 undoubtedly included general education as well as special education. This pair surely signals an important distinction among educators.

The need for ongoing dialogue among special education teachers and regular classroom teachers is essential. The days of "them" versus "us" are over, just as the phrase "my students" has been supplanted by newer language that focuses on *our students* in *our classrooms*. Nonetheless, the evidence is not so clear that each faction's role is well understood by the other. More than two decades ago Stainback and Stainback (1985) noted unique differences between regular and special education teachers, and attributed those differences to the preparation they had received for their roles. They felt that variations in teachers' specializations could be used to provide optimal opportunities for every student within one unified educational system. But in inclusive schools, general educators now are an integral part of education for students with disabilities, and many report still feeling unprepared for these responsibilities (Brownell, Adams, Sindelar, Waldron, & Vanhover, 2006).

Collaboration is becoming more widely recognized and promoted as an essential component in enhancing the ability of both general and special co-educators to get prepared. However, teachers whose perspectives differ most significantly are the least likely to collaborate (Brownell et al., 2006). This underscores the importance of having co-educators understand what their colleagues are thinking, feeling, doing, and bringing into the school environment for the instruction of *all* students. As Tiegerman-Farber and Radziewicz (1998) put it, from shared perceptions will come a set of shared expectations for schools and students. Mismatches between teachers, whether between general education and special education, or elementary and secondary, or fine arts and vocational programs, and so on, will create discord and stolidly independent thinking rather than shared problem solving.

Every educator needs to have a "big picture" of both general and special education curriculums, along with state and local standards, instructional approaches for diverse learning needs, ways of aligning goals with curriculum, teaching and behavioral management strategies for special needs, and assessment methods for grading and reporting on outcomes (McDonnell, McLaughlin, & Morrison, 1997; Walsh, 2001). A particularly volatile area is assessment of student achievement, and this has a domino effect on selection and development of curriculum. That said, curriculum for both special education and general education must guide assessment; assessment must *not* drive curriculum! Learning and behavioral goals and assessments are issues yet to be resolved in the backwash of NCLB and they must not be allowed to discourage co-educators from collaborating and co-teaching.

It is up to school administrators, counselors, school psychologists, experienced teachers, and parents to increase their own understandings of valid learning goals, assessment processes, scoring procedures, and grading philosophies, and promote the right practices for the right reasons. These understandings can be built through staff development activities, collaborative endeavors, and informal consultative dialogues. Walsh (2001) asserts that one major decision to be made by both general and special education teachers is what is *not* absolutely necessary for all students to learn in order to meet high content standards. The foundation for such understanding should be laid in teacher preparation programs before new teachers enter the hustle and bustle of school life and their first classroom where they will have immediate responsibilities for making decisions relevant to curriculum and assessment.

Novice teachers bring many assets to their first professional assignments. They are enthusiastic and eager to put into practice the ideas they have been accumulating for some time. They have been exposed to the most recent educational theories, methods, and materials. Many completed their student teaching assignments under the supervision of master teachers in excellent schools. But knowledge does not become wisdom without experience. A major difference between the novice and the veteran teacher, whether in general education or special education, is the experience that informs well so one can make decisions such as, "Yes, this is a promising plan," or "No, we don't want to try it with that student."

Grade Levels and Curriculum Areas

Grade-level differences among elementary and secondary teachers may be less likely than general and special education differences to interfere with collaborative enterprises; however, there are times that districtwide groups do come together for the purpose of aligning curriculum to state standards, or designing testing programs to comply with NCLB, or adopting a districtwide textbook series. Professional perspectives among preschool, elementary, middle school, and high school teachers also can vary considerably in regard to classroom organization and management of learning and behavior.

One timeworn cliché in comparing elementary and secondary teaching is that "secondary teachers teach content and elementary teachers teach kids." Perhaps this is a flawed assumption in need of revision. Young children are curious about the world and hunger for interesting subject matter, while teens crave interaction with peers, especially their friends. Professional development activities could be designed that provide K–12 curricular emphasis on richer content for elementary-age children and more creative use of social structures for adolescent learning.

Curricular-area differences also affect schedules in ways that impinge on collaboration and professional development experiences. Physical education teachers may request to be excused from much of the staff development because of their coaching duties and supervision of sports events. Vocational teacher classrooms and shops often are housed well apart from the other classrooms. Science projects and needed monitoring may spill over into other class periods, causing schedules and patience levels to fray. Music, debate, and academic competition groups are away several times during the year to take part in competitions and performances. Such realities make the scheduling of collaborative consultation and professional development activities especially difficult at the secondary level.

More Differences of Perspective

Other areas of variability among teachers that may surface when they gather to consult and collaborate, and particularly when they plan co-teaching strategies, include practices involving:

- Homework: how much, how often, and what kind
- Pull-out or pull-in sessions for students that deviate from normal classsroom procedures

- Whether to make up work missed during pull-out sessions
- Use of test accommodations and modifications for students with disabilities
- Grading policies
- Whether to allow do-over work for full or partial credit
- Time-out, positive and negative reinforcement, and contract contingencies
- Frequency and type of parent involvement in the classroom
- Noise and activity levels within the classroom
- Appearance and upkeep of classrooms, especially shared learning areas
- Being the only one on the teaching staff who is a teacher but *not* a parent too, or vice versa
- Styles of interfacing with co-educators and conducting classroom observations
- Affinity for using a system of student portfolios as a means of authentic assessment and involving students in development of the portfolio rubrics
- Spending personal money for classroom teaching supplies, a practice looked on with disfavor by some teachers who cannot or will not do it, with occasional fallout of parental requests to have their child assigned to the better-supplied classroom[3]

Principles of Learning

What to do, then, toward sorting out and managing differences in professional perspectives to compose a suitable plan for working together? At the outset there must be understanding among co-educators on two broad aspects of learning.

The first is simply this: *Variation in achievement among students cannot be eliminated.* The only ways in which it could be done would be to speed up less able students by artificial, unethical means, and to slow down very able students, again unethically, by withholding opportunities to learn. Both of these options are, of course, totally unacceptable. There are no Lake Wobegons where all students are above average, and no federal mandates, preschool programs, master plans for parent involvement, or rigorous teaching programs that can erase this reality of differences in achievement.

The second reality is this: *Good teaching will increase individual differences in achievement among students.* This is because students with less ability and those with disabilities *will* learn, while those with more ability will learn even more *if* not held back by teaching practices and school policies that pull performance expectations to the middle. When educators make peace with this reality, they are empowered to move on in constructive ways that will benefit all students (Hanna & Dettmer, 2004). However, if collaborating educators are not in congruence with these two principles, their efforts toward working together will be off balance from the start.

Educators must internalize, reflect on, accept, and teach within these two realities: differences in achievement cannot be eliminated, and good teaching will increase those differences.

---

[3]A National Education Association survey indicates teachers spend an average of $1,180 on classroom materials for a year, with current federal law (soon to expire) providing a $250 deduction for supplies (*Topeka Capital-Journal,* August 23, 2007).

Next to be considered are the eight areas that form an educator's day-to-day professional perspectives. Any one of the eight can introduce stumbling blocks on the road to successful consultation and collaboration. They are:

1. Types of learning theory
2. Kinds of subject matter
3. Types of instructional goals
4. Orientations in time and achievement levels
5. Kinds of tests
6. Types of scores
7. Interpretations of scores
8. Domains for learning and doing, with transfer of the learning

If co-educators differ markedly in these areas and do not work through their differences, well-meaning efforts to collaborate and co-teach will indeed cause them to falter in the rocky terrain. These perspectives most likely were formed in teacher preparation programs if not brought into the programs by students, and perhaps were fuzzily formed during school experiences as children. Then, too, experiences in parenting or being parented can affect outlooks on principles of teaching and learning.

Types of Learning Theory.   Learning theory frames expectations for achievement, construction of instructional objectives, and methods of assessment. For our purposes here, the focus will be on three predominant types of learning theory—cognitive, behavioral, and social. Each of these types is appropriate in some contexts and not so well suited in others (Hanna & Dettmer, 2004). This differentiation in suitability and usefulness is too often overlooked or, at the least, only minimally addressed in teacher preparation programs, especially at the undergraduate level.

Special education teachers have learned and practiced many behavioral principles. So have some general education teachers. However, many of the latter still prefer the cognitive theory or social cognitive theory approach to instruction for most students. Preservice teachers may have been swayed into an either-or situation to the extent that they profess they are a "behaviorist" or a "cognitivist." But when they collaborate with other educators to identify student needs and plan instruction for the needs, they may find that their "language" is not being used, or perhaps two "languages" are being spoken. One co-educator might focus on observation, reinforcement conditions for modifying behaviors, responses, prerequisite skills, instructional sequencing, and observable criteria for measurement as in behavioral theory. Another may feature mental constructs, active processing of information, reinforcement as a means of providing information, and construction of knowledge. A third may speak in terms of a co-constructed process in which people interact and negotiate to understand, apply, and problem solve, with intersubjectivity (to be addressed in Chapter 3) to guide the teaching and learning. The dissonance among these three perspectives (behavioral, cognitive, and social) and others that have been conceived can put even an experienced teacher off balance and may be especially confusing to a novice teacher who erroneously thinks the choice must be either-or.

Three Kinds of Subject Matter.   Subject matter can be channeled helpfully into one of three kinds—essential, developmental, or ideational. Each kind has its place in a well-designed curriculum at all age and ability levels and in all content areas. The distinctions among the three will mold teacher expectations for student achievement, and the goal setting, instructional strategies, and assessment methods to help fulfill those expectations. They also will influence markedly teacher-student, teacher-teacher, and teacher-family interactions. Here again, differences of perspective are molded to some extent by the educator's affiliation with a general or special education focus, the grade levels, curricular areas, preferred school of learning theory, teaching styles, and preferred assessment methods.

Essential subject matter is that which is at the most basic and clear-cut level within a closed, fixed sphere for learning. The objectives can be described with specificity and the material is to be mastered by students. This content is the basis for further learning; it can be used in similar situations through low-road transfer. Teachers instruct with well-defined material and students are to learn the material in its entirety. Time is allocated for mastery; if the material is not learned, compensatory activities are provided to help. Examples of essential content to be mastered include:

- Toilet training and recognition of colors for the preschool set
- Letters of the alphabet and simple sight words for kindergarten/primary grades
- Times tables and assigned spelling words for intermediate grades
- Traffic signs and symbols, standard keyboard position, procedure for setting up a microscope, music symbols and notation, target of completing a lap in a relay, or rules for baseball as examples for continuation of essential learning

Teachers of students with learning disabilities or developmental disability formulate many goals using this type of curriculum material. It is taught and learned for mastery.

The second kind of subject matter is *developmental*. It is specifiable but expansive to the extent that it either cannot be fully mastered or it need not be fully mastered in order to continue to learn and do. With developmental material, variable levels of achievement among students are to be expected. *All* students must have opportunities to learn many things at the developmental level. Examples of developmental content would be naming the capitals of all countries of the world (possible but is it essential?), listing all vice presidents of the United States (again, possible, but does it really need to be transferred to any other situation?), learning volleyball techniques (when can all possibilities ever be learned?), welding a metal joint (what is perfection?), or baking a soufflé (and who among the best chefs attains mastery at this?) This material is taught for only as much achievement as possible or deemed reasonable and necessary.

Lastly, *ideational* subject matter is neither specifiable nor masterable. This sphere of learning is broad, open-ended, and novel. Diverse outcomes and wide ranges of achievement among students are expected. Transfer of learning is at a high level; ideational material can be transferred to new situations calling for complex problem solving and innovation. Only a representation of the immense range of material is taught, and only some of what was taught is tested. Some instructed content is *not* tested, and some content that was not taught but is related to the topic *is* tested to find out if there is transfer of learning to more complex problems or new situations.

Educators with an orientation toward cognitive theory are quite comfortable with ideational subject matter and teachers of students with high aptitude "live here" when planning instruction for students' needs as dictated by their advanced abilities. The classrooms of such teachers are likely to provide learning centers and encourage independent studies. Group discussions with no predetermined outcomes are a vehicle for stimulating learning. Examples of ideational content would be to show in picture format how addition and multiplication are related, or to collect and record data from a square yard of ground in an outdoor area, or to illustrate an infringement on human rights that are provided by a particular amendment to the U.S. Constitution, or to plan a nutritional menu for a month on a given budget, or to apply principles of energy production and conservation to the concept of global warming. Material here is never masterable and learning is ongoing.

Differences in professional perspective emanating from general and education and special education, grade levels, learning theory orientations, and subject-matter realms can have significant effects on collaboration, consultation, and teamwork, and especially for co-teaching teams. These effects may be deleterious or, with respect, understanding, and accommodation, and perhaps a bit of humor mixed in, they can invigorate teaching practices and stimulate student efforts as well.

Annual Goals and Instructional Objectives.   Principles related to learning theories and subject-matter contexts will frame the kinds of goals and objectives that are formulated. They direct teachers in lesson planning and inevitably surface in arenas such as textbook selection meetings and IEP conferences, creating another distinct difference in professional perspective between special education and general education teachers.

Special education teachers are well schooled in Mager-type (Mager, 1997) behavioral objectives that indicate how attainment of goals and objectives will be sought and assessed, so they tend to construct annual goals that outline behaviors, conditions, and achievement levels to be met. The goals include: (1) an observable student behavior, (2) conditions for demonstrating the behavior, and (3) the minimal level of attainment expected.

General education teachers may have been exposed to Mager-based principles and they are required under the reauthorized IDEA legislation to attend some IEP conferences where this process for annual goal development is put into practice. But many prefer to use Gronlund-based instructional objectives (Gronlund, 2000) for instruction in developmental and ideational subject matter—those large, expansive bodies of content with no endpoint achievement levels. Because such goals are not easily measured, several indicants are provided for each instructional objective that have measurable verbs to sample behaviors for determining student progress. This distinction between goal types—Mager-based and Gronlund-based—has been sharpened by legislation such as P.L. 94-142 and by methods emphasized in teacher education literature. Much of the special education curriculum calls for mastery-type learning of essential subject matter, if only to ensure measurability of progress on IEP goals. This disadvantages students with disabilities unless they also have opportunities to learn and do with developmental and ideational subject matter as well. Effective teachers will make sure they provide those opportunities.

Achievement of broad instructional objectives with measurable indicants and measurable goals as called for in IEPs must be assessed by reliable and valid means to show progress—first and foremost to show the adequate yearly progress (AYP) as mandated by

NCLB, for each student and every school. But ideational goals and most developmental goals are not strictly measurable by efficient means such as paper-and-pencil tests. Evidence of achievement must be determined by authentic assessments carefully designed to demonstrate that progress has been made toward meeting the goals. Only basic, essential goals that can be met by recognition and recall of learned information are objectively measurable in reliable and practical ways. The rub in all of this is that to determine progress toward measurable annual *goals,* the curriculum needs to be simplistically masterable. Building curriculum only on easily measured goals severely shortchanges students in special education programs who need and are entitled to opportunities for learning broad, open-ended, interesting, and novel content.

What to do? As a start, to buy the needed instructional time for students who must learn apart from the class or leave the classroom periodically for remedial or practice sessions in a resource room, some of the IEP goals should be embedded into instruction for the general education curriculum. Then some broad, high-road transfer goals for students should be incorporated into both the general education and special education curriculum. If this does not happen, there will not be enough time in the school day to provide all the learning opportunities to which students with special needs are entitled. This reality makes collaboration between special education and general education teachers even more imperative. All students must have opportunities to achieve at deep levels regardless of disability or cultural or linguistic diversity; instructional objectives must be interpreted as *minimal* statements of expectations and not the outer limits of the learning (Hanna & Dettmer, 2004).

Students who learn differently or happen to have learning difficulties must not be *left* behind (NCLB), and students with high aptitude should not be *held* behind (NC*H*B). Consultation and collaboration, with linkage to other educational resources, can help ensure that all students have opportunities to learn, to develop their potential, and to explore their unique interests. Discussions among collaborative school consultants about this issue could have profound motivational influences and positive effects on higher-order learning of students with disabilities and behavioral problems. Collaboration becomes more and more valued and sought after when co-educators see it working to the benefit of students.

Time and Achievement Dimensions.   As teachers make decisions about the complexity of the subject matter to be taught and develop annual goals or instructional objectives for student learning, they must determine whether the instruction will be set in a time dimension or an achievement dimension. In other words, will all students be expected to master essential goals and be given time to do so before they can move on to other content? Will all students also have developmental or ideational goals that need not or cannot be mastered, with the expectation that achievement among students will vary? Here again, differences among cooperating teachers can have a fractious effect on collaborative efforts. But it need not be that way.

Essential material typically is framed in a time dimension, with correctives provided if and when students cannot master the material in the time allowed. In the past, this has often been the point at which the special education teacher assists with interventions in anticipation that the student can and must learn the material in order to move on with the class.

Conversely, developmental subject matter and most assuredly ideational material should be set in the achievement dimension. Students will *not* need to stay with that material until it is mastered because mastery is not sought and variance in student achievement is to be expected. This is the juncture at which co-educators must meet and plan learning opportunities for all students to have in learning developmental and ideational kinds of subject matter. Put another way and reiterating previous statements, no student with disabilities should be denied access to higher levels of thinking and doing; in fact, a case could be made that they need such instruction *more* than students who can function successfully in a more or less self-directed fashion. Collaborators must take such concerns into account when they plan instruction for students who have been achieving slowly or at low levels. Their collective aim must not be to expect students of lesser and greater ability to "come together at the middle," but rather to have high expectations for all students. Then design curriculum that helps all students master what is truly essential and move on to opportunities for learning at more complex levels to the greatest extent of which they are capable. Alas, NCLB has fueled much of the pressure to "teach so as to bring everyone to the middle" and then administer high-stakes tests to "see if they got there," much to the detriment of all students and the frustrations of teachers, parents, and school administrators, not to mention the deleterious effects on having a rich, broad-based curriculum. Once again, there is no Lake Wobegon.

Assessment and Evaluation Processes.   The next three types of professional perspectives are intertwined and therefore are grouped for discussion. They are purposes of tests, types of scores, and interpretations of scores. Professional differences in these components of assessment, along with political pressures from inside and outside the schools, are extremely important factors for working together successfully and in actuality they can be divisive without careful, collaborative exchanges of views.

Tests are administered to students in one of two manners, either to ascertain level of achievement on stated criteria, or to determine achievement in relation to others. So tests are either mastery tests or differentiating tests and they will yield scores that are criterion referenced or domain referenced. Criterion-referenced scores relate to specifiable content that was learned, while domain-referenced scores relate to broad spheres of learning and are compared with scores obtained by a well-identified and relevant group of people.

Teachers may teach to the test for mastery testing; in fact, they *should* inform students precisely what they will be tested on and then provide appropriate instruction so that every student has every opportunity to master the material and be prepared "to ace" the test. Students need to know what they will be accountable for and then they need to know whether they succeeded.

Conversely, teachers must *not* teach explicit content for a differentiating, or discriminatory, test. They must teach for learning and doing that extends beyond recall and comprehension (low-road transfer) so that students can apply broad, open-ended content (with high-road transfer) to new problems and novel situations. The instruction must be excellent, of course, and expectations for student achievement must be held high. But co-educators need to acknowledge that the tests are intended to differentiate between students who have learned (or, it must be said, in many instances already knew) the material, and those who have not, and then compare their achievement with that of others in an appropriate reference group. Comparisons are sought so that useful decisions can be made. These may be to determine class rankings, or facilitate entry to advanced programs or higher education, or award scholarships. But in a more immediate and practical vein, important decisions can be made about planning and pacing instruction, grouping or not grouping students, referring students to testing for special education programs, selecting appropriate materials for continued learning, and much more that could not be obtained from the limited information provided by mastery tests over specified material in closed content domains.

Interpretation of test scores can expose important professional differences among educators. In reality, many educators are not well enough acquainted with methods of score interpretation. Too many have never had formal instruction in measurement and testing; unfortunately this is especially true among preservice teachers who do not even have experience on which to rely for making their decisions.

Scores fall into two main types. First, there are raw scores and the closely related percentage scores that are suitable for interpreting scores on domain-referenced material where content is clear-cut and is to be mastered. Meaning can be ascribed to progress on such material by noting a raw score such as 8 out of 10 words spelled correctly, for example, or 90 percent of the 20 assigned arithmetic problems worked correctly.

Derived scores compare student achievement with that of others. They are discriminatory by design, to discriminate between those who have learned the material and those who have not. (Note that *discriminate* is a psychometric term referring to comparisons of *scores* and is not to be confused with the odious use of the word in stereotyping or prejudice toward *people*.) Scores on discriminatory, norm-referenced tests can be reported by several means, some more satisfactory than others: grade equivalencies (G.E.) or age equivalencies (A–E); ranks and percentile ranks; and standard scores such as deviation IQs, stanines, z-scores, T-scores, and normal curve equivalencies (NCEs).

Professional differences about scores and their interpretations can cause serious friction among co-educators because scores are used for evaluations, placements, grades, school reports to the public, communications with parents, and even assessments of teaching. Most school administrators would not look favorably on teachers who awarded all A grades for every student, nor would they do so on teachers whose composite of student grades never rose above D. They would begin to look at the teacher's planning and instruction as too limited or too demanding.

Unfortunately, score interpretations are often arrived at in a flawed manner and can result in quite misleading information. Just a few of the more flawed and sensitivity-laden issues include:

■ *Using percentages to score nonmasterable material.* The folly of this practice can be challenged by asking, "Let's see. That score is 70 percent of what?" which is of course unanswerable for open-ended subject matter. A score of 70 percent on the week's spelling list makes sense, but a score stating that a student achieved 70 percent on important, globe-encircling causes and effects of World War II does not. So a rigid system of percentage grading would lock content into the mastery mode where only simple, essential material is taught.

■ *Confusing percentile scores with percentages.* Percentiles put scores into rank file for comparison with others in a group selected for the comparison. That could be last year's similar classes, this year's multiple sections of the same class, districtwide classes of the same subject and grade level, national averages, and so forth. Percentiles are easily understood by students and their parents, but because they do represent ranks, they cannot be summed and averaged in grade books.

■ *Using grade and age equivalencies.* Most uses of G.E.s and A–Es are ill advised because they lead to serious misinterpretations by parents and sometimes even by teachers and administrators. As just one example, a parent might ask, "If my fifth-grader scored at the eighth-grade level in both math and reading, shouldn't she be advanced to the eighth grade, or at least elevated to eighth-grade math and reading curriculum?" This requires backpedaling and searching for reasonable explanations by the teacher to parents, so this score type is better avoided.

■ *Grading on the curve.* Some teachers cling to this very questionable but frequently employed practice for assigning letter grades, and alas, some school district policies dictate that it be used. Many school handbooks can attest to this practice although it is a misuse of student evaluation and an abuse of the learning process. The policy is harshly inappropriate because learning is not a zero-sum game with just so much learning to go around. When teachers announce before testing, and sometimes even before their instruction, that grade distributions will contain one or two As, for example, and X number of Bs, Cs, Ds, and perhaps Fs, effects on student learning will be many and mostly negative.

Achievement cannot be packaged into tidy, preordained "amounts" if students are to be interested and motivated to learn. Where there is grading on the curve, they will concentrate instead on competing and "taking away" from others. Some will withdraw from even trying to learn. The resultant peer pressure, not to mention the damper on learning, will be debilitating to motivation and interpersonal relations among students who feel they must compete to "bump" others for the few top grades and stay away from the inevitable bottom of the distribution. No clearer message for *not* collaborating and working together could be sent. Collaborating teachers can forget about demonstrating collegiality and shared effort if they adopt this evaluation perspective.

So again, what to do? One solution to the grading issue is to use a system such as modified percentage grading that does not link grades to the top student, but employs a covert kind of norm-referencing system instead. This process would anchor a class's scores to other groups, as was explained in regard to percentiles, and allow for adjustments to be made by the teacher so grade distributions come out as experienced teachers sense that they should. Preservice teachers typically have little assessment experience and they have no previous reference groups to draw on, but they can learn much in collaboration with veteran teachers to guide their novitiate grading processes. It could very well be that the entire teaching staff and perhaps even some interested parents would welcome an opportunity for consultation and professional development services directed toward the important teaching responsibility of assessment and evaluation.

■ *Assessment adaptations for students with disabilities.* Adaptations can be made through accommodations or modifications of testing procedures. Accommodations are changes in regular test conditions, and modifications are techniques that change the test to make it different from others in the group. These special education practices have important educational, social, and legal ramifications that must be understood by school administrators and general classroom teachers as well as special education and resource personnel. Collaborative consultation is a fitting process for examining all aspects of these complex issues and potential adaptations of professional perspective in order to make right decisions.

■ *Portfolios for assessment.* Portfolios have special appeal for teachers who value authentic data drawn from across a wide variety of curricular and behavioral areas. Some are especially keen on having student involvement in the portfolio assessment process. One could say that portfolios are evidence of what students *did* learn and do, rather than what they did *not* do correctly on a test. However, some educators are not so enthusiastic about this method of assessment for several reasons. A major concern is the need for well-designed rubrics to measure progress or goal attainment. As Bloom, Englehart, Furst, Hill, & Krathwohl (1956) found when working to develop good tests, they first needed to design good learning goals. In similar fashion, co-educators would find that development of rubrics and goal setting could be complementary processes in IEP conferences. It also would be good cause for having students involved in at least a portion of the IEP conference that is, after all, about them and their interests and needs.

To briefly summarize professional perspectives presented up to this point, seven of the eight main topics have been discussed: learning theory, subject matter, goals and objectives, time and achievement orientations, tests, scores, and score interpretations. A specialist in learning theory, curriculum, or assessment might be called on to help collaborating colleagues arbitrate differences in these seven areas and others that may come to light. The eighth topic just ahead will focus on taxonomies for domains of learning and doing. The process of talking about differing professional perspectives of co-educators can be stimulating and enlightening, and oftentimes discussants feel they have become more united in educational areas that really matter.

It must be said, however, that occasionally it will be necessary for collaborating colleagues simply to agree to disagree on one or more topics and then move on with confidence in the knowledge that their decisions have been made together after much thought and discussion, and represent the very best ones that could be made at that time under those circumstances for *their* students. This would not mean that collaboration and consultation failed and it should not discourage co-educators from seeking out other ways of coming together in the future to revisit the issues. Indeed, follow-through and follow-up processes, to be discussed in Chapter 5, may result in movement from extreme positions toward more collaborative perspectives with the passage of time and perhaps some well-targeted professional development activity.

Taxonomies for Thinking and Doing

People learn facts and comprehend material; then they apply their knowledge and understanding to accomplish what they need and want to do. The learning and doing occur within four domains—the cognitive domain of thinking, the affective domain of feeling, the physical domain of absorbing and performing, and the social domain of relating to others.

Activity in each of these domains can range from simple to complex, having potential for low-road transfer to similar material and situations or opportunity for high-road transfer to new material and novel situations.

The integrated domains of thinking, feeling, doing, and interacting provide a fertile field for co-educators to co-plan, co-instruct, and co-evaluate student learning. Understanding the hierarchical levels is requisite for designing differentiated curriculum for all students, and particularly those with exceptional learning needs. So they are addressed here in abbreviated form and with some alterations. To wit, the cognitive and affective domains are extended by two and three levels respectively, the physical domain is revised and becomes a sensorimotor domain, and a newly developed taxonomy for the social domain is added.

Taxonomy of the Cognitive Domain.   *Taxonomy of Educational Objectives, Handbook I: Cognitive Domain* (Bloom et al., 1956) is one of the most frequently cited publications in all of the educational literature. It was developed initially with an aim toward improving tests, but the developers soon realized that in order to do that they needed first to develop a classification system for instructional objectives.

The six categories of the very familiar cognitive domain are described briefly as (Hanna & Dettmer, 2004):

1. *Knowledge:* Recall or recognition of facts, principles, methods, and the like. This area of learning is essential, of course; however, recall is overemphasized in most classroom instruction.
2. *Comprehension:* Understanding of meaning as demonstrated by explaining or paraphrasing. This category does not facilitate deep understanding and also tends to receive an inappropriately large proportion of instructional time.
3. *Application:* Use of ideas, rules, or principles in new situations and to facilitate real-life problem solving.
4. *Analysis:* Taking apart components of a concept to find the relationships among those parts.
5. *Synthesis:* Putting elements together in new ways within limits set by the given framework.
6. *Evaluation:* Assessment and purposeful judgments of goals, ideas, methods, products, or materials.

Bloom's taxonomy for the cognitive domain has been helpful in making educators aware that a great proportion of instruction is directed toward simple recall of facts and explaining or restating learned material. Surprisingly, this is more characteristic of secondary schools than elementary schools. As much as 80 percent to 90 percent of high school learning can be classified as thinking at the very basic knowledge or comprehension levels, while content that has rich potential for transfer of learning, such as application, analysis, synthesis, and evaluation, is bypassed in favor of more simplistic and more easily assessed drill, practice, and regurgitation (Hanna & Dettmer, 2004). The emphasis on lower-level learning hampers development of complex skills of thinking and doing and stifles potential for creative thinking and production.

All students, regardless of disabilities or aptitudes, are entitled to be taught and encouraged to learn at levels of analysis and evaluation, and beyond that to synthesis and innovation. Educators must have high expectations for *all* students whether in general education, education of gifted students, or special education for students with disabilities and developmental delays.

Taxonomy of the Affective Domain.   In 1964 Krathwohl, Bloom, and Masia directed the development of the *Taxonomy of Educational Objectives, Handbook II: Affective Domain*. The original committee had recognized the need for addressing affective functions, but had been discouraged by the difficulty of designing ways to measure them.

It is logical that cognitive and affective domains are components of learning and doing. The classification scheme's five categories for the affective domain (Krathwohl et al., 1964), are again ordered from simplest to most complex. Briefly described, they are (Hanna & Dettmer, 2004):

1. *Receiving:* Being aware of something or someone in the environment and attending at least passively.
2. *Responding:* Reacting to the environment and responding to elements within that environment.
3. *Valuing:* Showing commitment by responding voluntarily and seeking out ways to respond.
4. *Organization:* Integrating knowledge and applying information to something regarded as important.
5. *Characterization by a Value or Value Complex:* Organizing values into a whole and acting in accordance with newly acquired values or beliefs.

Extending the Cognitive and Affective Taxonomies.   Developers of the cognitive domain taxonomy did not promote their work as the be-all and end-all for processes of thinking and doing. They disdained fragmentation of educational purposes and aimed to set the taxonomy at a level of generality that allowed for flexibility and growth. They hoped not to abort teachers' thinking and development of curriculum, and they surely did not wish for the taxonomies to be used as recipes, which nevertheless some teachers since that time have been prone to do. They thought of the taxonomies as fluid and unfinished, and encouraged more thought and development of the concepts.

Rereading the original works and pondering significances of their profoundly important ideas can be a rewarding professional development exercise or collaborative experience for educators that may lead to new ideas about teaching and learning. For example, since the original cognitive and affective domains were conceptualized, interest in creativity has expanded, generating increased research on having creative thinking and development of original products be an important part of school curriculum. Imagination is a cognitive and affective tool with which students explore how the world works in wonderful and mysterious ways (Dettmer, 2006). Therefore, stimulating the imagination should not be treated as a recreational activity left for that bit of extra time before the dismissal bell or as a reward for getting the "real work" done, but regarded as a means of enhancing the educational value of any lesson.

With this in mind, it follows that the cognitive taxonomy can be expanded appropriately to include categories for imagination and creativity. Then because cognitive activities of imagination and creativity are accompanied by affective components, the categories of *wonder* (in using one's imagination) and *aspire* (aiming for and accepting risks to create a new entity) fit well into the affective domain. Finally, a logical category to add to the existing affective domain as a parallel to evaluation in the existing cognitive domain is *internalize*. Parallelism of domain levels was not intended by the original developers, but it seems to be a natural condition in most, albeit not all, situations so as to seem balanced. Nor does one level have to precede or succeed another; for example, people often vote (evaluation) without doing much analysis and synthesis of information that could make their vote a more informed evaluation. And young people who are especially vulnerable to peer pressure may characterize and internalize affectively without carefully organizing their values.

The taxonomic levels need not be adhered to rigidly. However, a useful line of demarcation can be drawn between low-road thinking and feeling (knowledge and comprehension, receiving and responding) and high-road thinking and feeling (everything else).

Here is a brief listing of key words for categories in both domains as altered to include the enhancements:

- *Cognitive*—know, comprehend, apply, analyze, synthesize, evaluate, imagine, create
- *Affective*—receive, respond, value, organize, characterize, internalize, wonder, aspire

Taxonomy of the Sensorimotor Domain.   When Bloom et al. (1956) presented the cognitive taxonomy and later on the affective taxonomy that was developed by Krathwohl et al. (1964), these groups made little mention of physical development. But in the years since that time there has been increasing attention to motor skills needed for areas such as athletics, art, industry, and technology and to the sensing elements that are critical to the learning process. Several psychomotor taxonomies have appeared, including those developed by Simpson (1972) and Harrow (1972). However, such taxonomies did not emphasize the senses as integral components of motor skills. Senses are especially important to teachers of students who are challenged because of disabilities in hearing, seeing, smelling, touching, tasting, speaking, feeling, moving, being still, staying in balance, having highly elevated sensitivities and movements, and difficulties with other sensorimotor-based activities.

So a taxonomy for the physical realm should not be limited to motor activity. In the school curriculum a physical perspective needs to include sensory input, with attention to sight, sound, touch, taste, and smell, and perhaps other elements not yet included such as balance and sensitivity, in the school curriculum. Many teachers, particularly at the primary levels, do this already because they realize the importance of sensory input for learning. A taxonomic structure that moves beyond the psychomotor realm in order to include sensorimotor functions can be organized into eight levels (Dettmer, 2006):

1. *Observe*—Use the senses to notice
2. *React*—Show recognition with senses and/or movement

3. *Act*—Become involved by demonstrating physical and sensory response
4. *Adapt*—Adjust sensorimotor activity to fit unfamiliar situations
5. *Authenticate*—Assess validity of particular sensorimotor processes for conditions and purposes
6. *Harmonize*—Integrate sensorimotor activities into existing situations
7. *Improvise*—Develop new aspects of sensorimotor response for problem solving
8. *Innovate*—Construct new, self-expressive sensorimotor actions and solutions

Taxonomy of the Social Domain.   The social realm is an aspect of learning and doing that has been relegated to even greater benign neglect than the sensorimotor domain. Teachers and students relate to each other continuously in sociocultural settings. They develop networks of relationships in richly interactive in-school and after-school or extracurricular environments. Some of the most serious student behavioral problems occur in this domain. Layers of relationship are somewhat hierarchical; they can be arranged into an eight-category taxonomy for a social domain. The categories, described in more detail here than the previous three because they apply significantly to consultation, collaboration, and teamwork, are (Dettmer, 2006; Hanna & Dettmer, 2004):

1. *Relating.* Acknowledging the presence of others, making eye contact, attending to their words or actions, and showing acceptance of others.
2. *Communicating.* Sending or receiving messages from others to speak, gesture, call, sign, signal, listen. The most overlooked aspect of the communication process, to be discussed in Chapter 4, is *listening.* Messages are sent verbally and nonverbally, with body language often being the more powerful of these two types.
3. *Participating.* Joining in, volunteering for, going along with, or actively and willingly taking part in group activities. Much of school life previews later life and careers when belonging to and taking part in groups is a vital function.
4. *Negotiating.* Negotiating often takes place informally. Mediation and arbitration are extensions of negotiation and a means of setting aside singularly personal preferences to accommodate and assimilate those of others.
5. *Collaborating.* Working together for success of the group or the project. Teamwork conducted in a collaborative climate is a necessary quality in family, career, and community life for the twenty-first century.
6. *Adjudicating.* Conciliating with others and settling differences when they arise. Conciliation is an outcome of effective mediation and arbitration efforts. Those who collaborate, communicate, and negotiate effectively in social settings are more able to mediate differences to the benefit of all.
7. *Initiating.* Creating opportunities and processes for interactions, even if social risks are involved, in order to catalyze social action and change.
8. *Converting.* Constructing social transitions and convincing others to join in for social aims that can benefit all.

Contributions of the Four Taxonomies to Teaching and Learning.   Taxonomies in education are tools for focusing on levels of instruction that help educators plan for student learning in stimulating, challenging, future-oriented ways. Taxonomies guide the assessment process so as to be facilitative, not punitive. When teaching a concept at the basic (knowledge and comprehension) levels (for example, the times tables) and expecting students to attend to the lesson (by receiving it and responding to it), instructors will allow sufficient time for learning the material at preestablished, announced competency levels. If the material cannot be mastered and learners must move on, reteaching and correctives are employed. In this event *extending activities must be made available* for those who do not need to "mark time' or as one student described it, "rev my motor with my brakes on." Collaborative consultation among teachers and resource personnel is invaluable in these circumstances that call for curriculum differentiation.

As collaborating teachers plan together, they should discuss how to enhance student growth in critical thinking and creative thinking skills and help students develop tolerance for differing points of view. When lesson objectives are aimed at higher-order thinking, instructors should designate a level of achievement that is reasonable for open-ended, never-ending learning—for example, second-graders keeping logs of interesting words to use in creative writing activities, or high school students' evaluation of benefits of various power sources for an energy-hungry nation, or middle school students' comparisons of the needs for harvesting raw materials such as tree logs with the need to protect endangered species such as fish or owls. Then they determine the point in time at which the class must move on, thereby accepting the reality of varying levels of achievement among the group.

When the objectives for learning focus on creativity and innovation, with wonder and risk taking as affective components, teachers, mentors, and content-area specialists need to provide flexible time limits and suspend expectations for specific levels of achievement. If they feel inadequate to critique students' work and provide constructive feedback in specialized areas, they will want to call in experts and outside resources personnel to consult and collaborate with them and with the students. Students are major participants in planning the curriculum and assessing their performance at this level, with collaborative team effort taking place among all.

THINKING AND DOING TOGETHER BUT IN DIFFERENT WAYS

The previous section outlined and discussed several ways educators can differ markedly with regard to their professional perspectives. Educators do not need to think alike—they just need to think *together*. The process of thinking together divergently is not an oxymoron. It is an intriguing process that can be very productive. Understanding the unique orientations of others toward the world and the work they do in it, and valuing their individual preferences and perspectives, are key factors in having successful collegial relationships. Educators who make conscientious efforts to respect the individualism and independence of their students need also to respect and value these rights for their school-based colleagues and other co-educators including students' parents.

APPLICATION 2.2
WHAT IS YOUR PERSPECTIVE?

In groups of three or four persons, allow three minutes to discuss each of these questions. (All should expect to participate, but occasionally a person may wish to pass.)

Would you rather teach in a general education classroom or a special education resource room, and why?

In order to improve behavior, do you favor positive reinforcement techniques with contingencies or talking and reasoning with students to improve behavior?

Do you think students should be allowed to redo work and receive full credit or partial credit for the redo, or not be allowed to redo work at all?

Assuming both teachers would grade fairly, do you want to be perceived by students as "a tough grader" or as "an easy grader"?

What is your perspective on teaming up a student with disabilities and a student with advanced aptitude as study-buddies or tutor-tutee or members of a cooperative learning group?

Do you think teachers should supplement teaching materials with their own resources?

Then the whole group shares some interesting and helpful things they learned from the discussion. They may even generate more either-or questions to discuss.

One of the most overlooked but crucial factors in teacher preparation is the ability to relate constructively to others, including colleagues, by responding to differences among them with emotional maturity (Jersild, 1955). Well-known educator Madeline Hunter urged teachers to move toward dialectical thinking. This would not mean abandoning one's own position, but building correction into one's personal viewpoints by taking the opposing view *momentarily*. Hunter urged all to "come out of armed camps . . . where we're not collaborating, so that 'I understand why you think it's necessary for your students to line up while I think it's better for them to come in casually'" (Hunter, 1985, p. 3). She stressed that when educators show respect for others' points of view, they model the cooperation and resilience that students need to learn for their lives and careers in the future.

Several years later, in addressing the challenge of studying collaboration, John-Steiner, Weber, and Minnis (1998) asserted that if an account of collaboration fails to examine differences, especially ones related to tension and conflict of pivotal importance to successful collaboration, the process cannot be fully understood. Thinking back to some of the most potentially divisive issues within this chapter, educators should make efforts to respect different points of view even when they disagree, and to temper their interactions by *demonstrating* tolerance and *conveying* genuine interest in and appreciation for other ways of doing things.

Today's youth will be leaders in a global community that is shrinking, so to speak. A sense of urgency propels educators to prepare students for functioning successfully in societies that are increasingly diverse and multicultural. The most effective way of doing this is to model such skills and attitudes every day in the school context. Collaborative consultation and co-teaching are natural and appropriate vehicles for demonstrating the value of using individual differences constructively and ethically.

RECOGNIZING DIFFERENCES
IN PERSONALITY PREFERENCES

Personality is the sum total of physical, mental, and social characteristics of an individual—the embodiment of a collection of qualities (*Webster's New Collegiate Dictionary,* 1996). One's personality is a result of inner forces acting on and being acted on by outer forces (Hall & Lindzey, 1989).

Personality traits distinguish individuals and characterize them in relationships with others. Any one of a person's individual instincts is not more important than any one of another person's instincts; what *is* important is the person's own *preferences* for personal functioning.

As discussed earlier, professional perspectives may be developed and refined in teacher preparation programs and professional development programs, but personalities tend to be brought to the profession by individuals. During the 1970s, 1980s, and 1990s numerous methodologies and instruments were developed to help people understand personality and human behavior and to improve human relationships. In fact, analyzing personality became quite faddish for a number of years. Several of the instruments were used in such diverse social service areas as education, counseling for marriage and family, personal awareness, career needs, religion, and business and industry, among others. The emphasis here will be on self-study and a low-key look at various ways individuality is illustrated by personality.

Formal assessment of individual differences in personality can be done with one or more instruments selected from among a wide range of existing tools and techniques, including Gregorc's instrument for profiling learning style (Gregorc & Ward, 1977), aptitude–treatment interaction theories relating individual differences to instructional method, Kolb cognitive style concepts (Kolb, 1976), the McCarthy (1990) 4MAT system, the Dunn and Dunn learning style assessment (Dunn and Dunn, 1978), and the Myers-Briggs Type Indicator (Myers, 1962) to name only a few of the more traditional and prominent examples. Many such instruments are described online and some can even be accessed there. Others are available through the services of consultants and workshops.

Such assessments are used in a variety of contexts to increase awareness and understanding of human preferences that influence behavior. To balance the zeal of those who support each type of assessment for personality and personal styles, there are others who caution against generalizing and oversimplifying complex human attributes with dichotomous comparisons such as concrete/abstract, morning/evening, extrovert/introvert, quiet/music-filled, or impulsive/reflective comparisons. But Carl Jung, eminent Swiss psychologist on whose work the well-known Myers-Briggs Type Indicator (MBTI) is based, was quite convincing over many years with his premise that people do differ in fundamental ways even as they all have the same instincts driving them from within (Jung, 1923).

The collective sum of individual preferences is a prime example of the "patchwork quilt" of human interaction that can be so constructive and facilitative in collaborative enterprises. For instance, compare the personal style of a person who looks for action and variety, shares experiences readily, likes to work with others, and tends to get impatient with slow, tedious jobs, with the style of one who prefers to work alone, labors long and hard on one thing, and seeks abundant quiet time for reflection. As another example, compare the personal style of an individual who is interested in facts, works steadily and patiently, and enjoys being realistic and practical, as a helpful contrast during group work with one who likes to generate multiple possibilities, attends to the whole aspect of a situation, and anticipates what will be said or done.

Yet another example is a person who needs logical reasons, holds firmly to convictions, and contributes intellectually while trying to be fair and impartial, contrasted with the style of one who relates freely to most people, likes to agree with others, and enjoys cultivating enthusiasm among members of the group. Finally, an individual who likes to have things decided and settled, prefers to move along purposefully, and strives to make conditions as they "should be," does not demonstrate the same preferences in a group as one who has a more live-and-let-live attitude, leaves things open and flexible, and functions with attitudes of adaptability and tolerance.

The beauty of Jungian theory, as characterized in the work of Isabel Briggs Myers (1962, 1974, 1980a), is the concept that every person is equipped with a broad spectrum of attributes and can use them as needed, but typically *prefers* to focus intensively on one or the other at a time. E. Murphy (1987) explains this point by using the example of color. Just as red cannot be blue, one cannot prefer both polarities simultaneously. One might prefer having a red car, but could live with a blue one if circumstances necessitated it. If a person prefers to apply experiences to problems, that person cannot also prefer to apply imagination to those problems. But he or she can call forth imagination if need be, and may benefit from practicing the process of imagining or supposing in order to use that approach more productively.

Remarkably, one's less preferred functions often contribute to productivity and self-satisfaction because they provide balance and completeness. They are the well-springs of enthusiasm and energy. A person's least-preferred function is his or her most child*like* (not child*ish*—an important distinction) and most primitive function and as such it can be quite helpful in that it creates a certain awkwardness and unrest that sparks innovation. But people will continue to call on their most preferred functions when they feel that ease, comfort, and efficiency are most important.

■ ■ ■ ■ ■ ▬▬▬▬▬▬▬▬▬▬▬▬▬▬▬▬▬▬▬▬▬▬▬▬▬▬▬▬▬▬▬▬▬▬▬▬▬

APPLICATION 2.3

Compare and contrast the following pairs of characteristics and think about which one of the pair suits you best in most instances.

I offer my opinions to others readily.	*or*	I pause before responding.
I am very interested in facts.	*or*	I am interested in many possibilities.
I tend to hold firmly to my convictions.	*or*	I tend to compromise for agreement.

I like things decided and settled.	*or*	I like things open and flexible.
I like to work with others.	*or*	I like to work alone.
I work steadily.	*or*	I work in bursts and then slack off.

You may want to select another person who seems to differ from you in many ways, and each one talk about individual preferences. Then reflect on how these characteristics might surface in a school setting as co-educators.

Self-Study of Preferred Styles and Functions

Unless individuals study their personal preferences and how those factors guide their own functioning, they are apt to view others through the biased and distorted lenses of their own unrecognized needs, fears, desires, anxieties, and sometimes unreceptive impulses (Jersild, 1955). Collaborative and inclusive schools, in order to be successful, must develop and maintain superior working relationships. In an effort to develop collaborative norms for its school context, one district conducted enculturation activities that included getting-to-know-you activities using an instrument titled the Keirsey Temperament Sorter and a companion book *Please Understand Me* (Keirsey & Bates, 1984). Several years later the participants still remembered the activity as their first glimpses of their co-educators' uniqueness and the group's diversity (Roy & O'Brien, 1991).

Understanding and respect are crucial for nurturing a collaborative climate in which the group is more than the sum of its parts. In their studies of successful and less successful preservice teachers and personal characteristics of special education teachers, Lessen and Frankiewicz (1992) recommended that teacher preparation programs must strongly consider the personal attributes that seem to be needed for effective teaching. They also proposed that affective attributes can be determined and trained.

> As teaching is inevitably a human enterprise, to suggest that teachers' personalities have no effect on their teaching is to deny their humanity. (Lessen & Frankiewicz, 1992, p. 130)

SCENARIO 2.B

Comments by educators who have reflected on their own preferences and have now gathered to share them in a group discussion:

"I think I do have some good skills, but I don't seem to get them put together to do what I want."

"I get so fed up with the reports that have to be done on such short notice. If data are turned in hastily and carelessly, what is their value?"

"I worked really hard on a particular project and then when it came time to give out the recognition, everybody seemed to forget that the ideas were mine."

"I like to lead and get things organized and finished, and I guess I'm not timid about saying what I think."

"I'm always wondering if I should say what I think or wait and see what everyone else thinks and then fall in line if I'm totally out in left field."

"It seems like what I do mostly in my department is put out fires."

"If I didn't show up tomorrow, I'm not sure any of my colleagues would notice or care, so long as there is a substitute teacher here to corral the kids."

"I really like the way my co-teacher supports me; I don't feel at all like the first-year teacher that I really am!"

Collaborating co-educators should reflect on their personal values and preferences before attempting to work intensively with other people who have their own packages of values and preferences. This can be done informally if the stakes are not too high and the process is just exploratory, not mandatory. Self-study analyses and follow-up discussions can be undertaken through a variety of methods and settings, including group work, role playing, reading, conferences, and workshops. Tools for studying personality, temperament, and learning style such as those named earlier are useful when discussed in professional development sessions or department meetings that focus on small-group activities to highlight the rich variety inherent in human nature. Of course, no single journal article, book, conference, or training package will ever provide sufficient material to fully understand the sophistication and complexity of individual differences.

Self-study helps educators become more aware of their own attributes and weave their own best qualities into new combinations for helping students who have diverse interests and learning needs (Dettmer, 1981). Too few teacher preparation programs provide opportunities for this important self-exploration. Conoley (1987) and Dettmer (1981) were early advocates in promoting awareness of individual differences among collaborating adults as key to the theory and practice of school consultation. Safran (1991) criticized the shortsightedness of researchers who omit important factors in interaction such as personality, interpersonal affect, and "domineeringness," for example, from their research designs focusing on consultation and collaboration. Salzberg and Morgan (1995) report that while variability in personality is a key issue in human interaction, the topic was noticeably absent when they researched teacher preparation for working with paraeducators.

In the Special Education Consulting Project directed by Dyck, Dettmer, and Thurston (1985) at Kansas State University from 1985 through 1987 when the concept of collaborative consultation was emerging in the broad educational context, the researchers found, on analyzing pre- and post-test data, that an area of greatest gain among participants was in "Awareness of self as a rudimentary variable in the collaborative consultation process." High rates of improvement also were noted for "Ability to monitor and change my own behavior as needed to increase my effectiveness," and "Skill when communicating for problem solving."

As stated earlier, oversimplification and generalization of complex constructs such as personality are to be avoided. Conclusions should not become labels. Rigid interpretations must give way to open-mindedness and respect. With these cautions carefully in mind, teachers *can* begin to deal with their colleagues and students more effectively. As an additional incentive for the study of personality and preferences, it generally is lots of fun!

It is not necessary to use a formal personality assessment to explore the constructive use of individual differences. In fact, there is inherent value in keeping the process informal and somewhat fuzzy. The goals should be simple—to increase self-understanding in a non-threatening manner, then broaden one's ability to respect and truly value differences in others, and finally, use that wide range of differences constructively for the benefit of students. The Application activities and To Do and Think About activities for this chapter can be catalysts for implementing constructive use of adult differences in school settings.

Respecting Different Viewpoints and Different Inclinations during Collaborative Consultation

Teachers may differ dramatically from each other with regard to their perspectives and preferences so that a collaborative school consultation could involve one teacher, who pays close attention to detail, examining every test score and asking questions about particular assignments, and another teacher, who scarcely looks at the test scores, preferring instead to solicit verbal, generalized assessment of the student's capabilities from other professionals. A study by Lawrence and DeNovellis (1974) revealed that teachers with different preferences tend to behave differently in the classroom. Learning styles of teachers as well as students can contribute to these tendencies. Lawrence (1993) issues a broad analysis of such aspects:

- Cognitive style of preferred patterns of mental functions such as information processing and formulating ideas
- Attitudes and interests that influence what someone attends to
- Disposition to seek out learning environments to fit one's cognitive style and interests, and to avoid environments that do not fit
- Disposition to use certain learning tools and to avoid others

A person's perception of the environment reflects and is filtered through one's own stage of development (Oja, 1980). Because of learning style preferences and variations in ways of processing information, those who aim to collaborate should be ready to accept differences among co-educators. Such areas of difference can describe those who are (Garmston and Wellman, 1992):

- Looking for facts, data, and references
- Wishing to relate topics to themselves
- Wanting to reason and explore
- Would like to adapt, modify, or create new ideas and procedures

As teachers address their own preferences, they become more insightful about tuning in to student styles in ways that will help them plan together and provide the differentiation students need. They also will be more able and willing to relate to colleagues' personal preferences, not to do the same work in the same ways, but to understand the work of others and build on it together.

A number of years ago Carlyn (1977) studied the relationship between personality characteristics and teaching preferences of prospective teachers. Some were more interested in administrative functions and others had a strong need for independence and creativity. Some preferred planning school programs, whereas others enjoyed working with small groups of students. Some people liked action and variety more than quiet and reflection. Some liked to work in groups, whereas others preferred to work alone or with one person. Some people got impatient with slow jobs and complicated procedures. Others could work on one thing for a long time, and they resented interruptions. In this important study Carlyn concluded that teachers of different personality-type preferences also preferred different kinds of teaching situations. These kinds of preferences and values help explain why some teachers will experiment with modifications and materials, whereas others resist or just never seem to get around to doing it.

APPLICATION 2.4
SHARING A PROFESSIONAL EXPERIENCE

In a small group of four or five people, describe an experience from your teaching or school days in which you put forth significant effort but ended up feeling unappreciated, unaffirmed, and perhaps a bit of a failure in that instance. After all in the group have shared a personal example (with people having the option of passing if they wish), discuss how members of the group felt about each other's disappointing professional experience. To practice feeling empathy for one whose preferences differ from yours, show caring for their disappointment, especially if it was not something that would have bothered you all that much.

When a group of educators with different preferences collaborate, they have the opportunity to contribute a variety of strengths within the interaction. Those who like to bring up new possibilities and suggest ingenious ways of approaching problems will benefit from having other people supply pertinent facts and keep track of essential details. When some are playing devil's advocate in finding flaws and holding out for existing policy, others can contribute by conciliating and arousing enthusiasm to sell the idea (Myers, 1980b).

Opposite types may or may not attract, but they definitely need to be available in order to achieve maximum team productivity. Managing differences elegantly is a tremendous challenge for a collaborative consultant or co-teacher. As stressed earlier, the primary goal in consulting, collaborating, and working as a team is not to think alike, but to think together. Each one's personal preferences and professional perspectives are important elements in the effectiveness of interaction. Differences in schools and classrooms are not just role-related disagreements between adult and child, or teacher and student, or administrator and teacher, or paraeducator and supervising teacher. They reflect individual orientations to the world, unique learning styles, variability in personal values, and differentiated work styles. These differences, when understood and appreciated, can be quite constructive in finding ways to help those with exceptional learning needs.

USING ADULT DIFFERENCES
TO FACILITATE COLLABORATION

Some researchers and practitioners focus on the need for collaborators to view problems from mutual perspectives and shared frames of reference using a common language (Friend & Cook, 1990; Lopez, Dalal, & Yoshida, 1993). These mind-sets are assuredly important for rapport building and initiating exploration of a problem or need. However, greatest team success will come from making sincere efforts to respect members' differences, value the contributions, and communicate in ways that respect and accommodate a variety of verbal and nonverbal styles.

Needing to view matters through a shared "lens," yet doing so with different "eyes," may be a conundrum but nevertheless a useful one. (See Figure 2.2.) As Lopez et al. (1993) note, consultants and consultees must understand how divergent points of view may predispose them to see problems in conflicting ways. Divergence is an asset in problem solving and not a liability when utilized by skilled collaborators. Educators can learn a great deal from talking with (and listening to!) colleagues with whom they differ both in theory and in practice. If a common vocabulary is used and a framework of respect for individuality is in place, teamwork will be much more productive. When individuality is regarded as pleasant and interesting, teamwork will be much more enjoyable.

FIGURE 2.2   **Viewing Matters through Different Lenses**

Differences When Communicating

Many communication problems among team members are due to professional differences and personality differences. A statement that seems clear and reasonable to one person may sound meaningless or preposterous to another (Myers, 1974). One person may want an explicit statement of the problem before considering possible solutions. Another might want at least the prospect of an interesting possibility before buckling down to facts. Yet another may demand a beginning, a logically arranged sequence of points, and an end (*especially* an end, Myers cautions). Still another will really listen only if the discussion starts with a concern for people and any direct effects of the issue on people. Myers stressed that "[i]t is human nature not to listen attentively if one has the impression that what is being said is going to be irrelevant or unimportant" (Myers, 1974, p. 4). Communication is such a critical part of successful consultation and collaboration that it will be the focus of concern in Chapter 4.

Differences When Problem Finding and Problem Solving

Individual differences contribute to effectiveness of problem finding and problem solving. Some individuals proceed meticulously when identifying problems and working out possible solutions, while others earmark potential problems and propose possible solutions very quickly. One person may focus more on the problem and the facts, while another focuses on the process and meanings behind the facts. If someone has to solve a problem alone, he or she will want to approach it from multiple perspectives in order to have all the benefits of each type. Problem solving by a well-mixed team of individuals enables most perspectives to be represented efficiently. Again, the adage "Many heads are better than one" applies here. With pooled experiences, interests, and abilities, problem solving is enriched.

No specific personality preferences are predictive of success in communication or problem solving within groups; however, research shows that teams with a complete representation of types outperform virtually any single-type or similar-type team (Blaylock, 1983). The likelihood of having such team versatility in one's collaborative situation is better than might be expected, for a group of several individuals typically contains many various perspectives.

Differences When Evaluating and Reporting

Perhaps no area of teaching creates more tension and potential discord than testing and grading, whether it be among teachers, between teachers and students, between teachers and parents, between teachers and administrators, or even between teachers and coaches who need to keep athletes eligible to play. Consensus on evaluation methods will probably never be reached across all factions, but thoughtful and candid discussion sessions are a place to start.

Having an opportunity to express one's viewpoints and to explain professional perspectives on assessment, grading, and reporting results may defuse potential flare-ups of disagreement and quell discord between teachers, within departments, throughout the school, and among parents of students. Using consultation services in this area can be particularly productive. For the services to be successful, good questions, open minds, and forthright sharing of opinions are musts. Collaboration and teamwork to develop viable policies on assessment and evaluation for the entire school context can help the individual teacher, and especially the preservice teacher, feel less isolated and more involved.

■ ■ ■ ■ ■ ▬▬

APPLICATION 2.5
REFLECTING ON PLANS FOR A COLLABORATIVE ACTIVITY

Choose a favorite lesson or subject area and imagine that you and a consultee will be team-teaching this material. How would you go about this? Although it is important to know something about your co-teacher's style and preferences, are there things you should study about *yourself* first before embarking on this collaborative endeavor? Then how can you share that information pleasantly and agreeably with your colleague, and proceed to learn comparable information about that person, in order to co-plan and co-teach more effectively?

The phrase, "A little knowledge is a dangerous thing," must be heeded when reflecting on individual differences. As indicated earlier, educators can work from knowledge of personality assessment or learning style concepts without having the formal profiles of individuals in that group; in fact, they probably *should* do so. It is not always possible, necessary, or even desirable to ascertain people's preferences with a standardized instrument. (This chapter's numerous application sections are provided as a very informal and hopefully an enjoyable means of finding out interesting and useful things about oneself and one's colleagues.) The most important purpose is instilling the attitude that human differences are not behaviors acted out with intentions of irritating and alienating each other. Rather, they are systematic, orderly, consistent, often unavoidable realities of the way people prefer to use their perception and judgment. *Each set of preferences is valuable and at times indispensable in every field of endeavor.*

Well-researched personality theory does not promulgate labeling of individuals. Learning styles theory and right-left brain function research have fallen victim on occasion to unwarranted use of labels; "He's so right-brained, that he can't . . . " or, "She's a concrete sequential, so she won't. . . ." The world probably does not need any more labels for individuals, and this is particularly cogent in the field of special education where labeling has been problematic and opposed vigorously for many years.

■ ■ ■ ■ ■ ▬▬

APPLICATION 2.6
CONSIDERING PREFERRED RECOGNITION AND REWARD

Form groups of four to six and discuss ways in which you would like to be recognized, and perhaps rewarded, reinforced, or even praised, for something you did that required effort and skill. Then talk over with the group the variations in outcomes that different individuals prefer. How might this affect a work context such as the school and the teaching profession? How could you affirm professional perspectives and personal preferences of others with whom you will work?

Using Adult Differences to Facilitate Team Interactions

Individuals have far more potential than they use at any one time, and the power of this potential in team settings is exponential. Team building is articulated helpfully in Johnson and Johnson's (1987) description of helpful elements within teams (Welch et al., 1992). Elements are positive interdependence, individual accountability, face-to-face interaction, collaborative skills, and group processing. Such elements are particularly important in preparation programs of preservice teachers who need specific practice and modeling in interaction before they join experienced teachers in meetings and co-teaching activities.

A team of educators should use the strengths of each person to ferret out the problem or need, to generate ideas for serving that need, to organize and divide up what needs to be done, to prepare evaluation procedures, and to follow up with the evaluation and further planning if necessary. The variety of backgrounds and training can be rich sources of new ideas when conventional thoughts are not productive. However, it is not feasible and also not very helpful to contrive artificial arrangements that would provide a complete representation of types as featured in a personality assessment. As previously mentioned, variability among humans is rich enough that most groups of even a few will have a significant diversity of skills.

Some pertinent questions to consider when organizing teams or when discussing how each member can contribute best to the group are:

- Does our team have a mix of experiences, talents, and preferences? If we think we don't, is there something practical that can be done about it?
- Does the group appreciate the constructive potential of adult differences?
- Is everyone ready and willing to contribute in her or his own way?
- Is each person looking forward to having a good time together in finding ways to help our students learn, help teachers grow, and help school programs improve?

By valuing the contribution of each member on the team, the group can come to more fully formed, student-centered decisions to serve special needs. Valuing individual differences will require more than merely tolerating them. It means accepting the fact that people are different and the world is the better for the diversity (E. Murphy, 1987). Teacher preparation programs must be enterprising in preparing graduates to have superlative aptitude for understanding individual differences among co-educators. Much more research is needed on the constructive use of individual differences for collaborative consultation and working in teams.

■ ■ ■ ■ ■ ▬▬▬▬▬▬▬▬▬▬▬▬▬▬▬▬▬▬▬▬▬▬▬▬▬▬▬▬▬▬▬▬▬▬▬▬▬▬

APPLICATION 2.7
WHAT IS YOUR PREFERENCE?

In groups of three or four, discuss these sentences for about three minutes each.

Would you rather vacation in the Bahamas or in Alaska, and why?
Would you rather work in a rural area or an urban area, and why?

Would you prefer to explore deep ocean or deep space, and why?
Would you rather win a new car or a new, installed kitchen, and why?

Then with the whole group share some interesting and unusual things you learned about each other with this activity and, if time allows, with the other six activities in this chapter.

ETHICAL ISSUES CONCERNING INDIVIDUAL PERSPECTIVES AND PREFERENCES

Teachers who devote much attention to accommodating student individuality may still find it difficult to recognize, much less respect and adapt to, adult differences. Educators should give consideration to divergent points of view and be ready, willing, and able to change their minds when the evidence warrants it. This is particularly important when they will be co-teaching.

Some cautions must temper the study and use of information about individual differences. Self-study and ensuing group discussions can be quite interesting. Just about everybody likes to share their own viewpoints and react to those of others. But occasionally participants may become so enthused that they share inappropriately, generalize unadvisedly, stereotype inadvertently, or draw others out indiscriminately. So it is always wise for not only the leader, but also for each member of the group, to monitor events and do their part to keep discussions practical and helpful while appropriately personal and objectively impersonal.

The persuasive and personal aspects of consultative service require a close, careful monitoring of ethical concerns (Ross, 1986). Empathy for all, and an interactive manner of onedownsmanship, which is defined as de-emphasis of prior knowledge in order to maintain relationships (Henning-Stout, 1994), along with communication in a climate of parity as equal partners and agreement of mutual ownership, are essential behaviors for ethical collaborators. (See Figure 2.3.)

A collaborative school consultant must be open to new perspectives and ideas, giving colleagues every opportunity to share and letting them enjoy the benefit of contributing.

1. Talk and listen, really listen, together.
2. Describe own perspectives on the issue(s), giving objective examples if possible.
3. Express own preferences regarding the issue(s) if pertinent.
4. Explore resolutions or compromises together.
5. Summarize collective discussion points and any tentative agreements.
6. Seek input from other parties and information from other sources if the process is stalled.
7. Agree on a plan or procedure, with give-and-take arbitration if necessary.
8. Note who compromised more and who compromised less, so as to reverse next time if at all feasible.
9. Talk for a little while after concluding the plan to reflect on outcomes and discuss ways of improving next time.
10. Follow up on results emanating from the interaction.

FIGURE 2.3 Ten-Point Interaction Process Showing Respect for Professional Perspectives and Personal Preferences

Disagreements must not be taken personally. Co-educators must keep their channels of interaction open and friendly.

Groups can have profound influences on individual behavior; conversely, one principled person can exert considerable influence and good conscience on the group. Confident teachers demonstrate a willingness to learn from others. They draw others helpfully into productive sharing sessions. They promote strong respect for individual variability and work at deep understanding of human development and learning theory. They strive to nurture the cognitive, affective, sensorimotor, and social growth of co-educators as well as students.

Working together in harmony is a subtle and complex process to be developed over time within an attitude of respect. Each should strive to think and do with finesse as a consensus-building member of a collaborative team, having consideration for others on the team and demonstrating personal integrity in all matters.

TIPS FOR USING ADULT DIFFERENCES CONSTRUCTIVELY

1. Respect the rights of others to hold different beliefs. Even if people do not agree they must assume that others are acting in ways they believe are appropriate.
2. Reasons exist for things that people do or say, so try to discover them.
3. Try not to press for one's own favorite methods of serving school needs, educator needs, or student needs, but rather to encourage collaborative plans when problem finding and problem solving.
4. Have lunch, workroom breaks, and informal visits with other staff members often.
5. Ask others for their input when you are facing a problem, because it has a humanizing, rapport-building effect.
6. Listen to the other person's point of view and seek to understand that person's ideas and meaning.
7. Take time to assess preferences of others before deciding on a consultation method.
8. Appreciate perceptions and preferences that are different from one's own by engaging in a dialectical conversation. Do not feel that it is necessary to change your position or to convert the other person to your position.
9. Really care about other persons' feelings and ideas, and show it through actions.
10. Be available, available, available when others would like to share or just talk.

CHAPTER REVIEW

1. Most educators are attuned to the need for responding to individual differences of their students; however, much less attention has been given to individual differences among school personnel and ways in which those differences affect the school context and professional interactions. It is easy in the busy and public but relatively autonomous setting of school life to overlook the impact that differing personal preferences and professional perspectives of colleagues have on the process of working together. The study of adult differences and subsequent attention to constructive use of those differences is, for the most part, neglected

in teacher preparation programs and professional development experiences. Yet the school environment sparkles with variability among educators. Areas of variance among co-educators can include: age, years of teaching experience; type of teacher education program completed for certification; grade level(s) for teaching; curricular areas of teaching; general or special education focus; teaching experience in rural or urban areas, and small or large schools; personal preferences and professional perspectives regarding instruction for student learning and behavior; and much more.

2. Co-educator differences in professional perspectives can affect professional interactions when discussing students' needs and exploring ways of serving those needs. Types of learning theory and kinds of subject matter frame the intent of instruction. Goals and objectives guide educators and students in teaching and learning. Time and achievement dimensions gear instruction to students' needs. Types of assessments and scores are designed to measure achievement of mastery or status in a reference group. Methods of interpreting scores are selected to evaluate both learning and teaching. Co-educator differences in personality preferences can affect professional interactions when communicating, identifying problems, generating solutions to problems, and evaluating performance. Friction caused by disharmony among disparate types is reduced when the basis of disagreement is understood.

3. Educators instruct and students learn and do in four domains of functioning—the cognitive, affective, sensorimotor, and social domains.

Co-educators need solid grounding in learning theory, both special education and general education curriculum, and assessment, including measurement and testing for evaluation purposes.

4. When engaging in collaborative consultation and working together as co-teachers or team members, the more prickly areas of disagreement concerning professional perspectives and personal preferences can be discovered and discussed frankly in a spirit of camaraderie and collegiality. Co-educators do not need to teach in the same way; they simply need to understand and respect the work of others. Then teachers and students alike will benefit from the rich array of individual differences.

5. Adult differences can be used to significant advantage in teamwork and problem solving. When all aspects of team members' preferences are available to contribute diverse viewpoints and ideas, the multiple facets of problems can be analyzed and wide ranges of options generated. The most effective teams are those with the greatest variety of perspectives and the greatest tolerance for considering the views of others.

6. All educators must have high expectations for all students. They must understand the work of their colleagues and allow for individual differences among adults. They must accept all students as the responsibility of all educators. Finally, they need to value and use individual differences constructively without overgeneralizing or stereotyping characteristics of co-educators.

TO DO AND THINK ABOUT

1. Discuss ways in which provocative issues related to individual preferences and styles might be explored without endangering professional collegiality and school spirit.

2. Visit with colleagues or classmates about open-ended topics such as:
   - What do I think is good and not good about being a teacher?

- What changes do I hope will take place in education in the next ten years, and are there any ways that I will need to change if they do come about?
- What are my best attributes as a teacher?
- What do I need to work on most if I am to reach my potential as a teacher?
- What teaching strengths do I value in others?

- (If group members know and trust each other well at this time) What teaching strengths within this group do I value most?

3. Discuss with other participants your favorite perspectives and preferences that you are called on to use as an educator. Then discuss those that are not your best ones and solicit suggestions from the group on how you might modify them to best serve you and your students.

4. Participants seek out personality instruments they would like to study, using the Internet or books or publishing-house materials. School counselors and school psychologists could be approached about helping to find the instruments and then helping to interpret them in useful ways. A follow-up activity would be to share information that was learned and discuss potential benefits of the most promising ones.

ADDITIONAL READINGS AND RESOURCES

Brownell, M., Adams, A., Sindelar, P., Waldron, N., & Vanhover, S. (2006). Learning from collaboration: The role of teacher qualities. *Exceptional Children, 72*(2), 169–185.

This study examined how teachers who readily use strategies acquired in collaboration differed from those who do not and researchers contend that there is not much in-depth information on how the nature of teachers' individual beliefs might interact to facilitate or hinder innovations in teaching.

Jung, C. G. (1923). *Psychological types.* New York: Harcourt Brace.

Hanna, G. S., & Dettmer, P. (2004). *Assessment for Effective Teaching: Context-Adaptive Planning.* Boston: Allyn & Bacon.

Individual differences and variability among students, subject matter, learning theory, taxonomies, testing and grading, and other factors forming professional perspectives are discussed in detail.

Keirsey, D., & Bates, M. (1984). *Please understand me: Character and temperament types.* Del Mar, CA: Prometheus Nemesis.

Lawrence, G. (1993). *People types and tiger stripes: A practical guide to learning styles* (3rd ed.). Gainesville, FL: Center for Applications of Psychological Type.

Lessen, E., & Frankiewicz, L. E. (1992). Personal attributes and characteristics of effective special education teachers: Considerations for teacher educators. *Teacher Education and Special Education, 15*(2), 124–132.

Myers, I. B. (1980). *Gifts differing.* Palo Alto, CA: Consulting Psychologists Press.

Woolfolk, A. (2007) *Educational Psychology.* Englewood Cliffs, NJ: Prentice Hall.

A widely used, comprehensive book on educational psychology for preservice teachers.

CHAPTER THREE

CONTEXT:
History and
Models

Foundations and Frameworks for Consultation, Collaboration, and Teamwork

Consultation, collaboration, and teamwork probably began around cave fires ages ago, as humans discovered it was good to talk things over. It is likely that as they learned to explore wider territories, construct things, and then trade those things, they found it helpful to communicate by smoke signal and drumbeat. They formed connections of networks and began to consult and collaborate with those they trusted. Through social interaction they learned useful things from others and enjoyed expressing their own views as well. When they planned hunting and food-gathering forays and eventually began to plant and harvest, they developed methods for teamwork that gave them even more success as hunters, gatherers, and growers.

So it has been that throughout the ages people improved their quality of life by working together. Now, as our global world "shrinks," interpersonal skills are even more essential for progress and well-being in our increasingly complex, interconnected world. Individuals will continue to have their own professional perspectives and personal preferences, but those who interact and work together successfully will fare best.

Relating to others, communicating, and respecting the viewpoints of others should begin at an early age. Toddlers at home, in their neighborhoods, and perhaps in day care centers, are expected to outgrow egocentrism and learn how to interact with others. Preschool children are encouraged to work cooperatively with others. Schools become their next learning fields for interrelating. Educators who cooperate, negotiate, and model collaboration and productive teamwork are teaching students how to succeed in the world they will inherit and lead.

FOCUSING QUESTIONS

1. What school improvement and reform issues have influenced the growth of inclusive schools and collaborative teaching environments?

2. What legislation propels schools toward collaborative school consultation, instructional teams, co-teaching, and partnerships with families?

3. What, in brief, are the historical, theoretical, and research bases of collaborative school consultation?

4. What are the common structural components in collaborative school consultation methods?

5. What models of consultation, collaboration, and teamwork have evolved in education?

6. How might educators tailor methods for consultation, collaboration, and co-teaching to make them well suited to their school contexts?

KEY TERMS

Americans with Disabilities
  Act (ADA)
approach
collaborative consultation
  models
Conjoint Behavioral
  Consultation model (CBC)
consultee-centered
  consultation models
early intervention
free and appropriate public
  education (FAPE)
IDEA 1997, IDEA 2004
inclusion

Instructional Consultation
  model (IC)
intersubjectivity
least restrictive environment
  (LRE)
mainstreaming
method
mode
model
No Child *Held* Behind
  (NC*H*B)
No Child Left Behind
  (NCLB)
perspective

prototype
Public Laws 89-313, 94-142,
  99-457, and 101-476
regular education initiative
  (REI)
Resource/Consulting Teacher
  Program model (R/CT)
Schoolwide Enrichment
  Model (SEM)
semantics
system
Teacher Assistance Teams
  model (TAT)
triadic model

SCENARIO 3

The setting is a school administration office where the superintendent, the high school principal, and the special education director are having an early-morning conference.

Special Education Director: I've assigned five people on our special education staff to begin serving as consulting teachers in the schools we targeted at our last meeting.

Principal: I understand the high school is to be one of those schools.

Special Education Director: Yes, several classroom teachers will be involved. I've visited briefly with the English teacher who is getting a new student with learning disabilities and I'll work with one of the consulting teachers to collaborate and perhaps try some co-teaching.

Principal: I'm all for trying a new approach, but at this point I'm not sure my staff understands very much about how this method of service is going to affect them.

Superintendent: Are you saying we need to spend a little more time at the drawing board and get the kinks out of our plan before tossing it out to the teachers?

Principal: Yes, and I think the parents also will want to know what will be happening. They'll want us to tell them specifically how this will benefit their child.

Special Education Director: I've been compiling a file of theoretical background, research studies, program descriptions, even some cartoons and fun sayings, that focus on consultation and collaboration approaches and hopefully will lighten up some of the gray areas of their concerns. I'll get copies of the best of it to you and the principals of the other designated schools. Perhaps we should plan in-service sessions for teachers and some awareness sessions for parents, too, before we proceed, especially if we anticipate trying some co-teaching.

Superintendent: That sounds good. Draft an outline and we'll discuss it at next week's meeting. I'll get the word out to the other principals to be here.

MOVEMENTS FOR SCHOOL IMPROVEMENT

A little history from the past several decades will serve as background for the changing climate that led to the current educational environment. In the 1960s advocates representing special needs pressed for the right of those with mental retardation to have opportunities as similar as possible to those in mainstream society. In addition, the public's attention to needs of preschoolers from disadvantaged environments gained momentum.

In 1965, passage of the Elementary and Secondary Education Act (ESEA) authorized funding and made specific provisions for students with disabilities (Talley & Schrag, 1999). Reauthorizations of that legislation in 1988 and 1994 mandated parent involvement and coordination in early childhood programs such as Head Start, encouraging school and community-linked services through the Community Schools Partnership Act. Consultation and collaboration became essential factors in coordinating the array of services provided for students with special needs.

During the 1970s, 1980s, 1990s, and early 2000s, educators witnessed an explosion of reports, proposals, and legislative mandates calling for educational reform. Issues in the 1970s focused on accountability, lengthening of time in school, and increased investments in education. Demands for cost containment and growing concerns over labeling of students fueled interest in a merger of general education and special education. The primary impetus for the merger was the mainstreaming movement with its concept of least restrictive environment (LRE). This was catalyzed in 1975 by passage of Public Law 94-142 (that is, put forth by the 94th Congress as their 142nd piece of legislation). After that legislation was passed, educators could no longer arbitrarily place individuals with disabilities in a special school or self-contained classroom. A continuum of service options was to be available and the type of service or placement was to be as close to the normal environment as possible, with general education teachers responsible for the success of those students. In order to meet this new responsibility, general education teachers were to receive help from special education personnel. This was an important provision.

During the second wave of reform in the 1980s, the individual school became the unit of decision making. This movement promoted the development of collegial, participatory environments among students and staff, with particular emphasis on personalizing school environments and designing curriculum for deeper understanding (Michaels, 1988). One component of this second wave was school restructuring. Many states initiated some form of school restructuring; however, few schools were truly restructured. Where restructuring efforts occurred, they tended to be idiosyncratic in that they were carried out by a small group of teachers, creating only marginal changes (Timar, 1989).

A position paper issued by Madeline Will (1986), former director of the U.S. Office of Special Education and Rehabilitative Services, stated that too many children were being inappropriately identified and placed in learning disabilities programs. In that paper, Will called for *collaboration* between special education personnel and general education personnel to provide special services within the general classroom. This generated the regular education initiative (REI), referred to by some educators as the general education initiative (GEI), that caused major changes in the way education is delivered. All students, with the exception of those with severe disabilities, were from that time to be served primarily in a regular education setting. The rationale for the REI was that:

- The changes would serve many students not currently eligible for special education services.
- The stigma of placement in special education programs that were separate from age peers would be eliminated.
- Early intervention and prevention would be provided before more serious learning deficiencies could occur.
- Cooperative school-parent relationships would be enhanced (Will, 1986).

In 1986, P.L. 94-142 was amended by P.L. 99-457, which mandated free and appropriate public education (FAPE) for preschool children ages 3–5 with disabilities. An Individualized Family Service Plan (IFSP) was required for each child served, thus extending the concept of the IEP to provide support for child *and* family (Smith, 1998).

Early intervention programs for infants and toddlers with disabilities proliferated following the 1986 legislation. Parents and other caregivers outside the school now had an even more integral part in the education of these children. Because most disabilities of children in early intervention programs are severe, an array of services is essential.

Families are to have an integral part in the therapy through home-based programs. Families are described in a broad sense, not necessarily as a father-and-mother unit. Family includes parents, grandparents, older siblings, aunts and uncles, and others who function in the caregiver role. The IFSP is developed by a multidisciplinary team with family members as active participants. Children are served according to family needs, allowing for a wide range of services with parent training as one of those services. Family choices are considered in all decisions.

In 1990, early in the third wave of reform, Public Law 94-142 was amended with the passage of Public Law 101-476, the Individuals with Disabilities Education Act (IDEA). That legislation's primary elements were:

- All references to children as handicapped were changed to children with disabilities.
- New categories of autism and traumatic brain injury (TBI) were added, to be served with increased collaboration among all special education teachers, classroom teachers, and related services personnel.
- More emphasis was placed on requirements to provide transition services for students 16 years of age and older.

Two distinct groups emerged to advocate for REI—the high-incidence group (many cases) that included learning disabilities, behavioral disorders, and mild/moderate mental retardation, and the low-incidence group (fewer cases) that included students with severe intellectual disabilities. Both groups shared three goals:

1. To merge special and general education into one inclusive system
2. To increase dramatically the number of children with disabilities in mainstream classrooms
3. To strengthen academic achievement of students with mild and moderate disabilities, as well as that of underachievers without disabilities.

To attain these goals, total restructuring would be needed in schools. "Increasingly, special education reform is symbolized by the term 'inclusive schools,'" (Fuchs and Fuchs, 1994, p. 299).

Also passed in 1990 was the Americans with Disabilities Act (ADA). This law prohibited discrimination against people of all ages who have disabilities in matters of transportation, public access, local government, and telecommunications. It required schools to make all reasonable accommodations for access by students and it extended provisions concerning fairness in employment to employers who do not receive federal funds (Smith, 1998).

The *America 2000* report presented in 1991 by President George H. W. Bush and Secretary of Education Lamar Alexander, and the 1994 federal school reform package known as Goals 2000 that was signed into law by President Bill Clinton, identified goals to be met in the nation's schools by the year 2000. The latter report emphasized that home and school partnerships are essential for student success. After these reports were publicized, public pressure to improve schools escalated.

In 1997, after much study and discussion nationwide, reauthorization and amendments for IDEA were approved by Congress and signed into law by President Clinton. This legislation, known as IDEA 1997, contained the following:

- Provisions for improved parent-professional partnerships
- Requirement for states to provide mediation for parents and schools in resolving differences
- Requirement that states would have training for paraeducators to prepare for their roles
- Requirement for general education teachers to participate on IEP teams when students are or will be placed in a general education classroom
- Increased cost sharing among agencies with reduced financial burdens for special education locally
- Accountability of education for students with disabilities by way of participation in state and districtwide assessment programs
- Assurance that children with behavioral disorders who exhibit dangerous behaviors are not to be deprived of educational services, but educators could more easily remove them from their current educational placement if needed
- Tighter disclosure requirements, with families having greater access to their children's records and more information available in IEPs

A focus of IDEA 1997 was collaboration among general educators and special educators, parents, related services personnel, and other service providers; this inclusion meant that general educators in particular must be actively engaged in selecting program modifications and supports, alternative-grading procedures, and assistive technology devices (Williams & Martin, 2001). Transition services and interagency linkages were noted as being vital areas of assistance from collaborating consultants.

In general, the special education community was pleased with components of IDEA 1997. A few concerns remained, not the least of which was the *increase*, rather than a much hoped-for decrease, in the paperwork that so erodes the time and morale of special educators.

Inclusive Schools

The concept of inclusion that swept the nation in recent years did not suddenly emerge out of a vacuum. It emanated from the long line of special education movements and mandates briefly described above and summarized in Figure 3.1.

Inclusive schools *include* students with special needs in the total school experience, rather than exclude them by placement in special schools or classrooms. In full inclusion, support services come to the student in the general education setting. In partial inclusion students may be served in another instructional setting when appropriate for their individual needs, but receive most of their instruction in the general education setting.

From its rather quiet beginning, the inclusive schools movement snowballed into a popular position whereby special education and regular education were expected to merge into a unified school system. The merger was intended to modify many aspects of the rigidly compartmentalized, often stigmatizing, and very expensive special education structure. Furthermore, proponents of inclusive schools made the case that *all* students are unique individuals with special needs requiring differentiated individual attention; therefore, practices used effectively for exceptional students should be made available to all students (McLeskey, Henry, & Hodges, 1998).

In O'Neil (1994–1995), Sapon-Shevin made an appealing case that educators should not have to defend inclusion—rather, they should insist that others should have to defend *exclusion* if they are going to support that position. A collaborative climate with teachers working together for all students in inclusive settings is a realistic way to settle the debate. Collaborative consultation can be advocated for students with disabilities as providing better service, more time, greater levels of teacher attention, and more opportunities for socializing with age peers in natural settings.

The legislation did not define inclusion. But several useful definitions are available in the literature, including these:

- *Inclusion:* Educating each child to the maximum extent appropriate in the school and classroom he or she would otherwise attend (Rogers, 1993). The current focus for inclusion is on location of instruction and grouping of students, it is arbitrary across states and across districts within a state, and ideally it involves a regular education teacher and a special education teacher co-teaching in one classroom (Beakley, 1997).

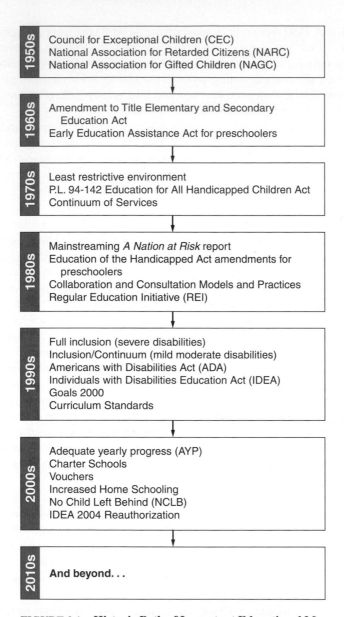

FIGURE 3.1   Historic Path of Important Educational Movements

- *Full (or Total) Inclusion:* Instructional practices and technological supports are available to accommodate all students in the schools and classrooms they would otherwise attend if not disabled (Rogers, 1993).
- *Inclusive Schools:* Schools where all members accept their fair share of responsibility for all children, including those with disabilities. Aids and resources are

utilized where needed regardless of official classifications of disability (Fuchs & Fuchs, 1994).

The National Center on Educational Restructuring and Inclusion (NCERI) conducted a study in 1994 to determine the status of the inclusion movement. The center found that inclusive programs were increasingly being implemented in many states across the country. At that time they identified six factors that are necessary for successful inclusion in schools: visionary leadership, collaboration, refocused use of assessment, supports for family and students, funding, and effective family involvement.

Collaboration is essential to inclusion because successful inclusion presumes that "no one teacher can or ought to be expected to have all the expertise required to meet the educational needs of all students in the classroom" (Lipsky, 1994, p. 5). All educators share responsibility for student achievement and behavior. There must be total commitment from principal to school custodian (Federico, Herrold, & Venn, 1999). Every inclusive school looks different, but all inclusive schools are characterized by a sense of community, high standards, collaboration and cooperation, changing roles and an array of services, partnership with families, flexible learning environments, strategies based on research, new forms of accountability, and ongoing professional development (Federico et al., 1999; Working Forum on Inclusive Schools, 1994).

A Continuing Dialogue about Inclusion.   Responses to inclusion have been complex; they are shaped by multiple variables, and these variables change over time (Salend & Duhaney, 1999). So while supportive educators may applaud the spirit of inclusion and the benefits of inclusive settings, others do not regard inclusion as everybody's panacea. Narrow definitions, myopic practices, and most of all, failure to prepare school personnel in collaborative and co-teaching strategies can short-circuit the well-meant intentions. Critics point to situations in which teachers receive little to no assistance and sometimes are not even informed about the nature of their students' disabilities. Some contend that special education teachers have difficulties managing educational programs of students scheduled among several classrooms.

In some schools several children with severe disabilities are assigned to the same classroom. This does not approximate a typical classroom situation because perhaps only 1 child in 100 will have severe disabilities. This situation can create an extremely frustrating environment for the classroom teacher (Rogers, 1993). Parents of students with disabilities sometimes make the case that their children have fewer services and, in particular, do not receive the direct services they may require. Problems can develop in inclusive settings for children with disabilities if they are "dumped wholesale" into classrooms where their teachers have no time or training for collaboration and teamwork. Sometimes special educators lament loss of control over the learning environment and fear loss of specialized services for students with disabilities (Salend & Duhaney, 1999), as do their parents. To add to the concerns, a backlash among some parents of children who do not have disabilities indicates that they feel their children's education is being compromised by the myriad demands on teachers in inclusive environments.

VanTassel-Baska (1998) notes that studies are limited for education of gifted and talented students within inclusive settings, but those that do exist reveal some troubling trends. Research shows that students with high ability and remarkable talents too often do not receive instruction intensive enough for their learning needs in inclusive classrooms. This concern will be addressed further in Chapter 7.

In a qualitative study of inclusive elementary school programs, Wood (1998) found that in the initial stages of inclusion, teachers maintained discrete role boundaries through an informal but clear division of labor. However, as the school year progressed, role perceptions became less rigid as the teaming process became more cooperative. More recent emphasis on collaborative climates, professional development activities, heightened interest and involvement by parents and communities, and intensive advocacy efforts toward inclusion by both general and special educators, have boosted the acceptance of inclusion throughout the land.

Reauthorization of the Individuals with Disabilities Education Act

Two significant pieces of legislation were due for reauthorization in the first decade of the new century. In 2004, the U.S. Congress reauthorized IDEA 1997 with passage of IDEA 2004. Areas targeted for improvement or change involved:

- High expectations for students with disabilities, to increase abilities for employment and independent living
- Professional development and training of all preservice and school personnel who work with children having disabilities, including skills and knowledge and use of scientifically based (research-based) instructional processes to the maximum extent possible
- Compatibility with No Child Left Behind performance goals for adequate yearly progress
- IEPs that include research-based methodology
- Elimination of short-term objectives and benchmarks except for students taking alternate assessments
- IEPs that provide clear, measurable annual goals, including academic goals and functional goals (routine activities of daily living having evaluation procedures that meet standards for all of the other evaluation procedures)
- Required parental consent for initial evaluation and before implementing services presented in the IEP
- Specification of the roles of school personnel to attend IEP conferences, including parents, not fewer than one regular education teacher, not fewer than one special education teacher, an individual who can interpret instructional implications of evaluations, and a representative of the school district who has supervisory responsibilities and is knowledgeable about the general education curriculum and outside agency resources
- Free and appropriate public education required for all, even those suspended or expelled
- Measurable goals with evaluation procedures that meet standards for all of the other evaluation procedures

Authorization of No Child Left Behind Legislation

The No Child Left Behind Act (NCLB) passed by the U.S. Congress in 2001 and signed by President George W. Bush on January 8, 2002, mandated requirements and added specificity to elements of the 1965 Elementary and Secondary Education Act. Purposes of this legislation were summarized under accountability, assessment, and high standards. Goals of the legislation were as lofty and most likely as undoable as President Clinton's Goals 2000 that mandated, among other things, having "All Children Enter School Ready to Learn."

NCLB unleashed a flurry of high-stakes testing in specific curricular areas (reading and math as first subjects to be tested), inclusion of children with disabilities in the testing scheme, intensive preparations for the tests, high-profile reports of schools that made or failed to make adequate yearly progress (AYP), higher standards for teacher certification, and more accountability of schools for student achievement. This legislation activated considerable discussion, much of it quite critical, in the professional literature, among school personnel, families, and in the Congress. Many educators stress that education is not conducive to high-stakes testing. Children do not learn the same amount at the same rate, as pointed out in Chapter 2. Success of schools cannot be measured by tests. Furthermore, test results should be used to guide instruction, not to signify school failure.

One of the harshest criticisms of NCLB has been that the emphasis on testing has narrowed the school curriculum considerably. Another is that the focus on students below proficiency has shifted attention and resources from very able learners who need challenge and advancement; consequently, they are being *held* behind (NC*H*B). Still another concern is that standardized tests and assessment of adequate yearly progress in cognitive areas do not assess student growth in the emotional, physical, self-expressive, and social areas that also are vital for student development (Dettmer, 2006). Children need development in fine arts, physical education, practical arts, problem solving, and working together collaboratively. All of these problems are compounded by failure of the federal government to adequately fund the legislation.

A number of revisions were proposed for a reauthorization of NCLB slated to happen during September 2007, but the process faltered under considerable controversy and debate during a politically volatile period. Changes considered for the reauthorization include, in a broad sense, making it more flexible and broad-based to serve its original purposes. Examples would be a wider selection of tests that provide more authentic assessment, supplemental education services for schools that are falling behind, limiting of students to be tested for whom English is a second or even a third language, and better data-processing systems to ascertain progress and diagnose needs.

Proponents of NCLB say the partnerships that are emerging have been encouraging and the resultant experienced-based information has been constructive. Most acknowledge that NCLB has caused a narrowing of the curriculum and some teaching to the test, but some schools are working to develop more flexible tests. They further believe that the responses to such concerns are providing new energy to work toward the accountability and high standards that were mandated.

Expanded goals for NCLB could include improving high school graduation rates, providing better tests to measure accountability, having stronger emphasis on preparing students for work and college, including assessments that reflect critical thinking and problem solving, and retaining excellent teachers by means of career ladders and mentors.

A BRIEF HISTORY OF COLLABORATIVE
SCHOOL CONSULTATION

The advent of special education in public schools probably dates back to the mid-nineteenth century, when state after state (Rhode Island in 1840, then Massachusetts in 1952, and followed in time by all others) passed compulsory school attendance laws mandating formal education for every school-age child regardless of disability, giftedness, or other special need. And now, in the twenty-first century, as school doors open each morning and school bells ring, students congregate and classes begin, students bring their special needs to school to be addressed. Up to one-third of all school-age children can be described as experiencing difficulties in school by reason of special needs. If the significant learning needs of gifted students were included, this figure would be increased substantially.

These realities, along with various social issues of the times, have spurred interest in school consultation, collaboration, and other forms of teamwork such as co-teaching, mentoring, cooperative learning, and peer tutoring. The result has been an escalating number of conferences, publications, research studies, pilot programs, federal and state grants, training projects, as well as development of several teacher preparation courses and programs, for understanding and applying collaborative practices in schools.

Collaborative School Consultation before 1970

School consultation probably originated in the mental health and management fields (Reynolds & Birch, 1988). Caplan (1970) had developed consultation programs to train staff members for working with troubled adolescents in Israel at the close of World War II. Building upon this Caplanian mental health consultation concept (Caplan, Caplan, & Erchul, 1995), mental health services escalated and moved into school settings, where consultation services of school psychologists produced promising results. The role of consultation in school psychology was broadened to encourage collaborative relationships (Gallessich, 1974; Pryzwansky, 1974). Such relationships were nurtured to help teachers, administrators, and parents deal with future problems as well as immediate concerns.

Examples of consulting in the areas of speech and language therapy, and in hearing-impaired and visually impaired programs, date from the late 1950s. Emphasis on teacher consultation for learning disabled and behavior-disordered students surfaces in the literature as early as the mid-1960s. At that time consultants for the most part were not special educators, but clinical psychologists and psychiatric social workers.

Also, by the mid-1960s the term *school consultation* was listed in *Psychological Abstracts* (Friend, 1988). School counselors began to promote the concept of proactive service, so that by the early 1970s consultation was being recommended as an integral part of contemporary counseling service. This interest in collaborative relationships on the part of counselors and psychologists reflected a desire to influence the individuals, groups, and systems that most profoundly affect students (Brown, Wyne, Blackburn, & Powell, 1979).

The behavioral movement had been gaining momentum in the late 1960s and it fueled interest in alternative models for intervention and the efficient use of time and other resources. This interest sparked development of a text by Tharp and Wetzel (1969) in which they presented a triadic consultation model using behavioral principles in school settings. The triadic model is the basic pattern upon which many subsequent models and methods for consultation have been constructed.

Passage of the Elementary and Secondary Education Act (ESEA) in 1965 authorized funding and made specific provisions for students with disabilities (Talley & Schrag, 1999). Reauthorizations in 1988 and 1994 mandated parent involvement and coordination in programs such as Head Start, encouraging school and community-linked services through the Community Schools Partnership Act. Consultation and collaboration became essential factors in coordinating the array of services provided for students with special needs.

By 1970 the special education literature contained references to a method of training consulting teachers to serve students in special education at the elementary level (McKenzie et al., 1970). The first direct explication of a consulting teacher service delivery model for students with mild disabilities was by McKenzie, Egner, Knight, Perelman, Schneider, and Garvin in 1970. This group described a program at the University of Vermont for preparation of consulting teachers and a plan for implementing a consulting teacher model in the state (Lilly & Givens-Ogle, 1981).

Collaborative School Consultation from 1970 to 2000

As noted earlier, the decade of the 1970s was a very busy time in the field of special education. Intensive special education advocacy, federal policy making for exceptional students, and technological advancements influenced special education practices for students who were at that time described as being handicapped (Nazzaro, 1977). The Education for All Handicapped Children's Act (EHA) was passed in 1975 and signed by President Gerald Ford, reauthorized in 1990 as the Individuals with Disabilities Education Act (IDEA), amended as IDEA 1997, and reauthorized in 2004. These legislative actions contained national guidelines on service delivery of education for students with disabilities (Talley & Schrag, 1999). One of the many guidelines was prescription of multidisciplinary and multidimensional services to be coordinated for maximizing student learning and development. By the mid-1970s consultation was being regarded as a significant factor in serving students with special needs. Special education became a major catalyst for promoting consultation and collaboration in schools (Friend, 1988).

Consultation became one of the most significant educational trends by the mid-1980s for serving students with special needs. To analyze the trend, West and Brown (1987) sent a questionnaire to directors of special education in the fifty states. Thirty-five state directors responded. Twenty-six of the respondents stated that service delivery models in their states included consultation as an expected role of the special educator. The 26 states reported a total of ten different professional titles for consultation as a job responsibility of special educators. About three-fourths of the respondents acknowledged the need for service delivery models that include consultation. However, only seven indicated that specific requirements for competency in consultation were included in their policies.

As interest in school consultation escalated during the 1980s, the National Task Force on Collaborative School Consultation, sponsored by the Teacher Education Division (TED) of the Council for Exceptional Children (CEC), sent a publication to state departments of education with recommendations for teacher consultation services in a special education services continuum (Heron & Kimball, 1988). Several guidelines were presented for development of consultative assistance options; definition of a consulting teacher role and recommended pupil-teacher ratio; and requirements for preservice, inservice, and certification preparation programs. The report included a list of education professionals skilled in school consultation and a list of publications featuring school consultation.

By 1990 a new journal focusing on school consultation, the *Journal of Educational and Psychological Consultation* (JEPC)*,* appeared. A preconvention workshop sponsored by the Teacher Education Division of the Council for Exceptional Children on school consultation and collaboration programs and practices was a featured event at the 1990 annual CEC conference in Toronto. Early leaders in school consultation reconceptualized models to fit more appropriately with inclusive schools and expanded roles of school personnel. Caplan's mental health consultation model evolved into mental health collaboration as a better choice of practice for school-based professionals (Caplan, Caplan, & Erchul, 1995). Bergan (1995) similarly described an evolution from the school psychologist's behavioral consultation focus on assessment, labeling, and placement activities to an expanded role of consultative and collaborative problem solving for students' needs. The framework for behavioral consultation was revised to become a case-centered, problem-solving approach that could be teacher-based, parent-based, or conjoint-based (parent-teacher) consultation in which the consultee's involvement is critical to success of positive client outcomes (Kratochwill & Pittman, 2002).

In the field of education for gifted students, discussion of collaborative consultation practices was minimal but gradually increased and promised to be one of the most viable fields for its extensive use (Dettmer, 1989). For more than two decades Dettmer and Lane (1989) and Idol-Maestas and Celentano (1986) stressed the need for collaborative consultation practices to assist with learning needs of gifted and talented students who spend most of their school day in regular classrooms. Dyck and Dettmer (1989) promoted methods for facilitating learning programs of twice exceptional, gifted learning-disabled students within a consulting teacher plan.

Collaborative School Consultation since 2000

The general public in the new millennium is aware that teaching is not just the responsibility of professional educators within the school's walls. Community members and resource personnel beyond school campuses are needed as collaborators and team members who can help plan and direct rich, authentic learning experiences for students.

Also gaining prominence is an awareness of the need for collaboration among general and special education teachers that will give students opportunities for learning and practicing skills related to standards set forth by governing bodies of each area. The practice of teaming across classrooms is being utilized by many dedicated teachers as an approach that can bring students closer to achieving the standards (Kluth & Straut, 2001).

The next several decades of this millennium are critical for professional educators as they learn to work together and to *enjoy* doing it. It will be very important for them to model such behaviors because their students also will be expected to work collaboratively as adults in their careers and community roles. Strong partnerships between home and school educators will be an increasingly essential part of helping students become capable, ethical leaders for the future.

THEORETICAL AND RESEARCH BASES OF COLLABORATIVE SCHOOL CONSULTATION

Is school consultation theory-based as a practice or an atheoretical practice related to a problem-solving knowledge base? Differing points of view exist.

School consultation is theory-based if identified across more than one literature source focusing on the relationship between consultant and consultee (West & Idol, 1987). On the other hand, if identified by problem-solving methods, then it is knowledge-based in the area of problem solving. At this point it would be good to bear in mind the adage that "there is nothing so practical as a good theory."

West and Idol identified ten prominent models of consultation, of which six are founded on a clearly distinguishable theory or theories: mental health, behavioral, process, advocacy, and two types of organizational consultation. They designated a seventh as a collaborative consultation model having the essential elements for building theory because it features a set of generic principles for building collaborative relationships between consultants and consultees.

During the 1980s when interest in collaboration and consultation escalated, many analyses and discussions of school consultation took place. Heron and Kimball (1988) identified an emerging research base that includes:

- Theory and models (West & Idol, 1987)
- Methodology (Gresham & Kendell, 1987)
- Training and practice (Friend, 1984; Idol & West, 1987)
- Professional preferences for consultation service (Babcock & Pryzwansky, 1983; Medway & Forman, 1980)
- Guidelines (Salend & Salend, 1984)
- Competencies for consultations (West & Cannon, 1988)

Fuchs, Fuchs, Dulan, Roberts, and Fernstrom (1992) share views stated by Pryzwansky (1986) that many studies on consultation are poorly conceptualized and executed. Consultation researchers must assess the integrity of consultation plans, since many plans are not implemented by consultees as designed (Witt & Elliott, 1985). Conducting the research effectively requires careful planning, attention to detail, interpersonal skills, flexibility, positive relationships with school personnel, and research skills (Fuchs et al., 1992). But West and Idol (1987) have pointed out that efforts to conduct research in the complex, multidimensional field of school consultation are impeded by lack of psychometrically reliable and valid instrumentation and controls.

Without question there should be more research to ascertain effects of collaborative consultation and to understand more about the variables related to those effects. Research can be improved by use of control or comparison groups, inclusion of more than one consultant and more than one dependent measure, including follow-up data, and making every effort to control experimenter bias (Bramlett & Murphy, 1998; Fuchs et al., 1992).

According to Slesser, Fine, and Tracy (1990), much of the research on school consultation heretofore has examined behaviors specific to particular models. They propose that further research is needed to examine specific behaviors and attitudes of more successful consultants compared with those who are less successful, because it is likely that many school consultants initiate their own integration of different models. Customization of models will be a recommendation given in this book.

One promising area for exploration is intersubjectivity. Since the 1980s and the rediscovery and analysis of Vygotsky's (1978) work, this aspect of social learning has captured the attention of educational psychologists. His intersubjective attitude of negotiation and joint construction of meaning is a commitment to building shared meaning by finding common ground and exchanging interpretations (Woolfolk, 2001). Colleagues with an intersubjective attitude assert their own positions while respecting those of others and working together to co-construct useful perspectives. Recall the discussion of adult differences and variety of styles in teamwork presented in Chapter 2.

Another area of collaborative and consultative processes that must be considered is disengagement. Winding down or ending a collaborative consultation relationship is likely to be an emotionally sensitive and stressful process. It is a joint decision in which participants feel comfortable applying things that have been learned during the collaboration to new situations. Communication skills are of utmost importance and proper timing is crucial. There is no textbook approach to this (Dougherty, Tack, Fullam, & Hammer, 1996); therefore, it is essential for those involved to prepare themselves for the feelings that come when professional and personal relationships must come to an end.

STRUCTURAL ELEMENTS OF COLLABORATIVE SCHOOL CONSULTATION

Overlapping philosophies of consultation have evolved from a blending of consultation knowledge and practices in several fields. This overlap creates a tangle of philosophy and terminology that could be problematic for educators. So it is helpful to sort out the myriad consultation terms, theories, research findings, and practices, and recast them into useful structures.

When communicating about educational issues, educators will want to avoid using "educationese" (convoluted and redundant phrases), "jargon" (in-house expressions that approximate educational slang), and "alphabet soup" (acronyms that appear to laypeople as a form of code). Communication must be presented in clear language and this requires careful attention to semantics, as discussed in Chapter 1. If the simple word *chair* cited in that chapter is problematic, consider words such as *progress* and its meaning in regard to NCLB, or *misbehavior* as discussed by parents, or *reinforcers* when co-teachers plan teaching strategies, or *homework* as defined by teachers, parents, and some high-profile educational experts. So when some would say, "Never mind, it's just semantics that are causing the problem," educators must keep in mind that it is quite possible semantics *are* the problem, and often a very serious one, in understanding and resolving issues.

Collaborative school consultation is a blend of six elements—system, perspective, approach, prototype, mode, and model. These six can be synthesized into a particular

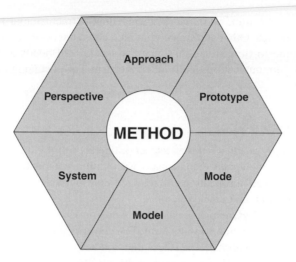

FIGURE 3.2   Structure for Collaborative School Consultation

method having a goodness of fit for a specific educational situation. (See Figure 3.2.) The six elements can be framed as:

1. *System*—entity made up of many parts that serve a common purpose
2. *Perspective*—a particular viewpoint or outlook
3. *Approach*—initial step toward a purpose
4. *Prototype*—pattern
5. *Mode*—form or manner of doing
6. *Model*—example or replica

For brevity and clarity the elements are designated by the uppercase form of their first letter—for example, system is marked with *S*. When two elements begin with identical letters, some other prominent letter in the word is used. Thus the six categories are *S* (system), *P* (perspective), *A* (approach), *R* (p**r**ototype), *E* (mod**e**), and *M* (model).

Systems

A *system* (S) is a unit composed of many diverse parts for a common purpose. The most natural system within which to conduct school consultation and collaboration is, obviously, the school context. However, educators are involved beyond the academic or cognitive aspects of student development, to address physical, emotional, social, and life-orientation aspects. Educators include not only teachers, but parents, related services and support personnel, other caregivers, and the community in general.

Systems (S) in which educators function to serve special needs of students include home and family, community, medical and dental professions, mental health, social work, counseling, extracurricular functions, and advocacy and support groups. Other systems with which consultants and collaborators might be involved from time to time in addressing very specialized needs are therapy, industry, technology, mass communications, cultural enrichment, and special interest areas such as talent development.

Perspectives

A *perspective* (P) is an aspect or object of thought from a particular viewpoint or outlook. Consultation perspectives that have evolved in education and related fields include purchase, doctor-patient, and process.

A *purchase* perspective is one in which a consumer shops for a needed or wanted item. The consumer, in this case the consultee, "shops for" services that will help the consultee serve the client's need. For example, the teacher of a developmentally delayed student might ask personnel at the instructional media center for a list of low-vocabulary, high-interest reading material with which to help the student have immediate success in reading. The purchase perspective makes several assumptions (Neel, 1981): (1) that the consultee describes the need precisely; (2) the consultant has the right "store" and stock for that need; (3) the consultant also has enough "inventory" (strategies and resources) to fill the request; and (4) the consultee can assume the costs of time, energy, or modification of classroom procedures.

As a consumer the consultee is free to accept or reject the strategy or resource, use it enthusiastically, put off trying it, or ignore it as a "bad buy." Even if the strategy is effective for that case, the consultee may need to go again to the consultant for similar needs of other clients. Little change in consultee skills for future situations is likely as a result of such consumer-type interaction. Thus the overall costs are rather high and the benefits are limited to specific situations.

The *doctor-patient* perspective casts the collaborating consultant in the role of diagnostician and prescriptor. The consultee knows there is a problem, but is not in a position to correct it. Consultees are responsible for revealing helpful information to the consultant. Again, this perspective makes several assumptions: (1) The consultee describes the problem to the consultant accurately and completely; (2) the consultant can explain the diagnosis clearly and convince the consultee of its worth; (3) the diagnosis is not premature; and (4) the prescribed remedy is not *iatrogenic* (a term from the medical profession meaning that the professionals' treatments turn out to be more debilitating than the illness they were designed to treat). An iatrogenic effect from educational services would create more problems for students, educators, or the school context than the initial condition did. For example, taking high-ability students from their general classrooms to meet with gifted program facilitators could result in resentment and antagonism from their peers and perhaps even from their classroom teachers, so that if pressed to choose, many students would reject academic enrichment in order to remain in good graces with their friends. Or having a restless, misbehaving toddler stay inside during playtime will make the child even more restless during the next quiet time.

Perspective
Approach
Prototype
METHOD
System
Mode
Model

A classroom teacher might use a doctor-patient perspective by calling on a special education teacher and describing the student's learning or behavior problem. The collaborative consultant's role would be to observe, review existing data, perhaps talk to other specialists, and then make diagnostic and prescriptive decisions. As in the medical field, there is generally little follow-up activity on the consultant's part with the doctor-patient perspective, and the consultee does not always follow through with conscientious attention to the consultant's recommendations.

In a *process* perspective, the consultant helps the client perceive, understand, and act on the problem (Neel, 1981; Schein, 1969). Consultative service does not replace the consultee's direct service to the client. In contrast to the purchase and doctor-patient perspectives, the consultant neither diagnoses nor prescribes. As Neel (1981) puts it, the consultee becomes the consultant's client for that particular problem.

Schein (1978) sorts process consultation into two types—a catalyst type in which the consultant does not know a solution but is skilled toward helping the consultee figure one out, and the facilitator type in which the consultant contributes ideas toward the solution. In both catalyst and facilitator types of process consultation the consultant helps the consultee clarify the problem, develop solutions, and implement the plan. Skills and resources used to solve the immediate problem may be used later for other problems.

All of these perspectives—purchase, doctor-patient, and the two types of process—have strengths; therefore, each is likely to be employed at one time or another in schools. One factor influencing the adoption of a particular perspective is the nature of the problem. For example, in a noncrisis situation the consultee may value the process approach. In crisis situations the consultee may need a quick solution, even if temporary, for the problem. In such cases the purchase or doctor-patient perspectives would be preferred. Situations that immediately affect the physical and psychological well-being of students and school personnel require immediate attention and cannot wait for process consultation.

When process consultation is employed regularly, many of the skills and resources that are developed for solving a particular problem can be used again and again in situations involving similar problems. This makes process consultation both time-efficient and cost-effective for schools.

Approaches

An *approach* (A) is a *formal* or *informal* preliminary step toward a purpose.

Approach

Perspective · Prototype · METHOD · System · Mode · Model

Formal collaborative consultations occur in preplanned meetings such as staffings, conferences for developing IEPs, arranged interactions between school personnel and support personnel, and organized staff development activities. They also take place in scheduled conferences with families, related services personnel, and community resource personnel.

In contrast, informal consultations often occur "on the run." These interactions have been called "vertical consultations" because people tend to engage in them while standing on playgrounds, in parking lots, at ball games, even in grocery stores. They are dubbed "one-legged consultations" when they happen in hallways with a leg propped against the wall (Hall & Hord, 1987; McDonald, 1989). Conversations also take place frequently in the teacher workroom. This aspect will be addressed more fully in Chapter 12 as a type of informal staff development. It is very important to note and record these informal interactions as consultations because they *do* require expenditures of time and energy on the part of both consultant(s) and consultee(s). Highlighting them as consultations will help establish the concept of school consultation and promote efforts to construct a suitable framework that includes allocation of quality time for interaction. Informal consultations should be encouraged because they can initiate more structured consultation and collaboration. Sometimes they become catalysts for meaningful inservice and staff development activities as well. In other cases they may initiate team effort that would have been overlooked or neglected in the daily hustle and bustle of school life.

Prototypes

A *prototype* (R) is a pattern. Consultation prototypes include mental health consultation, behavioral consultation, process consultation, and advocacy consultation. Only the first two will be featured here.

The *mental health* prototype has a long history (Conoley & Conoley, 1988). As noted earlier, the concept originated in the 1960s with the work of psychiatrist Gerald Caplan, who conceived of consultation as a relationship between two professional people in which responsibility for the client rests on the consultee (Hansen, Himes, & Meier, 1990).

Caplan (1970) proposed that consultee difficulties in dealing with a client's problems usually are caused by any one, or all, of four interfering themes:

1. Lack of knowledge about the problem and its conditions
2. Lack of skill to address the problem in appropriate ways
3. Lack of self-confidence in dealing with the problem
4. Lack of professional objectivity when approaching the problem

The consultant not only helps resolve the problem at hand, but enhances the consultee's ability to handle similar situations in the future. When the mental health prototype is used for consultation and the issue of theme interference is introduced, consultee change may very well precede client change. Therefore, assessment of success should focus on consultee attitudes and behaviors more than on client changes (Conoley & Conoley, 1988). School-based mental health consultation is characterized by consultant attention to teacher feelings and the meaning the teacher attaches to the student's behavior (Slesser, Fine, & Tracy, 1990).

The *behavioral consultation* prototype also purports to improve the performance of both consultee and client. It focuses on clear, explicit problem-solving procedures (Slesser, Fine, & Tracy, 1990). It is based on social learning theory, with skills and knowledge contributing more to consultee success than unconscious themes like objectivity or self-confidence (Bergan, 1977). Behavioral consultation probably is more familiar to educators, and therefore more easily introduced into the school context than mental health consultation. Indeed, it is the prototype on which the majority of collaborative consultation models are based. The consultant is required to define the problem, isolate environmental variables that support that problem, and plan interventions to reduce the problem. Bergan (1995) notes that his four-stage model of a consultative problem-solving process was grounded on successful identification of the problem as the first stage. Problem analysis, implementation, and evaluation followed this stage.

Conoley and Conoley (1988) regard behavioral consultation as the easiest prototype to evaluate because problem delineation and specific goal setting occur within the process. Evaluation results can be used to modify plans and to promote consultation services among other potential consultees. But behavioral consultation can fail to bring results when it focuses on problematic social behavior such as aggression or being off-task, if that behavior really emanates from poor or inadequate academic skills (Cipani, 1985).

Modes

A *mode* (E) is a particular style or manner of doing something. Modes for school consultation are direct consultation for the delivery of service to clients, or indirect consultation for delivery of service to consultees.

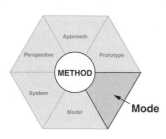

In a direct mode the consultant works directly with a special-needs student. For example, a learning disabilities consulting teacher or a speech pathologist specialist might use a particular technique with the student while a parent or classroom teacher consultee observes and assists with the technique. Direct service typically is provided to students subsequent to a referral (Bergan, 1977). The consultant may conduct observations and discuss the learning or behavior with the student (Bergan, 1977; Heron & Harris, 1987). The consultant becomes an advocate and the student has an opportunity to participate in decisions made pertinent to that need. Another example of direct service is teaching coping skills to students to use at home or at school (Graubard, Rosenberg, & Miller, 1971; Heron & Harris, 1987).

The *indirect* service delivery mode calls for "backstage" involvement among consultants and consultees to serve client needs. The consultant and consultee interact and problem-solve together. Then the consultee provides related direct service to the client. So school consultation is indirect service to students resulting from the direct service to teachers or parents.

Models

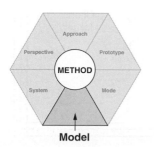

Models are many things—patterns, examples for imitation, representations in miniature, descriptions, analogies, or displays. But a model is not the real thing, just an approximation of it. A model functions as an example through which to study, replicate, approximate, or manipulate intricate things. Models are useful for examining things or ideas when they are too big to construct (a model of the solar system) or too small to copy (a DNA molecule). They help explain and illustrate things that cannot be replicated because they are too costly (a supersonic jet plane), too complex (the

United Nations system), or too time-intensive (travel to outer space). Such qualities make the model a useful structure on which to pattern the complex human processes of collaboration, consultation, and co-teaching in order to implement services that will help students who have exceptional learning needs.

A few of the many well-known models that have been adopted or adapted for collaboration and consultation in schools over the past twenty-five years are:

- Triadic model
- Resource/Consulting Teacher Program model
- Instructional Consultation model
- Conjoint Behavioral Consultation model
- Consultee-centered consultation model
- Teacher Assistance Teams model
- Responsive Systems Consultation model
- Collaborative consultation and its variant models

The *triadic* model, developed by Tharp and Wetzel (1969) and Tharp (1975), is the classic one from which many school consultation and collaboration models have evolved. It includes three roles—consultant, consultee (or mediator), and client (or target). In this most basic of the existing models, services are not offered directly, but through an intermediary (Tharp, 1975). The service flows from the consultant through the mediator to the target. The consultant role is typically, although not always, performed by an educational specialist such as a learning disabilities teacher or a school psychologist. The consultee is usually, but not always, the classroom teacher. The client or target is most often, but not always, the student with the exceptional learning need. An educational need may be a disability or an advanced ability requiring special services for the student. The triadic model requires that both consultant and consultee take ownership of the problem and share accountability for the success or failure of the program that is developed (Idol, Paolucci-Whitcomb, & Nevin, 1995). (See Figure 3.3.)

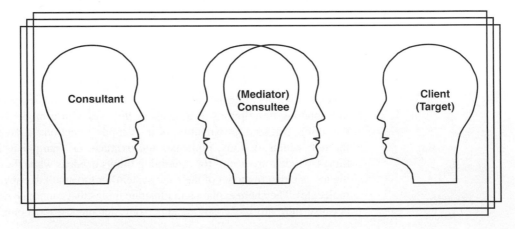

FIGURE 3.3   Example of a Basic Triadic Consultation

When studying the models, it is important to recall the discussion in Chapter 1 about roles. Roles are interchangeable among individuals, depending on the school context and the educational need. For example, on occasion a learning disabilities consulting teacher might be a consultee who seeks information and expertise from a general classroom teacher consultant. At another time a student might be the consultant for a resource room teacher as consultee, and parents as the clients who are targets for interventions intended to help their child. Tharp gives the following example:

> Ms. Jones the second-grade teacher may serve as mediator between Brown, the psychologist, and John, the problem child. At the same time, she may be the target of her principal's training program and the consultant to her aide-mediator in the service of Susie's reading problem. The triadic model, then, describes relative position in the chain of social influence. (Tharp, 1975, p. 128)

Tharp identifies several strengths of the triadic model, including the clarity it provides in delineating social roles and responsibilities, and the availability of evaluation data from two sources—mediator behavior and target behavior. However, it may not be the most effective model for every school context and content area given the process skills and resources that are available. Here is a summary highlighting the triadic model's strong points and possible concerns:

■ *Strong Points:* Appropriate in crisis situations; a good way to get started with the consultee; quick and direct; informal and simple; keeps problem in perspective; has objectivity on consultant's part; provides student anonymity if needed; is time efficient; can lead into more intensive collaborative consultation; may be all that is needed.

■ *Possible Concerns:* Has little or no carryover to other situations; probably will be needed again for same or similar situations; only one other point of view available; consultant will need expert skills; essential data may be unavailable; consultant may be held accountable for lack of progress; there is little or no follow-up.

The *Resource/Consulting Teacher Program* (R/CT) model was implemented at the University of Illinois and replicated in both rural and large urban areas (Idol, Paolucci-Whitcomb, & Nevin, 1986). It is based on the triadic model, with numerous opportunities for interaction among teachers, students, and parents. The resource/consulting teacher offers direct service to students through tutorials or small-group instruction and indirect service to students through consultation with classroom teachers for a portion of the school day. Students who are not staffed into special education programs can be served along with exceptional students mainstreamed into general classrooms. Parents are sometimes included in the consultation. (See Figure 3.4.)

In the R/CT model, emphasis is placed on training students in the curricula used within each mainstreamed student's general classroom (Idol-Maestas, 1983). Close cooperation and collaboration between the R/CT and the classroom teacher are required so that teacher expectations and reinforcement are the same for both resource room and regular class setting (Idol-Maestas, 1981). This accentuates the importance of sharing perspectives and preferences as discussed in Chapter 2.

■ *Strong Points:* Provides direct and indirect service; stipulates specific and relatively generous percentages of time for interaction when determining caseloads; includes

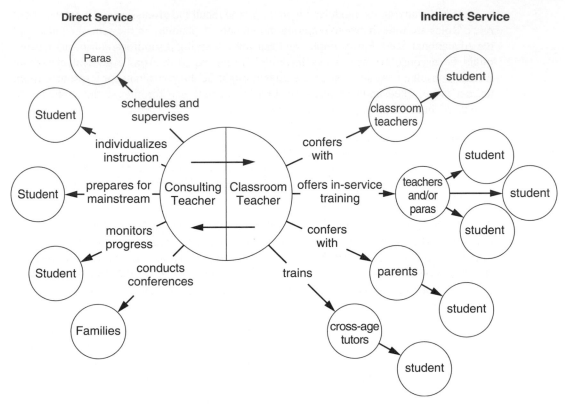

FIGURE 3.4   Interpretation of Resource/Consulting Teacher Program Model

parent involvement; is an "in-house" approach to problems; allows opportunity for student involvement; is compatible with interrelated methods; encourages ownership by many roles in problem solving; more closely approximates classroom setting; spreads responsibility around; provides opportunity for regular contact between consultant and consultee.

■ *Possible Concerns:* Energy-draining; caseloads can be high for the consulting teacher; indirect services are not weighted as heavily as direct services; provides delayed or no reinforcement for the consultant; requires strong administrator support and cooperation.

The *Instructional Consultation* (IC) model merges skill in collaborative consultation with expertise in specific areas of content. The model responds to several premises that have been offered by educational experts. First, teacher behavior does make a crucial difference to children's achievement (Rosenfield, 1995). Second, many tasks assigned to students are not well matched to their instructional levels. Bloom (1976) asserted that alterable variables, as opposed to such variables as IQ, are more important in planning instruction. Children should be regarded as having learning disabilities only if they fail to learn *after* having appropriate instruction (Rosenfield, 1995). Furthermore, when students are referred for special services, their classroom teachers should have ongoing assistance in developing and managing their learning programs.

The IC process begins with entry-level discussion between consultant and teacher about roles, expectations, and commitment. Consultants are case managers who have relinquished the expert role and configured their professional relationships to be collaborative and egalitarian. Steps proceed through problem identification and analysis, classroom observation, procedures such as curriculum-based assessment, implementation of interventions, ongoing evaluation, and termination of the consultation relationship. At termination, a written record of agreed-on findings is submitted to involved parties.

Rosenfield lays out challenges of providing continuing education to practitioners of this model. Online supervision and coaching are two supporting practices. Each team member is required to develop and apply consulting skills in order to create effective multidisciplinary teams. Another challenge is introduced by the variations in participants' preservice teacher preparation for applying consultation (Gravois, Knotek, & Babinski, 2002). Co-educators have to arrive at understandings and "be on the same page." This reinforces points about perspectives and preferences presented in Chapter 2. In addition, the goals and processes of this model are aligned with Vygotsky's social construction principles (Knotek, Rosenfield, Gravois, & Babinski, 2003). The interpersonal process of the consultation, problem-solving skills, language, and support personnel helps the consultee acquire new insight into the problem.

■ *Strong Points:* Follows the existing stage of consultation; removes attitudes that internal deficits within the child or the family create the learning and behavioral problems; focuses on the student-teacher-task interactions (Rosenfield, 1995); and helps transform schools into learning communities.

■ *Possible Concerns:* Does not relieve teachers of the responsibility for student learning; requires excellent communication skills; calls for teachers to have data-collection time and skill; needs consultant knowledge of high-quality instruction; is more problematic at the secondary level where a student has an array of teachers; must include a strategy for exiting from the consultation.

The *Conjoint Behavioral Consultation* (CBC) model offers home-school collaboration and shared problem solving (Wilkinson, 2005a). Behavioral problems in the classroom are intrusive and distracting to learning. Unfortunately, many classroom teachers have had little or no training in behavior management techniques. This relatively new model is an indirect, structured model of consultation service delivery for parents, teachers, and school personnel to join in and share responsibility for addressing academic, social, or behavioral needs (Wilkinson, 2005a). Home and school collaborators share problem solving as they work to pinpoint the problem or problems, develop a plan, and conjointly evaluate the success of the plan. A method of data collection for behaviors is conjointly developed.

■ *Strong Points:* Research on the model is ongoing; school educators and home educators respond well to the conjoint involvement of families, teachers, and school psychologists.

■ *Possible Concerns:* Some of the research is single-case study and a more robust design would help draw conclusions about attribution of improved behavior (Wilkinson, 2005a).

The *consultee-centered consultation* model is based on Caplan's work and is a non-prescriptive model that involves interaction between consultant and consultee, with the first task being to identify existing conceptualizations (Sandoval, 2003). Active listening and an attitude of onedownsmanship are important tools for the consultant. Next steps call for relationship building while maintaining rapport, problem identification, and generating a new theory. Some cognitive dissonance is expected as the participants ask questions and reframe facts. The goal is not to bring the consultee to an understanding that has been determined in advance by the consultant, but to construct together a concept that fits the situation and permits action (Sandoval, 2003). This model leaves the responsibility to accept or reject suggestions up to the consultee. Consultee-centered consultation is common in Swedish schools and is often used in preschools and childcare institutions (Hylander, 2003).

■ *Strong Points:* The learner (consultee) is actively participating and not passively receiving information; long-term and ripple-effect benefits in other situations can be expected; both consultant and consultee learn (Ingraham, 2003).

■ *Possible Concerns:* Needs more research on discourse of consultants; requires that consultants are calm and not shocked by a situation as presented for consultation; calls for self-disclosure by consultee (Ingraham, 2003); consultee must expect change and so may need to tolerate risks.

The *Teacher Assistance Teams* (TAT) model was developed in the 1970s as a way for classroom teachers to self-refer for assistance from a team of two or three skilled teachers in their building who have been elected as a problem-solving team (Pugach & Johnson, 1995). The team typically meets in problem-solving sessions for about thirty minutes. The approach also was intended as a means of reducing referrals to special education. It is regarded as a very nondirective approach to problem solving in which classroom teachers are regarded as professionals capable of using the problem-solving process effectively. The model also has been employed by special education pairs and others who have similar roles. As an in-house assistance plan it could be helpful for novice teachers who might otherwise be reluctant to ask for help due to apprehension that they might be regarded as less than competent.

■ *Strong Points:* Involves several teachers as experts; treats the consultee as a capable professional and not incompetent because of requesting assistance; reduces the number of inappropriate referrals (Pugach & Johnson, 1995).

■ *Possible Concerns:* Needs structure in the meetings even though it is a nondirective approach; requires teacher commitment to the recommended changes.

The *Responsive Systems Consultation* (RSC) model will resonate with co-educators who believe that learning and behavioral concerns result from the contexts and interactions experienced by the student. As some would put it, the problem is in the unsuitability of the environment for the student, not a misfit of the student in the environment. RSC takes a behavioral approach with collaborative consultation characteristics (Denton, Hasbrouck, & Sekaquaptewa, 2003). Parents and teachers work together in interview settings to achieve common goals.

Most *collaborative consultation* models are derived from Tharp and Wetzel (1969) and Tharp (1975) and include three components—(C) consultant, M (mediator), and (T) target (Idol et al., 1995). Collaborative consultation is a problem-centered approach requiring all parties in the consultation to participate in development of exemplary programs (Idol et al., 1995). The consultant and consultee are equal partners with diverse expertise in identifying problems, planning intervention strategies, and implementing recommendations that carry mutual responsibility (Idol et al., 1986; Raymond, McIntosh, & Moore, 1986).

The communication is not hierarchical or one-way. Rather, there is a sense of parity that blends the skills and knowledge of both consultant and consultee, with disagreements viewed as opportunities for constructive extraction of the most useful information (Idol et al., 1995). In addition, both consultant and consultee work directly with the student. In research to investigate teacher responses to consultative services, Schulte, Osborne, and Kauffman (1993) found that most teachers who were surveyed viewed collaborative consultation as an acceptable alternative to resource rooms. However, scheduling and congruence of teacher time slots can impose limits on success.

Idol, Nevin, and Paolucci-Whitcomb (1995) list six generic principles that participants need for success:

1. Situational leadership for guidance
2. Cooperative goal structures for conflict resolution
3. Appropriate interview skills
4. Active listening skills
5. Oral and written communication without "educationese" or jargon
6. Positive nonverbal language

Pryzwansky (1974) emphasized the need for mutual consent on the part of both consultant and consultee, mutual commitment to the objectives, and shared responsibility for implementation and evaluation of the plan. To reiterate, the collaborative school consultation process must be voluntary and nonsupervisory, and carried out with a demeanor of onedownsmanship. The consultant, mediator, and target have reciprocally reinforcing effects on one another and this encourages more collaborative consultation at a later date (Idol-Maestas, 1983). Each collaborator, as part of the team, contributes a clearly defined portion of the effort so that all come together to create a complete plan or solution.

Variations of collaborative consultation can be structured for particular contexts. For example, one teacher in a small rural school with as many as six different lesson preparations who is coaching a different sport each season finds a combination of the collaborative and triadic models very time efficient. It can be conducted informally to utilize both consultant and consultee knowledge efficiently. John-Steiner, Weber, and Minnis (1998) make the case for a theory of collaboration that promotes multiple definitions and multiple models of collaborative practice.

More Variations on Triadic and Collaborative School Consultation Models.   Many experts assert that the very best model is a combination of the best features from many models to create one that is tailor-made for a designated school context. Additional variations of collaborative consultation that lend themselves to further adaptation for local contexts are outlined in the section that follows.

Class-Within-a-Class (CWC). This is an innovative delivery model that reduces dependence on pull-out programs by serving learning disabled students full-time in general classes. Special education teachers go into the classrooms during instruction time to collaborate and consult with the teacher and provide additional support to students with exceptional learning needs.

Schoolwide Enrichment Model (SEM). This well-researched model (Renzulli & Reis, 1985) provides three types of challenging learning experiences for gifted and talented students in the regular classroom. It involves close collaboration between general education teachers and gifted program facilitators and includes intensive staff development to prepare all participants for their roles. Teachers and facilitators are co-educators in providing gifted and talented students with curriculum options and alternatives such as flexible pacing, enrichment, personalized instruction, and challenging group experiences.

Type 1 offers exploratory activities such as field trips, interest centers, demonstrations, and resource speakers for all students. Type 2 includes methods and materials designed to promote development of critical and creative thinking skills and problem-solving skills, again for all students. As many as 15 percent to 20 percent of students in the regular classroom can be declared eligible for enrichment and served by Type 1 and Type 2 learning experiences in general classrooms (VanTassel-Baska & Brown, 2007). Type 3 often takes place in the resource room or off-campus. It typically is provided for highly able students who become independent investigators and researchers and develop products that are critiqued by authentic audiences of professionals who have expertise in the student's area of investigation.

Resource Consultation Model. The concept was developed originally by Curtis, Curtis, and Graden (1988) and adapted for education of gifted students. The consultation is a problem-solving process shared by all school personnel in which the primary goal is to use limited and expensive resources more effectively and efficiently to better serve students (Kirschenbaum, Armstrong, & Landrum, 1999). It can occur at one of three levels—collaboration on a less formal and less structured basis; assistance from gifted education personnel (an option that turns out to be chosen 85 percent of the time); or team intervention if several school personnel will be affected, such as in a consultation matter involving radical acceleration.

■ *Summary of Strong Points for Collaborative Models:* In general, they fit current school reform goals; inspire professional growth for all through shared expertise; provide many points of view; focus on situations encompassing the whole school context; involve general *and* special education staff and often resource and support personnel as well; generate many ideas; maximize opportunities for constructive use of adult differences; allow administrators to assume a facilitative role; facilitate liaisons with community agents; are pleasing to families because many school personnel are working with their child.

■ *Summary of Possible Concerns:* Little or no training of educators in collaborative consultation and co-teaching; shortage of time and compatibility of schedules for interacting; working with adults not the preference of some educators; require solid, not token, administrator support; confidentiality harder to ensure with many people involved; could diffuse responsibility so much that no one feels ultimately responsible; can take time to see results.

Co-teaching as a team is one of the most powerful forms of consultation combined with collaboration, appearing on the educational scene in the 1960s and having a resurgence of interest among educators in the 1990s (Pugach & Johnson, 1995). Co-teaching and its variations will be the focal topic of Chapter 7.

DEVELOPMENT AND APPLICATION OF PLANS FOR COLLABORATIVE SCHOOL CONSULTATION

When planning for collaborative school consultation, it is helpful to use an informal, journalistic-style template that directs the discussion, such as:

- Why is this type of service best?
- What do we expect to occur?
- Who will be involved?
- When will it take place and for how long?
- Where will it be happening?
- How will we put the plan into operation and assess results?

Then, returning to the six components in Figure 3.3 for constructing a method, planners can decide which elements and to what extent they will be structured to help frame the plan:

1. System (school systems, other social systems)
2. Perspective (purchase, doctor-patient, process)
3. Approach (formal, informal)
4. Prototype (mental health, behavioral)
5. Mode (direct, indirect)
6. Model (triadic, Resource/Consulting Teacher Program, Instructional Consultation, Conjoint Behavioral Consultation, consultee-centered consultation, Teacher Assistance Teams, and other collaborative consultation variations).

Referring again to Figure 3.2, the Method area in the center draws from each of the six components to synthesize all into a method with goodness of fit for the particular school situation. Several practice situations that follow will provide opportunities to plan and implement school consultation, collaboration, and/or teamwork. To work through the situations, it is helpful to consider the why, who, what, when, where, and how, and choose among options for system, perspective, approach, prototype, mode, and model. It is not necessary to dwell on interaction and coordination processes at this time.

When thinking about a situation and one of the structures that could be useful, it is stimulating to address complex circumstances in the way that the eminent thinker Albert Einstein did, that is, as a thought problem to be explored in the mind and not in a laboratory or a classroom. The idea is to manipulate variables and concepts mentally, "seeing" them from all angles and withholding judgment until all conceivable avenues have been explored in one's mind. Thought problems are opportunities for intently reflecting on real problems and possibilities before presenting them for discussion and critique by others. This abstract way of pondering problems rather than manipulating elements in the real world, is a practice Einstein employed quite successfully. Indeed, much of the time this kind of thinking does occur informally when co-educators are contemplating multifaceted processes such as collaborative consultation and co-teaching.

■ ■ ■ ■ ■ ▬▬▬▬▬▬▬▬▬▬▬▬▬▬▬▬▬▬▬▬▬▬▬▬▬▬▬▬▬▬

APPLICATION 3.1
FORMULATING AN APPROPRIATE METHOD FOR SPECIFIC SITUATIONS

SAMPLE SITUATIONS
Before reflecting on one or more of the following sample situations, consider these combinations that have been used at one time or another for different circumstances:

■ One person or group may decide that the best way to address a situation is with the *triadic* model and a *purchase* perspective, using *indirect* service from the consultant to the client, in an *informal, mental health* prototype of interaction within the *school system.*

■ Another may address a client's need by choosing the *Conjoint Behavioral Consultation* model, with a *process* perspective, in a *formal* and *direct* way, using the *behavioral* prototype in the *social service* system.

■ Yet another individual or group may approach a particular problem through a variation of a *collaborative consultation* model, with a *process* perspective, using *direct* service to the client from both consultant and consultee, in a *formal* way that approximates a *behavioral* prototype, in a *community work setting* as the system.

Also, when thinking about possibilities, it is helpful to think about what might be major obstacles in carrying out the proposed method and also to consider what could emerge as major benefits and positive ripple effects beyond the immediate situation.

Situation 1: Ten-year-old Clarisse is new to the school and is placed in the TMR program. Her teacher quickly learns that she prefers to observe rather than participate, and will not join in group activities. In her previous school, according to her parents, Clarisse had been allowed to lie on the floor most of the day so she would not have tantrums about participation. Her new teacher and paraprofessional want Clarisse to demonstrate her capabilities, but do not want her to get off to a bad start in the new school and do not want parents to feel negative toward her new teachers. The teacher knows this is a crucial time for Clarisse and wonders what to do.

Situation 2: The speech pathologist has been asked by the gifted program facilitator to consult with her regarding a highly gifted child who has minor speech problems, but is being pressured by parents and kindergarten teacher to "stop the baby talk." The child is becoming very nervous and at times withdraws from conversation and play. How can the speech pathologist structure collaborative consultation to help?

Situation 3: A school psychologist is conferring with a teacher about a high school student she has just evaluated. The student is often a behavior problem, and the psychologist is discussing methods for setting up behavior limits with appropriate contingencies and rewards. The teacher makes numerous references to the principal as a person who likes for teachers to be self-sufficient and not "make waves." How should the school psychologist handle this?

Situation 4: A fifth-grade student with learning disabilities (LD) is not having success in social studies. The student has a serious reading problem, but is a good listener and stays on task. The LD resource teacher suspects that the classroom teacher is not willing to modify materials and expectations for the child. The teacher has not discussed this situation with the LD teacher, but the student has in a roundabout way. Parent-teacher conferences are scheduled for the following week. What should happen here, and who will make it happen?

Situation 5: Parents of a student with learning disabilities have asked the special education consulting teacher to approach the student's classroom teacher about what they think is excessive and too-difficult homework. The parents say it is disrupting their home life and frustrating the student. How can this situation be addressed?

Situation 6: A high school learning disabilities consultant is visiting with a principal at the principal's request. The principal expresses concern about the quality of teaching demonstrated by two faculty members and asks the consultant to observe them and then provide feedback. How should the consultant handle this situation?

Situation 7: A pediatrician contacts the director of special education and asks her to meet with a group of local doctors to discuss characteristics and needs of children with disabilities. How should this opportunity be structured for maximum benefit to all?

Situation 8: A middle school student has been failing in several subjects during the semester and has become more and more sullen and withdrawn over the past several weeks. Two of her teachers have arrived independently at the strong possibility that she is being abused by a male relative who is living with her family in the home. What actions need to be taken here?

Situation 9: Schoolwide achievement tests will be administered soon. According to IDEA regulations, special education students are to be included in these assessments or documentation must be made as to reasons for excluding them from the tests. The consulting teacher is conferring with a teacher who has several students with exceptional learning needs in her inclusive classroom about their ability to take these tests. The pressure of responding to demands of NCLB loom in the minds of both teachers. Where should these co-educators go with their concerns?

Situation 10: A fifth-grade boy with a quiet and sensitive nature who prefers to work and play with girls and shuns athletics, is not accepted by other boys in his class. He is being harassed and bullied by several of them on the playground, in restrooms, and on the way home from school. He has not talked about his plight to teachers, but two of his classmates have described some of the events to their classroom teacher. What should the teacher do about the boy, the alleged bullies, and the informers?

Situation 11: An energetic new teacher is full of ideas that often are initiated with little planning or step-by-step instruction for students. She allows the students to be self-directed and to move from one activity to another as their interests impel them. A slow-learning student is floundering in this unstructured setting. The special education director has been alerted to the situation by the school principal, who had been approached by the student's mother with her concerns. There is no other classroom at the student's grade level in this school to which the student might be transferred, and now that several weeks of school have gone by, it would be too late to consider such a step anyway. What might be done?

Situation 12: A teenage student went hunting over the weekend. He had lost his hunting knife with which he dressed out game, so he borrowed one from a friend. Now he drives to school on Monday with the knife in his backpack, intending to return it to his friend in the parking lot. But they do not connect and he is distracted by an altercation that is happening, so he forgets about the knife. But somebody learns about it later in the day and reports his backpack item. He is called to the principal's office. His special education teacher for learning disabilities and attention deficit disorder with hyperactivity (ADHD), his single mother, and law officers are summoned. Then his coach becomes involved because this student is a star athlete whose eligibility to play is crucial to the team's success. How should this situation best be addressed?

Situation 13: A preschool child with behavior disorders hits other children for no apparent cause in the inclusive day care center. The teacher has tried behavior management strategies and time-out periods. But the child impulsively strikes out whenever another child enters her physical "space." How should the Early Childhood Special Education (ECSE) teacher approach the grandparent caregiver and who else could be involved to help?

ETHICAL CONSIDERATIONS FOR DEVELOPING FOUNDATIONS AND FRAMEWORKS

Methods for collaborative consultation in schools are as varied as the school personnel who will use them and the school climates in which they will be used. Models may be drawn on for building the framework(s), but ultimately the development process will be a collaborative endeavor that is itself an example of the method to be developed for students.

If collaborative efforts markedly reduce the time and instruction needed for direct services to students with special needs, there will be a risk of diminishing returns (Friend & Cook, 1992). This is mentioned occasionally by parents as a reason for opposing interactive processes such as inclusive classrooms, and collaboration and co-teaching practices. This issue must be examined with objectivity (is it a valid point?), then discussed candidly with parents and resolved.

Cooperation is a facilitative endeavor, but not in the same way as collaboration. Cooperation often involves giving up something—changing one's perspectives to a degree or matters of one's preferences to a certain extent. Sometimes cooperation is a necessary engagement. Negotiation and arbitration impose similar demands and are complex social behaviors. But collaboration combines all three. It requires work, and more work, for relatively autonomous individuals to arrive at the same goal along different pathways.

Occasionally it is in the best interest of all concerned, and the student in particular, for co-educators to decide they must disengage from a collaborative endeavor or a shared teaching process. Having previously discussed a transition plan or an exit procedure can obviate feelings of inadequacy and failure among all concerned. The situation should be handled objectively according to the prior agreement and not taken as personal rejection.

TIPS FOR STRUCTURING FOUNDATIONS OF COLLABORATIVE ENDEAVORS

1. Be knowledgeable about the history and outcomes of school improvement and reform movements.
2. Keep up-to-date on educational issues and concerns.
3. Be informed about educational legislation and litigation.
4. Be on the alert for new methods or revisions of existing methods through which consultation and collaboration can occur in your school context.
5. Read current research on school consultation and collaboration, and highlight references to these processes in other professional material you read.
6. Visit programs where models different from those in your school(s) are being used.
7. Find sessions at professional conferences that feature different models and methods, and attend them to broaden your knowledge about educational systems.
8. Create specific ways that teachers can get your help and make those ways known.
9. Clarify expectations by having dialogue with people in all roles in the school context. Expectations will vary from person to person, and the first question must be, How important are these differences?
10. Be flexible and adaptable. Change takes time, and it must be preceded by awareness of the need to change.

CHAPTER REVIEW

1. Every decade from the 1960s on has had important movements and legislation that address the welfare of students with special needs. These efforts have sparked educational accountability, restructuring, mainstreaming in a least restrictive environment (LRE), assurance of free and appropriate public education (FAPE), the regular education initiative (REI), inclusion, and increasing interest in collaborative consultation among co-educators.

2. The reauthorization of the Individuals with Disabilities Act in 2004 and pending reauthorization of the No Child Left Behind Act contain mandates for ensuring student achievement and directives for managing environments so students can succeed. IDEA stipulates high expectations for students with exceptional learning needs as well as professional development and training of all preservice and school personnel who work with the students, replacement of IEP objectives and benchmarks with measurable annual goals, compatibility with NCLB performance goals, and parental consent for evaluation and services. NCLB focuses on accountability of schools and teachers for student learning, assessment of learning with high-stakes testing, and high standards for student learning and teacher credentialing.

3. School consultation evolved from practices in the mental health and medical services fields. Differing points of view are held about the existence of a theoretical base of school consultation. Some researchers consider school consultation theory-based if the relationship between consultant and consultee can be identified across more than one literature source. Research in school consultation and collaboration has been conducted to assess situational variables, outcome variables, and organizational change. There is need for more reliable and valid instrumentation, more specific definition of variables, and more careful control of variables during the research.

4. Structural elements to develop effective methods of school consultation can be categorized as: Systems (institutions and contexts); Perspectives (purchase, doctor-patient, problem-solving); Approaches (formal, informal); Prototypes (mental health, behavioral); Modes (direct, indirect); and a variety of Models.

5. Several collaborative consultation models are the triadic model (the basic model for most collaborative consultation models), Resource/Consulting Teacher Program model, the Instructional Consultation model, the Conjoint Behavioral Consultation model, the consultee-centered consultation model, the Teacher Assistance Teams model, the Responsive Systems Consultation model, and numerous other variations of the collaborative consultation model.

6. Educators should introduce into their school context one or more structures combining opportunities for consultation, collaboration, and co-teaching that will be well suited to the local schools, co-educators, families, and most of all taking into account students' needs and what will serve them best.

TO DO AND THINK ABOUT

1. Pinpoint several changes that have occurred in special education during the past several decades, and suggest implications they have for school consultation methods. For example, if you decide on inclusion, it could be analyzed as follows:

Select an article or book on inclusion. Before reading it, put your "knows" in Column 1 on the left and your "wants" in Column 2 in the middle. After your reading, complete Column 3 on the right. Return to your paper periodically as you study more about students with special needs, adding more information to the respective columns.

COLUMN 1	COLUMN 2	COLUMN 3
What I KNEW about Inclusion	What MORE I Want to Know about Inclusion	What I HAVE learned about Inclusion NOW

2. Locate articles focusing on consultation, collaboration, and teamwork. Summarize the highlights, and prepare a "fact sheet" or information bulletin for other school personnel such as building administrator or school board member.

3. Have the complete articles from which you shared information in #2 available for any who might ask to read the entire work.

4. Brainstorm with a group to list current issues and major problems in education. After generating as many ideas as possible, mark those that seem most amenable to solutions afforded by consultation, collaboration, and teamwork. You might want to asterisk those that in the past have "belonged" to special education, and discuss what part general education plays in dealing with those issues now.

5. Visit schools where consultation and collaboration play an integral role in serving students' special needs. Observe the consultation systems, perspectives, approaches, prototypes, modes, and models that appear to be in use in those schools. Then summarize the results into brief, innovative descriptions of the methods that seem to have evolved from the synthesis of these components. If you feel inspired to do so, sketch a graphic to illustrate your description.

6. Just as in most fields of human endeavor, stereotypes are "out there" regarding consultation and collaboration. Here are a few of the more pejorative phrases about collaboration and consultation. Propose some ways these negative perceptions could be dismantled with some collaborative consulting among teaching colleagues.

"A consultant drives over from the central office and borrows your watch to tell you what time it is."

"Collaboration is just the latest buzzword."

"The consultant is someone from two counties away wearing a suit and carrying a briefcase."

"A consultant is a big-bucks speaker who just pulls in, pops off, and pulls out."

"Collaboration is where we convene a meeting and then we take minutes to waste hours."

"Expert? Oh, yes, X marks the spot of the little spurt under pressure."

ADDITIONAL READINGS AND RESOURCES

Bassett, D. S., Jackson, L., Ferrell, K. A., Luckner, J., Hagerty, P. J., Bunsen, T. D., & MacIsaac, D. (1996). Multiple perspectives on inclusive education: Reflections of a university faculty. *Teacher Education and Special Education, 19*(4), 355–386.

Denton, C. A., Hasbrouck, J. E., & Sekaquaptewa, S. (2003). The consulting teacher: A descriptive case study in Responsive Systems Consultation. *Journal of Educational and Psychological Consultation, 14*(1), 41–73.
A case study analysis illustrating the consulting teacher's role in implementing the Responsive Systems Consultation (RSC), a behavioral approach that features relationships within contexts. The

consultation case involves two consulting teachers and a novice second-grade teacher addressing behavioral and academic problems of a student.

Erchul, W. P., & Martens, B. K. (1997). *School consultation: Conceptual and empirical bases of practice.* New York: Plenum.

For more information about the models described in this chapter, consult the following sources.

Idol-Maestes, L., & Ritter, S. (1985). A follow-up study of resource/consulting teachers: Factors that facilitate and inhibit teacher consultation. *Teacher Education and Special Education, 8,* 121–131.

Illsley, S. D., & Sladeczek, I. E. (2001). Conjoint behavioral consultation: Outcome measures beyond the client level. *Journal of Educational and Psychological Consultation, 12*(4), 397–404.

Descriptions of five children and their families illustrate the effectiveness of Conjoint Behavioral Consultation in reducing conduct problem behaviors.

Pugach, M. C., & Johnson, L. J. (1995). *Collaborative practitioners, collaborative schools.* Denver, CO: Love.

This source describes the Teacher Assistance Teams model.

Renzulli, J. S., & Reis, S. M. *The schoolwide enrichment model: A comprehensive plan for educational excellence.* Mansfield Center, CT: Creative Learning Press.

Rosenfield, S. (1995). Instructional consultation: A model for service delivery in the schools. *Journal of Educational and Psychological Consultation, 6*(4), 297–316.

Scruggs, T. E., & Mastropieri, M. A. (1996). Teacher perceptions of mainstreaming/inclusion, 1958–1995: A research synthesis. *Exceptional Children, 63*(1), 59–74.

Sheridan, S. M., Kratochwill, T. R., & Bergan, J. R. (1996). *Conjoint Behavioral Consultation: A procedural manual.* New York: Plenum.

Smith, J. D. (1998). The history of special education: Essays honoring the bicentennial of the work of Jean Itard. *Remedial and Special Education, 19*(4), entire issue.

Tharp, R. (1975). The triadic model of consultation. In C. Parker (Ed.), *Psychological consultation in the schools: Helping teachers meet special needs.* Reston, VA: Council for Exceptional Children.

Welch, M., Sheridan, S. M., Fuhriman, A., Hart, A. W., Connell, M. L., & Stoddart, T. (1992). Preparing professionals for educational partnerships: An interdisciplinary approach. *Journal of Educational and Psychological Consultation, 3*(1), 1–23.

Wilkinson, L. A. (2005). Bridging the research-to-practice gap in school-based consultation: An example using case studies. *Journal of Education and Psychological Consultation, 16*(3), 175–200.

Wilkinson, L. A. (2005). Supporting the inclusion of a student with Asperger's syndrome: A case study using conjoint behavioral consultation and self-management. *Educational Psychology in Practice, 21,* 307–326.

Williams, J. M., & Martin, S. M. (2001). Implementing the Individuals with Disabilities Education Act of 1997: The consultant's role. *Journal of Educational and Psychological Consultation, 12*(1), 59–81.

In addition, the following references may be helpful for other topics in the chapter.

Journal of Educational and Psychological Consultation, all issues.

The journal, as noted in this chapter, was initiated in 1990 and is published four times a year for the purpose of improving scientific understanding of consultation and offering practical strategies for effective, efficient consultation to individuals and organizations. Central administrators of schools would do well to subscribe to this journal that includes research, theory, and practice across all school role groups from speech pathologists to school psychologists to preservice teachers to parents and much more.

Educational Leadership. (December 1994/January 1995), *52*(4).

Topical issue on the inclusive school.

PART **II**

PROCESS

PROCESSES FOR WORKING TOGETHER AS CO-EDUCATORS

Part Two, the processes section, includes three chapters. Chapter 4 focuses on instruction and practice in communication skills; Chapter 5 on problem finding, problem solving, and planning skills; and Chapter 6 on skills for managing, organizing, and evaluating consultative and collaborative activities in schools.

Communication takes place within the context of a school's philosophies and practices. The communication process is influenced greatly by preferences and perspectives of school personnel and by the collaborative model(s) in place within that context.

Problem finding, problem solving, and planning in collaborative settings depend on the educational contexts and diverse styles of the co-educators. The type of problem-solving structure to be used will be determined to some extent by the consulting or collaborative model(s) the co-educators select or develop.

Management, organization, and evaluation of consultative, collaborative, and co-teaching efforts must fit the school context, perspectives and preferences of school personnel, and the structures that are formulated for working together.

CHAPTER FOUR

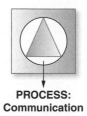

PROCESS:
Communication

Communication Processes in Collaborative School Consultation and Co-Teaching

Communication is one of the greatest achievements of humankind. A vital component of human relationships in general, it is also the foundation of cooperation and collaboration among educators. Communication is not simply delivering a message. Communication involves talking, listening, managing interpersonal conflict, and addressing concerns together. Components of successful communication are understanding, trust, autonomy, and flexibility. Effective communicators withhold judgment and minimize efforts to control the path of communication.

While problems and conflicts are unavoidable elements of life, good communication skills facilitate problem solving and resolution of conflicts. Ineffective communication creates a void that breeds misunderstanding and distrust. Elements of trust, commitment, and effective interaction are critical for conflict-free relationships. Effective communication becomes a foundation for cooperation and collaboration among school personnel, parents, students, and others involved in education.

FOCUSING QUESTIONS

1. What is a primary reason people fail in collaborative efforts?
2. What are key components of the communication process?
3. How does one establish rapport in order to facilitate effective communication?
4. What are major verbal and nonverbal skills for communicating effectively?
5. What are the primary roadblocks to communication?
6. How can a school consultant be appropriately assertive and cope with resistance, negativity, and anger to manage conflict?

KEY TERMS

anger	conflict management	resistance
assertiveness	empathy, empathic	Responsive Listening
body language	negativity	Checklist
communication	nonverbal communication	roadblocks to
computer-mediated	paraphrasing	communication
communication (CMC)	rapport	verbal communication

SCENARIO 4

The setting is the hallway of a junior high school in midafternoon, where the general math instructor, a first-year teacher, is venting to a colleague.

Math Teacher: What a day! On top of the fire drill this morning and those forms that we got in our boxes to be filled out by Friday, I had a disastrous encounter with a parent. Guess I flunked Parent Communication 101.

Colleague: Oh, one of those, huh?

Math Teacher: Jay's mother walked into my room right before fourth-hour, and accused me of not doing my job. It was awful!

Colleague: (frowns, shakes head)

Math Teacher: Thank goodness there weren't any kids around. But the music teacher was there telling me about next week's program. This parent really let me have it. I was stunned, not only by the accusation, but by the way she delivered it. My whole body went on "red alert." My heart was pounding, and that chili dog I had for lunch got caught in my digestive system. Then my palms got sweaty. I could hardly squeak out a sound because my mouth was so dry. I wanted to yell back at her, but I couldn't!

Colleague: Probably just as well. Quick emotional reactions don't seem to work very well when communication breaks down. I found out the hard way that it doesn't help to respond at all during that first barrage of words. Sounds like you did the right thing.

Math Teacher: Well, it really was hard. So you've had things like this happen to you?

Colleague: Um-humm. I see we don't have time for me to tell you about it, because here come our troops for their next hour of knowledge. But I can tell you all about it later if you want. Come to my room after school and we'll compare notes—maybe even plan some strategies for the future just in case. And, by the way, welcome to the club!

COMMUNICATION FOR EFFECTIVE SCHOOL RELATIONSHIPS

Teachers manage many kinds of relationships in their work with children who have special needs. Some relationships grow throughout the year or over several years, others are established and stable, while still others are new, tentative, and tenuous. No matter what the type of relationship, and no matter whether it is with families, colleagues, paraeducators, or other human service providers, communication is the key to successful relationships. Furthermore, communication in the twenty-first century has become paradoxically more simple and more complex due to the effects of modern technology.

In the chapter "Enter Technology, Exit Talking" of her 2006 book, Sonya Hamlin says that "even hello has changed" as a result of modern technology (p. 3). Her discussion lists examples of how technology has changed the ways we communicate:

- We e-mail the person in the office next door.
- We have a list of 15 phone numbers to reach our family.
- We pull up in our driveway and use our cell phone to see if anyone is home to help carry in the groceries.
- We get up in the morning and go online before getting our coffee.
- We don't stay in touch with friends because we don't have their e-mail addresses.

Computers, cell phones, the Internet, and even television have changed communication in the last decade. However, while all these media may be part of our repertoire when it comes to collaborating with school, home, and community partners, face-to-face interactions are still the standard and most effective type of communication for most collaboration. People typically communicate in one form or another for about 70 percent of their waking moments. Unfortunately, lack of effective communication skills is a major reason for work-related failure.

A supportive, communicative relationship among special education teachers, general classroom teachers, and parents is critical to the success of children with exceptional learning needs in inclusive classrooms. Trends in education emphasize the necessity for greatly strengthened communication among all who are involved with a student's educational program. Special educators who are to serve as consultants and team members for helping students with special needs succeed, must model and promote exemplary communication and interaction skills.

Consulting is not a one-person exercise. A consultant will pay a high price for a "Rambo" style of interaction ("My idea can beat up your idea," or "I'm right and that's just the way it is."). Communication that minimizes conflict and enables teachers to maintain self-esteem may be the most important and most "delicate" process in consulting (Gersten, Darch, Davis, & George, 1991.) Unfortunately, development of communication skills is not typically included in teacher education programs. Because the development and use of "people skills" is the most difficult aspect of collaboration for many educators, more and more educators are stressing the need for specific training in collaboration and communication skills to serve special needs students.

Challenges of Communication

Communication requires four elements:

1. A message
2. A sender of the message
3. A receiver of the message
4. The medium

Semantics play a fundamental role in both sending and receiving messages. As stressed earlier, a person who says, "Oh, it's no big deal—just an issue of semantics" is missing a major point. The semantics frequently *are* the issue and should never be taken for granted. The vital role of semantics in consultation, collaboration, and teamwork cannot be ignored.

Body language also plays a key role in communication. Studies of kinesics, or communication through body language, show that the impact of a message is about 7 percent verbal, 38 percent vocal, and 55 percent facial. The eyebrows are particularly meaningful in conveying messages.

Placing, or removing, a physical barrier would be another aspect of communication. We communicate nonverbally much of the time and in many more ways than we tend to realize. Nonverbal modes of communication include use of space, movements, posture, eye contact, attention to the clock, positions of feet and legs when sitting, use of furniture, facial expressions, gestures, mannerisms, volume of voice, rate of voice, and level of energy (Gazda, Asbury, Balzer, Childers, Phelps, & Walters, 1999).

In order to communicate effectively, the message sender must convey the purpose of the message in a facilitative style with clarity to the receiver. As the noted theologian John Powell put it, "I can't tell you what you *said,* but only what I *heard.*" Miscommunication breeds misunderstanding. A gap in meaning between what the message sender gives and what the message receiver gets can at best be described as distortion, or as communication trash in extreme cases. A person may send the message, "You look nice today," and have it understood by the receiver as, "Gee, then I usually don't look very good." A classroom teacher wanting to reinforce efforts of the learning disabilities teacher might say "Gerry seems to get much better grades on tests in the resource room," but the resource teacher may hear, "You're helping too much and Gerry can't cope outside your protection." (See Figure 4.1, which graphically illustrates a potential range of distorted communication.)

Vague semantics, distorted messages, and psychological filters disrupt the message as it passes (or doesn't pass) between the sender and the receiver. Examples of filters are differing values, ambiguous language, stereotypes and assumptions, levels of self-esteem, and personal experiences. Preconceived ideas constantly filter the messages we receive, prevent

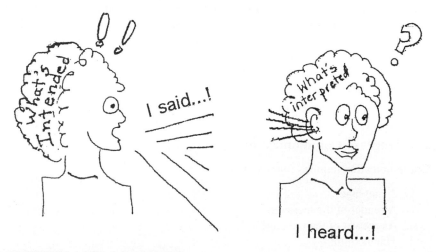

FIGURE 4.1   Miscommunication

us from hearing what others are saying, and provide only what people want to hear (Buscaglia, 1986). This can be demonstrated with the well-known game of "Gossip." Players stand in a long line or a circle, while one of them silently reads or quietly receives a message. Then that person whispers the message to the next one, and that message continues to be delivered to each one in turn. After passing through the filters of many people and stated aloud by the very last one, the message in most cases is drastically different from the original message. The game results are usually humorous. Real-life results are not always so funny.

■ ■ ■ ■ ■ ▓▓

APPLICATION 4.1
SENDING, RECEIVING, AND SHARING MESSAGES

In groups of three, with one person designated as Interviewer, another as Interviewee, and the third one Responder, conduct three-minute interviews to learn more about each other. After each interview change roles, so that each person has a turn to serve in all three capacities. Each Responder may make brief notes to use during a one-minute Share Time to introduce his or her Interviewee to the whole group. Use questions of this nature, or others given by the convener: What are your special talents? Apprehensions? Pet peeves? Successes you have had? Long-range goals? Things you want to learn more about?

Ethnic and Gender Differences in Communication

Language is the window through which the reality of others' experiences is revealed. Gender and ethnicity are other factors that may cloud that window and lead to systematic misjudgments in interpreting communication. Misunderstanding may not be due simply to miscommunication. Other factors such as the sex or cultural background of the sender or the receiver may be responsible. Examples of gender differences in conversational style affecting both sender and receiver of the message are discussed by sociolinguist Deborah Tannen and others (Tannen, 1991, 1994; Banks & Banks, 2007). Tannen's research describes differences in communication styles between females (both girls and women) and males (both boys and men):

- Amount of time listening versus talking
- Interrupting
- Physical alignment during conversation
- Use of indirectness and silence
- Topical cohesion

For example, men and boys' conversations tend to be diffuse, while those of women and girls are more tightly focused with minimal topics. Educational consultants should be aware that such types of communication style differences might lead them to be misunderstood or cause them to misunderstand their consultees.

The caveat for gender also applies to cross-cultural interactions. Most consultants are aware that different languages or different dialects may have different words for the same object. Some languages have no words for terms we use in education. For example, there is no word in Spanish for assertiveness or self-advocacy.

Verbal and nonverbal communication must be attuned to ethnic, racial, linguistic, and cultural differences. Because language and culture are so inextricably bound together, communicating with potential collaborative partners who are from different cultural and linguistic backgrounds is a very complex process (Lynch & Hanson, 1998). Chisholm (1994) has these suggestions for educators as they develop cross-cultural communication competencies:

- Develop awareness of your own cultural perspective and realize that your cultural perspective is not a universal norm.
- Develop mechanisms to cope with the stress of dealing with the unfamiliar.
- Understand that cultural context and personal experience have meaning. For example, the word *wedding* will convey a different meaning to persons from different cultural contexts, because the gender and familial role expectations, ceremonial traditions, and shared values vary across these cultures.
- Realize that logical reasoning and discourse styles are culture-specific.
- Learn about cultural aspects of nonverbal communication. For example, eye contact in a classroom may signal disrespect and inattention in one culture but may mean respect in another culture. There are cultural differences in use of space, touch, appearance, voice tone, and body language. Unwary educational consultants in such cases could lose much esteem for engaging in consultations in the same manner as they might do elsewhere.

As will be discussed specifically in Chapter 9 and elsewhere throughout the book, consultants will continue to be challenged by the cultural diversity of collaborators. Increasing diversity among colleagues, families, and communities requires that educational consultants recognize and continuously consider the impact of culture on communication in their work.

Computer-Mediated Communication

It is estimated that more than 147 million people across the country use e-mail daily. All told, people dash off millions of e-mails a day for work and pleasure, and most do not stop to consider how those hurried messages are being received or interpreted. Even in school settings, educators are sending e-mail instead of writing letters, phoning, or meeting face-to-face. In the case of school-based collaboration with colleagues, community organizations, and families, e-mail can greatly facilitate or hinder ongoing collaborative efforts. Because Internet communication, like other forms of written communication, lacks "tone of voice" and other nonverbal elements, this type of communication may make it more difficult for educators to get a message across clearly and result in miscommunication. Extra time and work are required to repair damage caused by an unread e-mail, a misinterpreted message, or an unclear communication related to an e-mail or classroom Web site.

Computer-mediated communication (CMC) is the process of human communication via computers. CMC includes task-oriented and personal communication and involves communication via both personal and mainframe computers. It includes both asynchronous communication via e-mail or electronic bulletin boards, and synchronous communication such as chat rooms or instant messaging (IM). Finally, CMC refers to all types of communication such as the World Wide Web, e-mail, message boards, and blogs (web logs or online journals).

CMC is an excellent tool for collaboration. It has the potential to provide a range of opportunities for interaction, information, and community among people of all ages, cultures, and socioeconomic classes. It also holds the potential for individuals to interact as peers and to overcome the physical constraints of communication (Gold, 1997). With the appropriate technology, collaboration among those in a virtual community is not hindered by language, culture, or disability.

However, just as with social etiquette rules that are designed to help people "think before they act," network etiquette ("netiquette") is designed to make communication easier and unlikely to cause harm by a stray or misguided comment or action via the Internet. Strawbridge (2006), in *Netiquette: Internet Etiquette in the Age of the Blog,* suggests a total of 157 netiquette rules that include rules for e-mail, mail lists, blogs, online services, and Web sites. Several of these suggestions are especially relevant to educators and others in team-building and collaborative work. Recommendations from Strawbridge, other experts, online communicators, and consulting teachers' experiences stress ten major points:

1. When sending an e-mail to a group, use "BCC" (blind copy) rather than listing all those addressed in the "To" line, because when a group e-mail is received and all addresses are in the "To" line, they are visible to all recipients. Often people do not like to have their e-mail address given to people they don't know or don't wish to have receive it; doing so could be considered a breach of privacy. Also be very careful about "Forward to" and "Reply to All" and other "group-send" buttons. There are horror stories about sending messages inadvertently to the wrong recipients!

2. E-mail greetings are not as formal as those for written letters. Start with the recipient's name or "Hello." If it is someone you don't know well, using a first name may come across as overly familiar. When sending an e-mail to a group of people, use such greetings as "Colleagues," "After-School Grant Proposal Team," or "Dear Families."

3. Each line should contain no more than 65 characters, allowing software to wrap sentences to the next line without making short lines and long lines in the same message. Use short, well-written sentences, with a space between paragraphs.

4. Use standard English and avoid abbreviations or popular contractions of text messaging. Most people can figure out that "pls hlp" means please help, but recipients whose language is not primarily English will have trouble with some of these expressions. E-mail is meant to be helpful and efficient, not puzzling and time-consuming. Written communication presents enough challenges without receivers having to interpret text shorthand!

5. Keep the writing style professional. Avoid "emoticons" and hone your writing and vocabulary skills rather than using such things as smiley faces. Use a readable font and remember that colors and special formatting can make your message difficult for the recipient to read. Sending hard-to-read messages is not a good practice for teachers of those with special (visual or learning) needs! Do not write in all capital letters or in all small letters.

6. Use a signature block for your professional e-mail that is about 4 lines long with 70 or fewer characters per line and includes information to help the recipient contact you.

7. Although e-mails should be short and to the point, an appropriate level of small talk lightens the mood and shows that you are accessible. But tailor it to the individual and remember that brevity is best. Mark Twain is said to have told a recipient, "If I'd had more time, I would have made this message shorter." Shorter may be harder, but it is more effective.

8. Reread for grammar and spelling, and for parts that could be confusing or embarrassing to anyone, even the sender. Never say in an e-mail what you wouldn't say in a crowded room, suggests Strawbridge (2006).

9. Whenever possible, don't deal with conflict, bad behavior, or negative comments in an e-mail. If you need to convey bad news, a face-to-face meeting allows both parties the full range of nonverbal cues given out by the other person.

10. Don't send attachments unless they are absolutely necessary. Many people are wary of attachments because of viruses; plain text e-mails without attachments do not carry viruses. When you do feel the need to send an attachment, use formatting that can be read regardless of the software readers might have on their computers. It is frustrating to receive an important attachment that cannot be opened in a timely fashion.

Computer-mediated communication is a great tool but in general it is not well used. Many organizations, businesses, and more and more schools are adopting and implementing etiquette rules for use of the Internet by their employees so there will be more efficiency and better protection from liability. Netiquette is an important consideration when educators use e-mail or other types of electronic communication. The overall purpose is to provide more effective communication.

Nonverbal Communication

The successful collaborative consultant models facilitative nonverbal communication, or body language, during interactions and attends carefully to the body language of others. Nonverbal communication can be organized into six categories: Eye contact; gestures; paralanguage (volume, rate, pitch, and pronunciation of the verbal communication); posture; overall facial expression; and as a new category to be added to the traditional five already named, clothing and setting for the interaction (White, 2000).

Eyes and the brows above them are expressive instruments for conveying thoughts as well as feelings. Gestures send signals, and facial expressions disclose thoughts and feelings. When gestures and facial expressions do not match verbal content, mixed signals result. For example, teachers send mixed signals when they smile as they outline class rules and procedures, but display stern faces when introducing a learning activity. A consulting teacher might err similarly when interacting with parents or co-teachers. Voice tone, pitch, volume, and speed can affect the receiver of a message in positive or negative ways.

Slouching posture or turning away will imply lack of interest or rejection. Clothing worn by educators should be comfortable, of course, but also should be chosen to suit the environment. A consulting teacher was told by her colleagues at one school that she "dressed to supervise, not to work," so she learned to "dress down" for that setting, with sneakers and no jewelry. For her afternoon schedule in a school with a more dressy style, she changed to heeled shoes, a blazer, and a scarf or necklace. Not expecting to notice much difference, she was amazed to find more acceptance for her role at both schools.

SKILLS FOR COMMUNICATING

In order to be effective communicators, senders and receivers of messages need skills that include rapport building, responsive listening, assertiveness, tools for dealing with resistance, and conflict-management techniques. With well-developed communication skills, consultants and consultees will be able to engage more effectively in collaborative problem solving.

Five major sets of skills are integral to successful communication:

1. Rapport-building skills
2. Responsive listening
3. Assertion skills
4. Conflict management skills
5. Collaborative problem-solving skills

Rapport building is the first step in establishing a collaborative relationship. Responsive listening skills enable a person to understand what another is saying and to convey that the problems and feelings have been understood. When listening methods are used appropriately by a consultant, the consultee plays an active role in problem solving without becoming dependent on the consultant.

Assertion skills include verbal and nonverbal behaviors that enable collaborators to maintain respect, satisfy their professional needs, and defend their rights without dominating, manipulating, or controlling others. Conflict management skills help individuals deal with the emotional turbulence that typically accompanies conflict. Conflict management skills also have a multiplier effect of fostering closer relationships when a conflict is resolved. Collaborative problem-solving skills help resolve the conflicting needs so that all parties are satisfied. Problems then "stay solved," and relationships are developed and preserved. Problem solving is discussed in Chapter 5.

Rapport-Building Skills

Collaboration with other professionals that is in the best interests of students with special needs often means simply sitting down and making some joint decisions. At other times, however, it must be preceded by considerable rapport building. Successful consultation necessitates good rapport between the participants in the consulting relationship. It is important to keep in mind that both the consultant and the consultee should provide ideas toward solving the problem. Respect must be a two-way condition for generating and accepting ideas. Rapport building is vital for building an appropriate consultation climate.

When we take time to build positive relationships with others that are based on mutual respect and trust, others are more likely to:

- Want to work with us
- Care about our reactions to them

- Try to meet our expectations
- Accept our feedback and coaching
- Imitate our behavior

We are more likely to:

- Listen to and try to understand their unique situations
- Accept them as they are and not judge them for what they are not
- Respond appropriately to their concerns and criticisms
- Advocate for, and support and encourage them in their efforts on behalf of, students with special needs

What behaviors are central to the process of building a trusting, supportive relationship? When asked this question, many teachers mention trust, respect, feeling that it is okay not to have all the answers, feeling free to ask questions, and feeling all right about disagreeing with the other person. People want to feel that the other person is *really* listening. Trust is developed when one addresses the concerns of others and looks for opportunities to demonstrate responsiveness to others' needs.

Respecting differences in others is an important aspect of building and maintaining rapport. Although teachers and other school personnel are generally adept at recognizing and respecting individual differences in children, they may find this more difficult to accomplish with adults. Accepting differences in adults may be particularly difficult when the adults have different values, skills, and attitudes. Effective consultants accept people as they really are rather than wishing they were different. Rapport building is not such a formidable process when the consultant respects individual differences and holds high expectations for others.

Responsive Listening Skills

Plutarch said, "Know how to listen and you will profit even from those who talk badly." Shakespeare referred to the "disease" of *not* listening. Listening is the foundation of communication. A person listens to establish rapport with another person. People listen when others are upset or angry, or when they do not know what to say or fear speaking out will result in trouble. People listen so others will listen to them. Listening is a process of perpetual motion that focuses on the other person as speaker and responds to that other person's ideas, rather than concentrating on one's own thoughts and feelings. Thus, effective listening is *responsive listening* because it is responding, both verbally and nonverbally, to the words and actions of the speaker.

Successful consultants listen responsively and empathically to build trust and promote understanding. Responsive listening improves relationships, and minimizes resistance and negativity. Although most people are convinced of the importance of listening in building collegial relationships and preventing and solving problems, few are as adept at this skill as they would like or need to be. There are several reasons for this. First, most people have not been taught to listen effectively. They have been taught to talk—especially if they are teachers, administrators, or psychologists. Educators are good at talking and regard it as an essential part of their roles. But effective talkers must be careful not to let the lines of communication get tangled up in a tendency to talk too much or too often.

According to Thomas Gordon, one of the early promoters of effective communication, listening helps keep the "locus of responsibility" with the one who owns the problem (Gordon, 2000). Therefore, if one's role as a consultant is to promote problem-solving without fostering dependence on the part of the consultee, listening will keep the focus of the problem-solving where it belongs. Listening also is important in showing empathy and acceptance, two vital ingredients in a relationship that fosters growth and psychological health (Gordon, 2000).

Responsive, effective listening makes it possible to gather information essential to one's role in the education of children with special needs. It helps others feel better, often by reducing tension and anxiety, increasing feelings of personal well-being, and encouraging greater hope and optimism. This kind of listening encourages others to express themselves freely and fully. It enhances your value to others, and often contributes significantly to positive change in others' self-understanding and problem-solving abilities.

If listening is so important, why is it so hard? Listening is difficult because it is hard to keep an open mind about the speaker. People may be hesitant to listen because they think listening implies agreeing. Openness certainly is important in effective communication. However, listening is much more than just hearing. Consultants must demonstrate tolerance toward differences and appreciation of richly diverse ideas and values while they are engaged in consulting relationships. A consultant's own values about child rearing, education, or the treatment of children with special needs become personal filters that make it difficult to really listen to those whose values are very different. For example, it may be hard to listen to a consultee parent who thinks it is appropriate for a very gifted daughter to drop out of school at the age of sixteen to help on the family farm because "She'll be getting married before too long and farm work will prepare her to be a wife better than school-work ever can." It takes discipline to listen to comments such as this when your mind is reacting negatively and wants to put together some very pointed arguments. A good thing to remember in such cases is that "when we add our two cents' worth in the middle of listening, that's just about what the communication is worth!" (Murphy, 1987).

Listening is indeed hard work. If the listener is tired or anxious or bursting with excitement and energy, it is particularly hard to listen carefully. Feelings of the listener also act as filters to impede listening. Other roadblocks to responsive listening are making assumptions about the message (mind-reading), thinking about our own response (rehearsing), and reacting defensively.

Improving listening skills can help establish collaborative relationships with colleagues, even those with whom it is a challenge to communicate. When consultants and consultees improve their listening skills, they have a head start on solving problems, sidestepping resistance, and preventing conflicts.

There are three major components of responsive listening:

1. Nonverbal listening (discerning others' needs and observing their nonverbal gestures)
2. Encouraging the sending of messages (encouraging others to express themselves fully)
3. Showing understanding of the message (reviewing what they conveyed), or paraphrasing

Nonverbal Listening Skills.   Responsive listeners use appropriate body language to send out the message that they are listening effectively. Nonverbal listening behavior of a good listener is described by Tony Hillerman in his 1990 best-seller *Coyote Waits:* "Jacobs was silent for awhile, thinking about it, her face full of sympathy. She was a talented listener. When you talked to this woman, she attended. She had all her antennae out. The world was shut out. Nothing mattered but the words she was hearing" (Hillerman, 1990, pp. 148–149).

Nonverbal listening may be less than effective for those people who do several things at once, such as watch a television show and write a letter, or talk to a colleague and grade papers, or prepare supper while listening to a child's synopsis of the day. This is because nonverbal components of listening should demonstrate to the speaker that the receiver is respecting the speaker enough to concentrate on the message and is following the speaker's thoughts to find the *real* message. Careful listening conveys attitudes of flexibility, empathy, and caring, even if the speaker is using words and expressions that cloud the message. A person who is attentive leans forward slightly, engages in a comfortable level of eye contact, nods, and gives low-key responses such as "oh," and "uh-huh," and "umm-humm." The responsive listener's facial expression matches the message. If that message is serious, the expression reflects seriousness. If the message is delivered with a smile, the listener shows empathy by smiling.

The hardest part of nonverbal listening is keeping it nonverbal. It helps the listener to think about a tennis game and remember that during the listening part of the "game," the ball is in the speaker's court. The speaker has the privilege of saying anything, no matter how seemingly silly or irrelevant. The listener just keeps sending the ball back by nodding, or saying "I see" or other basically nonverbal behaviors, until he or she "hears" the sender's message. This entails using nonverbal behaviors and "listening" to the nonverbal as well as the verbal messages of the sender. The listener recognizes and minimizes personal filters, perceives and interprets the filters of the sender, and encourages continued communication until able to understand the message from the sender's perspective. Responsive listeners avoid anticipating what the speaker will say and *never* complete a speaker's sentence.

After listeners have listened until they really hear the message, understand the speaker's position, and recognize the feelings behind the message, it is their turn to speak. But they must be judicious about what they do say. Several well-known, humorous "recipes" apply to this need.

- Recipe for speaking—stand up, speak up, then shut up.
- Recipe for giving a good speech—add shortening.
- It takes six letters of the alphabet to spell the word *listen*. Rearrange the letters to spell another word that is a necessary part of responsive listening.[1]
- In the middle of listening, the *t* doesn't make a sound.

Verbal Listening Skills.   Although the first rule of the good listener is to keep one's mouth shut, there are several types of verbal responses that show that the listener is following the thoughts and feelings expressed by the speaker. Verbal responses are added to nonverbal listening responses to communicate that the listener understands what the other is saying from that speaker's specific point of view. Specific verbal aspects of listening also keep the speaker talking. There are several reasons for this which are specific to the consulting process:

- The consultant will be less inclined to assume ownership of the problem.
- Speakers will clarify their own thoughts as they keep talking.

[1]Did you get *silent?*

- More information will become available to help understand the speaker's point of view.
- Speakers begin to solve their own problems as they talk them through.
- The consultant continues to refine responsive listening skills.

Three verbal listening skills that promote talking by the speaker are inviting, encouraging, and questioning cautiously. Inviting means providing an opportunity for others to talk, by signaling to them that you are interested in listening if they are interested in speaking. Examples are "You seem to have something on your mind," or "I'd like to hear about your problem," or "What's going on for you now?"

Verbal responses of encouragement are added to nodding and mirroring of facial responses. "I see," "uh-hum," and "oh" are examples of verbal behaviors that encourage continued talking. These listener responses suggest: "Continue. I understand. I'm listening." (Gordon, 1977).

Cautious questioning is the final mechanism for promoting continued talking. Most educators are competent questioners, so the caution here is to use minimal questioning. During the listening part of communication, the message is controlled by the speaker. It is always the speaker's serve. Intensive and frequent questioning gives control of the communication to the listener. This is antithetical to the consulting process, which should be about collaboration rather than power and control. Questions should be used to clarify what the speaker has said, so that the message can be understood by the listener—for example, "Is this what you mean?" or "Please explain what you mean by 'attitude problem.'"

Paraphrasing Skills.   Responsive listening means demonstrating that the listener understands the essence of the message. After listening by using nonverbal and minimal verbal responses, a consultant who is really listening probably will begin to understand the message of the speaker. To show that the message was heard, or to assess whether what was "heard" was the same message the sender intended and was not altered by distortion, the listener should paraphrase the message. This requires the listener to think carefully about the message and reflect it back to the speaker without changing the content or intent of the message.

There is no simple formula for reflecting or paraphrasing, but two good strategies are to be as accurate as possible and as brief as possible. A paraphrase may begin in one of several ways: "It sounds as if . . ." or "Is what you mean . . . ?" or "So, it seems to me you want [think] [feel] . . ." or "Let me see if I understand. You're saying. . ." Paraphrasing allows listeners to check their understanding of the message. It is easy to mishear or misinterpret the message, especially if the words are ambiguous. Correct interpretation of the message will result in a nod from the speaker, who may feel that at last someone has really listened. Or the speaker may correct the message by saying, "No, that's not what I meant. It's this way. . ." The listener may paraphrase the content of the message. For example, "It seems to me that you're saying . . ." would reflect the content of the message back to the speaker. "You appear to be very frustrated about . . . " reflects the emotional part of the message. It is important to use the speaker's words as much as possible in the paraphrase words and to remain concise in responses. By paraphrasing appropriately, a listener demonstrates comprehension of the message or receipt of new information. This aspect of hearing and listening is essential in communication, and in assertion, problem solving, and conflict management as well.

Just by recognizing a consultee's anger, or sadness, or frustration, a consultant can begin to build a trusting relationship with a consultee. The listener doesn't necessarily have to agree with the content or emotion that is heard. It may appear absurd or illogical. Nevertheless, the consultant's responsibility is not to change another's momentary tendency; rather, it is to develop a supportive working relationship via effective communication, paving the way to successful cooperation and problem-solving while avoiding conflict and resistance.

Parents often comment that they have approached a teacher with a problem, realizing that they didn't want a specific answer, but just a kindly ear—a sounding board, or a friendly shoulder. Responsive listening is important in establishing collaborative relationships and maintaining them. It is also a necessary precursor to problem solving in which both parties strive to listen and get a mutual understanding of the problem before a problem is addressed.

So when is responsive listening to be used? The answer is—*all* the time. Use it when establishing a relationship, when starting to problem-solve, when emotions are high, when one's conversation doesn't seem to be getting anywhere, and when the speaker seems confused, uncertain, or doesn't know what else to do.

This complex process may not be necessary if two people have already developed a good working relationship and only a word or two is needed for mutual understanding. It also may not be appropriate if one of the two is not willing to talk. Sometimes "communication postponement" is best when you are too tired or too emotionally upset to be a responsive listener. When a consultant cannot listen because of any of these reasons, it is not wise to pretend to be listening, while actually thinking about something else or nothing at all. Instead, a reluctant listener should explain that he or she does not have the energy to talk about the problem now, but wishes to at a later time, for example: "I need a chance to think about this. May I talk to you later?" or "Look, I'm too upset to work on this very productively right now. Let's talk about it first thing tomorrow." Figure 4.2 summarizes responsive listening skills that help avoid blocked communication.

Assertiveness

By the time the consultant has listened effectively and the collaborative relationship has been developed or enhanced, many consultants are more than ready to start talking. Once the sender's message is understood and emotional levels are reduced, it is the listener's turn to be the sender. Now the consultant gets to talk. However, it is not always easy to communicate one's thoughts, feelings, and opinions without infringing on the rights, feelings, or opinions of others. This is the time for assertiveness.

Assertiveness skills allow consultants to achieve their goals without damaging the relationship or another's self-esteem. The basic aspects of assertive communication are:

- Use an "I" message instead of a "you" message.
- Say "and" instead of "but."
- State the behavior objectively.
- Name your own feelings.
- Say what you want to happen.
- Express concern for others (empathy).
- Use assertive body language.

FIGURE 4.2   Responsive Listening Checklist

	Yes	No
A. *Appropriate Nonverbals*		
1. Good eye contact		
2. Facial expression mirrored		
3. Body orientation toward other person		
B. *Appropriate Verbals*		
1. Door openers		
2. Good level of encouraging phrases		
3. Cautious questions		
C. *Appropriate Responding Behaviors*		
1. Reflected content (paraphrasing)		
2. Reflected feelings		
3. Brief clarifying questions		
4. Summarizations		
D. *Avoidance of Roadblocks*		
1. No advice giving		
2. No inappropriate questions		
3. Minimal volunteered solutions		
4. No judging		

Open and honest consultants say what they want to happen and what their feelings are. That does not mean they always get what they want. Saying what you want and how you feel will clarify the picture and ensure that the other(s) won't have to guess what you want or think. Even if others disagree with the ideas and opinions, they can never disagree with the feelings and wishes. Those are very personal and are expressed in a personal manner by starting the interaction with "I," rather than presenting feelings and opinions as truth or expert answer.

In stating an idea or position assertively, consultants should describe the problem in terms of its impact on the consultant, rather than in terms of what was done or said by the other person. "I feel let down" works better than "You broke your part of the agreement". If a consultant makes a "you" statement about the consultee which the consultee thinks is wrong, the consultant will only get an angry reaction and the consultant's concerns will be ignored.

Concern for Others during the Interaction.   Expressing concern for others can take many forms. This skill demonstrates that although people have thoughts and feelings which differ from those of others, they can still respect the feelings and ideas of others. "I realize it is a tremendous challenge to manage thirty-five children in the same classroom." This statement shows the consultant understands the management problems of the teacher. As the consultant goes on to state preferences in working with the teacher, the teacher is more likely to listen and work cooperatively. The consultee will see that the consultant is aware of the problems that must be dealt with daily. "It seems to me that . . . ," "I understand . . . ," "I realize . . . ," and "It looks like . . . " are phrases consultants can use to express concern for the other person in the collaborative relationship. If the consultant cannot complete these sentences with the appropriate information, the next step is to go back to the listening part of the communication.

How to Be Concerned and Assertive.   Assertive people own their personal feelings and opinions. Being aware of this helps them state their wants and feelings. "You" sentences sound accusing, even when that is not intended, which can lead to defensiveness in others. For example, saying to a parent, "You should provide a place and quiet time for Hannah to do her homework," is more accusatory than saying, "I am frustrated when Hannah isn't getting her homework done, and I would like to work with you to think of some ways to help her get it done." Using "and" rather than "but" is particularly important in expressing thoughts without diminishing a relationship. This is a particularly difficult assertion skill. To the listener the word *but* erases the preceding phrase and prevents the intended message from coming through.

It is important to state behavior specifically. By describing behavior objectively, a consultant or consultee sounds less judgmental. It is easy to let blaming and judgmental words creep into language. Without meaning to, the speaker throws up a barrier that blocks the communication and the relationship.

■ ■ ■ ■ ■

APPLICATION 4.2
COMMUNICATING POSITIVELY

Compare the first statement with the second one:

1. "I would like to have a schedule of rehearsals for the holiday pageant. It is frustrating when I drive out to work with Maxine and Juanita and they are practicing for the musical and can't come to the resource room."
2. "When you don't let me know ahead of time that the girls won't be allowed to come and work with me, I have to waste my time driving and can't get anything accomplished."

In reflecting on these statements, which one is less judgmental and accusatory? Can these two contrasting statements create differing listener attitudes toward the speakers? For many listeners the judgmental words and phrases in the second sentence ("you don't let me know," "won't be allowed," "waste my time") sound blaming. They introduce a whole array of red flags.

Assertive communication includes demonstrating supportive body language. A firm voice, straight posture, eye contact, and body orientation toward the receiver of the message will have a desirable effect. Assertive body language affirms that the sender owns his

FIGURE 4.3   Assertiveness Checklist

	Usually	Sometimes	Never
1. Conveys "I" instead of "you" message			
2. Says "and" rather than "but"			
3. States behavior objectively			
4. Says what he or she wants to have happen			
5. States feelings			
6. Expresses concern			
7. Speaks firmly, clearly			
8. Has assertive posture			
9. Avoids aggressive language			

or her own feelings and opinions but also respects the other person's feelings and opinions. This is a difficult balance to achieve. Body language and verbal language must match or the messages will be confusing. Skills for being assertive are listed in Figure 4.3.

What we say and how we say it have tremendous impact on the reactions and acceptance of others. When consultants and consultees communicate in ways that accurately reflect their feelings, focus on objective descriptions of behavior and situations, and think in a concrete manner about what they want to happen, assertive communication will build strong, respectful relationships. Assertive communication is the basis for solving problems and resolving conflicts.

The Art of Apologizing.   Sometimes, despite good communication skills and careful relationship building and problem solving, consultants make errors and mistakes. Good consultants never blame someone else for communication breakdowns; they accept responsibility for their own communication. This is demonstrated when a consultant says, "Let me explain in a different way" instead of "Can't you understand?" Good consultants also use the art of apologizing.

One of the biggest misconceptions in the area of consultation and collaboration is that apologizing puts consultants and teachers at a disadvantage when working with colleagues and parents. It is simply not true that strong, knowledgeable people never say they're sorry. In fact, apologizing is a powerful strategy because it demonstrates honesty and confidence. Apologizing offers a chance to mend fences in professional relationships. Some suggestions from psychologist Barry Lubetkin (1996) about how to apologize include allowing the person you've wronged to vent her or his feelings first, apologize as soon as possible, don't say "I'm sorry, but. . . .," and say it once and let that be enough. Most importantly, apologies are empty if you keep repeating the behavior or the mistake.

Roadblocks to Communication

Roadblocks are barriers to successful interaction, halting the development of effective collaborative relationships. They may be verbal behaviors or nonverbal behaviors that send out messages such as, "I'm not listening," or "It doesn't matter what you think," or "Your ideas and feelings are silly and unimportant." Responsible school consultants most assuredly do not intend to send blocking messages. But by being busy, not concentrating, using poor listening skills, or allowing themselves to be directed by filters such as emotions and judgment, well-meaning consultants inadvertently send blocking messages.

Barriers to communication among educators and families may sometimes take the form of specific conditions such as learning disabilities of the adults involved. When education consultants work with parents, paraeducators or other adults who may have a learning disability themselves, some suggestions for improving communication are:

- Break large tasks or bodies of information into smaller ones
- Give information in a very structured manner
- Offer "organizational tools" such as notes, colored files or flyers for color coding, paper for taking notes or printed notes
- Be very careful about being critical
- Offer plenty of positive feedback, when warranted
- Encourage them to tape meetings or instructions
- Communicate frequently and offer information in smaller segments
- Frequently test the accuracy of communication by asking them to repeat or rephrase what was said

Nonverbal Roadblocks.   Nonverbal roadblocks include facing away when the speaker talks, displaying inappropriate facial expressions such as smiling when the sender is saying something serious, distracting with body movements such as repetitively tapping a pencil, and grading papers or writing reports while "listening." Interrupting a speaker to attend to something or someone else—the phone, a sound outside the window, or a knock at the door—also halts communication and contributes in a subtle way toward undermining the spirit of collaboration.

Verbal Roadblocks.   Gordon (1977) lists 12 verbal barriers to communication. These have been called the "Dirty Dozen," and they can be grouped into three types of verbal roadblocks that prevent meaningful interaction (Bolton, 1986):

1. Judging
2. Sending solutions
3. Avoiding others' concerns

The first category, judging, includes criticizing, name-calling, and diagnosing or analyzing why a person is behaving a particular way. False or non-specific praise and evaluative words or phrases, send a message of judgment toward the speaker. "You're not thinking clearly," "You'll do a wonderful job of using curriculum-based assessment!" and "You don't really believe that—you're just tired today" are examples of judging. (Notice that each of these statements begins with the word *you*.) Avoiding judgment about parents or others helps teachers avoid deficit-based thinking which hurts everyone it touches (Lovett, 1996). Nonjudgmental communication conveys equity in the relationship, a critical factor in teamwork.

Educators are particularly adept with the next category of verbal roadblocks—sending solutions. These include directing or ordering, warning, moralizing or preaching, advising, and using logical arguments or lecturing. A few of these can become a careless consultant's entire verbal repertoire. "Not knowing the question," Bolton says (1986, p. 37), "it was easy for him to give the answer." "Stop complaining," and "Don't talk like that," and "If you don't send Jim to the resource room on time . . . " are examples of directing or warning. Moralizing sends a message of "I'm a better educator than you are." Such communication usually starts with "You should . . . " or "You ought to. . . . " When consultees have problems, the last thing they need is to be told what they *should* do. Using "should" makes a consultant sound rigid and pedantic. Avoid giving the impression that you are more concerned with rules or shoulds than with the relationship with the consultee.

Advising, lecturing, and logical argument are all too often part of the educator's tools of the trade. Teachers tend to use roadblock types of communication techniques frequently with students. The habits they develop cause them to overlook the reality that use of such tactics with adults can drive a wedge into an already precarious relationship. Consultants must avoid such tactics as assuming the posture of the "sage-on-the-stage," imparting wisdom in the manner of a learned professor to undergraduate students, lecturing, moralizing, and advising. Unfortunately, these methods imply superiority, which is detrimental to the collaborative process.

Avoiding others' concerns is a third category of verbal roadblocks. This category implies "no big deal" to the message-receiver. Avoidance messages include reassuring or sympathizing, such as "You'll feel better tomorrow" or "Everyone goes through this stage," or interrogating to get more than the necessary information, thereby delaying the problem solving. Other avoidance messages include intensive questioning in the manner of The Grand Inquisition, and humoring or distracting, "Let's get off this and talk about something else." Avoiding the concerns that others express sends the message that their concerns are not important.

Other powerful roadblocks to communication are too much sending, not enough receiving; excessive kindness (Fisher, 1993); reluctance to express negative information (Rinke, 1997); and inadequate feedback, that is, the sender does not find out if the message has been received, acknowledged or understood (Fisher, 1993). When consultants use roadblocks, they are making themselves, their feelings, and their opinions the focus of the interaction, rather than allowing the focus to be the issues, concerns, or problems of the consultee. When they set up roadblocks, listeners do not listen responsively or encourage others to communicate clearly, openly, and effectively. Because it is so easy to inadvertently use a communication block through speaking, it is wise to remember the adage, "We are blessed with two ears and one mouth, a constant reminder that we should listen twice as much as we talk." Indeed, the more one talks, the more likely a person is to make errors, and the less opportunity that person will have to learn something.

Terms, Labels, and Phrases as Roadblocks.   Inappropriate use of terms and labels can erect roadblocks to communication. Educators should adhere to the following points when speaking or writing about people with disabilities:

■ Do not focus on the disability, but instead on issues affecting quality of life for them, such as housing, affordable health care, and employment opportunity.

- Do not portray successful people with disabilities as superhuman, for all persons with disabilities cannot achieve this level of success.
- Use people-first language, such as "a student with autism," rather than "an autistic student."
- Emphasize abilities and not limitations, such as "uses a wheelchair," rather than "wheelchair-bound."
- Terms such as *physically challenged* are considered condescending, and saying "victim of" is regarded as sensationalizing.
- Do not imply disease by saying "patient" or "case" when discussing disabilities.

Acceptable, contemporary terminology facilitates active listening and improves verbal communication.

MANAGING RESISTANCE, NEGATIVITY, ANGER, AND CONFLICT

Communication is the key to collaboration and problem solving. Without back and forth discussions, there can be no agreement. Problem solving often breaks down because communications break down first, because people aren't paying attention or because they misunderstand the other side, or because emotions were not dealt with as a separate and primary issue.

In problem solving it is critical to separate the person from the problem. Collaborative consultants will find themselves often needing to deal with emotions, as well as any errors in perceptions or communication, as separate issues which must be resolved on their own. Emotions may take the form of resistance, anger, negativity, or outright conflict. If emotions are not recognized and dealt with skillfully, they may become barriers to effective communication when they are experienced by the consultant or consultee. Sometimes, regardless of how diplomatic people are in dealing with the emotions of others, they run into barriers of resistance in their attempts to communicate.

It is estimated that as much as 80 percent of problem solving with others is getting through the resistance. Resistance is a trait of human nature that surfaces when people are asked to change. Researchers have found that people resist change for a number of reasons. They may:

- Have a vested interest in the status quo
- Have low tolerance for change
- Feel strongly that the change would be undesirable
- Be unclear about what the change would entail or bring about
- Fear the unknown

A wise person once suggested, "How can we ask others to change when it is so hard to change ourselves?" Resistance often has nothing to do with an individual personally, or even with the new idea. The resistance is simply a reaction to change of any kind. Change implies imperfection with the way things are being done, and this makes people defensive. However, it is good to remember the adage from another wise person, "Change is the only thing that is permanent."

Many people get defensive or resistant or just stop listening when others disagree with them. This often happens because they feel they are being attacked personally. Parents who are asked what time a sleepy student goes to bed at night may feel defensive because they feel you are attacking or questioning their parenting, even though you may just want to rule out lack of sleep for some of the behaviors the child is exhibiting in the classroom.

Why Collaborative Partners Resist

It is human nature to be uncomfortable when another person disagrees. It is also human nature to get upset when someone resists efforts to make changes, implement plans, or modify systems to be more responsive to children with special needs. The need for change can generate powerful emotions. Most people are uncomfortable when experiencing the strong emotions of others. When someone yells or argues, the first impulse is to become defensive, argue the other point of view, and defend one's own ideas. Although a school consultant may intend to remain cool and calm and collected in the interactions that involve exceptional children, occasionally another individual says something that pushes a "hot button" and the consultant becomes upset, or angry, or defensive.

Special education consulting teachers who have been asked to describe examples of resistance they have experienced toward their roles provide these examples:

- Consultees (classroom teachers) won't share how they feel.
- They act excited about an idea, but never get around to doing it.
- They won't discuss it with you, but they do so liberally with others behind your back.
- They may try, but give up too soon.
- They take out their frustrations on the students.
- They are too quick to say that a strategy won't work in their situation.
- They dredge up a past example where something similar didn't work.
- They keep asking for more and more details or information before trying an idea.
- They change the subject, or suddenly have to be somewhere else.
- They state that there is not enough time to implement the strategy.
- They intellectualize with a myriad of reasons it won't work.
- They are simply silent.
- They just prefer the status quo.

When resistance spawns counter-resistance and anger, an upward spiral of emotion is created that can make consulting unpleasant and painful. Bolton (1986) describes resistance as a push, push-back phenomenon. When a person meets resistance with more resistance, defensiveness, logical argument, or any other potential roadblock, resistance increases and dialogue can develop into open warfare. Then the dialogue may become personal or hurtful. Nobody listens at that point, and a potentially healthy relationship is damaged and very difficult to salvage.

How to Deal with Resistance and Negativity

An important strategy for dealing with resistance and defensiveness is to handle one's own defensiveness, stop pushing so that the other person will not be able to push-back, delay reactions, keep quiet, and *listen*. This takes practice, patience, tolerance, and commitment.

It is important to deal with emotions such as resistance, defensiveness, or anger before proceeding to problem solving. People are not inclined to listen until they have been listened to. They will not be convinced of another's sincerity and openness, or become capable of thinking logically, when the filter of emotions is clouding their thinking.

Negative people and negative emotions sap the energy of educational consultants. Reactions to negativity, to conflict, and to resistance can block communication and ruin potentially productive relationships. It is important to remember that negative people are not going to change. The person who has to change is the consultant.

The first point is to refrain from taking negativity personally. Such individuals just may be having a bad time at that point in their lives. A positive approach would be to deal with negativity as a challenge from which much can learned about working with people. When there is a breakthrough in the communication and problem solving, such folks can become one's staunchest allies and supporters.

Accommodating negative or resistant school colleagues or family members of students at their best times and on their turf can be a first step toward this alliance. Communicate in writing in order to diffuse emotional reactions and convey the message one wishes to send. Following up later and remaining patient will model a spirit of acceptance that is spiced with invincibility yet grounded in purpose.

For application of practical techniques, William Ury of the Program on Negotiation at Harvard Law School, stresses that one of the keys to working with difficult people is controlling one's own behavior (Ury, 1991). The natural reaction to resistance, challenges, and negativity is to strike back, give in, or break off the communication. A negative reaction to resistance leads to a vicious cycle of action and reaction and leads to communication and relationship breakdowns. Instead of reacting, seek to regain a mental balance and stay focused. So his suggestion is, don't react.

Ury (1991) provides two strategies for curbing one's own natural reactions to resistance and negativity. The first is to "go to the balcony". This means distancing oneself from the action-reaction cycle. Step back and take a deep breath and try to see the situation objectively. Imagine yourself climbing to the balcony overlooking the stage where the action-reaction drama has been taking place. Here, you can calmly look at the situation, with a detached or third-party perspective. Going to the balcony means removing yourself from your natural impulses and emotions. Remember, when your "hot buttons" get pushed or when you find yourself getting emotional and reacting instead of acting, go to the balcony!

Another strategy Ury (1991) suggests is to keep your eyes on the prize. Dealing with emotional and difficult situations in collaborative efforts usually diverts us from our goals and causes distress, so always keep your mind on the larger picture. In the collaborative consultant's case, the prize is optimal developmental and educational outcomes for students with special needs. If we remember that the communication process is crucial to the relationships among the stakeholders in a student's education, we will remember that diversions are worth dealing with and the eventual outcome is well worth the process.

Roger Fisher, director of the Harvard Negotiation Project and a collaborator with William Ury, co-authored a book with Sharp titled *Getting It Done: How to Lead When You're Not in Charge* (Fisher & Sharp, 1999). The book has been called the definitive book on collaboration, which they term "lateral leadership." Their formula to improve collaboration is: Ask, offer, and do. First, ask good questions, that is, questions that get others collaboratively thinking about a problem and looking for a solution. Open questions encourage others to be full and equal participants in the process. Second, offer your own thoughts, data, ideas, or suggestions. Contribute one piece of the puzzle. Third, model the behavior you would like to see. This method lessens resistance and helps create a climate of mutual support and feedback.

Yankelovich (2001), a social scientist and advisor to large corporations and government factions, believes that there are several "potholes that make the road to dialogue difficult to travel" (p. 130). These potholes are common causes of resistance and defensiveness. Yankelovich targets five potholes and then offers suggestions for avoiding them:

1. *Holding back.* Reasons people hold back are usually that trust has not been built, or they feel latent hostility, or they sense the potential for embarrassment. Try building trust with such strategies as breaking the ice by talking about personal experiences and by doing a small amount of self-disclosure.

2. *Staying in the box and not thinking or acting outside traditional boundaries.* This can be seen as resistance to change or to creative suggestions for solving problems. Focus on common interests, not divisive ones. Respect all suggestions; and bring assumptions out into the open.

3. *Prematurely moving into action.* We tend to act quickly on our problems. This, according to Yankelovich (2001), is one of our culture's great strengths as well as a limitation. Work to achieve mutual understanding before rushing into action.

4. *Listening without hearing.* The three core requirements of collaborative communication are equality, empathic listening, and treating the surfacing assumptions nonjudgmentally.

5. *Showboating.* Although we live in an era that values self-expression, subordinating one's personality to a certain extent is needed to empathize fully with someone else's point of view.

■ ■ ■ ■ ■ ▬▬▬▬▬▬▬▬▬▬▬▬▬▬▬▬▬▬▬▬▬▬▬▬▬▬

APPLICATION 4.3
MANAGING RESISTANCE

Construct a problem situation involving another person that could happen, or has happened, in your school context and interact with a colleague to try these communication techniques:

Dismiss the negativity with "You may be right," and keep moving forward. Be assertive (e.g., "I am bothered by discussing the negative side of things"). Ask for complaints in writing (because some people don't realize how negative they sound). Ask for clarification, also, by suggesting that the person describe the problem and clarify the desired outcome. This leads people to thinking about positive actions. Don't defend attacks, and invite criticism and advice instead. Ask what's wrong. Look for interests behind resistance, negativity, and anger by asking questions. Tentatively agree by saying "that's one opinion."

Switch roles and try another episode. Then have a debriefing session to critique the interactions.

Consultants must "hear their way to success" in managing resistance. This may take five minutes, or months of careful relationship-building. Colleagues cannot always avoid disagreements that are serious enough to create anger and resistance. A comment or question delivered in the wrong manner at the wrong time may be the "hot button" that triggers the antagonism. Consider remarks such as these:

> "If you want students to use good note-taking skills, shouldn't you teach them that?"
> "Not allowing learning disabled students to use calculators is cruel."
> "Why don't you teach in a way to accommodate different learning styles?"
> "You penalize gifted students when you keep the class in lockstep with basal readers."

Such remarks can make harried, overworked classroom teachers defensive and resentful. If an occasion arises in which a teacher or parent becomes angry or resistant, responding in the right way will prevent major breakdowns in the communication that is needed.

Why People Get Angry

Anger is felt when a situation is perceived as unfair or threatening, and the person angered feels helpless to rectify that situation (Margolis, 1986). Differences of opinions, values, and behaviors exacerbate these feelings. Coyle (2000) explains anger as a secondary feeling that follows frustration, unmet expectations, loss of self-respect, or fear. The anger is accompanied by anxiety and powerlessness, changing into feelings or actions of power and fight. Anger is directly proportional to a person's feeling of powerlessness. If you ask angry people to tell you what they want, you give them power, thereby reducing their feeling of powerlessness. And sometimes "people vent their anger at those giving them the most help because they feel comfortable directing it there. In most instances, angered people feel unjustly victimized and blame others for their pain and anguish" (Coyle, 2000, p. 43).

How to Deal with the Anger.   Unresolved conflict leads to anger, which undermines morale and thwarts productivity. It is important for the collaborative consultant to respond appropriately to angry people. A first rule is to address the problem rather than the person, then seek to find a shared goal with the angry person. Defer judgment and together explore options. When an angry person is loud and belligerent, speak more softly and calmly. Listen intently with responsiveness, not reaction.

Margolis (1986) recommends that educators learn about those who are angry and get to know them as people, not problems. When they meet with the angry person, they should succinctly state a general and slightly ambiguous purpose for the meeting and ask if that purpose is satisfactory. The tone must be empathic, with careful phrasing of questions and brief summaries at key points during the problem solving phase. The final summary with agreements and commitments should be written down to provide a record for later referral if necessary. Margolis reminds educators to congratulate all for what they have accomplished during the interaction.

Griffin (1998) has these suggestions for dealing with anger:

- Do nothing. Let the person vent. This will drain off some of the energy. Avoid telling the person to calm down; this only makes matters worse. Avoid telling the person to do anything to feel or behave in a certain way.
- After the first wave of rage is over, play it back, minus the rage. Try to understand the person, even if you are uncomfortable with the strong emotion.

■ Ask: "How would you like to resolve this?" Do what you can to transform an "I versus you" conversation into a "We versus the problem" dialogue.

Why Conflict Occurs in School Contexts

Conflict is an inevitable part of life. It occurs when there are unreconciled differences among people in terms of needs, values, goals, and personalities. If conflicting parties cannot give and take by integrating their views and utilizing their differences constructively, interpersonal conflicts will escalate. School consultants and collaborators are not exempt from the dysfunction that often accompanies conflict. So it is important for them to develop tools for transforming vague and ambiguous sources of conflict into identified problems that can be solved collaboratively. Lippitt (1983) suggests that conflict, as a predictable social phenomenon, should not be repressed, because there are many positive aspects to be valued. Conflict can help clarify issues, increase involvement, and promote growth, as well as strengthen relationships and organizational systems when the issues are resolved. Gordon (1977) contends it is undesirable to avoid conflict when there is genuine disagreement, because resentments build up, feelings get displaced, and unpleasantries such as backbiting, gossiping, and general discontent may result.

Teachers, administrators, and parents face many possible occasions for conflict when they are involved with educating children who have special needs. Some conflicts occur because there is too little information or because misunderstandings have been created from incorrect information. These instances are not difficult to resolve because they require only the communication of facts. Other areas of conflict arise from disagreement over teaching methods, assessment methods, goals, and values. Parent goals and teacher goals for the exceptional student may differ significantly, and support personnel may add even more dimensions to the conflict. For example, if a child is instructed by the reading specialist to read more slowly, urged by the learning disabilities teacher to read more rapidly, required by the classroom teacher to read a greater amount of material, and ordered by the parent to get better grades or *else,* effective communication is tenuous or nonexistent, and conflict is inevitable. Some conflict can even be beneficial if it clears the air of lingering disagreement and doubt so that conflicting parties can move ahead. But if differences cannot be resolved through formal or informal conflict-resolution processes, then relationships will surely disintegrate

Perhaps the most difficult area of conflict relates to values. When people have differing values about children, education, or educator roles within the learning context, effective communication is a challenging goal. As discussed earlier in this chapter, rapport-building, listening, and paraphrasing are significant in building relationships among those whose values conflict. The most important step is to listen courteously until a clear message about the value comes through, demonstrating respect for the value even if it conflicts with yours. Then it is time to assert one's own values, and along with the other person try to reach a common goal or seek a practical issue on which to begin problem solving.

How to Resolve School-Related Conflicts

Some conflicts, particularly those involving values, are difficult to prevent and may seem at the time to be irresolvable. However, if all can agree to common goals or common ground for discussion, conflicts can be resolved.

When emotions or conflict inhibit the communication process, first listen responsively and acknowledge what is being said. The other side appreciates the sense of being heard and understood, and the consultant will gain a vivid picture of their interests and concerns. A useful strategy is to focus on interests rather than positions as a way to circumvent potential conflicts during the communication process.

"Always think win/win" is one of Stephen Covey's (1989) seven habits of highly effective people and is a crucial element of effective relationships and problem solving in educational and community settings. If you can't come to a true win/win agreement, Covey suggests, it is better to go for no deal at all. This allows you to preserve the relationship and the possibility for a win/win pact in the future. Win/win agreements flow from solid relationships and taking time to develop a strong level of trust is essential for mutual collaboration. We must resist the urge to succeed at the expense of the other person. This forms a relationship that is open to success on both sides in the future.

Covey (1989) suggests a four-step process for the win/win approach:

1. Try to see the situation from the other person's perspective.
2. Identify the key issues and concerns involved.
3. Make a list of the results that you would consider a fully acceptable solution.
4. Look for new options to get those results.

Resolving conflicts within an "everybody wins" philosophy requires listening skills described earlier in the chapter to find common ground. In dealing with emotions of the speaker, the listener must concentrate with an open mind and attend to the speaker's feelings as well as the facts or ideas that are part of the message. The listener must strive to hear the whole story without interrupting, even if there are strong feelings of disagreement. Conflict usually means that intense emotions are involved. Only by concentrating on the message with an open mind can all parties begin to deal with the conflict. Emotional filters often function as blinders. If the emotions cannot be overcome, the best tactic is to postpone the communication, using assertive responses to do so.

Listening establishes a common intent and develops a starting attitude. Listening to one who is upset helps that person focus on a problem rather than on an emotion. Listening lets people cool down. Bolton (1986) calls this the spiral of resistance, suggesting that if one listens with empathy and does not interrupt, the speaker's anger or high emotion will dissipate. Without saying a word, the listener makes the speaker feel accepted and respected.

It is hard to argue with someone who does not argue back. It is hard to stay mad or upset with someone who seems to understand and empathize. Each time a person listens, a small victory for the advancement of human dignity has been achieved (Schlinder & Lapid, 1989). Only after emotions are brought into the open and recognized can all parties involved move on to seek a common goal.

The initial intent for resolving a conflict should be to learn. This enables all factions to increase mutual understanding and think creatively together. Most people could agree to such a start because it does not address goals or values. It does not even require agreement that a problem exists. It simply establishes the intent to learn by working together. Establishing intent for dialogue should follow the reduction of emotional responses. Of course, as discussed earlier, it is important to avoid roadblocks at all stages of the process.

Consultants and consulting teachers must put aside preconceived notions about their own expertise and learn from those who often know the student best—family members and classroom teachers. Such consultees respond positively to open-ended questions that let them know they are respected and needed. When consultants open their own minds, they unlock the potential of others.

APPLICATION 4.4

PRACTICE MAKES PERFECT, OR EASIER AT LEAST!

With a partner, practice the following ten uncomfortable or embarrassing situations. Use the Figures in this chapter as checklists to monitor verbal and nonverbal communication, for both sending and receiving.

 1. Ask a person who drops by to come back later.
 2. Say "no" to someone who is urging you to help with a project.
 3. Answer the phone when you have about three things going on (voice tone and rate being particularly pertinent here).
 4. Receive a compliment graciously.
 5. Deliver a compliment so that it is not a distorted message.
 6. Ask a colleague to please (for once!) be on time.
 7. Enter a roomful of people who are probably unknown to you.
 8. Respond when someone has interrupted you.
 9. Break into the conversation when someone has monopolized the discussion to everyone's frustration.
 10. Apologize for an oversight or ill-chosen remark you made.

Now, as you feel more confident in these real-life "peak" and "pit" situations, practice using them until they become second nature.

After listening constructively, consultants need to help establish ground rules for resolving the conflict. The ground rules should express support, mutual respect, and a commitment to the process. Again, this requires talking and listening, dialoguing, and keeping an open mind. It is important not to dominate the dialogue at this time, and by the same token not to let the other person dominate the conversation. This part of the communication might be called "agreeing to disagree," with the intent of "agreeing to find a point of agreement." It is important to share the allotted interaction time equitably and in a way that facilitates understanding. Consultants must use precise language without exaggerating points, or, as discussed earlier, flaunting educationese or taking inappropriate shortcuts with jargon and alphabet soup acronyms.

Dealing with conflict productively also requires asserting one's ideas, feelings, or opinions. While listening enables the consultant to understand the speaker's perspectives, wants, and goals, assertion skills allow consultants to present their perspective. This often follows a pattern of listen—assert—listen—assert—listen, and so on, until both parties have spoken and have been heard.

FIGURE 4.4   Checklist for Managing Resistance and Conflict

A. *Responsive Listening*

   1. Had assertive posture   _____

   2. Used appropriate nonverbal listening   _____

   3. Did not become defensive   _____

   4. Used minimal verbals in listening   _____

   5. Reflected content   _____

   6. Reflected feelings   _____

   7. Let others do most of the talking   _____

   8. Used only brief, clarifying questions   _____

B. *Assertiveness*

   9. Did not use roadblocks such as giving advice   _____

10. Used "I" messages   _____

11. Stated wants and feelings   _____

C. *Recycled the interaction*

12. Used positive postponement   _____

13. Did not problem-solve before emotions were controlled   _____

14. Summarized   _____

15. Set time to meet again, if applicable   _____

Although there may be resistance after each assertion, it will gradually dissipate so that *real* communication and collaboration can begin to take place. Only after this process has happened can collaborative goal setting and problem solving occur. Figure 4.4. summarizes useful steps for managing resistance and conflict.

There is a well-known story of a man who had three sons. He stipulated in his will that the oldest son should inherit half his camels, the middle son should get one-third of the camels, and the youngest should be the new owner of one-ninth of his camels. When the old man died, he owned seventeen camels. But the sons could not agree on how to divide the camels in accordance with their father's will. Months and months of bitter conflict went by. Finally the three young men sought the advice of a wise woman in the village. She heard their complaints and observed their bitterness, and felt sorry that brothers were fighting and putting the family into turmoil. So she gave the brothers one of her camels. The estate then was divided easily according to the father's wishes. The eldest took home nine camels, the second put six camels beside his tent, and the youngest took home two camels. The men were happy, the father's last wishes were honored, and the wise woman took her own camel back and led it home.

Conflict management is the process of becoming aware of a conflict, diagnosing its nature, and employing an appropriate problem solving method in such a way that it simultaneously achieves the goals of all involved and enhances relationships among them. If the consulting relationship is treated as a collaborative one in which each person's needs are met (the win/win model), then feelings of self-confidence, competence, self-worth and power increase, enhancing the overall capacity of the system for responding to conflict in the future. The win/win relationship is based on honesty, trust, and mutual respect—qualities stressed earlier as vital to a successful consulting relationship. Win/win allows all involved parties to experience positive outcomes. The model works best when all parties use effective communication skills (Fisher & Ury, 1991).

The opposite of successful conflict management is avoiding conflict, ignoring feelings, and bypassing the goals of others. The relationship becomes adversarial, if it is not already so, because for someone to win, another must lose. When conflicts are approached with responsive listening and dealt with honestly and openly, the underlying problem or need can be resolved.

What to Do When Communication Goes Wrong

Fisher and Sharp (1991) also have suggestions for diagnosing setbacks in the collaboration process. Many collaboration setbacks can be traced to four problems:

1. *Telling others what to think or do.* Telling does not inspire others to learn new behavior or adopt new attitudes. Telling someone what to do implies they have a lower status, and in fact, some see it as an accusation. They might respond, "Are you telling me how to do my job?" Telling your collaborators what to do fails to promote understanding of the problems and the perspectives involved. Team members who have not participated in the thinking about a problem have no ownership in the solution. Empower others by helping them see they can make a difference.

2. *Mistaking the person for the problem.* Collaborators must separate the person from the problem and acknowledge good reasons for the other's behaviors. Often this can be an empathic response such as "I know you've been swamped with all those IEP meetings as well as getting ready for the Special Olympics. We really need your input on this grant proposal."

3. *Blaming others.* There is a universal human tendency to blame others for problems; but this is a dead-end attitude for the consultant. Focus on your own actions; if partners don't react the way you want or expect, start with the assumption that you are doing something wrong.

4. *Having faulty working assumptions.* Some consultants make assumptions when working with teachers, community agencies, or families. Examples of working assumptions that inhibit successful collaboration include ideas like: the problems are someone else's fault; there's not much I can do to change the behavior of others; the situation is impossible, so it's best if I just ignore it; and if it didn't work before, don't try again. Successful consultants work to identify faulty working assumptions and to change them to healthier and more positive assumptions, such as: perhaps I can make a difference; the easiest way to change the behavior of others is to change my own; I can choose to help; and thoughtful persistence pays off.

When engineers stress collaboration, they often use the bumblebee analogy. According to the laws of aerodynamics, bumblebees cannot fly. But as everyone knows, they do. By the same token some might say that groups cannot function productively because of the conflicts, personal agendas, and individual preferences that exist among the members. But they do. Groups of people play symphonies, set up businesses, write laws, and develop IEPs for student needs. An understanding of adult individual differences, styles, and preferences, as discussed in Chapter 2, will encourage participants in consultation and collaboration to listen more respectfully and value differences among colleagues. This knowledge, when combined with responsive listening, avoidance of roadblocks, and assertiveness, will enable consultants to deal with resistance and conflict productively. Conflict management puts these skills to practical use in educational settings of school and home.

Educational consultants maximize their effect on the lives and education of children with special needs by using good communication skills. They should always keep in mind the ancient rule we instill in children for crossing the street: "Stop, Look, and Listen." For the collaborative school consultant it means:

- Stop talking, judging, and giving advice.
- Look at the long-term outcome of good communication (keep eyes on the prize).
- Listen to parents, colleagues and others who work in collaboration for children with special needs.

The stop, look, and listen rule sets up consultants for success—in establishing collaborative relationships, in developing rapport, in dealing with conflict and emotions, and in solving problems.

COMMUNICATING ETHICALLY IN COLLABORATIVE WAYS

Effective communication skills form the basis of respectful, egalitarian relationships within an ethical climate that best serves students with special needs. Verbal and nonverbal skills pave the way to effective problem solving and mutual collaboration.

It is often helpful to write down what one plans to say to a teacher or a parent, and note what the effects of different options might be (Laud, 1998). Novice teachers and more experienced teachers who are still honing their communication skills could keep a log for recording selected interactions, analyzing them, and reflecting on alternative ways to communicate if those interactions were not productive.

Along similar lines, when sending written communication, select words and expressions carefully. When in doubt, it is a good idea to have a colleague read your communication before it is sent on its way. A helpful recipe to keep in mind is to set aside anger or frustration, begin the note on a positive tone, state the problem or concern carefully and objectively in the middle of the communication, and conclude with additional positive words.

Listening instead of arguing, establishing ground rules that are considerate of the values and opinions of others, and working toward common goals and expectations for student success will help bring teams to the problem-finding and problem-solving stages with parity and respect. Consultants who remain calm and listen—always listen—will be "hearing their way to success" and helping to create an ethical and collaborative climate.

TIPS FOR COMMUNICATING EFFECTIVELY

1. Avoid communication roadblocks. Research shows that positively worded statements are one-third easier to understand than negative ones (Rinke, 1997).
2. Listen. This helps dissipate negative emotional responses and often helps the other person articulate the problem, perhaps finding a solution then and there.
3. Use assertion. Say what you feel and what your goals are.
4. Be aware of your hot buttons. Knowing your own responses to certain trigger behaviors and words will help you control natural tendencies to argue, get defensive, or simply turn red and sputter.
5. Attend to nonverbal language (kinesics, or body language) as well as to verbal language when communicating.
6. Don't "dump your bucket" of frustrations onto the other person. Jog, shout, practice karate, but avoid pouring out anger and frustration on others. Instead, fill the buckets of others with "warm fuzzies" of empathy and caring.
7. Develop a protocol within the school context for dealing with difficult issues and for settling grievances.
8. Deal with the present. Keep to the issue of the current problem rather than past problems, failures, or personality conflicts.
9. Use understanding of individual differences among adults to bridge communication gaps and manage conflicts in educational settings.
10. Advocate for training that focuses on communication, problem solving, and conflict management.

CHAPTER REVIEW

1. The primary reason people fail in collaborative efforts is because of communication problems. It is too often assumed that communication skill develops with no special attention to the complexities of social interaction.

2. The sender, message, receiver, and medium are four key components of the communication process. Each component is vital. When a message is missent or misheard, many distortions occur which prevent open, honest communication. This happens because of differences in values, language, attitudes, perceptions, gender, ethnicity, and history of sender and receiver.

3. Rapport building requires respect for differences in others, trust, feeling all right about not having all the answers, and being comfortable even when there is disagreement.

4. Major skills in effective communication are responsive listening, asserting, managing conflict, and collaborative problem solving. Both verbal and nonverbal components are included in these skills.

5. Communication can be hampered by verbal roadblocks and nonverbal roadblocks. Verbal roadblocks include responses that are judging, responses that send solutions, and responses that avoid the concerns of others. Nonverbal roadblocks include body language that conveys lack of empathy and concern.

6. Assertive communication allows speakers to state their own views, feelings, and opinions without impeding the ongoing consulting process. Assertiveness means stating one's wants or feelings by starting sentences with "I," using "and" rather than "but," and showing

concern for the other person. Resistance can be managed by using a combination of assertiveness and responsive listening. Resistance, anger, and negativity are residuals of disagreements and unwanted change. Conflict arises when members of educational teams have different feelings, values, needs, and goals. Conflict resolution should follow a win/win model if collaborative efforts are to be maintained.

TO DO AND THINK ABOUT

1. Discuss the following:
   What type of roadblock does each of these comments set up?

   > What you need is more activity. Why don't you develop a hobby?

   > You are such a good friend. I can count on you.

   > Let's talk about something more positive.

   > I know just how you feel.

   > Why did you let her talk to you that way?

   Which of these lines create resistance and defensiveness?

   > What you should do is . . .

   > Do you want to comment on this?

   > Everyone has problems like that.

   > That's a good thought.

   > You mean you'd actually do that?

   > Let's change the subject.

   > What should I do?

   What assertive statements could be made for each situation?

   > A colleague talks to you about his personal problems and you can't get your work done.

   > The paraeducator comes in late frequently.

   > During a committee meeting one member keeps changing the subject and getting the group off-task.

   > A colleague wants to borrow some material but has failed to return things in the past.

   > During a phone conversation with a wordy parent, you need to get some information quickly and hang up soon.

   > The class next door is so rowdy that your class can't work.

2. Discuss these basic assumptions about communication for consultation and add more to the list.

   > The reactions of others depend on your actions, word choices, body language, and listening skills.

   > People generally want to do a good job.

   > People have a powerful need to "save face."

   > No one can force another person to change.

   > Learning to communicate, be assertive, and facilitate conflict resolution is awkward at first.

3. Make a list of phrases that can be "hot buttons" in the school context. Then practice reacting to each one with a colleague who understands your purpose and will say them to you. Note your body language and the body language of your partner. Then discuss how these phrases might help or hinder the collaborative process.

4. Practice the following situations:

   > Expressing anger in constructive ways

   > Getting the interaction back on-task

   > Stating a contrasting view to a supervisor

   > Recommending a better way of doing something

   > Asking again, and again, for materials you loaned some time ago that you need now

5. Restate the following messages so the language is assertive but nonthreatening to the receiver.

   > "You penalize gifted students when you keep the class lockstepped in the basal texts and the workbooks."

   > "If you want students to use good note-taking skills, you should teach them how to take notes."

   > "Not allowing students to use calculators is terribly outmoded."

   > "It is not fair to insist that students with learning disabilities take tests they cannot read."

ADDITIONAL READINGS AND RESOURCES

Bolton, R. (1986). *People skills: How to assert yourself, listen to others, and resolve conflicts.* New York: Simon & Schuster.

Fisher, R., & Sharp, A. (1999). *Getting it DONE: How to lead when you're not in charge.* New York: HarperCollins.

Fisher, R., Ury, B., & Patton, B. (1991). *Getting to YES: Negotiating agreement without giving in.* Boston: Houghton Mifflin.

Lynch, E. W., & Hanson, M. J. (1998). *Developing cross-cultural competence: A guide for working with children and their families* (2nd ed.). Baltimore: Paul H. Brooks.

Stone, D., Patton, B., & Heen, S. (1999). *Difficult conversations: How to discuss what matters most.* New York: Random House.

CHAPTER FIVE

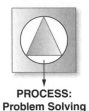

PROCESS:
Problem Solving

Problem-Solving Strategies for Collaborative Consultation and Teamwork

Using a structured process for collaborative school consultation is like preparing food according to a recipe. After the fundamentals of cooking have been mastered, one can adapt those procedures to just about any setting, preference, or creative impulse. In similar fashion, a basic "recipe" for consultation and collaboration can be adapted to any school context, grade level, content area, or special learning need. Just as a recipe should be adaptable for individual preferences, so should a collaborative consultation structure be flexible and adaptable to fit the needs of individual students in their school contexts.

A collaborative style is based on valuing and trusting one another. When educators exercise ingenuity in constructing teaching and learning strategies collaboratively, schools are better contexts in which all can perform at their best. Collaborative school consultation is an ideal scenario for incorporating problem-solving techniques that cultivate flexible, divergent thinking. Teamwork builds esprit de corps.

FOCUSING QUESTIONS

1. What are fundamental components in a problem-solving process?
2. Why is problem identification so important in collaborative consultation?
3. What basic steps should be included in the collaborative school consultation process?
4. What kinds of things should consultants and consultees say and do during their professional interactions?
5. What problem-solving techniques are particularly helpful for collaborative consultation and teamwork?
6. What are interferences and hurdles that must be overcome when problem solving with co-educators?

KEY TERMS

brainstorming	jigsaw	problem-solving process
concept mapping (webbing)	lateral thinking	SCAMPER
follow through	metaphorical thinking	Six Thinking Hats
follow up	multiple intelligences	synectics
idea checklist	Plus-Minus-Interesting (PMI)	synergism
Janusian thinking	problem identification	TalkWalk

SCENARIO 5.A

The setting is the office area of an elementary school, where a special education staff member has just checked into the building and meets a fourth-grade teacher.

Classroom Teacher: I understand you're going to be a consulting teacher in our building to work with learning and behavior disorders.

Consulting Teacher: That's right. I hope to meet with all of the staff very soon to find out your needs and how we can work together to address those needs.

Classroom Teacher: Well I, for one, am glad you're here. I have a student who is driving me and my other twenty-four students up the wall.

Consulting Teacher: How so?

Classroom Teacher: Well, since she moved here a few weeks ago she's really upset the classroom system that I've used for years, and used quite successfully, I might add.

Consulting Teacher: Is she having trouble with the material you teach?

Classroom Teacher: No, she's a bright child who finishes everything in good time, and usually does it correctly. But she's extremely active, almost frenetic as she "busy-bodies" around the room.

Consulting Teacher: What specific behaviors concern you?

Classroom Teacher: Well, for one thing she tries to help everyone else when they should be doing their own work. I've worked a lot on developing independent learning skills in my students, and they've made good progress. They don't need to have her tell them what to do.

Consulting Teacher: So her behavior keeps her classmates from being the self-directed learners that they can be?

Classroom Teacher: Right. I have to monitor her activities constantly, which means diverting my attention from all the other students. She bosses her classmates in the learning centers and even on the playground. At this rate she will soon be having serious difficulties with peer relationships.

Consulting Teacher: Which of those behaviors would you like to see changed first?

Classroom Teacher: Well, I need to get her settled into some activities by herself rather than bothering other students.

Consulting Teacher: What have you tried until now to keep her involved with her own work?

Classroom Teacher: I explain to her what I expect, and then try to reinforce appropriate behavior with things she likes to do.

Consulting Teacher: We could make a list of specific changes in behavior you'd like to see, and work out a program to accomplish them. In fact, the technique of webbing might help us explore the possibilities. How about doing one together on this chart paper? Then we will have a record of our ideas. (Consultant and teacher work together to make the web and begin a plan.) . . . There's the bell. Want to meet tomorrow to add any second thoughts to our chart and finalize this plan?

Classroom Teacher: Sounds good. I'd like to get her on track so the class is more settled. Then other children will like her better and she'll be able to learn other things, too. We could meet right here tomorrow, if that's OK with you. It helps a lot to have someone to talk with about this and work out a plan.

THE PROBLEM-SOLVING PROCESS

Educators must exercise perception and judgment in order to ascertain student needs, set reasonable goals, and select the most efficient means addressing those needs and goals. This requires development and implementation of effective problem-solving skills. Problem-solving ability comes more naturally and easily to some than to others. There is no one specific formula or "recipe." Furthermore, problem-solving strategies, particularly as used by groups, can be improved with training and practice.

Pugach and Johnson (1995) suggest that co-educators configure two general categories for problem solving in the context of teacher collaboration: (1) schoolwide problems, and (2) specific student problems. Full inclusion is an example of schoolwide problem solving undertaken in a collaborative way by all school staff. The second category, that of specific student needs, is more commonly dealt with by teachers in a problem-solving mode. Both categories of problems provide an opportunity to broaden the educational options for students with special needs.

In order to address both schoolwide problems and specific student needs, it is helpful to begin with a study of the fundamental problem-solving process. These components are key steps in solving problems effectively and they frame most problem-solving models:

- Data-gathering as guided by the "mess" for which a solution is being sought
- Identification and definition of the problem (*extremely* important)
- Generation of possible actions toward solution
- Critique of proposed actions
- Decision making to select best option(s)
- Implementing the elements of the decision
- Following up to evaluate the outcome(s)

Key problem solving steps.

Communicating in Problem-Solving Teams

A problem-solving process that encourages high levels of communication and collaboration will allow educators to share their expertise related to the problem. Learning and behavior problems are not always outcomes of student disabilities. Many students are simply "curriculum-disabled" (Conoley, 1985), requiring a modified or expanded approach to existing curriculum in order to function successfully in school (Pugach & Johnson, 1990). To modify the settings for learning and make accommodations in the educational environment, educators must identify those aspects of students' educational curriculum that are impeding their development.

Delineating the Problem.   The first and most critical step in a problem-solving process is to identify the problem (Bolton, 1986). The most sophisticated teaching methods and the most expensive instructional materials are worthless if student needs are misidentified or overlooked. It can even be argued that inaccurate definition of the problem situation has potential for iatrogenic effects. These effects hurt more than help, just as identifying an illness incorrectly can result in inappropriate treatment and delay or deny use of a better treatment, or perhaps even introduce a harmful one.

Problem identification requires special emphasis if the consultation process is to produce results. Bergan (1995) stresses that when problem identification is successful, the consultation is much more likely to come to a successful conclusion.

Multisourced information about student needs provides a more accurate perspective on learning and behavior problems, along with information about the settings in which they are demonstrated, the severity and frequency of the problems, and the persons who are most affected by those behaviors (Polsgrove & McNeil, 1989). Obtaining information from multiple sources requires effective communication skills by all who can contribute information. See Figure 5.1 to identify sixteen possible data sources.

Communication is such an important aspect of successful school consultation that it was addressed separately in Chapter 4. Expressing thoughts and feelings with clarity and accuracy requires effective listening and appropriate assertiveness. A problem will never be solved if all parties think they are working on different issues. Problems are like artichokes—they come in layers. Only after the outside layers are stripped away can problem solvers get to the heart of the matter. Good listening facilitates movement to the heart of the problem.

Co-educators must examine their own perspectives and preferences to identify any potential aspects that will impede their abilities to problem-solve for the student's needs. The four major interfering themes outlined by Caplan (1970) and introduced in Chapter 3 are revisited here to stress their potential impact on the educator's ability to listen effectively and think divergently on the student's behalf. They are:

1. Lack of understanding about the problem and relevant processes of instruction and learning
2. Lack of skills in posing options for courses of action that could be taken
3. Lack of self-confidence in addressing the situation and dealing with it
4. Lack of professional objectivity when former experiences or beliefs get in the way and have undue influence

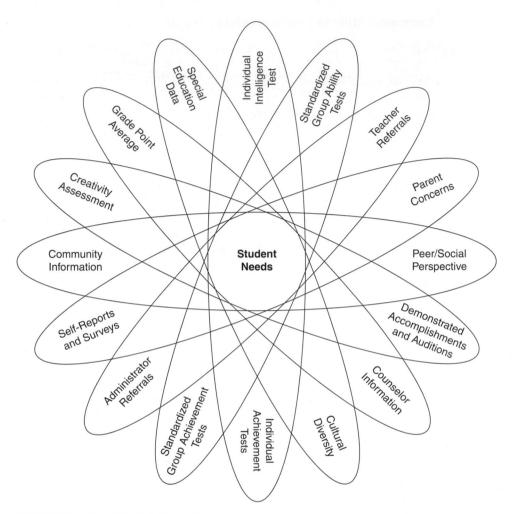

FIGURE 5.1 Case Study Information

Generating Possibilities. Problem solving also involves generating ideas for solutions. Divergent thinking is important to avoid getting stuck in routines and answers. Some consultants find it helpful to encourage the person who "owns" the problem to make the most suggestions. For example, if the problem is making a decision about postsecondary education for a student with learning disabilities, the student and the parents should be encouraged to generate the most options. This is important for several reasons. When people participate in decision making, they feel more ownership of the results than when the decision is forced on them. People are more apt to support decisions they helped create than those imposed on them.

An important second reason for prompting the owner of the problem to give initial suggestions is that consultants should avoid giving advice and being perceived as the expert. Several researchers have shown that a nonexpert approach to educational consulting is especially effective in special education (Idol-Maestes, Lloyd, & Lilly, 1981; Margolis & McGettigan, 1988). The suggestions and opinions of all others need to be listened to with respect and fully understood before additional suggestions are offered.

Problems that come up in school consultation often reveal the need for changes in classroom practices. (Recall that resistance was discussed in Chapter 4.) Advice giving and hierarchical structure may be unintentionally communicated if consultants promote the options generated as being their ideas. Furthermore, if a consultant is regarded as *the* expert, there is pressure on that consultant and false expectations are created. It is hard to win in this kind of situation. The best practice for the collaborating consultant is to communicate equality, flexibility, and a sharing attitude. Three questions assess the equality that is or is not present in a professional consulting relationship:

1. Does the consultant give recognition to the consultee's expertise and opinions?
2. Does the consultant encourage the consultee to generate ideas and make decisions?
3. Do consultees feel free to *not* do as the consultant might recommend?

Eager, competent consultants, who are ready to solve problems and produce quick results, instant cures, and dramatic increases, too often jump in and try to solve problems alone. Consultees may react with resistance or negativism, or perhaps even hostility, by hiding their feelings and withdrawing, blaming others if things do not work out.

It can be difficult for consultants to avoid the "quick fix." But a quick fix is inappropriate (DeBoer, 1986), and it is demeaning to the person who has been struggling with the problem. Others need to feel that the consultant fully understands their unique situation and the source of their frustrations before they are ready to participate in problem solving and listen to the suggestions of colleagues. Consultants must listen before they can expect to be listened to and treated with parity or approached voluntarily by consultees.

All learning situations and all students are unique. In response to a question about classroom management, a wise high school teacher replied, "I don't know all the answers, because I haven't seen all the kids." While students and situations may appear similar in some ways, the combinations of student, teacher, parents, and school and home contexts are unique for each problem. Furthermore, in many cases, people with problems already have their answers. They just need help to clarify issues or an empathic ear to face the emotional aspects of the concern. If people keep talking, they often can solve their own problems. Joint problem identification and idea generating ensures that professional relationships are preserved. Then professional communication is enhanced and professionals maintain a greater feeling of control and self-esteem.

Good collaborative consultants do not "solve" problems—they see that problems get solved. So they facilitate problem solving and "nix the quick fix." As Gordon (1977) asks, Whose problem is it? Who *really* owns the problem? Busy consultants do not need to take on the problems of others, and such action would inhibit consultees from learning and practicing problem-solving skills. Everyone who owns a part of the problem should participate in solving it. That may involve collaboration among several people—teachers, administrators, vocational counselors, social workers, justice system personnel, students, parents, and others. Consultants and consultees should focus on the problem rather than on establishing

FIGURE 5.2   Problem-Solving Process Guide Form

Problem: _____

Expected Outcome: _____

Options	*Consequences*
1. _____	_____
2. _____	_____
3. _____	_____
4. _____	_____
5. _____	_____
6. _____	_____

Chosen Solution: _____

Responsibilities and Commitments: _____

Follow-Up Date and Time: _____

Source: Linda P. Thurston. Used with permission.

ownership for the problem. All individuals will need to attend carefully to minimizing roadblocks and maximizing assertion and listening skills.

A record sheet for taking notes on the ideas generated can help collaborators communicate effectively and think divergently. Notes taken on problem, options, and consequences are a problem-solving guide and the responsibilities section is a record of expectations and commitments. (See Figure 5.2.) Also, Garmston (1995) recommends providing a rationale to participants in collaboration before initiating the group activity, then inserting a few moments for reflection and journaling after the activity and before the summarizing group discussion.

Implementing Agreed-On Plans.   The problem-solving group selects a workable solution all are willing to adopt, at least on a trial or experimental basis. The consultant promotes mutual participation in the decision. Group members more readily accept new ideas and new work methods when they are given opportunity to participate in decision making (Gordon, 1977). Many times a complex problem can be solved as each person in the group discovers what the others really want or, perhaps, dread. Then proposed solutions can be formulated to meet the goals and protect the concerns of all involved.

Better decisions are made with a cool head and a warm heart (Johnson, 1992). Johnson suggests asking oneself if the decision helps meet the *real* need. Real needs are based on reality, not illusion or wishful thinking. Co-educators should ask, Did we have enough information to create options we may not have realized before this? Have we thought through the consequences of each option? Have we *really* thought through all the options? Taking time to ask all the necessary questions is a key to the decision-making process. Asking many questions helps make options and choices obvious.

Effective consultants facilitate problem solving in such a way that all members of the group feel their needs are being satisfied, and an equitable social and professional relationship is being maintained (Gordon, 1977). Members of the problem-solving team work together to evaluate all the suggestions made, with each presenting disadvantages and merits of the suggestions from their own perspectives. Agreement is not necessary at this point, because the barriers and merits important to each person are taken into account. Honest and open communication, using good listening skills, and an appropriate level of assertiveness are vital at this step.

Following Through and Following Up.   After sorting through data, scheduling and arranging meetings, planning agenda, facilitating and participating in the meeting, it is tempting to breathe a sigh of relief when the agreed-on plan is ready for implementation and go on to other things. But collaborators, busy as they are, must follow through on the progress of the plan and follow up with co-educators who are carrying it out and students for whom the plan was made. If the follow-up process suggests no progress has been made or unexpected problems have surfaced, the problem-solving activity should be repeated.

Problem-Solving Roles

In collaborative problem solving, the role of the consultant is to facilitate interaction and teamwork with understanding, skill, objectivity, and self-confidence. Collaborative school consultation encourages collective thinking for creative and imaginative alternatives and allows all who are involved to have their feelings and ideas heard and their goals addressed in practical ways. The ultimate goal is to provide the best learning opportunities possible for students with special needs. At this point it may be helpful to review the descriptions of consultation, collaboration, and teamwork as personified through several examples differentiating these three interactive processes.

Problem Solving through Consultation.   A preschool teacher is concerned about a child in the group who is not fluent in speech. So the teacher asks the speech pathologist to help determine what to do about it. The speech pathologist consults with the teacher and the child's family, getting more information about the observed behavior, and makes additional observations. The consultant then uses his expertise in speech pathology to address the questions and concerns of the teacher and the family.

In another instance, a physical therapist provides individual therapy for a preschool child who has cerebral palsy. The therapist wants to know about the child's social development as well as performance in preacademic skills such as letter recognition and sound discrimination. The therapist asks the teacher to serve as a consultant regarding this issue, and the preschool teacher provides the information requested.

Problem Solving through Collaboration.   The kindergarten teacher and the music teacher are both concerned about a child's tendency to masturbate during group time while sitting on the rug. The two teachers meet to discuss their mutual concern. Both parties discuss their observations and engage in problem-solving activities to identify the problem clearly and select possible actions. Both parties agree to make some changes in their respective settings to address the problem. If the solutions do not work, they are committed to try other possibilities, including consultation with the child's parents. the school psychologist, and the health nurse.

In another situation, a teacher of students with behavioral disorders, along with the school counselor, three classroom teachers, and a student's parents, meet to discuss the behavior of that student. The individuals involved in the meeting engage in collaborative problem solving to formulate a plan for addressing the problem. Each individual has a role to play in defining the problem, generating possible actions, and implementing the plan.

Problem Solving through Teamwork.   A special education teacher and a general classroom teacher engage in co-teaching, a form of teamwork unique to classroom settings. The teachers meet weekly to engage in co-planning. During the co-planning they decide when, where, and how to share responsibilities for meeting the instructional needs of all students in the classroom during a specified class period each day. Each teacher uses his or her areas of expertise and strength whenever feasible. The co-teachers come to consensus on evaluation systems and assign grades for all students by mutual agreement. They no longer speak of "my students" or "your students" and instead they speak of, plan for, and teach "our students."

In another situation, a team of professionals provides services for infants and toddlers with severe or profound disabilities. Each professional has an area of expertise and responsibility. The social worker has the leadership role because she is responsible for most family contacts and often goes into homes to provide additional assistance for families. The nurse takes responsibility for monitoring the physical well being of each child and keeps in close contact with other medical personnel and families. The speech pathologist works with the children to develop speech and language skills. The occupational therapist is responsible for teaching the children self-help skills. The physical therapist follows through with the medical doctor's prescribed physical therapy. Special education teachers provide language stimulation and modeling, coordinate schedules, and facilitate communication among the team that meets twice weekly to discuss individual cases.

TEN-STEP PROCESS FOR COLLABORATIVE PROBLEM SOLVING

Now that the fundamentals of a typical problem-solving process have been discussed, and distinctions have been made among (1) problem solving with a major focus on consultation, (2) problem solving that emphasizes collaboration, and (3) problem solving as a team, a ten-step process for collaborative school consultation will be introduced. This process,

FIGURE 5.3   The Ten-Step Process for Collaborative School Consultation

1. *Prepare for the consultation.*
   1.1 Focus on major topic or area of concern.
   1.2 Prepare and organize materials.
   1.3 Prepare several possible actions or strategies.
   1.4 Arrange for a comfortable, convenient meeting place.

2. *Initiate the consultation.*
   2.1 Establish rapport.
   2.2 Identify the agenda.
   2.3 Focus on the tentatively defined concern.
   2.4 Express interest in the needs of all.

3. *Collect and organize relevant information.*
   3.1 Make notes of data, soliciting from all.
   3.2 Combine and summarize the data.
   3.3 Assess data to focus on areas needing more information.
   3.4 Summarize the information.

4. *Isolate the problem.*
   4.1 Focus on need.
   4.2 State what the problem is.
   4.3 State what it is not.
   4.4 Propose desirable circumstances.

5. *Identify concerns and realities about the problem.*
   5.1 Encourage all to listen to each concern.
   5.2 Identify issues, avoiding jargon.
   5.3 Encourage ventilation of frustrations and concerns.
   5.4 Keep focusing on the pertinent issues and needs.
   5.5 Check for agreement.

6. *Generate solutions.*
   6.1 Engage in collaborative problem-solving.
   6.2 Generate several possible options and alternatives.
   6.3 Suggest examples of appropriate classroom modifications.
   6.4 Review options, discussing consequences of each.
   6.5 Select the most reasonable alternatives.

7. *Formulate a plan.*
   7.1 Designate those who will be involved, and how.
   7.2 Set goals.
   7.3 Establish responsibilities.
   7.4 Generate evaluation criteria and methods.
   7.5 Agree on a date for reviewing progress.
   7.6 Follow through on all commitments.

8. *Evaluate progress and process.*
   8.1 Conduct a review session at a specified time.
   8.2 Review data and analyze the results.
   8.3 Keep products as evidence of progress.
   8.4 Make positive, supportive comments.
   8.5 Assess contribution of the collaboration.

9. *Follow through and follow up on the consultation about the situation.*
   9.1 Reassess periodically to assure maintenance.
   9.2 Provide positive reinforcement.
   9.3 Plan further action or continue the plan.
   9.4 Adjust the plan if there are problems.
   9.5 Initiate further consultation if needed.
   9.6 Bring closure if goals have been met.
   9.7 Support effort and reinforce results.
   9.8 Share information where it is wanted.
   9.9 Enjoy the pleasure of having the communication.

10. *Repeat or continue consultation as appropriate.*

outlined in Figure 5.3, will help consultants and consultees communicate effectively and coordinate their efforts efficiently so that they can identify educational problems and design programs for students' needs.

Step 1: Preparing for the Collaborative Consultation.   As consultants plan and prepare for consultation and collaboration, they focus on the major areas of concern. They prepare helpful materials and organize them in order to use collaborative time efficiently. It is useful to distribute information beforehand so that valuable interaction time is not consumed reading new material. But they must take care to present that material as tentative and still open to discussion. It is not always expedient to plan in great detail prior to consultations.

Sometimes consultations happen informally and without notice—between classes, during lunch periods, or on playgrounds. While educators usually will want to accommodate colleagues on these occasions, they also need to look beyond them for opportunities to engage in more in-depth sessions.

Consultants need to give each collaborator enough advance notice and time to prepare. They will want to provide convenient and comfortable settings for the interaction, arranging seating so there is a collegial atmosphere with no phone or drop-by interruptions, and privacy is ensured. Serving coffee and tea can help set congenial, collegial climates for meetings. (See Figure 5.3.)

Step 2: Initiating the Collaborative Interaction.   Consultants need to make a significant effort in this phase. When resistance to consulting is high, or the teaching staff has been particularly reluctant to collaborate, it is difficult to establish first contacts. This is the time to begin with the most receptive staff members in order to build in success for the consulting program. Rapport is established by addressing every consultee as special and expressing interest in what each one is doing and feeling. Teachers should be encouraged to talk about their successes. The consultant needs to display sensitivity to teachers' needs and make each one feel important. The key is to *listen.*

The consultant will want to identify the agenda and keep focusing on the concern. It is helpful to have participants write down their concerns before the meeting and bring them along. Then the consultant can check quickly for congruence and major disagreements. (Again, and with the remaining eight steps, consult Figure 5.3.)

Step 3: Collecting and Organizing Information.   The data should be relevant to the issue of focus. However, data that might seem irrelevant to one person may be the very information needed to identify the real problem. So the consultant must be astute in selecting appropriate data that include many possibilities but do not waste time or resources. This becomes easier with experience, but for new consultants, having too much information is probably better than having too little. However, time is limited and must be used judiciously.

Since problem identification seems to be the most significant factor in planning for special needs, it is wise to gather sufficient data from multiple sources. A case study method of determining data sources and soliciting information is particularly effective in planning for students who have special learning and behavior needs. Refer again to Figure 5.1 for identifying up to sixteen data sources of information for problem solving to address a student's needs. The more of the sixteen that are tapped, the more easily and clearly the need is understood.

Step 4: Isolating the Problem.   As discussed earlier, the most critical aspect of problem solving involves identifying and defining the problem at hand by focusing on the need, not the handy solution. Without problem identification, problem solving cannot occur (Bergan, 1995; Bergan & Tombari, 1976). The most common problem-solving error is to short-circuit the problem definition step and hasten to traditional solutions rather than developing individually tailored solutions (Conoley, 1989, p. 248). Henning-Stout (1994) notes that less experienced consultants in particular tend to spend insufficient time with the consultee on the nature of the problem and proceed too quickly to developing "the plan."

Step 5: Identifying Concerns and Stating Realities Relevant to the Problem.   All concerns and viewpoints related to the problem should be aired and shared by each participant. A different viewpoint is not better or worse, just different. An effective consultant keeps participants focusing on student needs by listening and encouraging everyone to respond. However, a certain amount of venting and frustration is to be expected and accepted. Teachers and parents will demonstrate less resistance when they know they are free to express their feelings without retaliation or judgment. Consultants should remain nonjudgmental and ensure confidentiality, always talking and listening in consultees' language.

As information is shared, the consultant will want to make notes. It is good to have everyone look over the recorded information from time to time during the consultation as a demonstration of trust and parity, as well as a check on accuracy. (A log format for recording information and documenting the consultation will be provided in Figure 6.8, on p. 199.)

Step 6: Generating Options.   Now is the time for creative problem solving. If ideas do not come freely, or if participants are blocking productive thinking, the consultant might lead the group in trying one or more of the techniques described later in the chapter. A problem-solving technique not only unleashes ideas, it also sends a message about the kind of behavior that is needed to solve the problem. Straw votes can be taken periodically if that helps the group keep moving toward solutions. Thinking outside the box and combining ideas are desirable processes at this stage. Two productive activities are to have brief discussions focusing on benefits and on concerns. These two sharing periods should be initiated with the word stems such as "I like. . ." (where the benefits are shared), and "I wish. . ." or "How to. . ." (where the concerns are shared). At this stage the group should modify, dismiss, or problem-solve for each concern.

Step 7: Formulating the Plan.   After options have been generated, wishes and concerns aired, and modifications made, the revised option is ready to be formulated into a plan. Participants must remain on-task. They need to be reinforced positively for their contributions. Consultants will want to be ready to make suggestions, but they should defer presenting them so long as others are suggesting and volunteering. They must avoid offering ideas prematurely or addressing too many issues at one time. Other unhelpful behaviors are assuming the supervisor/expert role, introducing one's own biases, and making suggestions that conflict with existing values in the school context.

As the plan develops, the consultant must make clear just who will do what, and when, and where. Evaluation criteria and methods that are congruent with the goals and plan should be developed at this time, and arrangements made for assessment and collection of data on student progress. A vital element to success in collaborative problem solving will be the commitment by *all* participants to follow through with the plan, an activity that will appear as Step 9.

Step 8: Evaluating Progress and Process.   This step and the final two steps frequently are overlooked. Consultation and collaborative decision making should be followed by assessment of student progress resulting from the collaborative plan, and also by evaluation of the collaborative consultation process itself. (Several figures in Chapter 6 are useful for this purpose.)

The consultant will want to make positive, supportive comments while drawing closure to the interaction, and at that time can informally evaluate the consultation with consultee help, being careful to record the information for later analysis, or formally evaluate by asking for brief written responses. This is also a good time to plan for future collaboration.

Step 9: Following Through and Following Up.   Of all ten steps, this may be the most neglected. Unsuccessful consultation outcomes often result from lack of follow-up service. It is in the best interest of the client, consultee, consultant, and future opportunities for consultation to reassess the situation periodically. Participants will want to adjust the student's program if necessary, and initiate further consultation if the situation seems to require it. Informal conversations with consultees at this point are very reinforcing. During the follow-up, consultants have opportunities to make consultees feel good about themselves. They can make a point of noting improved student behaviors and performance, as well as positive effects that result from the collaboration. Also, they may volunteer to help if things are not going as smoothly as anticipated, or if consultees have further needs. The sweetest words a consultee can hear are, "What can I do to help you?" However, this question *must* be framed in the spirit of: "What can I do to help you *that you do not have the time and resources to do?*" and *not* implied as, "What can I do for you that you do not have the skill and expertise to accomplish?" Consultants should follow through immediately on all promises of materials, information, action, or further consultation, and take special steps to reinforce things that are going well. Figure 5.4 is an example of a form that could be used.

Step 10: Repeating Collaborative Consultation If Needed.   Further consultation and collaboration may be needed if the plan is not working, or if one or more parties believe the problem was not identified appropriately. On the other hand, consultation also may be repeated and extended when things are going well. The obvious rationale here is that if one interaction helped, more will help further. This is very reinforcing for processes of consultation, collaboration, and teamwork. It encourages others to participate in consultation and collaboration processes.

The ten-step consultation procedure, committed to memory or stapled into one's plan book, is a good organizational tool and a reassuring resource for every co-educator, particularly for those engaging in their first consultations. When implemented, the scenario might go something like Scenario 5.B that follows.

FIGURE 5.4   Memo to Follow Through on Collaborative Consultation/Teamwork

From: _____ to _____
                    (consultant)   (consultee/s)

Date: _____ Re: _____

I am eager to follow through on the plan which we developed on the date above, and also to assist in other ways that may have occurred to you since then.

How do you feel things have progressed since that time? Please be forthright.

_____

_____

What else may I do to help?

_____

_____

                                        (List here any times, descriptions, etc., that would
                                        help me respond specifically to your needs.)

_____   Information   _____

_____   Resources   _____

_____   Meet again   _____

_____   Classroom visit   _____

_____   Conference with: _____

Thank you so much! I enjoy working with you to serve our students and schools.

SCENARIO 5.B

A special education teacher asks to meet with the classroom teacher of a student with hearing impairment. Implementation of instructional strategies and curricular adaptations made to address the student's IEP goals are going well. However, she believes more could be done in the school environment beyond cognitive development to help this student fit in socially, emotionally, and physically. In a quick "one-legged" conference during hall supervision with the student's classroom teacher, she senses that he has some concerns as well, and she suggests a meeting before contacting the parents to see if adjustments to the IEP are warranted.

She prepares for their meeting with an agenda and a summary of ideas and examples for adaptations. She asks to meet in the classroom on the teacher's "turf." This promises to be a very amiable collaboration, but as a novice teacher she wants to use her most polished collaborative consultation skills with this veteran teacher. She knows that as an intuitive thinker with her problem-solving style she has a tendency to gloss over facts and move too hastily to looking at ideas for solutions. This is something she has been working on and that awareness will serve her well today because she has observed that her co-worker has an opposite style of stating problems, issues, and factual data succinctly. These differences can work to their advantage, and the ultimate benefit for the student.

During the interaction she listens and waits appropriately. She uses verbals such as "we" and "How can I assist you in addressing the student's needs?" She asks the teacher about his concerns and uses reflective listening until the teacher concludes. She suggests items from her prepared list of ideas for modifications and accommodations. They review the student's IEP and then they begin to brainstorm based on both teachers' concerns and suggestions as a launch pad. This is where the novice teacher can shine. Next they generate a description of modifications that first focus on the areas of student need, and then outline what would be each teacher's responsibilities. Each shares expertise in how these modifications can be integrated into general curriculum and other parts of the student's school day. This includes more thoughtful placement in the music room, in assemblies, at lunch, and in playground games, to target the needs that go beyond academics into social, emotional, and sensorimotor areas.

The two teachers work out the details of the plan and they include an early conference with the student's family members to present the plan and be sure all facets are in compliance with their student's IEP and have their support. They make a special note to solicit additional ideas from input by the family members. They also plan the means by which they will engage support from other personnel including music teacher, physical education teacher, bus driver, cafeteria personnel, and school nurse.

This meeting carries the joint consultation through Steps 1–7 of the problem-solving process. Steps 8–10, namely evaluation, following up/following through and repeating if necessary, will have to wait until after discussing their ideas with the family members. But both co-educators leave the meeting on this day feeling very good about their collaborative effort and the event was a special boost to the first-year teacher's confidence. (See Figure 5.5.)

What to Say during the Consultation

Of course, the consultant does not want to parrot points from an outline as though reading from a manual for programming a video machine. But by practicing verbal responses that are helpful at each step, it will become more natural and automatic to use facilitative phrases when the need arises. Each number for the phrase sets below corresponds to a numbered step of the ten-step consultation process outlined earlier.

1. *When planning the consultation.* (Comments in this step are made to oneself.)

    (What styles of communication and interaction can I expect with these consultees?)
    (Have I had previous consultations with them and if so, how did these go?)

FIGURE 5.5   First, Identify the Problem

(Do I have any perceptions at this point about client needs? If so, can I keep them under wraps while soliciting responses from others?)

(What kinds of information might help with this situation?)

2. *When initiating the consultation.* (In this step and the rest of the steps, say to the consultee—)

You're saying that. . . .

The need seems to be. . . .

May we work together along these lines . . . ?

So the situation is. . . .

I am aware that . . .

What can we do in regard to your request/situation . . . ?

3. *When collecting information.*

Tell me about that. . . .

Uh-huh. . . .

What do you see as the effects of . . . ?

Let's see now, your views/perceptions about this are. . . .

> Tell me more about the background of. . . .
> Sounds tough. . . .
> To summarize our basic information then. . . .

4. *When isolating the problem.*

> The major factors we have brought out seem to be. . . .
> Are we asking the right questions?
> What do you perceive is the greatest need for . . . ?
> What circumstances have you noted that may apply . . . ?
> Are there other parts to the need that we have not considered?
> So to summarize our perceptions at this point. . . .
> Are we in agreement that the major part of this issue is . . . ?

5. *When identifying the concerns and stating the realities.*

> You say the major concern is. . . .
> How do you feel about this?
> But I also hear your concern about. . . .
> You'd like this situation changed so that. . . .
> How does this affect your day/load/responsibility . . . ?
> You are concerned about other students in your room. . . .
> What are some ways to get at . . . ?
> You're feeling . . . because of. . . .
> This problem seems formidable. Perhaps we can isolate part of it. . . .
> Would you say that . . . ?
> Perhaps we can't be sure about that. . . .
> The major factors we have brought out seem to be. . . .
> If you could change one thing, what would you change first?

6. *When generating possibilities.*

> How does this affect the students/schedule/parents . . . ?
> Do we have a good handle on the nature of this situation?
> We need to define what we want to happen. . . .
> How would you like things to be?
> What has been tried so far?
> What happened then?
> Is this the best way to get it done? The only way?
> How could we do this more easily?
> Could we try something new such as . . . ?
> Could you add to what has been said?
> What limitations fall on things we might suggest?
> Let's try to develop some ideas to meet the need. . . .
> Your idea of . . . also makes me think of. . . .

7. *When formulating a plan.*

> Let's list the goals and ideas we have come up with.
> So, in trying . . . you'll be changing your approach of. . . .
> To implement these ideas, we would have to. . . .

We have considered every possibility brought forth, so which shall it be?

The actions in this situation would be different, because. . . .

We've discussed all of the alternatives carefully and now it's time to choose.

We need to break down the plan into steps. What should come first? Next?

When is the best time to start with the first step?

8. *When evaluating progress.*

Have we got a solid plan?

One way to measure progress toward the goals would be. . . .

Some positive things have been happening. . . .

How can we build upon these gains?

Now we can decide where to go from here. . . .

In what ways did our getting together help?

I can see [the student] progress every day. . . .

You're accomplishing so much with. . . .

How could I serve you and your students better?

9. *When following up and interacting with colleagues.*

How do you feel about the way things are going?

We had set a time to get back together. Is that time still OK, or should we make it sooner?

I'm interested in the progress you have observed.

I'm following up on that material/action I promised.

I just stopped by. . . .

I wondered how things have been going for you.

How are things in your corner of the world these days?

I'm glad you've hung in there with this problem.

You've accomplished a lot that may not be apparent when you're with it every day.

You know, progress like this makes teachers look very good!

10. *If repeating the consultation.*

Should we have another go at discussing . . . ?

Perhaps we overlooked some information that would help. . . .

We got so much accomplished last time. How about getting together again to. . . ?

That's a great progress report. Would another plan session produce even more of these fine results?

▪ ▪ ▪ ▪ ▪ ▬▬▬▬▬▬▬▬▬▬▬▬▬▬▬▬▬▬▬▬▬▬▬▬▬▬▬▬▬▬

APPLICATION 5.1
USING THE 10-STEP CONSULTING PROCESS

Select one or more of the following situations and simulate a school consultation experience, using the ten-step process and any of the "What to Say" phrases that seem appropriate:

Situation A: A middle school student is vision-impaired. Her IEP includes modifications of paper-and-pencil tests. What are the ramifications of this for classroom teacher preparations, grading issues, and NCLB-mandated testing?

Situation B: It is the first week of school. A high school student new to the area has Tourette's syndrome and even though he has medication that keeps the syndrome under control, he has asked if he may speak briefly to his classmates during class to explain his condition "just in case." He believes that few in the public know much about the condition and one of his causes is to spread awareness. Who should meet about this and what should their agenda be?

Situation C: A ninth-grade student is considered lazy by former teachers, has failed several courses, and cannot grasp math concepts. He has difficulty locating information but can read and understand most material at his grade level. He is never prepared for class, seldom has pencil and paper, and loses his assignments. Yet he is pleasant, seemingly eager to please, and will try things in a one-to-one situation. His classroom teachers say he will not pass, and you have all decided to meet about this. How will you, the learning disabilities consulting teacher, address the situation?

Situation D: You are attending an IEP meeting on behalf of a third-grade student who is emotionally disturbed and classified as having borderline educable mental retardation. You believe she should be placed in a general classroom with supportive counseling service and reevaluated in a year. The other staff participants feel she should have been in special education placement with mainstreaming into music, art, and physical education. The mother is confused about the lack of agreement among school personnel. How will you address the concerns of all in this situation, particularly the mother?

Situation E: A sixth-grade student's mother is known as a perfectionist. Her son, who has been identified for the gifted program, did not receive all As on the last report card, and she has requested a conference with you as the classroom teacher, the principal, and the school psychologist. How will you address this situation?

Situation F: A first-year kindergarten teacher has learned that one of her students will be a child with cerebral palsy. Although the child's history to date has included continuous evaluation, home teaching, group socialization experiences, special examinations, and therapy sessions as well as family counseling for three years, the teacher is nervous about her responsibilities with this child. As the speech pathologist, how will you build her confidence in caring for the kindergartner's language needs, and her skill in helping the little girl to develop her potential?

Situation G: The special education director and middle school building administrator have been asked by a group of general education teachers and special education teachers to meet with them. The director and the principal sense that this group has been chosen informally by the entire teaching staff to be their spokespersons. They know that these teachers and their colleagues are caring and conscientious educators. The representative group wants to discuss the grave concerns they have about including all students with special needs in the high-stakes standardized tests to be given in a few weeks. As they voice the concerns, ask how best to prepare the students for these tests, and question what is to be done with the results of the tests, how might the special education director and building administrator react and respond?

What to Consider If Group Problem Solving Is Not Successful

There is no universal agreement on what makes consultation effective, and little empirical support exists to guide consultants as to what should be said and done in consultation (Gresham & Kendell, 1987; Heron & Kimball, 1988), However, the ten steps outlined above have worked well for many consultants and consulting teachers. If this method of ten steps does not work, consultants should ask several questions.

- Were feelings addressed?
- Was the problem defined accurately?
- Did all parties practice good listening skills?
- Were the nitty-gritty details worked out?
- Were any hidden agendas brought to light and handled?
- Were all participants appropriately assertive?
- Was the consultation process evaluated and then discussed?
- Could any other problem-solving tools facilitate the process?
- Was there follow-up to the consultation?
- Should we convene in groups to practice problem-solving techniques?

■ ■ ■ ■ ■

APPLICATION 5.2
FOR A FURTHER CHALLENGE

As a team effort in a group with several colleagues who share your grade level and subject area, construct a scenario to demonstrate the ten-step collaborative school consultation process at your teaching level and in your content area(s). Role play it for other groups, stopping at key points—for example, after problem identification, and again after formulating the plan, and then perhaps just before following through—to ask the observing group what they might do at that point. If several promising alternatives are suggested, try each one and follow it to its conclusion, in the manner of the choose-an-adventure books that children like to read.

What techniques worked best? How did individual differences influence the consultation? Were these individual differences used constructively, and if not, what could have been done instead? Did participants become better collaborators as they tried more scenarios?

TOOLS FOR GROUP PROBLEM SOLVING

The collaborative format of working together and drawing on collective expertise to solve problems is widely practiced in the business and professional world. In their efforts to use the best ideas of bright, innovative minds, astute leaders employ a number of group problem-solving techniques. These techniques allow individuals to extend their own productive thinking powers and enhance those of their colleagues by participating in structured group problem-solving activities. However, such techniques are yet to be relied on to much extent for adults in educational settings, where autonomy and self-sufficiency have traditionally been more convenient than collaboration and teamwork.

One of the most frequently occurring activities of problem-finding and problem-solving in schools is the IEP process. The shared thinking in which the interactive IEP team engages is a collaborative method of finding solutions to problems (Clark, 2000). So simulated IEP conferences can be used as development tools for enhancing consultation and collaboration skills of co-educators. A group could be assigned to develop an IEP for a graduate student colleague who wants to do an advanced, independent study on the subject of autism and then will share the information with other students and instructors. Her colleagues could collaborate in assigned roles—student, facilitator for the study, representative of school administration, instructor for the subject area (autism in this case), and "parent" (that could be her spouse who had to leave work to attend). It would be illuminating to have the student *not* participate in the meeting so as to simulate the reality of most IEP scenarios in which students are not present for their own IEP planning. As the group prepares a statement of level of performance (citing the student's capability and motivation toward completing the program while working full-time), justification for placement (ability and need to do an independent study), annual measurable goals, due dates with persons responsible for facilitation and support, and evaluation methods, they would be collaborating as a co-educator team. IEP development for very capable students who are doing independent studies typically do involve the student; however, by conducting the simulation without her participation, the team could experience the feelings that young students have when IEPs are developed *for* them rather than *with* them.

Too many general educators have expressed dissatisfaction with the IEP development process, citing terms, forms, and paperwork as factors, and also concern that student input was not valued. As noted by Menlove, Hudson, and Suter (2001), dissatisfaction was higher for secondary teachers than for elementary teachers. Reasons given included team disconnect, time and preparation involved, training needed for pertinent knowledge and skills, and IEP relevance to their school context. General educators had the view that the IEP meeting is a special education teacher's meeting, not a team meeting, and when parents were present they did not like to push issues. But on the positive side, general education teachers have been seeing improvement. Potential solutions speak to the issues of time, information, communication, and preparation. This is a promising area in which both IEP participatory skills and collaborative skills can be improved simultaneously through well-targeted training programs.

Another instructive simulation as a group is rubric development for a specific purpose, such as learning and behavior expectations for a class trip, or procedures and assessment for a cooperative learning activity. Development of rubrics might lead to setting up a portfolio system in the classroom.

Yet another exercise could be problem solving collaboratively to use technology for developing differentiated curriculum plans for exceptional learning needs. After generating lists of technological tools, the group could evaluate the lists using the Plus-Minus-Interesting technique described later in this chapter.

A great number of easy-to-use problem-solving techniques suitable for group participation are available. These include, but certainly are not limited to, brainstorming, lateral thinking, Six Thinking Hats thinking, concept mapping, idea checklists, and metaphorical thinking. Others are jigsaw, reciprocal teaching, compare-and-contrast, SCAMPER, Plus-Minus-Interesting, role play, TalkWalk, and more. Some teachers have often incorporated these kinds of group problem-solving activities into their curriculum-planning for students, but have overlooked the potential that the techniques have for collaborating with adults more effectively and pleasurably. Here are a few brief descriptions and application activities.

Brainstorming

Brainstorming is a mainstay of creative problem-solving methodology. It facilitates generating many unique ideas. When a group is brainstorming, participants should be relaxed and having fun. There are no right or wrong responses during the process, because problems seldom have only one right approach. No one may critique an idea during the brainstorming process. All ideas are accepted as plausible and regarded as potentially valuable. Each idea is shared and recorded. In large-group sessions, it is most efficient to have a leader for managing the oral responses, and a recorder for getting them down on a board or chart visible to all.

The five well-known rules developed by Osborn (1963) for brainstorming are:

1. Do not criticize any ideas at this time.
2. The more wild and zany the ideas, the better.
3. Think up as many ideas as possible.
4. Try to combine two or more ideas into new ones.
5. Hitch-hike (piggyback) on another's idea. A person with a hitchhike idea should be called on before those who have unrelated ideas.

Note that when coaching others (children in particular) in brainstorming techniques, it is good to introduce them to the "humanitarian principle" before the very first session. This means that no idea will be accepted if it is obviously harmful to others. So, a response to "What are new ways to use old bricks?" that came out as "To drown kittens," (typically accompanied by its contributor with a pause for chuckles or shocked expressions from peers along with quick glances to observe teacher reaction), would be answered by a brief but firm "Sorry, but as you know, we abide by the humanitarian principle here." Then the teacher could move quickly on without accepting that idea, and yet would remain true to rules 1 and 2 of a brainstorm activity.

Brainstorming is useful when a group wishes to explore as many alternatives as possible and defer evaluation of the ideas until the options have been exhausted. People who cannot resist the urge to critique ideas during brainstorming must be reminded that evaluation comes later. Leaders should call on volunteers quickly.

When the flow of ideas slows, it is good to persevere a while longer. Often the second wave of thoughts will contain the most innovative suggestions. Each participant should be encouraged to contribute, but allowed to pass if wished.

Individual brainstorming can be a very productive precursor to group brainstorming. Recall that personal preferences often have effects on instruction in unexpected ways, and this is one example. Some people like to brainstorm privately, rather like an incubation process, before joining in a group effort. Others enjoy just getting right to it. If an agenda that states topics to be discussed is provided ahead of meeting time, with the "heads-up" suggestion that brainstorming might be used as a tool for gathering ideas, those who wish to reflect on the matter will be better prepared to contribute enthusiastically.

Reverse brainstorming is an unusual technique that sometimes proves helpful if the group is stuck and needs to find another approach. With this technique, participants propose what would be considered the opposites of good ideas, such as, "If someone wanted to *increase* bullying and extortion on the school grounds, how would that be best accomplished?" Or, "If we *didn't* want Jaime to contribute to the cooperative learning group, how would we discourage him from doing so?" On a cautionary note, participants need to know exactly what the purpose of this technique is, and bring closure to the activity in a positive way by agreeing that "these are things we must avoid having happen in the instances for which we brainstormed." Any eavesdroppers on this activity would need to be informed forthwith about the purpose of this exercise.

Using the Brainstorm Technique.   A brainstorming session would be appropriate for this situation: A first-grade student has read just about every book in the small, rural school. The first-grade teacher and gifted program facilitator brainstorm possibilities for enhancing this student's reading options and augmenting the school's resources as well.

Lateral Thinking

The conventional method of thinking is vertical thinking, in which one moves forward mentally by sequential and justifiable steps. Vertical thinking is logical and single-purposed, digging down more deeply into the same mental hole or rising along the same line of thought. Lateral thinking, on the other hand, digs a "thinking hole" in a different place. It moves out at an angle, so to speak, from vertical thinking to change direction, attitude, or approach so that the problem can be examined in a different, unique, perhaps even bizarre, way (deBono, 1986).

   Lateral thinking should not replace vertical thinking, but complement it. While many educators emphasize vertical thinking at the expense of more divergent production, both are useful to arrive at creative solutions for complex problems. The ability to use a lateral thinking mode by suspending judgments and generating alternatives should be cultivated by school personnel.

Using the Lateral Thinking Technique.   Lateral thinking could be helpful in this situation. A high school student with learning disabilities has a serious reading problem, but teachers in several classes are not willing to make adjustments. The teachers have not discussed any problems with you, the resource teacher, recently but the student has. How might you as consultant, and student as consultee, think of ways to approach the situation and modify classroom practices to help this student succeed? To think laterally, the consultant might regard the teachers as clients, and consult with the student about ways of reinforcing teachers when they *do* make things easier. The student would be modifying the behavior of teachers, in contrast to a vertical thinking tactic of asking teachers to modify student behavior. Recall the earlier comment that students sometimes are curriculum-disabled.

Six Thinking Hats

This thinking tool also was developed by deBono as a nonargumentative and creative way to think through issues (deBono, 1985). Six colored hats—white, yellow, black, red, green, and blue, are "put on" as a way to encourage helpful kinds of thinking about a problem from many different angles. With the white hat on, participants gather information. The yellow hat is for looking at positives, values, and benefits. The red hat allows sharing of emotions and feelings about the issue. With the green hat, one can think outside the box for new possibilities. The blue hat is a management and procedures reminder. Finally, the black hat provides a devil's advocate perspective.

Thinking with Six Hats.   In a group, co-educators explore all sides of a problem, for example, the pros and cons of the NCLB legislation, or the use of a particular technology with students who have disabilities, using the Six Thinking Hats approach. They make paper hats to wear or simply hold up colored sheets of paper to make a point when the leader calls for a particular hat-color perspective.

The hats are assembled into a bulletin board collage for display as a reminder to maximize different styles of thinking and responding to issues. This is another practical example of the constructive use of adults' individual differences.

Concept Mapping

Concept mapping (referred to by some as mind-mapping, semantic mapping, webbing, or trees of knowledge or information) is a tool for identifying concepts, showing relationships among them, and reflecting on the degree of generality and inclusiveness that envelopes them (Wesley &Wesley, 1990). The technique allows users to display ideas, link them together, elaborate on them, add new information as it surfaces, and review the formulation of the ideas. The process begins with one word, or issue, written on paper or the chalkboard and enclosed in a circle. Then other circles of subtopics, ideas, words, and concepts are added to that central theme by lines or spokes that connect and interconnect where the concepts relate and interrelate. More and more possibilities and new areas open up as the webbing grows. Relationships and interrelationships that can help verbalize problems and interventions are recorded for all participants to see. If the concept map is left on display, the process can go on and on as more ideas are generated and added.

Concept mapping is being taught to students for purposes such as reading comprehension at all grade levels. Buzan (1983) offers strategies for mind-mapping in which learning techniques such as note-taking can be structured to show interrelationships easily. Many students in gifted programs have been introduced to the concept of webbing to focus on a problem of interest and plan an independent study. Sometimes college students are encouraged to try mind-mapping by combining lecture notes and text reading to study for exams. Concept-mapping is a powerful tool for enhancing individual learning. It also can lead to more meaningful and productive staff development (Bocchino, 1991).

Using Concept Mapping.   A classroom teacher has agreed to work with a student new to the district who has been diagnosed with Asperger's syndrome. The student has acceptable social skills in some instances, and is friendly and cooperative. But he also requires individual instruction, is working about two years below grade level, and makes threats impulsively to other students. During previous visits the teacher had indicated to the special education teacher that things were going well. Now, in the middle of November, she asks for a consultation immediately. She is upset, saying things such as, "It just isn't working," and "I've tried so hard," but she has not really described the problem. How might concept-mapping or webbing help in this situation? What word or phrase could go into the center to begin the webbing?

Idea Checklist

Checklists to help identify problems and determine ways to solve them can be created from sources such as college texts, teaching manuals, and instructional media manuals. More unusual checklists include referral agency listings, gift catalog descriptions, instructional resource center guides, and even Yellow Pages sections of various directories. By asking a question such as, "How can we help Shawn improve in math proficiency?" and scanning a Yellow Pages section or an off-level teaching manual, new ideas may emerge.

Using the Idea Checklist.   A high school sophomore, seventeen years old and in the educable mental retardation program, is ready for a vocational training program. The EMR resource teacher believes the Vocational Rehabilitation Unit's four-month job training program would be the most appropriate program for the student. However, the parents feel very protective of their son and are concerned that the environment will be non-caring. They resist suggestions that he leave their home. How might an idea-checklist process help during this consultation?

Synectics, Metaphors, and Janusian Thinking

As an example of synectics, one secondary teacher of students with developmental delay listened with much interest and an open mind when his colleagues for the school's gifted program voiced their perspectives on incorporating complex thinking skills into curriculum for all students in the general classroom. The EMR teacher began processing this with the facts and his feelings—making the familiar strange ("What if my students could take this perspective and run with it?") and making the strange familiar ("What if I take something that's appropriate for very bright, unchallenged students and design it for my students?") After much thought, planning, trial and error, revision, and preparation of a procedural plan, he set up a catering system in which his students provided snacks at first, then full-fledged meals after the plan was going well, for special events in the schools. The results for students' academic skills, social skills, practical skills in running the business, and feelings of self-confidence and self-esteem were immeasurable and the program became the talk of not only the school but also the entire community.

Metaphors are mental maps that permit the connection of different meanings through some shared similarity. They appear often in spoken and written communication. For example, the sentences "Life is a loom," "The fog swallowed the ship," and "Last June my flower garden was a paint box of colors" are metaphorical. They connect in order to explain. Many creative people in various fields have broken with conventional thinking by engaging in metaphorical thinking.

The metaphor uses one subject to strengthen and deepen the understanding of another. Metaphors can guide groups for activating change processes. They are useful to generate new ideas and teach new concepts (Garmston, 1994). Pollio (1987) suggests that some of the most important scientific, philosophical, and technical insights were conceived from an imaginative image. One of his examples is Einstein seeing himself as a passenger on a light ray and holding a mirror in front of him, an image that helped him form the theory of relativity. People use metaphors to sort out their perceptions and reflect on the meanings of things. Einstein broke with old facts and feelings related to Euclidian geometry to create metaphors that became his theory of relativity. In art, Picasso broke with familiar metaphors of looking and painting to show the world a new way of seeing. In similar, but perhaps more subtle fashion, educators can use metaphors to connect two different viewpoints so one idea can be understood by means of the other.

APPLICATION 5.3
EXPLORING THE POWER OF METAPHORICAL THINKING

With a group of your colleagues generate free-association responses to open-ended phrases such as, "Life is a _____" (e.g., zoo, journey, pressure cooker, bank, car lot, battle, or party) and "School is a _____" (e.g., prison, twelve-act play, family, game). A second part of the activity is to continue on from that image, e.g., "If life is a *zoo,* then teachers are _____, and students are _____" "If school is a twelve-act play, students are _____, teachers are _____, principals are _____." Open-ended phrases then could move to topics such as, "Team teaching is like _____, and teachers are the _____." "Inservice days are a _____ (battery charge?) and teachers are the (dead batteries now all charged up?)." (Metaphors can be served as tart lessons sweetened with humor and a twist of wry!)

Janusian thinking was recognized by Rothenberg & Hausman (1976) who studied the Eugene O'Neill play *The Iceman Cometh.* The term for the concept was coined from the Roman god Janus who looks backward into the old year and forward into the new (January). The process involves using two or more contradictory or opposite ideas *simultaneously*—for example, sweet and salty. This simultaneous consideration of opposites creates tension that can spark original thought. As an example, Mozart told aspiring musicians that the rests in between the notes are as important, if not more so, than the notes themselves. Frank Lloyd Wright valued the concept of Janusian thinking because architects need to conceptualize the inside and outside of a building simultaneously. The key element in the process is simultaneity; thus, convex outer shapes must be reconciled with concave inner shapes in order for the architect to conceptualize the structure.

APPLICATION 5.4
EXPLORING THE POWER OF JANUSIAN THINKING

With colleagues, use the technique of group brainstorming, permitting no judging of the ideas, and having a disposition in which the strange becomes familiar, such as in Sweet Tarts, dry ice, jumbo shrimp, and snow blanket, to generate more examples of Janusian thought. Then shift to a socially focused mode and try for ideas such as win/win, and friendly fire. After thinking of several clever product-type examples, the power of the process becomes evident. But that is the easy task! Now strive for new, Janusian-based concepts that can help students, such as creative homework, innovative drill, elementary/secondary student mentorships, and more. Not so many years ago some considered collaborative consultation to be a Janusian phrase, but no more.

More Techniques for Collaborative Problem Solving

A number of other collaborative activities that are used to nurture creative thinking can be employed to facilitate exchanging information and generating ideas among co-educators for the ultimate benefit of their students. Many of them can be retrieved at Web sites under their descriptive names or under key words such as creative problem solving, creative thinking, and even creative collaboration. These include: reciprocal teaching, random word technique, In What Ways Might We? (IWWMW), visualization, and attribute listing. A brief summary of just a few follows.

Jigsaw.   Participants in this learning method developed by Aronson (1978) undertake independent, collaborative research on a topic of mutual interest. A school faculty, school district staff, or other group of teachers and area specialists seek out background material in small groups and bring it back to share with the full group in order to agree on possible solutions to academic and behavioral problems. The whole group begins by deciding on the central theme(s) of the issue and several subtopics. Then the group divides into smaller groups. Each small group conducts research on one subtopic and shares that knowledge by teaching it to others. In this way all have a part in the problem solving. Time and energy of busy professionals are used to maximum benefit. Redundancy of effort is minimized. Most importantly, a collaborative synergism[1] develops that improves their ability to problem-solve in other situations.

One topic for a jigsaw procedure could be how to construct differentiated learning plans for the inclusive classroom. Others might be how to ensure appropriate behavior and decorum on school buses, or how to provide safety of equipment and student activity on school playgrounds, or making plans to deal with potential acts of violence or the aftermath of a student suicide.

A particularly useful and too often neglected area for developing educational awareness and expertise is school law. This deep and wide topic would focus on careful examination of numerous issues in the state and local school context, such as privacy of confidential information, accountability of school personnel in supervisory matters, use of corporal punishment, intervention and referral procedures, safety in the classroom or field environment, and much more. It is obvious that these jigsaw-based problem-solving experiences should include all school personnel and related and support personnel such as social workers, parents, and perhaps on occasion and for some topics, student participation as well.

Reciprocal Teaching.   In reciprocal teaching, six or so participants form a group and each member takes a turn leading a discussion about an article, video, position paper, staff development presentation, or other material they have read and want to understand more fully. The leader begins with a question and summarizes the discussion at the end. Clarification for understanding and predictions about content for the future can be requested by the leader when appropriate (Brown, 1994). With this technique, group cooperation helps ensure understanding by all members, with the less well-informed learning from those who are more knowledgeable.

---

[1]Interaction of elements that when combined produce a total effect greater than the sum of the parts (*Webster's College Dictionary,* 1996).

One example of using reciprocal teaching could be to have a team of teachers read relevant material and then explore possibilities for adapting classroom settings to accommodate students with attention deficit and hyperactivity disorder or perhaps those with obsessive compulsive disorder. The synergistic discussion may open new avenues for addressing this complex concern.

Compare and Contrast.   Each small group identifies terms and phrases that define differing perspectives of an issue—for example, reading methods, math methods, tracking or mainstreaming, inclusion or pull-out programs, graded or ungraded systems. One compare-and-contrast session might draw out aspects of the two-part item, "what general classroom teachers don't know about special ed curriculum, and what special ed teachers don't know about general curriculum." An organization of the results completes the exchange, with all participants leaving the session more informed and reflective about the issues. A technique such as brainstorming or POCS could be employed during a later staff development event to make use of compare-and-contrast findings.

SCAMPER.   The SCAMPER technique was developed by Eberle (1984) as a built-in mnemonic device to brainstorm in practical situations. For example, using SCAMPER to preplan a transition program for a teen with mental retardation from school into a work area could create a number of possibilities: S, what can be substituted?; C, what can be combined?; A, what adaptations?; M, how modified, magnified, multiplied, or minified?; P, how put to other uses or purposes?; E, what could be eliminated?; and R, how could things be rearranged or interchanged?

Plus-Minus-Interesting.   This simple process can be completed in a half-hour or so, often stimulating rearrangement of perspectives and sometimes recasting values placed on those perspectives. As an example, in a school considering the use of active senior citizens as reading aides, the collaborative team would generate a three-part list of the pluses, the minuses, and things that are interesting and that the team would like to investigate further before making a decision. It is not necessary that the pluses exceed the minuses, and sometimes the interesting feature may ultimately be determined as the most promising. The discussion which PMI instigates can assist problem solving (deBono, 1973).

Role Play.   A fundamental purpose of role play as a problem-solving practice is to produce new perspectives. For example, in a teacher-parent conflict, the teacher would take the role of the parent, and the parent that of the teacher. Participants have specific parts to play. At a critical part in the interaction the leader stops the players and has the whole group explore options that would be possible from that point. Then new solutions may emerge (Torrance & Safter, 1999). In role-playing the convener must be skilled and facilitative, so that the players participate intently without self-consciousness.

Concentric Circle or Fishbowl.   A small circle of participants discusses an issue while a larger circle on the outside of that one listens and then discusses. This technique encourages participation by members usually reticent to respond, and stimulates lively discussion. Issues must be well-chosen and articulated clearly to the group.

In-Basket Techniques.   These are simulations of situations that may come to the consulting teacher's mailbox or message board. The basket contains requests or questions that need action. Because there are typically no right or wrong answers, the technique is good for engaging in a multiperspective discussion in which the teacher describes the situation and invites input. This technique could be one option offered during a staff development day when teachers choose the sessions they want to attend. In that case, some "teaser" topics should be provided in the promotional material as examples so participants would know what to expect. General issues that do not require confidentiality would be most suitable for this approach.

Case Studies.   Problems gleaned from professional literature or composed by participants are given to the group. Members react to the question "What seems to be going on here?" and then prepare individual plans or one group plan for next steps. One member coordinates discussion of the various plans to enhance the group's flexibility in problem solving. This is another promising activity for a professional development session.

Role Rotation.   Here the participants have the opportunity to consider the issue in question from a completely different perspective. For example, a classroom teacher might participate as an administrator. A learning disabilities consultant could take the role of a parent. Figure 1.2 and relevant discussion in Chapter 1 could be useful for role rotation.

TalkWalk.   In this unique form of small-group interaction the participants engage in collegial dialogue focused on instructional and curricular issues while they walk together in an open environment (Caro & Robbins, 1991). The fresh air, physical and mental exercise, and exploration of ideas lead to free thinking and expression. This technique can be used as part of a workshop or simply as an informal arrangement among colleagues.

Caro and Robbins suggest that groups of two or three work best. TalkWalk provides educators with 4 Es for problem solving—*expertise* from collective experience; *enrichment* to improve sense of self-worth and problem-solving capacity; *expediency* to obtain rapid solutions through assistance; *exercise* to bring a fresh attitude and perspective to the problem. One walk, for example, might focus on the group's vision for students who are in transition from school to work and independent living. Another might be to join preschool teachers and primary teachers in a TalkWalk to discuss that transition period for very young children. An outcome of such talks just might be a plan that will help make the vision become real.

Use of Multiple Intelligences

One unique way to generate many perspectives and perhaps arrive at some clever solutions for problems is to frame the questions in terms of Gardner's (1993) well-known multiple intelligence categories. For example, to build interest, rapport, and skills for team teaching among staff with no experience doing it, these questions could help with planning efforts:

> *Linguistic:* How can we use words and stories to describe team teaching?
>
> *Logical–mathematical*: How might we measure the benefits and drawbacks of a team-teaching approach in our school?
>
> *Musical:* Should we create a team song or cheer?

Spatial: Should we make a physical map of where everything will be and what more, or less, we should include in the spaces we will share?

Interpersonal: What kinds of differences in interests, preferences, values, and personal habits would be important to discuss before embarking on a team-teaching mission?

Intrapersonal: How would I describe my feelings about giving up some of my professional autonomy, and sharing many of my ideas and techniques?

Bodily–kinesthetic: How can we move throughout the room, arrange materials, and get students' attention when we are teaching together in the same spaces?

Naturalistic: Will our school environment accommodate this team teaching so that students are comfortable, parents are satisfied, and teachers are positive about the experience?

Interaction Formats

Collaborating consultants will want to know how to set up a variety of group formats for stimulating interaction among professionals. (See Figure 5.6.) Some of the most useful ones are as follows:

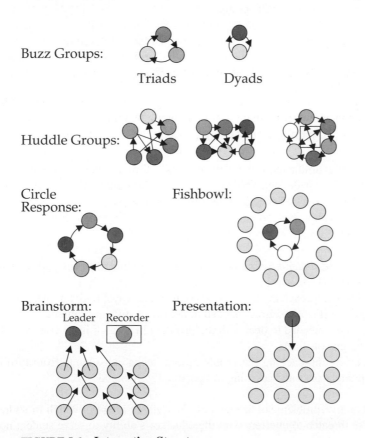

FIGURE 5.6   Interaction Structures

Buzz groups.   Buzz groups work well in a group of 50 or fewer. This format ensures total participation and is easy to set up. The leader presents a topic or problem, provides minimal directions for subgrouping by twos or threes, and invites everyone to consider all aspects of the problem in the time allowed. The main disadvantage is a high noise level if the physical space is small.

Huddles.   Huddles work best with groups of five or six discussants. The leader arranges the groups, defines the topic, announces the time limit (six minutes works well), and gives a two-minute warning that time is expiring. Each group designates its own reporter. The leader usually passes from group to group facilitating and encouraging if needed. In this structure the participants tend to build on colleagues' contributions. The reporting process can vary, from a simple "most important points" to ranking of major points, to a written summary that is collected by the leader. Some know this technique as the 6-6 method (Kohm, 2002) or the "Six Points of View" method.

Circle Response.   Small groups of collaborators sit in a circle. The designated leader begins by stating or reiterating the topic. The response pattern moves to the left, with each taking a turn or saying "I pass." At the end of a stipulated time, the leader summarizes the ideas and integrated thinking of the group.

Others.   An enterprising consultant also could consider structured role play, a structured or unstructured interview forum, reader's theater, research-and-report, round-robin (Kohm, 2002), and a film talk-back session as ways of encouraging interaction and information exchange among educators.

INTERFERENCES AND HURDLES TO OVERCOME

Co-educators must examine their own perspectives and preferences to identify any potential aspects that will impede their abilities to consult and collaborate on behalf of the student. A lack of four major aspects of teaching, as suggested by Caplan's (1995) four interfering themes, can reduce co-educators' ability to be divergent thinkers and problem solvers (Sandoval, 1996). These aspects are:

1. *Knowledge and understanding* needed to address student needs and related factors helpfully
2. Right *skills* to approach the problem in appropriate ways; for example, a teacher may not have the skills or resources needed to deal with student problems
3. *Self-confidence* needed to deal with the problem in spite of inexperience, self-doubt, or even fatigue or illness
4. *Objectivity* in approaching the problem, that keeps consultants from turning away inappropriately or from becoming too personally involved

A collaborative problem-solving process is a viable arena in which to address these four themes that threaten to interfere with the educator's ability to serve student needs. For example, some teachers might show lack of knowledge by over- or under-identifying students for special education because of stereotypical thinking. Others may show lack of skill by failing to modify curriculum for those with disabilities, or by inappropriately using a strategy such as cooperative learning. Lack of objectivity is evident when educators equate student situations to another situation in their own lives or to former students and their situations. Lack of confidence can generate resistance to new plans and inflexibility toward new ideas.

When collaborating, consultants should use every opportunity to reinforce the efforts and successes of classroom teachers and also to convey a desire to learn from them and their experiences. Too often classroom teachers, as ones occupying a non-specialist role among specialists, and parents, who know their child best, can be somewhat removed from the school setting and overlooked when ideas for addressing learning and behavior problems are explored.

When communicating and cooperating with consultees to identify the learning or behavior need, it is important that consultants avoid sending messages intimating that classroom teachers and parents are deficient in skills that only special education teachers can provide (Friend & Cook, 1990; Huefner, 1988). Communication skills and cooperative attitudes will encourage feelings of parity and voluntarism among all school personnel and parents during the problem-solving process.

Students assigned to resource settings in other schools for part of the week or school day may have teachers there who never communicate about them and their work. This is a serious drawback of some cluster group arrangements where students travel from one school to another with no planned interaction among school personnel taking place. Coordination of collaborative effort is vital.

Special education teachers who cannot identify basal reading curriculum used in various levels, and classroom teachers who cannot identify the nature of instruction taking place in the resource room, make problem identification more difficult (Idol, West, & Lloyd, 1988). Their lack of shared knowledge may even intensify the problem. All parties must think about their own roles in the problem situation, and endeavor to learn from each other by interacting, deferring judgment, and coordinating their services.

A team approach is a productive way to assess the context, conditions, interfering themes, and circumstances surrounding the student's needs and the school programs designed to meet those needs. It has been noted that astronomers from all parts of the world collaborate often because there is no one place from which every part of their "work area," the sky, can be observed. This analogy applies to educators and parents as they address each child's total needs in the cognitive, affective, physical, and social domains to develop learning and behavior goals.

Those goals become building blocks for decision making. Without goals, decision making is like a hammer without nails. Educators have long-range and short-term goals. Students have IEPs with yearly goals and short-term goals. Schools have mission statements and educational aims. Both school aims and student goals should be used for making decisions in educational environments. A goal motivates action and provides direction for that action. Reviewing goals helps educators stay focused and sort out the things that are important from those that are not.

Educators with experience as consultants describe several problems that can interfere with the success of consultation, collaboration, or teamwork among educators. By recognizing them as possibility but not necessarily expecting them to occur, consulting teachers can be ready to sidestep or step over potential hurdles such as:

- Loss of touch with the students when not in direct service with them
- Uncertainty about what and how to communicate with those who resist or resent collaboration
- Being regarded as a teacher's aide, "gofer," or quick-fix expert
- Having consultation regarded as a tutorial for students
- Territoriality of school personnel
- Rigid curriculum and assessment procedures
- Unrealistic expectations (either too high or too low) toward the role
- Not having enough information or appropriate materials to share
- Being perceived as a show-off, or a bossy expert, or an interloper
- Running into veils of professional politeness that shield consultees from genuine commitment
- Difficulty managing time and resources, which often happens
- Lack of training for the role
- An excessive caseload that short-circuits effectiveness
- Too many "hats" to wear in the role
- Most of all, resistance of colleagues toward change of any kind

Knowing potential hurdles can help educators keep them from becoming insurmountable barriers by ensuring that there is role delineation, a consultation framework, adequate evaluation of the process, and careful preparation to develop the necessary skills. Some of the mystique surrounding special education and support services is reduced when classroom teachers become familiar with the techniques and are led to appreciate and understand special education roles.

Positive and Not-So-Positive Consultations

Some collaborative consultations are more successful than others. In a few instances, they turn out rather discouragingly. Collaborators have reported positive outcomes in the following situations:

- "Primary-level teachers and I sat down and discussed what materials they thought would be good to order and place in the resource room, for their use as well as mine. Everyone had a chance to share needs, express opinions, and make recommendations."

- "An undergraduate asked me about my student teaching and substituting days. She was feeling very down and unsure of her teaching abilities. I reassured her by telling of some things that had happened to me, and why. I encouraged her to find a dependable support system, and gave her some ideas and things to think about."

- "One of the teachers I have spent several weeks with stopped me in the hall yesterday to ask for an idea to use in her class that next hour. Before she finished putting her question into words, she had thought of an idea herself, but she still thanked me!"

■ "I participated in a parent conference in which the parent wanted to kick the daughter out of the house and into a boarding school. It ended with the daughter agreeing to do more work at home, and the mother agreeing to spend one special hour of togetherness a week with just her daughter."

And now some not-so-positive situations:

■ "A kindergarten child was staffed into my program, but the teacher wouldn't let me take her out of 'her' class time. So I arranged to keep the child after school. The first night I was late coming to fetch the child, and the teacher blew up about it."
■ "The music teacher asks students who cannot read well to stand up in class and read, and then pokes fun at them. I approached the teacher about the situation, but the teacher wanted nothing to do with me, and after that made things even worse for the students."
■ "In visiting with the principal about alternatives in altering classroom assignments, it ended with his speaking harshly and suggesting that I was finding fault with the school staff, which I had not done."
■ "I give a sticker every day to a student who has learning disabilities if he attends and does his work in the resource room. His classroom teacher complained to the principal about it because 'other students work hard and don't get stickers.'"

ETHICS FOR COLLABORATIVE AND CONSULTATIVE PROBLEM SOLVING

An ethical climate and impeccably ethical behavior are keenly important in special education. Howe and Miramontes (1992) remind us that the actions of special educators have lifelong ramifications and must be taken very seriously. Many of the proposed actions require judgment to deal with potential consequences. As an example, consider the dilemma of a church-school teacher alone in her room preparing for class when a student entered the room and grabbed her from behind in an inappropriate and forceful way. After backing him off and calming him down, to whom should the teacher go first? She was virtually certain that the parents' harsh and peculiar child-rearing practices were the root of his alarming behavior. Should she report to social services, the school administrator, or the church pastor? As Kaufmann (1993) notes, teachers have little training in thorny issues such as these. But, as co-educators in inclusive settings with joint responsibility for students, they must pool their expertise and collaboratively make decisions for the welfare of the student and others.

When groups of co-educators gather (and in some IEP conferences the number of adults in attendance may be as many as a dozen), there is more risk in handling confidential material. A collaborative ethic guides such groups in discussing sensitive matters calmly, objectively, and respectfully. It empowers the professionals to support and motivate each other toward best instructional and management practices. Collegial problem solving must be valued and promoted as a tool to help students who need to succeed (Phillips & McCullough, 1990).

Collaborative consultants must not assume that all colleagues have the necessary information and skills to collaborate successfully. They need to be watchful for negative outcomes resulting from "groupthink," in which incompleteness, bias, failure to examine risks of proposed choices, and failure to work out plans carefully can result in quite negative outcomes (Murray, 1994). They must respect the right of every individual to hear and be heard, and they must also resolve to be responsive, accountable, and vigilant toward recognizing and refraining from unethical practices.

TIPS FOR PROBLEM SOLVING THROUGH COLLABORATIVE CONSULTATION

1. Have materials and thoughts organized before consultations and develop a list of questions that will help ferret out the real problem.
2. Be prepared for the meeting with a checklist of information typically needed. Do not be reluctant to say that you do not have *the* answer. If it is something you should know, find out when you can and get back to the person who asked.
3. Have strategies and materials in mind that may be helpful to the situation, but do not try to have all the answers. This discourages involvement by others.
4. Do not offer solutions too readily, and try not to address too much or too many topics at once.
5. Avoid jargon, and shun suggestions that conflict with policies or favored teacher practices.
6. Make it a habit to look for something positive about the teacher, the class, and the student, and comment on those things. Use feedback as a vehicle that can provide *positive* information, not just negative comments.
7. Don't try to "fix it" if it is not "broken."
8. Don't wait for the consultee to make the first move. But do not expect that teachers will be enthused or flattered to have questions asked about their classrooms and teaching methods.
9. When a teacher asks for advice about a student, first ask what the teacher has already observed. This gets the teacher involved in the problem and encourages ownership in serving the student's special need. Whenever possible, use the terms *we* and *us,* not *I* and *you.*
10. Know how to interpret test results and how to discuss those results with educators, parents, and students.
11. When possible, provide parents with samples of the child's schoolwork to discuss during the conference. Refrain from talking while they peruse the materials. Have a list of resources ready to share with parents for help with homework, reinforcements, and study tips. When providing materials, explain or demonstrate their use, and then keep in touch so that no problems develop.
12. Maintain contact with teachers during the year. You may find that the teacher has detected an improvement that is directly related to your work, and this reinforcement will be valuable for you and your own morale.
13. Remember that minds, like parachutes, work best when they are open.

CHAPTER REVIEW

1. Fundamental components of problem solving, practiced in fields as diverse as business, industry, science, entertainment, health care, education, and more, include gathering data, finding and defining the problem, generating ideas for action, making a plan, implementing the plan, and following up on success of the plan.

2. Problem identification is the most critical phase of problem solving. Information from multiple sources and collaborative input by a team of educators will help identify the real problem and facilitate its solution.

3. There are ten important steps in a problem-solving consultation: planning, initiating the consultation, collecting information, identifying the problem, generating options and alternatives, formulating a plan, evaluating progress and process, following through and following up, interacting informally, and repeating if necessary.

4. Collaborative consultants will benefit from practicing active listening and formulating key phrases to use during each phase of the consultation. They should monitor their own skills for rapport building, onedownsmanship, appropriate body language, avoidance of jargon, and active listening.

5. Divergent production of ideas during problem solving can be enhanced by the use of techniques and tools such as brainstorming, idea checklists, lateral thinking, Six-Hat thinking, concept mapping, idea checklists, synectics, metaphorical thinking, and Janusian thinking. Other tools for interaction include jigsaw, reciprocal teaching, compare-and-contrast, role play, TalkWalk, and more. Teachers may have used these techniques with students from time to time, but in too many cases have overlooked their potential for enhancing professional interactions. Collegiality and collaboration are cultivated by the use of a variety of interaction formats such as buzz groups, huddle groups, circle responses, role play, panels, and interviews.

6. Many of the interferences and hurdles to circumvent and overcome when collaborating and consulting emanate from the "lack of" themes identified by Caplan (1995)—lack of knowledge about general and special education and other education roles; lack of skills in applying differentiated curriculum, interventions, and adaptations; lack of objectivity by becoming too involved or not involved enough; and lack of self-confidence in managing special needs situations.

TO DO AND THINK ABOUT

1. When consultants introduce themselves to consultees, what are four or five things they can mention about themselves in order to develop rapport?

2. Discuss at least five things a consultant does *not* want to happen while consulting and collaborating, along with the conditions that might cause these unwanted events, and how the conditions might be avoided or overcome. Who has the most control over whether these unwanted events will or will not happen?

3. For a challenging assignment, select a school issue or student problem and create a method for engaging in consultation by designating a system, perspective, approach, prototype, mode, and model, as discussed in Chapter 3. Carry out the consultation as a role play or simulation, using the ten steps and verbal responses provided in this chapter. In a "debriefing" session with your colleagues, discuss which parts of the consultation process were most difficult, some possible reasons, and what could be done to make the consultation successful.

4. Choose a TV program that shows meetings—for example, committees for congressional hearings or locally televised school board meetings. Note the body language exhibited during meetings and make some inferences about possible effects this can have on progress and outcomes of the meeting. Examples would be fiddling with a pencil, looking at a watch or clock, crossing arms, pulling corners of mouth apart, leaning back, talking with hands, writing notes while spoken to, looking sideways without a focus, and so forth. Monitor your own personal body language and make efforts to modify anything you found disconcerting by others during the observation exercise.

5. As coordinator for a meeting to discuss a particularly sensitive educational issue, identify preparations that should be made for efficient, effective communication among all participants.

6. Complete the following partial statements with a variety of possible responses. Then generate ideas for developing mutual understanding of roles and responsibilities and eliminating these potential impediments to collaborative activity,

■ Special education teachers often are not able to _____.

■ General education teachers often are not able to _____.

ADDITIONAL READING AND RESOURCES

Clark, S. G. (2000). The IEP process as a tool for collaboration. *Teaching Exceptional Children, 33*(2), 56–66.

DeBoer, A. (1997). *Working together: The art of consulting and communicating.* Longmont, CO: Sopris West.

DeBoer, A., & Fister, S. (1998). *Working together: Tools for collaborative teaching.* Longmont, CO: Sopris West.

deBono, E. (1973). *Lateral thinking: Creativity step by step.* New York: Harper & Row.

deBono, E. (1985). *Six thinking hats.* Boston: Little, Brown.

Gardner, H. (1993). *Multiple intelligences: The theory in practice.* New York: Harper Collins.

Giangreco, M. F. (1993). Using creative problem-solving methods to include students with severe disabilities in general classroom activities. *Journal of Educational and Psychological Consultation, 4*(2), 113–135.

Provides specific examples of using the Osborn-Parnes Creative Problem-Solving process for instructional inclusion relevant to students with intensive educational needs.

Haynes, M. E. (1988). *Effective meeting skills: A practical guide to more productive meetings.* Los Altos, CA: Crisp.

Hobbs, T., & Westling, D. L. (1998). Promoting successful inclusion through collaborative problem solving.

TEACHING Exceptional Children, Sept./Oct. 1998.

Presents five key components of a structured problem-solving process and a number of professional practices to maximize success of the process.

Menlove, R. R., Hudson, P. J., & Suter, D. (2001). A field of IEP dreams: Increasing general education teacher participation in the IEP process. *Teaching Exceptional Children, 33*(5), 28–33.

Mills, G. E., & Duff-Mallams, K. (2000). Special education mediation: A formula for success. *Teaching Exceptional Children, 32*(4), 72–78.

Morris, A. (1999). *Teamwork.* New York: Lothrop, Lee, & Shepard.

A delightful children's book describing teamwork as a group from any culture or walk of life that works together and plays together. Photos from fifteen different countries and descriptions of activities as diverse as college students laying sandbags to contain a river in the United States, to whitewashing a temple roof in Thailand. The book could be a useful prelude to a group problem-solving meeting, or with students to explain the concept of team-teaching when it is introduced into their classroom.

Osborn, A. F. (1963). *Applied imagination: Principles and procedures of creative problem-solving.* New York: Scribner.

Starko, A. (2001). *Creativity in the classroom: Schools of curious delight* (2nd ed.). Mahwah, NJ: Erlbaum.

CHAPTER SIX

**PROCESS:
Management and
Evaluation**

Management and Evaluation of Collaborative School Consultation

Schools are bustling arenas of activities that often seem to have little to do with books and studies. Not only do school personnel teach students in academic settings, they also feed them, transport them, keep records, counsel and advise, dispense materials and resources, address social and health problems, and much, much more. If the services of various school-related roles such as librarian, speech pathologist, school psychologist, social worker, nurse, were included, the list of responsibilities would be even more daunting.

In this complex hubbub, the demands on educators can be overwhelming. Stress and fatigue take a toll, with burnout and attrition from the teaching profession an all too frequent result. The challenge of accountability is a heavy burden. High-stakes testing takes its toll on teachers as well as on students. But role-related stress can be minimized and heavy responsibilities controlled by managing time and resources wisely and by assessing outcomes of services provided.

FOCUSING QUESTIONS

1. What aspects of being educators can make school personnel vulnerable to stress and burnout?

2. What management and organizational techniques can help consultants and collaborators perform their roles effectively?

3. What procedures for conducting meetings, interviews, and observations contribute to consultation and collaboration success?

4. How can collaborating school consultants manage records and resources efficiently?

5. When and how should evaluation plans for collaborative school consultation be developed and implemented?

6. What are important ethical issues in management and evaluation of collaborative consultation in schools?

KEY TERMS

attrition	consultation log or journal	stakeholders
authentic assessment	evaluation	stress management
behavior observations	formative assessment	summative assessment
brief-agenda meetings	interview	time management
burnout	observation	
caseload	self-assessment	

SCENARIO 6.A

The setting is a coffee shop in a university's student union. Three faculty members in the College of Education—including one who teaches educational psychology for elementary education majors, another who teaches educational psychology for secondary education majors, and a third who teaches a class called Exceptional Child in the Inclusive Classroom—are sharing views about their new classes for the semester.

First Ed Psych Professor: I am impressed with the new group of students we have this semester in our teacher education program.

Exceptional Child Professor: I haven't been here as long as you have, but from what I have observed during my first two class sessions, I agree that they seem to be strong and very capable as a whole.

Second Ed Psych Professor: They're so idealistic. They just know that they will be able to inspire kids and excite them toward learning. Most of all they want to make a positive difference in their students' lives. I hope they'll be well-prepared and strong enough to deal with all the challenges out there, especially if they accept positions in tough schools with many difficult students.

Exceptional Child Professor: Yes, or all too soon they'll join the ranks of teachers who burn out after just three or four years in the profession. I'm alarmed at the attrition rate for new teachers in this country.

Second Ed Psych Professor: I think we should all be alarmed about those figures. The statistics are an urgent message to us in teacher education programs to prepare them as best we can. Of course we all think our classes are vital toward that effort! But besides knowing their subject matter well, new teachers will need to be competent in many kinds of things. I think a key area of competence that novice teachers need to develop is included in the objectives of our college's course in collaboration and co-teaching.

First Ed Psych Professor: You raise a good point. Even though it's a graduate-level course, it provides knowledge and practices that beginning teachers need to know from day one.

Exceptional Child Professor: Yes, several years ago our undergrads caught on to the value of working our assessment course into their program or taking it in the summer even though it is a graduate-level course. Some said it even helped them clinch the job they wanted when they interviewed and could discuss that area competently. So here's an idea. How about if we seek out our colleague who teaches the collaboration course and put our heads together to talk about preservice teachers' need to learn many of the concepts in that course? I certainly don't want students from our university's teacher education program to fall among those in the ranks of early attrition from the profession.

STRESS AND BURNOUT AMONG EDUCATORS

Teacher retention is a burning issue in education, particularly in science, math, the arts, and special education. Levine (2006) points out that population increases, immigration of students, and teachers reaching retirement age create disparity between rising numbers of school-age population and decreasing numbers of teachers. "Recruiting and preparing strong, effective teachers must be a top priority for those concerned about public education" (Levine, 2006, p. 220). But several factors erode preparation of teachers and support for teachers after they enter the profession: expanding costs of maintaining schools, public criticism as reflected in polls and the media, low morale among educators, and an avalanche of regulations and paperwork. During the 1999–2000 school year, 500,000 public and private school teachers left the profession; nearly one-fourth of new teachers leave after only two years, and one-third leave within five years (Ingersoll, 2002; Millinger, 2004).

Shortages of special education teachers continue to plague school districts. As demand for special education teachers has been mushrooming, the number of educators who prepare for special education and then enter the field has been dwindling. The demands imposed on classroom teachers by the NCLB mandate are weighing heavily on teachers and making it hard for them to feel good about what they do. One fourth-grade teacher put it this way, "I wanted to be a teacher, and I'm glad to be a teacher, but it's just not fun anymore." Professional satisfaction is a key variable in the effort to increase retention and enhance the work settings of special education personnel. Management of time and other resources, structures for some of the more burdensome tasks, targeted evaluation with careful analysis of the outcomes, and astute use of electronic technology are four areas that can minimize stress and hopefully reduce attrition from the profession.

Some educators remain in the profession and juggle their daily routines within a burgeoning agenda of reform and mandates. Others burn out and leave the profession. Still others simply "fizzle out," "rust out," or "coast out." The latter tend to go through the motions of their profession in lackluster fashion, just getting by until retirement age arrives or a better opportunity comes along. These educators create situations that are particularly detrimental for students who have special needs and are the most vulnerable to effects of uninspired teaching.

One of the most difficult aspects of the No Child Left Behind Act is its requirement that schools staff all classrooms with highly qualified teachers, even as it is becoming harder and harder to keep teachers who are prepared. Attrition in the first few years of teaching is high, especially among new teachers, with many leaving the profession within five years (Darling-Hammond, 2003). Sadly, teacher turnover is 50 percent higher in high-poverty schools than in low-poverty schools (Ingersoll, 2001).

As advocates for children with special learning and behavior needs, special education teachers may set unreasonably high expectations for themselves and others. Ambiguous roles and a discrepancy between their own role perceptions and the expectations of others contribute to this situation. Lack of recognition and reinforcement for their work, along with heavy responsibilities without much decision-making authority, are additional stressors for special education personnel. (See Figure 6.1.)

Teacher education programs must be strong preparation centers for preparing preservice teachers to succeed as novice teachers so that they will want to remain in the profession. Undergraduate students, when queried about their greatest concerns for their first

FIGURE 6.1   "I Need A System Here."

years in the profession, target areas that fit remarkably into Caplan's "lack-of" themes—knowledge, skill, objectivity, and self-confidence. The students cite as major concerns preparing good, motivating lessons; managing classroom discipline appropriately; working with parents; serving all students' special needs; being confident that they can handle it all and not fail; knowing all of the subjects well enough; and managing the classroom effectively.

Minimizing Stress of Professional Responsibilities

Burnout can arise from physical and emotional exhaustion. Prolonged stress or the buildup of stressors causes fatigue and frustration. According to Maslach (1982), who has researched burnout among service professionals for many years, there are three basic components of burnout:

1. Emotional exhaustion ("I'm tired and irritated all the time. I am impatient with my students and colleagues.")
2. Depersonalization ("I am becoming emotionally hardened; I start to blame the students or their families for all the problems.")
3. Reduced accomplishment ("I feel like I'm not making a difference for my students.")

The result can be attrition, alienation, cynicism, and physical problems such as heart disease, hypertension, ulcers, headaches, and psychosomatic illnesses.

Factors that cause stress reactions are many and varied. For the consultant, stressors could be a new special education regulation, a change in job description, too much paperwork, too many meetings that seem to go nowhere, an angry parent, or a student who is behaving in a violent manner. Most educators do have a vast repertoire of coping skills, and we all know that stress in general is a normal life event. In fact, eustress (Schultz, 1980), a proactive, positive response to a stimulus such as that experienced by artists, entertainers, athletes, speakers, and yes, teachers, before going "on stage," helps us perform at our best. It can even help us learn and grow. People who have experienced some stress probably are more likely to have good coping skills and to be understanding of others under stress than people who have not.

On the other hand, distress (anxiety, sorrow, pain, trouble) wears us down physically and emotionally. People become less capable of recognizing and responding to the needs of others in supportive ways when they are distressed. Busy, committed educators will never be able to reduce or eliminate all the stressors in their lives, but they can develop some specific strategies to achieve a balance between stress and coping and avoid burnout.

Developing positive adaptive strategies is crucial to maintaining emotional and physical health. The techniques individuals use depend on their preferences, lifestyle, and skills. Consultants and consultees must learn to "work smarter, not harder" to accomplish goals for students who are at risk of failure in school. Consultants also must take care of themselves so they do not lose their commitment and enthusiasm, and students with special needs do not lose their good, caring teachers. Recall the words of the flight attendant who instructs, "First put on *your* oxygen mask and *then* put on the baby's mask." We cannot take care of others if we are in no condition to help.

Building mutually supportive networks will minimize, if not eliminate, feelings of isolation and helplessness in the demanding role of school consultant. It helps to talk things out with others and get a new perspective when tackling complex responsibilities inherent in meeting special needs. This is another useful aspect of collaboration among co-educators! A support system is an effective outlet for frustration and provides a backup in times of crisis. One group of special education staff makes a commitment to meet each Friday at a centralized place for lunch and lively conversation. Ground rules stipulate there will be no talking about students, schools, or staff in that public place. The camaraderie and conviviality of the weekly event, looked on favorably by district administrators, provide an effective support system for teachers whose roles invite stress.

Strategies for Reducing Stress

What if burnout has happened or is at least in the glowing embers stage? What if you feel low self-esteem, and emotional and physical exhaustion now? The following ten strategies may help.

1. Talk to someone, give a positive comment, share ideas.
2. Find a former teacher who was very important in your life and tell her or him how much you learned with that person's guidance.
3. Schedule some time to be alone and reflect. Then stick to it.
4. Laugh out loud. Each person should have his or her "laugh ration" every day for mental and physical health. Listen to a comedy tape. Read a joke book. Watch children play.

5. Move, stretch, walk, jog. Mild exercise gets the blood flowing and transports more oxygen throughout the body, helping you feel alert and alive, and sunlight and fresh air help body and mind function well.

6. Play energetic, happy music. Classical music is best. Listening to sixty-cycle music such as that by Bach, Handel, and Mozart has been shown to increase alpha brain waves, the relaxation wave length (Douglass & Douglass, 1993). On the other hand, rock music is tiring and tends to drain energy away.

7. Break the routine. Take a different route when driving to work. Let others' cars cut in front of your car and feel smug about it. Rearrange your schedule or your furniture. Take a vacation if you can and when you do, leave worries and cares behind. Give yourself over to relaxation and rejuvenation.

8. Keep a jar of little treats in a handy place, such as encouraging statements, chocolates, or envelopes with a $5 bill inside, to be good to yourself every now and then. Positive reinforcement is not just for kids.

9. Use reminders to help remember these and other prevention and intervention strategies. They could be colored ribbons, stick-on happy faces, ads from magazines, letters to yourself. Put the reminders on your tote bag or briefcase, on your watch, calendar, or rearview mirror.

10. Remind yourself often that prevention and remediation of stress and burnout are the concern of the individual, not family or friends or colleagues. Each person must become aware of the factors and variables in his or her own unique formula of strategies for keeping the flame of motivation alive.

TIME MANAGEMENT

When school consultants are asked about the biggest obstacle to performing the important aspects of their role, the majority respond, "Time!" A study released by the Council for Exceptional Children in October 2000 (*CEC Today,* 2000) reported that special education teaching conditions have pushed teachers into crisis mode. Time required to complete overwhelming paperwork, pressure of high caseloads, lack of administrator support, and shortage of qualified special education teachers are major issues. Teachers stress that they need more time for collaborative planning, and 15 percent of the respondents reported that they have *no* time for individualized instruction. Only 26 percent have more than three hours daily for individualized instruction. When administrators are not attuned to the responsibilities and demands of special education, the unfortunate result can be failure to allow time for the planning and collaborating that are vital components of instructional accommodations and modifications.

Studies have shown that school consultants chafe under considerable time pressures from attending meetings, preparing and planning, administering tests, communicating, observing, evaluating, and problem solving. Many are prone to "timelock" that is, claims on time have grown so demanding that it seems impossible to wring one more second out of the crowded calendar (Keyes, 1991).

Caseload is a key factor in managing time and arranging schedules. Those having both direct and indirect service roles should have their ratios classified for each category, and students receiving consultation services as well as direct services should be counted twice. The solution, if there is one, lies in how we choose to use the time available to us.

Time is a nonrenewable resource; it is not adaptable, but people are. An ancient Chinese proverb says, "You cannot change the wind, but you can adjust the sail." Time-management skills can be learned and improved. Because the time-management "sail" is primarily about choices, it is very personal, and the best management plan for one may not be the best for another. A basic five-step plan is useful for practicing time management:

1. Analyze one's current use of time.
2. Establish professional and personal goals and priorities.
3. Plan time and work as arranged by priorities.
4. Use positive time-management techniques.
5. Review results and reinforce successes.

Most consultants, when asked specifically how they use their time, rely on memory or perceptions. However, to make significant improvements in time management, busy consultants must accurately observe *and record* their use of time. Time logs are a valuable way to observe personal use of time and they ultimately save time rather than waste it. Consultants may choose to use a diary time log, recording everything they do, when they do it, and how long it takes. Another option is to record time in fifteen-minute segments, or use a matrix which lists times of the day in segments and lists elements of the consulting role. The matrix can be used to check off quickly those responsibilities that were being done in each segment, and time spent on each activity can be totaled at the end of the day. When recording use of time, remember to begin recording your activities early in the day, not waiting until the end of the day and trying to remember it all.

It is helpful to review long-term goals daily. They should be posted on the desk, the wall, or in a planner. This simple activity, according to Douglass and Douglass (1993), helps one stay focused. Long-term goals should be subdivided into short-term goals, weekly goals, and daily goals. To minimize the gap between long-term and short-term goals, Douglass trying Douglass (1993) suggest:

- Keeping a master To Do list with priority codes that match the items to your goals.
- Assigning a due date to each project. Due dates keep tasks from being put off and foster a sense of completion when accomplished.
- Estimating time required to complete the task or the project.

Putnam (1993) offers a number of practical tips for making every minute count, including:

- Think of oneself as a time manager.
- Establish goals, stay focused, and make long-range plans.
- Take time to make time, so that there are fewer time-management issues later on.
- Delegate routine tasks to students, aides, or parent volunteers when possible.
- Minimize procrastination.
- Learn to say "no." *Practice* saying "no" until it feels firm, sincere, and guilt-free.

WEEKLY ORGANIZER

Dates: _____ to _____

Week at a Glance				
Monday /	Tuesday /	Wednesday /	Thursday /	Friday /

To Do (Priority)	To See	
	Person/Place	**Time**

To Do (Eventually)	To Phone/E-mail	
	Person	**Phone number/E-mail address**

☺ Notes & Reminders ☺

FIGURE 6.2   A Weekly Organizer Form

© Jane Jacquart 2003. Reproduced with permission.

Time-management practices encourage efficient use of abilities and strengths. The purpose of time management is not to get *everything* done, but to meet high-priority and personal goals successfully. Being busy is not the same as being productive. Time management is a skill that can be learned and improved. (See Figure 6.2 for one consulting teacher's weekly organizer form.)

Burdened with the paperwork of IEPs, contacts with families, reports, and lesson plans, special education teachers can feel overwhelmed. Add to that the ever-increasing demands of NCLB and other requirements for general education teachers, and the blizzard of paper becomes a whiteout in which it is hard to find time to collaborate, consult, and work in teams.

But hoped-for relief has come for some educators in the technology tools that are now available. When early childhood teachers are faced with transitioning responsibilities for preschool children, Benz (1997) suggests generating computer formats for reports, databases for frequently used terms and phrases, additional databases for preparing student goal sheets, comprehensive report forms for students with several therapies, developmental checklists, and observational record forms.

More recently, Meyers, Meyers, and Grogg (2004) described the technological tools featured at the 2002 Futures Conference for school psychologists that promise to be enhancers of change in schools—tools that seem complicated and out of reach now but are likely to be available for connected consultations in the near future. Streaming video of the conference and the subsequent Web site underscore possibilities for Internet participation, videoconferencing, electronic consultation and staff development, e-Forums for posting questions and answers, exchanges of information through networked computers and arrangements of time and schedules via e-mail. Such advancements hold exciting promises for reducing the stress and workloads of collaborative educators.

■ ■ ■ ■ ■ ▬▬▬▬▬▬▬▬▬▬▬▬▬▬▬▬▬▬

APPLICATION 6.1
USING TIME WISELY

Physicists define time as nature's way to keep everything from happening at once! By planning time and managing time-wasters, educators can be more productive and less stressed. The following seven strategies can be helpful:

1. Make a To Do list—monthly, weekly, and/or daily lists. Make each list at the same time of day on the same kind of paper. Write down all that needs to be done and plan all activities, even those such as talking with friends or playing with the family. Then prioritize the list. Lakein (1973) suggests "ABC-ing" the list, with A as top priority for only those things which *must* be done. Designate B priorities as "nice if done," and C jobs as "maybe later." You might even end up with a D or "so what?" list. Handle the C tasks sensibly. If they can't be delegated or ignored, try putting them on an "extra-minutes" list. If that is not an option, consider bartering, pooling resources, and consolidating activities.

2. Say "no" when you need to. Avoid saying "Well . . . ," or "I'll think about it." Certainly avoid, "I will if you can't find anyone else," because they won't. Responding with "This is so important that it needs more attention than I can give it now," is often very effective.

3. Delegate. This is the perfect solution for C priorities, if a helper is available. Teachers are habituated into functioning autonomously, but others may just be waiting for a chance to contribute and develop their own skills.

4. Set deadlines and time limits. Plan a treat for accomplishing a task by deadline. Time limits help get things done efficiently and prevent simple tasks from becoming major projects. It prevents letting the intentions to clean out one drawer become major cleaning of the whole desk, file cabinet, and book shelves.

5. Organize desk and office area. MacKenzie (1975) describes the "stacked desk syndrome," in which the desk is so cluttered with things-not-to-forget that one cannot find things, concentrate, or work efficiently.

6. Get a Do Not Disturb sign, and use it without guilt. Some teachers have had great success making and using work-status cubes for their desk *and* even encouraging their students to do the same. Faces on one's cube can convey messages such as "Please Do Not Disturb Right Now," "I need help," "This is not a good day for me, so be patient, please," or "May I help someone?"

7. Plan time for yourself. Busy educators often devote so much time and energy to taking care of others that they neglect themselves. Take time to relax, visit with others in the building, talk to a child, read a book, go for a walk, sketch a picture.

Finding Time for Collaboration and Teaming

Managing time and schedules in order to conduct consultation and collaborate effectively is indeed one of the biggest challenges for school consultants. According to Cawelti (1997), teachers report their instruction improves when they work in teams. But they need to have the time available in order to do that. Many educators believe outcomes-based education and performance-based assessment are promising innovations for schools, but acknowledge that each plan requires additional teacher time. How to accomplish that is as yet unresolved. Three examples from comments by teachers as reported by Voltz, Elliott, and Cobb (1994) more than a decade ago are still being experienced in schools:

> Our schedules are so tight, there is no time during the regular school day for planning together or discussion.
>   Timing is the greatest problem. There is just no time for classroom teachers and resource teachers to communicate. . . .
>   . . . when the resource teacher and I needed to confer and we had to do it on our own time . . . we had an essential conference with the resource teacher in the lavatory and me on the floor outside the door, talking through the door. . . . (p. 534)

Such comments are consistent with a number of other studies investigating barriers to consultation, collaboration, and teaming. Time emerged as the key issue inherent in every school-change analysis for many years (Raywid, 1993), with successful schools differing from unsuccessful ones in the frequency and extent to which teachers interact and collaborate about materials and instruction. Raywid (1993) found that approaches to finding time included freeing up existing time, restructuring or rescheduling time, using existing time better, or buying time. Examples from this research include:

- Teachers sharing the same lunch period with their plan period after lunch, which results in ninety minutes of shared time per day
- Teachers interacting while students leave the building a few hours weekly to perform community service
- Substitutes hired with money saved by increasing class sizes by one or two students

- Day-long staff development for three to five days per year in some districts
- Compensatory time for teachers participating in two- to three-day planning sessions during breaks between terms
- Staff development days, from as many as five or more instructional days waived by state legislatures
- Lengthened instructional days
- Special talents and skills programs provided by specialists, or hobby days for students while teachers meet to collaborate and plan
- University personnel working in partnership to provide activities that free up teachers to interact

Raywid stressed that teachers cannot be expected to give up time for working together when they are exhausted at the end of the school day, or when they have their own personal activities, or just because they are uncomfortable about the way their class might be handled in their absence. Teachers do not want collaborative time to be tacked on to a school day; they want it integrated into their school day (Mann, 2000).

Building administrators must be the driving force to make this happen. In some areas, teachers meet to develop rubrics, tests, teaching ideas, and the like. They are not required to make reports or write summaries as justification for time spent. They are just asked to show the products that resulted from the shared time. Other faculties brainstorm in an initial collaborative effort to come up with unique ideas for carving out more extensive collaborative time. Still others have grade-level or departmental plan time on a regular basis during some music, art, and physical education periods.

In one district teachers were convinced their high school students didn't get enough sleep. These teachers also were looking for ways to collaborate. So a policy was put into place to have late-start days every other Wednesday, moving school starting time from 8:00 A.M. to 8:30, to allow teachers an extra forty-five minutes to meet and students an extra thirty minutes to sleep in, visit, or study. Administrators and paraprofessionals supervised students who showed up early. The meeting time was guided by the Professional Learning Communities model first implemented in Adlai Stevenson High School in Lincolnshire, Illinois. Even experienced teachers reported learning many useful things during their time together.

In another district three building administrators made it possible for teachers to form interdisciplinary teams and meet on their own time—Saturdays for breakfast or before or after school, to work on instruction that would use authentic achievement criteria (Stewart & Brendefur, 2005). The trade-off was that they were excused from regular inservice days. As they participated in the learning team, they adjusted to the reality that their work was available for scrutiny by others. An interesting outcome was one administrator's remark that a master teacher had commented how much she learned, so she could only imagine how much a new teacher might have learned. The administrator was convinced that learning teams could improve instruction.

Other educational leaders offer additional strategies for creating time to collaborate. Some work with the parent-teacher organization to implement volunteer substitute-teacher programs that free up teachers. Others revise schedules to provide shared planning time, and still others release teachers from school duties such as lunch and bus supervision, and student activities and assemblies. Peer-tutoring programs across classes can free up time for team meetings, although start time and monitoring time must be factored in. Many innovative ideas are available, but generating and implementing the ideas requires time to plan and coordinate them.

West (1990) offers a number of strategies for increasing collaboration time that have been used successfully at elementary, middle, and junior and senior high levels, including:

Strategies for Increasing Collaboration time

- Bringing large groups of students together for speakers, films, or plays
- Using volunteers such as grandparents, parents, community leaders, and retired teachers
- Hiring a permanent "floating substitute"
- Having the principal set aside one day per grading period as "collaboration day," with no other activities on this day
- Having the principal or another staff supervisor teach a period a day regularly
- Having students working on independent or study activities while clustered in large groups under supervision
- Having faculty vote to extend the instructional day twenty minutes for two days a week in a collaboration period

In an education update from the Association for Supervision and Curriculum Development (ASCD, 2000), finding time for collaborating is described as "not a question of know-how, but of want-to." One thing teachers do want is for collaborative time to be part of the school day, not after school or on Saturdays. The sharing of materials and ideas, asking big questions, doing joint planning, and making presentations to one another is good staff development activity. When teachers focus on producing rubrics, creating strategies for improvement, and analyzing assessment data, they refrain from using their collaborative planning time for routine activities such as grading papers.

Much of the research on issues such as caseloads and allocations of time for collaboration and consultation in inclusive schools was conducted more than a decade ago. Newer research is needed to ascertain if there has been improvement in this major element that affects partnerships and networking. Research is needed to determine the contributions that technology has made to saving time, travel, and stress. Researchers also would want to note the interest many schools have displayed in recent years for having teachers work together. Energetic, inquisitive teachers could make a study of this topic using well-designed action research that would ultimately benefit all educators.

Techniques for Meetings, Interviews, and Observations

Who has not winced at the thought of yet another meeting? Meetings, interviews, and classroom observations take precious time as well as drain physical and mental energy. Tremendous amounts of collective time and energy are wasted when people are trapped in unproductive meetings. Educators who want to work smarter, not harder, should set goals for conducting group interactions that are efficient and productive for all.

Conducting Efficient Meetings.   Consulting educators are busy, but classroom teachers may be the most overextended of all. Many classroom teachers find that the total time for having all their students together for a class period is appallingly short. Consultation and collaboration will be accepted more readily when consultees know that consultants respect their time and their students' time. So a meeting should be planned only if it promises to contribute significantly in serving client needs.

The first rule in planning an efficient meeting is to ask, "Do we really need to have this meeting?" If the answer is *not* a resounding "Yes," then the business probably can be handled a more efficient way, perhaps by memo, phone, e-mail, or brief face-to-face conversations with individuals. Good reasons for having a meeting are:

- Meeting legal obligations (such as an IEP conference)
- Problem-solving with several people representing a variety of roles
- Brainstorming so that many ideas are put forth
- Reconciling conflicting views
- Providing a forum for all to be heard
- Building a team to implement educational decisions

Good reasons for having a meeting

Unnecessary meetings waste school time. They also erode participants' confidence in the value of future meetings that may be called. Sigband (1987) recommends that meetings be held only when there is verifiable need, basing each meeting on an overall purpose and series of objectives. Only people who can make a definite contribution need to be there. An agenda should be prepared, and the meeting room and any needed equipment should be ready. Most important, the meeting must begin on time and end on time, or early if possible.

Preparing for the Meeting.   Leaders or chairs of meetings will be more prepared and organized if they follow a planning checklist. (See Figure 6.3 for an example.) The sheet should include general planning points such as date, time, participants, and goals. Checklists designed to stipulate preparations for the room and to note participant needs also will be useful.

Participants.   After determining a need for a meeting, leaders and chairs will want to request attendance from only those who can contribute. They should keep the group as small as possible, adhering to the rule that the more people involved, the shorter the meeting should be. Experts on group interaction recommend that the maximum for problem-solving is five, for problem identification about ten, for hearing a review or presentation as many as thirty, and for motivation and inspiration as many as possible. If a problem-solving group includes more than six people, it is likely that not everyone will have an opportunity to speak.

Agenda.   Chairpersons for meetings should develop an agenda that reflects the needs of all participants. Sometimes e-mail can be used to solicit agenda items from those who will participate. It is often helpful to send out an e-mail agenda in advance and to solicit suggestions for additional items. The agenda items could be given in question format as a variation now and then. For example, rather than "Scheduling for the Resource Room," the issue might be "How can we craft a fair, workable schedule for use of the resource room on M-W-F?"

FIGURE 6.3   Checklist to Prepare for Meetings

Date: _____   Place: _____

Time: _____   Topic: _____

Participants: _____

Goals for Meeting: _____

_____

_____

Preparation of Room: Preparation for Participants:

_____ Overhead projector   _____ Nametags

_____ Screen, bulbs, cord   _____ Pads and pens

_____ Chalkboard, chalk   _____ Handouts

_____ Charts, pens, tape   _____ Agenda

_____ Tape recorder, tapes   _____ Ice-breaker activity

_____ Podium, lectern   _____ Map of location

_____ Tables, chairs   _____ Refreshments

_____ Breakout arrangements   _____ Follow-up activity

_____ Other?   _____ Other?

Room Arrangement: _____

_____

_____   (Sketch of Room)

_____

_____

With an agenda distributed beforehand, participants will be more productive and less apprehensive. Sometimes leaders of large-group meetings draw on a teaching technique of placing a short, high-interest activity, relating to the topic but needing little explanation, on the chalkboard or overhead screen. Participants focus on the task as they arrive, thereby becoming centered on the meeting topic as they do so. Meetings are more effective when participants can anticipate the task. (See Figure 6.4 for an example of a premeeting communication to prepare participants.)

It is important to allocate time for each item on the agenda. Estimating the time needed for each item will allow the chair to monitor progress during the meeting. It is counterproductive to focus too long on early items and fail to get to the last ones. If more important items are placed far down the agenda and time becomes short, it might even

FIGURE 6.4   Checklist to Prepare Participants

Date: _____   Place: _____

Time Start: _____   Time End: _____   Topic: _____

Roles: Facilitator: _____

Recorder: _____

Timekeeper: _____

Other Participants: _____

Agenda for Meeting: _____

_____

_____

_____

_____   Minutes of Prior Meeting Attached _____

_____   Advance Preparation Needed _____

_____   Next Planned Meeting _____

At the Meeting

Action	Person(s) Responsible	Target Date	Done

appear that they have been put there by the convener to avoid action or decision making. Consultants seeking to build collaborative interactions among their colleagues will not want that to happen.

Seating Arrangements.   Comfortable chairs and seating arrangements that facilitate interaction are important factors in the success of a meeting. Full-size chairs (not kindergarten furniture) with a little padding, but not too much, should be provided. For best interaction, there should be an arrangement where all can face each other. A circle for six to ten people, a U-shape with peripheral seating if there is to be a visual presentation, and a semicircle of one or more rows for large groups work well (Lawren, 1989).

Participant Responsibilities.   Along with the responsibility of each participant to interact and help problem-solve, brainstorm, or decide, three other responsibilities are important— chair, recorder, and timekeeper. In many cases the consultant will take care of all three roles, particularly if the meeting includes only two or three people. However, if the meeting is long, or the issues are complex and there is much discussion and brainstorming, it is efficient for the chair to ask another participant to record the plans and decisions. One potentially useful strategy for getting the most out of a meeting is to take notes, whether or not they are required. This focuses attention and keeps the writer active yet still. Even adults sometimes find it hard to sit still and listen when there are so many other things vying for one's energy and attention.

During the Meeting.   The first order of business is to make sure that all participants are introduced by name and role. Whether the meeting involves two or twenty persons, all participants should be made to feel that they have important contributions to make. All should listen attentively to each other, think creatively and flexibly, and avoid disruptive communication such as jokes, puns, sarcasm, or side comments (Gordon, 1974). Talking and whispering in subgroups can be particularly distracting. Ironically, some teachers who will not tolerate such behavior by their students in the classroom are the biggest offenders. Astute group leaders have various ways of handling this disagreeable occurrence. They might go over to the offenders and stand alongside or between them, direct a question to one of them, or request a response from them. Each participant in a meeting should be thinking at all times, "What will help move us ahead and solve the problem," and "What does the group need and how can I help?" (Gordon, 1974).

Compromise for consensus is not always the best solution. It may reflect a weak decision, a watered-down plan, or failure by some participants to express their concerns as firmly as they should. During the meeting leaders should encourage opposing views so that they do not surface later when the matter has been closed. If any participant wishes to dissent, the time to do so is in the meeting, not in hallways after the matter has been decided. Of course, many consultations and collaborations involve only two individuals—consultant and consultee. But procedures recommended for groups of several or more are often pertinent to interactions between only two individuals as well.

Winding Up the Meeting.   The timekeeper should be consulted frequently but quietly, so the meeting can end on time. When time is nearly up, the leader should review any key decisions and, if needed, set the time and place for the next meeting, perhaps with a preliminary overview of that agenda. If a meeting's agenda and progress become sidetracked, leaders should redirect the group's attention by making a point to refocus the discussion (Raschke, Dedrick, & DeVries, 1988).

Minutes of the Meeting.   Sometimes committees are faulted for keeping minutes to waste hours! Minutes should reflect the group's decisions about what is to be done, by whom, and by what date, but need not include each point of the discussion. Minutes are a record for naming those who will have a responsibility, for describing plans and decisions, and for listing projected dates for completion of tasks. This is an important aspect of the consultation which must not be slighted.

Assessment of the Meeting.   Some time should be reserved at the end of the meeting to discuss progress made and to evaluate the effectiveness of the meeting. A brief checklist like the one in Figure 6.5 can be distributed or sent by e-mail to be completed online and

FIGURE 6.5   Checklist to Evaluate Meetings

	Yes	No	Don't Know or DNA
1. All participants were prepared in advance with an agenda.	_____	_____	_____
2. The meeting began on time.	_____	_____	_____
3. Facilities were comfortable and pleasant.	_____	_____	_____
4. Privacy was ensured.	_____	_____	_____
5. Participation was evenly distributed with everyone contributing.	_____	_____	_____
6. Time was used well and the agenda was completed.	_____	_____	_____
7. A summary of decisions was made, listing those responsible.	_____	_____	_____
8. Follow-up activities and any needed repeats were planned.	_____	_____	_____
9. The meeting ended on time.	_____	_____	_____
10. Participants evaluated the meeting's structure and outcome(s).	_____	_____	_____

Additional Comments: _____

_____

_____

returned. Participants should be thanked for coming and for their active participation. Finally, there should be follow-up on any actions assigned.

Brief-Agenda Meetings.   When collaborators have a single topic that can be handled in a quick meeting before or after school, they can structure the meeting with a brief-agenda conference. After becoming familiar with this process, team members will be able to have these 30-minute meetings without much ado. However, they should not try to squeeze a large agenda or issue into the brief-agenda format. (See Figure 6.6.)

FIGURE 6.6   Brief-Agenda Conference

Date, Time, and Participants

Data reporting: _____

_____

_____

_____ 3 minutes

1. Problem finding	5 minutes
2. Idea generating	5 minutes
3. Solution finding	12 minutes
4. Follow-through planning	5 minutes

Conducting Effective Interviews.   School consultants often need to interview school personnel, community resources, and family members to plan programs for helping students with special needs. Interviewees can provide information for case studies and formulation of learning goals. They help generate options and alternatives for special needs, and provide data for program evaluation.

Successful interviews require effective communication skills, and postures of one-downsmanship, parity, and cooperativeness. Queries such as "Tell me more," "Could you expand on that?" and "Let me see if I understand what you are saying" are examples of the responsive listening and paraphrasing that help to elicit the most useful information.

The interviewer should take notes, allowing interviewees to look them over at the conclusion of the interview. If a tape recording is desired, the interviewer must ask permission beforehand to make one. Some feel it is best to avoid taping, because respondents are often less candid if their comments are being recorded.

Interviews must be conducted ethically, collegially, and for a purpose not attainable by less intrusive, time-consuming methods. Keys to a successful interview by the school consultant are asking the right questions and valuing the expertise of the interviewee. A follow-up interaction soon after the interview session is affirming and reassuring, thus facilitating further collaboration.

Making Prudent Observations.   Consultants often need to observe a student, groups of students, or an entire program in operation. This is not an easy professional task. Consultants who go into classrooms to observe can expect some discomfort and anxiety on the teacher's part. There may be latent resentment because the consultant is free to visit other classrooms, something many teachers would like but are rarely given the opportunity to do.

Consultants can facilitate the process of observation and ease the minds of those being observed in several ways. First, they should provide a positive comment upon entering the room, and then sit unobtrusively where the teacher has designated. They should avoid getting involved in classroom activities or helping students. Effective observers can blend into the classroom setting so they are hardly noticed. Regular visits minimize the likelihood of having students know who is being observed and for what reason. It is a sad thing to hear a student say, "Oh, here's that learning disabilities teacher to check up on Jimmy again." Records of behaviors must be done in code so that the physical aspects of writing, watching, and body language of the consultant do not reveal the intent of the observation. Each consultant should develop a personal coding system for recording information. Sometimes observers watch the targeted student for one minute, and then divert their attention to another student for one minute, continuing the process with other peers. In this way the student's behavior can be compared with that of classmates. The consultant may teach a lesson and have the classroom teacher observe. This can be helpful for both consultant and consultee. (See Figure 6.7 for a sample observation form.)

An observer should exit the room with a smile and a supporting glance at the teacher. Then very soon after the observation, the observer will want to get back to the classroom teacher with positive, specific comments about the classroom, feedback on the observation, and suggestions for entering into problem solving. Although consultants do not observe in classrooms for the purpose of assessing teacher behaviors and teaching styles, it would be myopic to assume that they do not notice teaching practices which inhibit student success

FIGURE 6.7   Classroom Observation Form

Classroom Observation Form
for Social and/or Academic Assessment

Student's Name _____ Teacher's Name _____

School _____ Grade _____

Date _____ Time _____   To _____

Consulting Teacher/Observer _____

_____

Location of Student in Room _____

Percent of Time Student Is: In Seat _____ In Group Activity _____ On-Task _____

Attends to Instruction of Teacher or Aide_____

Responds/Follows Directions _____

Complies with Teacher/Aide Requests _____

Complies with Class Rules _____

Works Independently _____

Completes Work _____

Seeks Help Appropriately _____

Is Distracted _____

Seems Confused/Unfocused _____

Distracts Others _____

Participates in Discussions _____

Participates in Group Activities _____

Shows Respect for Teacher(s) _____

Shows Respect for Other Students _____

Helps Others Appropriately _____

Other Observations _____

_____

Summary/Comments _____

in that classroom. When the practices seem to be interfering with student achievement, the consultant might ask the consultee in a nonthreatening, onedownsmanship way whether the student achieved the goals of the lesson. If not, is there something the teacher would like to change so this could occur? Then what might the consultant do to help?

To avoid gathering inaccurate information, consultants will want to make repeated observations. In doing so they can use the opportunity to obtain additional information on antecedents to the problem (Cipani, 1985).

Achieving rapport with a consultee, while targeting a teaching strategy for possible modification, requires utmost finesse by consultants. The observer should make an appointment as soon as possible for providing feedback and continuation of the problem solving.

MANAGEMENT OF CONSULTATION RECORDS AND RESOURCES

A prominent space scientist commented that physicists can lick anything, even gravity, but the paperwork is overwhelming. Special education teachers can relate to that. They cite excessive paperwork and record-keeping, along with insufficient time in which to do it, as major causes of stress and burnout. Writing and monitoring IEPs, individual pupil record-keeping, and completion of records and forms rank high as major usurpers of their personal and professional time (Davis, 1983).

When asked to estimate the amount of time they spend performing their responsibilities, resource teachers often overestimate the time spent on direct pupil instruction and staffings and underestimate their preparation for instruction and clerical duties such as record-keeping. If teaching is to be an important service profession, careful record-keeping is essential. Record-keeping must be written into the consultant's role description as an important responsibility, with time allowed for its accurate completion. Who would want to be treated by a doctor who did not write down vital information after each visit, or served by a lawyer who failed to record and file important documents? The key for educators is to manage their paperwork so that it does not manage them. Developing efficient systems and standardized forms for record-keeping will help educators, and consultants in particular, work smarter and not harder.

Using a Consultation Journal or Log

One of the most important formats for consultants to develop is a consultation log or journal. Consultants can record the date, participants, and topic of each consultation on separate pages, along with a brief account of the interaction and the results agreed on. Space should be provided for follow-up reports and assessment of the consultation. (See Figure 6.8 for a sample format.) Records should be kept for the time spent in consultation and any positive results accomplished, if consultation is to gain credibility as an essential educational activity. Although consultants cannot control the type of records required, they can exercise a good bit of control over processes and procedures for collecting and using information (Davis, 1983).

One caution is due in regard to consultation logs. Important points of the discussion about student needs and progress might be entered in the log. However, no diagnostic classification or plan that necessitates parent permission should be recorded (Conoley & Conoley, 1982). Confidentiality of the information must be preserved. Consultants will want to develop procedures for coding that will ensure confidentiality, yet identify pertinent information efficiently and accurately.

FIGURE 6.8   Consultation Journal Format

Client (coded): _____ Consultee (initials): _____

Initiator of Consultation: _____

General Topic of Concern: _____

_____

Purpose of Consultation: _____

_____

_____

Brief Summary of Consultation: _____

_____

_____

_____

Steps Agreed On—by Whom, by When: _____

_____

_____

_____

Follow-Up: _____

_____

Most Successful Parts of Consultation: _____

_____

Consultation Areas Needing Improvement: _____

_____

Satisfaction with consultation process (1 = least, 5 = most)

1. Communication between consultant and consultee _____

2. Use of collaborative problem solving _____

3. Consultee responsiveness to consultation _____

4. Effectiveness of consultation for problem _____

5. Impact of consultation on client _____

6. Positive ripple effects for system _____

Memos and Professional Cards

A consultation memo is a communication tool and also a record of that communication. It should be as brief as possible and very clear, or it will confound rather than convey the message (Cleveland, 1981). Receivers will pay more attention to a memo that synthesizes the information and expresses it in simple terms. Jargon, acronyms, excess verbiage, and cryptic sentences are to be avoided. Contrary to some practice, memos should be drafted and then rewritten in best form, rather than dashed off hastily and flung into a mailbox. This is particularly relevant to electronic memos. The writer should put the message simply, tell just enough and no more, state facts (times, dates, meeting rooms, descriptions, names), stick to the point, and make the memo as grammatically correct and aesthetically pleasing as possible without spending hours at the task.

Consultants will find it helpful to include a personalized logo on the memo forms they use to communicate with consultees. This logo identifies the consultant at a glance. A busy recipient immediately recognizes its source and can make a quick decision about the need to respond now or at a later time. It personalizes professional interaction by providing a bit of information about the consultant, a humorous touch, or the creative element that educators enjoy and appreciate. A carefully designed logo can promote consultation, collaboration, and team effort in a positive light.

Another item that improves consultant efficiency is the professional card. Business cards have been a mainstay for communicating basic information in many professions and can be useful in education as well. Administrators can increase the visibility of their staff and enhance staff morale by providing them with attractive, well-designed professional cards. Educators find these cards helpful when they interact with colleagues at other sites, or when they attend conferences and conventions. The cards are convenient for quickly jotting down requests for information. They help build communication networks among colleagues with similar interests, and even promote one's own school district.

Organizing a Consultation Notebook

Consultants often use a looseleaf notebook divided into sections with index tabs. The sections can be categorized by buildings served, students served, or teachers served. One very organized consulting teacher had a section of "Best Times to Meet with Teachers," listing days and times available for every teacher with whom she collaborated. Each consultant will want to develop the style that works best in his or her school context and role. Figure 6.9 is a list of suggestions for a special education consultant's notebook sections. Figure 6.10 on page 202 shows a different format used by a consulting teacher for learning and behavioral disabilities. Consultants may not want or need all of these sections, and may come up with others of their own they would like to include. Personalization for the role and school context again determines its usefulness.

A primary responsibility of the consultant is to ensure confidentiality of information for both student and staff. This can be accomplished in at least two ways—coding the names with numbers or symbols while keeping the code list in a separate place, and marking person-specific files as confidential. A "Confidential" rubber stamp prepared for this purpose can be used to alert readers that the information is not for public viewing. These

FIGURE 6.9   Consultation Notebook Format

Appointments:	One for week, one for year.
"To-do" lists:	By day, week, month, or year as fits needs. List commitments.
Lesson plans:	If delivering direct service, outline of activities for week.
Consultation logs:	Chart to record consultation input and outcomes (Figure 6.8)
Phone call log:	Consultation time by phone.
Observation sheets:	Coded for confidentiality.
Contact list:	Phone numbers, school address, times available.
Faculty notes:	Interests, social and family events and dates, teaching preferences of staff.
Schedules:	For faculty, paras, support staff, regular school events.
Student list:	Coded for confidentiality, birth dates, IEP dates, other helpful data.
Student information:	Anecdotal records, sample products, events, awards, interests, birthdays, talents.
Medication records:	If part of responsibilities.
Materials available:	Title, brief description with grade levels, location.
Services available:	School and community services for resources.
State policies:	Guidelines, procedures, names and phone numbers of agencies/ personnel.
School policies:	Brief description of school policies regulations, handbook.
Procedural materials:	Forms, procedures, for standard activities.
Evaluation data:	Space and forms to record data for formative and summative evaluation (discussed later in this chapter) and coded if confidential.
Idea file:	To note ideas for self and for sharing with staff and parents.
Joke and humor file:	To perk up the day, and for sharing with others.
Three-year calendar:	For continuity in preparing, checking, and updating IEPs.
Pockets:	For carrying personalized memos, letterhead, stamps, hall passes, paper, professional cards.

practices, along with the usual protection of information and data, and the practice of seeing that the recorded information is as positive and verifiable as possible, are common-sensible rules that should be sufficient for handling all but the most unusual cases.

An itinerant consulting teacher who serves several schools may want to prepare a simple form stating the date, teacher's name and child's code, along with the topic to be considered, for each school. The list can be perused quickly before entering the building, so that no time is lost in providing the consultative or teaching service. Some consulting teachers block off and color-code regular meeting times and teacher responsibilities. This practice permits a clearer picture of available consultation times. Another helpful strategy is development of a comprehensive manual that includes standard procedures and forms used in the school district and required by the state.

FIGURE 6.10   Consulting Teacher's Notebook

Table of Contents

1. Student Information
   1.1 Personal Information
   1.2 Student Profiles
   1.3 A Quick Look at IEPs
   1.4 Student Schedules
   1.5 Medication Records

2. School Information
   2.1 Faculty-Staff Roster(s)/Faculty Notes
   2.2 Master Schedule(s)
   2.3 School Calendar(s)
   2.4 School Policies/School Handbook(s)

3. Calendars
   3.1 Daily To-Do Lists
   3.2 Personal Calendars (Weekly, Yearly)
   3.3 IEP Review Dates
   3.4 Three-Year Evaluation Dates

4. Forms
   4.1 Personal Motif Memos
   4.2 Consultation/Collaboration Request

   4.3 Observation Sheets
   4.4 Weekly Teacher Progress Report
   4.5 Consultation Logs

5. Lesson Plans
   5.1 Weekly Lesson Plans
   5.2 Student Matrix Worksheet
   5.3 Class Co-Planning Sheet
   5.4 Unit Co-Planning Sheet
   5.5 Co-Teaching Planning Sheet
   5.6 Para schedule and responsibilities

6. Consultation/Collaboration
   6.1 Advantages of Consultation/
       Collaboration
   6.2 Tips for Consultation/Collaboration
   6.3 Completed Consultation Logs
   6.4 Consultation Evaluation Forms
   6.5 Personal Journal

7. Resource Listing

Consultation Schedules.   The consultant schedule is a vital tool. It not only allows the consultant to organize time productively, but also demonstrates to administrators and other school personnel by its very existence and the records it contains that the school consultant is goal-directed, productive, and facilitative. Schedules should be left with secretaries of all buildings assigned to the consultant, and posted in teacher workrooms so that colleagues have easy access to the information. School secretaries should be asked to refer to these schedules if consulting teachers have phone calls, and report their location to the caller. Saying, "Gee, I don't know. I can't keep up with those people," does not present collaborative consultation in a positive way.

Consultations and collaborative experiences can be keyed on the consultant's schedule with code letters for efficiency. One consulting teacher uses this code in her notebook:

- ID   informal discussion, spontaneous meeting
- PM   planned, formal meeting
- PC   phone conversation
- MM   major meeting of more than two people
- FT   follow-through activity
- SO   scheduled observation

Standardized forms are helpful for collecting and using basic information. The forms that produce multiple copies may be more expensive in the short run, but can save valuable time and energy in the long run. The time spent on developing systems and standardizing conventional forms will be well spent. It frees up more time and energy for individualizing and personalizing the instruction for special needs of the students.

Commercial resources are available that provide sample letters and forms adaptable to a variety of educational purposes, from writing a letter of congratulations to thanking a resource speaker for a presentation. Although educators will not want to use these patterns verbatim, they can use them to jump-start preparation of some of the more difficult communications.

Coordination and organization of student files, consultation logs, school procedures, and schedules will necessitate more time for paperwork at the outset, but once the procedures are set up, they will be time-efficient and cost-effective in the long run.

Organizing and Distributing Materials

Many school districts now have extensive instructional resource centers where school personnel can check out a variety of material for classroom use. Even with the busiest resource center in full operation, consultants usually have their own field-related materials and information about special areas that teachers want and need. With little or no clerical help, and often little storage space available beyond the seats, floor, and trunk of their own vehicles, traveling school consultants need to develop a simple, orderly checkout system for loaned materials, or soon the consultant will have little left to use and share.

Materials belonging to a school should be marked with the school stamp, and consultants' personal materials should be labeled with a personal label. The consultant will want to keep an up-to-date inventory of available materials within both personal and school libraries that are loanable and specific to student needs. In some school situations, library pockets and checkout cards will facilitate checkout and return. But the inventory can be most efficiently managed, updated, and loaned out if it is organized in an interactive electronic file arranged by subject of the material that includes grade levels for which it is appropriate, is alphabetized by name of the item, notes the recommended loan period, and includes space for a requester to enter name, date, and item borrowed for what length of time.

Before traveling to a school, the consultant can scan the checkout file for due dates, and stop by classrooms or put memos into message boxes asking for return of overdue material. Efficient consultants leave request cards so school staff can let them know of their needs. They also periodically assess the usefulness of their materials by querying teachers and students who used them. These kinds of interactions build positive attitudes toward collaboration and teamwork, promote the effectiveness of school consultation, and extend the ripple effect of special services.

EVALUATION OF COLLABORATIVE SCHOOL CONSULTATION

Why do collaborative school consultants need to know about evaluation? Here are some examples of how evaluation is used in school settings:

■ The school district received a year of funding from the state library to develop a parent-teacher center for families of children with disabilities. Future funding for the center depends on evidence that the center is having a positive impact on children, parents, siblings, and neighborhoods. An evaluation of the program can provide evidence needed to receive further funding.

■ The local school board wants useful information so they can make a decision to continue, eliminate, or expand the school's after-school bilingual special education program.

■ Every year the theater department of the local community college works with parents of all fifth-graders and their fifth-graders to write and produce a play based on current events. Special education teachers and general education teachers work collaboratively with the theater department for this activity. There is a new chairperson of the theater department, and she wants to know if the project is worth all the time and effort her students and faculty put into this joint effort.

■ Co-teaching in inclusive classrooms in the school district takes time and energy. With all the mandated testing and programs, the middle school principal wants to know if the method is worthwhile. Program evaluation will help the principal and others made decisions about staffing integrated classrooms.

Indeed, evaluation is particularly important for programs in which there is a strong focus on process skills and outcomes that can affect students in profound ways. Consultants cannot know if the consultation activities are effective unless they conduct evaluation; administrators and policy makers are not eager to support programs for which there are no meaningful data. Engaging in an ongoing systematic assessment process is the best way to be more confident that appropriate decisions are made. Consider the following scenario:

SCENARIO 6.B

The setting is the conference room of a special education program office where the principal, the director of special education, the special education consulting teacher, and a parent are seated.

Principal: Mrs. James, I have asked Mrs. Garcia, our director of special education, and Mr. Penner, our special education consulting teacher, to meet with us today to help address your questions. I've explained to them that you're concerned about the new program for your daughter. As I understand your concerns, you feel she is not learning as much as she did last year when she went to the resource room for special help. Is there anything you would like to add?

Parent: Well, I don't like to complain, but I just don't understand this new way of doing things for her. I was glad when she qualified for special education, because I thought she would finally get some help. Now she isn't getting it any more. Besides that, I wonder how this consulting program affects the other children. As you know, I am president of the local Parent Teachers Association, and questions about the special education program have come up at several of our meetings. I told parents I would try to get more information from you.

Consulting Teacher: I've been working closely with your daughter's classroom teacher this year, and we've worked out some special learning activities in the classroom such as cooperative learning. She loves that, and when she needs a little extra help we've arranged for a sixth-grade girl to tutor her. Besides that, she goes to the resource room for math.

Special Education Director: I understand the placement team agreed to all these special experiences at the IEP meeting last spring.

Parent: Yes, I know we agreed to try them, but I don't think they are working. I'd like more evidence that this is the right way to educate children who have learning problems.

Principal: Mr. Penner, do you have data that we can show Mrs. James?

Consulting Teacher: Well, I could get some test scores from teachers, I guess.

Special Education Director: Our collaborative consultation program is rather new. I believe it is already producing some positive outcomes, but it's evident that we must provide more documentation of the results. We'll need a more structured evaluation plan to get the appropriate data for assessing our results.

Principal: I agree. Thank you for being involved with your daughter's program, Mrs. James, and thanks for helping us think through what we need to do. After we do some further work on this topic, may we call on you to collaborate with us on developing a more specific plan? Your input will help us improve this facet of the program for other students as well.

What Is Evaluation?

In general, evaluation means to fix a value or determine the worth of something. In most education settings, evaluation relates to determining the worth of an educational program, such as an IEP, a peer tutoring program, an after-school program, a co-teaching arrangement, or a family involvement program.

Program evaluation is defined here as an activity directed at collecting, analyzing, interpreting, and communicating information about the workings and effectiveness of designated educational programs (Rossi, Lipsey, & Freeman, 2004). Evaluation of collaborative activities and programs is important for three reasons:

1. If the program is to be continued as an item in the school district budget and funded and staffed adequately, school administrators need to know about the impact of the program.
2. School personnel will want to know whether their hard work is paying off. They will want to continue successful practices and discontinue or modify activities that do not have an impact. Thus, evaluation data will help to continuously improve the program.
3. Evaluation results are an excellent source for explaining, validating, and providing accountability for collaborative consultation programs and efforts. Evaluation results provide justification for the time used to invest in these kinds of efforts. This is especially important when some are skeptical about indirect services and are pushing for more direct services to students with exceptional learning needs.

A school or district may have an assigned evaluator whose job it is to assess programs and activities within the school. Local universities may also have faculty or graduate students who can assist in evaluation activities. Whether schools are working with outside professional evaluators or in-district evaluators, the process is a collaborative activity. Those involved in the program or who are invested in the expected outcomes of the program are called stakeholders; a good evaluation involves stakeholders in all aspects of program assessment.

Participatory or collaborative evaluation is organized around a team, usually an evaluator and key stakeholders (Patton, 1997). Stakeholders are other educators, parents, community members, students, and school administrators. In educational settings, stakeholders are directly involved in all phases of the evaluation (Rodriguez-Campos, 2005). The consultant may provide leadership for evaluation, or may simply be a stakeholder who is active in the process. Regardless of the role of the consultant in program evaluation, she or he should be familiar with evaluation designs, methods, and models.

When collaborative consultants organize in leadership roles or as participants on evaluation teams, they should always communicate the purpose and importance of soliciting involvement by all stakeholders, working to establish relationships with them and to achieve buy-in from participants. In fact, many evaluators involve stakeholders at the evaluation design phase of a project and ask them to help design the evaluation questions. For example, if school personnel want parents to believe in the home-tutoring program, they should find out what questions parents have about the program. Then they can design the evaluation to elicit responses for the questions. In interviewing parents or asking teachers to fill out a survey, evaluators should always make sure people know why they are being asked to participate in an evaluation and how the resulting data will be used.

Types of Program Evaluation

Many types of program evaluations and methods for evaluation are in use by professional evaluators (Mertens, 2005; Rossi et al., 2004). But most educational evaluation features the accumulation of information for one of two primary purposes—formative evaluation or summative evaluation.

Formative evaluation provides information for making decisions to modify, change, or refine a program during its implementation. If a program is not producing expected outcomes, then program staff and administrators want to know that so they can make immediate changes. The process of formative evaluation often suggests the need for specific program changes; thus, formative evaluation provides important information to assist with ongoing program improvement. Evaluators use quantitative or qualitative methods, or both, for formative evaluation. (See Figure 6.11.)

Summative evaluation provides documentation for the attainment of program goals and is used most often by administrators in determining whether programs should be started, maintained, ended, or chosen from among several alternatives. It is conducted to determine the collective impact of a project on students, teachers, parents, schools, and communities. Summative evaluation takes place at the end of the program. It is expected to provide information about the viability of the program, to test the effectiveness of a completed new program, or to indicate if a product or process is ready for dissemination or

FIGURE 6.11   Purposes of Assessment and Evaluation

	Focus on:	**FORMATIVE** Change/improvement	**SUMMATIVE** Accountability
Context	*Program success*	*Development/change* What program aspects should be changed to fit this school and community?	*Status decisions* Should the consulting program continue next year?
Process	*Consultation skills*	*Growth/development* What interpersonal management skills need to be changed?	*Self-analysis* Do I have the skills to be an effective consultant?
Content	*Student/client progress*	*Growth/progress* Are achievement and behavior improving?	*Placement decisions* Does the student need more or less restrictive service?

replication. Summative evaluation indicates the short-term and long-term outcomes of the project and should relate program activities to these outcomes. (Refer to Figure 6.11.)

DESIGNING EVALUATION PROCESSES

Some collaborative programs in schools are evaluated using either formative evaluation or summative evaluation processes. But many are evaluated using both formative and summative methods. When planning program evaluation, the evaluators need to review the questions they intend to have the evaluation address. Usually these questions are related to the expectations of school districts and families. If the questions concern how the program is progressing and what improvements are needed to make it better, then formative evaluation is appropriate. If the questions are more about what impact the program is having on participants, then summative methods are called for.

The Logic Model

Evaluators should design the evaluation as early in the process of program planning as possible to help ensure that planning and implementation are congruent with expected outcomes and that evaluation has been built into the program from the outset. Many evaluators use a logic model to design their method and to communicate program processes to stakeholders. The Kellogg Logic Model (Kellogg, 2004) is a systematic way to depict visually relationships among resources for operating the program, activities that have been planned, and outcomes the program is geared to achieve. In addition, this model provides stakeholders with a roadmap that shows the sequence of related events connecting the need for the program to the desired outcomes. The Kellogg Logic Model can show the relationship

FIGURE 6.12   Logic Model Evaluation Model Template

RESOURCES	ACTIVITIES	OUTPUTS	SHORT- & LONG-TERM OUTCOMES	IMPACT
In order to accomplish our set of activities we will need the following:	*In order to address our problems or assets we will accomplish the following activities:*	*We expect that once accomplished these activities will produce the following evidence or service delivery:*	*We expect that if accomplished these activities will lead to the following changes in 1–3, then 4–6 years:*	*We expect that if accomplished these activities will lead to the following changes in 7–10 years:*

W. K. Kellogg Foundation. 2004. *Logic Model Develoment Guide.* Battle Creek, MI: Author. Illustration courtesy of The W. K. Kellogg Foundation, Battle Creek, Michigan.

between planned work (resources and activities) and intended results (outputs, outcomes, and impact). (See Figure 6.12.) Figure 6.13 shows an example of the Kellogg Logic Model prepared for a collaborative family-school program of information exchange activities (Hughes & Greenhough, 2006).

Phases of the Evaluation

An evaluation process uses evaluation questions to design a high-quality evaluation. Four major phases are essential for the evaluation of a collaborative school consultation program:

1. *Match expected outcomes with goals and activities of the program.* In matching expected outcomes with goals and activities of your program, each collaborative program will have its own particular goals and specific activities to help meet those goals. Assign specific measurable objectives or outcomes to each program activity.

2. *Ensure that the measures relate directly to the expected outcomes.* Select or design measures that do this. For example, if working on a volunteer community program, measure achievement gains for tutees, and possibly look at subject-matter grades. Interview students and parents about their thoughts about the impact of the program (see Bodgan & Biklen, 2003, for methodology). Survey community volunteer tutors (see Dillman, 2007, for methodology). The evaluation measures may use qualitative methodology (Bodgan & Biklen, 2006; Patton, 1997), quantitative methodology (Posavac & Carey, 2006), or mixed methods (Creswell & Plano-Clark, 2006; Mertens, 2005). Examples of quantitative data are surveys, enrollment figures, attendance figures, dropout rates, and test scores. Qualitative methods include interviews, focus groups, checklists, rubric scores, and open-ended survey questions.

FIGURE 6.13   Logic Model Evaluation Plan for Home-School Collaboration Project

RESOURCES	ACTIVITIES	OUTPUTS	SHORT- & LONG-TERM OUTCOMES	IMPACT
In order to accomplish our set of activities we will need the following:	*In order to address our problems or assets we will accomplish the following activities:*	*We expect that once accomplished these activities will produce the following evidence:*	*We expect that if accomplished these activities will lead to the following changes:*	*We expect that if accomplished these activities will lead to the following impact on home-school collaboration:*
■ Government policies (Every Child Matters: Change for Children) ■ Primary and secondary schools in Bristol and Cardiff ■ Teachers and administrators in target schools ■ Students and parents in target schools ■ Funding of the Home-School Knowledge Exchange (HSKE) Project	■ Video Activity—Video based on literacy teaching to inform parents of new literacy methods used at school and to encourage parents to do literacy activities at home (school-to-home communication). ■ Shoebox Activity—Students filled shoeboxes with items from home that were special to them; contents were used as part of the curriculum across all subjects (home-to-school communication).	■ Feedback from parents ■ Feedback from teachers ■ Demonstrated evidence of teachers' knowledge of out-of-school lives of their students ■ Demonstrated increased parent-child school-related interactions ■ Demonstrated increased parent-teacher interactions	■ Better communication between school and home ■ Increased parental appreciation and support of school learning activities ■ Parents learning about how reading and writing were taught ■ Teachers providing curriculum enrichment that is relevant to students' out-of-school lives ■ Improved trust and mutual understanding between teachers and parents	■ Increased trust between parents and teachers ■ Increased willingness to listen to parents and their priorities ■ Increased parental appreciation of educational methods ■ Increased parental support of school activities ■ Students see link of out-of-school lives with classroom and curriculum ■ Ongoing exchange of "funds of knowledge" between school and home

Based on Hughes, M., & Greenbough, P. (2006). Boxes, bags, and videotape: Enhancing home-school communication through knowledge exchange activities. *Educational Review, 58*(4), 471–487. Illustration courtesy of the W. K. Kellogg Foundation, Battle Creek, Michigan.

3. *Collect data, get good data, analyze data.* When the goals have been determined, list the types of data needed and decide collaboratively on ways of obtaining the data. Much of the data will exist within classrooms, or student files, or school computer data banks. The challenge is to determine what is needed and then plan a strategy for collecting and summarizing the data in a meaningful, time-efficient way.

Instrumentation and data collection should be put into place at the beginning of a project. Thereafter at the start of each new school year, the ways and means of evaluation should be reassessed and revised if necessary. A consultant who does not decide how to evaluate the program until the end of the school year will be working harder, not smarter, and opportunity for formative evaluation will be lost. Evaluators need to be assured that important aspects of the program get measured, and that the evaluation instruments are sensitive enough to pick up all outcomes that result from the project. An evaluation is only as good as the data. Incomplete, flawed, out-of-date, or irrelevant data lead to results that are not valid and in some instances just might be harmful. "Garbage in, garbage out" is a phrase frequently used by evaluators.

Summative evaluation procedures should be extensive enough to document achievement of each annual program goal. This language probably sounds familiar, for that is exactly what is required when an IEP is developed for a student. The similarity is not coincidental. Principles guiding IEP development must guide all good program development.

The evaluation should include at least one measure to document achievement of each program objective and a projected timeline for gathering the information. Many different sources of information should be used, including but not limited to:

- Direct observations of behavior
- Portfolios of student work
- Long-term projects
- Parent input
- Reports by related services personnel and support personnel reports
- Student self-assessment records
- Logs and journals of consultation activities
- Progress charts
- Interviews
- Videotaped conferences
- Anecdotal records
- Student grades
- Input from counselor and school psychologist
- Teacher portfolios
- Professional development activity evaluation data

Evaluation instruments and procedures must be as objective and unbiased as possible. Unfortunately, unbiased opinions and objective information are not easily obtained. For example, a consultant might ask consultees to complete checklists such as the ones presented in this book, but respondents may not be willing or able to offer objective opinions. As noted earlier, lack of objectivity can interfere in working with the special needs of students. Consultees may give high ratings indiscriminately to avoid losing a colleague's friendship or to cloak the reality of not knowing enough about the issue to provide a constructive response. Exaggerated ratings are of little benefit for evaluation purposes and if inaccurate they may be another example of an iatrogenic effect that compounds problems rather than creates solutions. For these reasons, consultants need information from multiple sources, in different circumstances within the school and home context, and at varying times throughout the school year.

Data collection activities must be congruent with the type of data to be collected. For example, evaluators could use a survey to obtain information about teachers' perceptions of the new parent-teacher center in the district. Or they could use an online survey system such as SurveyMonkey.com to e-mail a survey to teachers. It is essential to let teachers know why they are being asked for feedback about the center, and to inform them that their names will not be used in any reports that may be prepared using the data. Questions should relate to information that is important for improving or testing the program; co-educators will be more forthcoming if they are asked only for information that will indeed be used. Timing of data collection is a key element. Periods just before holidays or during the last week of school are not good for requesting information from busy educators and families. All who participate in the evaluation process must be thanked generously and sincerely.

The data analysis method must fit the chosen methodology. Some complex programs may require extensive databases and statistical programs. Evaluation personnel should check with the school district to find out what types of database and statistical programs are available. Stakeholders may be interested only in pre-post comparisons, tables with collected information, or charts that visually represent the results of the evaluation. Most common software packages have database programs that will convert databases to charts or tables. Involving stakeholders in making decisions about the representation of the data will help ensure that they remain interested and involved through the entire process so that the hard work of evaluation pays off with smart decisions.

4. *Using data for decision making about programs.* The final element of evaluation involves communicating or reporting the results of the evaluation in a manner that is useful. Evaluation has value only if the results will be used to facilitate improvement of programs or to develop better programs, lower the costs of the program, or improve methods of operation. Evaluation findings should be used to discover what works and what doesn't work. The data should promote self-reflection and evidence-based thinking, and point out actions that need to be taken—for example, curriculum revisions and adaptations, testing modifications and accommodations, reassignment of school personnel, reconfiguration of schedules, reallocation of funds, and so forth.

The report of evaluation findings should be constructed to answer the evaluation questions in specific ways. Providing graphs, tables, and a brief summary of the results of the evaluation is often sufficient to make the report useful for those reading it. Many evaluations include a request for input about the types of evaluation and kinds of reporting that the participants would find useful.

The following ten points summarize key elements to consider in the design of an effective evaluation plan for collaboration, consultation, and co-teaching activity:

1. The evaluation process should be ongoing.
2. Multiple sources of information should be used.
3. Valid and reliable methods of gathering information should be used.
4. It should be limited to gathering data that will answer pertinent questions and document attainment of consultation goals.
5. It should be realistic, diplomatic, and sensitive to diversity issues.

6. Legal and ethical procedures, including protection of privacy rights must be followed.
7. Anonymity of respondents should be maintained whenever possible, and they should be informed whether the data are to be reported as grouped data.
8. It needs to be cost-effective in terms of time and money (for example, whenever possible, use existing data).
9. Data that are collected must be put to useful purpose; if not, data should not be collected.
10. Formative evaluation should result in program change; summative evaluation should result in decision making about the program.

Self-Evaluation of Collaborative Consultation Skills

Important reasons for conducting self-evaluation are to examine one's own collaborative work and processes used, as well as to glean information for professional development. Self-evaluation, self-assessment, reflection, and self-direction are excellent methods of professional development for teachers. Without some type of self-evaluation, a consultant may perpetuate ineffective processes and the quality of the consultation may decline over time. The following suggestions for conducting a self-assessment are adapted from the work of Bailey (1981).

Gain a Philosophical Overview of Self-Assessment.   Understand that self-assessment is not synonymous with the accountability required by administrators. Its purpose is personal change and improvement and the results are not to be shared with supervisors unless you want to. Data should be collected in several consulting sessions with different types of consenting consultees and various problem situations.

Use Media for Self-Assessment.   An objective way of gaining feedback about one's behavior is to monitor it through use of audio- or videotaped material. These tips for preparing and analyzing videotapes are helpful:

- Set the consultee at ease by explaining the purpose of the videotape recording.
- Do a few trial runs before involving a consultee in order to become comfortable with the video camera and accustomed to seeing yourself on tape.
- Don't focus on traits that have nothing to do with the quality of consultation. Voice and visual image on tape are distorted, so don't worry about it.
- Observe or listen to the tape several times, each time focusing observations on just one or two behaviors.
- Tabulate behavior using a systematic observation method so the information can be interpreted meaningfully and progress followed objectively.
- Be sensitive to the rights of privacy of the consultee. Arrange the seating during a videotape recording session so that you face the camera and the consultee's back is to the camera.
- Do not show the tape without receiving signed permission from the consultee.

Identify the Important Consultation Skills to Be Observed.   Merely watching and listening to oneself with the help of media will not provide enough information to guide personal development. Specific skills must be targeted for recording the observation.

Checklists and rating forms such as the Consultant Behaviors Checklist, can be used to identify behaviors to observe while viewing or listening to the taped consulting sessions. These checklists were developed from lists of important consulting behaviors described by researchers in the field. (See Figures 6.14 and 6.15.)

View or Listen to Taped Consulting Sessions and Tabulate Observation Data. Systematic behavioral observation techniques discussed later in this chapter are useful for observing consultant behavior, just as they are useful in observing student behavior in the classroom. Tabulate only one or two behaviors in each viewing, perhaps starting with a

FIGURE 6.14   Collaborative Consultant Behaviors Checklist

Consultant _____   Observer _____   Date _____

	Yes	Needs Work	Does Not Apply
1. *Welcome*			
Sets comfortable climate	____	____	____
Uses commonly understood terms	____	____	____
Is nonjudgmental	____	____	____
Provides brief informal talk	____	____	____
Is pleasant	____	____	____
2. *Communication Exchange*			
Shares information	____	____	____
Is accepting	____	____	____
Is empathic	____	____	____
Identifies major issues	____	____	____
Keeps on task	____	____	____
Is perceptive, providing insight	____	____	____
Avoids jargon	____	____	____
Is encouraging	____	____	____
Gives positive reinforcement	____	____	____
Sets goals as agreed	____	____	____
Develops working strategy	____	____	____
Develops plan to implement strategy	____	____	____
Is friendly	____	____	____
3. *Interpretation of Communication*			
Seeks feedback	____	____	____
Demonstrates flexibility	____	____	____
Helps define problem	____	____	____
Helps consultee assume responsibility for plans	____	____	____
4. *Summarizing*			
Is concise	____	____	____
Is positive	____	____	____
Is clear	____	____	____
Sets another meeting if needed	____	____	____
Is affirming	____	____	____

FIGURE 6.15   Consultee Assessment of Consultation and Collaboration

Please evaluate your use of the consulting teacher service provided in the _____ program by providing the following information. Respond with:

1 = Not at all   2 = A little   3 = Somewhat   4 = Considerably   5 = Much

1. The consulting teacher provides useful information.   _____

2. The consulting teacher understands my school environment and teaching situation.   _____

3. The consulting teacher listens to my ideas.   _____

4. The consulting teacher helps me identify useful resources that help my students'   _____
    special needs.

5. The consulting teacher explains ideas clearly.   _____

6. The consulting teacher fits easily into the school setting.   _____

7. The consulting teacher increases my confidence in the special programs.   _____

8. I value consulting and collaborating with the consulting teacher.   _____

9. I have requested collaboration time with the consulting teacher.   _____

10. I plan to continue seeking opportunities to consult and collaborate with the   _____
    consulting teacher.

Other comments: _____

_____

verbal behavior such as the number of "OKs" or a nonverbal behavior such as looking away from the consultee. After tabulating the targeted behaviors, summarize strengths and note behaviors that should be improved.

Write Down Goals and Objectives.   Prioritize the behaviors needing change and write behavioral objectives for them. Remember to state some type of criterion such as saying "OK" no more than two times in a 20-minute consultation session. Include dates for achievement of each objective.

Select Strategies to Help Make Needed Changes.   Formulate the strategies from material presented in other chapters of this text.

Gather Feedback and Chart Progress in Achieving Goals.   Periodically check to determine whether there is progress in the self-selected area for change. It is very easy to believe erroneously that the change has taken place if this step is bypassed. If goals focus on verbal skills, audiotapes probably will be sufficient for follow-up data, but if they include nonverbal skills, use of videotapes should continue.

When a Criterion Is Met, a Self-Reward Is Due for a Job Well Done!   The objective data can be shared with a supervisor. The consultant may wish to chart consultation growth just as student progress is documented. Self-assessment should be an ongoing process propelled by realistic expectations.

The value of engaging in self-evaluation of one's consultation is illustrated by this journal entry of a graduate student in collaborative consultation:

Before involvement in the consulting project at this university, I had never seriously examined my communication skills. The videotaping assignment has been the hardest for me; however, I have come to realize the importance of it and I have gained a better insight into areas that can be improved.

The first videotape recording I made with a consultee was a real eye-opener, revealing my lack of skill in handling resistance. The second recording surprised the consultee, as she realized that during the consultation she had thought of a solution to the problem for herself. The third videotape revealed more areas I needed to work on: conflict resolution, assertiveness, and controlling my facial responses. I feel I did a good job of using a problem-solving technique, and the best part was to hear two consultees say they were going to use it themselves in problem situations. They felt it helped them focus on the problem and think of practical solutions. It gave them a base from which to work.

Setting time limits is something I'm not comfortable doing. I would rather allow the consultee enough time to work through feelings and identify the issues. However, looking back over my consultation log, I see that six of the consultations took more than forty-five minutes and might well have concluded earlier if I had set time limits. Such lengthy consultations probably will not work on an everyday basis. Realization of this is an example of reflective thinking!

Now that I have identified this baseline of strengths and weaknesses, I have set the following goals I want to achieve by the end of the school year:

1. *Reduce resistance from consultees to no more than one time in twenty*
2. *Resolve conflicts at least 80 percent of the time*
3. *Engage in active listening 100 percent of the time*
4. *Use assertive behavior during consultation 100 percent of the time*
5. *Eliminate inappropriate facial responses*
6. *Practice more problem-solving techniques so I will have a variety from which to choose the most appropriate one for the situation and context*

I will videotape consultation episodes every nine weeks and tabulate the target behaviors to see if I am making progress in reaching my goals. In addition, I will use an assessment checklist to get feedback from my consultees every nine weeks. I will periodically interview consultees after consultation episodes to gather more immediate feedback about the target behaviors I am trying to improve. (See checklists provided in Figures 6.14 and 6.15.)

Teacher Portfolios for Self-Assessment

Portfolio assessment is a vehicle for authentic assessment that educators can use to assess their own skills and continuing development. A teacher portfolio focuses on the educator's learning. It is useful vehicle for evaluating progress in collaborative experiences and team interactions, as well as in co-teaching and partnerships with co-educators. It is multidimensional and authentic in purpose and task, and contributes to an ongoing learning process. The material can be evaluated, streamlined, and added to from year to year as visible evidence of growth and improvement.

When educators develop professional portfolios they demonstrate the value and importance of authentic assessment to evaluate their own professional growth and development. A portfolio can be presented as an example of productivity when it is time for an educator to be evaluated by supervisor or administrator. Portfolios can be tools for sharing ideas during team meetings and professional development activities and sparking discussions about reforms needed in education and excellent practices to be replicated. They might also be shared with students and parents as models for student-developed portfolios. Their value as a record of professional activities and experiences has not been fully plumbed. Last but not to be overlooked—they can be fun to design and maintain.

The mainstay of assessment by portfolio is development of sound rubrics. This could be accomplished with several colleagues who want to prepare their own teaching portfolios. As suggested in Chapter 5, designing a rubric for a collaborative activity is a good way to engage in meaningful collaboration.

Possibilities for teacher portfolio products abound. A few are lesson plans that worked well; videotapes of classroom activity highlights; sample tests; particularly effective worksheets or packets; an original teaching or grading technique; sketch of an unusual bulletin board so it won't be forgotten; list of professional books read; any articles published in newsletters, newspapers, or other professional outlets; photos of special class sessions; original computer software that worked well; a highly effective management technique; and notes from parents or students that were reinforcing. Inclusions in the portfolio that are especially relevant to collaborative consultation and teamwork are documentation of consultation episodes (coded for confidentiality); descriptions of team-teaching activities; stimulating discussions or collaborative activities with co-educators; interesting contributions made to one's teaching and student learning by related services and support personnel;[1] special achievements by students; the list could go on and on.

■ ■ ■ ■ ■ ▬▬

APPLICATION 6.2
DEVELOPING A TEACHER PORTFOLIO

Develop a plan for your own teacher portfolio. Include a table of contents and a rubric for showing growth and progress toward your professional goals. Be sure to record a number of collaborative experiences in your collection. Decorate the folio in your personal style. It could be fun as well as rewarding to engage in this project in collaboration with co-educators, discussing elements to put in the portfolio, and in particular developing the rubric for the portfolio assessment and perhaps some parts of it such as co-teaching skills.

[1]One teacher of students with learning and behavioral disorders learned that the school custodian was an expert on bees. Several of her students were keenly interested in a science project on apiaries and apiarists. The teacher consulted with the custodian and together they made plans for a classroom presentation by the custodian. Multiple positive outcomes resulted from this collaboration and were entered into her portfolio.

Records of Collaborative Consultation Activities

Administrators are interested in more than how effectively consultants communicate or engage in problem solving. They want to know about practical issues such as how the consultant uses time, how many consultees have been helped, the types of problems addressed, and whether the consultation services were helpful to the consultees. Consultants should keep records of consultation activities in order to answer these types of questions. The consultation journal format in this chapter (Figure 6.8) is useful for documenting these data. It may be productive also to check with one's administrator to find out what specific information would be best. Busy consultants should not spend time collecting information that is not wanted or needed.

BENEFITS FROM EVALUATION OF COLLABORATIVE SCHOOL CONSULTATION

Teacher involvement in consultation and collaboration must not be perceived as a sign of weakness or inadequacy. Instead, consultees should be commended for taking advantage of services provided to help both educators and students succeed. Involvement in consultation and collaboration must be rated as a strength on the performance evaluations of school personnel by administrators and supervisors. School personnel should be involved in developing and implementing consultation practices and assessing their outcomes, and should conduct self-assessment of their consultation and collaboration. Self-assessment is sometimes a painful but always a necessary practice for the consultant. The consultation log earlier in this chapter includes a brief self-assessment.

Videotaping, having a colleague observe and report, and often just reflecting on one's habits are all potentially helpful ways of growing professionally. Reflection leads to insights about oneself, prompting changes in self-concept, changes in perception of an event or person, or plans for changing some behavior (Canning, 1991). One speech/language pathologist analyzed her emerging consultation skills this way:

> In my early perception of consulting I viewed myself as the expert. Experience has taught me I am not. Expert language usually is understood by very few. Knowing how to frame good questions is an invaluable tool. I used to think I knew what was best for the child. Experience again has shown me this is not so—we must all get our respective "what's best" on the table and mediate. I felt that I needed to have all the workable solutions to the problem at hand, but this was assuming too much. I thought everyone likes and respects the "expert" and wants his or her help. I now perceive my task as one of earning the right to become part of the planning for any child. This means I must be as knowledgeable as possible, not only in my own field, but about the total environment (physical and mental) of each child. I am still learning that effective intervention takes time and careful planning.

Figures 6.15 (on page 214) and 6.16 provide tools for assessing the collaborative consultations. Other self-assessment questions the consultant can ask include:

- What solutions have I offered for discussion?
- What documentation have I gathered to support my opinions?

FIGURE 6.16   Checklist for Evaluating Collaborative Consultation

Dear _____,

Please take a few minutes to help me improve my consulting skills by completing this checklist. Any additional comments you wish to make will be greatly appreciated. Thank you!

_____(name)_____

	A Strength	OK	Needs Improving
1. Helped me to be comfortable collaborating	____	____	____
2. Communicated clearly	____	____	____
3. Used our time productively	____	____	____
4. Listened well	____	____	____
5. Asked facilitating questions	____	____	____
6. Showed understanding of my role	____	____	____
7. Demonstrated flexibility	____	____	____
8. Presence/time not disruptive	____	____	____
9. I want to work together again	____	____	____
10. Other comments:			

- Can I list the questions I want to ask the consultee?
- Can I listen and work cooperatively on the problem?
- Can I be honest about my feelings toward the student, the problem, and the personnel involved?
- Will I follow through on the plan?
- Will I document the efficacy of the plan?
- Will I try new methods and strategies?
- Will I persist in the plan?
- Will I give feedback to the consultee about the situation?
- Am I willing to ask for help or advice?

ETHICS FOR MANAGING AND EVALUATING COLLABORATIVE SCHOOL CONSULTATION

When co-educators engage in interactive situations, they will want to keep the needs of their colleagues in mind. Ethical climates for collaboration will nurture teachers who are experiencing stress and perhaps verging on burnout from the profession. It is often the accumulation of mountains of little things, not big crises, that push professional educators into disillusionment. Caring, supportive colleagues can make all the difference. Many of the tips in this chapter, when carried out with camaraderie and team spirit, will convey caring and respect for the overwhelmed novice teacher, the burdened administrator, or the discouraged veteran teacher.

Co-educators must respect the views and the rights of their colleagues who do not want to collaborate and prefer not to co-teach. They must tolerate kindly the "fly in the ointment"—perhaps the teacher in the building who does not want to be involved in a student portfolio plan or who will have no part of a teacher-developed block schedule that allows for co-teaching. The saying "you can catch more flies with honey than vinegar" comes to mind, and a hesitant teacher just might be won over eventually.

When collaborative consultants visit a teacher's classroom, they should conduct their observations discreetly and without judgment. Many teachers find it hard to carry on comfortably when they and their classroom environment are under observation by other professional educators. Respect for privacy and confidentiality of information are essential characteristics of the collaborative environment.

More evaluation of collaborative consultation programs and better research to ascertain the outcomes of the programs are very much needed. Ethical practices in this field demand them.

TIPS FOR MANAGING AND EVALUATING COLLABORATIVE SCHOOL CONSULTATION

1. At the end of the year, write thank-you notes to school personnel you have worked with, including principals, secretaries, and custodians. When writing notes to colleagues, sign your name in a distinctive color on pads of an individualized design. Send a note on a "reminder" memo, and staple a treat such as a bag of nuts, or a Valentine cookie, or a doughnut, to it. Remember those who collaborate with you in special ways by delivering a treat to their room along with a brief note of appreciation.

2. Color-code folders for schools if you serve several. Use a file box with a card for each day to list reminders, and a schedule book. Keep an idea file of filler activities.

3. Use tubs for storage of materials. Plan ahead and put materials in the tub for one week, one month, a season, or a thematic unit.

4. Have a retrieval box in a certain place for receiving borrowed items that are returned. Keep a checkout catalog so you will know where your materials are. When materials are due, remove due-cards for the buildings where you will be that week and collect the materials while there.

5. Listen to conversations in the workroom, lunchroom, and faculty meetings. When a topic surfaces for which you have materials, offer to share them. Prepare a list of instructional material that is for loaning and distribute it. Make sure grade level and sample objectives of the material are given.

6. Don't schedule yourself so tightly that you have no time for informal interactions and impromptu consultation. These can open the door for more intensive and productive collaboration. Also, be even more protective of colleagues' time than you are of your own, and make good use of it.

7. Furnish treats often. (For very nutrition-conscious schools, make the treats vegetables or fruit.)

8. Make concise checklists for procedural activities, such as general items to tell parents at conferences, or items to tell new students and their parents.

9. If doing a demonstration lesson, give the classroom teacher a paper stating the activity name, type of activity it is, and learning objectives. State your name at the bottom and specify that it comes from "Consultant ___'s Lesson Plan," thereby establishing your identity.

10. Go to classroom teachers and ask *them* for help in their area of expertise. Ask for a copy of something you have seen that would be a good addition for your file, but be sure they mean for you to use it or share it before you do so.

11. Generate alternatives to having more and more meetings, try them out, and get input from colleagues on their value. When a meeting *is* needed, and it promises to be a difficult one, on the night before the meeting try visualizing a successful one in which everything goes very well.

12. Visit other schools and make notes on organizational systems and management techniques that could be incorporated into your system. Then prepare a summary sheet for colleagues on your return.

13. Find time to collaborate by exploring innovative ways of "making" more time and using it wisely. Schedule common lunch or preparation periods; in large districts increase class size by just one and use surplus funds to hire substitutes; have teachers match a period of early dismissal time with their contribution of equal time; have students involved in community service one afternoon a week while teachers meet.

14. Develop ways of working smarter, not harder, such as having information-exchange pools with other teachers, sharing learning centers and packets with colleagues in other attendance centers, and gathering free resources from commercial business and industry.

15. Promote instances of high-quality consultation and collaboration, not just the frequency and time spent in the activities.

16. As a consultant, portray yourself as assistant to the teacher.

17. Become more visible, visiting each classroom and making positive comments about what is going on there.

18. Always have an ear open to opportunities to help out, and spin off helping situations to become more established as a consulting teacher.

19. Be realistic and understanding about the demands that are placed on classroom teachers, administrators, and parents in fulfilling *their* roles.

20. Be realistic about what consultants can do, and celebrate even small successes.

21. Keep school personnel wanting more consultation services, making services so valuable that if they were taken away from the schools, the role and its services would be missed.

22. Keep providing benefits for them. Again, "What can I do for you and your students that you do not have time or resources to do?" is the operative question.

23. Identify successful, exemplary consultation and collaboration practices, *especially* when they occur in your school district!

24. Work with a group of collaborating colleagues to write a guide on the use of consultation and collaboration. Present it to new faculty members, and periodically conduct refresher sessions for all professional development activities.

25. Send notes of appreciation to consultees regularly.
26. Do not expect a uniformly high level of acceptance and involvement from all, but keep aiming for it.

CHAPTER REVIEW

1. Stress that is encountered in many human service roles can lead to burnout and subsequent attrition from the field. Positive attitudes, health maintenance, supportive networks, realistic goals, relaxation, environmental changes, and taking control of one's life will minimize stress and help prevent burnout, fizzle-out, rust-out, and coast-out among consultants and teachers.

2. Careful management of time and energy decreases stress and increases productivity for those in consultative roles. School personnel will want to establish goals to manage their resources, identify and remediate time-wasters, use positive time-management strategies, and take very good care of themselves.

3. Meetings, interviews, and observations must be kept as efficient and positive as possible for both productivity and morale. With careful planning each of these activities can be more productive for consultants and collaborators. It is important to provide a comfortable meeting environment, prepare an agenda, keep minutes of decisions and plans, and assess the success of the meeting. When consultants observe in classrooms, they should demonstrate caring attitudes and provide positive support for those being observed.

4. Systems for record-keeping and resource management are necessary for busy consultants who serve many schools. Consultants must keep records and materials in order, maintain confidentiality, and be on the lookout for helpful material with which to consult and collaborate. Consulting journals and notebooks are tools that facilitate management of complex responsibilities. Personalized touches for memos and messages help develop rapport with consultees.

5. An evaluation program is essential for documenting the effectiveness of any educational program, making improvements, and defending the quality of the program to administrators and other decision makers. During the initial stages of program development, consultants should create a plan for ongoing evaluation. Formative and summative information of the context, processes, and content of consultation must be gathered throughout the program and the school year in the most efficient manner possible. Methods of gathering data should come from multiple sources and should be as objective and unbiased as possible. Consultants need to engage in systematic self-assessment, in order to gain information for improving their consultation skills. They should also keep careful records of their activities, to justify the program to decision makers.

6. Ethical concerns include caring, valuing, respecting, and supporting collaborative colleagues. Evaluation of collaborative school consultation can show needed change and justify the approach for serving exceptional learning needs.

TO DO AND THINK ABOUT

1. Discuss some record-keeping and managerial tasks that most people really do not like to do, such as preparing income tax returns, and consider ways that activities such as these could be made less unpleasant and more manageable. Then consider how these techniques could be used creatively by school consultants.

2. Describe the "perfect" meeting. What would need to be done in order for this meeting to transpire?

3. Design a weekly and daily planning sheet that has space for stating goals, listing activities in categories, prioritizing the list, and estimating times for accomplishing the activities. Try your planning sheets, and share them with others if you found them helpful.

4. Conduct a time analysis to diagnose time-management problems you may have. Use one of the methods described in this chapter or develop your own.

5. Create ideas for the following management tools, and if your present situation warrants, construct them and try them out:

   ■ A logo for personalized note pads or memo sheets that will identify you and feature school consultation in a positive, collaborative spirit

   ■ An observation checklist that would work in your school situation

   ■ A consultation log or journal format to record the consultation and follow-through, as well as a brief assessment of the consultation

   ■ A table of contents for a notebook in which to organize information, data, and material needed to carry out the school consultation role

   ■ A system for cataloging materials to be shared with consultees, and for checking the material in and out

6. Name several consumer and decision-making target groups within a school district who are likely to ask for data to support a consultation program. What would be the most effective formats for presenting the data to each stakeholder group for its purposes?

7. Develop an evaluation plan for consultation service during the coming school year in your school setting.

8. Conduct a self-assessment of your own consultation skills. Give careful attention to each step of the process. Make an effort to videotape the consultation in a real or simulated experience periodically. Chart behavioral data to demonstrate progress on at least two specific objectives.

9. Use the consultation log in Figure 6.8 for at least six weeks. Meet with other consultants to modify the forms as needed, and then use the revised forms for the remainder of the school term.

10. Once a week, make it a point to take ten or fifteen minutes at the end of the day to reflect on all the important things that happened in the classroom that day. Notice how observant one becomes after engaging in this practice for a while.

ADDITIONAL READINGS AND RESOURCES

Bogdan, R., & Biklen, S. (2006). *Qualitative research for education: An introduction to theory and methods* (5th ed.). Boston: Allyn & Bacon.

Dillman, D. A. (2007). *Mail and Internet surveys: The tailored design method* (2nd ed.). Hoboken, NJ: Wiley.

Haynes, M. E. (1998). *Effective meeting skills: A practical guide for more productive meetings.* Los Altos, CA: Crisp.

Kozoll, C. E. (1982). *Time management for educators,* Fastback #175. Bloomington, IN: Phi Delta Kappa Educational Foundation.

Sapolsky, R. (1994). *Why zebras don't get ulcers: A guide to stress, stress-related diseases, and coping.* New York: W. H. Freeman.

Stewart, R. A., & Brendefur, J. L. (2005). Fusing lesson study and authentic achievement: A model for teacher collaboration. *Phi Delta Kappan, 86*(9), 681–687.

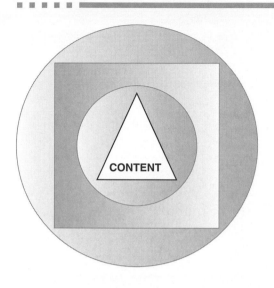

PART III

CONTENT FOR WORKING TOGETHER AS CO-EDUCATORS

CONTENT

Part III, the content section covers the following topics: Chapter 7 outlines techniques for collaborative instruction of students with exceptional learning needs in a consultative, collaborative, or co-teaching mode; then, Chapter 8 addresses working as co-educators with families of students who have special needs; and finally, Chapter 9 considers productive interactions with many types and configurations of culturally and linguistically diverse groups.

Co-teaching takes place in school contexts that adopt a supportive philosophy, adhere to preferences and perspectives of the teachers, and emanate from a sound model for collaborative endeavor. Communication skills are an integral component, as are problem finding and problem-solving techniques, and organization and management skills. Evaluation is vital to determine the success of co-teaching.

Family partnerships with parents as co-educators are best developed in supportive school contexts with acceptance and commitment by all as important elements for success. Excellent process skills help to assure that success. Family members also must be encouraged to participate in evaluation of collaborative services.

Respect for diverse populations is a major aspect of effective collaboration. Recognizing and valuing diversity promotes successful interactions. This catalyzes effective problem solving and efficient implementation of educational plans and resources.

CHAPTER SEVEN

CONTENT:
Co-Teaching

Collaborating and Co-Teaching for Students Who Have Special Needs

Over the years educators have increasingly recognized and accepted as reality that student abilities and needs lie along a continuum of learner differences rather than fall into discrete, separate categories. It follows that there is no uniform instructional strategy for every student's needs; alternatives must be available in order to provide accessible curriculum and appropriate instruction for variations among individual learners. Educators are challenged to differentiate learning goals for students' special needs and to find or generate adaptations when necessary. Adaptations can be in the form of accommodations (aids and supports) or modifications (altered goals and expectations).

Co-planning and co-teaching are effective processes for providing differentiated curriculum in inclusive classrooms. Such curriculum may be remedial, review, student-interest based, accelerated, enriched, or a combination of differentiations. Regardless of the intervention or interventions to be used, it is important for special educators and general educators to work together so that appropriate differentiated curriculum and alternatives for learning are developed and made available to fit *all* students' needs.

FOCUSING QUESTIONS

1. How does planning for co-teaching differ from planning for typical lessons?

2. What effect can the Universal Design for Learning (UDL) have on teachers who are working together for students with disabilities?

3. What are some common approaches to co-teaching?

4. Why is it important to inform all persons involved in the student's instruction about the goals, adaptations, enrichments, and assessments included in the student's IEP?

5. What are appropriate accommodations and modifications for students with disabilities?

6. What other instructional strategies and supports will benefit students with disabilities and students with advanced abilities in general classrooms?

KEY TERMS

acceleration
adapted outcomes
adapting tests
adapting text materials
co-planning
co-teaching
curriculum accommodations
curriculum adaptations
curriculum compacting
curriculum modifications
differentiated instruction

digital text
enhanced outcomes
enrichment
facilitator
flexible pacing
functional outcomes
Interactive Lesson Planning
    model
parallel teaching approach
peer tutors
remedial instruction

Response to Intervention
    (RTI)
scaffolding
self-advocacy
Station Teaching approach
study strategies
Teach and Monitor
    approach
team teaching approach
Universal Design for Learning
    (UDL)

UNIVERSAL DESIGN FOR LEARNING

The Universal Design for Learning (UDL) paradigm features flexible curriculum development, teaching, learning, and assessment to accommodate individual differences. Rather than providing remediation for students so that they can learn from a set curriculum, UDL recognizes that there is no one optimal solution for everyone. It includes alternatives that make curriculum accessible and appropriate for individuals with different backgrounds, learning styles, abilities, and disabilities in widely varied learning contexts (Center for Applied Special Technology, www.cast.org). With such a curriculum, special educators and general educators must work together to ensure that they select appropriate alternatives that address unique needs of students. When curriculum alternatives are insufficient for individual students, or when non-UDL curriculum is used, the special educator has an additional challenge of finding or creating adaptations to accommodate, and in some cases modify, the learning goals for students in accordance with their Individualized Educational Plans (IEPs).

Whether or not the classroom educator is using UDL curriculum, co-planning and co-teaching are important roles for collaborating consultants. This chapter presents five aspects of working together for students with special needs who learn differently:

1. Planning and delivering differentiated instruction
2. Planning individualized alternatives for certain students
3. Planning and making adaptations
4. Planning remedial instruction
5. Planning for other instructional strategies and supports

SCENARIO 7.A

Lori (Secondary Classroom Teacher):   Mark, you were going to fill me in on last week's staff development session about Universal Design for Learning that I missed. Is this a good time?

Mark (Secondary Classroom Teacher):   Sure. It'll be good for me to collect my thoughts and try to explain it, because I think you and I might want to work together to give some of its aspects a try with our classes. It was presented as a collection of best practices that are to be strategically placed at each phase of the teaching and learning process. They maximize learning and give all students access to the curriculum. Thinking about the needs in our inclusive classes, that has appeal, don't you think?

Lori: So we wouldn't make adaptations for certain students after the fact, but plan lessons at the front end so that they're accessible to the broad spectrum of students we have?

Mark: That's the main idea I took away from the session. The overall concept is an outgrowth of the universal design movement in architecture. As you know, architecture is my true love, so I really related to that. As a result of the Americans with Disabilities Act, the universal design movement shelved the "one size fits all" mentality about architecture and the environment to one that's precisely the opposite—multiple ways of getting in, out, and around buildings and functioning successfully in the environment. Regardless of whether someone can see, hear, walk, read, or speak, appropriate alternatives are provided so that anyone who can't do what others might be able to do can experience the environment in a fair and equitable way.

Lori: So this brick-and-mortar plan for using physical space became a concept that works for curriculum. That's interesting.

Mark: Yes, UDL provides supports for students in the classroom and reduces the barriers curriculum often throws up that shut them off from learning. It maintains high achievement standards for all learners, too. Here, I have an extra copy of the handout from the session that explains what the presenters called multiple means for using UDL.

Aspects of Universal Learning Design

The paradigm for teaching, learning, assessment, and curriculum development that emerged in the 1990s when the Center for Applied Special Technology (CAST) coined the term *Universal Design for Learning* (UDL) is a refinement of differentiated instruction (Pisha & Coyne, 2001). It calls for:

■ *Multiple means of representation,* meaning that whatever content or information is to be learned can be represented in different ways. For example, a teacher can have many books or Web sites at different reading levels to deliver the same information. Or a teacher can use lecture to deliver information, but also provide visuals of main points, guided notes, and/or an audio file for students to access at a later time.

■ *Multiple means of engagement,* tapping into learners' interests and offering practice opportunities that provide appropriate challenges for each student. Just like when a child is learning to ride a bike for the first time and the supervising adult needs to determine the right amount of support—when to remove the training wheels and how long to hold on while running alongside—teachers need to find and implement a scaffold that provides the right amount of support students need while they acquire and practice new skills. This involves creating many pathways for students to actually learn the material presented. Some students may benefit from small-group learning opportunities, others may require more focused practice with precise feedback, and still others may benefit from working independently. Some students will need to write, some will need to talk through ideas before they understand, and others may need to represent their learning physically.

■ *Multiple means of expression,* providing learners with alternatives for demonstrating what they have learned. Again, the creation of many paths is key. Some students are good test-takers, whereas others are not. Some students write well and other students express themselves better orally. Most learning objectives can be manifested in multiple ways. Giving choices within a framework of options will likely provide increased motivation for students to participate meaningfully and demonstrate what they have learned.

The flexible UDL curriculum provides alternatives to address the broad range of learner differences. With this type of curriculum, it is imperative that special educators and general educators work together to ensure that appropriate alternatives are selected to address unique student needs. General education teachers are often the content and grade-level experts, whereas special education teachers possess advanced training in matching specialized teaching methods and learning strategies to specific student learning needs. In other words, general educators are in the best position to determine the big ideas that all students need to learn in their content area or grade level and special educators can help determine if those goals are appropriate for individual students and suggest alternatives to teaching, practicing, and demonstrating their knowledge when necessary. As noted earlier, if curriculum alternatives are insufficient for individual students, or if non-UDL curriculum is used, then the special education teacher has the additional challenge and responsibility of finding or creating accommodations, and in some cases modifying the learning goals for students with disabilities in accordance with their IEPs and sharing that information with others directly involved in the students' education.

PLANNING AND DELIVERING DIFFERENTIATED INSTRUCTION

Co-teaching (two or more teachers planning and delivering instruction) by special education and general education teachers creates new challenges for planning lessons in general classrooms. Without co-planning, co-teaching often involves a special educator helping the classroom teacher, or the classroom teacher helping the special educator, or "turn-taking" at best. This arrangement brings little satisfaction to either teacher and is not likely to result in the high-quality student outcomes that educators and parents want. Reinhiller (1996) proposes that co-teaching is both art and talent, and is now widely accepted as an appropriate model for collaboration.

Typical Lesson Planning

Special educators and general educators in traditional roles typically plan lessons differently from one another. General classroom teachers usually plan for groups of students whereas special education teachers tend to plan for individuals. Research conducted by a

Joint Committee on Teacher Planning for Students with Disabilities (1995) indicated that general education teachers do not individualize instruction as a rule, although they might differentiate by planning for *all, most,* and *a few* students. They do not typically engage in a linear planning process of going from objectives to activities followed by determining evaluation methods, even though they may know how to use that type of planning. They tend to start by selecting a theme or topic for a lesson and then planning content and activities for the entire class or large group.

Special educators, on the other hand, are trained, even required by federal law, to base lesson plans on individualized learner goals. Federal laws for individuals with disabilities require multidisciplinary teams to develop plans for individuals (IEPs). The planning steps are based on traditional, linear lesson planning models—goals, objectives, activities, and evaluation. This linear process may not be the best way for co-teachers to plan lessons, nor does it reflect the way teachers typically plan lessons (Joint Committee on Teacher Planning for Students with Disabilities, 1995). General classroom teachers obviously are concerned about student learning, but they must keep their groups of students engaged in activities throughout the school day for the sake of classroom order and whole-group learning. The challenge for co-teachers is to reconcile the individualized and group planning processes for the benefit of *all* students.

Stewart and Brendefur (2005), in their study of collaboration among teacher teams, were told by participants that they found power in collaborative planning and found value in observing colleagues teach. Collaboration helped to organize teachers' thoughts about teaching a lesson and to bring instruction to a higher level with more student-centered lesson planning.

Co-Planning Lessons

An interactive model for planning differentiated instruction that reflects the realities of current classroom contexts and students with special needs who are included in the classroom is shown in Figure 7.1. This interactive lesson planning model provides for three groups—one with nearly all students, another with most students, and a third with just some students. As a result, the model can help co-teachers plan lessons (Dyck, Pemberton, Woods, & Sundbye, 1996).

This model (Dyck et al., 1996) does not follow the linear approach of many planning models. It allows teachers to plan activities, objectives, and assessments concurrently or in varying orders depending on the situation. Co-teachers can begin planning at any point in the model or they can choose to use only parts of it. Therefore it does not require that each objective must be tied to a separate activity, as is usually the case in a linear planning mode. An activity can address several objectives and assessments. Likewise, one objective can be addressed by several activities and assessments. In all instances, the lesson theme, topic, or goal, often determined by the textbook, is the common element in the plan.

Co-teachers using the model answer the following questions when planning a lesson:

- What is the theme, topic, or goal of the lesson?
- What content is in the textbook and/or printed curriculum guide that addresses this theme, topic, or goal?

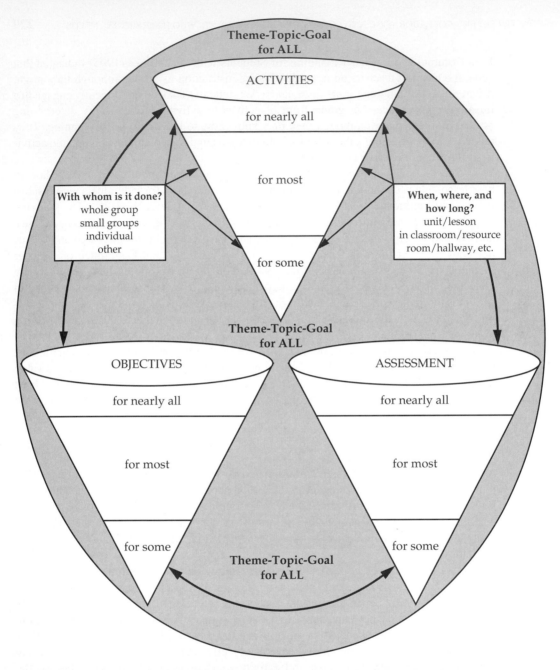

FIGURE 7.1   Interactive Lesson Planning Model

- What parts of that content are useful to and can be learned by *all* or *nearly all* students in the class?
- What parts of that content are useful to and can be learned by *most* students in the class?
- What parts of that content are useful to and can be learned by only *some* individual students in the class?
- Which students are not likely to benefit from any of that content?

- How will the activities take place—whole group, small groups, or individual, etc.?
- Who will be in each group or activity?
- What activities will keep *each* student motivated and busy?
- When, where, and for how long will this lesson plan be taught?
- Who is primarily responsible for each of the activities and for the assessments?

The answers to these questions form a basis for differentiating activities, objectives and assessments.

Delivering Differentiated Instruction

A key element of co-teaching is the shared responsibility of the teachers in both planning and delivering instruction. Co-teaching usually occurs for a set period of time such as one class period each day, certain days of the week, or for one lesson topic. Some teachers have been misled to believe that co-teaching is necessary for every inclusion situation and that students should never be taken out of the general classroom for special help. However, co-teaching should only be used when it is the best option for meeting the needs of a significant number of students. Friend and Bursuck (1996) note:

> It is relatively expensive (that is, the cost of two teachers with one group of students) and should be reserved for situations in which the number of students with disabilities in a class justifies the presence of two teachers, or the class is one in which all students with disabilities enroll (for example, in high school, it may be U.S. history). (pp. 86–87)

Preparation for Co-Teaching

Teachers need to prepare the classroom before implementing co-teaching. They need to discuss their views on teaching and learning and resolve any major differences. (Refer to Chapter 2 for that discussion on differences in perspectives and preferences.) They also need to agree on classroom rules and routines during co-teaching. In addition, they should agree on how grades will be assigned to students. Other matters to discuss are the role of paraeducators and substitute teachers during co-teaching, how to inform parents of the new approach, and most importantly, a schedule for planning time together at least once weekly.

■ ■ ■ ■ ■ ▬▬▬▬▬▬▬▬▬▬▬▬▬▬▬▬▬▬▬▬▬▬▬▬▬▬▬▬▬▬

APPLICATION 7.1
VARIATIONS IN TEACHER PERSPECTIVES

With colleagues or classmates, brainstorm to compile a list of the kinds of classroom misbehaviors that bother teachers and disrupt student learning. For starters, put on the list: Getting out of seats; talking; making noises; clowning; calling out; milling around after the bell; calling names; dropping things intentionally; passing notes; using put-downs or sarcasms; cursing; being habitually late; and so forth. Then discuss the importance of those on the list through the lenses of teachers' perspectives. What differences surface about importance and possible responses or actions to take? Then discuss how these variations in teacher perspective might affect co-teaching relationships.

Selecting the Best Co-Teaching Approach

Co-teachĬers can use one of several approaches to present their lessons to heterogeneous groups and they should vary the approaches often. Some examples of approaches are One Teaching and One Assisting; Teach and Monitor; Parallel Teaching; Station Teaching; and Team Teaching. Vaughn, Schumm, and Arguelles (1997), Bauwens and Hourcade (1997), and Reinhiller (1996) provide descriptions of other co-teaching arrangements.

Teach and Monitor.   One of the most common approaches is for both teachers to be in the classroom during instruction, but one of them takes primary responsibility for lecturing or presenting the lesson. The other teacher helps monitor performance of students and provides additional assistance to the students who need it. This approach does not require as much advanced planning as other approaches and is simple to implement. However, the teacher who circulates around the room could easily begin to feel like a "teacher's aide." One parent recently reported that her child came home from school saying they had a new "student teacher" in her room. In reality, the "student teacher" was the special education teacher who was co-teaching in the classroom. This observation is not provided to minimize the role of "student teachers" but to illustrate the point that both teachers might not be recognized as co-equals by the students and as such may not be equally effective in providing instruction. So in order to minimize potential limitations of the Teach and Monitor approach to co-teaching, the teachers should alternate roles regularly.

Variations of this approach are Speak and Chart or Speak and Add. With Speak and Chart, one teacher lectures while the other writes the outline or notes on the chalkboard. With Speak and Add, one teacher lectures while the other jumps in to add or clarify points from time to time. Duet is a planned variation of Speak and Add in which each teacher takes turns presenting portions of the material in a coordinated fashion. These co-teaching structures often become blended, as the example of Lori and Mark's co-teaching experience later in this chapter will illustrate (see Scenario 7.B on pp. 234–236).

Parallel Teaching.   A second form of co-teaching is parallel teaching. Both teachers plan a lesson, but they split the class and each delivers the lesson to a smaller group at the same time. Parallel teaching might also require parallel curriculum, that is, both teachers teach a similar topic but one teacher teaches it at a more advanced level than the other. For example, after having read a story to the entire class, one teacher takes the highest achievers and works on a dramatization of the story while the other teacher works with the other students on vocabulary meaning and retelling the story sequence.

Station Teaching.   A third method of co-teaching is Station Teaching. This approach occurs when teachers co-plan instructional activities that are presented in "stations" or learning centers. Each station presents a different aspect of the lesson and allows teachers to work with small groups of students. This way each teacher works with all students in the class as they rotate through the stations.

Team Teaching.   This approach is sometimes used as a synonym for co-teaching. However, it can be a variant approach whereby the special education teacher joins with one or more other special education teachers to form a team. The team is responsible for all of the children in the classroom or at a particular level. A variation of team teaching was observed in one school that involved ignoring categorical labels for service of students. Instead, all students identified for special education services were assigned to special educators according to their age or grade-level placement. The special educators, regardless of categorical specialization, were assigned to grade-level teams and assumed primary responsibility for all students with special needs at the assigned grade level. In addition, the special educators met weekly to discuss matters of concern. Each special educator was a member of a grade-level team and met regularly with that team to discuss common issues. The special educators moved in and out of the classrooms at that grade level to co-teach as needed, to adapt materials, or sometimes to present a special lesson. The teaming processes to manage such a system are extensive. According to the teachers involved in the approach, it will not work unless there is *trust* among all the teachers and efficient *teaming* practices. This underscores the need for general and special education teachers to understand and resolve issues of differing instructional strategies and curriculum.

A high school math teacher described a pre-algebra class that she and the teacher for learning disabilities co-teach. They have a shared planning time every other day, because the school uses block scheduling. Within that time they usually are able to set out a general plan for the week and then attend to specific problems or coordinate activities as needed. They share actual teaching responsibility more than they use a Teach and Monitor approach. This is purposeful, so students perceive them *both* as math teachers, and not one as math teacher with the other as special education teacher for certain students. What one of the co-teachers likes best about the approach is the camaraderie she shares with another adult. It lessens her feelings of isolation. However, she is quick to point out that co-teaching in situations when partners do not share a similar philosophy of classroom management, or do not appreciate and value temperament differences, will be challenging.

Other, More Informal Examples of Co-Teaching.   Co-teaching occasionally transpires almost spontaneously. Two third-grade teachers had adjoining classrooms and early in the school year they could see that some students' math skills had slipped during summer vacation. So one teacher worked on basic skills with a blended group of students from both rooms because she was very good at that, while her colleague provided enrichment activities for students who were ready to move on because she enjoyed working with them and challenging them. Then one day they had a "lightbulb moment": The curriculum and students were mismatched! So the co-teachers exchanged the curriculum plans. The enrichment group did modified bundling to grasp the concept of huge numbers after they complained about hearing adults on TV stammer over words like billion and trillion because the amounts were almost beyond comprehension. The other group was more enthusiastic about math after constructing geo boards and building birdhouses and figuring out recipes, and they began to understand tens and ones through these construction activities. The teachers continued to monitor, co-plan, and move students back and forth among groups from time to time.

Meanwhile, at the high school, a history teacher and a literature teacher took advantage of a trend—block scheduling—to request a double classroom with two classes of students coming together for a two-hour period integrating history and literature by using a timeline-based curriculum. They studied historical periods—for example, the Renaissance—through the lenses of history and literature but wove into those core subjects much period-relevant art, music, science, sports, and other interesting historical and literary content.

Yet another instance of serendipitous co-teaching occurred when a student teacher arrived in her assigned classroom for her first day of practice teaching and within a half hour had engaged in animated conversation a withdrawn child with severe socioemotional needs that caused him to speak only rarely. She assumed much responsibility for working with this reluctant student that semester and co-taught many lessons in a Teach and Monitor approach with teacher supervision. When the teacher took maternity leave in midyear, her newly graduated student teacher was hired for that teaching position.

At the university level, team teaching is generally voluntary and instructors select their partners, unlike K–12 team teaching which typically is set up to facilitate inclusion of students with special needs (Winn & Messenheimer-Young, 1995). Even so, preservice teachers can learn about co-teaching in a university environment. Winn and Messenheimer-Young (1995) recommend allowing students significant time for reflection on the experience. They also emphasize that one matter to be handled carefully is dual grading; therefore, some co-teachers find that a workable strategy is to divide assessment responsibilities by assignment rather than by students.

SCENARIO 7.B

Lori and Mark decide to co-teach an American History lesson about the Battle at Gettysburg during the Civil War. They will use the Interactive Lesson Planning form in Figure 7.2.

■ First, Mark provides his lecture materials from past lessons. They review the lecture outlines, textbook materials, and assignments and discuss what could be eliminated or added to the original lecture and textbook material. They decide that everyone could benefit from the lecture, even Randy who is developmentally delayed. Most students can read the textbook assignment, which is ten pages, except Colin who needs it read aloud and Randy who cannot read it at all.

■ They decide that most students, with the exception of Randy, will benefit from two of the assignments in the textbook.

■ Mark is concerned about the ability of some students with learning difficulties to benefit from some of the content. Lori wonders if students with high ability will be challenged. They decide to use cooperative learning methods to deal with some of those concerns. Lori will prepare "challenge tasks" that will be required for the students with high ability although anyone can try to do them. Mark has group-study worksheets they could use, but Lori recommends several changes. Mark thinks of some other items that could be eliminated or added to help the students in the class who have learning difficulties.

■ Mark then volunteers to make the revisions since he has the original study worksheets on his computer.

■ Although Lori is the teacher assigned for the course, they decide Mark should present the lecture since he has done it many times previously. However, Lori will be in the classroom and can add information whenever it seems appropriate to help clarify a point.

■ Lori will direct the cooperative learning activities. She has already established teams in the class and this content fits in well. Mark will have his para come into the classroom during that time, freeing him up to consult with another teacher.

FIGURE 7.2   Interactive Lesson Planning Form

Theme, Topic, or Goal: *Battle at Gettysburg*   Date(s): *4/5 – 4/10*

ACTIVITIES

WHEN	WHAT	FOR NEARLY ALL	FOR MOST	FOR SOME	WITH WHOM
Mon. & Tues.	*Lecture* *Read pages 254–263*	*all for lecture*	*Reading all but Randy*	*Read aloud to Colin*	*Mark*
Tues. & Wed.	*Assignments 1 and 3 on page 263 of the textbook*		*all but Randy*		*Lori & para.*
Tues. & Wed.	*Draw picture showing important people in the battle*			*Randy*	*Mark*
Thurs.	*Cooperative Learning—revised study guides*	*all*		*challenge tasks for high achievers*	*Lori & Mark*
Fri.	*Independent Test*		*all but Randy*	*read to 3 LD*	*Lori*
Fri.	*Test in resource room*			*Randy*	*para.*

OBJECTIVES

WHEN	WHAT	FOR NEARLY ALL	FOR MOST	FOR SOME	WITH WHOM
by 4/10	*State the primary events leading up to the Battle at Gettysburg*		*all but Randy*		
by 4/10	*State primary people and events during the battle*		*all but Randy*		
by 4/10	*Answer questions about the important outcomes of the battle*			*orally for LD and Randy*	
by 4/10	*Identify pictures of key persons and events in the Battle at Gettysburg*			*Randy*	
by 4/10	*Create a product showing the important outcomes of the Battle at Gettysburg*			*high achieving students*	

ASSESSMENT

WHEN	WHAT	FOR NEARLY ALL	FOR MOST	FOR SOME	WITH WHOM
Fri.	*Independently take written test*		*all but 3 LD & Randy*		*Lori*
Fri.	*Take oral test*			*3 LD*	*Mark*
Fri.	*Draw picture of key people and events*			*Randy*	*para.*

Source: Dyck, N., & Thurston, L. P. (1998). *Getting the Message Across: A Para's Guide to Communication.* San Antonio, TX: PCI Educational Publishing. © 1998, permission granted by PCI Educational Publishing.

SCENARIO 7.B   CONTINUED

■ Lori thinks the students need a summative experience requiring them to demonstrate individual accountability. Mark and Lori discuss what the activity could be and Lori agrees to prepare it (a test this time). They will divide the tests, each grading half. When the tests are graded, Lori will record the scores in her grade book and Mark will give team rewards. Mark will give the test orally to the students with learning disabilities and prepare a modified test for the para to administer to Randy in the resource room.

THE PLAN IN ACTION

No matter how well the teachers plan, some co-teaching actions must be spontaneous. This reality became obvious as Lori and Mark put their plan into action. Mark presented the lecture while Lori monitored as planned. Lori spontaneously "jumped in" from time to time to clarify information. At one point she went to the chalkboard and drew a diagram to more clearly illustrate a point that seemed confusing to students. The next day, as planned, Lori took over when the class began team study in the cooperative learning format. She instructed students to get into their teams, gave instructions for team activities and told how they could earn bonus points. Now the para was monitoring and noticed Randy needed more explanation so he wrote out the steps for Randy. Once students were engaged in teamwork, Lori and the para "cruised" the classroom, stopping to help individuals or teams as needed and providing positive reinforcement for team effort. Later they met to reflect on results of the plan.

On Friday, both teachers were present while students took individual tests. The para took Randy to the resource room to help him take his special test while Mark read the test to the students with learning disabilities. He read questions orally for them when needed. He noticed two students having difficulty writing their answers and pulled them aside one-by-one to let them dictate answers to him. Then he asked them to do an additional task while the rest of the class finished their tests. Lori involved the students with high ability in other activities after they finished their tests. Mark continued to monitor the test-takers. Lori and Mark divided the tests to grade as planned. Later they met to reflect on results of the plan.

DESIGNING CURRICULAR ADAPTATIONS COLLABORATIVELY

Federal law requires accommodations for individuals who qualify for certain types of carefully defined disabilities. Section 504 of the Rehabilitation Act of 1973 calls for public agencies to provide reasonable accommodations for individuals with disabilities, even those who do not qualify for IDEA, such as students with attention deficit disorders or health impairments. The intent of both laws is to provide access to participation in school programs. Although Section 504 provisions and IEP plans may specify accommodations needed by individual students, consultants should help all parties who are involved in teaching these students to plan and to prepare accommodations. Many authors use the terms *adaptations, accommodations,* or *modifications* interchangeably. For purposes here, curriculum adaptations are delineated as accommodations and/or modifications.

Curriculum *accommodations* are assistive aids and supports that help a student achieve the same outcomes as most other students in the class by adjusting the requirements. Therefore, an accommodation changes the path the student takes and the way he or she demonstrates learning, but it doesn't modify the initial learning goal or the final learning outcome. Examples of accommodations include reading a test to the student, writing answers dictated by the student, putting text in a digital format so a screen reader can be utilized, putting text into Braille, or providing sound amplification.

Curriculum *modifications* involve changing the goals or the content and performance expectations for what the student should learn. This might be, for example, reducing the number of spelling words for a student to master or allowing a student to create an outline of the major points rather than writing an essay.

The key to effective accommodations and modifications is the word *appropriate*. Today, with the special education population included in high-stakes testing, accommodations must be appropriate without reducing the minimal objectives expected of all students. Accommodation strategies—for example, "Read tests aloud and provide extended time"— should be individualized to meet the learner's needs and not generically applied to all special education students.

Consulting teachers might want to draw on the concept of scaffolding rather than accommodations. Scaffolding, as presented by Vygotsky (1978) is a structure for learning on which adults or more expert peers can help develop a student's independent problem-solving skills with collaboration and guidance that facilitates cognitive growth. The scaffolding is used temporarily for enabling a student to benefit from classroom learning and then it is faded once the student no longer needs it. While that is the goal of general educators and is reasonable for some students with disabilities, many individuals with disabilities will need scaffolding or accommodations for a lifetime. Consider the special needs of students who are deaf or hard of hearing.

Making Text Accessible

No reasonable person would question the need to convert printed text for someone who is blind to another format such as Braille or audio format in order for the person to access the text, yet some expect students who are challenged by printed text for other reasons such as having a learning disability or being an English language learner (ELL) to struggle through using grade-level text. Hehir (2007) argues that school time devoted to activities focusing on changing the disability may take away from valuable time needed to learn academic material. Academic deficits may actually be exacerbated by ingrained prejudice against performing activities in more efficient, nontraditional ways, such as reading with Braille or text-to-speech software. For example, many older students with dyslexia and other specific learning disabilities who are in inclusionary classrooms have been required to handle grade-level or higher text rather than having the book made available in an audio file format.

In the era of No Child Left Behind, all students are expected to be reading at grade level by the end of third grade. However, some students still fail to acquire skills necessary to read independently and comprehend information in print formats. Disabilities such as dyslexia that affect ability to handle print, can pose grave consequences for student success if accommodations aren't made. Concerted efforts are needed to help children gain access to text when they do not have independent reading skills for reading text at grade level.

National Instructional Materials Accessibility Standard (NIMAS)

Until recently few students with disabilities had access to books they needed. Sometimes the problem was technical—schools did not have the technology they needed to provide accessible versions to students even if they were available. In other cases, the problem was lack of awareness; many teachers and schools did not understand the issue of access or potential solutions. But for too many students the problem was the result of a frustrating distribution system; students couldn't get the materials in a timely fashion. The dissemination of accessible materials was inefficient, and raised barriers rather than opportunities.

One of the most frustrating barriers to accessibility is created by multiple formats. Adoption of a common, or standard, format is a simplifying step that has been crucial to progress in many other fields—from railroad transportation (adopting a common track gauge) to video technology (adopting a common format for DVD and HDTV). Similarly, progress in addressing the needs of students with disabilities has been enhanced by the U.S. Department of Education's endorsement of a common National Instructional Materials Accessibility Standard (NIMAS). New to IDEA with the 2004 amendments, NIMAS is designed to maximize access to the general education curriculum for blind or other print-disabled students through timely provision of accessible instructional materials created from NIMAS source files. NIMAS has been a long time coming. It established, for the first time, an efficient and cost-effective means by which blind or other print-disabled children could receive instructional text materials in the alternate, accessible formats that meet their needs in a timely manner. NIMAS was included as the standard to be used in preparation of all electronic files suitable for conversion into specialized formats such as Braille, audio, or digital text. As a result of the standard, printed instructional materials, including textbooks, are to be made available free of charge by publishers in the NIMAS-specified format to blind and other persons with print-related disabilities in elementary and secondary schools. Prior to NIMAS, converting print textbooks into specialized formats was complex and time consuming, often taking months to complete. But now, students who need materials in accessible formats will receive their textbooks and other instructional materials at the beginning of the instructional period right along with their classmates. The adoption of the NIMAS not only improves the speed of the process, but also the quality and consistency of books converted into specialized formats.

RESPONSE TO INTERVENTION

The 2004 reauthorization of IDEA also changed federal law concerning identification of children with specific learning disabilities. Schools are no longer required to consider whether a child has a severe discrepancy between achievement and ability. Because of this change, the Response to Intervention (RTI) method of determining student eligibility for special education programs has received increased attention. This three-tiered prevention model works to support students with varying instructional needs (Brown-Chidsey, 2007):

1. In Tier 1, the students at risk are identified and monitored using universal screenings and group interventions.

2. In Tier 2, targeted small group interventions are provided to students not making adequate progress in the general classroom and they are assessed more frequently. Those making too little progress are considered for Tier 3 interventions.

3. In Tier 3, students receive individualized, intensive interventions targeting their skill deficits. Those not responding at this level are considered for eligibility under IDEA.

RTI has many beneficial features. It helps ensure that all students have equal opportunity to learn (Brown-Chidsey, 2007). It can help at-risk students who have endured hard times and delays to catch up. It is a data-based, systematic method that lets co-educators know what is and what is not working. A summary feature is that it reduces the number of children and youth who are referred for special education. Not surprisingly, it does require much collaboration between general education and special education teachers.

RTI also comes with cautions. It must be implemented by educators who have considerable training in the model. Identification of students for special education must focus on assessments that directly relate to instruction and services must focus on intervention, not eligibility. However, as a preservice teacher noted while participating in team, RTI was a very helpful in improving a teacher's lessons and being able to learn from watching others teach. A number of Web sites, such as www.wrightslaw.com/info/rti.index.htm, feature explanatory material, articles, and links additional Web sites that present the pros and cons of RTI for intervention and identification.

Other Ways to Adapt, Extend, and Enrich Text Materials

In addition to converting printed text to specialized formats such as digital text, Edyburn (2006) suggests that teachers compensate for a student's difficulty with printed text in a number of different ways, including altering the size of the text, translating the text to a different language when English is a second language, providing vocabulary and concept development to scaffold for student understanding, providing similar text at different reading levels, decreasing the amount of reading, or teaching students learning strategies in order for them to become more strategic in their interaction with the text. For example, free web-based applications such as Babel Fish (http://babelfish.altavista.com) provide a quick and easy tool for translating text or web pages from one of several languages into another. These can provide helpful scaffolds for students who are English language learners struggling to comprehend text used in classroom instruction.

Other strategies such as concept-teaching routines or analogical anchoring developed at the Center for Research in Learning at the University of Kansas also can help support struggling readers with vocabulary and concepts encountered in grade-level materials (Deshler et al., 2001). Using tools like the concept diagram for helping students grasp critical concepts will go beyond simple text adaptations to deepen their understanding (Bulgren, Schumaker, & Deshler, 1993). Unit and lesson organizers can enhance learning for students by providing a graphic organizer to help them transform content into a learner-friendly format (Boudah, Lenz, Bulgren, Schumaker, & Deshler, 2000). Teaching routines and organizers such as these enhance content learning rather than watering it down.

As another strategy, Rotter (2006) suggests applying basic rules of graphic arts and design to all written materials. These simple guidelines can be applied to almost any type of written materials including everything from graphic organizers, commercially prepared materials, tests, overheads, PowerPoint presentations, and guided notes. Elements of design have a direct relationship on how well the message of the material will be transferred to the reader and how clear visual signals can help the reader grasp concepts more readily. Rules of graphic design help teachers prepare their instructional materials to make them easier for students to read, organize information more clearly, and improve comprehension.

Dyck and Pemberton (2002) recommend that in deciding whether to adapt a particular text for an individual student, the teacher must ask, "Can the student read and understand the text with sufficient speed and accuracy?" If the answer is yes, no adaptation is needed, but, if the answer is no, text adaptation should be considered. Figure 7.3 shows a decision tree for making adaptations.

Addressing Misbehavior Collaboratively

When a student misbehaves, school professionals are faced with the challenge of finding an effective way to respond. Federal law (IDEA, 2004) mandates the use of functional behavioral assessments and positive behavior supports to address inappropriate behaviors of students. Functional behavioral assessment (FBA) is a multidimensional problem-solving approach to analyzing student behavior within the context of the setting in which the behavior occurs. It is a proactive approach to program planning that teachers who share students with behavioral concerns find useful. The purpose is to decide the function of the behavior and a way to address it (Erickson, Stage, & Nelson, 2006). FBA should yield information to help design effective positive behavior support plans. It can provide links to developing interventions based on the purpose of the student's behavior and it focuses on keeping the problem behavior from reoccurring.

FBA is based on two assumptions (Ryan, Halsey, & Matthews, 2003). The first is that inappropriate behavior occurs in context; that is, it is influenced by the setting in which it occurs. Therefore, the setting must be considered when developing a plan for changing the behavior. The second assumption underlying FBA is that problem behavior serves a function for the student. Although there may be many reasons students engage in problem behaviors, they generally fall into one of four major categories: (1) to receive attention from others; (2) to gain a desired activity or item; (3) to avoid or escape something unpleasant such as an academic or social demand; or (4) to meet sensory needs (Barnhill, 2005).

Educators must identify functions the behavior is serving for the student before attempting to develop an intervention plan. For example, the student may be trying to escape from a difficult task or assignment by becoming disruptive in class in order to be removed from the setting. In another situation, a student may try to engage a teacher in a confrontation in order to gain attention from the teacher or class peers. Functional behavior assessment involves five steps:

1. *Identify the problem behavior.* A clear, specific, detailed description of the behavior is required. The behaviors must be stated in observable ways and prioritized. To ensure that selected target behaviors are the right ones, team members should ask themselves questions such as: Does the behavior negatively impact this student's or other students' learning? Does the behavior occur in only one place or in multiple settings?

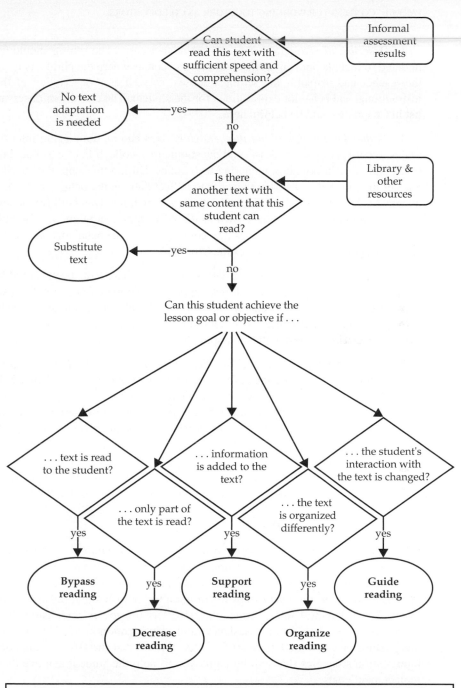

FIGURE 7.3   The Decision Tree for Adaptations

Source: Dyck, N., et al. (1998). *Getting the Message Across: A Para's Guide to Communication.* San Antonio, TX: PCI Educational Publishing. © 1998, permission granted by PCI Educational Publishing.

2. *Describe the setting(s) where the behavior occurs.* The setting should be described in detail to include both environmental factors such as where the child sits in proximity to the teacher and demands the setting imposes, as well as a description of the teacher's instructional and behavior expectations for the student. The classroom observation checklist in Chapter 6 could be helpful here.

3. *Gather information about the behavior.* This can be done using interviews, rating scales, record reviews, checklists and questionnaires, collection of baseline data, observations, and other information-gathering techniques. During this step, the special education teacher might ask the classroom teacher to collect data on the behavior, documenting frequency of the behavior, duration, and intensity, which involves both frequency and duration. An observation technique known as the ABC approach might also be utilized. ABC stands for antecedents (what comes immediately before the behavior), behaviors, and consequences (what happens a result of the behavior).

4. *Review the data.* Once all the data have been gathered, the team should look at various sources of information to see if they support one another. For example, based on interview information from the parents and observational data from the teacher, does the behavior occur both at home and school? Or do the data show that the behavior is more likely to occur in one setting than in another?

5. *Form a hypothesis about the function of the behavior based on data gathered.* The co-educator team analyzes the information gathered about the student's behavior, and makes an educated guess about what function the behavior is serving. Which variables are most likely to be supporting the student's behavior? This information is used to develop a hypothesis describing factors that can assist in determining the occurrence (frequency, duration, and/or intensity) of the problem behavior. The same behavior could serve any number of functions depending on the child and all the related environmental factors. For some, the behavior may be a way to get attention; for others, it serves to get them what they want; and in another situation, it may help remove them from a situation they want to avoid.

Behavior Intervention Plans

When team members have completed the functional behavioral assessment (FBA) and are confident that they have identified a reasonable and probable hypothesis statement for the purpose of the problem behavior, a replacement behavior goal should be determined. Teams will find many steps in common to both FBA and behavioral intervention plans. The behavioral intervention plan (BIP) is the logical extension of FBA. Both processes involve behavioral assessment and identification of target behaviors. The primary factor that sets the BIP apart from the FBA is that the BIP contains details of the intervention strategies that will be employed to help the student achieve the behavioral replacement goals.

An implementation plan should be created as a management strategy to ensure effective communication for team-based, positive behavior support planning by documenting the actions needed and who will be responsible for each task. The BIP should also include assessment methods to measure behavioral progress. These methods most likely would be similar to those used in collecting the baseline data for the FBA. A description of what will happen when the student achieves the behavioral goals, as well as what will happen if the goals are not reached, also should be included. For example, the plan should clearly lay out what will happen if the student commits a specific behavioral violation such as fighting or running away from authorities. Family involvement in development of the BIP is crucial to its success.

Using IEP Information Collaboratively

When teachers and other instructional support personnel such as paras collaborate with shared students, it is important to use sensitive information from IEPs in a way that is useful but also maintains the confidentiality of the information. General education teachers with a classroom full of other students can't be burdened with sifting through massive IEP documents to keep track of goals and objectives of shared students relative to their class or content areas. Likewise, paras need the big picture of what goals the student is working toward and clear directions and guidance in terms of what they are to do while working with the student.

Consultants should devise a way to provide IEP highlights to teachers and paras in a format that will be useful to them without violating a student's rights. This might be in the form of a document called "IEP at a Glance" or "IEP Snapshot." To protect this information, it could be shared in a password-protected computer file or a paper copy placed in a locked file cabinet. Only individuals who know the password or who have been given access to the locked file can access the information. The limitation of putting information in locked files is that it is too easily forgotten—out of sight, out of mind. Perhaps a periodic e-mail message with the relevant information and a personal note about the student's progress or lack of it would be a way to keep everyone informed about progress toward meeting IEP goals and objectives.

PLANNING AND MAKING ADAPTATIONS

Classroom teachers may believe they do not know how to adapt instruction, but the most plausible explanation is that they do not have time to do it. Consultants and collaborators must consider whether their suggestions for classroom modifications are reasonable and feasible for the situation. (See Chapter 4 for ways of dealing with consultee resistance.)

Many of the resources available for helping teachers make classroom modifications represent the views of special educators rather than the collaborative views of classroom teachers and special education teachers. However, Figure 7.4 contains a list of adaptations taken from materials prepared jointly by elementary classroom teachers and special education collaborating teachers. The list is a helpful resource for sharing with classroom teachers during collaborative consultations.

Digital Resources to Assist in Adaptations

When text is available in digital format, teachers can use it in a variety of ways to meet individual student needs. Digital formats can be used in computers so the teacher can adapt the

FIGURE 7.4   Suggestions for Adaptations

Instructional Level
Let student work at success rate level of about 80%.
Break down task into sequential steps.
Sequence the work with easiest problems first.
Base instruction on cognitive need (concrete, abstract).

Curricular Content
Select content that addresses student's interest.
Adapt content to student's future goals (job, college. . .).

Instructional Materials
Fold or line paper to help student with spatial problem.
Use graph paper or lined paper turned vertically.
Draw arrows on text or worksheet to show related ideas.
Highlight or color-code on worksheets, texts, tests.
Mark the material that must be mastered.
Reduce the amount of material on a page.
Use a word processor for writing and editing.
Provide a calculator or computer to check work.
Tape reference materials to student's work area.
Have student follow text as listening to taped version.

Format of Directions and Assignments
Make instructions as brief as possible.
Introduce multiple long-term assignments in small steps.
Read written directions or assignments aloud.
Leave directions on chalkboard during study time.
Write cues at top of work page (for example, noun = . . .).
Ask student to restate/paraphrase directions.
Have student complete first example with teacher prompt.
Provide folders for unfinished work and finished work.

Instructional Strategies
Use concrete objects to demonstrate concepts
Provide outlines, semantic organizers, or webbings.
Use voice changes to stress points.
Point out relationships between ideas or concepts.
Repeat important information often.
Use color-coded strips for key parts.

Teacher Input Mode
Use multisensory approach for presenting materials.
Provide a written copy of material on chalkboard.
Demonstrate skills before student does seat work.

Student Response Mode
Accept alternate forms of information sharing.
Allow taped or written report instead of oral.
Allow students to dictate information to another.
Allow oral report instead of written report.
Have student practice speaking to small group first.

Test Administration
Allow students to have sample tests to practice.
Teach test-taking skills.
Test orally.
Supply recognition items and not just total recall.
Allow take-home test.
Ask questions requiring short answers.

Grading Policies
Grade on pass/fail basis.
Grade on individual progress or effort.
Change the percentage required to pass.
Do not penalize for handwriting or spelling on tests.
Use scoring templates and rubrics.

Modifications of Classroom Environment
Seat students according to attention or sensory need.
Remove student from distractions.
Keep extra supplies on hand.

text for the class in a variety of ways. The print can be enlarged and printed out for students with low vision. It can be read aloud by the computer if it has the appropriate software. Teachers can request that publishers provide digital versions of CD-ROM materials for specific learners. Although publishers are not required by law to provide the digital versions, many do so as a courtesy to schools. Digital versions of text can also be found online. One of the best sources is the eText Spider at the CAST Web site (www.cast.org). The site provides tools to search selected online sources in order to find electronic text in the public domain and that can be adapted without fear of copyright infringement. For example, one teacher entered "Mark Twain" and received a list of about thirty publications written by Mark Twain. The teacher then selected one title that was shown on the site, allowing a download of the entire text free of charge.

Making Modifications

Students whose cognitive disabilities prevent them from benefiting from the general classroom curriculum, even with accommodations, need curriculum modifications. Students with mild or moderate cognitive disabilities may need adapted outcomes while students with severe cognitive disabilities will need different goals or outcomes. Whenever possible, a theme or topic being studied by the rest of the students in the classroom should also be studied by these students.

Adapted Outcomes.   Students with moderate learning and behavior problems can succeed very well in most classrooms but may need modified outcomes such as reduced number of practice problems or highlighted text. Other examples: in math, the student works on the same concept but the number of required practice problems may be reduced; in social studies, the teacher might mark certain parts of the text material that must be read and the remainder skimmed; in science, the teacher might limit the number of concepts within a domain to be mastered. In short, these students are expected to master most but not all of the content. Most of the items listed in Figure 7.4 are adapted outcomes.

Functional Outcomes.   For students with severe cognitive challenges, curriculum goals may focus on areas such as social/behavioral development, language development, concept development, basic skills, or self-help skills. For example, if the class is studying plants, but a certain student's goals have to do with counting and language development, that student may count, sort, and talk about seeds. These students may also need accommodations to help them attain their goals. The primary reason for inclusion in the class is to participate in the social context and culture of the group.

Enhanced Outcomes.   Students with high ability also need modified curriculum. Cooperative learning is an effective instructional strategy for a variety of reasons. However, it should not be justified for gifted students through inference that they require remediation in social skills. Nor should it be used to make gifted students available as handy tutors (Robinson, 1990). While occasional peer tutoring can be challenging and rewarding for the gifted student, collaborative activities are not intended to set very able students up as surrogate teachers for other students.

When gifted students are included in general classrooms, as the majority are for most of their school day, their learning needs also must be considered. Providing appropriate learning environments for them necessitates intensive collaboration and consultation among gifted program facilitators, classroom teachers, and resource personnel so that classroom modifications and resource adaptations help gifted students develop their learning potential. This is discussed in more detail later in the chapter.

PLANNING REMEDIAL INSTRUCTION AND OTHER SUPPORTS

Many special education programs have put all their resources into co-teaching, accommodations, and modifications while overlooking the special needs of students with significant basic skill disabilities who need remedial instruction. Some parents turn to private remedial services, conduct home schooling, or employ private tutors to help their children who are not getting remediation in the schools. Special educators in public schools must provide this type of instruction for students who need it.

Collaborating teachers must develop remedial plans indicating what skills to remediate, what teaching techniques to use, who will provide the instruction, and when and where it will be provided. Harris and Sipay (1990) give the following guidelines for planning remedial instruction:

- Tutoring from one to three children at a time produces best results.
- Some students must be given one-to-one tutoring to make any progress.
- A minimum of about fifty instructional hours is necessary for significant improvement.
- Three times a week will produce results, but every day is even better.
- Remedial periods should usually last from thirty to forty-five minutes.

Resources for Remedial Lessons

Most special educators will not have time to provide extensive remedial instruction given all their other responsibilities. They can plan the remediation and direct a paraeducator, peer tutor, or volunteer to provide the instruction with their supervision. Special educators need to acquire a library of resources that provide explicit guidelines for tutors to follow. An excellent resource for this task is *Helping the Struggling Reader: What to Teach and How to Teach it* (Sundbye & McCoy, 1997). This resource provides thirty-nine teaching plans that address varying student needs from learning about sounds and letters, to using print and meaning together, to comprehension. The teaching plans are designed for one-on-one, intensive teaching, but can be adapted for use with small groups as well. An easy-to-use grid helps the teacher match types of reading difficulties with the teaching plans that are most likely to be helpful. Tutors can easily follow the teaching plans selected. The performance records for each teaching plan will help the consultant monitor student progress and make adjustments when needed.

Another resource that goes beyond reading is *Tactics for Teaching* (Lovitt, 1995). Some 105 tactics are categorized into six sections: reading, writing, spelling, mathematics, classroom management, and self-management. Each tactic provides a brief rationale for the tactic, describes the type of student with whom it would be most appropriate, an outline of procedures for implementing the technique, procedures for monitoring its use, and ways the tactic can be modified in special situations.

Consultants and collaborating teachers cannot be present in every inclusive classroom for all instruction that takes place but they can support classroom teachers in many other ways. They might help plan for tutors and other instructional assistants assigned to the classroom; or teach students study strategies and classroom survival skills; or adapt tests and other text material; or coach students in self-advocacy behaviors; or monitor student progress.

Planning for Peer Tutors and Other Instructional Assistants

Classroom teachers sometimes are reluctant to implement peer tutoring programs despite obvious benefits, because they must spend time and effort in gaining successful results. Since time, energy, and resources for establishing effective peer tutoring programs are considerable, consulting teachers can collaborate with teachers to develop the programs. Peer tutoring programs could be buildingwide or limited to one or a few classrooms.

Jenkins and Jenkins (1985) identified the following seven critical components of a successful peer-tutoring program:

1. Provide highly structured lesson formats for tutors to use during the tutoring session, such as packaged programs with teacher instruction.
2. When possible, use content that correlates with the classroom content. Do not expect the tutor to teach material that has not already been presented by the teacher.
3. A mastery model of instruction is preferred because it provides satisfaction to tutor and tutee.
4. Schedule tutoring sessions frequently for moderate lengths of time (about one-half hour every day at the elementary level and daily one-hour sessions at the secondary level).
5. Provide tutor training and supervision, including feedback and reinforcement to tutors and classroom teachers.
6. Keep daily performance data on instructional objectives. Other types of information can include daily assignment record, monthly calendar, diary, or log book.
7. Carefully select and pair tutors with learners. The most important selection criteria are individual characteristics such as dependability, responsibility, and sensitivity.

Consideration should be given to personalities and compatibility of the tutor and tutee, congruence of schedules, gender differences (not a critical issue, but perhaps pertinent at the secondary level), tutor knowledge of content to be tutored, interests, and eagerness to participate. More highly skilled tutors are often placed with more difficult-to-teach students (Jenkins and Jenkins, 1985).

One of the most important elements of a good peer-tutoring program is tutor training. The amount and type of training will vary depending on the ages and abilities of the tutors and learners. Training usually addresses topics such as information about the program, tutor responsibilities, measurement procedures, lesson structure, teaching procedures, and personal behavior. The training should include personal relationship skills such as responsive listening, conversing, and praising good effort. It is important that the tutors be instructed in specific procedures that have been experimentally validated to assure maximum learning and minimum frustration.

An example of peer tutoring at the high school level is the H.E.L.P. room in a midwestern high school. The program (Here to Encourage the Learning Process) was developed for students who had difficulties keeping up in general education classrooms, but who did not qualify for special education programs. Although a teacher and a para staffed the program, peer tutoring was the principal methodology. Tutors were trained over a period of several weeks in communication skills, study skills, observation skills, writing of behavioral objectives, and tutoring skills. Evaluations of the H.E.L.P. program showed positive results. Parents reported that their children are more interested in school, and teachers welcomed the assistance. Students said they were less frustrated and more successful in the classroom (Thurston & Dover, 1990).

Teaching Study Strategies

Students with learning difficulties often show marked improvement in general education classrooms after they have been taught strategies for using information presented in the classroom. Many learning strategies resemble processes more commonly recognized as study skills.

Strategies Intervention Model.   Special educators in high schools can support classroom teachers by teaching all students to use a technique such as the Strategies Intervention Model (Deshler and Schumaker, 1988). These strategies are techniques, principles, or rules that enable students to learn, solve problems, and complete tasks independently. Deshler and Schumaker (1986) stress the importance of deliberately teaching for generalization across settings. If the special education teacher is collaborating with the classroom teacher, this generalization process will be much more effective than other delivery options. Perhaps the special education teacher will teach the strategies in the resource room, but the regular classroom teacher will want to take over monitoring the generalization. The classroom teacher provides explicit cues that will help the student know when to use a particular strategy and gives periodic probes to determine whether the student continues to use the strategy.

> Central to the entire generalization process just described are regular cooperative planning efforts between the resource and regular classroom teacher. Regular communication is essential to determine the degree to which the newly-acquired learning strategies are being used in the regular classroom. In addition, in such meetings classroom teachers can be encouraged to cue students to use the strategy at the appropriate time. (Deshler & Schumaker, 1986, p. 586)

Teaching Self-Advocacy

Students with special needs should be taught how to communicate their special needs to teachers, employers, and others. The self-advocacy form in Figure 7.5 was prepared by Dyck (1997) to use with secondary-level students in general classrooms. Under ideal circumstances, the special education teacher would prompt the student to take responsibility to give the form to each of her teachers and pick it up once the teacher has filled in the right-hand column. This responsibility is especially important for students with learning and behavior problems. A good variation is for the classroom teacher to hand out the form the first day of class and ask every student to complete the left-hand column and return it. The teacher then looks over each form, writes responses in the right-hand column and returns them to the students shortly thereafter. (It is a good idea for the teacher to photocopy the completed forms before returning them to the students.) This process provides an efficient and confidential way for teachers and students to communicate regarding special needs and preferences.

FIGURE 7.5   Self-Advocacy Form

Name _____   Course _____

What Works for Me:	What Teacher Accepts:

Class Presentations
- Allow me to tape-record lectures.
- Hand out lecture outlines or objectives in advance.
- Give me copies of overheads.
- Let me sit where I can see and hear the presenter.
- _____

Tests
- Give me oral tests.
- Record test on tape.
- Allow someone to read test to me.
- Allow extra time for me to take tests or shorten the test.
- Put plenty of space for me to write on tests.
- Provide short-answer and multiple-choice questions.
- _____

Study Methods
- Allow more time for reading or shorten assignments.
- Let me read an easier book (_____ level).
- Provide explanations for acceptable homework form (typed, etc.).
- Check to make sure I understand directions.
- I need frequent breaks.
- I need a quiet area for study.
- Explicitly instruct me to write down my homework assignment in my notebook.
- Type handwritten teacher materials.
- Use written backup for oral directions.
- Allow me to use a calculator.
- Allow me to use a word processor with spell check.
- Break down long assignments into smaller sections for me to complete.
- I learn well in small groups.
- I don't learn well in small groups.
- I learn well in whole-class presentations.
- I need to learn with a "study buddy."
- _____

Source: Dyck, N., et al. (1998). *Getting the Message Across: A Para's Guide to Communication.* San Antonio, TX: PCI Educational Publishing. © 1998, permission granted by PCI Educational Publishing.

Adapting Tests

Many students with learning and behavior problems have difficulty taking tests about subject matter they have learned. As a student progresses to higher grade levels, the ability to demonstrate knowledge through tests becomes more and more important. Consultants at upper grade levels will need to give careful attention to the test-taking skills of students with learning and behavior difficulties.

When students have difficulty taking teacher-made tests in content subjects, consultants should give attention to a number of elements about the nature of the tests and ways to either help students take the tests as written, or collaborate with the teacher to make test adaptations. Lieberman (1984) suggests the first week of each school year, beginning at about the seventh-grade level, should be devoted to teaching study skills and test-taking strategies. This is a particularly relevant suggestion in the climate of NCLB-mandated high-stakes testing.

Other suggestions to consider when consulting with classroom teachers about alternative test construction and administration are:

- Give frequent, timed mini-tests
- Give practice tests
- Have students test one another and discuss answers
- Use alternative response forms (multiple-choice, short-answer, essay)
- Back up the written tests with taped tests
- Provide extra spacing between discussion or short-answer items
- Underline key words in test directions as well as test items
- Provide test study guides featuring a variety of answer formats
- Provide additional time for students who write slowly
- Administer tests orally (Mercer & Mercer, 1993)

Teachers are likely to be more resistant to test adaptations than to adaptations of classroom materials. Likewise, even when they believe it is a good thing to do they are not very likely to make the adaptations themselves. Consultants can assist classroom teachers in:

- Adapting their tests by adjusting the content to be directly related to the objectives of the class
- Changing the format so the items are easy to read, more space is allowed for discussion, or the order of items is rearranged to make them more predictable
- Rewriting directions or providing cues such as highlighting, underlining, and enlarging
- Providing prompts such as "Start here" or "Look at the sign on this row"
- Adjusting the readability level of the questions
- Providing outlines or advance organizers
- Providing spelling of difficult words
- Allowing students to use outlines, webs or other visual organizers (Salend, 1994)

As teachers become proficient in using more authentic assessment procedures the need for test modification will lessen. Even then, some type of accommodation is likely to be needed for some students with disabilities.

Adapting Text Materials

Many of the guidelines for adapting tests apply when adapting other text material such as textbooks, study guides, or activity sheets. Before getting started with textbook adaptations the consultant and collaborating teacher should answer the following questions:

- What are the outcomes or objectives?
- What chapters will be covered and in what order?
- When will the chapters be covered, and in what depth?
- In what setting will the text be used?
- How will the objectives be assessed?
- What is the student's reading problem—decoding, comprehension?
- What are the student's interests, strengths, and prior experiences?

Adapting text can be the most powerful accommodation teachers make but it is also the most difficult and time-consuming. "Text adaptations are not for the faint-hearted. They tend to require more time and effort on the part of the teacher than other instructional adaptations, and consequently, are less likely to be done by general classroom teachers" (Dyck, 1999, p. 3).

Characteristics of students who are most likely to benefit from adapted text fall into five broad categories. These are students who cannot do one or more of the following:

1. See print
2. Read many words in the text
3. Understand content in the text material
4. Attend to long texts
5. Write print

Once the type of adaptation needed has been determined, specific selection can be based on the student's abilities, the lesson goals, and available resources. Figure 7.3, shown earlier, is a decision tree for selecting the type of text adaptation most likely to help an individual student. In general, the simplest adaptation requiring the least resources such as time and money that will help the student meet curriculum goals should be selected.

Bypass Reading.   Perhaps the most common way to adapt a text is to change the modality of text input, usually reading it aloud in person or on audio file. Many teachers ask students to take turns reading text material aloud in a round-robin manner. This form of adaptation may not be best on a regular basis, but we recognize that teachers use it because it is an easy way to bypass reading for certain students. Although relatively easy to accomplish, reading text aloud is not without problems. Recorded text material, peer tutoring, and computer adaptations are often better ways to bypass reading.

Decrease Reading.   Students who can decode text, but at a very slow rate, or who have difficulty with the vocabulary meaning or concepts presented in a text need the amount or density of content decreased. Such adaptations include selecting another text with similar content but using easier vocabulary, highlighting key concepts, omitting unnecessary or distracting parts of text, or writing abridged versions of text.

Support Reading.   Sometimes students need more information than is provided in the text to help them understand it. Examples include adding definitions of key terms, adding interest to important content, and adding cues, signals, and questions that will help the student focus on the most relevant information.

Organize Reading.   Many students who are not thought of as "struggling readers," as well as those who are, will benefit from the use of graphic organizers. Much has been written about teaching students to create graphic organizers, but struggling readers may benefit most when the teacher provides such organizers before making the reading assignment.

Guide Reading.   Teachers often use study guides to help students focus on and review important content in reading assignments. They can use previews and summaries, fill-in graphic organizers, framed outlines, and structured notes as alternatives to traditional study guide formats.

Keep in mind, if a decision is made that a text needs to be adapted, then the student's work products and tests should be similarly adapted. For example, if a student needs the amount of reading decreased by eliminating portions of the text, the student also will need decreased written product assignments. In some cases the student's IEP goals will also need to be revised to reflect the use of adapted text. An elaborated discussion of these concepts is available in *How to Adapt Text for Struggling Readers* (Dyck, 1999).

Monitoring Student Progress

Frequent monitoring is essential when the special education teacher is not providing all of the direct instruction to students with special needs. In fact, it might be the most important function performed by the special educator in inclusive schools. Consider the example of Debbie:

> Debbie was now in her second year at an inclusive school. She had sixteen students in her caseload—mostly fourth- and fifth-graders. Debbie spent at least one hour each day in each classroom where her students were included. In addition, she taught math to several small groups in which her students were included. Although she felt fairly confident her students were making satisfactory progress in basic skills, she wasn't sure. She began using curriculum-based measurement (CBM) procedures, taking reading and math probes once each week. After a few weeks of charting data she realized four of her students were not making progress in reading. She had not been working directly with these students in reading and did not realize the problems they were having. She immediately took steps to make changes in those students' reading instruction.

Monitoring Classroom Grades.   Secondary-level teachers can monitor student progress by number of completed assignments and grades in general classroom courses. This information must be interpreted cautiously however, because teachers' grading standards vary greatly. Special educators in inclusive schools should discuss with each teacher their grading philosophies and plan a system for grading students with adapted curriculum. (Refer again to Chapter 2 for teacher perspectives on grading policies.)

COLLABORATING AND CO-TEACHING FOR STUDENTS WITH HIGH ABILITIES

Too many educational policy makers, school administrators, and even teachers, believe that students with high ability for learning do not have special educational needs; *they can get by on their own* and most of them will do just fine. Those with such views point out that many other students have immediate, major problems to be addressed by overworked teachers in busy, crowded, underfunded schools full of students with serious learning and behavioral problems. They believe that students who *cannot* succeed without intensive special services must be served first and foremost.

But many students mastered much of the material well before it was formally introduced in school. Or, they quickly learned it in a fraction of the time the instructor had allocated for learning it. Some already knew it. These students, bound by compulsory education laws to be in school, gain little if anything while "marking time in place." For the students this is frustrating. For the world at large, it is a tremendous waste.

So many educators, parents, and members of the general public have been concerned over the past half-century about failure to challenge very bright students, that a majority of states include education for gifted students in their special education mandates and regulations. In many, although not all, this accesses special education funding and the special education requirement that an IEP will be in place.

Educators face the challenge issued by legislated mandate to have No Child Left Behind (NCLB). Schools must show adequate yearly progress (AYP) by students or be tagged as "needs improvement." However, there is no counterbalancing mandate that calls for having No Child *Held* Behind (NC*H*B). School boards and administrators are pressed to focus their attention and resources on NCLB to ensure adequate yearly progress in the standard curriculum by the majority of students, especially those with English language learners and children of families who are poor (Christie, 2004). The requirement for high-stakes academic testing in order to be accountable to the NCLB mandate erodes education directed toward more broad, deep, and creative kinds of learning (Allen, 2004). Therefore, collaborating co-educators must find ways of working together to provide the learning challenges and intellectual stimulation needed by the very able.

SCENARIO 7.C

Vinny is frustrated. He loves to high-jump and he shows great promise in this activity as well as other related track-and-field events. But his elementary physical education teacher says that the high-jump bar can be set no higher than what is a comfort level for most of the class. "Why not?" asks Vinny. "Well, I guess there are lots of reasons," the teacher responds. "The other kids can't go as high as you, and they need to work where they can be successful. So we all need to stay at that height for the limited time we have to practice. We do have only so much time to spend on the high jump. And you know, it might discourage them to see you do lots better than they can. Then, too, think about this. They might not even like you as much if you 'show them up.' So we need for you to just go along with everyone else, and we'll wait till you get older to set the bar higher."

Ironically, if this were a sports-focused matter, accommodations would be recommended and be made. A precocious Vinny* would not have the high-jump bar (note the adjective *high*) frozen at a designated low level until everyone else grows into his skill; he would be given time, equipment, space, instruction, and encouragement to develop his special talents. A tall, precocious freshman basketball player would not be relegated to the bench for the next one or two years if she could contribute to school victory and pride now. It is unfortunate when schools and the public forgo age/grade-level constraints for performance areas that don't really matter all that much in the overall aims of education (meaning development of skills needed primarily for competitive sports events, not fitness skills needed for quality of life), but then "throttle down" bright minds that could contribute so much to quality of life for all.

*Some would call Vinny an overachiever. That is a misnomer because one cannot achieve more than one does; the "overachiever" is being mislabeled as such by persons who are *underexpecters*.

Reviewing the Reality of Individual Differences

As pointed out in Chapter 2, students differ, and the magnitude of these differences can be great. Some educators ignore this reality and strive to treat all students alike. They take very seriously the concept of equality and fail to consider that "there is nothing so unequal as equal treatment of unequals. Eisner (2003) questions the widely accepted assumption that the aim of schooling is to get all students to the same place at about the same time. His critical analogy of schools as railroads delivering students for expected arrival at a common destination by the time they reach age eighteen is sharply descriptive. He asserts that the *good* school:

> does not expect all students to arrive at the same destination at the same time. Indeed, it provides conditions in which variability among students can be increased. What we ought to be doing in schools is increasing the variance in student performance while escalating the mean. In an ideal approach to curriculum and instruction—an approach in which every aspect of teaching is ideally suited to each student, and each aspect of curriculum is appropriate for the abilities students possess—variability among students will increase, not decrease. (p. 650)

Good teaching practices require educators to make every effort to maximize the achievement of all students; in other words, we should strive to have No Child Left Behind, but we must also make every possible effort to have No Child *Held* Behind.

CHARACTERISTICS OF LEARNERS WITH HIGH APTITUDE AND TALENT

Definitions of high abilities vary greatly among schools and are often more attuned to the programs a school has decided to offer than to a particular definition of giftedness or talent. So, then, how do school personnel decide which students have needs that should be served with special programming of curriculum? The simplest methods are often best.

Elementary teachers have opportunities to observe student work in a variety of content areas. However, there *is* a major problem. Observations and evaluations of student potential, if they are to be of value, must be predicated on a condition that many schools fail to provide—that of making available the means by which students can *reveal* their potential. Clark (2002) aptly describes this as creating responsive, nurturing school environments so that children's abilities will "bubble up." It does not take too much imagination to recognize that such environments for learning also would give educators a head start on the infusion of differentiated curriculum!

Identifying Exceptional Ability and Talents through Checklists and Interest Inventories

One of the attributes of programs about which planners do not get bogged down on identification issues is a philosophy of serving a flexible number of students if, when, and how the students need such curriculum differentiation. In such programs school personnel are called on to provide data about students' academic achievement and also to contribute information emanating from the "hidden curriculum," or that part of school life which includes participation in extracurricular activities, behaviors in settings such as hallways and lunchrooms, leadership abilities, demonstrations of innovative and creative abilities, zest for learning evidenced by attendance and completed assignments, and more. They also have input from families and students *if they seek it out*. This can be a start toward a more formal assessment of student abilities and curricular needs.

Checklists.   In a very responsive learning environment, obtaining teacher perceptions of student ability is often the best place to begin. The collaborative consultant, often the facilitator for the gifted education program, can introduce co-educators to the purpose and procedures of the process in a one-on-one conference, a brief inservice, or during a regularly scheduled faculty meeting. It is extremely important for the building administrator(s) to support this activity and highly desirable that one or more attend if it is a group meeting.

An example of a teacher checklist for considering high performance potential is provided in Figure 7.6 on page 256. The form can be used as is, or better yet, modified to fit the school setting. It also can be a tool for framing and presenting a staff development activity on characteristics and needs of high-ability learners. It may be duplicated and completed for only one or a few targeted students, or even better, for the entire classroom. High scores on items 1–7 reflect the kinds of mental processes measured by standardized individual aptitude tests. Items 8–12 target learning styles and items 13–19 performance styles. Items 20–25 predict creative thinking and doing. Items 26–30 are indicants of social preferences that relate to learning. The seven lettered items at the end of the numbered list are factors that, if present, provide even more evidence of exceptional ability.

Figure 7.7 on page 257 provides an alternate checklist for building administrators. They know all students but perhaps not as many facets of student performance as do classroom teachers. They see the bigger picture and sometimes have interesting interactions with families regarding student capabilities and school programs. Administrators tend to prefer brief, succinct fact sheets, information bulletins, and in this case, short checklists. A written formal note of explanation and request should accompany distribution of the form to them. If they have participated in meetings where teacher checklists were introduced and explained, they will be especially well-informed for their part in the process.

Teacher forms and administrator forms should include space for making additional comments. Confidentiality of the information during distribution and collection processes must be ensured.

Secondary teachers often respond well to checklists that are in question format and describe specific (and sometimes annoying) behaviors, such as:

Do you have a student (or more than one) who:

- Finishes what should have been a 20-minute assignment in 5 minutes?
- Volunteers off-the-wall comments or suggestions during discussions?
- Is highly intolerant of stupidity, especially when perceived in an authority figure?
- Is impatient with sloppy or disorganized thinking to the point of rudeness?
- Recognizes sophisticated punch lines and gets more out of humor?
- Plans activities efficiently but can procrastinate to the point of desperation?
- Would rather argue than eat?
- Has probably read every book available on subjects of personal interest?

FIGURE 7.6   Teacher Referral Checklist

The following criteria are useful in assessing high potential of students. Please use one form per student to assign a value of *3* (to a considerable degree), *2* (to some degree), or *1* (to little if any degree) for each characteristic.

1. Learns rapidly and easily _____
2. Uses much common sense and practical knowledge _____
3. Retains easily what has been presented _____
4. Knows about many things of which other students are unaware _____
5. Uses a large number of words easily and accurately and appreciates word power _____
6. Recognizes relationships, comprehends meanings, and seems to "get more out of things" _____
7. Is alert with keen powers of observation and responds quickly _____
8. Likes difficult subjects and challenging tasks for the fun of learning _____
9. Asks penetrating questions and seeks out causes and reasons _____
10. Is a good guesser with an intuitive sense _____
11. Reads voraciously well beyond age level, and sets aside time for reading _____
12. Questions the accepted ways of doing things _____
13. Prefers to work independently with minimal direction _____
14. Has a longer attention span than age peers _____
15. Has little patience for routine drill and practice _____
16. Tends to be critical of self and others, with high standards and seeking perfection _____
17. Seldom needs more than one demonstration or instruction in order to carry out an activity _____
18. Perseveres on projects and ideas _____
19. Is withdrawn yet very capable when pressed _____
20. Demonstrates remarkable talent in one or more areas _____
21. Uses materials in innovative and unusual ways _____
22. Creates unusual stories, pictures, examples, models, or products _____
23. Has many interests and follows them with zeal _____
24. Makes extensive collections, with sustained focus _____
25. Invents contrivances, gadgets, and new ways of doing things _____
26. Prefers to be around older students or adults, communicating effectively with them _____
27. Has an advanced sense of humor and "gets it" when others may not _____
28. Influences other students to do things _____
29. Is serious-minded and intolerant of prolonged foolishness _____
30. Shows much sensitivity toward people, social issues, and right and wrong _____

Please check any of the following factors which apply. If present along with a number of the attributes above, they may provide additional validation of high ability.

A. A disability that affects learning and/or behavior _____
B. Living in a home where English is the second (or third) language _____
C. Transience (three or more moves) during the elementary school years _____
D. Social or educational isolation from resources and stimulation _____
E. Home responsibilities or employment that interferes with school _____
F. Irregular school attendance _____
G. Little or no interaction between school personnel and family _____

Additional comments:

FIGURE 7.7   Building Administrator Referral Checklist

The following criteria are useful in assessing high potential of students. Please use one form per student to assign a value of *3* (to a considerable degree), *2* (to some degree), or *1* (to little if any degree) for each characteristic.

1. Is quite advanced in academic areas   _____
2. Shows superior leadership qualities   _____
3. Demonstrates a high degree of critical thinking and prefers intellectual challenge   _____
4. Is motivated by curiosity and seems to be self-directed   _____
5. Has many interests and is involved in many activities and projects   _____
6. Is full of ideas and demonstrates flexibility, originality, and resourcefulness   _____
7. Is keenly observant and questioning   _____
8. Is usually serious-minded and intolerant of foolishness   _____
9. Has a high energy level with unusual perseverance   _____
10. Has family members who are intensely concerned with enrichment and acceleration
    in the curriculum and with the learning environment of the school   _____

Please check any of the following factors which apply. If present along with a number of the attributes above, they may provide additional validation of high ability.

    A. Irregular school attendance   _____
    B. Limited contact between school personnel and family   _____

Additional Comments:

Educators who work with preschool children and kindergartners, and parents of preschool children who observe signs that lead them to think their child is precocious, will relate to lists that contain characteristics such as these:

- Asks many questions, often on topics typically interesting to older children
- Demonstrates early use of a large vocabulary and multiple meanings of words
- Understands abstract concepts such as time, coins, larger numbers, calendars
- Relates experiences with great detail and makes up vivid, dramatic stories
- Has a long attention span and deep concentration level for such an early age
- Learned to read at a very young age with little or no instruction
- Expressed self in complete sentences at an early age
- Shows precocious interest in values, purposes, and right-and-wrong issues

Space and reminders must be left on the forms for noting characteristics that signal more than one exceptionality. Students with high potential may have physical disabilities or behavior disorders. Attention deficit with hyperactivity disorder (ADHD) is not uncommon among the high-ability population. Cultural differences such as deference to authority or reluctance to compete against friends can force talents underground. Conditions of illness may prevent students from demonstrating their capabilities. There also may also be chronic underachievers; but there is no such phenomenon as "overachievement," in spite of the unfortunately frequent use of that contrived word by people who are underexpecting. Students causing the most concern among school personnel in regard to their progress will be those in subgroups such as students with disabilities, English language learners, and children of families who are poor and disadvantaged (Christie, 2004).

Identification of potential among such populations of special need can be masked by problems that do not allow their abilities to "bubble up." Conversely, their abilities to compensate may mask problem areas so that those do not become apparent. Thus the student loses both ways. Ability is not served and disability is not remediated. Collaborative consulting teachers, special education personnel, school counselors, and school psychologists must be vigilant in watching for these circumstances.

Interest Inventories.   As a part of the identification process, or after selections have been made for service in special programs and curriculum is being designed, rich data can be obtained from individual interviews in which collaborating co-educators use an inventory format to gather information about student interests and goals. Sometimes the interest inventory is supplemented with a learning styles inventory to determine likes and dislikes in regard to structures for the learning process. Figure 7.8 presents an informal instrument that includes both interests and learning styles to obtain rudimentary information about a student's learning wants and needs. Educators must bear in mind, however, that the best interest survey for any school's personnel is one that has been designed by the user(s) to fit that school setting.

Much more information will be obtained from a personal interview in which a collaborating consultant or the classroom teacher serves as recording secretary or at least shares the writing responsibility, than one in which a form is just given out for the student to fill out then or later. Sometimes, to save time, the teacher may solicit the information from students in a group. One drawback to this approach however is that students, especially younger ones, may mimic others' preferences rather than concentrate on making their own wishes known.

Case Study Information.   The case-study format in Chapter 5's Figure 5.1 (p. 146) presented sixteen data sources for gathering information about student interests and needs. The figure can be visualized as a "daisy" of opportunities to know students better. If each explored "petal" source is shaded with a graphite pencil or covered with a tissue paper overlay, an increasingly dark center indicates a growing assurance that student characteristics and needs will require differentiated curriculum. The daisy tool is instructive for staff development and is useful in planning sessions that include school psychologists, school counselors, family members, related services personnel, and most importantly, the student.

CURRICULAR NEEDS OF LEARNERS WITH HIGH APTITUDE AND TALENT

A simple equation can guide educators in providing special services for students:

Characteristics + Needs = Curriculum Implications

Tomlinson's (1999) prompt that "one size cannot fit all" emphasizes the need for differentiated curriculum that is tailored for the individual. Tailored curriculum includes these four conditions:

1. Release from repetition of material already learned. (Why waste precious learning time redoing what one already has mastered?
2. Removal of ceilings on prescribed curriculum. (Why always have to stop and wait until the rest of the class or group catches up?

FIGURE 7.8   Interest Inventory Format

INTEREST INVENTORY

1. Name _____ Age _____ Grade _____
2. Gender _____ Brothers/Sisters _____
3. Community type (rural, urban, small town) _____
4. School(s) attended _____
5. My favorite subject(s) in school _____
6. What I like to read about _____
7. What I like to access on the Internet _____
8. My hobbies and collections _____
9. Lessons I take _____
10. What I like to watch on TV _____
11. My favorite recreation/sport _____
12. Where I have been on trips _____
13. Where in the world I would go if I could _____
14. What I would do in the world if I could _____
15. What I like best about school _____
16. When I have free time at school I like to _____
17. What I would like to learn more about _____
18. What careers I find most interesting _____
19. What I want to think about doing as a career _____
20. What I wish _____

Rate the next set of activities by putting:

1 = "Like very much," 2 = "It's OK," 3 = "Just so-so," or 4 = "Don't like."

_____ Doing things with a group
_____ Doing things on my own
_____ Reading assignments
_____ Writing reports
_____ Doing experiments
_____ Constructing things
_____ Drawing pictures
_____ Acting out things I'm learning
_____ Listening to teachers and speakers
_____ Watching films or television
_____ Working quickly in order to get done
_____ Working at a leisurely pace
_____ Being a leader most of the time
_____ Being a follower most of the time
_____ Planning my own learning activities
_____ Evaluating my own progress and development

3. Flexible pacing for progress through curriculum that allows time and space for accelerative, enriching learning experiences, and provides time for learning activities with mental peers. (If just marking time in class, why not go on to learn more about the subject in more breadth and depth or advance to another level of study with mental peers?)

4. Engagement in self-directed learning and self-assessment processes. (Why not continue learning in a self-selected topic of keen interest, setting personal goals for achievement?)

These conditions can be addressed through general strategies that match the conditions just described, to include:

1. Release from repetition by curriculum compacting
2. Removal of ceilings by setting appropriate open-ended goals and objectives
3. Flexible pacing through the use of alternative instructional strategies, learning options, and planned learning experiences with mental peers
4. Student engagement in learning through participation in goal setting and planning conferences, design and production of portfolios, and student-engaged assessment processes

These conditions are easy to put into words, but harder to accomplish. Collaborators must exercise considerable skill in communicating with all parties including parents, to plan the enriching and accelerating curriculum, coordinate all facets of it, and assess the outcomes carefully with attention to ever-expanding needs. Gifted education facilitators must acknowledge the concerns of classroom teachers when they worry that bright students who are allowed to move faster or skip material may have some gaps in learning later. Wide ranges of educational experiences must be available that demonstrate students did or will meet general instructional objectives while appealing to their interests, talents, and goals.

All students in school have the right to a challenging school-based curriculum that allows them to learn, and educators and policy makers have the unequivocal responsibility to provide it. Collaborative consultation and working in teams are key processes in making it happen.

Differentiating School-Based Curriculum

As teachers struggle with management and coordination issues, students often languish waiting for something interesting and challenging to happen. Some "sleep through" their classroom situations only to "wake up" later and find that they have missed important elements needed for understanding key concepts. Other students tune out and create their own personal diversions during the school day, sometimes by acting out. But most simply bide the time by reading, daydreaming, playing little games such as writing class notes backward or with the other hand, analyzing and charting their teachers' idiosyncrasies, or surreptitiously interacting with friends. So how can teachers engage these students in learning?

Acceleration or Enrichment?   There is no need to debate the choice of accelerated curriculum over enriched curriculum, or vice versa. Curricular content that accelerates student learning *is enriching,* and curriculum that enriches *will, by its purpose,* be accelerative. Enriching, accelerating instructional strategies call for careful organization and coordination among general education teachers, special education personnel, resource personnel, school administrators, and families, with intensive student collaboration in their own learning programs. Classroom teachers are responsible for delivering content in differentiated, alternative, accelerated, enriched formats. They should introduce fundamentals at the levels and paces (note the plurals) that can be accomplished by each student. No one should have to repeat, repeat, and repeat again content that has already been learned. The key is *flexible pacing,* with movement through the curriculum at speeds, breadths, and depths that stimulate and challenge exceptionally able minds.

Co-Educator Roles for Students of High Ability and Talents

A task force commissioned by the National Association for Gifted Children (NAGC) to investigate linkage of general education and gifted education (more appropriately described as education of the gifted but colloquially referred to as "gifted education") has presented three rationales that signal the need for school collaboration (Tomlinson, Coleman, Allan, Udall, & Landrum, 1996):

1. Collaboration between general and gifted education would facilitate balancing equity and excellence, to the benefit of all students.
2. Collaboration between the two fields would reinforce the reality of shared goals, namely, better schools, richer curriculum content, and robust learning experiences for all students. (It is important to remember that very able students spend most of their school time in general classrooms.)
3. Collaboration between the two fields would maximize strengths of both generalists and specialists to the benefit of the total school community. (Both have important roles; they are not the same roles and they ought not to be.)

As stressed earlier in the book, the "my kids/your kids" and "us/them" attitudes undermine collaborative efforts and working as teams. The NAGC task force recommends thinking of collaborative consultation metaphorically as an orchestra with full expression of the music possible only when all parts do their best to blend and harmonize.

Roles of General Classroom Teachers.   Classroom teachers are responsible for delivering curriculum content in basic, differentiated, compacted, accelerated, and enriched forms. But they should have assistance from special services personnel such as gifted program facilitators who may co-teach, provide resources, coordinate out-of-school learning experiences, direct mentorships, and so forth. Teachers need to understand and appreciate the characteristics, needs, and curricular implications of those with high learning ability, provide a learning environment in the classroom that nurtures high ability, draw on the assistance of special services personnel, and release students from assignments for which they have demonstrated competence. This requires that they use curriculum compacting to remove unnecessary repetition and to "buy time" for more challenging assignments.

Curriculum Compacting.   Just as teachers condense daily lessons and assignments for children returning to school after an illness, they can compact curriculum for students who learn more quickly and easily than the majority of students (Renzulli & Reis, 1985). This "buys time" for students to pursue individual interests and independent study in more challenging areas of regular or accelerated curriculum.

Reis, Burns, and Renzulli (1992) suggest starting the compacting process by targeting a small group of students for which it seems especially appropriate. Then:

■ Select one content area in which student(s) seem most successful and in which the most resources are available.

- Try different methods of finding out what students already know.
- Compact the material by unit, chapter, or topic rather than by schedule.
- Document the rationale for the compacted material and define proficiency based on staff consensus and district policy.
- Request help from collaborating co-educators in order to create a wide range of opportunities and alternatives for replacing the eliminated content.

Very able students need not always accelerate at a fast pace through the curriculum. On occasion they may welcome the opportunity to slow down and study a subject in depth and detail, catching up with the class later by completing regular assignments on a compacted basis. The principle of curriculum compacting could still apply.

If teachers want students to think and perform at more complex and individually expressive levels than recall, recitation, explanation, and translation, they must convey that intent to students. Very able students will accept readily the challenge to analyze, synthesize, evaluate, imagine, and create. With encouragement they can become partners in curriculum development rather than passive recipients. Recall the Chapter 2 discussion that well-known educational taxonomies are powerful tools for focusing on levels of instruction that enable students to learn in increasingly complex, challenging ways. Figure 7.9 can be introduced to students as early as the primary grades. It is a tool for explaining high-order thinking and doing that builds on the categories of knowing and understanding. Growth in higher-order processes as depicted on the taxonomic "plant" illustration is readily grasped by most students, high-achieving or not. By striving beyond rote recall and explanation of basic things learned, they will be able to "bloom" into the most knowledgeable and productive persons they can be.

Gifted Program Facilitators.   Specialists in the education of highly able students have responsibility for coordinating alternate learning activities, freeing up options, gathering resources, and designing responsive learning programs to challenge students appropriately. They must familiarize themselves with classroom content of all grade levels they serve—a daunting assignment but important for building rapport with classroom teachers and being contributive in collaborative conferences. They function as team members in classrooms, as consultants out of the classrooms, as communicators with administrators, and as partners in learning with students and their families. They keep records on student needs and accomplishments, and are in close contact with school counselors and school psychologists. Sometimes they provide professional development experiences for school personnel or awareness sessions for families, school boards, or community groups.

On occasion it is good for them to exchange roles, as discussed in Chapter 1, by working with a classroom teacher's students while that teacher guides a small group in a complex learning activity in or out of the classroom. This lets the special education facilitator observe other students for manifestations of exceptional ability and allows the classroom teacher to have time away from the classroom to direct accelerative, enriching activities with a single student or a small group of students.

Enrichment Triad Model.   Renzulli's Enrichment Triad model, as one of most long-standing and successful gifted education programs, promotes general education and special education teacher collaboration and schoolwide professional development to support the model. It was introduced in the models section of Chapter 3, but will be reviewed here.

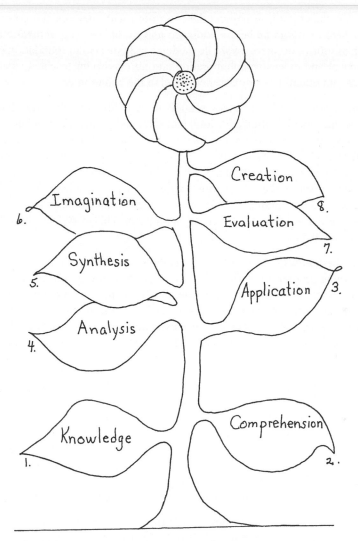

FIGURE 7.9   Blooms for Thinking and Doing
© Peggy Dettmer, 1997.

All students in the general classroom participate in Type 1 exploratory activities on topics of interest through learning centers, field trips, resource speakers, learning packets, and more. All students in the classroom also participate in Type 2 process-building activities to develop skills in problem solving, creative thinking, inquiry, and more. Students who are of above-average ability, motivated to learn and do, and show signs of creativity are encouraged to participate in Type 3 enrichment activities such as independent studies, research, and project development as would be done by professionals. Interest inventories and learning styles surveys guide construction of these intense activities. The Type 3 experiences may take place in the classroom, in a resource room with other students identified for the talent pool, or beyond the classroom with mentors and content experts. The work is shared with an authentic audience and evaluated with authentic assessment methods such as rubrics or interviews. The model is built on a solid foundation of intensive staff development and extensive collaboration among classroom teachers, special education personnel, and oftentimes resource personnel in the community.

Resource Consultation Model. In many schools there is little collaboration between general classroom teachers and gifted education teachers, with classroom teachers making few efforts to modify their curriculum for highly able students. The resource consultation model calls for teachers to work in ways that may be different from ways they have worked in the past (Kirschenbaum, Armstrong, & Landrum, 1999; Ward & Landrum, 1994). Staff development for activating the model allows gifted education teachers to learn more about the general education program, and classroom teachers and other school personnel to become more familiar with the gifted education program. This model was introduced in the models section of Chapter 3.

Building Administrators.   In important ways the school principal has a vital role in differentiated learning programs for students with exceptional ability. If principals do not support tailored curriculum and encourage accelerated, enriching instruction, little is likely to happen that benefits students *or* their teachers. Administrators must provide the support and safety that very able students need to use extended resources productively. They have responsibility for reinforcing teachers who make efforts to collaborate with colleagues and design differentiated curriculum strategies and materials.

School Counselors and School Psychologists.   These roles are integral in identifying student capabilities and ferreting out any problems occurring from failure of schools to meet those needs. In IEP conferences they often fill the required administrator role when the principal cannot attend. They can be helpful with practical suggestions for resources to optimize learning if encouraged to do so, and with information in staff development activities if asked to do so. Secondary-level counselors can be so much more assistive to highly able students than as "card shufflers" who schedule drop/adds; they can help by overseeing students' cognitive, emotional, and social needs in what are often explosive peer environments for them.

IEP Conferences. A major area of team contribution by school psychologists is in the individual education planning conference or, if IEPs for gifted students are not mandated in that state, then any similar goal-setting conference for a student. IEP goals must be open-ended, aimed at complex learning and the high-road transfer of learning that calls for application to new areas. Objectives should be developed with input from the student and not remedial in tone, but directed toward those strengths for which the IEP is warranted. The student also should help plan the assessment process.

Learning Options in and beyond School. School personnel feel the brunt of parental pressure to provide advanced opportunities, and some become defensive when the school's most able students complain that lessons are "boring."[1] Some educators, including school

[1]The "b word" as delivered by impatient students (and sometimes parents) tends to be overworked. It is likely that everyone benefits at one time or another from feeling bored, for it causes us to fall back on our own resources and develop them. But atrophy (of mind and ability) is another thing altogether. Atrophy shrinks one's capability and productivity for present and future.

counselors and school psychologists, become defensive on hearing that schools are not prepared to teach children who may be as knowledgeable or more so in subjects than they and often can pass tests over subject matter before they open the texts. These situations call for a meeting of the minds among all parties for collaborative resolution of curricular and extracurricular issues that can impede student progress and dampen enthusiasm for learning. A study by Purcell and Leppien (1998) highlights two facets of the collaborative process that can tap into its power for providing challenging instruction.

1. Expectations for student learning must be discussed and made congruent.
2. Interactions among school personnel must facilitate differentiated curriculum.

Some arrangements that would benefit very capable students can take place in the general classroom. Others require a resource room or laboratory or library setting. (See Figure 7.10.) Still others are accessible only outside the school setting. When students leave their school campus for enrichment, or for accelerated coursework, group learning experiences, or individual arrangements, special educators, classroom teachers, counselors,

---

FIGURE 7.10   Learning Opportunities in the School Setting

- Differentiated curriculum in the classroom
- Curriculum compacting
- Use of books from the library as basal readers for both comprehension and skill building
- Telescoped curriculum where a course of study is collapsed into a shorter time frame
- Continuous progress courses, moving ahead as content and skills are acquired
- Grade skipping
- Early entrance to school (however, not permitted in some states)
- Test out
- Cross-age tutoring, with very able students teaching younger students of high ability
- Programmed instruction packages for rapid progress in areas of keen interest
- Seminars within schools or in collaboration with other schools or universities
- Advanced placement
- Mini-replications of existing research studies
- Conversations with/observations of book authors, artists-in-residence, scientists, etc.
- Enrichment activity calendars for classroom teachers with a daily enriching activity
- Resource room time for independent study, research, or project development
- Honors classes
- Dual enrollment
- Discussion groups for moral dilemmas, great books, or current issues
- Special units of study that have a concentrated international perspective
- Biographies and autobiographies, to study great leaders of past and present
- Collection and analysis of the world's wisdom (proverbs, fables, maxims, credos, etc.)
- Summer school enrichment courses
- International baccalaureate program
- Extra classes for extra credit
- Cluster grouping to work with mental peers on advanced topics
- Extended library, lab, practice, or computer time, or more time to work on projects
- Small-group discussions and investigations with mental peers (and more)

FIGURE 7.11   Learning Opportunities Beyond the School Setting

- Early graduation from high school
- Early entrance to the university, with or without a high school diploma
- Career shadowing
- Academic competitions—regional, state, national, international
- Community service (sometimes for high school credit)
- Student exchange programs—urban to rural, west to east, U.S. to other countries, etc.
- Mentorships
- Tutorials with experts in a field of keen interest or exceptional talent
- Travel study programs
- Concurrent enrollment in high school courses and college courses
- Part time enrollment in vocational-technical schools to learn a trade
- University credit by examination
- College correspondence courses
- Field trips
- College level independent studies
- Internships and apprenticeships
- Periodic contributions of writing and reporting for newspaper and media
- Presentations and performances of advanced work, to audiences outside the school (and more . . .)

and principals must collaborate to ensure that the students accomplish school district and state academic requirements and continue to be involved in the life of the school. They also must deal with scheduling, student supervision, and liability issues. (See Figure 7.11.)

Mentors and Resource Personnel.   Mentors have opportunities for such profound influence on others that the relationship must not be left to chance happening. Mentorships allow students to apply and extend their learning beyond available school curriculum. Key steps in setting up and facilitating a mentorship are:

1. Designate student(s) who will participate in mentorships.
2. Ascertain student interests and learning styles.
3. Locate mentors who may be matches for those interests and styles.
4. Discuss mentorship with the potential mentors to ascertain their feelings about it.
5. Temporarily match mentor with mentee and initiate casual interaction between them.
6. When a match is established, involve parents and develop a very general study plan, including a plan for eventual termination of the mentorship; this is important so that neither party is offended or let down when the mentoring relationship concludes.
7. Continue to monitor progress, from a distance if possible, handling any problems immediately.
8. Evaluate the experience, with input from student, mentor, parents, and facilitator, and bring closure as previously planned in Step 6.

For evaluation of their products and performances, and as a means of authentic assessment, students can be encouraged to solicit critique from outside experts, favorite former teachers, the principal, or even older students who are budding experts in that field. An example of a form for critique is provided in Figure 7.12.

FIGURE 7.12   Request for Assessment

I, _____, would like for you, _____, to critique my _____

    (student name)   (evaluator's name)   (type of work)

It is included with this form. I have proofread, edited, revised, and improved it, and I now present it for critique and feedback from the evaluator I have chosen—You!
I am asking that you:

_____ provide comments on merits and strengths of this work.

_____ suggest any additions, deletions, revisions that could improve the work.

_____ comment on weaknesses, inaccuracies, errors, or misjudgments in the work.

_____ suggest resources I missed that would have added value to work.

_____ offer any ideas that come to mind for an extension of this work.

I will use your critique and feedback to:

_____ redo this work for the purpose of _____

_____ work more effectively on my next project which is _____

Thank you very much for your assistance! My teacher(s) and I value your help very much.

_____   _____

(student signature)   (facilitating teacher signature)

_____   _____

(date of request)   (date of returned assessment)

Other Important Roles for Education of Students with High Ability.   Librarians, media specialists, and technology specialists are often the best resources for locating materials to lift students beyond mundane basal texts or to delve into an independent study or research project. They know where things are! They can help teachers build core skills practice into rich subject-matter investigations rather than rely on workbooks of mundane basal materials. They should be part of any team that is targeting curriculum modification, independent study, research projects, individual study for testing out of courses, and other individual education plans. One way they could help is to collaborate with teachers on analyses of textbooks and accompanying instructor manuals to determine which ones provide the most useful enrichment instruction strategies and ideas for student projects and activities.

Ensuring Differentiated Curriculum in Inclusive Schools

An inclusive school increases responsibilities of classroom teachers to provide for learning needs of highly able students. VanTassel-Baska (1989) notes several mistaken beliefs that need to be altered regarding differentiation for highly able students. First, consultants and consultees should not assume that curriculum must *always* be different from what all learners have. Nor do all learning experiences need to be product oriented. Then, too, one curriculum package or a single learning strategy will *not* provide all that is needed.

It cannot be denied that many teachers feel negatively toward acceleration, telescoping, or compacting of content for very able students. Some of their concerns must be heeded, such as the possibility that vital content and needed practice will be skipped; however, most such concerns are not justified. The research is clear that acceleration is *not* harmful as a general rule to the academic, emotional, or social well-being of students who already may be tuned out, bored, or discouraged. Far worse is to languish for years craving more challenging work.

Research by Gerber and Popp (2000) indicates that collaborative programs should be explained thoroughly to those affected by them prior to the initiation of the programs. Students in particular need carefully presented, clear explanations about the purposes and potential benefits of consultation, collaboration, and co-teaching.

SCENARIO 7.E

Oliver, a high school senior and aspiring playwright but a lackluster student in most classes, had never participated in a gifted program. He did not care to be tested with the district's standardized measure of aptitude and as for the program, he commented to the facilitator, "Activities like riding in a bus 100 miles to tour the aircraft plant are not what I need." But when his drama teacher, after consultation with the gifted program facilitator and the building administrator, suggested that perhaps gifted program enrollment could make him eligible for curriculum adaptations in his senior year, he agreed to the testing. He tested very well, and after eleven years of "revving his motor with his brakes on" in many of his classes, he was given relatively free license to write the senior class play, cast, stage, and direct it, conduct rehearsals, and even advise the art department as to type of publicity material he wanted.

This was truly a co-teaching and collaborative consultation experience, involving school principal, gifted program facilitator, general classroom drama teacher, art teacher, school psychologist, custodian, evening security guard, and family/consumer science teacher whose class made refreshments for the performance. Some teachers expressed doubts about the latitude given to this student in their small-town, rural high school, but the principal endorsed the idea with only two stipulations—the consulting facilitator could edit any objectionable parts of the script and there must be teacher supervision at all rehearsals. The play, though not well attended, was interesting and innovative, and Oliver graduated deeming his senior year a personal success.

ETHICS FOR CO-TEACHING STUDENTS WITH EXCEPTIONAL LEARNING NEEDS

Many positive benefits result from consulting, collaborating, and co-teaching to tailor the curriculum and manage classroom procedures for students who learn differently, whether it is because of disabilities, behavioral disorders, or high abilities. As teachers work together, they have time and input from colleagues for getting to know students' interests, strengths, and areas of need.

However, not all teachers wish to co-teach and those wishes should be respected. Some classroom teachers are uncomfortable with having other teachers in the classroom as they teach. Then, too, teachers must not be expected to hand off their personal best ideas to others even when engaging in collaborative activities.

Accomplishments and innovative ideas should be recognized and credited in a manner that is sincere and not patronizing. Building trust among collaborating teachers, families, and students as partners is a major determinant of success in co-teaching, and effective communication is a major tool in building that trust.

Classroom teachers and special education teachers may want to co-teach a lesson or perhaps even a unit. They might exchange roles for a time, to gain new perspectives on the students and the material. They can work together with a particular student as a partnership of three or more to plan, implement, and evaluate differentiated learning experiences. As they collaborate to design personalized programs and free up time for learning alternatives, they can more readily provide seamless attention to special needs. Schools become more lively places for learning, staff members more enthusiastic, and families more supportive in a collaborative, ethical climate. When allowed, students are delighted to have a "voice" in their learning. Teachers model interpersonal skills for their students and they also find outlets for expression of their best and most creative ideas, which affirms and reinforces their decision to be an educator.

TIPS FOR COLLABORATIVE PLANNING AND TEACHING

1. Co-teaching requires careful planning. Planning time must be built into the restructured school day.
2. Co-teachers will want to discuss their philosophies about teaching.
3. When co-teaching, clarify classroom rules and procedures such as routines for leaving the room, discipline matters, and division of chores such as grading or making bulletin boards.
4. Devise a way to keep track of individuals who are providing services for students so that monitoring does not become a problem.
5. Rather than just telling classroom teachers about materials modification, *show* them. Give some examples or do one for them.
6. Request demonstration lessons from classroom teachers featuring *their* most outstanding teaching techniques.
7. Offer to retype a test for a teacher (to double space, type in large print, or organize it differently) for use with any student who has a learning problem.
8. Before ordering computer software, have students try it out first. This gives them an opportunity to be consultants for teachers and cultivates student ownership in educational planning and evaluation.
9. When preparing and distributing materials for classroom use, don't just drop them off and run. Help the teacher or student get started, and stay awhile to see how it goes.

10. Keep a supply of materials to send to classrooms for students who need reinforcement, even those with whom you don't work who could benefit.

11. Have a favorite dozen or so of successful strategies available for demonstration teaching or sharing.

12. Be understanding of classroom teachers' daily trials with some mainstreamed students. Celebrate with classroom teachers even the smallest student progress.

13. Talk with school librarians and public librarians, asking them to order books and periodicals about needs of students that would appeal to families and community members. Give them the name, author, publisher, and if possible, the ISBN.

14. Drop off samples of periodicals such as *Educational Leadership, Phi Delta Kappan, Early Childhood Today, Journal of Emotional and Behavioral Disorders, Journal of Learning Disabilities,* and *Gifted Child Today* at offices of pediatricians, obstetricians, and dentists for their waiting rooms. If possible, briefly visit with the medical staff about potential value of these materials to families and community members.

15. Build networks of interaction among school personnel, parents, and community members who could serve as tutors, monitors, mentors, and independent study facilitators for special needs.

CHAPTER REVIEW

1. Co-teaching (two or more teachers planning and delivering instruction) by special educators and general educators requires co-planning, which differs from group planning models used by general educators and the linear, individual planning models of special educators. Most special educators will not have time to provide extensive remedial instruction given all their other responsibilities. Most will need to plan the remediation and direct a peer tutor or volunteer to provide the instruction. Special educators need to acquire a library of resources that provide explicit guidelines for tutors to follow.

2. Universal Design for Learning is a system of best practices to have in place at every phase of learning and teaching to maximize access to the curriculum and maximize learning of all students. Until the ideals of UDL become a reality in all classrooms, special educators need to assist classroom teachers in planning, adapting, and delivering lessons.

3. The Interactive Planning model addresses nearly all students, or most students, or some individual students, as needs dictate. As a result, the model can be successful when co-teachers plan and co-teach lessons using one or a combination of various approaches for presentation of lessons. Other co-teaching approaches are Parallel Teaching, Team Teaching, Station Teaching, and Teach and Monitor.

4. Without information about a student's IEP goals and objectives, classroom teachers, paraeducators, and other persons involved in a student's instruction can only assume the student should meet the same goals and objectives as most students in the inclusive classroom. Federal laws specify who should be eligible for reasonable accommodations in schools.

5. Curriculum adaptations involve accommodations (assistive aids and supports) and modifications (changed activities, goals or outcomes). Students whose cognitive disabilities prevent them from benefiting from the general classroom curriculum, even with accommodations, need curriculum modifications. Students with

mild or moderate cognitive disabilities may need adapted materials while students with severe cognitive disabilities will need different goals or materials. For the very able, curriculum adaptation can be acceleration and enrichment, curriculum compacting, flexible pacing, mentorship, and learning opportunities beyond the school campus.

6. Consultants and collaborating teachers cannot be present in every general classroom for all instruction that takes place, but they can support classroom teachers in many other ways such as planning for tutors and other instructional assistants assigned to the classroom; teaching students study strategies, classroom survival skills, and self-advocacy behaviors; adapting tests and other text material; locating or constructing resource materials; preparing challenging, enriched, and accelerated content; and monitoring student progress with authentic assessments as well as tests.

TO DO AND THINK ABOUT

1. Plan a lesson with another teacher. Then co-teach the lesson with students or with a group of adult colleagues (which could be fun!). After teaching, evaluate the process and think about what you need to do to improve.

2. Interview teachers who co-teach to find out how they make it work. If possible, visit in their classrooms.

3. Develop a plan for implementing a peer tutoring program that could be used in your school.

4. Construct a profile for a hypothetical student with disabilities and provide adaptations (accommodations or modifications) for the student during a lesson in the general classroom when you are not present.

5. Prepare a co-teaching plan for one week (or one month, if that is more appropriate). Determine how you and your co-teacher(s) will move on from the inevitable articulation of differences to a compatible and cohesive plan. Decide, and practice, how you will explain the plan to students and their family members. To really benefit from this activity, develop a scheduling template and a co-teaching lesson plan template that you could use for planning and organization.

6. Develop a co-teaching evaluation checklist that could be completed by each co-teacher as a self-evaluation and by each collaborating co-teacher for the process, without singling out individual co-teachers.

7. In collaboration with another teacher, co-plan a lesson at the elementary level that addresses needs of a student with behavioral disorders in a typical classroom. Describe resources that will be needed and who will obtain them. Determine how you will assess the learning (entire class and smaller group) and how you will evaluate the success of the co-teaching process.

8. Develop a hypothetical situation at the secondary level in which you consult with a potential mentor about a student with high ability and/or talents. Draft ideas that might come up for discussion regarding planning, resource gathering, coordinating, and assessment. The ideas should be consistent with school policy, acceptable to the student's family, and above all, appealing to the student.

9. Select a textbook for a grade level and curricular area that interests you. Analyze it and its instructor's manual for qualities that would make it suitable for use with students of high ability.

10. As an extension of #9, have a colleague select a contrasting text, and then each one describe merits or demerits of the material as if one of you were a member of a curriculum selection committee and the other were a marketing representative for the text's publisher. (Suggestion: This is more productive if the text has desirable qualities, so be choosy and look until you find one that seems promising.)

ADDITIONAL READINGS AND RESOURCES

Center for Applied Technology (CAST). *Resources to help implement UDL and make curriculum adaptations*. www.cast.org

Fennick, E. (2001). Co-teaching: An inclusive curriculum for transition. *TEACHING Exceptional Children, 33*(6), 60–66.

Describes how co-teaching in high school life skills classes can provide instruction for transition, job skills, and daily living skills in inclusive environments.

Friend, M. (2007). The coteaching partnership. *Educational Leadership, 64*(5), 48–52.

Hughes, C. E., & Murawski, W. A. (2001). Lessons from another field: Applying co-teaching strategies to gifted education. *Gifted Child Quarterly, 45*(3), 195–204.

Offers a new definition of collaboration within the context of gifted education and expands on co-teaching as a collaborative strategy. Descriptions and examples of adaptations of five models for co-teaching originally developed for students with disabilities are provided.

Kirschenbaum, R. J., Armstrong, D. C., & Landrum, M. S. (1999). Resource consultation model in gifted education to support talent development in today's inclusive schools. *Gifted Child Quarterly, 43*(1), 39–47.

Mastropieri, M. A., Scruggs, T. E., & Berkeley, S. L. (2007). Peers helping peers. *Educational Leadership, 64*(5), 54–58.

Morocco, C. C., & Aguilar, C. M. (2002). Co-teaching for content understanding: A schoolwide model. *Journal for Educational and Psychological Consultation, 13*(4), 315–347.

A model for co-teaching involving collaboration between a content-area teacher and a special education teacher. Success is dependent on collaborative school structures, equal status rules for teachers, commitment to all students' learning, and strong content knowledge.

Pisha, B., & Coyne, P. (2001). Smart from the start: The promise of universal design for learning. *Remedial and Special Education, 22*(4), 197–203.

Reinhiller, N. (1996). Co-teaching: New variations on a not-so-new practice. *Teacher Education and Special Education, 19*(1), 34–48.

Co-teaching approaches as a collaborative model, a special education instructional strategy, and an activity are discussed. Challenges, barriers, and benefits to these innovations are delineated.

Renzulli, J. S., & Reis, S. M. (1985). *The schoolwide enrichment model: A comprehensive plan for educational excellence*. Mansfield Center, CT: Creative Learning Press.

Stewart, R. A., & Brendefur, J. L. (2005). Fusing lesson study and authentic achievement: A model for teacher collaboration. *Phi Delta Kappan, 86*(9), 681–687.

VanTassel-Baska, J. (1991). Gifted education in the balance: Building relationships with general education. *Gifted Child Quarterly, 35*(1), 20–25.

This article focuses on the relationships among gifted education, special education, and general education and discusses the importance of establishing links with general education and educational reform movements.

Vaughn, S., Schumm, J. S., & Arguelles, M. E. (1997). The ABCDEs of co-teaching. *Teaching Exceptional Children, 30*(2), 42–45.

CHAPTER EIGHT

CONTENT:
Family
Partnerships

Working Together with Families and Communities

Education must be a shared responsibility. Education of the whole child requires solid, well-functioning partnerships among school, community, and family. In a 2003 Delta Kappa-Gallup poll of attitudes toward public schools, 94 percent of respondents declared that home life, parent involvement in education, student interest in education, and the community environment are crucial to improving student achievement (Blank, 2004).

Family members are a child's first and most influential teachers. The nature of education makes families and schools partners in educating children with special needs. Too often the conventional pattern of relationships between schools and parents is limited to having parents as donors, classroom volunteers, or passive recipients of information. This pattern should be altered by joining family members and community members in partnerships to prepare students for their future. Cultivating home-school collaboration allows school educators and home educators to fulfill their commitments toward developing each child's potential.

FOCUSING QUESTIONS

1. How does involvement by families in home-school partnerships benefit students, their families, teachers, their schools, and communities?

2. What legislation has mandated parent involvement and supported family empowerment in schools?

3. In what ways has family involvement matured into family partnership and collaboration?

4. What are barriers to home-school collaborative partnerships?

5. How can educators examine their values and attitudes toward families in order to build collaborative relationships?

6. How can school personnel initiate and individualize partnerships with families and involve students in planning for their own learning?

KEY TERMS

cultural and linguistic
   diversity (CLD)
empowerment
equal partnerships model

family-focused collaboration
home-school collaboration
Individualized Family Service
   Plan (IFSP)

parent involvement
parent partnerships

SCENARIO 8.A

The setting is a junior high school. The learning disabilities teacher has just arrived at the building, hoping to make some contacts with classroom teachers before classes begin, when the principal walks out of her office briskly, with a harried look.

Principal: Oh, I'm glad you're here. I believe Barry is part of your caseload this year, right? His mother is in my office. She's crying, and says that everybody's picking on her son.

LD Consultant: What happened?

Principal: He got into an argument with his English teacher yesterday, and she sent him to me. After he cooled down and we had a talk, it was time for classes to change, so I sent him on to his next class. But he skipped out. The secretary called and left word with the babysitter to inform the mother about his absence. He must have really unloaded on her, because she's here, quite upset, and saying that the teachers do not care about her son and his problems. Could you join us for a talk?

LD Consultant: OK, sure. (Enters the principal's office and greets Barry's mother.)

Mother: I am just about at my wit's end. It's not been a good week at home, but we've made an effort to keep track of Barry's work. Now this problem with his English teacher has him refusing to come to school. Sometimes I feel that we're at cross purposes—us at home and you at school.

LD Consultant: We certainly don't want this to happen. I'd like to hear more about your concerns, and the problems Barry and his teachers are having. Is this a good time, or can we arrange for one that is more convenient for you?

Mother: The sooner, the better. I don't want Barry missing school, but with the attitude he has right now, it wouldn't do him any good to be here.

LD Consultant: Sounds like you are eager to work on this! I would like us to move into the conference room and talk about Barry's problems here at school. We may want to involve others in our discussions later. Would that be OK with you? We are all concerned about Barry, and we need for him to know that.

MANDATES FOR FAMILY INVOLVEMENT

School partners need to be aware of several legislated mandates intended to ensure and strengthen educational partnerships between home and school. The Education for All Handicapped Children Act of 1975 (P.L. 94-142) prescribes several rights for families of children with disabilities. Succeeding amendments have extended those rights and responsibilities.

Legislation mandating family involvement is part of EACHA, the Handicapped Children's Protection Act, Early Intervention for Infants and Toddlers (Part H of P.L. 99-457), and the Individuals with Disabilities Education Act (IDEA, P.L. 101-476). Passage of P.L. 94-142 in 1975 guaranteed families the right to due process, prior notice and consent, access to records, and participation in decision-making. To these basic rights the 1986 Handicapped Children's Protection Act added collections of attorney's fees for parents who prevail in due process hearings or court suits. The Early Intervention Amendment was part of the reauthorized and amended P.L. 94-142. Passed in 1986, it provides important provisions for children from birth through five years and their families. Part H addresses infants and toddlers with disabilities or who are at-risk for developmental delays. Procedural safeguards for families were continued and participation in the Individualized Family Service Plan (IFSP) was added.

The IFSP is developed by a multidisciplinary team with family members as active participants. Part B, Section 691, mandates service to all children with disabilities from ages three to five, and permits noncategorical services. Children may be served according to the needs of their families, allowing a wide range of services with parent training. This amendment fosters collaboration based on family-focused methods. The legislation speaks of families in a broad sense, not just a mother and father pair as the family unit. Families' choices are considered in all decisions.

The 1990 amendments under P.L. 101-476 increased participation by children and adults with disabilities and their families. An example is the formation of community transition councils with active participation of parents in the groups. Subsequent court decisions and statutory amendments have clarified and strengthened parent rights (Martin, 1991). The spirit of the law is met when educators develop positive, collaborative relationships with families.

The Individuals with Disabilities Education Act (IDEA) Amendments of 1997 were signed into law in June of 1997 after two years of analysis, hearings, and discussion. This reauthorization of IDEA, as Public Law 105-17, brought many changes to P.L. 94-142. Parent participation in eligibility and placement decisions, and mediation as a means of resolving parent-school controversies are two critically important areas of change. P.L. 105-17 strengthens the involvement of parents in all decision making involving their children (National Information Center for Children and Youth with Disabilities, 1997).

The 1997 amendments were reauthorized in 2004 as P.L. 108-446, the No Child Left Behind (NCLB) legislation. NCLB mandates that schools give parents the tools they need to support their children's learning in the home and that they communicate regularly with families about children's academic progress, provide opportunities for family workshops, and offer parents chances to engage in parent leadership activities at the school site.

EDUCATIONAL RATIONALE
FOR FAMILY INVOLVEMENT

School, family, and community provide overlapping spheres of influence on children's behavior and achievement. All spheres should be included for involvement by the collaborative team for partnerships that operate with students at the center of the model. Student development and learning at all levels of education are supported by strong home-school relationships within which they improve academic behavior and social behavior, achieving higher attendance rates and lower suspension rates.

Families make a difference in the academic and social lives of children and youth. At all phases of schooling, strong home-school relationships are critical for children's learning and development. Extensive research demonstrates that family involvement can enhance a student's chances for success in school and significantly improve achievement. Students have higher attendance rates, more pro-social behavior, better test scores, and higher home-work completion rates. Level of family involvement predicts children's academic and social development as they progress from early childhood education programs through K–12 schools and into higher education (Caspe, Lopez, & Wolos, 2007).

For preschool children, family involvement means improved cognitive and social development. Frequency of parent-teacher contact and involvement at the early childhood site is associated with preschool performance (Weiss, Caspe, & Lopez, 2006). In their study of experimental research on parent involvement at the early childhood level, the Harvard Family Research Project found that participation in school activities is associated with child language, self-help, social, motor, adaptive, and basic school skills (Weiss et al., 2006).

Home-school relationships have positive short-term and long-term benefits for elementary school students, too (Caspe et al., 2007). Barnard (2004) showed that when low-income African American families maintained continuously high rates of parent participation in elementary school, children were more likely to complete high school. Dearing, Krieder, Simpkins, and Weiss (2006) conducted a longitudinal study that showed consistent family involvement was predictive of gains in children's literacy performance. In a meta-analysis of studies examining the relationship of parent involvement with student academic achievement in urban elementary schools, Jeynes (2005) discovered that continuous and consistent parent involvement shields and protects children from the negative influences of poverty; it may be one approach to reducing the achievement gap between white and nonwhite students.

At the middle and high school levels, family involvement is a powerful predictor of various positive academic and social outcomes. Because of the adolescent's increasing desire for autonomy and changes in school structure, family involvement in education tends to decrease in middle and high school (Kreider, Caspe, Kennedy, & Weiss, 2007). However, family involvement in learning remains important in the adolescent years. Parents can monitor their children's academic and social progress and acquire information they need to make decisions about their children's future, then engage in positive relationships with school staff (Hill & Taylor, 2004). They also have the opportunity to learn skills that help with their child's needs, such as behavior management techniques and communication strategies.

As parents work with teachers, they can provide input about their children's histories and experiences and express their own wisdom about their children's interests and needs. Teachers learn more about students' backgrounds and receive support from family members who can provide encouragement to their children as they study and learn.

School systems benefit from home-school collaboration through improved attitudes toward schools and advocacy for school programs. A positive home-school relationship helps others in the schools and the community. Family involvement increases positive communication among all who are involved on the education team.

All in all, substantial research supports family involvement, and a growing body of intervention evaluations demonstrates that family involvement can be strengthened with positive results for children and youth (Caspe & Lopez, 2006). Therefore, it is crucial for encouraging optimal outcomes by students.

Family Empowerment

A significant goal of family and community involvement with education is empowerment of families. The old way of working with families of children with disabilities often meant "helping them into helplessness." Well-intentioned educators and other professional helpers provided services and solved problems, and families were deprived of the experience of learning to solve their own problems. But families are the constant in children's lives and family members need the knowledge, skills, and motivation to become advocates for themselves and their children. Empowerment means that family members take action to reach goals for their children, satisfying their wants and needs and building on their strengths. Empowered people have the means and knowledge to act; they know what they want and take action to get it (Turnbull, Turnbull, Erwin, & Soodak, 2006).

True educational partnerships support empowerment of families. Educators should provide families with some of the means they need to become empowered. Turnbull and Turnbull et al. (2006) describe an empowerment model of collaboration. In their empowerment framework, family resources, professional resources, and education context resources are all involved in collaborating for empowerment. Family resources include motivation, expectation, energy, and persistence. Families often need additional skills and knowledge to become empowered as strong advocates for their children and partners with their children's teachers. This knowledge includes information, problem solving, life management strategies, and communication skills. Teachers can use their resources to empower parents and support development of their skills. Providing this support for parents, families, and siblings of children with exceptionalities also means fostering community support and advocacy (Fiedler, Simpson, & Clark, 2007). Resources for studying the interests and needs of siblings of people with special health and developmental needs are available online at Web sites such as www.siblingsupport.org.

Several program attributes can help assure consultants that school-home-community programming will result in family empowerment. Those listed here are based on principles of Family Support America (Dunst, 2002):

- Educators and families work together in relationships based on equality and respect.
- Educators enhance families' capacities to support growth and development in all family members.
- Families are recognized as resources to their own members, to other families, to programs, and to communities.
- Schools affirm and strengthen families' cultural, racial, and linguistic identities and enhance their ability to function in a multicultural society.
- Educators and communities advocate for services and systems that are fair, responsible, and accountable to the families served.
- School personnel work with families to mobilize formal and informal resources to support family development.
- Programs are flexible and responsive to emerging family and community issues.

Broadened Conceptualization of Family

Changing times and changing families require new ideas, new languages, and new models. The first step in these changes is to think in terms of family rather than parent. Many children do not live with both parents, or with either biological parent. Part H and Section of 619 of IDEA refer to families rather than parents. Consultants who are collaborating with adults for development and well-being of children with special needs should have a broad, inclusive definition of *family*.

This new, inclusive definition for family was suggested to the Office of Special Education and Rehabilitation Services (OSERS) by the Second Family Leadership Conference:

> A family is a group of people who are important to each other and offer each other love and support, especially in times of crisis. In order to be sensitive to the wide range of lifestyles, living arrangements, and cultural variations that exist today, family . . . can no longer be limited to just parent/child relationships. Family involvement . . . must reach out to include mothers, fathers, grandparents, sisters, brothers, neighbors, and other persons who have important roles in the lives of people with disabilities. (Family Integration Resources, 1991, p. 37)

Consultants need to help school personnel accommodate differences in families—families of children with disabilities, poverty-level families, CLD families—and recognize that they are not homogeneous groups. Educators need to respond in individually relevant ways rather than to make assumptions about families based on their language, ethnicity, or background. Educators need to learn more about full-service models and collaborate actively with related service providers and community networks. If they become knowledgeable about services and advocate for broader services and access, collaborative efforts with parents will be more successful, to the benefit of students, families, and school personnel.

MOVING FROM PARENT INVOLVEMENT
TO PARTNERSHIPS WITH FAMILIES

Educational consultants and their colleagues must be aware of the realities and new legislation facing today's families. Increases are evident in poverty levels, births to unwed adolescent parents, and the rise of nonbiological parents as primary caretakers (foster care, grandmothers, extended family, adoptive parents, and so on). In addition, there are increasing numbers of families with cultural minority backgrounds, single-parent families, parents with disabilities, gay and lesbian parents, and blended and extended families.

Many families are overwhelmed by family crises and normal life events. Others face multiple stressors such as long work hours, illness and disability, and overwhelming responsibilities. Many are discouraged and burned out. Such situations make family collaboration a challenge for collaborative consultants and many families. Educational legislation and social reality result in an inclusive school context that gives educators the opportunity and flexibility to work collaboratively with persons who may be helpful and supportive of the child's success in school.

It is possible for families to be involved in the school life of their children but not be collaborative. Collaboration goes beyond involvement. Educators may provide families with information, parenting classes, and advocacy groups. However, this kind of involvement does not ensure that family needs and interests are being heard and understood. It does not signify that educators are setting program goals based on family members' concerns and input. It might involve parents in a narrow sense, but not in the larger sense of *working together* to form a home-school partnership.

It is important to distinguish between parent involvement and family collaboration in two ways:

1. Parent involvement is parent participation in activities that are part of their children's education—for example, conferences, meetings, newsletters, tutoring, and volunteer services.
2. Family collaboration is the development and maintenance of positive, respectful, egalitarian relationships between home and school. It includes mutual problem solving with shared decision making and goal setting for students' needs.

Values Inherent in Home-School Collaboration

Collaboration with families adds a dimension to home-school relationships. Not only should family members be involved with schools, educators must be involved with families. Metaphorically speaking, a one-way street becomes a two-way boulevard to provide an easier road to "Success City" for students. Family-focused home-school collaboration is based on these principles:

- Families are a constant in children's lives and must be equal partners in all decisions affecting the child's educational program.
- Family involvement includes a wide range of family structures.
- Diversity and individual differences among people are to be valued and respected.
- All families have strengths and coping skills that can be identified and enhanced.
- Families are sources of wisdom and knowledge about their children.

Central to family-centeredness is the respect for family concerns and priorities, issues of family competence and assets, and utilization of family and community resources and supports. Hammond (1999) lists other characteristics of family-centered programs: flexible programming, individualizing services for families, communication, developing and maintaining relationships, building family-staff collaboration, and respecting the family's expertise and strengths. This is a tall order for educational consultants, but new, empowering relationships and better outcomes for students depend on this shared sense of respect and care.

BARRIERS TO COLLABORATION WITH FAMILIES

Changing family structures make traditional methods of recruiting parent participation somewhat problematic. Historical, attitudinal, or perceptual factors in regard to work, transportation, and child care can influence family participation. Major changes in immigration patterns and in the diversity of the U.S. population add to the complexity of collaboration with families (see Berger, 2008; Lynch & Hanson, 1998; and Chapter 9 in this book). Collaborative consultants who recognize potential barriers to home-school partnerships will be better prepared to use successful and appropriate strategies in bridging the gap between home and school.

Most educational consultants recognize the importance of family involvement, but going beyond the "what can parents do for the school" presents a barrier to some educators. Christie (2005) believes it is often easier to talk about what parents can do for the school than it is to listen to parents about what they know their children need to be successful. Sometimes when parents appear not to care, Christie says, it is because they know that what they have to say probably will not be heard.

The success of family collaboration activities is based on partnerships developed and maintained by using the relationship and communication skills such as those described in Chapter 4. However, other barriers overshadow the need for effective communication. They surface as formidable challenges to educators even before lines of communication are established. Examples of such barriers are time limitations, anticipation of negative or punishing interactions, denial of problems, blaming, or a personal sense of failure in parenting and teaching.

Parents of children with learning and behavior problems can be effective change agents for their children; therefore, the question is not whether to involve them, but *how* to do it (Bauer & Shea, 2003). Although family members may want very much to play a key role in encouraging their children to succeed in school, they may be inhibited by their own attitudes or circumstances. Many parents, while very concerned about their child's education, are fearful and suspicious of schools, teachers, and education in general (Hansen et al., 1990). They may fear or mistrust school personnel because of their own negative experiences as students. Or they may have experienced an unfortunate history of unpleasant experiences with other professionals, so that current school personnel fall heir to that history.

Parents of children with special needs face many economic and personal hardships such as work schedules and health concerns. Low-income families may have difficulty with transportation and child care, making it hard to attend meetings or volunteer in school even when they would like to do so (Thurston & Navarette, 1996). Also, families stressed by poverty or substance abuse will be less available to consult and collaborate with school personnel.

The single parent, already burdened with great responsibilities, is particularly stressed in parenting a child with special needs. The role can be overwhelming at times. For collaborative efforts to produce results, the interaction must fit the single parent's time and energy level. When working with the single parent, school personnel will need to tailor their requests for conferences and home interventions, and to provide additional emotional support when needed (Conoley, 1989).

The two-parent, two-home student also struggles with repercussions from family strife leading to the divorce, breakup of the family, and passage back and forth between parents, oftentimes with stepparents and new brothers and sisters in the mix. Educators at school and at home must organize a cooperative and collaborative team for managing the academic and emotional needs of the students. As just one example, homework assignments can be problematic for the child who will be with one parent for only a short time. Teachers need to partner with the noncustodial parent to integrate homework and other school activities into visitation periods (Frieman, 1997). School counselors, support personnel from community mental health centers, and social workers should be included as part of the team for assisting the student torn between two or more homes.

The same can be said for children in foster care, who often fall behind academically, fail classes, neglect homework, or are truant. Some students do not know how to ask their foster family for help with homework or other school problems. Many have low self-esteem and associate school with fear and anxiety, so validating self-esteem through small successes and acquiring problem-solving skills can be first steps toward succeeding in school (Noble, 1997).

Many types of disability are very expensive for families, and the impact on the family budget created by the special needs of a child may produce formidable hardships. Sometimes families arrive at the point where they feel their other children are being neglected by all the attention to the child with exceptional learning needs. This adds to their frustration and stress. In addition, children with special needs and their families are vulnerable to stereotypes of society about disabilities. The ways in which families cope with the frustrations and stress influence their interaction with school personnel. Providing support networks can help them cope with the situation (Dunst, 2002; Turnbull et al., 2006).

Family members may avoid school interactions because they fear being blamed as the cause of their children's problems. Sometimes teachers do blame parents for exacerbating learning and behavior problems—"I can't do anything here at school because it gets undone when they go home!" But blaming does not facilitate development of mutually supportive relationships. Family members are very sensitive to blaming words and attitudes from school personnel. A teacher who is part of a therapeutic foster family reported that he felt "blame and shame" after a school conference about the child with emotional and behavior problems who had been his foster child for two months.

Judging attitudes, stereotypes, false expectations, and basic differences in values also act as barriers and diminish the collaborative efforts among teachers and families. It is difficult to feel comfortable with people who have very different attitudes and values. Families and teachers should make every effort not to reproach each other, but to work together as partners on the child's team. Educators, including teachers and parents, must abandon any posture of blaming or criticism, and move on to collaboration and problem solving. It is important to remember that it does not matter where a "fault" lies. What matters is who steps up to address the problem.

Culturally and Linguistically Diverse Families

Active parent and community involvement in educational programs for culturally and linguistically diverse (CLD) students is essential. Yet the growing differences among cultural and linguistic backgrounds of school personnel and their students makes home-school collaboration a challenge. The unfortunate portrayal of CLD families as deficient in skills necessary to ready children for school is a huge barrier to active parent participation. Misconceptions about parental concern for their children's schooling are all too prevalent among school personnel (deValenzuela, Torres, & Chavez, 1998).

Too often programs for parent involvement are based on middle-class values. Effective collaborative consultants recognize that sometimes there are differing views between home and school educators about the involvement of families in education of their children and varying levels of visibility for that involvement. August and Hakuta (1997) researched patterns of parental involvement (parent behaviors that support education) among Puerto Rican families, Chinese American families, and Mexican American families and found that parent behaviors nurturing child learning may not always be visible to school personnel or recognized as such.

Classrooms today have increasing numbers of students from culturally and linguistically diverse backgrounds. It is important to note that the concept of *disability* is culturally and socially constructed. Each society's culture defines the parameters of what is considered normal, with some cultures having a broader or different definition of disability from that in U.S. schools (Linan-Thompson & Jean, 1997). This may be one reason ethnically diverse parents tend to be less involved and less informed about their child's school life than mainstream parents. It is important to learn from family members how their beliefs and practices will affect programs for children with special needs. Educational consultants who work with families must be aware of the family's perceptions of disability. Linan-Thompson and Jean (1997) suggest taking time to learn about family perceptions of special needs, carefully and thoroughly explaining the whole special education process, using informal assessments in addition to formal assessment tools (which helps explain the disability on other than formal terms), and discovering and using parents' preferred forms of communication (written, informal meetings, video- or audiotapes).

Collaborative consultants need to help other school personnel accommodate differences in families—families of children with disabilities, poverty-level families, CLD families—and consider that they are not homogeneous groups. Educators should respond in individually relevant ways rather than make assumptions about families based on language, ethnicity, or background. Educators need to learn more about full-service models and collaborate actively with related service providers and community networks. If they become knowledgeable about services and advocate for broader services and more access, collaborative efforts with parents will be successful to the benefit of students, families, and school personnel.

Traditional approaches to reaching out to families are not always appropriate for families from cultural and other minority groups. Educators must develop cultural competence that demonstrates acceptance and respect for cultural diversity and differences (Cross, 1996; Lynch & Hanson, 1998). This allows individualization of educational programs for students and individualization of parent interactions to be done in a manner that respects the family's culture. Cross (1996) recommends that educators learn about cultures they serve by observing healthy and strong members of different groups. Other recommendations include spending time with people of that culture, identifying a cultural guide, reading the literature (professional as well as fiction) by and for persons of the culture, attending relevant cultural events, and asking questions in sensitive ways.

Bruns and Fowler (1999) recommend that educators give special recognition to cultural preferences in transition planning. Traditional parental roles of teacher, information source, decision maker, and advocate for transition planning may not be appropriate for or sensitive to all families. They suggest transforming these roles to be that of guide, information specialist, decision maker, and ally. They also recommend inviting extended family members, friends, and community members to take part in education-related decisions as a way to meet diverse values and traditions of cultural groups. As educators develop cross-cultural competencies and increasingly collaborate with families culturally or linguistically different from themselves, they need to remember that one approach does not fit all ranges of diversity (Parette & Petch-Hogan, 2000).

The following ten strategies are helpful when collaborating with families from diverse cultural groups:

1. Acknowledge cultural differences and become aware of how they affect parent-teacher interactions.
2. Examine your personal culture, such as how you define family, and your desired life goals and perceived problems.
3. Recognize the dynamics of group interactions such as etiquette and patterns of communication.
4. Go out into the community and meet the families on their own turf.
5. Adjust collaboration to legitimize and include culturally specific activities.
6. Learn about the families. Where are they from and when did they arrive? What cultural beliefs and practices surround child rearing, health and healing, and disability and causation?
7. Recognize that some families may be surprised by the extent of home-school collaboration expected in the United States.
8. Learn and use words and forms of greetings in the families' languages.
9. Work with cultural mediators or guides from the families' cultures to learn more about the culture and facilitate communication between school and home. Examples are relatives, church members, neighbors, or older siblings.
10. Ask for help in structuring the child's school program to match home life, such as learning key words and phrases used at home.

Well-publicized policies at the district level encouraging home-school collaboration are vital in providing opportunities for minority family members to become full partners with teachers. Traditional methods of parent involvement such as PTA meetings, open house, or newsletters seldom permit true collaboration, constructing instead a "territory" of education that many parents are hesitant to invade. Concern, awareness, and commitment on the part of individuals in the educational system are beginning steps in challenging the limitations that inhibit collaboration between teachers and families who have language, cultural, or other basic differences.

BRIDGE BUILDING FOR SUCCESSFUL HOME-SCHOOL COLLABORATION

Friendly, positive relationships and honest, respectful communication can help bridge the barriers that might exist to home-school collaboration. The goal of collaboration is to promote the education and development of children by strengthening and supporting families.

Keeping this in mind, consultants will remember that collaboration is not the goal but the means to the end. Strategies that have proved to be sturdy bridges to circumvent barriers are building trust, focusing on family strengths, using appropriate communication skills, and promoting positive roles for family members.

Focusing on Family Strengths

Family-focused services and collaboration emphasize an empowerment approach rather than focusing on what is going wrong. Instead of focusing on a child or family's problem, collaborators focus on family members and the strength of their experiences. An effective partner-educator provides support and reinforcement for family members in their family roles. In addition to listening to family members and acknowledging their expertise, it is crucial to empower families by giving them positive feedback about their efforts to support their child's education. Families often get very little reinforcement for parenting, particularly for the extra efforts they expend in caring for children with special needs. They should be encouraged and commended for providing three types of parental engagement at home that are consistently associated with student performance at school (Finn, 1998):

1. Organizing and monitoring the student's time
2. Helping with homework
3. Discussing school matters with their child

Too few families hear positive comments about their children. They may feel guilty or confused because of their children's problems. Examples of support and reinforcement that teachers can use include thank-you notes for helping with field trips; VIP (very important parent) buttons for classroom volunteers; supporting phone calls when homework has been turned in; and Happygrams when a class project is completed.

Using Appropriate Communication Skills

Bridges to circumvent language and communication barriers are difficult to construct. Chapter 4 describes communication skills that are important in building and maintaining collaborative relationships with adults in the lives of students with special needs. Consultants will want to use rapport-building skills to build trust and confidence in the collaborative relationship, and to recognize and reduce their own language and communication barriers. Those who communicate with family members should use these guidelines:

- Be aware of voice tone and body language.
- Be honest and specific.
- Give your point of view as information, not the absolute truth.
- Be direct about what is wanted and expected.
- Do not monopolize the conversation.
- Listen at least as much as talk.
- Do not assume your message is clear.

- Avoid educational or psychological jargon.
- Attack the problem, not the person.
- Focus on positive or informational aspects of the problem.
- Have five positive contacts for every negative one.
- Always be honest; do not soft-pedal reality.
- Attend to cultural differences in verbal and nonverbal communication.

Providing Social Support

Families rely on informal and formal social support networks for information and guidance they need to carry out responsibilities for child rearing, children's learning, and child development. Schools can provide a rich array of child, parent, and family support in the form of information and environmental experiences to strengthen family and child competence and influence student outcomes. Parenting supports include information and advice that can strengthen existing parenting knowledge and skills and facilitate acquisition of new competencies (Dunst, 2000).

For families of children with disabilities, supports are a crucial aspect of family-focused collaboration. Workshops, newsletters, informational meetings, provision of emotional support, and multigenerational gatherings are examples of formal supports needed by families. Schools are also instrumental in promoting informal support systems for families. According to extensive research by Dunst (2000) and his colleagues, informal support demonstrates a stronger relationship to many child, parent, and family outcomes than does formal support. Fiedler, Simpson, and Clark (2007) suggest that providing support for all family members and siblings also benefits children with special needs, as does fostering community advocacy and support. Thus, consultants should encourage activities that help families develop informal support networks such as parent-to-parent groups and informal multiple-family gatherings.

Promoting Positive Roles for Family Members

Family members play a range of roles from purveyor of knowledge about the child to advocates for political action. No matter what role is taken by individual family members, educational consultants should remember that families are:

- Partners in setting goals and finding solutions
- The best advocates and case managers for the child with special needs
- Individuals with initiative, strengths, and important experiences
- The best information resource about the child, the family, and their culture

Within any role along the wide continuum of family members, the consultant must respect and support the courage and commitment of family members to struggle with the challenges of daily living faced by all families. Recognizing, supporting, and reinforcing interventions on behalf of the child with special needs will promote an increased sense of competency and help create a safe, nurturing environment for children, while maintaining

FIGURE 8.1   Suggestions for Building Bridges to Successful Home-School Collaboration

- Keep in mind that the family usually has concerns and issues that have nothing to do with you personally and that you may not know about.
- Be sensitive to the language levels, vocabularies, and background of the family and adjust your language, but be yourself.
- Get enough information, but not more than you need. You don't want to appear "nosy."
- Focus discussions on factors you can control.
- Find out what has been tried before.
- Listen so that you are completely clear about the family's concerns.
- Honor confidentiality.
- Remain open to new approaches and suggestions. Each family is different.
- Set concrete, measurable goals. Communication is clearer and measures of success are built in and promote collaboration.
- Wait until the family asks for help or until a good relationship is established before making suggestions.
- Help families solve their own problems and allow them to become, or develop the skills to become, their child's own case manager.

Source: Adapted from PEATC. (1991). *Partnership series.* Alexandria, VA: Parent Educational Advocacy Training Center.

the unique cultural and ethnic characteristics of their family unit (Barbour, Barbour, & Scully, 2008; Caspe & Lopez, 2006; Turnbull et al., 2006).

Supporting and reinforcing families in their chosen roles is not always easy. Members in multiproblem families often are viewed as having defective or faulty notions of parenting, no problem-solving skills, and mental health problems. Even for families having different values and expectations, and risk factors such as poverty mental illness or drug/alcohol involvement, focusing on strengths and providing positive supports is the best approach for collaborators. Figure 8.1 lists other suggestions for developing bridges to overcome potential or real barriers in collaboration.

DEVELOPING HOME-SCHOOL PARTNERSHIPS

There is great variation in individual practices for home-school collaboration. Effective collaboration efforts depend on attitude of teachers, their beliefs about the family roles and the efficacy of family involvement, and their comfort level and communication skills. When school personnel collaborate with family members, they nurture and maintain partnerships that facilitate shared efforts to promote student achievement. As families and teachers plan together and implement plans of action, they find that working as a team is more effective than working alone. Each can be assured that the other is doing the best for the child and each can support the other, thus producing positive educational outcomes for children with special needs. Families that are stressed by poverty or substance abuse will be less readily available to consult and collaborate with school personnel, so educators must be resourceful in developing strategies for encouraging their participation.

Family involvement is usually conceptualized from family member perspectives (Wanat, 1997). In her study with fifty-seven parents, Wanat (1997) found that parents did not distinguish between involvement at school and at home and they had specific ideas about what constituted meaningful involvement. One parent summarized legitimate parent involvement as "everything you do with the child because education involves a lot more than just sitting at school." It would be good for education consultants to remember this statement when they work collaboratively with parents.

■ ■ ■ ■ ■

APPLICATION 8.1
READING CENTER FOR FAMILIES

Visit a school library, or revisit your own school library, and find a corner that could be outfitted as a "Parent/Family Reading Center." (Try to find a quiet, pleasant place but not *too* out-of-the-way.) Display an attractive painting, a plant, perhaps a snapshot display of recent school events, along with a small table, comfortable chairs, and, of course, books and periodicals. These should be focused on interests and needs of families, parents, day care providers, grandparents, and home-school projects. Promote the center at parent-teacher meetings and parent conferences. Perhaps meet with a group of parents there on a nonconfidential matter (planning the yearly social event, initiating a coupon drive for playground equipment, and so forth.) Work into the plan the school personnel who would be responsible for upkeep, checkout and returns, and materials acquisition. Some of this might even be accomplished by students.

Five Steps for Collaborating with Families

Five basic steps will assist school personnel in developing successful home-school partnerships:

Step 1: Examining personal values
Step 2: Building collaborative relationships
Step 3: Initiating home-school interactions
Step 4: Individualizing for parents
Step 5: Evaluating home-school collaboration

Step 1: Examining Personal Values.   Value systems are individualistic and complex. They are the result of nature and the impact of experiences on nature. People need to apply information and logic to situations that present values different from their own. Kroth (1985) provides an example. He notes that a significant amount of research indicates a positive effect on children's academic and social growth when teachers use a daily or weekly report card system to communicate with parents or guardians. This information provides logical support for interaction among teachers and family members on a regular, planned basis.

School personnel must guard against valuing teacher knowledge and experience over family knowledge and experience. As stated earlier, it is vital to recognize that parents are the experts when it comes to knowing about their children, no matter how many tests educators have administered to students, or how many hours they have observed them in the classroom. If professional educators are perceived as *the* experts, and the *only* experts, false expectations may create unrealistic pressure on them. Some family members find it difficult to relate to experts. So a beautiful "boulevard of progress" becomes a one-way street of judging, advising, and sending solutions.

The first step in collaborating with families is to examine one's own values. Figure 8.2 is a checklist for examining one's values and attitudes toward parents and other family members.

Communicating messages of equality, flexibility, and a sharing attitude will facilitate effective home-school collaboration. The message that should be given to parents of students with special needs is, "I know a lot about this, and *you* know a lot about that. Let's put our information and ideas together to help the child."

The checklist in Figure 8.3 on page 290 serves as a brief self-assessment to test congruency of attitudes and perceptions with the two-way family collaboration discussed earlier. Inventorying and adjusting one's own attitudes and perceptions about families are the hardest parts of consulting with them. Attitudes and perceptions about families and their roles in partnerships greatly influence implementation of the consulting process.

School personnel also must keep in mind that family members are not a homogeneous group; therefore, experiences with one family member cannot be generalized to all other parents and families. Resources for examining values and for increasing cultural sensitivity are found in the Additional Readings and Resources section of this chapter and in Chapter 9.

Step 2: Building Collaborative Relationships.   The second step in collaborating with families is building collaborative relationships. As emphasized in Chapter 4, basic communication and rapport-building skills are essential for establishing healthy, successful relationships with family members. To briefly review, these are the most important skills for educators in interacting with families:

- Responsive listening
- Assertive responding
- Mutual problem solving

Prudent teachers avoid words and phrases that may give the impression that a disability or a person with a disability is undesirable. They listen for the messages given by parents and respond to their verbal and nonverbal cues.

In communicating with families, school personnel must avoid jargon that can be misunderstood or misinterpreted. Parents often feel alienated by professional educators and one common cause is words (*program, site*) and acronyms (IFSP, ITBS) that pepper the conversation without explanation of their meaning (Soodak & Erwin, 1995). Some professional educators seem unable, or unwilling, to use jargon-free language when they communicate with laypeople (Schuck, 1979). Choices of words can ease, or inhibit, communication with parents, and professional educators must respect language variations created by differences in culture, education, occupation, age, and place of origin (Morsink et al., 1991).

Teachers and administrators often find that one of the most important, but difficult, aspects of developing relationships with parents is listening to them. The challenge lies in

FIGURE 8.2   Examining Own Values

Instructions: Rate belief or comfort level, from 1 (very comfortable or very strong) to 5 (very uncomfortable or not strong at all).

How comfortable do you feel with each?

____ Parents or others who are overly protective

____ Teachers who think they are never wrong

____ Families who send their children to school without breakfast

____ Teachers who get emotional at conferences

____ Teachers who do not want mainstreamed students

____ Open discussions at family meetings

____ Parents who have lost control of their children

____ Volunteers in the classroom

____ Conflict

____ Being invited to students' homes

____ Using grades as a behavior management tool

____ Family members who call every day

____ Teachers who do not follow through

____ Students attending conferences

____ Principals attending conferences

____ Parents who do not allow their children to be tested

____ Different racial or ethnic groups

____ Family members who do not speak English

____ Others who think special needs children should be kept in self-contained classrooms

____ Teachers who think modifying curriculum materials or tests is watering down the lessons

____ Family members who drink excessively or use drugs

____ Administrators who do not know your name

____ Criticism

How strongly do you believe the following?

____ Family members should be able to call you at home.

____ Newsletters are an important communication tool.

____ Family members should volunteer in the classroom.

____ General classroom teachers can teach students with special needs.

____ All children can learn.

____ Family members should come to conferences.

____ Resistance is normal and to be expected in educational settings.

____ Children in divorced families have special problems.

____ Family resistance is often justified.

____ Teacher resistance is often justified.

____ Family influence is more important than school influence.

____ Medical treatment should never be withheld from children.

____ Children with severe disabilities are part of a supreme being's plan.

____ Sometimes consultants should just tell others the best thing to do.

____ Consultants are advocates for children.

____ Teachers should modify their classrooms for children with special needs.

____ It is a teacher's fault when children fail.

____ Consultants are experts in educating special needs children.

____ Some people do not want children with special needs to succeed.

Do you think all teachers, administrators, counselors, psychologists, parents, grandparents, social workers, and students would have responded as you did? What happens when members of the same educator team have different views?

FIGURE 8.3   **Self-Assessment of Attitudes and Perceptions Concerning Families and Family Collaboration**

Rate yourself on the following, from 1 (very little) to 5 (always).

1. I understand the importance of parent involvement.   1 2 3 4 5
2. I recognize the concerns parents may have about working with me.   1 2 3 4 5
3. I recognize that parents of students with special needs may have   1 2 3 4 5
   emotional and social needs I may not understand.
4. I recognize and respect the expertise of families.   1 2 3 4 5
5. I feel comfortable working with families whose values and attitudes   1 2 3 4 5
   differ from mine.
6. I am persistent and patient as I develop relationships with families.   1 2 3 4 5
7. I am comfortable with my skills for communicating with families.   1 2 3 4 5
8. I am realistic about the barriers for me in working with families.   1 2 3 4 5
9. I find it difficult to understand why some families have the attitudes   1 2 3 4 5
   they have.
10. I recognize that some family members will have problems interact-   1 2 3 4 5
    ing with me because of their experience with other teachers.

listening to parents' messages even though they might disagree strongly with family members, and their attitudes and values might differ significantly from those of the families. Although the quality of the interaction should be a primary focus in parent relationships, the numbers and variety of initiated communications are important as well. Phone calls, introductory and welcoming letters, newsletters, teacher-to-parent calendars, and notepads with identifying logos all have been used effectively by educators to initiate partnerships. Each note, phone call, conversation, or conference, whether taking place in a formal setting or on the spur of the moment at the grocery store, should reflect the willingness and commitment of school personnel to work with parents as they face immense responsibilities in providing for the special needs of their child.

It is important for teachers to arrange and encourage more regular, informal contacts with parents. Family members often report being put off by the formality inherent in some scheduled conferences, particularly when they are limited to ten minutes, as they often are, with another child's family waiting just outside. (Lindle, 1989). Ask parents for preferred modes of communication. Phone calls are appropriate for positive reports, but should not be used to discuss weighty concerns. Notes sent home can promote consistency in expectations and help teachers and family members develop a common language (Bos, Nahmias, & Urban, 1999). Some consultants have found e-mail and school Web site access an effective way to communicate with families. However, many families do not have access to this technology. Chapter 4 has important recommendations for using e-mail in collaborative efforts.

Step 3: Initiating Home-School Interactions.   Parents want their children to be successful in school. Even parents who are considered "hard to reach," such as nontraditional, low-income, and low-status families, usually want to be more involved (Davies, 1988). Most, however, wait to be invited before becoming involved as a partner in their child's educa-tion. Unfortunately, many have to wait for years before someone opens the door and pro-vides them the *opportunity* to become a team member with others who care about the educational and social successes of their children. Parent satisfaction with their involve-ment is directly related to perceived opportunities for involvement (Salisbury & Evans, 1988). They are more motivated to carry on when they are aware that the results of their time and energy are helping their child learn. School personnel who are in a position to observe these results can provide the kind of reinforcement that parents need so much.

When parents are welcome in schools and classrooms, and their child's work and experiences are meaningful to them, parents often experience new aspirations for them-selves and for their children (St. John, Griffith, & Allen-Hayes, 1997).

Step 4: Individualizing for Families.   Special education professionals are trained to be competent at individualizing educational programs for students' needs. Nevertheless, they may assume that all family members have the same strengths and needs, thereby over-looking the need to individualize family involvement programs (Turnbull et al., 2006). By using the assessments discussed earlier, and taking care to avoid stereotypes and judg-ments, they will be more successful in involving parents as partners in their child's learn-ing program. Another helpful instrument is the checklist for determining family interests in Figure 8.4 on the next page.

Successful work with parents calls for establishing respectful and trusting relation-ships, as well as responding to the needs of all partners. The degree to which parents are placed in an egalitarian role, with a sense of choice, empowerment, and ownership in the education process, is a crucial variable in successful collaboration.

Step 5: Evaluating Home-School Collaboration.   Evaluation of efforts to provide opportunities for collaboration in schools can indicate whether or not families' needs are being met and their strengths are being utilized. Evaluation also shows whether needs and strengths of educational personnel are being met. Assessment tools used after a workshop, conference, or at the conclusion of the school year allow school personnel to ask parents, "How did we do in facilitating your learning of the new information or accessing the new services?" Some teachers use a quick questionnaire, to be completed anonymously, to see if the activity or program fulfilled the goals of the home-school collaboration. If data show that the activity gave families the information they needed, provided them with the resources they wanted, and offered them the opportunities they requested, educators know whether or not to continue with the program or modify it.

Educators also should evaluate their own involvement with families. This means assessing the use of family strengths and skills to facilitate educational programs with chil-dren who have special needs. Did teachers get the information they needed from families? How many volunteer hours did parents contribute? What were the results of home tutoring on the achievement of the resource room students? What changes in family attitudes about the school district were measured? Chapter 6 contains information about procedures for evaluating collaboration efforts. Note again that the purpose of family collaboration is to utilize the unique and vital partnership on behalf of their children.

FIGURE 8.4 Ascertaining Family Interests

Families! We want to learn more about you so that we can work together helping your child learn. Please take a few minutes to respond to these questions so your voice can be heard. It will help the Home-School Advisory Team develop programs for families, teachers, and children.

Check those items you are most interested in.

_____ 1. Family resource libraries or information centers

_____ 2. Helping my child learn

_____ 3. Support programs for my child's siblings

_____ 4. Talking with my child about sex

_____ 5. Helping with language and social skills

_____ 6. Mental health services

_____ 7. Talking with another parent about common problems

_____ 8. Respite care or babysitters

_____ 9. My role as a parent

_____ 10. Classes about managing behavior problems

_____ 11. Making my child happy

_____ 12. Managing my time and resources

_____ 13. Making toys and educational materials

_____ 14. Reducing time spent watching television

_____ 15. What happens when my child grows up

_____ 16. Recreation and camps for my child

_____ 17. State wide meetings for families

_____ 18. Vocational opportunities for my child

_____ 19. Talking to my child's teacher

_____ 20. Talking with other families

_____ 21. Learning about child development

_____ 22. Things families can do to support teachers

_____ 23. Home activities that support school learning

_____ 24. Information about the school and my child's classes

_____ 25. Helping my child become more independent

_____ 26. Others?

_____

_____

_____

Thanks for your help!

Name of family member responding to this form:

_____

Child's name: _____

■ ■ ■ ■ ■

APPLICATION 8.2

First, meet in groups of four or five teachers to discuss the situation below:

A fifth-grade girl is having difficulty with her schoolwork, especially math and spelling. Family members try hard to help, but they and the child become frustrated and little progress is made. Tension within the family is palpable. The mother feels her daughter needs more instructional attention at school to relieve strain on the family at home. She has requested a conference with the girl's teachers and related services personnel.

As you discuss this, make a list of things you would *not* want to have happen during any ensuing home-school conference. Make another list of things that you would want to have happen. Then combine and arrange all lists into overall "Do and Don't" help sheets for home-school involvement in students' learning programs and study strategies. Embellish with illustrations if appropriate. Find practical uses for these help sheets.

Family Partners in IEP, ITP, and IFSP Planning

The Individualized Education Plan (IEP), Individualized Family Service Plan (IFSP), or Individualized Transition Planning (ITP) conference can be a productive time or a frustrating experience. Parents may be emotional about their child's problems, and teachers can be apprehensive about meeting with the parents in emotion-laden situations. A number of researchers have found that too little parent involvement in team decision making, particularly relating to IEP, IFSP, and ITP development, is a major problem in special education programs (Boone, 1989).

School consultants will improve school-home collaboration in these areas if they provide family members with information for the meeting. Consultants can communicate with family members by phone, letter, or informal interview to inform them about names and roles of staff members who will attend; typical procedure for meetings; ways they can prepare for the meeting; contributions they will be encouraged to make; and ways in which follow-up to the meeting will be provided.

Turnbull and Turnbull (2006) list eight components that an IFSP/IEP conference should include:

1. Preparing in advance
2. Connecting and getting started
3. Sharing visions and great expectations
4. Reviewing formal evaluation and current levels of performance
5. Sharing resources, priorities, and concerns
6. Developing goals and objectives (or outcomes)
7. Specifying placement and related services
8. Summarizing and concluding

Figure 8.6 (Dettmer, 1994) to be presented later in this chapter outlines specific ways parents can be involved in IEP, ITP, or IFSP development and implementation before, during, and after the IEP conference. These lists could be printed in the school handbook.

When parents and teachers work together as equals, they have more opportunities to express their own knowledge and can come to respect each other's wisdom. Siblings need information about disabilities, opportunities to talk about their feelings, time to hear about the experiences of other siblings of children with disabilities, people with whom to share their feelings of pride and joy, and ways to plan for the future (Cramer, Erzkus, Mayweather, Pope, Roeder, & Tone, 1997; Fiedler, et al., 2007).

Equal Partnership Model

Parents have much to communicate to school personnel about their children—the "curriculum of the home," and the "curriculum of the community" (Barbour et al., 2008). This information can include parent-child conversation topics, how leisure reading is encouraged, deferral of immediate gratifications, long-term goals, how homework is assisted and assessed, what TV is watched and how it is monitored, and how affections and interests in the child's accomplishments are demonstrated. If school personnel do not understand (or attempt to understand) the curriculum of the home and the community, equal partnerships are difficult to establish. Educators can use checklists, conversations, home visits, and community involvement to learn about the strengths, interests, and needs of parents and the communities in which the families live. If school personnel offer workshops and materials that are not based on family interests and needs, a message is communicated that educators know more about their needs than they do; and then the family involvement is not a true partnership. An example of a needs and interests assessment is included in Figure 8.5.

The equal partnership model stresses not only respect for the curriculum of the child's home and community, but also the importance of providing opportunities for family members to use their strengths, commitment, and skills to contribute to the formal education of their children. This relationship is not based on a deficit model of blame and inequality. Families appreciate having their special efforts recognized, just as teachers do. Multiyear research by St. John and colleagues (1997) showed mixed results when parents were not treated as full partners in the education of their children.

Tools for assessing parent strengths are similar to those for assessing needs. Interviews and checklists are useful in determining what types of contributions families can bring to the partnership. These assets can be conceptualized along four levels of involvement (Kroth, 1985), from strengths that all family members have, to skills that only a few family members are willing and able to contribute. For example, all parents have information about their children that schools need. At more intensive levels of collaboration, some family members are willing and able to tutor their children at home, come to meetings, help make bulletin boards, and volunteer to help at school. At the highest level of collaboration, only a few parents can be expected to lobby for special education, serve on advisory boards, or conduct parent-to-parent programs. A number of parent advocates of children with learning and behavior disorders have made impressive gains in recent decades toward state and national focus on the rights of children with special needs. They have formed organizations, identified needs, encouraged legislation, spoken for improved facilities, and supported each other through crises. In many instances they have involved pediatricians, community agency leaders, and businesses in special projects for children with special needs.

FIGURE 8.5   Family Member Participation Checklist

Families! We need your help. Many of you have asked how you can help provide a high-quality educational program for your children. You have many talents, interests, and skills you can contribute to help children learn better and enjoy school more. Please let us know what you are interested in doing.

_____ 1. I would like to volunteer in school.

_____ 2. I would like to help with special events or projects.

_____ 3. I have a hobby or talent I could share with the class.

_____ 4. I would be glad to talk about travel or jobs, or interesting experiences that I have had.

_____ 5. I could teach the class how to _____.

_____ 6. I could help with bulletin boards and art projects.

_____ 7. I could read to children.

_____ 8. I would like to help my child at home.

_____ 9. I would like to tutor a child.

_____ 10. I would like to work on a buddy or parent-to-parent system with other parents whose children have problems.

_____ 11. I would like to teach a workshop.

_____ 12. I can do typing, word processing, phoning, making materials, or preparing resources at home.

_____ 13. I would like to assist with student clubs.

_____ 14. I would like to help organize a parent group.

_____ 15. I want to help organize and plan parent partnership programs.

_____ 16. I would like to help with these kinds of activities:

At school _____

At home _____

In the community _____

Your comments, concerns, and questions are welcome. THANKS!

Name: _____

Child's Name: _____

How to Reach You: _____

By considering family member strengths as well as needs and interests, educators will be focusing on the collaborative nature of parent involvement. An example of a strengths assessment form is provided in Figure 8.6.

Utilizing the strengths and interests of family and community members to engage them with the education of infants and toddlers, preschool and kindergarten students, primary, middle, and secondary students can be approached in many creative ways. Teachers Involve Parents in Schoolwork (TIPS), developed by the National Network of Partnership Schools (Van Voorhis, 2003) as an interactive process for encouraging homework, used strength and motivation of middle school families to help sixth- through eighth-graders

FIGURE 8.6   Checklist for Families in Developing IEPs

Throughout the year:

Read about educational issues and concerns.

Learn about the structure of the local school system.

Observe your child, noting work habits, play patterns, and social interactions.

Record information regarding special interests, talents, and accomplishments, as well as areas of concern.

Before the conference:

Visit the child's school.

Discuss school life with the child.

Talk with other families who have participated in conferences to find out what goes on during the conference.

Write down questions and points you would like to address.

Review notes from any previous conferences with school staff.

Prepare a summary file of information, observations, and products that would further explain the child's needs.

Arrange to take along any other persons that you feel would be helpful in planning the child's educational program.

During the conference:

Be an active participant.

Ask questions about anything that is unclear.

Insist that educational jargon and "alphabet soup" acronyms be avoided.

Contribute information, ideas, and recommendations.

Let the school personnel know about the positive things school has provided.

Ask for a copy of the IEP if it is not offered.

Ask to have a follow-up contact time to compare notes about progress.

After the conference:

Discuss the conference proceedings with the child.

Continue to monitor the child's progress and follow up as agreed on.

Reinforce school staff for positive effects of the planned program.

Keep adding to the notebook of information.

Be active in efforts to improve schools.

Say supportive things about the schools whenever possible.

complete more accurate homework and get better grades. At the early childhood level, Mayer, Ferede and Hou (2006) used storybooks to successfully promote family involvement. The online Family Involvement Storybook Corner promotes awareness and practice of family involvement through storybooks (www.gse.harvard.edu/hfrp/projects/fine/resources/storybook/index.html). Another example is the Raising a Reader Program, based on the work of Judith K. Bernhard (www.ryerson.ca/~bernhard/early.html). She and her colleagues built their Early Programs on parents' strengths to benefit children by giving parents a prominent role as their children's literacy teachers. Raising a Reader is a nonprofit organization in California whose purpose is engaging parents in a routine of daily "book cuddling" with their children birth through age five (www.pcf.org/raising_reader/research.html).

As stated earlier, involvement is not synonymous with collaboration. Developing a workshop on discipline or a volunteer program without assessing strengths, needs, and goals demonstrates failure to respect the partnership between school and home. True partnership features mutual collaboration and respect for the expertise of all parties.

STUDENT PARTICIPATION IN CONFERENCES

The student has the greatest investment and most important involvement in constructing an individual education plan for learning. Indeed, it is counterproductive to formulate goals and objectives without involving students in their conferences as a member of the planning team.

Having students help plan a student-led conference with family members will give them a sense of ownership in their own learning process. Students and their teachers should talk beforehand about the purpose of their conference and then set some goals for the meeting. Teachers should convey to students that family members like this kind of parent-teacher conference and it will be fun.

The student will want to decide which samples of work to show and what learning activities to describe. Developing a sample rubric to evaluate the conference after it takes place will add to the learning process. The classroom teacher or special education teacher, or both, may want to have a brief practice session so the process feels familiar and comfortable when the conference takes place. See the summarized ten-step process on page 298.

Teachers should prepare family members for the student-led conference with a phone call or a brief letter, focusing on the contributions it can make to their child's confidence and pride in achievement.

Parent partnerships can be particularly difficult to cultivate at the secondary level. Much of the difficulty stems from attitudes of teenage students who would just "die" of humiliation if their parents were seen at school by their peers. Other teens might head off a teacher's efforts to have involved family members with "Go ahead, but they won't care/come/participate," "They have to work," "They don't care," and so on. Parents pick up on these attitudes and acquiesce to them, and teachers are hard-pressed to find time for and ways of addressing them (McGrew-Zoubi, 1998).

In some middle school settings where traditional parent-teacher interactions and conferences have been perceived as more problematic than problem-solving, an innovative student-centered model for conferencing has been developed and tried. In this model, a structure is created by which students are helped to prepare for their own conferences. The new format is communicated to parents and colleagues and procedural operations are developed (Countryman & Schroeder, 1996). In the planning, development, and evaluation phases of this new approach, teachers find that students should have more participation in preparing conference scripts. They need a log to help them organize their products, and they must not overlook bringing to the discussion such classes as art, family and consumer science, and modern languages or those subjects will not get discussed. Students reasonably express the need to see how teachers have evaluated them before it is revealed at the conference.

Hanna and Dettmer (2004) provide a detailed, ten-step plan for getting students ready to guide their parent-student-teacher conference. Student and teacher should discuss these steps and prepare for them, even rehearse them, in advance of the scheduled conference:

1. Determine the purpose(s) of the conference.
2. Formulate goals for the conference and prepare the invitation to family members. In the invitation, family members should be clued as to what to expect and ways to contribute.
3. Develop an agenda and determine location, seating plan, format for introductions, and possible opening and closing remarks.
4. Select samples of work and pertinent information that focus on accomplishments, interests, and any major concerns. Anticipate questions or concerns parents might bring up and think of responses to give.
5. Rehearse a simulated conference.
6. At conference time, explore ideas for further learning and achievement.
7. Set reasonable goals.
8. Adhere to the time schedule, summarize, and close on a positive note.
9. Determine follow-up and follow-through procedures for attaining the planned goals.
10. Have all participants evaluate the event with rubrics designed specifically for the purpose.

A student-guided conference must not be hurried. A thirty-minute segment of time might be reasonable. Busy teachers, particularly those at the secondary level with dozens of students, will need strong administrator support and innovative scheduling ideas to make student-guided conferences effective. But for a courageous, energetic school staff, student-guided parent conferences can promote meaningful ownership by students in their own learning. Students and other participants also can benefit from an assessment of conference outcomes by using a rubric designed for the purpose. (See Figure 8.7.)

Benefits from having students participate in conferences for their individualized programs include receiving information about their progress, feeling involved in their own education, being motivated to improve, and having awareness that both parents and teachers are interested in working collaboratively on their behalf.

MAINTAINING HOME-SCHOOL COLLABORATION AND PARTNERSHIP

Home-school collaboration is mandated, it is challenging, and it is rewarding. Educators have two choices in collaborating with families—to see school as a battleground with an emphasis on conflict between families and school personnel, or to see school as a "homeland" environment that invites power sharing and mutual respect, with collaboration on activities that foster student learning and development (Epstein, 1995). The goal for educators and their partners is to integrate family involvement as part of the school instructional strategy, that is, as part of the curriculum rather than added on to school activities. Successful models for home-school-community partnerships are those that:

FIGURE 8.7   Rating Form, Student-Led Conference on Portfolio Achievement

Name: _____

Criterion	Needs Improvement		Fair	Good	Outstanding
1. Was prepared for the conference	0	1	2	3	4
2. Participated enthusiastically	0	1	2	3	4
3. Presented material in organized way	0	1	2	3	4
4. Explained learning process effectively	0	1	2	3	4
5. Assessed achievement realistically	0	1	2	3	4
6. Submitted ideas for next work/studies	0	1	2	3	4
7. Credited resources accurately	0	1	2	3	4
8. Involved all participants in discussion	0	1	2	3	4

Total: ____ of 32

Areas of strengths:

Areas which need more work:

- Respect the family as the child's first teacher
- Empower families and communities to support and advocate for all students
- Understand learning as a lifelong endeavor involving families and communities
- Recognize that all families want the best for their children and can have a positive, significant impact on their children's education

Students, schools, and families are strengthened by appropriate outreach efforts and partnership activities that are based on values and practices of a family-focused approach. Educators who empower and support families of their students recognize that they are part of a powerful partnership and the work they do with parents is part of the educational legacy they leave with the student and with the family. (See Figure 8.8.)

RESOURCES FOR SCHOOL EDUCATORS AND FAMILIES

The library and Internet are excellent sources of information about successful home-school-community collaborative efforts. Many state and national organizations are dedicated to providing helpful information about disabilities, special education, legal issues, and successful parent-as-partner strategies. For example every state has least one parent center that is funded by the U.S. Department of Education (www.taalliance.org). Most states have a Parent Training and Information Center and a Community Parent Resource Center; they provide training and information to families of children and young adults from birth to age twenty-two who have physical, cognitive, emotional, or learning disabilities. They help families obtain

FIGURE 8.8 Good Meeting of Home and School Educators

appropriate education and services for children with disabilities and function to improve education results for all children. They train and inform parents and professionals on a variety of topics, resolve problems between families and schools or other agencies, and connect children with disabilities to community resources that address their needs. Other resources include:

National Association for the Education of Young Children (www.naeyc.org)

Harvard Family Research project (www.hfrp.org)

National Network of Partnership Schools and the Center on School, Family, and Community Partnerships (www.csos.jhu.edu/P2000/center.htm)

National Dissemination Center for Children with Disabilities (NICHCY; www.nichcy.org)

Children, youth and families education and research network (CYFERNet; www.cyfernet.org)

Most of these resources have both Spanish and English versions of their Web sites and are excellent resources for both parents and educators.

ETHICS FOR WORKING TOGETHER WITH FAMILY AND COMMUNITIES

In an ethical climate for home-school collaboration, educators will demonstrate keen awareness of realities facing today's families. Challenges in working with families today are very different from those of past decades due to significant changes in society. Many families are overwhelmed by specific family crises as well as everyday life events. And many face multiple and prolonged stressors such as poverty, long work hours or multiple jobs, health issues without insurance, and bi- or multilingual communication between home and school. Families might include a single parent, a blended family, gay or lesbian parents, unwed adolescent parents, nonbiological parents serving as primary caregivers, foster care, grandparents, extended families, and adoptive parents.

Collaborative consultants must avoid judging attitudes, overtones of blaming, stereotyping, holding false expectations, and dwelling on basic differences in values. They must be tolerant if parents want to obtain second or even third opinions. It is important to have empathy with families with the awareness that parents may be having considerable difficulty in coming to terms with their child's disability or disabilities. Confidentiality of information and privacy pertaining to family matters must be honored and preserved.

In an ethical climate families and school personnel will make every effort not to reproach each other, but work together as partners on the child's team. They will be honest with each other and willing to listen and empathize, acknowledging anger and disappointment with patience and calmness. In potentially explosive situations the teacher will want to include the principal, remain calm and open-minded, and listen to learn exactly what the family members' views are. Teachers who find out that they are wrong should acknowledge that before stating their views. They will want to stress that all parties have the welfare of the child in mind. Teachers and administrators will want to keep in mind that most families are doing the best they can; parents of students do not start out the morning saying, "I think today I will be a poor parent." Collaboration will not require total agreement in values or educational method, but school personnel and families must focus on needs and interests of children and their families.

TIPS FOR HOME AND SCHOOL COLLABORATION

1. Establish rapport with families early in the year. Call right away, before problems develop, so that the first family contact is a positive one.
2. Invite families in to talk about their traditions, experiences, hobbies, or occupations.
3. Send home "up slips," putting them in a different format from the "down slips" that families sometimes receive, and have conferences with families because the student is performing *well* in the classroom.
4. When sharing information with families, "sandwich" any necessary comments about problems or deficits between two very positive ones.
5. During interaction with families, notice how your actions are received, and adapt to that.
6. When interacting with families, never assume anything.

7. When several staff members will be meeting with family members, make sure each one's role and purpose for being included in the meeting will be understood by the parents.

8. Introduce families to all support personnel working with the child.

9. Build interpersonal "bank accounts" with frequent deposits of good will to families. The "interest earned" will be better outcomes for students.

10. Send out monthly newsletters describing the kinds of things the class is doing, and school news or events coming up. Attach articles families would be interested in. Have a Family Corner occasionally, for which families provide comments or ideas.

11. Encourage volunteering in the classroom to read stories, help with art lessons, listen to book reports, or give a lesson on an area of expertise such as a job or hobby.

12. Ask families about their educational expectations for their children. Develop a climate of high expectations in the home, school, and community.

13. Send follow-up notes after meetings. Put out a pamphlet about home-school collaboration in IEP planning conferences.

14. Provide classroom teachers with handouts that can be useful during conferences.

15. Have a Home Book notebook of pictures, activities, and stories about class that students take turns sharing at home.

16. Put a Family Board at the entrance of the building for posting ideas of interest to families, examples of class activities, and pictures.

17. Involve parents and siblings, babysitters, and grandparents to all class parties.

18. Write the right notes. Say thanks, confirm plans, ask for opinions, praise work, give good news, give advance notice of special events and classroom needs.

19. Have families from other countries or culture groups talk to students about their customs and culture.

20. Ask families what their family goals are, and respond with how those goals are being met by the classroom curriculum.

CHAPTER REVIEW

1. The variable with the most significant effect on children's development is family involvement in the child's learning. Educational professionals are integral parts of children's lives, but families are the link of continuity for most of them. Parents and other family members and caregivers are the decision makers for their children, whose futures are largely dependent on the continued ability of their parents to advocate for them. Numerous mandates and passages of legislation have recognized this relationship and provided for involvement by families in the educational programs of students who have special learning and behavioral needs. Educators must be partners with families of students with special needs. This is a demanding and challenging responsibility; however, educators are committed to such a partnership because it fulfills a legal right of families.

2. Legislation codifies the benefits of the partnership for children, families, and schools. Important mandates include P.L. 99-457, P.L. 101-476, P.L. 94-142, and P.L. 105-17.

3. Educational consultants have begun to focus successfully on family strengths by broadening the concept of parent involvement to parent partnership, by using appropriate communication skills, and by promoting positive

roles for family members. These enhanced perceptions recognize family needs and promote family competence.

4. Educators and families encounter numerous barriers to home-school collaboration, including underutilization of services, lack of organizational cultural competency, and differing attitudes, history, values, culture, and language. Examining their own culture and values as potential barriers to understanding will enable them to address the diversity they experience during collaboration.

5. Educators must clarify their own values in order to respect the values of others. Check-

lists, structured value-clarification activities, or thoughtful consideration help educators identify their specific values about education, school, and home-school collaboration.

6. Educators should provide a variety of opportunities for families to become involved with the school. These opportunities should be based on family strengths, expertise, and needs. Family strengths represent contributions that they can make to the partnership. The needs of parents are those interests and needs they have concerning their families.

TO DO AND THINK ABOUT

1. Put yourself in the place of a parent of a student with a disability. Reflect on:

   ■ What you would expect to find in a climate of family partnership at your child's school
   ■ What you would want in terms of knowledge about services and opportunities to be involved in the educational process
   ■ What questions you would have for your child's teacher(s)
   ■ What kinds of school environment or teacher behavior would encourage you to engage in partnership with the school and teachers

   Then summarize these thoughts into a set of do's and don'ts for family school partnership.

2. Brainstorm to identify family characteristics or strengths that would be encouraging to a consultant or teacher who has students with learning or behavior disorders. Then develop a set of guidelines for interaction and involvement between school educators and home educators that would cultivate those characteristics.

3. Plan a booklet that could be used by consultants to improve home-school communication and collaboration. Determine who would compose it, how it could be distributed and used, and how it would be helpful for involving families as collaborative partners in their child's education. In the booklet include either the do's and don'ts of #1 above, or the guidelines from #2, or both.

ADDITIONAL READINGS AND RESOURCES

Berger, E. H. (2008). *Parents as partners in education: Families and schools working together* (7th ed.). Upper Saddle River, NJ: Prentice Hall.

Caspe, M., & Lopez, M. E. (2006). *Lessons from family-strengthening interventions: Learning from evidence-based practice.* Cambridge, MA: Harvard Family Research Project. Available at www.gse.harvard.edu/hfrp.html

Caspe, M., Lopez, M. E., & Wolos, C. (2007). *Family Involvement in elementary school children's*

education. Cambridge, MA: Harvard Family Research Project. Available at www.gse.harvard.edu/hfrp.html

Fiedler, C. R., Simpson, R. L., & Clark, D. M. (2007). *Parents and families of children with disabilities: Effective school-based support services.* Upper Saddle River, NJ: Prentice Hall.

Harry, B., Kalyanpur, M., & Day, M. (1999). *Building cultural reciprocity with families: Case studies in special education.* Baltimore: Paul H. Brookes.

Hildebrand, V., Phenice, L. A., Gray, M. M., & Hines, R. P. (2000). *Knowing and serving diverse families*. Upper Saddle River, NJ: Merrill.

Kreider, H., Caspe, M., Kennedy, S., & Weiss, H. (2007). *Family Involvement in middle and high school students' education*. Cambridge, MA: Harvard Family Research Project. Available at www.gse.harvard.edu/hfrp.html

Soodak, L. C., & Erwin, E. J. (1995). Parents, professionals, and inclusive education: A call for collaboration. *Journal of Educational and Psychological Consultation, 6*(3), 257–276.

Researchers found that parents want more meaningful collaboration with educators because they do not necessarily support the goals of the schools' philosophy and practices in special education.

Turnbull, A., Turnbull, R., Erwin, E. J., & Soodak, L. C. (2006). *Families, professionals, and exceptionality: Positive outcomes through partnership and trust* (5th ed.). Upper Saddle River, NJ: Pearson.

Weiss, H., Caspe, M., & Lopez, M. E. (2006). *Family Involvement in early childhood education*. Cambridge, MA: Harvard Family Research Project. Available at www.gse.harvard.edu/hfrp.html

CHAPTER NINE

CONTENT:
Diversity

Working Together for Students from Diverse Populations

The United States is a multicultural society. This diversity of cultures, races, ethnicities, and languages found within our boundaries represents an ever-expanding richness of perspectives, attributes, talents, skills, and styles that epitomize our country in the twenty-first century.

The imagery of a mosaic is illustrative of our broad spectrum of cultures. Each socioeconomic, racial, ethnic, religious, age, gender, and ability group offers unique pieces to the picture, with shared values and institutions of the whole providing the frame and the adhesive. Or, we could construct a tapestry in which threads of many textures, hues, and sizes would be woven into a colorful, interesting picture. Of course there would be occasional knots, ravelings, and frays, but every thread would be valuable in providing purpose and significance to the whole design.

Many other colorful metaphors and illustrative concepts have been proposed to discuss diversity. But no matter which ones collaborative school consultants prefer, recognition of cultural differences and respect for diversity is a key element in serving special needs of all students.

FOCUSING QUESTIONS

1. How does the changing demography of contemporary classrooms relate to school consultation and collaboration?

2. What is meant by *cultural diversity,* and what terms are used for various school programs that serve culturally diverse learners?

3. What is the collaborative consultant's role for working with diverse populations and how can supportive attitudes, sensitivities, and skills for the role be developed and assessed?

4. Why should consulting teachers strive to first know their own culture before they set out to consult, collaborate, and work on educational teams in multicultural settings?

5. What are some differences in culturally diverse communication styles and belief systems that teachers may find among their students and their colleagues in education?

6. How can collaborative consultants team with educational partners to serve needs in culturally and linguistically diverse school settings? In rural and isolated areas? Areas with high rates of mobility? Military dependent contexts? Settings where students are home schooled? With gay or lesbian families? With educators who have disabilities? With children having disabilities who are abused?

KEY TERMS

culture
cultural and linguistic diversity (CLD)
cultural and linguistic diversity with exceptionality (CLDE)
diversity

English language learners (ELLs)
ethnic group
home-school settings
military dependent students

mobile students
multicultural education
rural and isolated students
sexual orientation

SCENARIO 9.A

The instructor of a course that includes awareness and appreciation of cultural diversity distributes an activity to class members, and says, "Please move about the room to obtain a different autograph on each blank line of your paper. You may use your own name once if you qualify for that item. When your autograph form is complete, or the signal is given to stop, please sit down and interact with others near you by telling some things about your own cultural background, sharing memorable multicultural experiences you have had, and discussing places and peoples you would like to know more about.

AUTOGRAPH FORM
Obtain autographs from:

1. Someone who speaks Spanish.   _____
2. Someone who has been in more countries than you have.   _____
3. A person who owns a world atlas.   _____
4. Someone who has eaten blubber (or sushi, grasshoppers, or some other local delicacy of a culture not your own).   _____
5. A person who has driven on roads (legally) left of center.   _____
6. A person who has seen a movie in a foreign language.   _____
7. Someone who knows the time in Sweden right now.   _____
8. A person who has studied the French or German language.   _____
9. One who has or did have an international pen pal.   _____
10. Someone with a friend or a relative from another culture.   _____

As participants collect the autographs, and especially as they begin discussing their own experiences with other cultures and languages, the instructor is aware of the wide range of multicultural experiences within the group. Sharing these backgrounds and learning more about their experiences will be helpful in expanding multicultural understanding.

DIVERSITY AND EDUCATIONAL COLLABORATION AND CONSULTATION

Respecting cultural differences and cultural similarities fosters collegial interactions and relationships. Understanding other cultures is not an easy task, but it is a cornerstone for successful collaboration. Consultants need to understand the implications of cultural diversity within our society as it affects the educational system because according to March 2004 Census Bureau projections, by the year 2050 (Armas, 2004):

- The total population of the United States will be about 420 million, minority groups will account for 49.9 percent of that number, and over 20 percent of residents will be 65 years of age or older.
- The non-Hispanic white population is expected to be 210 million, just over 50 percent of the population.
- The population of those with Hispanic ethnicity will increase by 188 percent to 102.6 million or about one-quarter of the total population.
- The Black population is expected to rise some 71 percent to become 15 percent of the total population and the second-largest minority.
- The Asian population will more than triple to about 33 million.

What Is Culture?

Banks and Banks (2007) describe culture as knowledge, concepts, and values shared by group members. Although different cultures have different tools, dress, language, food, housing, and other artifacts, it is the values, symbols, interpretation, and perspectives that most distinguish one culture from another. Culture is a dynamic framework that provides guidelines and bounds for life practices. T. L. Cross, of the National Indian Child Welfare Association, describes culture as an organized response to human needs. Food, safety and security, love and belonging, esteem and identity, and self-actualization are all shaped by culture (Cross, 2003).

All members of a cultural group are not the same and individuals are not fixed in their attitudes, beliefs, or behaviors. Therefore, consultants should think about cultural differences as a continuum. This helps us to avoid stereotyping and to develop accurate perceptions of the diversity of our collaborators. Lynch and Hanson (1998) suggest several cultural continua to consider:

- Family constellation
- Interdependence/individuality
- Nurturance/independence
- Time
- Tradition/technology
- Ownership
- Rights and responsibilities
- Harmony/control

Resources such as Lynch and Hanson and others listed at the end of this chapter are recommended for consultants who want to learn more about these continua and about the development of cultural identity, immigrant culture shock, and culture-specific information, as well as important caveats, for gathering this type of information. It is beyond the scope of this book to delve into the issues more fully, but it is extremely important for educators who collaborate with adults from different cultural backgrounds to study and reflect on the reality of diversity.

For educational consultants, it is appropriate to define diversity broadly, because many demographic variables (age, gender, residence), status variables (social, educational, economic), and affiliations (formal, informal) contribute to identity as well as to issues related to collaborative relationships. Current uses of the word *diversity* in education settings have come to relate to ethnicity, language, religion, sexual orientation, demographic indicators such as economic level, geographic locations, age, gender, and many other indicators of group uniqueness. Educational systems will be called upon more and more during the next several decades to serve new pluralities with sensitivity to and understanding of multicultural issues.

Cultural Diversity in the Teacher Population

The teaching force does not reflect cultural diversity and it never has. Profiles of prospective teachers continue to be primarily white females from small towns or suburban communities who attended colleges or universities not far from home and plan to return to places similar to home for their teaching career. These teachers reflect middle-class backgrounds and values and have limited travel experience in which to become acquainted with diverse cultures. Eighty percent of teachers surveyed by Futrell, Gomez, and Bedden (2003) felt unprepared to teach a diverse student population. Discrepancy between teacher and student backgrounds argues forcibly for parent and community collaborative efforts.

It is essential for educators to become familiar with the cultures of the students and families with whom they work and to have preparation in interpersonal communication and problem solving with culturally diverse populations. Deans and department chairs of teacher education programs are well aware that a critical element in gaining national accreditation for their programs is demonstration of diversity in student enrollment, instructional faculty, and sites for student teaching and field experiences. Once preservice teachers are placed in schools for that first year of teaching, experienced consulting teachers have an important role in mentoring and coaching them to work effectively with culturally and linguistically diverse students. (The mentor teacher is discussed in Chapter 12.)

Diversity-Related Terminology for Educational Collaborators

Changes in the language used in various professional circles to describe programs, students, and instructional strategies related to diversity may be confusing to consultants and consultees. Definitional uncertainties must be tolerated by consultants, who may need to ask questions or research the meaning of terms used in various local school programs related to diversity. Terms include English language learner (ELL), English language development (ELD), multicultural education, English for speakers of other languages (ESOL), cultural and linguistic diversity (CLD), and culturally and linguistically diverse students with exceptionalities (CLDE).

The term *English language learner* (ELL) is used to refer to students who are less than proficient in English. *English language development* (ELD) refers to all types of instruction that promote the development of either oral or written English language skills and abilities. This term replaces ones such as English as a second language (ESL) or English for speakers of other languages (ESOL; Gersten & Baker, 2000).

However, cultural competence is not always one of an educator's strengths. As an example of just one teacher's experience, Dorris (1979) describes a printed program that was brought home from school by a third-grade American Indian boy. On the program was an illustration of "The Pilgrims' First Thanksgiving." This child's father was not amused when he read the caption "informing" readers "the Pilgrims had served pumpkin, turkey, corn, and squash to the Indians, *a feast the likes of which the Indians had never seen before*" (emphasis added).

The phrase "minority group" is used less frequently than in the past decades unless it is in a numerical sense. The more acceptable term, *ethnic group,* is a microcultural group that shares a common history and culture, values, behaviors, and other characteristics that cause members of the group to have a shared identity (Banks & Banks, 2007). Multicultural education refers to an educational reform movement designed to change the total educational environment so that students from diverse racial and ethnic groups, gender groups, exceptional students, and all social classes will experience equal educational opportunities across all educational settings (Banks & Banks, 2007).

CULTURAL AWARENESS BY COLLABORATIVE CONSULTANTS

Some students, because of their particular racial, ethnic, gender, and cultural characteristics, have a better chance of succeeding in educational institutions as they currently are structured than do students who belong to other groups with different cultural and gender characteristics (Banks & Banks, 2007). Efforts to become more inclusive in education must include expanded knowledge about cultural diversity. Educators must foster positive attitudes toward cultural pluralism and cultivate skills for arranging multiple learning environments that enable individuals from every culture to realize their potential. In addition to their roles of working directly with students from diverse backgrounds, collaborative consultants work daily with other adults who are integral to providing the best education possible for all students. Being sensitive toward cultural differences and knowledgeable about cultural practices will enhance relationships and the process of collaboration.

Lynch and Hanson (1998) compare culture to looking through a one-way mirror; everything we see is from our own perspective and limited view. It is only when we join the observed on the other side of the mirror that it is possible to see others and ourselves clearly. However, getting to the other side of the glass is difficult. Cultural competence is the ability to function comfortably in cross-cultural settings and to interact harmoniously with people from cultures that differ from our own. Cultural competence brings a set of skills and attitudes that help collaborators move to the other side of the one-way mirror. There are many different perspectives on specific skills, attitudes, behaviors, and policies for cultural competence, but whatever definition is used, the bottom line is acknowledging, respecting, and building on the strengths of ethnicity and cultural and linguistic diversity.

Developing Cultural Competencies

How educators interact with diverse groups of people, demonstrate behavior that respects and responds to cultural diversity, and integrate cultural diversity into their curriculum and teaching strategies has an impact on the process and outcomes of collaborative consultation. To develop cultural competencies, consultants should:

- Increase self-awareness of cultural and linguistic diversity
- Cultivate appreciation for diversity
- Increase knowledge and understanding of specific cultures
- Promote multicultural education for all students
- Develop skills to work effectively with a variety of students and parents

Increase Awareness of Diversity.   Only after we have assessed our own attitudes and values toward cultural and linguistic diversity will we be able to develop and strengthen our skills for working with diverse populations. When we hone our cross-cultural competencies, we are better consultants for consultees from diverse backgrounds. In addition, we are better equipped to promote understanding and appreciation of diverse cultural groups in the school setting. Therefore, we must examine our attitudes and practices about cultures different from our own, taking care to ferret out any narrowness in our thinking.

Sample items for assessing one's multicultural attitudes and practices are provided in Figure 9.1. The items can be used for personal reflection and self-study. Discussion and expansion of the list can form the framework for staff development or be administered as part of a study module for a teacher preparation course on consultation and collaboration. Additional items might be added after discussions about multiculturalism and cultural diversity in schools and communities.

■ ■ ■ ■ ■

APPLICATION 9.1

SETTING PERSONAL OBJECTIVES FOR APPRECIATION OF DIVERSITY

After completing the checklist in Figure 9.1, select two or three of the items that you would like to incorporate into a plan of personal awareness development for the school year. Set target dates and on those dates evaluate the outcomes. For making significant progress, treat yourself to something special!

Cultivate Appreciation for Diversity.   Recognition and acceptance of diversity allows individuals and groups to interact effectively (Berger, 2008). Clare (2002) suggests that a person's worldview and perspectives of diversity expand as a result of multicultural experiences and proximity to other diverse groups. Recall the taxonomy for the social domain in Chapter 2 with the increasingly complex levels of social interactions. These experiences create avenues for personal reflection and shift the way consulting teachers frame collaborative efforts and educational practices.

The first step in cultural awareness is to understand one's *own* culture, beliefs, and values. Recognizing characteristics of one's own culture is especially important for

FIGURE 9.1   Examples of Multicultural Assessment Items

A = Always; U = Usually; S = Sometimes; R = Rarely; N = Never

Personal Sensitivity

_____   1. I realize that any individual in a group may not have the same values as others in the group.

_____   2. I avoid words, statements, expressions, and actions that members of other culture groups and orientations could find offensive.

_____   3. I read books and articles to increase my understanding and sensitivity about the hopes, strengths, and concerns of people from other cultures.

_____   4. I counteract prejudicial, stereotypical thinking and talking whenever and wherever I can.

School Context Efforts

_____   5. I include contributions of people from diverse populations as an integral part of the school curriculum.

_____   6. I strive to nurture skills and develop values in students and colleagues that will help members of minority groups thrive in the dominant culture.

_____   7. I know where to obtain bias-free, multicultural materials for use in my school.

_____   8. I have evaluated the school resource materials to determine whether or not they contain a fair and appropriate presentation of people in diverse populations.

Parent/Community Relations

_____   9. I invite parents and community members from various cultural backgrounds to be classroom resources, speakers, visiting experts, or assistants.

_____   10. I value having a school staff composed of people from different cultural backgrounds.

_____   11. I exhibit displays showing culturally diverse people working and socializing together.

_____   12. I advocate for schools in which all classes, including special education classes, reflect and respect diversity.

European Americans because of their tendency to view culture through an ethnocentric lens, often believing somewhat naively that theirs is the primary or prevailing culture (Banks & Banks, 2007; Lynch & Hanson, 1998).

■ ■ ■ ■ ■

APPLICATION 9.2

REFLECTING ON ONE'S OWN CULTURAL ORIENTATION

Think about your own cultural background. What language did your great grandparents, or more distant ancestors, speak? When did they come to this country? Why did they come? What family customs, such as holidays, food, and traditions reflect the culture of your ancestors?

Then practice effective communication skills by listening to descriptions from others about their cultural heritage. Share your cultural background information with others so that they may practice their active listening skills and get to know *you* better.

After consultants reflect on their own culture, they should work to enhance their abilities for acknowledging cultural differences in responding and relating to others. When considering methods for improving cross-cultural awareness and sensitivity, the best way for consultants to learn about other cultures is by learning from the people themselves, rather than learning about them secondhand as belonging to a particular cultural group. Communication skills and interpersonal skills are important for collaboration with educational partners. Awareness of differences and respect for customs within diverse cultures are major factors for interacting within school settings and engaging in collaborative efforts with school personnel.

Consulting teachers and collaborators must model respect for diversity and assist other school personnel in cultivating ethnic identities of students through classroom activities that range from more traditional through contemporary approaches. One Chinese student studying special education in the United States, who was enrolled in a university course with authors of this book, wrote:

> Since I came to the United States, I have been involved in a totally different circumstance I have never confronted before. . . . I really observe and analyze a life with different implications and features. I was puzzled at the scene in which American students rushed in and out of the classroom each day, while in China we may have more leisure time chatting or discussing among students. Classmates in China usually stand for [sic] close friends, who take years to study, work, play, and live together. Here in America, only a few faces are familiar to me as one semester passed. . . . I sometimes feel myself retiring, quietly friendly, sensitive, modest about my abilities. This in fact reflects some aspect of culture in our society. I was nurtured to become "good"—courteous and modest. Thus, I, like many other Chinese students, shun disagreements, do not force my opinions or values on others.

Increase Knowledge and Understanding of Specific Cultures.   One of the biggest challenges for consultants in diverse settings is understanding the consultee's frame of reference, or "entering the consultee's world" and viewing things as the consultee (or client) sees them (Soo-Hoo, 1998). Home communication patterns of students or consultees may be quite different from those they hear and see in school. Expectations between family members and teachers may be at variance.

Collaborators require a deep understanding of the co-collaborator's frame of reference. Sometimes general characteristics of cultural groups provide preliminary insights for consultants as they strive to develop and maintain collaborative relationships. These characteristics include cultural norms for the style of communication behavior and beliefs about families, and their spirituality and nature. For example, some individuals in the Asian culture expect one-way communication from the authority figure to another person. Silence signifies respect and there are well-defined, concrete patterns of interaction. Members of the Hispanic culture may have a different time perspective, strong emphasis on the extended family, and a bilingual background. Members of the African American culture often are action oriented and place importance on nonverbal behavior. Values within the Native American cultures tend to stress cooperation over competitive individualism; working toward immediate, short-range goals; and respect for creative and intuitive approaches.

Hispanic, Asian, and Native American cultures promote respect for elders and authority figures, and the expectation of not speaking until spoken to. Therefore, a consulting teacher hoping to engage the family in collaborative problem solving may be met with silence or short phrases as a sign of respect, and may erroneously interpret this response as being negative or disengaged.

One cautionary note: Generic cultural characteristics are not the be-all and end-all of cultural diversity. *Any person or family may differ markedly from these generalities.* Although many researchers provide lists of generic cultural characteristics of specific diverse groups, consultants must guard against the myopic perspective that culturally diverse families are a homogeneous group. Educators must respond in individually relevant ways to those with whom they collaborate rather than make assumptions based on group characteristics of microcultures. Descriptions of characteristics provide only broad brush strokes for initiating multicultural interrelationships.

Furthermore, brief descriptions of cultural characteristics of specific cultures may imply that cultural differences are simple and easy to understand. Cross (2003) gives us an example from his own Seneca teachings. For this Native American group from the U.S. Northwest, the theoretical model for their culture is a relational worldview; and this world-view, Cross says, is different from that found in most educational institutions. For the Senecas, human existence is understood in the form of a four-quadrant circle encompassing mind, body, spirit, and context. Health and well-being depend on the balance among the quadrants. Balance is a constant human process, and the Senecas rely on their culture to provide the resources within each quadrant to stay in balance. Cross points to this relational worldview as being different from a culture that relies heavily on linear thought and the scientific process to understand and solve problems in terms of causal relationships. So cultural perspective is far from simple.

Communication and Culture. Effective intercultural communication for consultants means coping with stress of dealing with the unfamiliar, establishing rapport with others, sensing other people's feelings, and communicating effectively with people from varying backgrounds. Collaborative consultants benefit from understanding interrelationships between language and cultural meaning.

Bogdan and Biklen (2006) caution that not all cultures share middle class values and American definitions of terms. Examples of ethnic-based values and behaviors that can affect group interaction are preferences regarding (Adler, 1993; Sue & Sue, 1990):

- Personal space, such as physical distance between communicants and arrangement of furniture for seating
- Body movement, including body orientation, gestures, and facial expressions
- Time orientation
- Eye movement and position
- Touch

Cultures have differing rules about human communications and relationships. For example, it is not acceptable in some cultures to share beliefs and opinions with people outside the group. Another example is the proclivity in some cultures for being quiet in the presence of authority figures. This can be disconcerting to school personnel when trying to solicit input from parents who think of the teacher as an authority.

In some cultures the way to respond to a question with finesse is to skirt the subject and arrive at it indirectly, while in another culture being direct and forthright is admirable. Public congratulation in certain cultures is offensive because group accomplishment is valued more than individual achievement, whereas in other cultures public congratulation would be an incentive to continue excelling.

Knowledge of cultural differences in nonverbal communication is important for educational collaborators. For example, knowing that avoiding eye contact is a sign of respect in some cultures will help consultant and consultee avoid interpreting this as disrespect and rudeness. Although it is the opposite of the cultural norms in most educational settings, in some cultures, looking away from the speaker indicates paying attention. Variations of actions involving handshakes, head nods, eyebrow raising, and finger-pointing have widely different meanings in different cultural settings. The socioeconomic variable that includes class, status, position, and prestige has many ramifications for teaching and learning, and may be even more obvious during collaborative endeavors.

Language and Colloquialisms.   Consultants will want to avoid negative words, using language that instead indicates a desire to help students expand their abilities, not to help them "get better." They need to exercise caution in discussing poor work, bad behavior, or poor attitudes because what is perceived as mild criticism or simply suggestion in one culture may lead to severe punishment of the child or disillusionment about the student's ability from a family of another culture. Idioms should not be used that might be misunderstood in another language—for example, "He will work his way out of this," or "Let's put this on the back burner for now," or "We need to get her to up to speed in that," or "Students need to toe the line in his classroom," or "That's a Catch-22." Consultants should listen carefully to family members to learn more about the student and capitalize on strengths, which, for that matter, is good strategy for any situation involving any student.

Gendered language also affects interactions, particularly when they intersect with characteristics of some cultural groups. Collaborators must monitor their own behavior for use of fair and balanced gender-specific languages, for example:

- Use *persons* or *women and men,* not *men* or *mankind.*
- Use the term *homemaker*, not *housewife.*
- Avoid saying *female* doctor, *male* nurse, saying simply doctor or nurse.
- Instead of saying, "He adds the balances," say, "The accountant adds the balances."
- Do not avoid recognizing same-sex partnerships. Same-sex partners are typically referred to as "partner" rather than "significant other."
- Avoid *man* and *wife*; instead saying *the couple* or *husband and wife.*
- Refrain from terms like *the fair sex, woman's work, man-size job.*
- Say "Susan is a successful executive," not "Susan is a successful lady."
- Identify someone as a "supervisor" rather than a "foreman."
- Say "students," or "class," instead of "boys and girls."

Promote Multicultural Education.   Multicultural appreciation and understanding evolve from direct interpersonal contact and from knowledge of the history and culture of diverse groups, including their stories, values, myths, inventions, music, and art. Many consultants report that "hitting the streets" to become involved with families, communities, and cultures not only improves their work with students and families, it also enriches their own lives. When consultants learn about the cultural heritages of their students and the adults with whom they collaborate and honor those heritages, they can help mitigate the negative impact of prejudice and racism and utilize cultural traditions as strengths. Cross (2003) challenges us to "help our children find the strengths, positive emotions, and mental wellness that are a part of every culture" (p. 359).

Banks and Banks (2007), Glasgow and Hicks (2003), Chisholm (1994), and others offer suggestions for promoting multicultural education for all students. When consultants integrate these suggestions into their work with CLD children, families, and other school personnel on the education team, the process of collaboration is greatly enhanced, as in the following examples:

- Think beyond content. English language learners come with a variety of challenges and needs, as well as strengths.
- Use technology in ways that are sensitive to cultural and individual differences. Technology is not culture-free because it reflects the cultural perspective of software developers.
- Develop a critical understanding of the social-cultural context of interactions and instruction in your setting and allow this understanding to guide your work.
- Promote a positive ethnic identity, because all cultures add value to schools and to society and are a powerful resource for group members.
- Develop multicultural connections in your discipline and your community.
- Prepare for an increasingly likely cultural and linguistic mismatch in this country among school personnel, students, and their families.

COLLABORATION AND CONSULTATION IN DIVERSE CULTURAL SETTINGS AND WITH DIVERSE TEAM MEMBERS

Consultants have an instrumental role in bringing together diverse groups of educators, including teachers, administrators, related services personnel, families, and community members. Consultants use communication and collaboration skills to help the educational team address and resolve problems and to work for creative solutions.

Collaborative consultation and a true collaborative environment, rather than an expert model of consultation, comprise the current preferred mode of education for CLDE students (Baca and Cervantes, 1998). In this approach the expertise of one partner in the team working is not valued over that of another; all are recognized as vital to the collaborative process and the education of students.

Collaboration with Partners for CLDE Students

Students who are culturally and linguistically diverse with exceptionality (CLDE) are served by a variety of educational professionals and specialists in the school and the community. There are several models of bilingual special education. In the coordinated services model, students are served by a team composed of a special educator and a bilingual educator.

Whatever model is utilized in your school, collaboration and consultation are essential for quality services for CLDE students.

Teacher assistance teams are a common strategy for serving exceptional CLD students. This team should include individuals with expertise in appropriate assessment and instructional options related to the cultural and linguistic background of the students as well as the exceptionality. Bahamonde and Friend (1999) suggest that co-teaching is a promising alternative to current practices of bilingual education. By applying best practices and knowledge from special education to bilingual education, improvements can be documented in student-student, student-teacher, and teacher-teacher relationships. Collaborative consultation is a key feature of co-teaching.

Harris (2004) describes a set of consultation competencies needed by educators who consult for CLDE students:

- Understanding one's perspective
- Using effective interpersonal, communication, and problem-solving skills
- Understanding the role(s) of collaborators
- Using appropriate assessment and instructional strategies

McCardle, Mele-McCarthy, and Leos (2005) suggest that not only should teachers and practitioners become familiar with the cultural norms of the children and families with whom they work, they should also be familiar with the phonological, syntactic, and morphological parameters of the student's first language. These parameters may interact with the learning of English. English language learners' linguistic performance cannot be fully or appropriately evaluated separated from their culture because culture influences how people use language to express themselves and how language is used in a social context.

Consultants need to learn about language and literacy because there is a close link between language and literacy abilities and disabilities (McCardle et al., 2005). Bilingual students are often lost between these two levels of proficiency in their first language (L1) and their second language (L2), usually English. For example, the ways that children develop study habits, reading practices, and writing skills are influenced by home and culture (Maldonado, 1994). The native literacy approach advocated by many in the field means that the children's native language and culture are acknowledged and are the main focus of instruction. This chapter does not address these important issues in working with ELL children; however, collaborative educators should understand that such issues are vital to the education of many of the children they serve, and should be an area of collaboration and consultation among special educators, bilingual educators, and others.

Those who work together for CLDE students should remember that students in the throes of acculturation may find the learning environment in public schools to be stressful and confusing (Baca & Cervantes, 1998). It is necessary to consider the interaction of culture and language within the acculturation context and the possible effects of a disability on this interaction (Baca & Cervantes, 1998). Success for CLDE students can be maximized by attending to practices that have been proven effective. Several suggestions for further reading about using appropriate assessment and instructional strategies can be found at the end of this chapter.

Collaboration and Consultation in Rural and Isolated School Settings

Rural schools in remote areas are characterized by geographic isolation, cultural isolation, too few students for some kinds of grouping, too few staff members covering too many curricular and special program areas, resistance of students toward being singled out, limited resources, and most of all, distance that necessitates great amounts of personnel time spent in travel. The traveling consulting teacher has become a mainstay of school districts in which miles and more miles separate students who have special learning and behavior needs.

In rural areas communication is more likely to be person-to-person rather than written or phoned as in urban settings. In rural settings teachers tend to be highly visible, therefore more vulnerable to community pressure and criticism. Rural educators are left much to themselves to solve problems and acquire skills for their roles. These qualities of rural school life create advantages for consulting teacher approaches, yet there are certain disadvantages inherent in indirect service delivery. Few rural schools are fully prepared and able to meet the needs of special needs students without consultation and other indirect services. Therefore, it is necessary for consulting teachers to become intensively involved in providing learning options and alternatives for students. Consulting teachers can coordinate collaborative effort among teachers, administrators, parents, and other community members so that few resources seem like more. (See Figure 9.2.)

In a comparative study of consultant roles and responsibilities in rural and urban areas, Thurston and Kimsey (1989) found several major obstacles to consultation and collaboration activities. Rural teachers have less formal recognition of their consulting roles. They seem less confident in their consulting skills than their urban counterparts. Major obstacles include:

- Too many other responsibilities
- Not enough time

FIGURE 9.2   Here to Help, There to Help

- Lack of administrative support
- Too much paperwork
- Minimal professional interaction due to sparse population (although electronic communication has become increasingly helpful in this aspect)
- Long distances to travel and often poor roads and weather conditions for driving
- More lesson preparations and extracurricular duties
- The reality that differentness is more noticeable among smaller populations

Contrasting obstacles reported by urban area consulting teachers include too many other responsibilities, too much paperwork, and disinterested parents.

Rural area students tend to be resourceful, open to a wide range of experiences, somewhat independent, and capable of self-direction. These pluses can be used to advantage by consultants in designing collaborative arrangements for special needs. Since students in rural areas often dislike being singled out, it is important to involve them in planning learning programs in which they are comfortable and interested.

Rural teachers do have advantages in carrying out their consulting roles. They often function as influential change agents. They tend to be creative and innovative problem solvers (perhaps paralleling the farmer/rancher who can fix most anything with improvisation and what is on hand.) In no other setting is the multiplier effect more useful than in rural areas having limited access and resources. These multiplier benefits can be maximized by playing on the strengths of the rural community, including smaller class sizes, more frequent interaction between students and staff, greater involvement of parents in the school and its activities, and students who participate in most phases of school life.

Collaborating with Families Who Move Frequently

With up to 20 percent of the population in the United States on the move each year, many school-age children's educational programs are disrupted. Moving and the events leading up to and following it can be traumatic for anyone; for the student with disabilities they may be particularly troublesome. Records must be forwarded, new teachers and texts and classmates assimilated, and adjustments made to home conditions of sleep, meals, and schedules while the child is getting settled in. In some communities, the predominant language may be different.

Wallings (1990) describes several characteristics and some major effects on mobile families. Such families tend to be younger with young, school-age children, and they are more apt to rent than own a home. The older the student, the more difficult a move seems to be, because adolescents are quite peer-oriented. Boys in particular are often less adept than girls at making new friends, and may be teased, bullied, or rejected. Children may feel they cannot measure up to expectations in the new school. One whose disability was accepted by peers in the former school has to begin all over again to win friends and influence adults.

Single-parent families have a particularly difficult time because there is no other adult with whom to share responsibilities and repercussions of the move. The school-age individual may be put into the position of that other needed adult without having the coping skills and maturity to manage the stress. Belonging to a minority group (for example, an African American student in a white majority classroom, or a white student in a primarily

African American classroom) is another factor in feeling welcome and being accepted. Limited ability with English will add yet another dimension to acclimation and academic success.

Neighborhood ties are disrupted by moves, and parents are adjusting to new jobs in many cases. Families who are forced to move due to eviction, ethnic or racial tension, or economic deprivation, will be particularly stressed. Children and teens of agricultural workers whose work takes them to different areas with regular frequency (and many of whom participate in that work themselves), may arrive late after school has begun. They often must catch up in academic areas due to constant moves, necessitating that they forego enrolling in classes such as art, drama, and debate. Gaining English language fluency can take five to seven years; young children can achieve it sooner, but transience remains a big hurdle. Those with disabilities and other special needs beyond these apparent ones are in particular need of consultation and collaboration by those who can provide the array of services they require. Mobility affects not only the students and families who move, but also the institutions they use.

Newly arriving students with special needs should be assisted by the collaborative team in handling any stress and disorientation as soon as they arrive at the new school. Collaborative teams in the new school can help ease their transition through such plans as:

- Synchronous curriculum for smooth transitions between schools
- Peer support groups, particularly helpful when there is seasonal influx such as migrant worker employment
- Class emphasis on teamwork and cooperation, which will help the new students and all others in the process
- A buddy system, which could involve matching the student with an older, confident, and popular student
- Inclusion of a variety of learning styles and methods
- Mentors (best if adult) to serve as the new student's advocate and confidant
- Parent support groups
- Periodic orientation programs at various times of the year
- In-service programs for school personnel that focus on the needs of transient students, particularly those with disabilities, in their adjustment to the new school and neighborhood

Students with special needs due to advanced abilities also can be affected by family moves. This area has not seen much research activity; however, one study revealed that gifted students were much more concerned about making new friendships and adjusting to their new school climate than they were about their academic success (Plucker & Yecke, 1999). There seemed to be little difficulty in sustaining their academic performance, but organizational difficulties such as different qualifications for programs and reluctance of school officials to accept test scores were barriers to smooth transitions (See Figure 9.3). The researchers noted that in order to overcome these kinds of administrative hurdles, parents frequently relied on assertiveness in their interactions with school personnel. Collaborative consultants should take this into account without being judgmental and overreacting.

FIGURE 9.3   "This isn't like what I had at the other three schools."

Collaborating with Gay and Lesbian Families

The increasing diversity of family structures means that educators interact with those whom students consider to be their family, whether it be a single parent, grandparents, foster parents, multigenerational living groups, or gay or lesbian parents. Families headed by gay and lesbian parents are becoming more common and more visible (Ray & Gregory, 2001). Therefore, educators who are committed to inclusive schools and active parent-educator collaboration are likely to be interacting with family members who are gay or lesbian.

Many educators are from homogeneous community backgrounds and may have biases or lack of knowledge about issues related to families with gay or lesbian parents. To establish crucial home-school ties and to understand more about a child's out-of-school context, educators must do two things:

1. Examine personal beliefs and feelings about families and family diversity in all its many facets (Koemer & Hulsebosch, 1996)
2. Become educated about the context of gay and lesbian families and their children

Examining one's own beliefs and feelings is not always a comfortable activity. No matter what our personal beliefs, values, and experiences, as educators we understand that it is not possible to be *for* children but against their families. Inclusiveness is a moral imperative in schools, as well as in family and community relationships.

Educators seek to develop relationships with parents so they can understand the lives of their students. School staff need to have comfort, understanding, and effective skills for promoting and maintaining an inclusive environment for learning for all children in all types of families. Educators should work out their own feelings and clarify their own values on the issue. Casper and Shultz (1999) suggest reflection by individuals or groups on such questions as: What types of family differences fit into my borders of tolerance? Do gay and lesbian families fit into this circle? Is discomfort associated with fear or other deep-seated feelings? In what ways can conscious awareness of my feelings help me question them, and help me become more inclusive in my interactions with the adults in my students' lives?

Educators need to recognize that lesbian and gay parents represent a range of diverse social, ethnic, and economic class backgrounds, as do any other group of parents. Along with questioning stereotypes, school personnel who strive for inclusive and respectful home-school relationships should strive to learn more about the families with whom they work.

Golombok and colleagues (2003) offer three important findings that help educators understand the reality of families with gay or lesbian parents:

1. The only clear difference between heterosexual and homosexual parents' child-rearing patterns is that co-mothers in lesbian-mother families are more involved in parenting than are fathers in two-parent heterosexual homes.
2. A longitudinal study of adults who had been raised as children in lesbian-mother families found that as young men and women they continued to function well in adult life and maintained positive relationships both with their mothers and their mothers' partners.
3. Research has consistently failed to find differences between children of gay and lesbian families and children in heterosexual families with respect to gender development or psychological well-being. Sexual orientation of parent is not a predictor of successful child development.

Research shows that children in gay and lesbian families have similar psychological adjustment to children growing up in more traditional family structures (Ray & Gregory, 2001).

Research by Ray and Gregory (2001) identified common concerns of gay and lesbian parents. First, their type of family structure was not included in the curriculum about homes and families, thereby making their children feel isolated. Also, their children were apt to be teased or bullied, and were asked difficult questions by teachers or other children such as, "Why do you have two mommies?" Educators should take note of these very real concerns as they work with gay and lesbian parents.

Although debates take place at both national and local levels about the definition of family and the parameters of a "legitimate" family, educators have an ethical responsibility to collaborate with *all* significant adults in the lives of their students. Educational collaborators should help schools develop the ability to set a comfortable tone within which all parents can feel welcome in classrooms and comfortable with taking an active role in home-school interactions.

Educators play a powerful role in demonstrating that they believe in treating everyone with dignity and respect. Lamme and Lamme (2001–2002) offer several concrete suggestions for making schools more inclusive and friendly to gay and lesbian parents. Four of the most important to include here are:

1. Refer to families or parents rather than mothers and fathers.
2. Refuse to tolerate harassment and use of homophobic teasing, just as racist remarks and behavior are not tolerated. None of the children of gay and lesbian parents whom Lamme and Lamme (2001–2002) interviewed had heard an adult intervene when a homophobic remark was made in school.
3. Model and teach respect for all.
4. Examine special parent-focused activities. Emphasizing a stereotypical father's day or mother-daughter breakfast may stigmatize children in homes with gay or lesbian parents.

In addition, educational collaborators can provide leadership in improving a school climate of accepting diversity. Part of diversity training or professional development regarding community-home-school relationships and programs should include the concerns expressed by families with gay or lesbian parents.

Another aspect of sexual orientation affecting school personnel is the increasing number of young gay and lesbian students who are coming out about their sexual orientation, especially those in their early teens who live in urban areas. Some educators might deny that this could be a problem, but others recognize the need that students with sexual-orientation differences have for sensitivity from school personnel. A few states are mandating sensitivity training in their teacher certification programs and developing guidelines and materials for making schools more inclusive places of learning (Anderson, 1997). When caring teachers and administrators provide support to gay and lesbian parents and gay and lesbian students, there is less abusive language, harassment, and evidence of homophobia (Edwards, 1997). In years past little information on this subject was available, but now educators, parents, and students talk more openly and share information that can help students feel safe in their school environment.

Collaborating with Partners in Educating Military-Dependent Students

Children and youth who are military dependents, a group whose families tend to move frequently and live with considerable stress and anxiety, are too often overlooked as a population with special needs who can benefit significantly from consultation services. Most are quite resilient; they make friends easily but also know how to say good-bye and move on. However, their lives do put demands on those qualities of flexibility and their personable nature. When they arrive at a new school they may be behind their age peers in achievement. Others are ahead of their class and need academic challenge. The less frequent the moves, the better the achievement. The earlier in the school year the move occurs, the higher the academic success rate (Keller & Decoteau, 2000). One concern that is often overlooked is that their moves frequently take them farther away from their extended families and lifelong friends who could have provided some of the support they need (Tovar, 1998).

When families move from site to site, they frequently become frustrated with the tangled web of records (or having *no* records until they do arrive), referrals, screenings, and conferences. When school records and student information are slow to catch up with the student or are misplaced, then the students are at risk of being misplaced in the school programs. Parents need quick forwarding of accurate, clear student records to ease their child's transition from school to school. Coordinators for the Army's Exceptional Family Member Program in Hawaii advise parents of exceptional children to deliver copies of program records personally, especially those related to their child's IEP (Keller & Decoteau, 2000). They also recommend that parents get a personal letter from former teachers to new teachers on how they worked with that child. Consultants can become a lifeline for students and their families by assisting busy classroom teachers with organization of student records and coordination of orientation activities and conferences. Consultants also can facilitate integration of students into activities with their new peers.

Much can be done in the way of making military dependent and transitory students feel welcome in new environments. Local partnerships among home, community, and military establishment are a first step that benefits all groups. Institutional partnerships among schools, military installations, and colleges and universities have brought research and programs that help students succeed academically and socially (Keller & Decoteau, 2000).

In their schools, students can be assigned to buddies who help with orientation to the school and integration into peer groups. Selected classmates might interview the "new kid on the block," focusing on things their new peers like to do. Teachers can plan activities in which all students participate in making a class album or collage mural, highlighting unique qualities of everyone in the class. Ethnicity is addressed by reminding students that everyone has a cultural heritage (German, Finnish, Korean, Samoan, Irish, Nigerian, and so on.) Each could research his or her own heritage, and a variety of project extensions are possible.

Curricular units and learning centers that highlight a student's travels and former experiences will be instructive for other students even as they make the military family's child feel more welcome. New students' strengths can be drawn on to help remediate gaps that may have resulted from dissimilar educational programs and frequent adjustments to new situations. In addition, students who have traveled widely can be valuable resources for their classmates and teachers and they should be encouraged to do so.

As more families are separated by the deployment of fathers, mothers, or sometimes *both* parents to trouble spots and active war zones around the world, consulting teachers can become sources of assurance for anxious families who have students with special needs. These caring professionals can provide continuity in learning programs and support for the social and emotional needs of students who may feel afraid, lonely, and confused. Working in a team with families, school administrators, teachers, social service personnel, and military staff who oversee family and school life concerns will help ensure a stable learning environment for military-dependent students.

Collaborating on Behalf of Students Schooled at Home

Homeschooling has increased steadily throughout the past two decades. The number of homeschoolers has been estimated as 1.5 million students (*CEC Today,* 2000). More recently, other reports suggest that as many as 2 million students are homeschooled and tens of millions of families are becoming more and more interested in it for their children.

Parents' reasons for homeschooling have been cited as academic, value-driven, or religious, aiming for flexibility, wanting to keep their student's problems such as suspension or pregnancy at home, or the desire to serve special needs such as disabilities or giftedness more intensively than programs in public schools typically do. It is believed that approximately 10 percent of homeschooled students have disabilities.

As homeschooling is becoming more accepted and prevalent, educators are seeing the need to develop collaborative partnerships with families who homeschool. Some parents request the use of school services, including speech therapy, foreign language classes, extracurricular activities including sports, enrichment programs, and the use of libraries and other materials. As taxpayers they are entitled to these resources and by law they are entitled to special education services for their exceptional children.

Evidence that homeschooling is successful for most of the students has been documented through such means as success rates in university classes and scores on standardized tests. However, there are few safety nets for the students if home schooling does not work. Good homeschool experiences are built upon tremendous commitments of time, effort, and often a lost second-income source by families, particularly when there are disabilities that require special attention.

The homeschool process has benefited greatly from distance learning curricula and from resources available on the Internet. Many homeschooling families also take advantage of nearby community colleges and universities. Some parents do not want to commit to homeschooling as a full-time activity, preferring instead to send their children to school and supplement their education with downloaded curricula or community-based experiences to give them additional opportunities for learning.

Many homeschooling families want to remain a part of the public school community, and many educators adhere to the policy that all private school and homeschooled students are eligible to receive services (Council for Exceptional Children, 2000). A growing trend is one in which personnel from public schools and homes work together to educate children. By collaborating with school personnel for a child's special needs, families can be assured that they have taken advantage of everything the home and school have to offer in order to maximize their child's opportunity for success. Collaborative partnerships will allow both home and school educators to provide the utmost benefits available for students in whom they have a common interest.

Working with Educators Who Have Disabilities

One diverse group that seldom is discussed in educational literature is educators who have disabilities. The teaching ranks undoubtedly include individuals with disabilities—physical, learning, perhaps behavioral—but this is not a widely investigated or talked-about topic. Adults with physical disabilities such as missing limb, hearing or visual impairment, disfigurement, or impaired mobility do occasionally prepare for and enter the teaching profession. Young children, and sometimes socially awkward adolescents, can be quite blunt, as when a group of seventh-graders queried a former war veteran, now a teacher who has a prosthesis for the right arm, by asking, "Where'd you get that thing?" At the same time children can be remarkably accepting as they get their papers handed back to them with the prosthesis, or shake hands with their teacher in greeting.

Teachers who have learning problems with memory, spelling, or comprehension have opportunities to model tenacity toward achievement and to share learning strategies that have helped them be successful. They can inspire children with anecdotes about how hard it was for them to succeed in college, but that by having solid goals and good habits to nudge them forward, they succeeded in their aim of earning a degree and obtaining teacher licensure. Adults who have overcome anxiety disorders, eating disorders, obsessive-compulsive disorders, or alcohol and other drug dependency also have much to offer children and youth by modeling attitudes of coping, resilience, a regimen of good habits, and a conquering spirit.

Media cite data sources estimating that 6 to 9 million adults have ADHD, or attention deficit with hyperactivity disorder ("Adults and Attention Deficit Disorder," 1997), and some of these individuals surely are in the education profession. However, many adults with ADHD tend to excel in crises and have learned adaptive strategies for dealing with paperwork and details. One former salesman said he could not keep an accurate count of his merchandise, so he left that job and found fulfillment working in a restaurant and teaching reading to those with disabilities.

The incidence of disability among school personnel, the objective analyses of their abilities to handle the conditions, and discussions of the impact this has on schools and students are topics for which more information is needed. School collaboration is an arena in which these topics can be discussed openly rather than left to linger below the surface and adversely affect communication and problem solving. Interference with problem solving because of one's own problems would be an example of lack of objectivity, one the four interfering themes (Caplan, 1970) that were cited earlier in the book as impediments to effective teaching.

Other cultures throughout the world have very different perceptions of disability from those of Anglo-Americans ("Adults and Attention Deficit Disorder," 1997). In some cultures those with "disabilities" are accepted as having a place in the community with no stigma or problem because they are viewed as having a talent or uniqueness to contribute. This is a challenging concept for educators to address as they work diligently to provide appropriate services for students with special needs.

Collaborating on Behalf of Students with Disabilities Who Are Abused

Newspapers and television newscasts occasionally report extremely disturbing accounts of abuse toward children with disabilities. Research indicates that these children are abused more often than other children (Cosmos, 2001). Furthermore, many cases are not reported; if all were, the incidence rate would be even greater. In her own thought-provoking report, Cosmos points out that some children with disabilities are not capable of telling others about their plight and alarmingly, some who do tell are not believed.

Most abusers are family members, but nonfamily abusers include, sadly, some teachers, health care and residential care workers, transportation personnel, volunteers, babysitters, and peers (Cosmos, 2001). Types of abuse are many and complex, defying brief descriptions, but they include major trauma, such as injury to the brain, and neglect, which could be lack of basic needs or being held in isolation. Neglect is the most common form of abuse toward children with disabilities. Special education teachers are in an ideal role to detect child abuse, but even more importantly they often have an opportunity to notice conditions that lead to abuse and help prevent its occurrence.

The National Clearinghouse on Child Abuse and Neglect Information (NCCAN) and other researchers cite symptoms teachers can be aware of, such as stealing, hoarding things, missing school, appearing to be unsupervised, and displaying emotional trauma in their art and writing, along with being dirty, hungry, and needing proper clothing and medical care. In the NCCAN research summaries, recommendations for addressing these situations include working with the school psychologist, requesting help from an outside consultant, and seeking services from related services personnel who can be helpful such as physical and occupational therapists. Families in which there is abuse are stressed and a major aspect of intervention is reducing the stress. Collaboration by a number of agencies will undoubtedly be needed. At school, special education teachers and paraeducators should use positive behavioral supports and nonaversive forms of behavior modification. Experts also recommend avoidance of physical restraint.

One of the most troubling aspects of detecting abuse is when and to whom it should be reported. According to NCCAN personnel, all fifty states have a mandatory reporting law and most states include teachers as persons who must report abuse. So they advise teachers to know their school policy and abide by that. If the policy is not available or not clear, then they should follow reporting procedures for that state. The teacher is not responsible for affirming the abuse, but only to report suspicions of abuse or neglect. Teachers will want to know the policies and then think things through in order to do the right thing in the right way.

CULTURALLY RESPONSIVE AND ETHICAL COLLABORATIVE CONSULTATION

If a consultant is not familiar with cultural similarities and differences, the collaborative process is likely to lack mutual goals and successful outcomes. Then both consultant and collaborative partner(s) will experience frustration, disappointment, and, in some cases, disenfranchisement. On the other hand, culturally sensitive consultants can initiate meaningful cross-cultural collaborations, and instigate activities that draw out contributions from culturally diverse groups.

Multicultural education is *not* an activity for the last thirty minutes of school on Friday. Awareness and acceptance of cultural and linguistic diversity must be infused throughout the entire school program. Consultants can be particularly facilitative and supportive in this endeavor as they assist in assessing the instructional environment and designing effective instruction for culturally diverse groups.

Collaborative consultants also are in a position to encourage fuller use of diversity-focused resources within the entire community. They might bring in eminent citizens representing culturally diverse groups to tell about their heritage, interests, and roles in society, and pair them with students having special needs, particularly if they have the same cultural background as the student.

Awareness and appreciation of individual differences and cultural diversity are vital attributes for consultants as they work with a wide range of resource and support personnel, teachers, parents, and the students themselves. An educational consultant's respect for diversity demonstrates and models acceptance of individuals and their cultural heritage. Culturally competent and sensitive collaborative consultants can elicit brilliant textures and hues in the tapestry of diversity as they work with students, families, and communities to achieve success for all.

TIPS FOR WORKING WITH DIVERSE POPULATIONS IN SCHOOL SETTINGS

1. Learn about the values, beliefs, and traditions of other cultures in your school by attending community activities sponsored by those cultural groups.
2. Read fiction about people, families, and communities that are very different from your own.
3. Get to know the families of culturally and linguistically diverse students by making special efforts to reach out to them. Let them know you want to learn more about them because you care about their children.
4. Sit in on classes in bilingual education programs.
5. Develop collaborative relationships with teachers of English language learners or culturally and linguistically diverse students with exceptionalities, even if you are not working with any of the students at the present time.
6. Make the most of opportunities to travel to new places, interact with people from other cultures, and learn at least a rudimentary part of a new language.
7. Attend professional conferences that feature speakers and presentations focusing on diverse populations.
8. Have families from other countries or cultures talk to students about customs in their culture.
9. Ask families from diverse groups what their family goals are and discuss with them a variety of ways those goals could be addressed in the school curriculum.
10. Be realistic about what collaborative consultation can do and celebrate even the smallest successes.

CHAPTER REVIEW

1. Cultural and linguistic diversity is increasing dramatically in public schools. Demographic trends are presenting major new challenges for school personnel. This will require that consultants work closely with families, community members, and professionals of diverse cultural and linguistic backgrounds.

2. Cultural diversity is reflected in the variety of customary beliefs, social norms, and ways of living built up by groups of people and transmitted from one generation to the other. Culture must be defined broadly because many demographic variables contribute to this construct.

3. Collaborative school consultants have key roles in bringing together diverse groups of educators from schools, families, and communities. Self-assessment, preceded by examination of one's own cultural affiliations, can be a basis for ongoing professional and personal development concerning diversity and self-awareness issues. In addition, assessments or checklists can be used for staff development and individual consultation work.

4. Consultants need to develop cultural competencies for collaboration with adults from diverse backgrounds. Cultural competence is the ability to function comfortably in cross-cultural settings and to interact harmoniously with people from cultures that differ from our own. It involves specific skills, attitudes, behaviors, and policies that show respect for and valuing of all ethnicities. Although some generalities about cultural characteristics may be initially helpful to the educational consultant, understanding that individuals within a culture vary across several cultural continua ensures that we individualize our collaborative efforts for each of our educational partners and treat them as unique individuals.

5. There are many variations in the meaning and use of language and body language that impact interactions with diverse collaborative partners. The use of nonverbal language, colloquialisms, gender and family references, and silence are all examples of cultural differences that impact the consultation process.

6. Consultants should learn as much as possible about best practices for CLD, CLDE, and ELL students and combine these with best practices from special education. This will be most likely to produce the best outcomes for the student, and such commitment demonstrates true collaboration between professionals from various fields of expertise. School consultants and consulting teachers are in ideal positions to infuse appreciation and recognition of diversity into the school context. They can facilitate greater parent involvement, coordinate instruction with ELL and bilingual education teachers, and collaborate in system changes that help schools meet the needs of CLDE students. Coordination of services and collaboration among school personnel and support personnel in diverse settings and from diverse backgrounds requires knowledge of issues and strategies for rural and isolated areas, military families, highly mobile families, homeschooled families, gay and lesbian families, students who are gay or lesbian, adults with disabilities, abused students, and collaborators for CLDE students.

TO DO AND THINK ABOUT

1. Visit a family or attend an event that is culturally or linguistically different from your own background. Ask questions that will help you develop an understanding of that family's or group's values, beliefs, and customs. Learn some words in their language.

2. Think about this statement and discuss its possible meanings for consultants in educational settings: "You can walk in another's shoes, but you still have to walk on your own feet."

3. Interview teachers from schools with significant multicultural populations, asking them to suggest ways in which consultation and collaboration might help meet students' special needs. What steps should be taken to carry out these ideas?

4. Visit with colleagues or classmates about open-ended topics such as:

- What do I think I would do if I were in a school where I was the only teacher whose native language was English?
- What are my best attributes as a teacher of children with cultural and linguistic differences?
- What cross-cultural strengths do I have? What could I improve?

ADDITIONAL READINGS AND RESOURCES

Baca, L. M., & Cervantes, H. T. (2004). *The bilingual special education interface* (4th ed.). Upper Saddle River, NJ: Merrill.

Banks, J. A., & Banks, C. A. M. (Eds.). (2006). *Multicultural education: Issues and perspectives* (6th ed.). Hoboken, NJ: Wiley.

Chisholm, I. M. (1994). Preparing teachers for multicultural classrooms. *Journal of Educational Issues of Language Minority Students, 14,* 43–68.

Harris, K. C. (2004). The relationship between educational consultation and instruction for culturally and linguistically diverse exceptional (CLDE) student: Definitions, structures, and case studies. In L. M. Baca, & H. T. Cervantes, *The bilingual special education interface* (4th ed., pp. 337–359). Upper Saddle River, NJ: Pearson.

Lynch, E. W., & Hanson, M. J. (1998). *Developing cross-cultural competence: A guide for working with children and their families* (2nd ed.). Baltimore: Paul H. Brookes.

Russell, N. M. (2007). Teaching more than English: Connecting ESL students to their community through service learning. *Phi Delta Kappan, 88*(10), 770–771.

Students develop relationships and improve English language abilities in working and communicating with businesses and community leaders.

National Association for Bilingual Education: www.nabe.org

National Association for Multicultural Education: www.name.org

Northwest Regional Educational Laboratory: www.nwrel.org

(A guidebook called *Culturally Responsive Practices for Student Success* is available on the NWREL Web site.)

Teaching Tolerance: www.teachingtolerance.org

(*Teaching Tolerance* is an excellent periodical that is available free for teachers. Sign up on their Web site.)

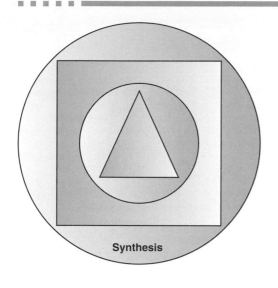

Synthesis

SYNTHESIS FOR WORKING TOGETHER AS CO-EDUCATORS

Part IV, the synthesis section, completes the book. Chapter 10 emphasizes the roles of paraeducators, early childhood educators, and preservice teachers; Chapter 11 addresses the support that can be provided by related services and support personnel, interagency collaboration, technology, and funded grants; and Chapter 12 encourages leadership and mentorships, stresses the roles of school administrators and school board members in collaboration, addresses professional development and networking among co-educators for the future, provides a competencies checklist, and summarizes ethical principles that were interspersed throughout the book.

Teachers want to make a positive difference in the world by helping all students grow and develop to their fullest potential. Educators believe they have chosen a noble profession; nevertheless, they know their work will continue to be challenging and demanding and they will strive to grow in their profession.

Schools are becoming more and more complex and multifaceted. But more and more ways are being found to bring support services to the schools for the benefit of both students and teachers. Teachers must engage in self-improvement by continuing their own professional development. They should serve as mentors to preservice and novice teachers who need leadership and collegial interaction. There is no more important calling than being a co-educator with other dedicated members of this noble profession.

CHAPTER TEN

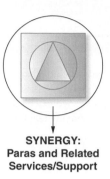

SYNERGY:
Paras and Related
Services/Support

Paraeducators, Teachers, Early Childhood Educators, and Preservice Teachers as Collaborators

Much of the discussion about school consultation and collaboration to this point has been in reference to classroom teachers and special educators. Now the focus will shift to three other important roles in the collaborative school environment. First is that of paraeducators (sometimes referred to as paraprofessionals, or shortened to "paras").

Paraeducators and teachers have an important interactive relationship. They are partners in accomplishing the tasks inherent in the teacher's role; however, the teacher has responsibility for supervising the para's work and assessing outcomes of the para's performance. In short, teachers supervise and direct the work of paraeducators.

Early childhood educators and early childhood special educators have important collaborative roles in interfacing with school personnel. They are involved in collaborative consultation especially during transition periods from preschool to school.

Preservice teachers in teacher preparation programs are readying themselves to become novice teachers, and to collaborate and co-teach with experienced professional colleagues. Postsecondary instructors and advisers are major influences on the kinds of interactive and collaborative experiences that preservice teachers will put into practice from day one of their first teaching position.

FOCUSING QUESTIONS

1. Why is it important for the paraeducator role to be defined clearly?
2. How should teachers plan for and communicate about the para's responsibilities?
3. How are paraeducators selected and prepared for their roles?
4. In what ways do teachers supervise and direct para activities?

5. How do early childhood educators (ECE) and early childhood special educators (ECSE) connect and blend their services with elementary school educators?

6. When, where, and how can preservice teachers prepare to collaborate with their teaching colleagues-to-be?

KEY TERMS

early childhood education (ECE)

early childhood special education (ECSE)

early intervention

Head Start

Individualized Family Service Plan (IFSP)

novice teachers

paraeducator (para, paraprofessional)

preservice teachers

supervising teachers

PARAEDUCATORS AS PARTNERS

Paraeducators are essential partners in providing special education services; therefore, teachers and consultants to whom these partners are assigned must give special consideration to their needs. Many of the concepts and skills presented in other parts of this book apply to working with paraeducators. This section emphasizes special skills that relate specifically to supervising and communicating with paras.

SCENARIO 10.A

Latisha, a nontraditional student in a university with an elementary school nearby, learned that the elementary school had implemented inclusionary classrooms. Part of the implementation plan for the school was getting assistance from volunteers to provide more help for classroom teachers. These assistants were to be called "volunteer paraprofessionals" and would do what paras typically do, but without salary.

As mother of two school-age children, Latisha had been considering teacher preparation as her field of study. She decided to volunteer for one afternoon of service each week at the school. This would give her a way to better understand the role of an educator as well as the inclusionary process in schools. It would help her decide if she wanted to apply now for a job as a paraeducator or enter a teacher education program at the university.

The building principal of the elementary school had made it clear to general classroom teachers that the volunteers were to be involved in instructional help, just as the school's paras were, not mundane clerical tasks. Teachers could request assistance on a form and turn it in to the principal each Friday. The principal would approve these requests and forward them to a special education teacher charged with responsibility for matching requests with volunteers.

So it was that Latisha was sent into a first-grade classroom to assist with a writing lesson. The teacher had presented a lesson earlier and Latisha's task was to help the students with disabilities write in their journals. It sounded simple enough. Very quickly several questions came to Latisha's mind. She made this checklist:

- Where are the writing supplies for the children to use?
- How can I help this child whose desk is facing away from the board? That makes it really difficult for the student to copy what the teacher wrote on the board.
- Will the teacher mind if I change the instructions a little so the student can be more successful?
- Who are the children with disabilities, anyway?
- What is the goal of the lesson?
- How will I know when the lesson goal is met?

"This is not as easy as it first seemed," Latisha concluded. It got easier as she became more familiar with the teachers and the students, but she soon learned that at times she tended toward overstepping her assigned role and going beyond what was expected. Teachers were forgiving and were not upset when she did this. They seemed to welcome her help, and after all, there were so very many student needs. She did have a significant list of responsibilities; however, it was not the ones she was expected to do that concerned her, but those that were outside her role boundaries that she wanted very much to do. She was finding out that a paraeducator has a subordinate (by-the-side) role when it comes to planning content and instructing students.

Latisha had always been a take-charge person, directing others in her home, church, and community life. She was beginning to think that, even though the teachers and students were glad to have another adult to help out, a para role probably would not be one for which she was well-suited. A better personal goal for her might be to earn teacher certification and focus on being a excellent teacher and an effective supervisor of the paraeducators assigned to assist her. But for the moment, there was Randy's hand up, signaling his need for more help with the arithmetic assignment!

Since the early 1990s, significant changes in special education have fueled an increase in the reliance on paraprofessionals to support students with disabilities. In recent years schools have turned increasingly to paras because of large caseloads for special education teachers, the need for more individualized attention to students at risk due to economic disadvantage or other circumstances, and the cultural and linguistic fit with students by many paras who live right in the school's neighborhood (French & Pickett, 1997). Paras are particularly important members of the teaching team in rural communities. They may be the most constant element in the school life of students with special needs if they stay there when teachers move on (Ashbaker & Morgan, 1996; Demchak & Morgan, 1998).

Increasingly, paras are being utilized within general education settings, particularly for students with low-incidence disabilities such as autism, intellectual and multiple disabilities, and deaf-blindness. Giangreco, Edelman, Broer, and Doyle (2001) in their review of a decade of literature on paraprofessional support of students with disabilities, noted that when the Education of All Handicapped Children Act (P.L. 94-142) was first passed in 1975, there were discussions concerning training a whole new cadre of personnel, essentially paraprofessionals (now regarded as *paraeducators* in much of the literature), to meet the needs of the new population of students with more severe disabilities who would be entering the public schools. At the time, some believed these students did not need highly trained teachers with baccalaureate degrees. Others felt differently and assumed that given proper support and instruction, students with more severe disabilities were in fact educable, and needed specialized and individualized instruction from highly trained special educators. In the end, federal officials agreed with the latter group and advocated for professional teachers to serve students with severe disabilities. In looking at the landscape of services for students with moderate to severe disabilities in today's schools, one should note the increasing reliance on paraprofessionals to support students with more severe disabilities within the general education classroom. Some might ask, "Have we come full circle?

Paraeducator Requirements

As one outcome of the No Child Left Behind Act, all paras hired after January 8, 2002, must meet one of three requirements (Christie, 2002):

1. Complete two years of study (forty-eight semester hours) at an institution of higher education
2. Obtain an associate's degree or higher
3. Meet a rigorous standard of quality and be able to demonstrate, through a formal state or local assessment, knowledge of and ability to assist in instruction for reading, writing, and math

Until recent years, paras employed in special education typically worked under the close supervision and direction of a special educator who was present with them in a resource or self-contained classroom all or most of the time. Today, paras are more likely to be assisting students with disabilities within general education classrooms; and sometimes they have very limited contact with the professional special education teacher listed on the student's IEP who supervises them (Giangreco, Edelman, Broer, & Doyle, 2001). This raises many questions. Are the roles and duties that paras are asked to perform clearly delineated and appropriate? Do they have adequate training to carry out their duties? Are they being adequately supervised?

Under NCLB, teachers are held more accountable for supervising their paraeducators, and administrators are expected to give paras more support, avoid misassignments of their responsibilities, and provide professional development to help them perform their roles effectively. Neither paras nor teachers typically have had formal preparation for interacting with one another in productive ways. Frequently, the relationship is hampered by inadequate communication, lack of time for planning together, and lack of clear job descriptions.

A fine line often exists between paras' assistance to teachers in implementing their plans and functioning as instructor and decision maker. With more and more pressures evolving from inclusionary practices, paras are sometimes being asked to extend their roles inappropriately to include assessment, curricular adaptations, instruction, and communicating with families.

With these issues, and heavy caseloads and lack of time, paraeducators have many pressures. They may feel a lack of respect. Their salaries tend to be appallingly low. Some resent the absence of opportunity for advancement. Many articulate a need for more intensive clarification and preparation for the para role. Research by Giangreco, Edelman, and Broer (2001) identified six themes pertaining to how school personnel can respect, appreciate, and acknowledge paraprofessionals: nonmonetary signs and symbols of appreciation; adequate compensation; being entrusted with important responsibilities; having noninstructional responsibilities; being listened to; and having orientation experiences and support. Successful matches of role delineation, skill development, expectations, and support can help instill respect and appreciation for the role.

Delineating the Role of Paraeducators

Paraeducators may be found in virtually any educational setting, ranging from a preschool class for children with special needs, to a first-grade classroom having students with disabilities, to a grocery store where adolescent students with developmental disabilities are learning a new job, to a resource room for gifted adolescents with needs for advanced and expanded curriculum. Paraeducator responsibilities vary widely, from teaching a lesson, to grading homework and tests, to participating in classroom activities, to sometimes just "being there" for the students and teacher.

An extensive literature review by Giangreco, Edelman, Broer, and Doyle (2001) had already noted greatly expanding roles and duties for paraprofessionals during the 1990s, especially those who serve students with disabilities in general education settings. They found that paras continue to work with students who have the most challenging behavioral and learning characteristics and to engage in a broad range of roles, many of which they have not been prepared to assume. The researchers listed eight major role categories of such duties:

1. Providing instruction in academic subjects
2. Teaching functional life skills
3. Teaching vocational skills at community-based work sites
4. Collection and management of data
5. Supporting students with challenging behaviors
6. Facilitating interactions with peers who don't have disabilities
7. Providing personal care
8. Engaging in clerical behavior

The relationship between the special education teacher and paraeducator differs somewhat from the other collaborative roles. Unlike the consulting teacher and the consultee teacher, classroom teachers and paraeducators do not have parity in the school program because they are not equally responsible for decisions about student needs and instructional interventions. The teacher is expected to supervise and direct the paraeducator, who is employed to assist the teacher and, therefore, to follow the teacher's direction. Even so, the paraeducator is necessary as a partner to the teacher's success and to the success of the teacher's students. Indeed, the prefix *para*-means "to come alongside," or to help another.

Paraeducators are employed in schools to come alongside teachers and help them with the demands of their jobs. Some people use the term *instructional paraprofessional* to designate a person who helps with instruction of students. Nevertheless, paraeducators do not plan instruction nor are they responsible for evaluating student performance. But they can do a great deal to help students learn and gain confidence with their schoolwork.

Paraeducator Responsibilities

While every paraeducator position has its unique characteristics, there are four basic responsibilities to which virtually every paraeducator is assigned at one time or another (Kaff & Dyck, 1999):

1. Student support and monitoring (reading to students and listening to them read, helping students with health care and personal needs, assisting with small-group activities, supervising playground activities)
2. Preparing instructional materials (materials for specific lessons, duplication of materials, bulletin boards, arrangements for field trips)
3. Communication support (participation in team meetings, preparation of student performance charts, feedback about student progress)
4. Support of routine business (recording attendance, checking papers, filing materials)

The inclusion movement has created a situation that causes some concern among special education teachers because paraeducators sometimes do their work in a general education classroom with individual students or small groups of students, where the special education teacher is not present to oversee day-to-day activities. Paraeducators may assume a range of job responsibilities in that setting, such as providing instruction in academic and social skills; making curricular modifications; managing student behavior; and developing working relationships with others. Many of them appear to assume primary responsibility for the included students, even though they are aware that it is more appropriate for the classroom teacher to carry out these responsibilities (Marks, Schrader, & Levine, 1999). Explanations for this behavior include:

- Paraeducators do not want students to be a "bother" to the teacher.
- Paraeducators feel an urgency to meet a student's immediate academic needs.
- Paras may believe their own performance will be based on positive relations with the teacher.
- Paras are often faced with the need to make on-the-spot modifications when teachers are not readily available.

Some paraeducators have become the primary vehicle for accommodation for students with severe or multiple disabilities in inclusive schools. In most instances the paraeducators stay in close proximity to the students with disabilities, attending to their students' physical needs such as toileting, and to instructional needs such as reading aloud to students or recording their answers. Paraeducators may even adopt an advocacy role, taking it as their responsibility to work toward general acceptance of the included student, or to "represent" the student in ways that would support acceptance (Marks et al., 1999).

Supervision of paraeducators can be complex and challenging. Not many teacher education programs include the topic in their preparation programs. Salzberg and Morgan (1995) contend that few teachers were expecting to direct other adults and they have not been adequately prepared to supervise paraeducators. Even fewer have had practice in doing so.

One area of particular importance that Salzberg and Morgan (1995) target in regard to para and teacher relationships and success of the supervisory relationship is that of personality variables. (See Chapter 2 for a discussion of individual differences among adults in the work setting.) Individual differences also can be problematic when there are large discrepancies in age, culture, socio-economic group, or ethnic background.

In spite of challenges in addressing the roles and responsibilities of paras, there are positive effects. As suggested earlier, many paras can be supportive links to the community. Their positions cost the schools relatively little. Laudably, most paras are pleased to work patiently and caringly with students who can be difficult at times and they often tend to view these students in different and positive ways. They are able to contribute information that helps teachers and consulting teachers provide appropriate learning experiences. Much more effort should be made to prepare professionals to collaborate with and supervise paraeducators, and to recruit exemplary paras and prepare them well.

Roles and responsibilities must be delineated clearly so that there will be mutual understanding among all concerned. The paraeducator and teacher relationship can be likened to a couple on the ballroom dance floor. The two gracefully perform together to the rhythm of the music, one partner leading and the other following. Both partners use the same basic dance steps, but the unique timing of special moves, as guided by the leading partner, keeps them from impeding others or digressing from their areas.

The para-supervisor relationship becomes less obvious when a para is employed to work with a team. In that case it can be likened to having an orchestra: The para plays an important role in a group performance directed by a conductor. Co-teachers, in contrast, can be thought of as engaging in a musical duet. Each follows the same score, but with different, preplanned parts. All must maintain the rhythm and harmony to create a pleasant experience.

The co-teaching team will need to determine who is to assume supervisory responsibilities for paraeducators. The best selection will likely be a person who:

- Holds ultimate responsibility for the outcomes
- Is in the best position to direct the para
- Can provide training for the assigned duties
- Can observe and document para performance

Supervision requires specific, sophisticated skills and behaviors. A supervisor must plan, schedule, coordinate, and evaluate another person's actions. It is not unusual for special education teachers to be assigned as many as five or six paras whom they direct and supervise. The supervisor is responsible for the para's actions and the para is accountable to the supervisor. No matter how much education or preparation a person has before taking a position as para (and, according to French and Pickett, 1997, many of them do bring very little formal preparation), a supervisor should provide on-the-job training. For example, co-teachers may develop a teaching plan that includes the para for part of the implementation. For the plan to be successful, the supervisor or co-teacher must ready the para for implementing the pertinent parts of the plan.

French (1997) lists seven functions associated with para supervision:

1. Planning
2. Managing schedules (prioritizing tasks, preparing schedules)
3. Delegating responsibilities (assigning tasks, directing tasks, monitoring performance)
4. Orienting (introducing people, policies, procedures, job descriptions)
5. Providing on-the-job training (teaching, coaching new skills, giving feedback)
6. Evaluating (tracking performance, summative evaluation of job performance)
7. Managing work environment (maintaining communication, managing conflicts, solving problems)

The more individuals with whom the para works, the more complex the supervision processes. When paras are in the general classroom most of the school day, it is essential that the classroom teacher also is involved in the supervision. In some instances the classroom teacher may take major responsibility for the supervision. If communication processes among all parties are open, this arrangement can work well.

Selection and Preparation of Paraeducators

Many of the common difficulties between paraeducators and their supervising teachers can be minimized or avoided completely if the relationship begins with a well thought-out orientation session. The foundation for the relationship is built during the initial orientation. With development of a job description, trust can emerge along with high expectations and mutual support.

Supervisors are ultimately responsible for the actions of paraeducators in the classroom; however, a certain amount of leeway should be granted if the paraeducator has experience or insight into the behavioral or academic interventions that might be most beneficial. The para's ideas might improve effectiveness of the intervention. Ongoing communication, in which the teacher invites the paraeducator to provide input, will validate the para's ideas and knowledge gained from working with particular students in different classroom environments. Paraeducators should have differing assignments and responsibilities based on their experience, training, and confidence level.

The National Resource Center for Paraeducators (NRCP) (www.nrcpara.org) has established three levels of responsibilities for paraeducators;

- *Level I* responsibilities include basic supervision and monitoring of students, preparing learning materials, providing personal assistance to students, reinforcing learning experiences that are planned and introduced by teachers, and conducting themselves in a professional and ethical manner.
- *Level II* includes all of the Level I responsibilities as well as more autonomy in delivering lessons developed by the teacher. Other responsibilities in Level II include assisting students in completing projects assigned by the teacher, collecting ongoing

assessment data as directed by the teacher, implementing teacher-developed behavior management plans, and participating in regularly scheduled teacher and paraeducator meetings. These may include other team members for the purpose of planning and supporting students in the general education setting.

■ *Level III,* the highest level, includes additional tasks of collaboration and information sharing with teachers for planning purposes, modifying curriculum and instructional activities for individual students under the direction of teachers, and assisting teachers in maintaining student records, to name a few.

When training paraeducators, Pickett and Gerlach (2003) recommend that teachers provide a rationale for a given skill or strategy, explain why it is important, and give a clear, step-by-step description. Next, in good teacher fashion the teacher should demonstrate or model the skill in the setting where the para is to implement it. Then, observe the para practice teaching the skill or implementing the procedure, and provide feedback. Finally, the teacher should provide ongoing coaching unobtrusively while the para is working with students.

Supervisors should discuss roles, skills, and needed training on an ongoing basis. New federal and state preparation and training requirements for paraeducators created a need for documenting training and skill development activities. At the very least, all paraeducators should maintain a file folder documenting the training by means of certificates, transcripts, meeting/training agendas, products, or other evidence of completed activities. If some type of skill inventory has been completed and training modules are selected and completed based on that inventory that should be included in the documentation as well. The Project PARA: Paraeducator Self-Study Program (http://para.unl.edu/ec) is set up to include eight units of instructional resources for paras, including pretests for self-assessment of skills prior to beginning each unit. After completion of the unit, a post-test is taken. The ParaEducator Learning Network (www.paraeducator.net) is a commercial program used by many districts across the country to provide online training and documentation for paraeducators in a variety of skill areas.

The teacher's lesson plans should be explicit and provide a means for the paraeducator to communicate ongoing student progress and other daily and weekly anecdotal information from which lesson adjustments can be made. In the end, the supervising teacher needs to be informed and connected to each student who is working with a para in order to make knowledgeable and informed decisions regarding lesson and behavioral intervention plans.

A variety of ways are available for para and supervising teacher to communicate; the method chosen will depend on preferences of those involved. Logistics, access, level of comfort with technology, number of parties involved, caseload and supervision load are preferences to be considered. Some use an ongoing paper-and-pencil log within a student folder in which the paraeducator and teacher can share information such as data on student progress, anecdotal notes, questions about adaptations or adjustments to lessons, and so on. In other situations, a supervisor may have opportunity to touch base with paraeducators and debrief at the beginning or end of the day. Still others may find technology applications helpful for sharing lesson notes, changes in schedules, and other necessary communication. If e-mail is used for this purpose, it is important that paraeducators on the team be well informed about issues of confidentiality and how e-mail can and should not be used. Other devices such as personal digital assistants (PDAs) or even AlphaSmart devices commonly used in schools for students to take notes and do basic word processing can be utilized by the paraeducator to capture on-the-spot notes, which can be downloaded later by the supervising teacher or printed out and placed in a file for the teacher's review.

Most paraeducators bring many useful skills to the job. Some even have teaching experience. When selecting a paraeducator, the administrator should look for a person with:

- A high school diploma, at least
- Evidence of good attendance at work
- Adherence to teaching ethics and confidentiality
- Ability to follow the teacher's direction and written plans
- Ability to communicate effectively with students and adults
- Good relationships with students
- Willingness to learn new skills
- Flexibility
- A sense of humor always helps!

With the rapidly increasing cultural and linguistic diversity of students in special education, diversity among paraeducators who support them is important. Efforts should be made to create a staff of paraeducators who reflect the cultural and linguistic background of the students. This is especially crucial in communities where teachers may not be familiar with the culture and language of the students; paras have often fulfilled a role as a community partner in home-school relationships. They can serve as translators of the culture and language for both educators and families. Hispanic and Native American families especially rely on the interconnectedness of the extended family and informal community-based networks for emotional and social support (Geenen, Powers, & Lopez-Vasquez, 2001). Thus paras from the community may be able to facilitate meaningful collaboration with CLD families. Paras who are not familiar with cultural and linguistic diversity should participate in the same relevant staff development and self-assessment as other educators.

Although IDEA 1997 *requires* states to provide appropriate training, preparation, and supervision for paraeducators, the type and amount of training that is provided varies from state to state. Using more than twenty-five years of experience as staff developers and data from a nationwide survey validating guidelines on standards and skills required by paraeducators and teachers, Lasater, Johnson, and Fitzgerald (2000) make several recommendations for school district staff development:

- Communicate that paraeducators are valued and important to the instructional process by conducting professional development in settings similar to those used in training other professionals, and offering professional credits and stipends.
- Direct any needs assessments for the para role to paras in particular, rather than including them in teacher-focused sessions that may not be of major interest or appropriate for them.
- Provide ongoing, responsive support to answer questions and discuss issues.
- Include numerous opportunities for sharing, interacting, and problem solving.

- Allow for venting while ensuring refocusing and action.
- Build a solid knowledge base that reflects students' needs and goals.
- Do not provide unnecessary information but focus on the "best practices" they need to know.
- Offer concrete tools to take back to the classroom so they can implement them immediately.
- Offer practical alternatives for responding to implementation challenges. While both the teacher and the paraeducator partner should receive professional development together for most topics, there are instances where this would not be an effective use of time.
- Provide opportunities for partner teachers and paraeducators to experience professional development together. Include exploration of roles and responsibilities, team-building activities and communication skills.
- Celebrate their successes and recognize contributions made by the paraeducators.
- No matter how much advance preparation the paraeducator has received, teachers to whom a para is assigned must provide orientation and on-the-job training. The job of the supervising teacher is to provide training that will help the paraeducator function in the specific situation of the assignment.

The supervising teacher can create or obtain a guide that can be given to the paraeducator for self-study. One example of such a guide is *Essential Skills for Paras* (Kaff & Dyck, 1999). Topics addressed in this guide include responsibilities of most paraeducators; labels used to categorize students with disabilities; terms and phrases frequently used in schools; a discussion of ethics for paras; basic principles of direct instruction methods; and guidelines for reporting student behavior.

Marks, Schrader, and Levine (1999) recommend that training be provided for both teachers and paraeducators on the goals of inclusive practices, including specific skill areas such as curricular and academic modifications and positive behavioral support strategies. If behavior management is a primary responsibility of the para, the teacher should provide a good behavior management resource. One example is the *Behavior Management Guide for Paras* (Dyck, Zabel, & Zabel, 1998). For those whose paras have responsibility for making text adaptations, *How to Adapt Text for Struggling Readers* (Dyck, 1999) is a useful resource. *The Positive Para: Helping Students Develop Positive Social Skills* (Thurston, 2000) is another helpful resource for paraeducators who work with students having social skill deficits. Other resources are listed at the end of this chapter.

Need for Confidentiality by the Paraeducator

The Council for Exceptional Children (CEC) has published standards for paraprofessionals working in special education, and the National Resource Center for Paraprofessionals (NRCP) has also suggested standards for knowledge paras are expected to possess if they work in special education programs. One of the CEC standards for paraprofessionals specifically addresses professional and ethical practice. It includes knowledge about ethical practices for confidential communication and kinds of biases and differences that affect one's ability to work with others.

Since there is no single professional association for paraeducators, standards such as those proposed by CEC or NRCP are voluntary. No outside agency monitors unprofessional behavior, although school administrators can bring disciplinary action if a paraprofessional acts in a way considered inappropriate by school district standards. Ashbaker and Morgan (2006) target such criteria of professionalism as dress and appearance, health and safety of students and staff, communication and conflict resolution skills, collaboration with teachers and parents, and confidentiality in the use of information.

It is of utmost importance that paraeducators understand the necessity for confidentiality when working with students. Teachers need to impress on paraeducators the importance of keeping confidential and secure any information such as academic achievement, test scores, student behavior, attendance, family problems, and other information of a personal nature.

Kaff and Dyck (1999) offer the following guidelines to help paraeducators decide whether to share information with other teachers.

- Is the person requesting the information *directly involved* with the student's education?
- Will the *student* benefit if the person receives the information?

If the answer to both of these questions is yes, the para can share information. However, if there is any doubt, the para should be instructed to just say "no."

Likewise, teachers must plan ahead to ensure para confidentiality when substitute teachers are present. Fleury (2000) provides the following guidelines that can be helpful to the substitute teacher *and* the paraeducator when the regular teacher is absent:

- Discuss with paraeducators at the beginning of the year the guidelines for confidentiality and how to proceed when you are absent.
- Make sure paras know the limits on sharing more information than needed and the role they will have on days you require a substitute.
- Have a typed schedule of the day and duties you have for the day.
- Include notes on general information that will help the substitute.
- Point out the important role of the paras.
- Prepare a paper discussing the need for routine in your class and ways paraeducators can help the substitute with it.

Fleury (2000) makes these suggestions to help classroom teachers when a *paraeducator* is absent:

- Ask the para to call you at home to notify you personally that he or she will be absent.
- Go over the duties with the substitute assistant as soon as possible.
- Discuss issues of confidentiality at the beginning of the day.
- Provide the typed schedule of the day and methods you use, such as reinforcers and other classroom management routines. (Be class specific, not child specific, at this time.)

- If the absent para was assigned to a student with unpredictable behavior, consider reassigning that student temporarily to someone who does know the student.
- Encourage the substitute to ask questions about your teaching methods or behavior management tools. Be aware that sometimes you will not be able to fully answer the question because of the need to preserve confidentiality.

Framework for Working with Paraeducators

Para supervision requires skills beyond consulting, collaborating, or teaching. The supervisor is responsible for the para's actions and the para is accountable to the supervisor. Whereas collaborating teachers mutually develop a teaching plan, the supervisor will tell the para what parts of the developed plan to implement. Most paraeducators are assigned to one supervising teacher who is responsible for planning what paraeducators should do from day to day, and for scheduling where and when the paras will do it, as well as communicating this information to others.

French (2000) suggests a number of practical ways a supervising teacher can select classroom tasks for delegating to a paraeducator. She describes delegation as getting things done through another who has been trained to handle them, by giving that person authority to do it but not giving up teacher responsibility. Selection of the task is determined by considering it in the light of time sensitivity and the consequences of *not* doing it. A task that needs to be done soon and that has major consequences should *not* be delegated. Such tasks include student behavior crises; meetings regarding the crises; student health crises, and monitoring students in nonclassroom settings. Tasks that are not time sensitive but have major consequences also should not be delegated. They include designing individual behavior plans; assessing students' progress; developing curriculum; and co-planning instruction.

French (2000) recommends six steps for delegation of para responsibilities:

1. Analyze the task, and if it can be delegated, identify the steps it contains.
2. Decide what to delegate, keeping in mind the skills and preferences of those involved.
3. Create a plan that tells how to do the task, purposes of the task, student needs to address, and criteria for completion.
4. If more than one para is available, choose the one best for that task.
5. Direct the task, being available to answer questions and provide clarification.
6. Monitor performance without hovering over the para, and then document and reinforce good work.

French also reminds teachers to be tolerant of the reality that the para may not do some things exactly the way they themselves would have done those things.

Special educators responsible for supervising paras need to define clearly and monitor carefully the paras' responsibilities. Zigmond (1997) observed in her study of inclusion classrooms that the least trained person (para) often is responsible for helping and instructing the students who are hardest to teach. "Too often students with disabilities are placed in general education classrooms without clear expectations established among the team members regarding which professional staff will plan, implement, monitor, evaluate, and adjust instruction" (Giangreco, Edelman, Luiselli, & MacFarland, 1997, p. 15). These researchers suggest assigning paras as classroom assistants rather than as assistants for single students. They note that if co-teachers fail to plan instruction, the responsibility often falls on the para, which is clearly beyond reasonable expectation for them. Others recommend ongoing collaborative meetings for sharing expertise areas and for discussing and clarifying areas of responsibility, including strategies and a plan for "fading" the level of support provided by the paraeducator (Marks, Schrader, & Levine, 1999, p. 325).

Sometimes paras inappropriately take the students in their charge away from the general classroom group (Giangreco et al., 1997). Paras must be instructed that students are to be physically, programmatically, and interactionally included in classroom activities planned by qualified teachers. To help instill this awareness, teachers need to make sure they consider the para's role when co-planning lessons, and whenever possible include the para in the planning process.

■ ■ ■ ■ ■

APPLICATION 10.1
CLARIFYING THE PARA ASSISTANT ROLE

Jane is one of three paras assigned to Martin, a teacher of students with behavior disorders. Jane is an experienced para and has clear notions of what she should do in the inclusive classroom where Martin has assigned her. Martin told Jane simply to be in the classroom to intervene whenever a particular student, Bart, gets off task or refuses to do work. She is not to help him with his work, but only to take steps to keep him "under control." Jane doesn't think that is a good way to use her time. She wants to help this student and others who might be having difficulty with the assignment. She thinks she should help clarify confusing information and outline class lectures on the chalkboard as she did in the previous school where she was assigned. Is it appropriate for Martin to have these somewhat limited expectations for Jane even when she isn't comfortable with it? Does Bart's classroom teacher have a voice in this? How could this conflict be addressed?

Managing Schedules and Time.   We have discussed elsewhere the challenges of arranging consultant and co-teaching schedules. Those challenges are magnified when several paraeducators are part of the scheduling demands. Since schedules are likely to change from week to week, it is helpful for everyone to have a schedule each week that indicates who does what, and when, and where. The schedule should be available to all special service staff and the building secretary.

The challenge of finding time to plan and discuss student needs with a para mirrors those issues of time discussed elsewhere for collaborating teachers. Teachers and paras in self-contained special classes may have break periods at the same time, but that is not likely when the para is working in a different classroom, as is often the case in inclusive schools. In an ideal situation at least twenty minutes a day is set aside for para-supervisor planning.

The more individuals with whom a para works, the more complex the supervision process is. When paras are in the general classroom most of the school day, classroom teachers must also be in a supervisory role for them. If communication processes among all parties are open and ongoing, this arrangement can work well. Sometimes, however, much confusion can occur.

It is one thing to plan for oneself and quite another to organize and plan for another person such as a paraeducator. French (1997) provides several examples of forms teachers can use to plan for paras. Another type of plan would be a daily schedule that would list all time periods through the day, where the para is to be during each time period (e.g., "room 25," or "the work room"), and what activity or responsibility the para will have (e.g., co-teach the group with Martin or adapt the textbook for student Willy.) Plans of this nature can be printed on paper or put into a computer data base where the paraeducator and professional can easily add comments and provide feedback to one another.

Another challenging part of supervising paras will be to determine *when* the supervisory responsibilities will be performed.

> Most teachers report that they spend time outside the student-contact day to plan the schedule, design or prescribe appropriate learning activities for the paraeducator to use with students, and provide the paraeducator with on-the-job training, coaching, and feedback. In return for the investment of their time outside of the students' school day, the presence of a paraeducator will double the amount of instructional time that teachers have available during school hours. Teachers who fail to spend outside time for planning, training, coaching, and feedback with paraeducators report that they are dissatisfied with the performance of the paraeducators with whom they work. (French, p. 73)

Examples of other information to provide the paraeducator are:

- A copy of school handbook(s) providing school policies and regulations
- Information about the students included in one's caseload
- Teachers' guides for instructional materials that will be used
- First aid information
- Classroom rules and other expectations for classroom management
- Behavior management guidelines for specific students

Although supervising teachers are responsible for planning carefully and communicating responsibilities to paraeducators, it will not always happen. The following tips are useful to share with paraeducators who may be uncertain about their responsibilities (Kaff & Dyck, 1999, p. 32):

- Use common sense.
- Don't ask for help too soon, but when in doubt, please do ask.
- Request details about your designated tasks.
- Practice good communication skills.
- Maintain a sense of humor.

■ ■ ■ ■ ■

APPLICATION 10.2

APPROPRIATE OR INAPPROPRIATE?

For the following situations, label the paraeducator's actions as (a) inappropriate; (b) inappropriate; or (c) can't decide. Then discuss your viewpoints with your colleagues. There are no absolute answers to these situations. They can be interpreted differently within contrasting school philosophies.

1. A para works with a small group of students in the hallway every day. Students from another classroom walk past his group regularly on their way to music. The passing students sometimes make off-color jokes and comments about the para's small group of students. The para tells the offending students to stop talking in the hallway when he is working with students. If they do not stop, he says he will report them to the *principal* because they are breaking school conduct rules.

2. The special education teacher has set up a behavior management plan and the para is instructed to give the student a token every ten minutes if working independently at that time. The para does not favor giving rewards for only meeting the minimum expectations. So she decides to dispense tokens if, and only if, the student demonstrates good behavior by *her* standards for the *entire ten minutes*.

Evaluating the Paraeducator/Teacher Relationship

Extensive use of paraeducators has changed the role of teachers. Supervising and directing the work of paraeducators is now added to the teacher's role. "Even though teachers are no longer solely responsible for providing instruction, they remain wholly accountable for the outcomes of the instructional process" (French, 1999, p. 70).

Teachers may find evaluating paras neither easy nor particularly pleasant, especially when performance is substandard. However, the task may be made less discomforting by following three suggestions:

1. *Be clear and concise in telling paras exactly what you expect.* Preparing job descriptions will get you off to a good start. Say, "When you help co-teach in science, please refrain from responding to questions, and show the student instead how to find answers in the textbook or other resource materials," rather than, "Would you please help students in the science class during study time?"

2. *Tell paras what you like about the way they do their jobs.* Everyone likes to have good performance acknowledged.

3. *Tell paras if there are things they are not doing well.* Talking about what you don't like as well as what you do like is not only a teacher's responsibility, it also shows you care about the personal relationship. Many teachers do not feel comfortable talking about problems, so they dodge around troublesome issues far too long. But constructive feedback gives you and the para a chance to work out differences and misunderstandings. (Recall that Chapter 4 provided material to help with communication in sensitive areas.)

Feedback must relate to the task or action, not the person. Further suggestions provided by experts from the business world (GOAL/QPC & Joiner Associates, 1995, p. 22) are:

- Review the actions and decisions that led up to the moment.
- Give feedback sooner rather than later.
- Choose an appropriate time and place. Be selective about when you share negative reactions in particular. Do it one-on-one when you will be around to follow up with the person. Hit-and-run feedback is not fair.
- Start by describing the context. "I'd like to talk with you about what happened in the meeting today."
- Describe your reactions and reasons. ("I was distracted by your side conversation and couldn't follow what others were saying.")
- Ask for the change you'd like to see. ("You often have good points to make and I'd like it if you would share them with the whole group rather than talking with just a few people.")
- Allow time for the other person to respond.

It is never easy to discuss problems. Other suggestions that may be helpful include:

- Review the guidelines above and plan or rehearse what you want to say before you meet with the para.
- Select a place to meet where you won't be overheard or interrupted (which usually is *not* the teacher's lounge or workroom!).
- Remember, you can only control what *you* say and what *you* do. You cannot control the other person.

Supervising teachers should listen to the para's input and suggestions that result from her or his observations and knowledge of the students. They need feedback from the para for two different purposes. The first is to learn what is happening with students assigned to the para's responsibility, and the second is to learn how the teacher is affecting the para and others with whom they work. Most paraeducators will feel uncomfortable providing the latter type of feedback unless the teacher makes it clear that the input is important and will be accepted without negative consequences. Accepting feedback does not mean that one automatically agrees with the other person. It only means you will make an effort to understand the other person's concerns. Here are suggestions for accepting feedback (GOAL/QPC and Joiner Associates, 1995, p. 27):

- Breathe deeply. This can help you relax.
- Listen carefully.
- Make sure you understand what the other person is saying. ("Can you describe what I do or say that seems aggressive to you?")
- Acknowledge valid points even if you don't agree with the other person's interpretation.
- Acknowledge the feedback but take time to sort out what you heard. (A simple "thank you" is all that is needed right away. Ask for time to think about what you heard. If possible, schedule a time to get back together with the person.)

Equally important is feedback to learn what is happening to and for the students assigned to the para's responsibility. Sometimes the paraeducator is the only adult who observes what a student does during a particular activity. The para's observations and the way these are communicated to the supervising teacher are important factors in the decisions that will be made about that student. The supervising teacher should direct the para to report outcomes related to specific goals and objectives on students' IEPs such as learning outcomes, specific behaviors, and relationships with others. Ask the para to provide information to answer the following questions:

- What was the event?
- Who was there?
- When did it take place?
- Where did it take place?
- What was going on before the event?
- How did the event take place (what was said or done by all those mentioned in "Who" above)?
- What was the outcome (e.g., natural consequence) of your intervention?

Caution the paraeducator to avoid interpreting, judging, labeling, speculating about the student's motives, dwelling on covert behaviors, or making judgments about feelings. Ask for only the facts and get them written out if at all possible. Figure 10.1 shows examples of poorly written interpretations of behavior, followed by more objective behavioral descriptions suitable for an appropriate record of an event. Figure 10.2 provides a checklist that may be useful in guiding evaluation before or after instructional activities. Paraeducators should be encouraged to use a checklist such as Figure 10.3 as a way of

FIGURE 10.1   Behavioral Descriptions for Paraeducator Feedback

	Poor	**Better**
Motives	She was trying to get Marlene's attention.	She tapped Marlene's shoulder four times.
Feelings	She was embarrassed by the comment.	She looked down at the floor and her face turned red.
Covert behavior	He was daydreaming.	He stared at the bulletin board with a blank expression on his face.
Labels	His tone of voice was really obnoxious.	He answered, "No, why should I?"
Pseudodescription	She glared at Billy for a long time.	She stared at Billy for five seconds.
Dialogue	He said he didn't want to do his work.	He said, "This stuff is dumb. Nobody could do this."

Source: Dyck, N., Zabel, M. K., & Zabel, R. H. (1998). *Behavioral Management Guide for Paras.* San Antonio, TX: PCI Educational Publishing.

FIGURE 10.2   Paraeducator Teaching Checklist

Ask yourself the following questions before and after teaching students. Identify those areas in need of improvement. Reward yourself for areas well done.

Getting Ready to Teach

> Do I know the special instructional needs of all the students I will be teaching?
> Is the teaching environment comfortable with no distractions?
> Do I have all the necessary materials for this lesson?
> Have I asked the teacher to clarify any parts of the lesson I do not understand?
> Have I adapted material if needed?
> Do I know the content I am preparing to teach?
> Am I prepared to use at least three different activities related to the lesson goal?

While You Are Teaching

> Do I take a few moments to establish rapport with students each time?
> Have I verbally cued students to attend before starting the lesson (e.g., "Eyes up here")?
> Are my instructions concise and clear?
> Have I reviewed relevant past learning?
> Is the lesson goal clear to me and my students?
> Have I modeled a skill when appropriate?
> Do I keep the student(s) engaged in the task at least 70% of the time?
> Do I ask questions of selected students by name instead of calling on volunteers?
> Do I provide praise for effort?
> Do I give brief, immediate, corrective feedback to the student who errs?
> Does every student have an opportunity to respond many times during the lesson?
> Do I provide questions and cues to help students use what they already know to discover new information?
> Do students respond correctly 80–90% of the time?
> Do I check for skill mastery before closing the lesson?
> Do I change activities when it is clear a student is experiencing frustration?
> Do I keep the lesson interesting by changing activities?
> Am I using rewards for individual students correctly as instructed by my supervising teacher?

demonstrating ethical behavior. Regular rechecks can allow them to monitor their continued performance in this vital area.

Teachers should provide students with information about para responsibilities and roles related to matters of discipline and classroom management. It is very important for supervising teachers of paras to keep in mind that paraeducators typically work very hard and are woefully underpaid, and yet their dedication to student welfare in most cases is considerable. The difficulty in attracting and retaining paras in special education may be indicative of these realities. And, as discussed earlier, teachers often have little preparation for and, therefore, considerable reluctance toward supervising paraeducators (French, 1998).

Paraeducators, according to Ernsperger (1998), can play key roles in helping students avoid going to or have a smoother return from more restrictive settings. However, to maximize the effectiveness of paraeducators specifically and special education in general,

FIGURE 10.3   Paraeducator Ethics Checklist

Ask yourself the following questions to identify areas in which you can improve yourself as a paraeducator.

Accepting Responsibilities

- Do I recognize that the supervisor has the ultimate responsibility for the instruction and behavior management of children and follow the directions prescribed by him/her?
- Do I engage only in noninstructional and instructional activities for which qualified or trained?
- Am I careful to not communicate progress or concerns about students to parents unless directed to do so by the supervising teacher?
- Do I refer concerns expressed by parents, students, or others to the supervising teacher?

Relationship with Students and Family Members

- Do I discuss a child's progress, limitations, and/or educational program only with the supervising teacher in the appropriate setting?
- Do I discuss school problems and confidential matters only with appropriate personnel?
- Do I refrain from engaging in discriminatory practices based on a student's disability, race, sex, cultural background, or religion?
- Do I respect the dignity, privacy, and individuality of all students, families, and staff members?
- Do I present myself as a positive adult role model?

Relationship with the Teacher

- Do I recognize the role of the teacher as supervisor and team leader?
- Do I establish communication and a positive relationship with the teacher?
- When problems cannot be resolved, do I utilize the school district's grievance procedures?
- Do I discuss concerns about the teacher or teaching methods directly with the teacher?

Relationship with the School

- Do I accept responsibility for improving my own skills?
- Do I know school policies and procedures?
- Do I represent the school district in a positive manner in the community?

Source: Adapted from Dyck, N., & Kaff, M. (1999). *Essential Skills for Paras.* San Antonio, TX: PCI Educational Publishing. © 1999, permission granted by PCI Educational Publishing.

consultants and teacher teams should be keenly aware of the need for well-designed preparation programs, role clarification, appropriate supervision, and adequate compensation for their work.

Giangreco, Edelman, Broer, and Doyle (2001) suggest that education teams or schools strengthen paraprofessional support by examining their own status and priority needs and take constructive action to improve. This assessment could begin, the researchers suggest, with an examination of the six issues they noted in their extensive review of the literature: acknowledging paraprofessional work, orientation and training, hiring and assigning, interactions with students and staff, roles and responsibilities, and supervision and evaluation. Carrying out the assessment of progress with these six issues may be part of the special education administrator's role or it may be a responsibility of the school administrator.

EARLY CHILDHOOD EDUCATORS AND EARLY CHILDHOOD SPECIAL EDUCATORS AS COLLABORATORS

Concern for preschoolers with special needs has been gaining momentum since the 1960s. After passage of P.L. 94-142 in 1975, interest increased in identifying special needs among preschool children. P.L. 99-457, the Early Intervention Amendments to P.L. 94-142, extended free and appropriate public education to children from ages three to five by October 1991 in all states wanting to participate. It also phased in early intervention services for children from birth through two years of age (Council for Exceptional Children, 1997). Part H created a new program for preschoolers from birth to three years of age, and stipulated the development of an Individualized Family Service Plan (IFSP) for each child and family served. This amendment fostered collaboration based on family-focused methods and continued the procedural safeguards for families. The legislation reached beyond academic concerns to include family members, social workers, speech/language pathologists, medical personnel, and other professionals. It authorized funding for state grants and for multidisciplinary experimental, demonstration, and outreach programs. Such increases in services for preschool children with disabilities require cooperation among professionals, parents, and other caregivers, with collaboration at the heart of the programs.

Early Intervention for Special Needs

The earlier the attention to special needs of preschool children, the more successful the interventions and remediation programs in schools will be. Preschool programs with family involvement and emphasis on socialization, readiness for academic learning, language development, and emotional independence, will do much to ensure success in school. Tiegerman-Farber and Radziewicz (1998) contended more a decade ago that sweeping changes proposed for education will not happen without early intervention programs in inclusive settings. More recently, in discussing problems associated with meeting the goals of No Child Left Behind, Houston (2005) put it succinctly:

> If we really intended to leave no child behind, wouldn't we be worried about the kind of start children are getting? Wouldn't we see to it that those most likely to be left behind get reasonable pre- and postnatal heath care . . . ? Wouldn't we want to make sure that they are parented by people who can provide the kind of mental and emotional support a developing child needs? . . . Wouldn't we want to make sure that those most likely to fall behind get a better head start by having preschool programs available to them that develop their intellect . . . ? If we really wanted to leave no child behind, wouldn't we see to it that those most likely to fall behind have the best teachers we can find? (p. 470)

To press the point, education for special needs of students so they do not fall behind is most effective during the early childhood years. P.L. 99-457 requires family-centered and community-based direct services for all children from infancy to five years old with special needs that call for direct services. Early childhood education (ECE) and early childhood special education (ECSE) reduce special education costs and improve teaching environments. ECE programs can save school systems between $2,600 and $4,400 per child over the child's K–12 school experience (Carter, 2007). However, in order to have programs of high quality, there must be qualified and stable staff, low child-teacher ratios, curriculum that is aligned with local school district curriculum, and community collaboration with schools. Teachers need to be trained specifically in early childhood education and certified as such. There should be preparation and accreditation for early childhood teachers and a smooth transition plan in place for preschoolers from early childhood education to K–12 school.

Early intervention is cost-effective and educationally sound. Benefits to the child, the family, and the public are quite significant in reducing later academic failure and social problems such as teenage pregnancy, crime, and school dropout rates.

Teams for Early Childhood Special Education

Early childhood special education is moving toward full inclusion with consultation services provided by ECSE itinerant consultants who must have expertise across all disabilities including multiple disabilities (Harris & Klein, 2002). Settings include a variety of venues such as Head Start, family day care, child care centers, child education centers, and prekindergarten classes. The nature and responsibilities of educator roles can be clouded.

> One thing is clear, however: The successful delivery of inclusion support by the ECSE itinerant consultation is dependent on teamwork. To meet this challenge, ECSE itinerant consultants must receive intensive training not only in ECSE but equally important in consultation and effective teaming in ECSE contexts. (Harris & Klein, 2002, pp. 239, 245)

Teams for ECSE may differ from K–12 teams in that the child may receive services across a variety of settings such as placement in a special education preschool class *and* after-school care in an inclusive setting. Many resources may be required to address medical, financial, family counseling, rehabilitation, and other needs. Team leadership often falls to the ECSE itinerant consultant as case manager for services as varied as occupational therapist, audiologist, Head Start teacher, family members, and other caregivers. Programs may not be as structured and standardized as they are in K–12 schooling, and expectations of team members may range widely from basic social skills to meeting specific IFSP or IEP goals (Harris & Klein, 2002). Then, too, time is the enemy when complex, intensive interaction is needed for planning interventions and remediation. All team members must be knowledgeable about other members' roles and backgrounds, and communicate with all members' perspectives in mind and "on the table" for consideration.

Issues that permeate early childhood education in general can seriously affect early childhood for special education. Most prominent are costs to taxpayers, teacher credentialing, accreditation and oversight of centers, and need for an extended school day (Gill, 2007). Then, too, there may be hidden issues to bring out and resolve. As just one example, inclusive environments for preschool children with disabilities may not be well accepted by parents of preschoolers without disabilities who are paying for their child's early childhood education and would prefer that it not be an inclusive environment.

Early childhood special education consultants can help families determine their most needy areas and direct them to appropriate support groups. They can work with families and children on early intervention plans that facilitate transition in the critical time of movement from preschool to kindergarten. They can counsel families to keep files and records of materials accumulated in the care of their child so that resource personnel will have the information they need to provide those interventions thoughtfully. Early childhood educators have many responsibilities as collaborative consultants and members of teams where the stakes are high for very young children and their families.

PRESERVICE TEACHERS AS STUDENTS OF COLLABORATION, CONSULTATION, AND CO-TEACHING

Preservice teachers, as postsecondary students in teacher education completing their last few semesters of undergraduate education, are concentrating on curriculum, educational psychology, methods for teaching, development of professional portfolios, field experiences, practicum and/or student teaching, and professional organizations. Today's preservice teachers have grown up using the latest technology to connect and interact, and to some extent working with colleagues in cooperative groups. But it is not likely that their interactions and group work have involved being a bona fide advocate for a third party (a client) with exceptional learning and behavioral needs or a consultee who is teaching children with such needs. But in only months, if not weeks, they will be doing just that—working in parity with experienced co-educators and interacting with families of typical and special needs students.

The more modeling of collaboration that postsecondary teaching personnel can provide for preservice teachers, the better. The Professional Development School (PDS) movement is an example of collaboration at the institutional level in the United States. PDS partnerships around the country are multi-institutional endeavors to review teacher education and K–12 schools simultaneously. As one example, collaborative reconstruction is the process for the PDS work at Kansas State University in which arts and sciences faculty, education faculty, and K–12 public school educators work together in collaboration, inquiry, program assessment, and professional development experiences (Shroyer, Yahnke, Bennett, & Dunn, 2007). This exemplary collaboration on behalf of students has resulted in course modifications with curriculum redesign and development of new teacher education programs.

Preprofessional programs in teacher education must prepare preservice teachers for collaboration with co-educators. College and university instructors need to:

- Assign articles and textbooks on the "why" and "how to" of collaboration, consultation, and co-teaching
- Instruct students in the sociological principles that underlie professional interactions
- Model collaboration and consultation and teamwork such as co-teaching, participating in faculty meetings, and serving on curriculum and planning committees

- Arrange demonstrations of collaboration in authentic settings, such as observations of practicing teachers engaged in interactions with colleagues or family members of students, or IEP conferences (with permission of students' appropriate family members)
- Present situations in which preservice teachers respond to new scenarios that have collaborative consultation potential

Then novice teachers will be more prepared and comfortable with the collaborative consultation and co-teaching formats from their first moments in schools alongside more experienced teachers. Teacher education faculty in colleges and universities are vital links in assuring K–12 school personnel that the preprofessional graduates of their programs will be ready for their very first professional assignments.

Other universities are working with K–12 in PDS activities to improve teaching and learning at all educational levels. Professional development personnel have opportunities to be key members of PDS collaborations. Although these are promising trends, some argue that even when professors emphasize the importance of collaborative teaching and learning in K–12 schools, not many of them *model* collaboration in their courses (Jones & Morin, 2000). If projects intended for collaboration degenerate into turn-teaching, that does not help students develop a collaborative mind-set. Jones and Morin (2000) summarize characteristics for successful collaboration as:

- Voluntary participation for shared goals
- Mutual respect and parity
- Mutual support with sharing of expertise
- Administrative support

They target as barriers to collaboration:

- Turf issues
- Tradition
- Lack of trust
- Lack of time

Not all beginning teachers are young; some are second-career professionals or entering the profession after involvement in child rearing and homemaking. Their pragmatism and wider experience bases complement the exuberance and energy of younger teacher education graduates. But both groups have the need and share the desire to be well prepared for their first day, week, month, and full academic year inasmuch as possible. In some districts mentors and support groups have been established for new teachers to help ensure that novice teachers have a good first-year experience and do not join the ranks of teachers making early departures from the profession.

Novice Special Education Teachers

Although first-year teachers have been the focus of numerous studies, few studies have centered on first-year *special education* teachers. Whitaker (2002a, 2000b) speaks out on the difficulty of being a beginner in special education and reports on results of focus groups she conducted to explore concerns of these teachers. Categories of need that were volunteered by the groups included:

- Mentoring accompanied by emotional support
- Information about special education paperwork and IEPs
- Awareness of the school's policies and procedures
- Means of locating and accessing materials
- Methods of discipline
- Curriculum building (a standard responsibility and practice within the area of education for students' special needs)
- Management of routines
- Interaction with others on faculty and staff to work with them more effectively

To this list it would be realistic and practical to add interaction with families of students. Failure to designate this category may indicate a problem in and of itself.

One new educator called her initial teaching year "My First Year of Learning" (McCaffrey, 2000). Her school setting had class sizes of eight to twelve students, a teacher and three four paras, and students with needs ranging from physical disability to speech to occupational therapy throughout the day, moving in and out of the classroom. In preparation for this work she came in early and stayed late, but the result was, nevertheless, frustration on her part and confusion among her students. The situation improved dramatically when she began seeking advice from experienced educators, whom she described as the "*most underused and underappreciated resource* for beginning teachers" (emphasis added). New teachers often think that by discussing the problems they are having, they will be committing professional "suicide" (Carver, 2004). But it is not a sign of ineptitude or defeat to ask an experienced teacher, "Am I in about the right spot in the text for this time of year?" or "Is my instructional pace in this subject about right?" or "Have I set my expectations for students too high (or too low) or just about right?" In some areas after-school learning communities have been established, with attendance voluntary, to be "a lifeline for new teachers in a challenging urban setting" (Carver, 2004, p. 58). Attendees focus not only on instruction but also on how to "navigate the bureaucracy of a large urban district."

A top-ten-plus-one list of practical recommendations for first-year teachers could include these points:

1. While in the teacher education program, keep an idea journal.

2. If a teaching portfolio is required for graduation, plan the contents so they will be useful and generate ideas.

3. Save major teacher textbooks such as educational psychology, methods, content area, introductory special education, and assessment. (Also, taking an assessment course is highly recommended.)

4. When enrolled in courses such as educational psychology, look for ways of applying the material to future teaching situations; for example, when studying negative and positive

reinforcement, or developing class rules, create sample charts that you could modify a bit and reference later. Talking through these activities collaboratively with classmates will result in even better products to stow away for future use.

5. Tape yourself teaching, lecturing, conferencing, and interacting with students, then study the tapes just as a football team studies game footage to improve their playing. Older teachers may dislike videotaping, but the younger generation tends to be quite comfortable in front of video cameras. Of course, confidentiality and privacy must be assured.

6. Join a new-teacher support group; if none is available, start one.

7. Find a key "magnet-type" teacher in your first assigned building(s) and ask for some collegial time to study that person's expertise. In exchange for the time, offer to take that person's bus or lunchroom duty for double that length of time.

8. Return to your own early school days and visit with your favorite teachers, telling them how much you valued their guidance and asking them to talk about teaching with you. Most will be flattered and touched by your desire to do this. Perhaps you will receive such a visit from some of your own former students someday.

9. Take every opportunity to observe collaborative and co-teaching activities in schools during your field experiences or practicum. It might be permissible to attend an IEP conference—a very helpful activity, but only with parent permission and your assurance of preserving complete confidentiality.

10. Take notes when observing or working in schools. Sketch classroom layouts, catalog ideas for materials, and observe teaching procedures.

11. Make broad-stroke plans for your first day, month, week, and year. For example, a dedicated first-grade teacher would want to plan out that first day in ten-minute increments, with flexibility to tweak the plan, of course.

■ ■ ■ ■ ■ ▬▬

APPLICATION 10.3
COLLABORATING TO DEVELOP RESPONSIVE
LEARNING ENVIRONMENTS

In the manner of a jigsaw version of cooperative learning, divide the whole group into three subgroups for completing parts of this task. One group is to design and illustrate a layout for an ideal inclusive classroom, adhering to money and space limitations that ordinarily would be available. (Mark off the dimensions of a typical classroom to make the exercise more realistic.) Begin by planning for two high-traffic areas that often can create behavioral and management problems—wastebaskets and wall-mounted pencil sharpeners—and allocating space for coats and backpacks. Then proceed to the fun part of arranging the room with plants, books, artifacts, and personal touches that reflect one's teaching personality.

The second subgroup discusses conduct and behavior disorders that disrupt classroom decorum. Then, with the first group's room plan, point out any potential problem areas and suggest how the room arrangement can accommodate special needs so as to reduce misbehavior and increase high-quality academic learning time.

The third group examines sets of basal texts and instructor's manuals in core subjects to determine what, if any, accommodations and modifications are implied in the student books and specified in the instructor manuals. Some will be found sadly lacking and some may be quite good. Discuss how faculty could collaborate as curriculum committees to select the best of the best as basal texts. Then all groups meet to combine the work that in summary would showcase a responsive and adaptive physical, academic, and socioemotional environment for an inclusive classroom. So with room plan, management plan, and materials planned, voilà! Ready for that first day.

ETHICS FOR PARAEDUCATORS, EARLY CHILDHOOD EDUCATORS, AND PRESERVICE TEACHERS

Five areas in which it is important for paraeducators and their supervising teachers to create an ethical climate for students and school personnel are the para role, responsibilities in that role, relationships with students and parents, relationships with teachers, and relationships within the school. Confidentiality of information and rights of privacy for students and families are especially important. Paraeducators should be encouraged to use a checklist such as the one in Figure 10.3 to demonstrate ethical behavior. Regular checkups allow them to continue monitoring their performance and developing in these vital areas.

For early childhood educators, codes of ethics and practices have been developed by the National Association for the Education of Young Children and the Council for Exceptional Children's Division for Early Childhood that address needed knowledge and skills. Collaboration with colleagues is included, but guidelines for working with adults are not clear-cut. More effort is needed to focus on the challenges involved and to develop specific recommendations for meeting those challenges.

Preservice teachers become novice teachers upon completion of their teacher education program as they make the leap into teaching roles parallel with those of teachers who have taught for many years in a variety of circumstances. Instructors in teacher education programs can remind the preservice teacher that it is not only OK but also smart, caring, and completely professional for beginning teachers to seek advice from seasoned educators.

Paraprofessionals, early childhood educators, and preservice teachers, along with their teacher education instructors, have vital collaboration and consultation roles in helping students with special needs to succeed. Teamwork as partners at all stages is the key. (See Figure 10.4.)

TIPS FOR COLLABORATION WITH PARAPROFESSIONALS, EARLY CHILDHOOD EDUCATORS, AND PRESERVICE TEACHERS

1. Discuss the school district's mission statement, building(s) philosophy, and your own teaching philosophy and values with the paraeducators assigned to you before they begin working with you and the students.

FIGURE 10.4   Teacher, Para, and Preservice (Student) Teacher as Collaborators

2. Visit other schools where there are clear procedures for scheduling, directing, supervising, and evaluating the work of paraeducators. Implement practices that are promising for your school setting.

3. Encourage paras to share their ideas on student behavior and learning, and incorporate those ideas into the instructional plan when appropriate.

4. Introduce family members to the paraeducators who will work with their child.

5. When a para asks for advice, first ask what the para has observed. This gets the para involved and encourages active participation in observing students, deciding on a plan and implementing that plan.

6. Advocate for well-designed, well-conducted, and carefully evaluated staff development prepared specifically for paraeducators, and help them take place, if possible.

7. Continue to read, study, attend educational conferences, and take courses in collaboration, consultation, and co-teaching.

8. Strive to learn as much as possible about the work, environments, potential problems, and always the joys and satisfactions that your co-educators experience in their roles.

9. Keep remarks about teaching colleagues, staff, students, and families of students to a minimum, focusing only on instructional tasks.

10. Reach out to preservice and novice teachers to instill their confidence and to expand their skills.

11. Find and use opportunities to have beginning teachers mentor veteran teachers in areas such as technology, recent trends in curriculum, or new ideas for content areas.

12. Practice the adage we all learned as children, "If you can't say something good (respectful, appreciative, supportive) about a colleague or student or family, then say nothing at all."

CHAPTER REVIEW

1. When the paraeducator's role is clearly defined at the outset, the partnership between teacher and para is more likely to be smooth and productive. The paraeducator assists the special education teacher and follows that teacher's direction. The teacher directs and supervises the para. It is important that classroom teachers participate in supervising the work of paras as well.

2. Teachers must be permitted the time and space needed to plan effectively with paras. IDEA legislation requires training for paraeducators; also, teachers need to provide specific, on-the-job orientation and training in their own school contexts.

3. Paraeducators should have a high school diploma, a sense of ethics and understanding of the need for confidentiality, ability to communicate with children and adults, ability to follow verbal directions and written plans of teachers, willingness to learn new skills, flexibility, sense of humor, and a good attendance record. Preparation will involve staff development sessions, teacher-provided instruction, and use of numerous materials available in the literature and professional resources.

4. Teachers supervise and direct para activities by planning with them, managing their schedules, delegating responsibilities, orienting them to their roles and work settings, providing training, managing their work environment, and evaluating their performance.

5. Early childhood education is integral to future success of children with exceptional learning needs, and special education is particularly effective in early childhood. Early childhood teachers can collaborate with families to support them and direct them to assistive resources. All who interact must be knowledgeable about others' roles and respectful of their perspectives, keeping in mind that parents and caregivers know their child best.

6. Preservice teachers can begin to prepare themselves for collaborative and co-teaching roles by participating in group and team activities during their teacher education programs. College and university instructors, and supervising teachers in schools, should contribute by modeling co-teaching and other professional interactions. They could involve teacher education students in faculty meetings, department meetings, IEP conferences with permission of parents, participation in professional organizations, and other collaborative activities important to the profession.

TO DO AND THINK ABOUT

1. Discuss the following activities and determine whether they should be done by the paraeducator, only the teacher, or either person.

   - Read to students.
   - Prepare homework assignments.
   - Observe and record student behaviors.
   - Administer and score standardized tests.
   - Check student papers.

2. Discuss the following situations and propose next steps for each.

   - The general classroom teacher asks the paraeducator to help a student complete his algebra assignment. It has been a long time since the paraeducator studied algebra and she feels uncertain about some of the steps involved.

   - During his break period in the staff lounge, a paraeducator overhears two teachers talking about one of the students with whom he works. The paraeducator is aware that some of the information the teachers are sharing is not correct.

   - The paraeducator is attending a meeting at her social club when someone says, "These people with mental problems should be in separate schools. They shouldn't be in school with my child."

3. Interview parents of preschool children with disabilities to find out what kinds of preschool they want for their children before transition to kindergarten. Then interview early childhood special educators to learn the positive and not-so-positive aspects of their work. Assimilate your data and consider how you might use this information effectively.

4. As a preservice teacher, take a survey of experienced teachers, asking them to respond to four items: (1) good things about teaching; (2) things they would like to improve about teaching; (3) changes in education and schools that need to happen right away; and (4) long-term changes needed. Compare your findings with other preservice teachers and discuss what you could do to help bring about change during your years in the profession.

5. Make a "recruitment poster" for encouraging young people to enter the educational profession and become a teacher, then perhaps school administrator, school counselor, or other related personnel.

ADDITIONAL READINGS AND RESOURCES

Demchak, M. A., & Morgan, C. R. (1998). Effective collaboration between professionals and paraprofessionals. *Rural Special Education Quarterly, 17*(2), 10–15.

Doyle, M. B. (1997). *The paraprofessional's guide to the inclusive classroom: Working as a team.* Baltimore: Paul H. Brookes.

Dyck, N., & Pemberton, J. (1997). *A dozen tools for paras.* Lawrence, KS: Curriculum Solutions, Inc.

Dyck, N., & Thurston, L. P. (1998). *Getting the message across: A para's guide to communication.* Lawrence, KS: Curriculum Solutions, Inc.

French, N. K. (1997). Management of paraeducators. In A. L. Pickett & K. Gerlach (Eds.), *Supervising paraeducators in school settings.* Austin, TX: PRO-ED.

French, N. K. (2000). Taking time to save time: Delegating to paraeducators. *Teaching Exceptional Children, 32*(3), 79–83.

Giangreco, M. F., Edelman, S. W., & Broer, S. M. (2001). Respect, appreciation, and acknowledgement of paraprofessionals who support students with disabilities. *Exceptional Children, 67*(4), 485–498.

Marks, S. U., Schrader, C., & Levine, M. (1999). Paraeducator experiences in inclusive settings: Helping, hovering, or holding their own? *Exceptional Children, 65*(3), 315–328.

Mueller, P. H., & Murphy, F. V. (2001). Determining when a student requires paraeducator support. *Teaching Exceptional Children, 33*(6), 22–27.

A process is outlined that helps IEP teams determine when to assign paraeducators to support students with disabilities.

Riggs, C. G. (2001). Ask the paraprofessionals: What are your training needs? *Teaching Exceptional Children, 33*(3), 78–83.

Stanley, A. L., & Vasa, S. F. (1998). How paraeducators learn on the Web. *Teaching Exceptional Children, 30*(5), 54–59.

Thurston, L. P. (2000). *The positive para: Helping students develop positive social skills.* Lawrence, KS: Curriculum Solutions, Inc.

Wallace, T., Shin, J., Bartholomay, T., & Stahl, B. J. (2001). Knowledge and skills for teachers supervising the work of paraprofessionals. *Exceptional Children, 67*(4), 520–533.

Weiss, H., Caspe, M., & Lopez, M. E. (2006, Spring). Family involvement in early childhood education, No. 1. Harvard Family Research Project. Available online at www.gse.harvard.edu/hfrp/projects/fine/resources/research/earlych
Research review of the array of learning supports for young children's cognitive and social development. Studies the link between family involvement in early childhood and learning and developmental outcomes.

Whitaker, S. D. (2000b). What do first-year special education teachers need? Implications for induction programs. *Teaching Exceptional Children, 33*(1), 28–36.

CHAPTER ELEVEN

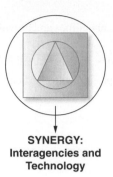

SYNERGY:
Interagencies and
Technology

Related Services, Interagency Networks, Resources, and Technology in Collaboration

An ancient proverb reminds us that a child's life is like a tablet on which every passerby leaves a mark. It is the responsibility of all members in every society to mark that tablet well. All children have individual needs, and all are entitled to a free and appropriate public education (FAPE) that addresses any special needs. In order to serve students in ways that are right for every child and productive for society, educators can look to many people, places, and things for help:

- People who can help are related services and support personnel.
- Places to seek help include agencies and intervention programs.
- Things can be selected from a wide array of materials and assistive devices, with significant contributions from technology.

Collaborations and networks among general and special education teachers, related services and support personnel, families, and the communities they live in are sure to increase learning and achievement by students. When people from many areas of work and community life consult and collaborate, educators can choose among a broad array of services from specialists and coordinate them to focus on students' interests and needs. As Helen Keller spoke so wisely, "Alone we can do so little, together we can do so much."

One area of service that has grown exponentially in recent years is technology. Technology helps co-educators in many ways to "work smarter, not harder." Another source of assistance comes from federal, state, or corporate funding, and grants for special projects.

FOCUSING QUESTIONS

1. What can related services and support personnel contribute as team members to teachers of students with special needs, and who will coordinate these efforts?

2. How can collaborative consultants facilitate communication and coordination among a variety of agencies for the diverse needs of students with learning and behavioral differences?

3. What transition services from early childhood to school, from middle school to secondary school, and from secondary school to work or postsecondary education should be provided for students with exceptional needs?

4. How can home-school-community collaboration maximize student abilities and provide service for their special needs?

5. In what ways can technology assist co-educators in schools, homes, and communities?

6. How are external funds requested and used to invigorate school programs for the benefit of students and schools?

KEY TERMS

Educational Resources Information Center (ERIC)	grant funds	request for proposal (RFP)
Federal Grants and Contracts Weekly	home-school-community collaboration	shell/template
Federal Register	interagency collaboration	support personnel
	related services personnel	technology
		transition services

Educators of the twenty-first century endeavor to develop connections and networks that provide opportunities for students with special needs. They reach out beyond traditional teaching roles within the school to find the right people, places, and things that can help students succeed. But it is not easy. It takes time, energy, communication skill, management ability, diplomacy, and of course, approval of school administrators. Inevitable barriers make the process more challenging, such as failure to identify the student needs appropriately, turf issues among personnel, potential liability issues, lack of clarity on fiscal responsibilities, and need for shared agreements involving personnel, facilities, and equipment.

As a process, collaboration is a means to an end rather than an end in itself. The primary goal is success in school for students with special needs. But schools are not alone in having responsibility to help students succeed; they cannot do it all. After all, typical students are in school less than 10 percent of the time from birth to their nineteenth birthday. This has been dubbed "the 9/91 factor," an amazing figure that is calculated by allocating 6 hours a day in school for 180 days, which is 1,080 clock hours a year, for 12.5 years of formal schooling within the first 18 years of a child's life. And this is only time *allocated* for learning; a measure of actual time students are *engaged* in academic learning would be much less. (This is also one of the shortest school years, if not *the* shortest, in the industrial world.) For the remaining 91 or so percent of the time, the child is at home with friends or relatives, or elsewhere in a community or alone or with others. Schools and communities can address their considerable responsibilities in helping students learn and do so by employing a wide spectrum of resources and collaborating with many agencies to help them stay in school as active, successful learners.

RELATED SERVICES PERSONNEL AS PARTNERS IN COLLABORATION AND CONSULTATION

Schools are required by the Individuals with Disabilities Education Act (IDEA) and Section 504 of the Rehabilitation Act of 1973 to provide an array of services for students with disabilities. IDEA 1997 mandated a free and appropriate education to all children that emphasizes use of special education and related services designed to meet their special needs. Special educators and related service personnel work together to prepare students for employment and independent living after transition from secondary schools. Related services are described in IDEA 1997 as facilitators of transportation and developmental, corrective, and other supportive services needed to help a child who has a disability benefit from special education. Figure 11.1 shows services that are included within this definition. The list is not exhaustive and does not include all services the school district may need to provide—for example, an interpreter. Other services might be those such as artistic and cultural programs, art, music, and dance therapy if they are needed in order for the child to benefit from special education and receive free, appropriate public education. Parents are not to be charged for these services.

To be eligible for related services, the student is assessed in areas of health, vision, hearing, social and emotional status, general intelligence, academic performance, communicative status, and motor abilities. A variety of assessment tools and strategies must be used to gather the information in order to have a complete picture of the student's needs. IDEA 1997 does not require that an IEP team meeting include related services personnel, but if a particular service is to be discussed, it is obviously important that such personnel be involved.

FIGURE 11.1   Related Services for Students in Special Education Programs

Audiology	Psychological services
Counseling services	Recreation services
Early identification and assessment services	Rehabilitation counseling services
Medical services	School health services
Occupational therapy	Social work services
Orientation and mobility services	Speech-language pathology services
Parent counseling and training	Therapy programs in art, dance, music
Physical therapy	Transportation

Other Services of Support for Students in Special Education Programs

Assistive technology	Reading specialists
Custodial and maintenance services	School aides
Food services	Secretarial/Receptionist services
Media/Library/Technology specialists	Security services
Mentors/Apprenticeship and career-shadowing supervisors	Senior citizens/Grandparents
Paraprofessionals	Special education administrators
Parent volunteers	Student teachers

Related services may be provided in the regular classroom, special education class, therapy room, or other locations in school, home, or community (see National Dissemination Center for Children with Disabilities, NICHCY). IDEA allows the use of trained, supervised educators and assistants to help provide related services, just as it allows their assistance in providing special education with appropriate supervision and training. Related services personnel can provide services that involve face-to-face interactions between educator or therapist and student, or teachers and consultants, or paras, or parents. The services are to be real and substantial. They are defined and determined by how they relate to the student's IEP.

SCENARIO 11.A

The setting is the kitchen of a home where an intermediate-level student and her mother are sitting at the kitchen table.

Mother: I see a note here from your teacher saying that you need to make up an important math test you missed yesterday.

Child: Uh-huh, I missed it because yesterday was Tuesday.

Mother: What does that have to do with the math test?

Child: Well, on Tuesdays I'm supposed to see Mrs. Evans, but she wasn't there. So I went to Mr. Bowman instead.

Mother: Who is Mrs. Evans?

Child: She's the reading teacher. I see her Tuesdays and Thursdays, from 1:30 to 2:30, but she was sick yesterday.

Mother: So you saw Mr. Bowman. Who is he?

Child: The special education teacher I see for more help with reading, but mostly with spelling and my workbooks. He got called to another school for a meeting, so he sent me to Jeanette.

Mother: Now wait a minute—who is Jeanette?

Child: Gee, mom, I thought you told the principal you and dad would keep up with my school program.

Mother: I'm *trying!*

Child: Anyway, Jeanette is the high school girl who tutors me in reading.

Mother: Oh?

Child: It's OK. She's nice. She wants to be a teacher someday. Mrs. Bagley helped me work it out.

Mother: And *who* is Mrs. Bagley?

Child: The counselor. She says working with Jeanette is good for me, and for her, too.

Mother: And just what does Miss Anderson think about all of this?

Child: Uh, who's she?

Mother: Your *classroom teacher!*

Child: Oh, yeah, I forgot all about her.

The child's schedule discussed during this little kitchen-table scenario underscores the complexity of the school day and accentuates the need for communication, cooperation, and coordination among an array of school personnel.

Adapted from Michelle Berg.

SUPPORT SERVICES PERSONNEL AS PARTNERS IN COLLABORATION AND CONSULTATION

Every school has many support personnel without whom school life for everyone would be uncomfortable and disorganized. They include people who are integral to all school programs and activities—food service staff, secretaries, bus drivers, paraeducators, custodians, and volunteer aides. Just as the roles of consultant, consultee, and client are interrelated and interchangeable according to the focus of the service, so the roles and responsibilities of support service personnel are interrelated and interchanging according to the part each plays in the teachers' instruction and the students' learning. For example, school bus drivers and cab drivers are involved in the lives of students in special education programs in ways that go beyond just picking them up and delivering them home again. One bus driver put it this way, "As drivers we realize that we are a traveling billboard for schools" (Geisler, 2004). They are a key link between home and school, being the first person to see the student in the morning and often the last of the school staff to see them in the afternoon. They transport students from school to school and program to program while adhering to tight schedules and facing unpredictable weather and traffic conditions. They can provide input for a special education referral process. Sometimes it is even appropriate for them to help with intervention programs as partners in reward-and-reinforcement systems for students, or in extending learning activities beyond the classroom in practical, real-world ways.

Transportation personnel also help students in ways that respect their differences and needs. One driver of a bus for students in special education classes displays their schoolwork in her bus. She also has a chart for the "Star" bus student of the week. She explains that because it is the "special education bus," she wants to make their bus ride special. She makes an effort to collaborate with teachers, adhering carefully to complicated schedules so students are not late or left stranded at a building. Transportation personnel might be called on to serve in the role of consultant for a teacher of a student with mental retardation who, as a consultee, needs information about the student's social interactions or neighborhood environment.

School psychologists, as related services staff, provide information about purposes, interpretation, and uses of tests. Counselors trained in individual guidance and group guidance techniques are important participants or presenters in staff development activities and problem-solving sessions. School nurses and social workers contribute valuable data in both informal consultations and IEP conferences. They are often able to target seemingly insignificant data toward meaningful problem identification.

An understanding custodian who is tuned in to both teachers' needs and students' needs has always been regarded as teacher's best friend and helpmate in the school setting. This is especially relevant to the special education teacher who can encourage custodians to be involved in planning and monitoring special programs for students with special needs.

Other school and community personnel can provide invaluable support services for unique needs of students. These include a multitude of roles: Boy/Girl Scout leaders, 4-H leaders, private music and art instructors, media representatives, interest-area speakers, mentors, tutors, judges of events and products, and community organization members. Enriching and extending services can be solicited from personnel in libraries, park systems, colleges, industries, businesses, and other professions. Community leaders can assist with career shadowing by students who express interest in specific vocational areas. (Refer to Figure 11.1.) Others might provide knowledge and experiences from their own lives as members of a cultural minority.

Special activities, managed through clubs, workshops, interests groups, travel, and the like, are an important component of special services arranged to accommodate special needs. Doctors and dentists can teach and advise within their professional roles. An added benefit of this service is that as they become involved, some ask for opportunities to gain more insight into children's needs and school-related development, creating a ripple effect of awareness and understanding. A frequently overlooked source of help that more and more schools are learning to value and call on is senior citizens, including grandparents of students, to instruct, demonstrate, comfort, relate their own experiences, and model and advocate for children and youth. Schools and universities house a variety of support personnel who can assist with student needs. These institutions are catalysts for the increasingly popular practice of using community resources to accentuate learning.

As another example, a librarian could be a consultant to help a gifted program teacher consultee select and locate useful resources for her students' research projects. Libraries and media centers are repositories of tremendous amounts of information. Conceivably, no other public service center has changed more than the library in the past half-century. It now is a teaching and learning system, a network for interactive learning, a storehouse for artifacts to enhance learning, a workplace for development of interests and skills, and much more. The "Shhhhh!" of librarians has been replaced with the hum and clicks of computers and microfiche readers, the queries and responses of information seekers and technical assistants, sliding of printed materials into organizers, and the buzz of small groups sharing information or problem solving. Corners and tables of libraries and media centers are set up for instructing students with special needs using modified curriculum materials and strategies. In order to access these rich educational resources most efficiently, consultants and collaborators should be familiar with several basic organizational units, including:

■ Educational Resources Information Center (ERIC), a federal information system of sixteen clearinghouses throughout the United States that provides access to educational information not appearing in journal articles (reports, conference papers, curriculum guides), and makes location of current information about almost any educational topic relatively easily

- *Education Index,* an index of titles and citations arranged by topic headings and author names
- Educational journals and reviews, both general and curriculum specific

Students-helping-students is a rich, in-house source for help and tends to be well received by the individuals receiving assistance. Cooperative and collaborative learning activities, peer tutoring, and coaching give students opportunities to share their own new knowledge and provide service to others. This is yet another example of Vygotsky's (1978) principles of social learning proposing that children learn ways of thinking and behaving during shared activities.

Collaborative consulting teachers find it helpful to have a notebook of potential resource personnel. A school-related group such as the Parent Teacher Organization (PTO) or a committee of teachers, or a student group seeking a service project, could develop a Community Resources Information Page format for the school and compile individual pages into a Community Resources Notebook. Persons or agencies targeted for inclusion in the notebook should be contacted to obtain their permission to be included and information from them to enter on the page. Figure 11.2 shows an example of a resource shell/template for recording information. The notebook must be reviewed and updated periodically to keep it current and useful; this in itself can be a rewarding collaborative activity for a cross section of school personnel.

Another project that some local or state educational organizations develop is a pocket-sized handbook for middle school and high school students with sources for help in times of crisis or felt need. Such booklets list phone numbers, Internet connections, and addresses of agencies that assist young people. Brief, to-the-point sections could include, for starters:

accidents; AIDS; alcohol and other drugs; animal care; Big Brothers/Big Sisters programs, camps, counseling; divorce; church/synagogue/mosque councils; driving and seat belt use; eating disorders; education; emergency hotlines; employment opportunities; environmental groups; gun laws for minors; health and dental care; interesting places to visit; international studies programs; juvenile justice and probation systems; law and legal issues; libraries; mental health agencies; pregnancy and prenatal care; rape and other sexual abuse; recreation centers and sports; running away from home; Salvation Army/YMCA, YWCA; scholarship programs; school-related support; self-improvement centers; sexuality, sex education, and sexually transmitted diseases; smoking and nicotine use; social and family services; special needs services; suicide; teenage parenting; testing agencies; truancy; vandalism; youth organizations such as Scouts and 4-H

Student involvement as collaborators in the project would enrich the booklet contents and improve the perceptions of co-educators about preteens and teens.

FIGURE 11.2   Community Resources Information Page

Name of Individual or Agency   _____

Phone Number _____   Fax _____   E-Mail _____

Address   _____

Occupation or Emphasis   _____

Area(s) of Expertise/Contribution _____

Preference for Grade Level or Staff Area   _____

Preference for Group Size with Which to Work _____

Time of Day Preferred _____

Preference for Day(s) of Week and Month(s) of Year _____

Maximum Times Would Care to Assist in a Year _____

Special Arrangements Needed _____

Special Equipment Required _____

Any Further Clarifications _____

Record of Dates Contributed, with Description of Activities of the Contribution:

_____

_____

For More Information Contact (Resource Personnel) _____

                                              (School Personnel) _____

APPLICATION 11.1

**IDENTIFYING ROLES TO HELP WITH STUDENT
INTERESTS AND NEEDS**

Think of other related services and support services roles beyond those listed in Figure 11.1 and described in this chapter that you might call on to assist with special needs and interests of students through consultation and collaboration with schools. Think outside the box to come up with roles such as county extension agents, museum curators, and more. You might find a

Yellow Pages Directory useful for this. Describe practical ways in which the sources could provide pertinent services to individual students or groups of students.

ORGANIZING RELATED AND SUPPORT SERVICES

When students need services such as physical therapy, occupational therapy, or speech therapy, a decision must be made about where to locate the service. In many inclusive schools the therapist removes the child from the group while providing the service directly in the classroom. This intervention can cause considerable apprehension on the part of some teachers (Schlax, 1994); having only one therapist at a time working with the child and integrating therapies with the classroom routine can reduce such apprehension. In reality, the majority of students with special needs are assigned to general classrooms, even though they may attend resource rooms or work with consulting teachers for a portion of the school day.

Support services and classroom extender services should be integrated into educational programs and school schedules. Pearce (1996) stresses the need to work with specialists in order to adapt curriculum to special needs. She suggests that special education teachers might have a plan to work with all students in the classroom on activities for which the classroom teachers may not have time or materials. This may take getting used to by some teachers, but is well worth the effort when they can get twice as much done. Furthermore, it may be a catalyst for rich co-teaching activities in the future. Sometimes therapists can engage in carefully selected, well-prepared learning experiences with all students in the class in order to avoid singling out those with disabilities or to observe students in typical academic and social classroom situations.

A group of teachers in a special project to include students with severe disabilities in their general education classrooms reported that the most helpful aspects of the specialist support they received included a shared framework and goals; physical presence of the collaborator; validation of the classroom teacher's contribution; and teamwork (Giangreco, Dennis, Cloninger, Edelman, & Schattman, 1993). If problems did appear, they tended to be caused by one or more of these:

- Separate goals by the related services specialist
- Disruption of the classroom routine
- Overspecialization in special education practices

In the project both teacher and consultant needed to consider more fully the context of the regular classroom and to respect values and needs of that classroom, its students, and its teacher. That notwithstanding, in this study to analyze the benefits of inclusion for students with severe disabilities, seventeen of the nineteen teachers reported that they were transformed by their experience. Not only were their attitudes toward the students changed; in some cases the teachers said they changed their attitudes about themselves as well (Giangreco et al., 1993).

Communication, cooperation, and coordination among general educators, special education teachers, support and related personnel, administrators, and ancillary staff will

FIGURE 11.3 Integrating Efforts through Collaboration

Collaborative consultants can integrate and collaborate with other educators in these ways:

With general education teachers:
1. Establish joint ownership of the student and the learning situation.
2. Respect the views of all.
3. Keep problems "in house."
4. Request regular interaction and feedback from them.

With other special education colleagues:
1. Openly deal with the discomfort of having others give critique and feedback.
2. Arrange and coordinate planned interactions.
3. Together develop support systems.

With support and related services personnel:
1. Become more knowledgeable about their roles and responsibilities.
2. Make sure to integrate major ideas they produce.
3. Plan and implement student programs that reflect coordinated involvement and not fragmentation.

With building administrators:
1. Inform them in as brief and practical a manner as possible.
2. Don't carry tales from a school/district to others.
3. Don't be a spy, or judge, even if asked.
4. Request regular feedback as to your own effectiveness.

With attorneys/hearing officers:
1. State your credentials, certifications, training, and experiences relative to the case.
2. State the nature and extent of knowledge about the student.
3. Discuss assessments, curricula, and modifications used, and their reliability, validity, and appropriateness.
4. Explain all terms, using no acronyms or jargon.
5. Remain calm, honest, and cooperative.

With legislators:
1. Be brief, accurate, and substantiating with all material delivered.
2. Thank legislators for their past interest and help.
3. State situations realistically without unreasonable demands.
4. Consider the whole picture, as the legislator must, and not just one's own primary interest.

With the public:
1. Be perceptive about issues of culture, diversity, and conflicting interests.
2. Demonstrate reasonable expectations while upholding standards and delivering challenges.
3. Express your dedication to students and commitment to excellent schools.

help ensure that collaboration has the best possible likelihood of success as an integral educational process. Several concrete steps can be taken. See Figure 11.3 on special education teacher efforts to integrate their roles with seven sample groups of potential collaborators.

Labels for the roles of school personnel are necessary; however, they are relatively unimportant within a collaborative climate. The service implemented to meet a child's need determines the role label. Schools and communities have many untapped pools of skills and interests across a wide range of unassigned areas. When teachers form teams and move among roles, positive ripple effects occur, such as increased adult-to-pupil ratio in learning programs and the ability of a school to provide more personalized instruction (Nevin, Thousand, Paolucci-Whitcomb, & Villa, 1990).

In order to facilitate appropriate support services for students, collaborative co-educators can do several things:

- Become knowledgeable about the roles, capabilities, and responsibilities of support personnel.
- Strive to have both IEPs and more informal learning plans include all facets of the student learning and involve all possible roles that can help the students succeed.
- Within the bounds of necessary confidentiality and ethical school practices, ask support personnel for their viewpoints and opinions about helping students with special needs.
- Inform support personnel about the collaborative consultation role, schedule, and responsibilities.
- Monitor student performance across all kinds of school, home, and community learning in a variety of situations.
- Provide time in teachers' schedules for co-planning, co-teaching, and following up on collaborative activities.
- Show ongoing support for professional staff development activities that focus on inclusion and collaboration, encouraging their involvement as co-educators.
- Have specific sessions during professional development programs for providing information about exceptional learning needs, and for encouragement to work as teams.

Lugg and Boyd (1993) caution against "contrived collegiality" that is administratively regulated and compulsory. They contend that such an environment erodes trust and communication, even that which may already be in effect. This is an important consideration. They recommend restructuring schools into schools-within-schools, where teachers and students are organized into teams that work and play together for sustained periods of time and perhaps over several years so that strong interpersonal relationships can flourish.

Along the lines of schools-within-schools, Murphy (1995) proposes a whole-faculty study-group concept as a way of implementing school improvement initiatives. Teachers can be organized into small study groups of four to six individuals who meet weekly for about an hour in a collegial interchange that focuses on whole-school improvement and how to help students learn more.

Staff developers LaBonte, Leighty, Mills, and True (1995) set up study groups of teachers, creating collaborative time for them to improve programs and share new practices, and to link whole-school improvement with increased student achievement. One focus team format consists of having the principal and four or more teachers from each participating school attend a week-long institute and develop a plan for leading their schools in implementation of whole-faculty study groups. These educators believe that whole-faculty study groups are promising vehicles for school improvement that increase both student and teacher learning. They assert that professional development personnel must create interagency collaboration in order to increase student achievement.

ORGANIZING INTERAGENCY COLLABORATION

Consultants must consider how to work together with different services agencies, different professional cultures, and different norms and standards (Shaver, Golan, & Wagner, 1996). Many of the strategies, skills, and attitudes addressed in previous chapters will guide educators in developing good working relationships with those who are not professional educators and in resolving major obstacles to collaboration and service integration.

The twenty-first-century Community Learning Centers in schools across the nation are examples of collaborative efforts that combine the resources of schools, universities, families, volunteers, and community-based organizations to serve students beyond the school day. Communities in Schools unites community resources such as health care and mental health professionals with teachers, parents, principals, and volunteers on behalf of children (Barbour & Barbour, 2001). Many highly successful outcomes have been realized for students and families. Business-school partnerships have also shown promise for impacting schools, communities, and students. Several student entrepreneurship programs have boosted student achievement and the local economy (SEDL, 2000a). Critical features of these partnerships include strong leadership and support from local power brokers; open communication; respect for differences in skills, ideas, cultures, and values of other partners; decision making based on common ground; long-range goals; careful planning; continuous assessment; and keeping the community informed (Barbour & Barbour, 2001).

The Southwest Educational Development Lab in Austin, Texas, suggests these steps for organizing and managing collaborative interagency projects (SEDL, 2000b):

1. Convene a group.
2. Assess student and community needs.
3. Establish purposes and priorities.
4. Study effective ways of working together.
5. Plan the project.
6. Implement the plan.
7. Assess the results.
8. Sustain the achievement.

How can groups study ways of working together? Suggestions involve efforts to:

- Cross-train in each others' procedures and norms
- Build a sense of community
- Obtain and maintain high levels of support at all organizational levels
- Develop joint procedures and eliminate conflicting ones
- Write policies that encourage integrated services and interagency collaboration
- Keep in mind that the more democratic the process is, the better
- Work to develop high levels of trust
- Define the decision-making process

School-community collaboration requires patience, effort, and new perspectives about what is important in teaching and learning. Cross-agency collaboration creates multiple opportunities for learning and enhances the diversity of experiences for students with disabilities. It utilizes and exploits the informal curriculum of the community. The results will be longer-term, consistent, and community-developed educational supports for student success. The challenges may be great, but there are resources in educators' own backyards that will benefit students.

Home-School-Community Collaboration

Schools, families, and communities are overlapping spheres of influence on children's learning (Epstein, 1995). Much of what students learn comes from the experiences, associations, and interactions they have outside and beyond scheduled school activities. This secondary curriculum may be a dominant part of any student's life (Barbour & Barbour, 2001), especially when traditional or formal school curricula are not compatible with the special needs of many students. Community settings offer many alternative therapies or learning environments that promote socialization, language, and cognitive and physical development. Nonschool facilities in the community provide the added component of parental involvement, and linkages to the community and to other institutions in the community. This "curriculum of the community" (Barbour & Barbour, 2001) has great potential for enhancing the social networks of students and families, inculcating natural resources into the education of students, and providing services such as entertainment, recreation, and informal education. In addition, this informal curriculum enables the involvement and collaboration of several organizations within a community (Barbour & Barbour, 2001).

Because family-school-community partnerships are often more difficult with parents of students who have disabilities (Plunkett, 1997), educational consultants must consider the community an integral part of the preparation of all students for a successful adult life. Family-friendly educational programs should contain nonschool elements.

It is a challenge for educators to form new paradigms that decompartmentalize services for students with special needs. In the past Guthrie and Guthrie (1991) stated that service providers must step outside the boundaries of their job descriptions on occasion to do what needs to be done for students. They suggested going to community centers, schools, and homes, devoting more time than usual to families and outside resources. These functions are compatible with the processes and content familiar to those in school consultation roles. Guthrie and Guthrie warned against "all-talk, no action" posture, excessive jargon, and failure to follow up. These points are readily recognizable to school consultants, who have developed skills in avoiding such pitfalls.

"If you think in-school and co-teacher consultation is challenging, wait until you try interagency collaboration!" says one experienced educational consultant. Turf issues, lack of clarity on fiscal responsibilities, and shared personnel, facilities, and equipment agreements are among the barriers to successful interagency collaboration. On the other hand, many educators have had experience with interagency collaboration while working with Interagency Coordinating Councils, as established under Part H of P.L. 99-457 (the Handicapped Infant and Toddler Program), and with Community Transition Councils, as established under P.L. 101-476. Others have valuable experience working with other human service agencies in developing programs such as "one-stop shopping" and "wrap-around" programs. These collaborative experiences, difficult though they may have been, will serve participants well as they assume new roles in interagency collaboration.

As a process, collaboration is a means to an end rather than an end in itself. The desired end is to engender more effective educational outcomes for students with special needs. Schools are not alone in their responsibility for removing barriers that keep students from succeeding in the adult world. Personnel in mental health, employment and training, child development, recreation, health, and welfare services, as well as education, have a vital interest in promoting school success for all children. (See Figure 11.4.)

Many families of children with special needs face a multitude of problems and require services beyond the school environment. The reality is that no one agency can provide all necessary services for children with disabilities and their families. Collaborative strategies can help provide better services to families who are part of several human service systems, and keep children and families from falling through the cracks by ensuring that they receive needed services.

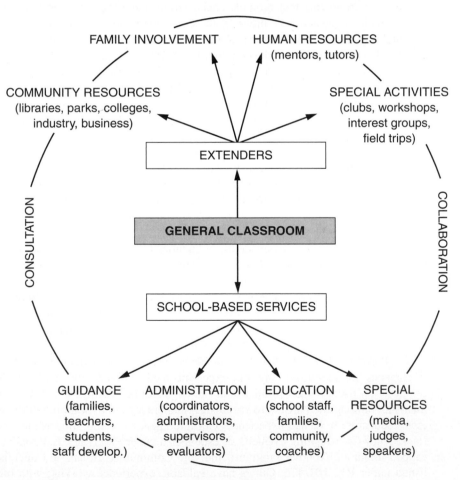

FIGURE 11.4   School-Based Extenders and Services

All in all, when personnel within various systems collaborate, they avoid service duplication, reduce the total cost of services, ensure fewer gaps in services, minimize conflict, and clarify responsibility. Interagency collaboration includes three elements (Bruner, 1991):

1. Jointly developing and agreeing to a set of common goals and directions
2. Sharing responsibility for obtaining the goals
3. Working together to achieve the goals, using the expertise of each collaborator

Identifying and implementing collaborative strategies and evaluating their impact can be challenging. The ultimate goal is ensuring the future success of students with special needs by eliminating or reducing difficulties that place them at risk—infant mortality, delinquency, violence such as school shootings and bomb threats, youth unemployment, child abuse and neglect, drug involvement, suicide, mental illness, and poverty. Interagency collaboration is not a quick fix. It is time-consuming and process-intensive. It takes commitment and flexibility to discover new roles and relationships. These new roles and responsibilities utilize collaborative skills that require wide knowledge and much practice.

SCENARIO 11.B

An informal conversation is taking place at City Hall before the monthly meeting of the City Council. Several council members and visiting citizens, including some school personnel, are talking about recent vandalism and several arrests that have occurred near their community.

Mr. Alvarez (Middle School Teacher):   You know, I've been teaching for many years, and I remember when our main discipline problems in schools were running in the halls and talking without permission. Today our problems are everything from drug abuse, sexual harassment, verbal abuse, to assault and destruction of property.

Ms. Cohen (Mother of an Elementary School Student):   Yes, I hear you loud and clear. I strongly believe that violence in schools and communities undermines our children's physical and mental health, and their readiness to learn. Furthermore, the incidence of young suicides across our nation is especially troubling.

Mr. Adamson (Council Member):   The pressure for safe and orderly schools is strong. I read in the latest national poll on public perceptions of schools that parents and community members name school safety as one of their top concerns.

Ms. Dinkens (High School Assistant Principal):   I can tell you this, teachers have concerns about the safety of their students and themselves right in their own classrooms.

Ms. Cohen: We need to have some community policies that help school officials set strong guidelines against violence and destruction, not to mention disruption of learning.

Mr. Adamson: Yes, absolutely. Then we all need to work together as a community and figure out some strategies for making this area as safe and healthy and productive a school environment as we can. Schools are our country's lifeblood and the showcases for communities. We want our community to shine so others will want to live here, and work and have businesses and raise their families here.

Schools are often the brokers and bridges for interagency collaborations aimed at eliminating threats in the school setting. In this collaborative process, all school personnel, parents, students, and community members must work together to adopt violence prevention measures that help make schools safe learning environments and communities safe places to live. These groups can work together in designing locally appropriate crisis intervention programs to be implemented in the unfortunate event that violent and destructive acts do occur.

Collaborative consultants are often called on to provide leadership for these activities. This approach requires ongoing dialogue among teachers, school counselors, administrators, related services personnel, community leaders, social workers, medical personnel, local justice officials, families, students, and other stakeholders in the educational process. Ongoing, proactive attempts to reach out to parents and community members will help make this collaboration successful. Positive parent and community relationships, and excellent communication and problem-solving skills are essential for prevention of violence and for crisis management. One effective organization for such tasks is a school advisory council. The council should meet regularly to discuss *big* issues, not mundane matters, that involve everyone in the community, even if they do not currently have children in school or never had children in school. After all, those with no children in school are the group that pays the most school taxes and typically does so without reservation because they value highly the presence of good schools in their communities.

Educators have a variety of resources available for collaborative discussions and planning related to school safety issues. The National Youth Violence Prevention Resource Center (www.safeyouth.org) and the Center for the Prevention of School Violence (www.ncdjjdp.org) have information and programs. Informative resources for schools, parents, and community members can be found at www.keepschoolssafe.org and others will appear when key words such as school violence, bullying, vandalism committed by teenagers, teen suicide, drugs in schools, and other similar terms are searched online.

Sources for Assistance

Every community, large or small, urban or rural, accessible or isolated, wealthy or poor, has agencies and potential resources that can contribute meaningfully to learning programs for special needs of children and adolescents. The consulting teacher will find it helpful to develop a directory of referral agencies, with addresses and phone numbers, to have available for consultations and staffings. As one example, a consulting teacher in a midsize town in the Midwest prepared a referral directory containing more than 100 sources of assistance. Some were national sources which could be called toll-free, such as the Missing Children's Network. Others were state-level agencies, such as the Families Together agency. Still others were county agencies, such as the County Family Planning Clinic. But within this average town, many sources were available "just down the street," including a crisis center and a community theater.

Another special education teacher in a large town with a land-grant university found more than 200 agencies, from Alcoholics Anonymous and LDA (Learning Disabilities Association of America) to a Living with Cancer group and MADD (Mothers Against Drunk Driving), to the World Friendship Organization and a Young Mom's group.

Resourceful consultants will involve personnel regularly from a variety of agencies to collaborate in planning and implementing student programs that provide assistance for students' special needs.

■ ■ ■ ■ ■ ▬▬▬▬▬▬▬▬▬▬▬▬▬▬▬▬▬▬▬▬▬▬▬▬▬▬▬▬▬▬▬▬▬

APPLICATION 11.2
SEARCHING FOR RESOURCES

Have a personal scavenger hunt, or go with a small group of your classmates or colleagues, to discover new resources for student and adult learning. Find people, places, and things that can enhance special abilities and serve special needs. As you do this, if someone asks what you are doing, explain and then engage them in conversation about education. Invite them to be advocates and collaborators in enterprises that will help students succeed in school.

COLLABORATION FOR TRANSITION SERVICES

Transition is an umbrella term for activities and opportunities that prepare students for significant changes in their lives. It can be described as the process of moving from one service delivery system to another (Fowler, Donegan, Lueke, Hadden, & Phillips, 2000). Such movements include transition into preschool and out to kindergarten, transition from elementary to junior high or middle school and junior high to high school, and transition from high school to work or postsecondary education (*CEC Today,* 1997).

Requirements for transition were modified by IDEA 1997. The IDEA amendments called for inclusion of a statement in the student's IEP by age fourteen that focuses on courses of study such as vocational education, and also a statement that the student has been informed of legal rights that transfer to the student when reaching the age of majority. Transition services are to be a coordinated set of activities including instruction, related services, community experiences, employment, and adult living objectives; therefore, extensive interagency collaboration is necessary. Schools now are responsible for generating Individual Transition Plans (ITPs) to assess students' career interests and help them focus on career possibilities. Community support is given through vocational transition liaisons, job coaching, work awareness classes, and school employment.

Transition from Early Childhood to Kindergarten

Early intervention programs for infants and toddlers with disabilities proliferated following the early childhood legislation. Parents and other caregivers outside the school now play a more integral part in the education and well-being of these children. Disabilities of children in the early intervention programs tend to be severe; therefore, services of specialists from several disciplines are essential. Families have an integral part in the therapy through home-based programs. In these programs, therapists go into the homes to provide stimulation for the children, and guidance and instruction for the parents. Staff and parents are in collaboration with all available resources, including health and medical personnel, social services personnel, public school personnel, and community resources such as preschool and day care centers. The programs typically are year-round, not nine-month programs.

Federal legislation (P.L. 102-119) requires that states develop interagency agreements to address roles and responsibilities for transition from early intervention services to preschool services and to provide guidance for local communities through specification of state level responsibilities (Fowler et al., 2000). Preparation of such agreements is a daunting task, requiring skillful collaboration by team members. Issues to be dealt with include transmission of information from one agency to another, preparation of child and family for services, provision of services in least restrictive environments, service delivery for children who turn three late in the school year or during the summer, use of Individualized Family Services Plans (IFSPs), and consideration of the way eligibility for services is determined (Fowler et al., 2000). The interagency agreement and its implementation should be monitored and evaluated on a regular basis.

Transition from the preschool settings to kindergarten school programs also calls for strong, continuous efforts in collaborative school consultation. Though formal programs such as Head Start and Follow Through for young children have been successful in and of themselves, as stated earlier P.L. 99-457 reaches far beyond classroom interventions. Preschool teachers should identify essential skills needed in the local kindergarten in order to prepare children for that setting (Beckhoff & Bender, 1989; Salisbury & Vincent, 1990). Their contributions to elementary school programs are invaluable for getting new kindergarten students off to a successful start. A search of Internet sources of information, and state departments of education in particular, can apprise families and early education teachers of current practices in interagency coordination—for example, interagency agreements, transition agreements, and models for preschool-focused partnerships.

Transition from Middle School to High School

Transition services for students should begin much earlier than high school level. The most pressing need for the preteen is to make a comfortable move from elementary school to the very different middle school climate and then to high school. If support systems are not in place for students with disabilities at these important junctures, students may drop out, become alienated, or experience failure in school (Council for Exceptional Children, 1997). Career awareness, social skills, money management skills, involvement in extracurricular activities, and development of portfolios are examples of directions that students in intermediate and middle school grades can take to prepare for setting their life goals. Assessment of student abilities and needs is key to successful transition, with careful data collection a vital part of that process. The assessments should be authentic in kind and scope, replicating the school-based and work-related challenges that students will encounter as they go through life.

A project by the National Association of Secondary School Principals, Phi Delta Kappa International, and the Lumina Foundation for Education to collect opinions of middle school students about their current school activities and their preparation for success in high school and college showed that the students were optimistic and positive but not necessarily attuned to the reality of American high schools (Bushaw, 2007). The Harris Poll Online database system was used in early 2007 to poll U.S. residents in grades 7 or 8 with weighting of gender, grade level, race/ethnicity, parents' highest level of education, geographic region, and urbanicity to align the sample with population proportions. Two major areas of their overestimation were confidence about graduating from high school (93% certain, compared with actual current rate of 83%) and confidence that they would attend college (92% certain, compared with 66% current rate).

Researchers for this study suspected that something must not be right in high schools, but when they asked questions, the discrepancy was explained as if somehow the students were to blame—"not ready," "not college material," and "having unrealistic goals." The researchers concluded that schools are operating on a "sort and select" mission. They urged that this mission be replaced with a goal of preparing *all* (emphasis added) students for postsecondary opportunities that are linked to their interests. The responses of polled students, when asked how much information they had about how to choose high school courses that prepare them to attend college, showed that 68 percent had "some or none." Only 11 percent had "a great deal." It does not take a giant leap of imagination to conclude where students with disabilities fit into this scene. Several suggestions by researchers can be summarized here as:

- Eliminating the sink-or-swim transition from middle school to high school, with the ninth grade in particular being the key link in the schoolchain where students begin to disengage
- Partnering with parents and caregivers to make more information available about postsecondary options, beginning in middle school
- Working to reduce financial burdens on low-income students who would attend and complete college
- Helping students better understand their interests and relate them to a program of study
- Enlarging perceptions of college to include community college, part-time study, work combined with study in the career environment, and study programs offered through distance learning

Transition from Secondary School to Postsecondary Opportunities

At the opposite end of the continuum from early childhood needs and continuing beyond those of the middle school child are the needs of students leaving school to enter the world of work and adult living. Heightened awareness of this important transition period for young people with disabilities grew in the 1980s, when program goals for serving students with disabilities were built on education services that could help them lead meaningful and productive lives. One of the realities was that no one parent, teacher, or school counselor could adequately provide all the necessary assistance. All school professionals and agencies with services for the welfare of students need to be involved in partnerships and team efforts to assist the student and the family.

As in transition from middle school to high school, comprehensive assessment of student interests and needs is vital. Curriculum and instructional strategies should include a variety of job explorations, along with skills needed to succeed in those areas of work and to enjoy that work. In model programs, students spend part of their day on academic subjects and the rest of the day at work sites (*CEC Today,* 1997). Some even allow students to earn academic credits at the work site. The recommendations of the NASSP/PKD/Lumina study group described in the previous section (Bushaw, 2007) could apply here.

Students with disabilities who plan to attend a college or university need transition services. They might visit campuses, or take precollege courses. Perhaps most important of all is that they be introduced to sources of assistance on campus to whom they can go for help in choosing appropriate classes and arranging for accommodations and modifications with their instructors.

Co-educators must be vigilant in assessing the best opportunities for their students with disabilities and orienting them to the right kind and amount of assistance that will enable them to be independent, productive, and full of self-confidence and strong self-esteem. They also must advocate for the legislative initiatives and funding that attend to the academic and social needs of preschool, school-age, and postsecondary students in school contexts.

TECHNOLOGY IN COLLABORATIVE SCHOOL ENVIRONMENTS

Collaborating educators in the twenty-first century have technology tools that educators in years past could not even envision, much less find and use. In 1990 many people had never heard of the Internet (Perkins-Gough, Snyder, & Licciardi, 2004); in 1993 fewer than 200 Web sites existed (Kantor, 2003). But by 2001 there were 30 million Web sites around the globe (Wright, 2002).

Many new forms of professional communities are developing that encourage interactions to take place on the Internet (Cummings, 2001; Cummings, Harrison, Dawson, Short, Gorin, & Palomares, 2004). New tools make electronic interfacing with colleagues possible asynchronously rather than face-to-face and at the same point in time. They reduce the tedium of many clerical tasks required of teachers. This increases available time for educators and energy for engaging in collaboration and co-teaching. An important but often overlooked benefit is being able to allot more school time for direct services to students.

Too many schools, however, are still not technologically up-to-date. Peck and Dorricott (1994) declared that business builds electronic highways while education creates electronic dirt roads. Indeed, the process for some districts is quite slow. Professional journals revisit this concern periodically, and some school districts have surged ahead to construct their own technology highways. But others lag behind due to lack of funds, lassitude about the issue, or the reality of location where one home in a rural area has a high-speed connection and the next home down the road must still use dial-up access. One umbrella question remains to be addressed in depth, Does state-of-the-art technology improve education? With the right answers to that question, stronger efforts will most likely be directed to making sophisticated technology for learning available to all schools.

Technology for Managing Educational Responsibilities

In the broad scope of teaching, learning, relating to others, and providing accountability for goals accomplished, computers and other forms of technology can facilitate:

- Access of information from online sources
- Software for handling forms such as IEPs, observation sheets, and records
- Programs and spreadsheets for data analysis and recording of student work
- Files for monitoring student progress and grades
- Curriculum applications for students such as drill-and-practice programs, tutorial programs, simulations, and instructional games
- Mechanisms for interacting with colleagues through chat rooms, e-Forums, and blogging
- Systems for communication with co-educators and families of students by e-mail, web-based grade book and student-information management systems
- Programs to aid with details such as word processing, spell checking, calculations of scores and grades, and statistical treatment of measurements
- Programs for record-keeping and efficient modification of lesson plans and assessment devices and storage for them
- Records of calendars, appointments, and other managerial activities
- Promotional and informational material for students and parents via web pages
- Wireless broadband Internet connections that allow access to the Web from virtually any location
- Digital cameras, recorders, and audio-listening supports for audio files such as podcasts and other digital audio applications such as e-books
- Social-networking tools that link and motivate students, such as MySpace and Facebook

Much more undoubtedly will be added to this list in future years as asynchronous communications become conventional practice for all educators and students. Technology experts describe even more innovations such as monitor-and-control systems, videoconferencing capabilities, and download and transmission of PowerPoint presentations. Such is the world that today's children live in, and educators must ensure that students with disabilities are prepared for their future. Many children and adolescents with learning and social differences have been helped with various types of technology during their preschool and school years. Others have contributed to the development of technology, with the stories of their amazing innovation and entrepreneurship told and retold in the media.

That said, however, school personnel know that technology as it is today, does not come without qualifications and restrictions, especially in the area of special education. It must be used wisely with keen attention to ethics and etiquette (in technology parlance called "netiquette"). Groundwork must be laid with continuous monitoring for structuring the ways in which technology will be used in schools. Needs and concerns include:

- Anxiety among some teachers over using computers and other devices, especially if their generation did not grow up with modern technology and they are still in a very steep learning curve with the devices that their students are so comfortable and proficient in using
- Strong need for every school district to have not only a technology specialist on staff, but an Internet Use Committee with wide representation across staff

FIGURE 11.5   "I need tech support!"

- Selection of appropriate hardware and well-proven software for both teachers and students
- Sufficient budget allocation for technology support *after* the hardware and software are acquired, because there *will* be bugs and glitches from time to time and nothing is more useless and frustrating than equipment that is "down" (See Figure 11.5.)
- Awareness of parents about the nature and purposes of technology being used and how they can be involved (one example being the monitoring of homework or progress in class work)
- Rigorous evaluation of software for suitability and practicality
- Training for staff who are not comfortable with the technology used in their contexts, and for all staff when new systems are acquired
- Last, but first in importance and particularly in special education situations, strict adherence to confidentiality and privacy issues

Above all, in the education profession as in the medical profession, the proposed technology must first do no harm. Issues to be studied very seriously by school personnel involve confidentiality of information, assurance of privacy, vigilance in constructing firewalls to shut out pornography and profanity, adherence to copyrights and intellectual property rights, fair use in regard to disability, gender, and socioeconomic level, and careful attention to feelings of inadequacy and reluctance by some educators. In regard to the latter, the younger generations of educators have strengths in using technology that can be a mentoring asset for less able veteran teachers who just might become their technology mentees. Young novice teachers who grew up using technology can be another source of help. When they assist veteran teachers with technology, positive ripple effects can promote even richer collaborations.

■ ■ ■ ■ ■

APPLICATION 11.3
SHOPPING CARTS OF HELPFUL TECHNOLOGY

Imagine you are online and looking for some new technology tools. Scan the following merchandise and check Yes for those you are familiar with and No those you know little or nothing about. Then place an asterisk (*) after any you would like to learn more about, and circle those you would like to have. Finally, what might be your next steps for your asterisked and circled items?

	Yes	No
e-mail		
web page construction		
e-Forums		
chat room (MUD, MOO)		
text messaging		
instant messaging		
podcasting		
listservs		
electronic bulletin board		
webcam		
hypertext		
PowerPoint		
videoconferencing		
newsgroup		
webcast		
web log		
wiki		
video streaming		
voice recognition software		
social networking		
virtual education		
others?		

Twenty Uses for Technology to Organize and Collaborate

Interactive teams that reach across organizational boundaries use technologies such as electronic mail, broadcast fax, teleconferencing, and videoconferencing to communicate with one another frequently and quickly. Digital pagers and cellular phones make team members accessible regardless of their location. Information is gathered rapidly and exchanged through databases and electronic networks or listservs.

Consider one of the most the common stumbling blocks to collaboration—the need for time. Computers and other technologies can be major time-savers:

1. *Messages.* Can be sent at the convenience of one party and others read and respond to them at their convenience.

2. *Databases and information on student progress.* Stored in a file-server and accessed by any team member at a convenient time.

3. *Notes.* Added on by team members to keep everyone on the team apprised of information or items of concern.

4. *Computer adaptation of assignments.* Developed by teachers or resource personnel for meeting students' needs.

5. *Copies of special instructions or worksheets.* Sent by a consultant in one building to a teacher in another place by fax. With electronic networks, a consultant prepares an adapted lesson or test and sends it to the classroom where needed. The adapted lesson or test is "waiting" for the teacher or students in the classroom to access at the appropriate time without requiring the presence of the consultant. Conversely, a student prepares a product in the classroom and sends it to the collaborating consultant for review and feedback. The network allows monitoring of student work and makes feedback to the student more timely.

6. *Facilitation of interaction among consultants, co-teachers, and team members.* In some systems users work simultaneously with the same program to develop a lesson plan, with each team member accessing the work of others and making changes or adding notes, much as wikis work on the Internet.

7. *Scheduling/appointment calendar.* Appointments and other commitments are entered into the computer calendar. One special advantage is the way the program can handle recurring appointments. For example, if a team planning meeting is scheduled for Friday afternoons at 2:00, the consultant can enter that information; the program will automatically write in meeting reminders on the appropriate dates. Another advantage is the ability to view and print out daily, weekly, or monthly calendars to be shared through the network if desired. Sharing privileges can be customized to give one or many individuals the right to view or schedule appointments for all or part of a colleague's calendar. Personal digital assistants (PDAs) and smartphones have made the work of many busy educators more efficient and less stressful. Thanks to online software that is available for scheduling meetings, finding dates and times and scheduling meetings between several parties becomes automatic and less labor intensive for busy consultants and teachers.

8. *Information centers.* Consultants, teachers, and students are connected to large host information systems that offer a variety of options ranging from electronic listservs to conferencing capabilities. Potential uses for consultants and teachers include library searches and information bulletins relating to special needs of students with disabilities. Special listservs can be created to address unique audiences. It is even possible to create local listservs that are used by teachers in a single building or school district. A consultant or teacher might consider developing such a bulletin board where ideas that have worked in other classrooms are shared with fellow teachers and consultants.

9. *Managing student records.* Databases can organize large amounts of information into electronic "filing cabinets." They allow great flexibility in sorting and retrieving data. For example, a consultant might set up a database file on a caseload of students with each individual record containing a separate entry for categories selected, such as name, address, phone, age, grade, type of disability, family members' name(s), address, and phone number. Once the format is established, the consultant or an assistant enters the information for each record. It then can be searched and sorted for different types of reports. This search-and-sort capability gives databases flexibility, an advantage over traditional paper filing systems. Confidentiality of data is, of course, essential.

10. *Recording student grades.* Programs allow teachers to enter students' scores, determine the weight of each assignment or quiz, and set standards for assigning grades. Final grades can be computed automatically. Many programs provide options for printing class rosters, grade reports by student or by assignment, and summary statistics and graphs. If special software is not available to a teacher or consultant, a standard spreadsheet can be used to accomplish many of these purposes. Many schools now use web-based grade books and student information systems, making it possible for parents and special education teachers to monitor student progress in general education courses and keep up with the students' grades and any missing work.

11. *Developing draft IEPs.* Software programs for producing IEPs have been developed and are available commercially. These programs are special types of databases tailored to the needs of special education professionals. The programs usually contain an IEP template and a collection of suggested annual goals and short-term objectives. Although computerized availability of goals and objectives can alleviate much drudgery of writing IEPs, it is also the source of most criticism about computerized IEPs. Critics argue that goals and objectives provided in the software are often isolated skills that are not relevant to the individual student or consistent with the local school curriculum. However, the IEP team can develop others if they wish. Some systems enable users to generate administrative reports and notices to teachers and parents. Margolis and Free (2001) note that computerized IEPs have been challenged successfully in court when they failed to individualize education to meet the student's special needs. They recommend that computerized IEP programs have three design features: efficiency and consistency; adherence to the key legal requirement that each child's IEP be personalized for the student's needs; and record-keeping for the IEP content that will satisfy requirements for federal and state reports. They recommend further that school personnel be trained adequately in preparing the computerized IEP.

12. *Managing assessment and evaluation data.* Data can be stored in database or spreadsheet applications and readily summarized in various formats, including meaningful graphs and charts. However, when educators store confidential information in computers, *careful steps must be taken to protect confidentiality of student information.* This issue is a big concern if data are to be shared with team members by way of computer networks. Computer technicians should be consulted to determine the safest and most efficient ways to make files secure.

13. *Test scoring.* Many test developers provide software programs to help educators administer tests and scoring probes to monitor student progress. The results can be graphed over time to compare progress with expected rate of improvement. The programs also analyze results and make recommendations about possible changes in instruction. Graphing of student data can be enhanced and simplified for interpretation with online programs such as ChartDog that set up graphs based on information provided by the teacher and then creates aim lines and data-based decision-making information to be viewed online or printed out for student files.

14. *Compiling portfolios.* Portfolios are popular among teachers in some school contexts. But organizing and maintaining portfolio information can be very time-consuming and space-guzzling. Products developed on the computer are easily filed. Other products and information can be scanned into the computer to be added to the portfolio. Many interesting possibilities exist for the innovative educator and students.

15. *Documenting consultations and collaborations.* Information is kept in electronic databases rather than paper-and-pencil format. It can be searched and sorted in various ways to provide valuable information for making decisions about students and collaboration processes. For example, if one wanted to know how many times a certain consultant or service provider worked with a student during the year, the data could be sorted to have all the entries for the service provider appearing together. Later, if one wanted to know who provided services on a particular date, the information could be sorted by the date field. Having a record of these activities helps validate the need for time and places to consult and collaborate. Communication between teachers and paraeducators can also be facilitated easily and captured through these electronic formats.

16. *Adapting materials and textbooks.* A work page may have too many items for students with attention deficit disorders to complete in one setting, or graphic material might distract students from relevant stimuli. The worksheet can be scanned into the graphics program and the "cut and paste" function of the program used to eliminate portions that are distracting or too difficult. Remaining portions are rearranged as needed and the "new" worksheet is printed out. This allows personalized adaptations for many students in a relatively short amount of time. A consultant might scan a teacher-made test, for example, and make adaptations as needed, such as enlarged print or more space between items. Even better, if a classroom teacher prepares the test on the computer, the file can be sent to consultants or co-teachers to adapt. Software programs are available for writing tests. Test banks often accompany classroom texts. Some software can produce several types of tests—matching, true-false, completion, and multiple-choice. When questions have been keyed into the program, they can be easily transferred from one format to another. Other software can create paper-and-pencil tests or quizzes that students take at the computer.

17. *Preparing reports and other written products.* Word processors and desktop publishing programs are a must for busy consultants and other team members. Once text has been entered in a word processor, it can be changed easily, edited, added to, modified, or reformatted. This capability is particularly useful for routine writing such as consultation logs, letters to parents, memos to other team members, assessment reports, newsletters, and classroom materials with adaptations made for specific students with disabilities.

18. *Computer contact between teachers and families.* Home educators and school educators can be in daily or weekly communication to monitor homework, assign work missed when a student is ill, report grades, and share classroom events that involve the student.

Many schools, especially at the high school level, have school-home connections so that parents are involved.

19. *Access to professional clearinghouses.* For example, the federal government funds a variety of clearinghouses that deal with specific topics, such as delinquency, drug use, child abuse, online libraries, student support groups, and much more. Putting key words or phrases into search engines such as Google, Yahoo!, and others can open up vistas of information for people who need assistance.

20. *Other innovations by resourceful teachers.* It is likely that every day a new way is found to use technology for working smarter, not harder, in addressing special needs of students.

Anticipated and Unexpected Effects of Technology

Technology can obviously save teachers time and labor, but there are many teaching responsibilities that involve working with people directly, and technology cannot take the place of face-to-face interactions with people. Consider the frustrations we all experience when waiting and slogging through and waiting some more for countless automated phone prompts to play themselves out when what we need is to be in touch with a real person. Teachers value having immediate and realistically helpful teaching and management tools even if those tools are low-tech and not quite state of the art. These include phones in every classroom; multiple fax machines to eliminate waits; automatic paper grading for uniform assignments in subjects like spelling and arithmetic; video- and teleconferencing capability to other schools; databases of student records to look up previous schools, grades, and scores; and a database of educational specialists organized by area of expertise with whom to confer for information and ideas.

It would be helpful if software designers sympathetic to the harried schedules and multiple responsibilities of school personnel could find ways to automate the most tedious chores in teaching and allow more time for "peoplework," not paperwork, to interact as collaborative consultants and co-teachers. Teachers do not feel that they must have the newest, most expensive technology outfit in the store; they simply want tools that help them work smarter and more efficiently, not harder and less effectively. They want technology to complement curriculum. Many are distressed when fancy computer labs replace art rooms and music teachers. They grimace when computers arrive with no accompanying technical support and no budget allocation for repairs and upgrades. It is counterproductive to have expensive machines stand idle in schools when they go "down" and help is not available to start them back up.

Teachers are no different from others who work in the digital-information-laden workplace. They can easily become paralyzed with what Hurst (2007) calls bit-literacy overload. It is important for consultants to know how to manage efficiently and effectively the ever-increasing amount of electronic data flowing in and out of their workplaces through their e-mail boxes, cell phones, web browsers, and more. The consultant can easily become a slave of the technology rather than its master using it in a productive way. (See Figure 11.6.)

Collaborative consulting teachers can provide leadership in schools to ensure effective use of technology for professional purposes and to accommodate the needs of students with disabilities in general classrooms in three important ways by:

1. Participating in schoolwide planning groups to determine what technology would be most useful for their school context

FIGURE 11.6   Technology is for working smarter, not harder

2. Being a role model in using technology collaboratively and productively
3. Engaging in activities that use technology collaboratively when possible

As one can see from the wide array of technology applications discussed in the pre-ceding pages, there are many decisions to make about what, when, where, and how to invest in emerging technology. Thoughtful planning and investment decisions are needed to ensure that team members have the right technologies in their schools for management and instructional purposes.

COLLABORATING ON GRANT PROPOSALS FOR EXTERNAL FUNDING

One of the most welcomed resources that school personnel can deliver is a funded grant proposal. Grant money is available from a wide variety of sources, including the federal government, state governments, private donations, foundations, local businesses, local clubs and organizations, donations to fund-raising activities, and corporations. These sources have programs and projects in mind that fit their philosophies and goals. They set their own procedures, which must be followed explicitly by entrants if they wish to be in the running to receive the grant.

Several benefits can result from submitting a collaborative grant proposal. The first is the collaboration experience gained by the team regardless of whether the grant proposal is funded. Few significant proposals are developed in these times that do not include a num-ber of colleagues interacting to conceptualize and develop the plan, and then carry out the project after it is funded. Some people have major roles and others serve in minor ways, but all can participate and ultimately profit in tangible and intangible ways. Another benefit is the collection of resources and support needed to meet the goals of the grant. When multiple resources are targeted and letters of support are generated, more people become involved as supporters of innovative school programs.

When a grant proposal is funded, the benefits soar. Money and resources become available for carrying out projects that were only dreams or wishes before funding. This has an energizing, morale-boosting effect that reverberates throughout a school system. The amounts of money do not need to be sizable for these positive outcomes to be realized. Some of the most invigorating projects have resulted from relatively small grant funds. The projects with highest payoffs are those that generate ripple effects well beyond the funded grant.

School consultants and collaborators, particularly those who have significant professional development responsibilities, are in ideal positions to seek grant funds. Even larger districts that employ grant writers can use the participation of these personnel productively. School districts should designate individuals to be trained in grant-seeking techniques, for there are some important procedures that are vital to success of the endeavor: (1) identifying a need; (2) targeting a funding source; and (3) preparing the proposal using the helpful ten-step procedure.

Identifying a Need.   Successful proposals emanate from an identified need. A good match must be found between that need and the philosophy and goals of an appropriate funding source. The proposed project may be wonderful, and the benefits for students very promising, but if it does not address the interests of the potential donor, it will be rejected.

Funding Sources.   Two general sources of funding are available—public agencies and private foundations. Most companies give some money away as part of their tax structure; the grant developer's challenge is convincing companies to give part of it to them (Zimet, 1993). Experts in grant production advise that requirements for proposals are somewhat different between public and private sources, so they must be studied carefully.

Preparing the Proposal.   Development of a proposal begins with the idea for the project and continues through two phases: (1) planning; and (2) preparation. The most productive strategy is to spend about 80 percent of time and energy on planning the project, and the remaining 20 percent on writing the proposal. Those who switch these priorities often end up with weak projects that are hard to carry out even if funded.

The proposal must be prepared carefully and correctly according to the guidelines given, and submitted on time. Grant writing is a combination of technical writing and creative writing (Zimet, 1993). Three mistakes must be avoided at all costs and proposal writers should check for them often: (1) failure to read instructions carefully; (2) failure to match grant goals with funding sources; and (3) missing deadlines.

Proposal preparation is hard work and astute grant writers follow these basic steps to avoid major pitfalls. They:

1. *Identify a need.* What is the problem that stems from that need? Is it potentially fundable? For example, high-priority topics for successful grant proposals in the mid-1990s included gangs, violence, drugs, world-class standards, teachers for providing education to meet those standards, math and science education, teen pregnancy, inclusion, integrated curriculum, diversity, and computer literacy for both young people and adults. Priorities shift as other issues surface to capture public attention and funding agencies' interests.

2. *Explore the research base* for information about the identified need. Watch for trends and for connections that link trends and fields.

3. *Get together a team* of productive people. Note the points in Chapter 2 about having a variety of skills and learning styles on the team. Having multiple perspectives and a wide range of competencies will vastly improve the proposal. Teams are particularly helpful for collecting the demographic data required for a properly executed proposal. Also, the more people who are involved in preparing the proposal, the greater the interest generated in the supporting and participating in the project after it is funded.

4. *Identify possible funding sources.* Federal funding sources are listed in the *Federal Register.* Find out if someone in your district has access to this document. If not, suggest that someone be in charge of that, because benefits might prove to be significant.

5. *Obtain the guidelines* for the selected funding source(s). A guidelines packet is called a "request for proposal," or RFP. From this point on, each step of the process carries an admonition—*Read the guidelines*! Read to be sure there is a good fit between your idea and the funding source. Look for the ability of that source to meet your budget request, for directions on how to submit the application, for criteria to be used in evaluating the proposal, and most of all, for the *application deadline.* A proposal, even a superior one, if submitted late, is no proposal at all. Late proposals are the first ones discarded by reviewers. Those that do not follow the guidelines are dismissed next.

6. *Design the project.* As stressed earlier, this phase should take up the major time and energy directed toward the project. Again, read the guidelines thoroughly and often and be keenly aware of the deadline date.

7. *Prepare a budget adequate for the project,* but not "padded." All items should be tied to the activities of the project and the key personnel costs involved. A budget set too low signals poor planning that could undermine the project. Budgets provide for indirect costs (overhead), any cost sharing or subcontracting for services, and, primarily, direct costs of the proposed project—salaries and fringe benefits, equipment, supplies and materials, travel (which is getting quite restrictive with many funding agencies), consultant fees, computer expenses, printing and duplicating, postage and telecommunication, along with other direct costs specific to the focus of the project.

8. *Interagency collaborative support* is a particularly desirable component of most grant projects, and a requirement of some agencies for submitted proposals. Collaboration and obvious teamwork usually result in a much stronger project in this day and age than do solo projects. (Recall the Application on page 32 of Chapter 1 challenging readers to listen for the word *collaborate* in a variety of venues; this is one example.)

9. *Establish contact with the funding agency* and put to good use any suggestions their program officers have for proposal development.

10. *Meet the deadline.* Again, this is the single most important step. If it is not met, the proposal is eliminated and the time, energy, and costs expended in producing it are wasted. Send in the application, with sufficient postage attached, postmarked to arrive on time.

When proposals are received by the funding agency, they are scanned for ten or twelve key elements, with the first four or five receiving the most attention (Shanteau, 1997):

1. *Identity.* Are the persons submitting well known to the agency?
2. *Topic.* Is it an appropriate topic for the program?
3. *Funding level.* Is the requested amount within the guidelines?
4. *Duration.* Is it within acceptable time limits?
5. *Plan.* What is the approach?
6. *Procedure.* What procedures will be used?
7. *References.* Who is cited, and in what related fields?
8. *Identity of the developer.* What is the background?
9. *Budget.* Do the categories and amounts make sense?
10. *Consultants.* Who are they, and do they add to the team?
11. *Format.* Does the proposal meet requirements?
12. *Thoroughness.* Is anything missing?

If a proposal is not funded, the developer(s) should ask to receive the reviews. Reading reviewer comments is a form of professional development and can help make any next attempt more productive. If the review marks were good, but not quite good enough for the proposal to be selected, the proposal might be revised or modified and resubmitted. Proposals that are not funded should not be cast aside in a spirit of disillusionment, but critiqued thoroughly for possible revision and resubmission.

Proposals are funded because of:

- The benefits they can deliver to a targeted population
- The uniqueness of the proposal if it is educationally sound
- A strong case for local need, often underscored by effort to help with funding
- Collaborative efforts exemplified in teamwork and networking with others
- The potential for ripple effects to other school contexts
- Strong evaluation plans and methods
- Justifiable and reasonable budget projections

When proposals are funded, grant recipients often find that they become more and more successful with future applications. It appears to be a phenomenon of "the rich getting richer," but there is a logic to this. The applicants have become more adept at preparing the proposals, and even more meaningfully, funding agencies believe that success of well-designed, funded projects will breed success for their contributed funds as well.

In summary, the ingredients for successful pursuit of external funds are an innovative idea, a team of qualified individuals, a close fit with the funding source, and a well-written, persuasive, potentially contributive proposal. The process does take effort, and some co-educators might want to pool their time and skills with each completing a part of the project.

■ ■ ■ ■ ■ ▬▬▬▬▬▬▬▬▬▬▬▬▬▬▬▬▬▬▬▬▬▬▬▬▬▬▬▬▬▬▬▬▬

APPLICATION 11.4
TRYING OUT THE PROPOSAL PLAN

When you have an idea for a project and begin to prepare a proposal, as you are developing it, try explaining your plan in no more than three minutes to some impartial, objective colleagues or better yet, to some individuals outside the profession whose perspectives you value. If they do not understand it and "catch your enthusiasm" for it, your plan probably needs more work or a different focus. (This activity also works well for developing a term paper theme, a master's thesis, or a doctoral dissertation.)

ETHICS FOR INVOLVING RELATED AND SUPPORT SERVICES PERSONNEL AND TECHNOLOGY IN COLLABORATIVE ACTIVITIES

If co-educators from a broad spectrum of roles are to collaborate successfully as team members in helping students with learning and behavioral differences grow cognitively, emotionally, socially, and physically, they must make every effort to respect and value the talents and skills of their colleagues. Collaborating professionals need to work diligently at understanding the perspectives and preferences of others. Awareness is growing in schools and communities that school systems alone cannot be expected to address learning and behavior problems of millions of children. Many collaborative initiatives are being explored that could expand services to help students learn and grow. Full-service schools, as interagency collaboratives that integrate schools and human services, are one example of these new initiatives (McMahon, Ward, Pruett, Davidson, & Griffith, 2000).

All service agencies have the same goal—making a difference in the world by helping those in the community grow, produce, and lead fulfilling lives. The pathways and means of each agency in helping children and youth, from social worker to music teacher to audiologist to security officer to special education administrator to Big Brother volunteer to school secretary and on and on, are important resources that can be tapped in many ways for students who find it hard to learn and to relate. Keen awareness and understanding of roles will nurture an ethical climate for collaboration. Respect, communication, coordination, cooperation, and consolidation of efforts by those in home, school, and community will make positive differences in students' lives.

The most important steps in interagency collaboration are for each entity, including the family, to know and relate to the work of the others and to understand how that entity can contribute to the welfare of children and youth. Clear, cogent communication is the mechanism through which this will happen. Next should be frank discussions about common goals, turf issues, ownership issues, accountability concerns, and possible agency contributions.

An ethical climate for using the wonders of technology can be described as one of maintaining confidentiality, having respect for intellectual rights, showing ultimate courtesy and consideration, and using good judgment. One blogger wrote about his dismay over the increasing level of rudeness that is evident on some web logs. He attributed it largely to anonymity, but found that could be seriously misleading when he recognized the source of a particularly vitriolic blog as the father of a very good friend.

When educators teach with and about electronically delivered communication and information, they have opportunities to model good practices and instill ethical principles in their students. As for the students, the adage "The child is the father of the man," comes to mind, for often in matters of twenty-first-century technology "the student is the instructor of the teacher." Perhaps teachers and students, in collaboration, can use technology in the richest, most ethical, and ultimately satisfying, manner possible.

TIPS FOR USING RELATED SERVICES PERSONNEL, RESOURCES, AND TECHNOLOGY

1. Don't try to do everything yourself.
2. Develop rapport with media specialists. Give them advance notice of upcoming topics and try not to make too many spur-of-the-moment requests.
3. Make friends with custodians and refrain from making excessive demands on their time and energy.
4. Keep public remarks about colleagues on a positive, professional level. If you must vent, try using a journal at home. Reviewing it now and then may show you the way to improve the situation.
5. Remember special things about the faculty in each school, and start a card file with comments that will be useful in personalizing the interactions. If you find a news article pertaining in a positive way to a colleague or a student, clip it out and send it along with a congratulatory note.
6. Advertise successes, both yours and those of classroom teachers. Sometimes teachers are amazed that a student or a situation has shown *any* progress at all.
7. Do not expect the same levels of involvement and commitment from everyone.
8. Before sending confidential information through electronic networks make sure steps have been taken to keep hackers and other would-be "technology thieves" from gaining access to the information.
9. Constantly monitor your methods of protecting confidential information. Make sure you do not leave information in files accessible to individuals who are not authorized to see them. When you use e-mail, be careful when selecting addresses for mail. It is very easy to accidentally include an unauthorized person. Most breeches of confidentiality result from carelessness of people, and not from lack of technology safeguards.
10. Consult a technology specialist on a regular basis to remain current in the ever-changing uses of technology.

11. Join or form a computer user's group to learn from one another about new uses for computers.
12. Write a proposal that results in resources for sharing among schools.
13. Do not try to "go it alone," but look to colleagues for support and counsel.
14. Remember Ralph Waldo Emerson's words, "It is one of the most beautiful compensations of this life that no man can sincerely try to help another without helping himself."

CHAPTER REVIEW

1. Related-services personnel and support personnel represent a wide variety of fields in education and beyond. They can contribute to learning programs for students with special needs by collaborating as a team with general and special education teachers to address special needs (disabilities and/or high abilities), interests, talents, transition to school or to work, and achievement. Coordination of services and collaboration among school personnel and support personnel is an important responsibility for the collaborative school consultant.

2. Successful schools of the future will engage in interagency collaboration, with collaborators working together to achieve goals for serving all students' needs effectively. Bringing about needed school change requires greater emphasis on collaboration and teamwork. School consultation will be an important tool for coordinating health, social, and educational services to help all students, particularly those with special needs.

3. Transition services help young children and adolescents make smooth adjustments at significant times in their education. The transition from preschool to kindergarten, from elementary to junior high or middle school, from junior high to high school, and ultimately from high school to work or postsecondary education can be eased for students with special needs through collaborative consultation.

4. Home-school-community networks build knowledge and understanding about students' special needs. With schools, families, and agencies working as a team, transition periods are smoother and students benefit from collaboration among a wide array of resources.

5. Telecommunications and electronic networks alter the way consultants and collaborating teachers engage in collaborative activities. Many time-consuming, routine tasks such as organizing schedules, keeping and sorting records, adapting materials, and developing IEPs are done more efficiently with the use of technology. Consultants should provide leadership in schools to ensure effective use of technology for professional uses and to accommodate the needs of students with disabilities in general classrooms by participating in schoolwide planning groups, being a role model in the use of technology, and engaging in collaborative activities when technology is being used. Planning should include applications for professional collaboration as well as instructional and student uses.

6. School personnel should seek out resources such as external funding to enhance school environments and learning programs for special needs. Such money, even if in small amounts, can be a strong motivational force in carrying out a learning project. Goals of the proposed project should match those of the funding source, and proposal writers must adhere stringently to the guidelines and deadline.

TO DO AND THINK ABOUT

1. Develop a plan for ways in which at least three related services and support personnel could work as a team with collaborating teachers to serve students with special needs.

2. Compile a reference list of referral agencies, support groups, and community resources in your area that could be helpful in meeting special needs of students. Preface the list with a brief description of the community where the school is located. Then compare your list with a colleague's list that represents a different type of geographic area.

3. Find out more about several related-services roles that you are not familiar with, for example, the occupational therapist, the audiologist, the social worker, or the school psychologist. What are their responsibilities? What preparation did their roles require? What does a typical day entail for each of them? Interview them and ask their views about consultation, collaboration, and working as a team with teachers.

4. Invite consultants from businesses and other professions to participate in a class discussion or panel presentation to describe their roles and the skills that are required.

5. Survey your school building to determine the extent to which staff members are using up-to-date technology to engage in their collaborative activities. Then think about how you can get involved in this type of collaboration in your building. Or interview a person who uses technology extensively and write a plan for yourself to adapt that use to your work.

6. Use computer software to adapt an instructional material or a test for a student who needs modification.

7. Describe what you would want in a technology-infused inclusive environment if money were no object and training and tech support were available.

ADDITIONAL READINGS AND RESOURCES

Carlson, M. (1995). *Winning grants step by step: Support centers of America's complete workbook for planning, developing, writing successful proposals.* San Francisco: Jossey-Bass.

Denham, A., & Lahm, E. A. (2001). Using technology to construct alternate portfolios of students with moderate and severe disabilities. *Teaching Exceptional Children, 33*(5), 10–17.

In this article the authors provide a plan, with accompanying forms, for performance-based evaluation through alternate portfolios that use a multidisciplinary approach and holistic scoring. The portfolios also serve as instructional organizers for students' daily educational programs and as teaching tools for students to learn self-management, planning, and self-evaluation skills.

Jason, L. A., Pokorny, S. B., Ji, P., & Kunz, C. (2005). Developing community-school-university partnerships to control youth access to tobacco. *Journal of Educational and Psychological Consultation 16*(3), 201–222.

Collaborative partnerships were an important element in putting policies into place to lower rates of tobacco use among youth. Researchers worked collaboratively with police, school officials, and other community leaders to develop preventive interventions.

Knapczyk, D., Rodes, P., Chung, H., & Chapman, C. (1999). Collaborative teacher education in off-campus rural communities. *Rural Special Education Quarterly, 18*(3/4), 36–43.

Provides an overview of a distance education program for special education in rural communities. Details are given about the technology used to support the program and helpful recommendations accompany the details.

McMahon, T. J., Ward, N. L., Pruett, M. K., Davidson, L., & Griffith, E. E. H. (2000). Building full-service schools: Lessons learned in the development of interagency collaboratives. *Journal of Educational and Psychological Consultation, 11*(1), 65–92.

Nelson, G., Amio, J. L., Prilleltensky, I., & Nickels, P. (2000). Partnerships for school and community prevention programs. *Journal of Educational and Psychological Consultation, 11*(1), 121–145.

Community-based, multicomponent approaches rooted in partnerships are described in context of work with immigrant and refugee children and families. Six steps outline the components that can ensure service to children who function within several systems—family, school, neighborhood, culture, media. Steps 4–6 are to define the problem collaboratively, develop it collaboratively, and research and evaluate it collaboratively.

An important factor is having *boundary spanners* (people who have experience in and can understand the worlds of both professionals and citizens who are disadvantaged).

Pianta, R. C., & Kraft-Sayre, M. (2003). *Successful kindergarten transition: Your guide to connecting children, families, and schools.* Baltimore: Paul H. Brookes.

Gives a framework for successful kindergarten transitions, featuring collaborative relationships as a key element in implementing transition practices and policies. Recommendations for a variety of formal and informal evaluation tools are provided.

Short, R. J., & Talley, R. C. (1999). Services integration: An introduction. *Journal of Educational and Psychological Consultation, 10*(3), 193–200.

CHAPTER TWELVE

SYNERGY:
Leadership, Competencies, Ethics

Leadership, Professional Development, and Positive Ripple Effects of Collaborative Consultation and Teamwork

Never in recorded history have so many facets of our world changed so rapidly and dramatically. We do not know for certain how these changes will affect schools and educators, but one thing is clear. Students now at risk with learning and behavior disabilities will be placed in greater jeopardy than ever by the accelerating demands on them to keep pace and measure up in competitive, high-pressure environments.

Teaching and learning are key elements in preparing students to meet such demands. Collaborative school consultation and teamwork among all educators in school, home, and community partnerships will be vital in preparing and enabling all students to be successful learners, self-assured individuals, and productive members of society.

FOCUSING QUESTIONS

1. How is a visionary perspective relevant to student needs and roles of collaborative consultants?

2. How do leadership skills and mentorships influence the effectiveness of collaborative school consultants?

3. How can school administrators and school boards cultivate collaborative arrangements in their school contexts?

4. How do professional development personnel promote collaborative consultation among a broad range of school personnel having multiple roles and assignments?

5. What competencies and ethical guidelines are needed to ensure the success of collaborative school consultation and team efforts?

6. What benefits and positive ripple effects result from successful consultation, collaboration, and co-teaching in schools?

KEY TERMS

advocacy	leadership	professional development
collaborative school	mentor/mentee	school administrators
competencies	multiplier effects	school boards
ethics	positive ripple effects	synergy

SCENARIO 12.A

Another school day is over. The events of the past week are history. What happens beyond this moment is the future. As teachers finish their bus duties and other supervisory tasks and head for their rooms to pick up work they will take home for the weekend, their glances fall on a poster that hangs beside the door. It delivers a short message:

"THE FUTURE IS NOW!"
Below the poster in smaller type is the familiar maxim, "If we continue to do what we have been doing, we will continue to get what we have been getting." Below that someone has penciled in a question, "Can we do better?" It is a good question to ponder over the weekend. . . .

CHALLENGES FOR COLLABORATIVE CONSULTATION AND WORKING AS TEAMS IN THE FUTURE

As co-educators work hard to establish themselves in school classrooms and buildings, they find that they are sometimes trailblazers and often pioneers in modeling consultation, collaboration, and teamwork. Establishing new collaborative roles is demanding but satisfying (Newmann, 1991). No simple solution exists for the complex issues and concerns of the future.

Now is the time for co-educators to have the visionary scope in education that looks inward to analyze in microscopic detail, scans in all directions with periscopic breadth and depth, focuses on kaleidoscopic colors and shapes that reveal the beauty and usefulness of diversity and individual differences, and finally peers telescopically toward lofty goals for students and their promising futures. Microscope, periscope, kaleidoscope, and telescope are metaphorically authentic ways of reflecting on what educators can do together. (See Figure 12.1.)

Collaboration will be more and more a process of the future. Those who accepted the challenge in Chapter 1 to watch and listen each day for the word *collaborate* most likely found an amazingly frequent occurrence of examples, in newspaper and news magazines, TV shows, science journals, sportscasts, music reviews, economic reports, diplomacy

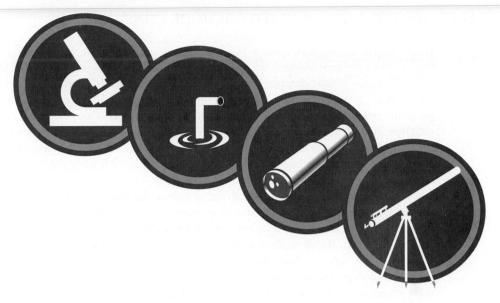

FIGURE 12.1   Education: A Visionary Scope

efforts, and much more. Working together is essential to school reform and restructuring, just as it is in all of these venues. As educators collaborate and consult within the school context, they build a framework for continued collaboration throughout the global world. This framework will serve our students well when they become citizens and leaders in their future.

But an unknowable, unpredictable future is not a sound basis on which to plan curriculum and instruction, so we must prepare students to deal effectively in the here and now (Eisner, 2003). Eisner, a noted educator at Stanford University, underscores this perspective by emphasizing that instruction must teach students to exercise judgment, think critically, acquire meaningful literacy, serve others, and collaborate with colleagues in all walks of life.

With school consultation and collaboration as a contributing process to teaching and learning, there is hope for creating the flexibility and individualization that students need. Collaborating educators can enhance the repertoire of instructional and counseling practices that will enable students to succeed. The best educators have always been those who expand, change, modify, and tailor requirements so that the important material is taught, but in a way and to the extent that serve each student's individual interests, needs and talents.

The challenge of thinking in new ways about school-based education is not a call to avoid accountability or to abandon our cherished values and history that have provided meaning and given us direction. Rather, it is a challenge to participate in creating a new vision of helping students to achieve their potential, not just crank out acceptable test scores. The time to begin is now. As that well-known adage reminds us, "A journey of a thousand miles begins with a single step."

LEADERSHIP FOR COLLABORATIVE SCHOOL CONSULTATION

Leadership is an enigmatic quality. For centuries sociologists, psychologists, and educators have tried to define leadership with only marginal success. It is another one of those constructs "we can't really describe, but we know it when we see it." Perhaps these words will be adequate: *Leadership* is the capacity to influence people and/or to represent them, and to perform responsibilities on their behalf. Some put it this way: Good leaders help others to progress in such a way that they think they did it all themselves. Strong leaders are not threatened by signs of leadership in others. By collaborating to combine strengths and efforts of others, and calling on theory and practices, school leaders can address concerns and lead toward success (Miller, Devin, & Shoop, 2007).

Another way of saying this is attributed to that eminent leader Harry Truman: "Great leaders have the ability to get others to do what they really don't want to do, and to like doing it." Effective leaders develop responsive followers. They make others feel more empowered. They thrive on the successes of followers. They take pleasure in seeing a collaborative team spirit coalesce and they constantly strive to help others improve and grow.

In the everyday work world, leaders use phrases and expressions that make others want to succeed. They avoid phrases such as " It'll never work in our district," and "That's been tried before with no success" and "We are too new/old/big/small/inexperienced/set in our ways, etc., to do that in our school." Five expressions that dampen enthusiasm (Annunzio, 2001) are:

1. It's impossible—that idea could never work.
2. We've done that before.
3. If you had more experience, you'd understand why we can't do that.
4. It doesn't look like you put any thought behind that.
5. I'll tell you what you have to do.

As Annunzio sees it, rephrasing such "wet blanket" comments in the following manner will get better involvement and results:

- Seems unworkable to me, so help me understand how it *could* work.
- I'll explain what we tried before, and you can explain how your idea is different.
- That sounds innovative, but there are some obstacles. How might we overcome those?
- Help me understand the reasoning behind your idea.
- We need to accomplish the goal within these restraints. How might we do that?

Not all leaders are openly active and dynamic. Some very successful leaders have reflective leadership styles, shaping others' values by teaching and modeling. Active leadership skills can be developed by putting people in situations in which they can lead; enhancing communication skills (including listening skills); honing creative problem solving and critical thinking skills; and practicing people skills of conflict resolution, management of meetings, and parliamentary procedure. Reflective leadership skills thrive on researching universal problems, learning how social policies are developed and implemented, and solving problems through interdisciplinary teamwork. In a collaborative environment, leadership often is diffused and passed around for individual contribution to what is needed for addressing the goals.

Envisioning collaborative environments is a relatively easy process; developing such environments and activating them require much more effort. The leadership role of wise school administrators and veteran teachers can be a catalyzing element in structuring the collaborative atmosphere. Administrators can steer researchers toward finding out why some students at risk *do* succeed, rather than dwelling on why students fail. Administrators as leaders can forge alliances with other social service agencies, with business foundations, judicial systems, library and media centers, colleges and universities, families, civic groups, and members of the community (Lugg & Boyd, 1993).

Leadership in schools is not a position, but a way of *doing* for everyone in the educational setting. Getting everyone involved in leadership builds leadership density in schools, which benefits all (McNulty, 2003). An educational and professional consultant with decades in New York City public education, Monroe (1997) cautions that leaders can't wait around for consensus before they begin making innovations. She proposes that "school should not reflect what society is, but rather school should model what society should be" (Monroe, 1997, p. 208).

Collaborative Consultants as Mentors

Effective leaders and enthusiastic followers are positioned well for roles as mentors and mentees (those who are mentored). The mentorship concept originated and was recorded many centuries ago in Greek literature to explain the relationship of Odysseus, son of Telemachus, and Mentor, chosen by Telemachus to be Odysseus' model and guide.

A mentor is part "parent" and part peer—model, guide on the side, expert, diagnostician, appraiser, and advocate—all taking place in the full press of conducting daily business and accommodating the mentor's own work. The relationship between mentor and mentee, based on shared talent and passion for the field of common interest, is special and personal. The mentor recognizes budding talent in the mentee, but does not campaign for commitments or push for greatness. However, the mentor has a sense of timing—when to bear down, or ease off, and take advantage of a teachable moment. The mentor coaches toward the bent of the mentee, modeling indirectly through experience rather than simply dispensing information to be ingested. This is an ideal situation for novice teachers to gain experiential learning from master practitioners. Mentor-mentee relationships can encourage beginning teachers early in their careers so as to *keep them there.*

In studies of special education teacher attrition, Whitaker (2000a) notes an alarming statistic that approximately 15 percent of new teachers will leave after their first year of teaching, and 10 percent to 15 percent more after the second year. This compares with an overall annual rate of 6 percent attrition for teachers nationally. Her studies show that effectiveness of mentoring correlates significantly with special education teachers' plans to remain in special education. Careful selection of a mentor as a special education teacher and a match with one who teaches students with the same disabilities are particularly relevant. Unstructured, informal, and frequent contacts are most important.

Marsal (1997) proposes that mentoring relationships, established between beginning teachers and experienced, effective colleagues can reduce the alarming rates of attrition from teaching during the first five years. She supports the CEC Guidelines for Developing a Mentorship for Beginning Special Education Teachers adopted at the 1997 Council for Exceptional Children (CEC) convention. She challenges each CEC member to find at least one person with possibilities and mentor that person in his or her local context. Knowledge and practice of consultation, collaboration, and co-teaching skills are superb conduits through which the model and mentoring can occur. Some interesting mentor programs have been developed using the services of retired teachers who welcome the opportunity to become involved just as grandparents are involved in grandparenting—loving every minute and sharing their years of experience and wisdom, then going home at the end of the day invigorated but with few-to-no responsibilities.

The experienced teacher's process of mentoring a beginning teacher should be somewhat like that of the resource co-educator mentoring a student, as was discussed in Chapter 7. First steps include matching mentor and mentee and determining mentee teaching styles, curricular specialties, and extracurricular interests such as sports or debate. Frequent communication about teaching successes and not-so-successful events, thinking recursively about teaching activities and the whole school day, discussing ideas and aspirations for students, analyzing texts and tests and techniques, and much more are middle steps in mentoring. (See Figure 12.2).

FIGURE 12.2   Mentorships Mean Sharing and Caring

In the collaborative process both mentor and mentee will gain. Both roles must be voluntary. An unstructured and informal mentorship is often most effective. One caution pertaining to this special relationship is that there must be advance preparation for the inevitable termination of the relationship. Mentorships do end, and if this is resolved at the outset, most often as an agreed-on limit of weeks or months, a way has been prepared for when and how it will be over. Then no one feels "stood up" or let down. Oftentimes mentorships have positive ripple effects and diffuse into satisfying friendships.

A different approach to new teacher education is the induction program (a highly organized and comprehensive form of professional development) that is taking place in five countries—Switzerland, France, Japan, New Zealand, and (Shanghai) China. The program lasts at least two years, involving new teachers in practice groups to network in learning effective problem solving, and including mentoring as a component of the induction process (Wong, Britton, & Ganser, 2005). The approach differs among countries, but all have three commonalities—high level of structure, focus on professional learning, and emphasis on collaboration. Collaboration is considered the strength of the model, contrasting with a common complaint of isolation that is expressed among new teachers in U.S. schools. Wong, Britton, and Ganser (2005) report that

> New teachers want more than a job. They want to experience success. They want to contribute to a group. *They want to make a difference.* Thus collegial interchange, not isolation, must become the norm for teachers. (p. 384; emphasis added)

This is remarkably reflective of the teachers' aspirations that were summarized in Chapter 1. A preservice language arts teacher spoke for her peers when she wrote this for her local newspaper:

> I've always wanted to help others, especially children . . . . What better way to combine my love for helping others and my passion for grammar, syntax, vocabulary and the like. I am finally pleased to answer that age-old question. When I grow up, I want to make a difference in children's lives, doing something I love. (Skinner, 2007)

THE SCHOOL ADMINISTRATOR'S ROLE IN COLLABORATIVE, INCLUSIVE SCHOOLS

The building principal's role and concomitant responsibilities are just short of overwhelming. So many school issues compete for a principal's time and energy that consultants need to make special efforts to accommodate their principals' heavily committed schedules when asking for their participation in consultation and collaboration.

But building administrators must be involved; they have key roles in allowing and encouraging collaboration and teamwork to happen. They make allocations of time, space, and materials that are so necessary for effective consultation and collaboration. They assign paraeducators and coordinate teamwork that takes place among building personnel. They also arrange and promote staff development for educational reform and new programs.

SCENARIO 12.B

Margo is the principal of an elementary school where a collaborative school reform approach is being implemented. The approach is a bold attempt to turn around a low-achieving school that failed the NCLB-required adequate yearly progress (AYP). Teamwork is central to success of the program's four distinctive features:

1. Family and community partnerships in education
2. Academic excellence with focus on reading, writing, math, and science instruction
3. Citizenship efforts where students are taught to develop responsible behaviors with emphasis on treating others with respect
4. Educator support that helps teachers make important decisions based on frequent reports throughout the year of each student's progress toward reading, writing, math, and science standards, which is in keeping with standardized testing requirements imposed by the NCLB legislation

In Margo's building the teachers are extremely resistant toward making any changes. She has the challenge of leading them to a more positive and supportive attitude and to successful implementation of the approach. She makes it clear to the teachers that the approach *will* be implemented in the building and she is 100% behind it. She asks teachers who feel they cannot be supportive to consider transferring to another building in the district by the next school year. She invites teachers to discuss their concerns individually with her. She remains positive and supportive, yet firm in her goals for the school. She is careful to follow through to see that each implementation activity is completed and nothing slips through the cracks.

Margo confers with district administrators, including the director of special education, to provide additional personnel and material support to the teachers during the transition time. With the help of the school counselor and music teacher, she organizes school-wide assemblies for Friday afternoons so teachers can have time for planning and teaming.

Margo also organizes a family-community night for interacting with each other and showcasing the school's aims. She seeks written evidence of support from children, teachers, family members and others. She continues to keep families informed of changes taking place in the school and requests their input for significant decisions.

How Administrators Can Encourage Collaboration and Teamwork

Administrators can assist staff immeasurably by freeing up teacher time and arranging for substitutes so consultation and collaboration among school personnel can take place. They can work with consultants to clarify collaborative consultation roles, and to ensure that such roles have parity among the school staff.

Another major contribution is encouraging interaction and staff development for all school personnel. When in-service and staff development are arranged, promoted, and *attended* by building principals, the positive ripple effects can be profound.

In a review of educational research on the principal's role in creating inclusive schools for diverse learners, Riehl (2000) notes that school leadership has moved well beyond application of knowledge and skills as a science of administration would suggest, and beyond finesse with processes as an art of administrative performance, to school administration as a form of *practice.* School administration as a practice "creates a 'horizon' that envisions what schools create and where they might lead" (Riehl, p. 69).

A study by Foley and Lewis (1999) indicated that the secondary administrator role of manager and primary decision maker for operation and function of the school, with responsibility for centralized control of school activities and resources, is not congruent with the principles of collegiality, parity, and shared decision-making that are underpinnings of collaborative-based structures. Foley and Lewis contend that a shift in authority is needed that allows the principal to be a team member and support others in leadership roles and collaboration.

In their handbook *A Principal's Guide,* Bateman and Bateman (2001) target the principal's role in special education and discuss what principals need to know in order to implement best practices in their schools. Topics covered include eligibility, assessments and evaluations; inclusive schools; special education laws; policy issues concerning discipline, due process, accommodations and adaptations; selection and evaluation of special education teachers; and more (Council for Exceptional Children, 2001). It is vital for all school administrators, along with general and special education personnel and related services and support personnel, to study and reflect on such issues.

■ ■ ■ ■ ■

APPLICATION 12.1
QUESTIONS FOR A BUILDING ADMINISTRATOR

Use these eight questions posed by a typical classroom teacher to draw school administrators into dialogue about consultation, collaboration, and teamwork among all school personnel, and with families of students who have special needs.

1. Do I *have* to have a student with disabilities in my classroom? If so, who has the responsibility of developing curriculum and lessons for him or her?

2. If I don't agree with what the special education teachers or support staff have asked me to do and I've discussed the issues with them but still there is no change, what do I do next?

3. Why does the special ed teacher have a smaller caseload than I do?

4. Whose responsibility is it to supervise and evaluate the special education staff and support personnel staff?

5. How may I request services for a student that are not available now in our school?

6. Where will I find time to confer and collaborate with consulting teachers?

7. How can I go about setting up co-teaching with a colleague? Then if it doesn't work out after a dedicated fair trial, what do we do?

8. What is my responsibility toward accountability for standardized-test scores of all students in my room, including those with disabilities?

Getting Off to the Right Start with Administrators

Recall that four guiding questions for collaborative school consultation were introduced in Chapter 1. It is time to reiterate those questions and focus on a plan to set goals as co-educators. The questions are:

1. Who am I [to be] in this role?
2. How do I carry out responsibilities of the role?
3. How do I know whether I am succeeding?
4. How can I prepare for such a role?

Sometimes just getting started is the hardest part of what has great potential for being a pleasant and fulfilling professional experience. Ten steps will put the co-educator on the right track to success:

1. First, read, study, think, interview others, and complete coursework or professional development sessions if possible to gain information and skills about collaborating and consulting as teams of co-educators.

2. Formulate your own personal philosophy of collaboration as a co-educator.

3. Observe the chain-of-command conventions in assigned school(s), meeting with a central administrator if feasible to learn administrators' perceptions of the collaborative consultant role or co-teacher role for the district.

4. If an advisory council is part of the administrative structure, engage members in discussion about consultation and collaboration roles. The council should include general and special education teachers, support personnel, administrators, families, and other community leaders, and perhaps a student or two.

5. Meet with all building administrators to whom assigned, using excellent responsive listening skills to learn their viewpoints. This is an extremely important step.

6. After meeting with principals of your assigned attendance centers, reorganize your thoughts and ideas, and gather more information if necessary.

7. Develop a tentative role description and goals based on views expressed by central and building administrators' views and advisory council's views as well as one's own perspective.

8. Return to central administration and/or building administrators, as appropriate in that district, conveying the description and goals to them and revising if necessary.

9. After honing the plan to a concise format, put it up for discussion, explaining it to teaching staff and nonteaching staff and refining it even further based on their comments.

10. Convey the essence of the plan to co-educators during a professional development or staff meeting, and to parents during a parent-teacher meeting or individually to family members.

SCHOOL BOARD MEMBERS AS PARTNERS IN EDUCATION

School districts in the United States are governed by boards of education. The school board is arguably the most influential group in a community because they oversee education for children and youth of the community; therefore, they are framing the future. Being a school board member in a community just may be the most significant responsibility that can be fulfilled by a citizen of that community.

A school board sets policies for operation of the district's schools, including the hiring of staff, approving curriculum, and taking care of school buildings and other property. Hiring duties include the all-important task of selecting a superintendent of schools. The superintendent is the agent of the school board, and the board is an agent of the state. The aggregate of individuals making up the board speak as one body to formulate policy for the community's schools, to enforce the policies, and to evaluate the outcomes of policies.

Effective boardsmanship calls for members to focus on policy and not become mired in regulations or procedural matters. Although the details of "buses, ballgames, buildings, and budgets" are very important, it is vital that school boards also discuss and make decisions about matters such as curriculum, student achievement, teacher contracts, and the structure and philosophy of inclusionary schools. Teacher leaders who aim to introduce concepts such as curriculum revision, changes in basal textbooks, block scheduling, collaboration among co-educators, or co-teaching arrangements should bring their plans to the school board's attention.

Board meetings are held monthly, and sometimes more often; they tend to be long, often arduous, and sometimes contentious because of the high stakes—the community's children—that are involved. Nevertheless, teachers should attend meetings now and then, even when their own topics of immediate concern are not on the agenda. This demonstrates to the board that teachers want to be involved. A group of co-educators, representing all grade levels and curricular areas, could collaborate on occasion to present a report to the school board about a current topic such as the efforts they are making to plan and teach together. Sometimes boards have additional meetings—typically a workshop session when there is a new educational trend or innovation they want to learn more about, or a public forum where parents and taxpayers can become more informed about their schools. Faculty and other school personnel should discuss news reports from board meetings, generally available in local newspapers.

When school personnel want the news to flow the other way—from school to board—they must remember that board members are typically some of the community's busiest people. So they will react most favorably to comprehensive, concise written reports or fact sheets. Examples of what teachers have done, and what students have accomplished, and how the schools can be showcased, provide solid support and rationale for proposed policy changes or innovative ideas.

Too few educators and the general public know very much about school boards—how they are selected, qualifications for running (which are surprisingly minimal), term of office, whether reimbursed or not, and perhaps most intriguing, reasons a candidate puts herself or himself up to run for the school board. Teacher education programs should provide preservice teachers with more knowledge about school boards and practicing teachers should become familiar with who is on the board, why they are members, and what transpires at board meetings.

School board members must be active listeners and skilled decision makers. They also must be attuned to the adage that no one can please all of the people all of the time, but they must give their best efforts in collaborating with fellow board members, articulating policies to their constituents as a body and not individuals, demonstrating creativity in problem identification and problem solving, arriving at consensus as decision makers, and providing service as change agents for their communities. Collaboration, consultation, and co-education are important tools for school boards as well as for school personnel in fulfilling their responsibilities.

ADVOCACY FOR STUDENTS WITH SPECIAL NEEDS

At a well-attended conference on special needs in schools, a legislator active on a key legislative education committee directed some strong remarks to participants who gathered to hear her speak. She asked pointedly from her place on the podium, "Can you name the representatives and senators who serve you in our state legislature? Do you know their positions on key issues?" She then charged each one there to not spend one more day without knowing such important answers to her questions. It gave the educators much to ponder, and homework to do!

Getting to know policy makers and elected officials, communicating with them about the needs of students, and building bridges of communication are responsibilities of collaborative school consultants and necessary steps of advocacy. When communicating, personal letters are more effective than form letters. *Many* letters, rather than copies of one letter *signed* by many, will get more attention. Letters that are short, concise, friendly in tone, and free of stereotyped phrases, derogatory comments, and unreasonable requests, make a positive impact. Thanking legislators for their interest in the past and support they have given, along with descriptions of specific ways that their support has helped communities, will be particularly powerful. Think of the letter as a vehicle of appreciation, information, and documentation, and as a message of ideas for action that would help, along with suggestions for ways in which they might be carried out. Examples of student work and achievement, and newsletters and clippings that commend students and schools, provide convincing evidence when included with the letters (with parent and administrator permission, of course).

Student Self-Advocacy

Self advocacy is knowing what one wants, what one is entitled to, and how to achieve one's goals (Kling, 2000). Students can be helped to become effective self advocates by teaching them self-advocacy skills. Kling offers a mnemonic acronym (ASSERT) to help students recall self-advocacy steps:

- *A*wareness of disability
- *S*tatement of disability
- *S*tatement of strengths and limitations

- *E*valuation of problems and solutions
- *R*ole playing a situation
- *T*rying advocacy efforts in authentic situations

The successful advocate knows her or his rights, needs, and best supports. It is important also to know the best time to approach others with requests that serve one's needs. Students who learn to do this can gain a sense of control and influence over their employment conditions and living situations. It is especially important for students who are in the transition phase between high school and postsecondary school or a vocation.

PROFESSIONAL DEVELOPMENT
FOR CO-EDUCATORS

Professional development is a prime factor in the success of school consultation, collaboration, and co-teaching. When carefully planned, well delivered, and constructively evaluated, it catalyzes these interactive processes. School personnel now in the profession, and preservice teachers preparing for careers in education, need professional development experiences to build scaffolding that will support their consultation, collaboration, and co-teaching efforts and further develop their skills. Furthermore, consulting teachers for students with exceptional learning needs often are called on to prepare material for staff development, and some are asked to present sessions for their professional colleagues.

Unfortunately, attitudes toward professional development often are anything but positive, ranging from indifference to resentment to disdain. Criticisms include lack of clear purpose and relevance, insufficient time and poor scheduling, and pointed questions about how the material will affect them and their students.

SCENARIO 12.C

Several teachers at a middle school are conversing in the teachers' workroom on Friday afternoon.

Social Studies Teacher: What a week! I feel like I've attended to everything this week but students and curriculum. Maybe things will slow down a bit next week.

Math Teacher: Guess you didn't look at your office memo yet, hmmm? There's a reminder about the staff development sessions next Tuesday and Thursday mornings before school. Something about collaborative consultation with special education.

Social Studies Teacher: Consultation? You mean visits by those people who drive over from the central office to borrow your clock and tell you what time it is? Or do you mean the imported experts breezing in from more than fifty miles away with their briefcases and stacks of transparencies?

Math Teacher: I believe this group involves our own special education staff. We're supposed to find out about what we all can do together now that so many students with learning and behavioral problems are in our classrooms most of the time.

Art Teacher: Oh, great. How does that involve me? I had my required course in special ed. What I *really* need is a bigger room and more supplies.

Social Studies Teacher: And if we're supposed to collaborate with these people, where will we find the time?

Physical Education Teacher: Uh–huh. It will be hard enough just carving out the time to go to the *meeting* about it.

Math Teacher: Now you know you'll just *love* congregating en masse to try and concentrate on some new-fangled proposal when you'd rather be in your classroom getting set for the day.

Social Studies Teacher: Well, let me put it this way. If they're not through by 8:20 sharp, I'm gone!

—Adapted from Dettmer, 1990

In order to provide the most constructive professional development experiences possible, the planners and presenters must address five points:

1. How do adults respond to and acquire new information about teaching?
2. What should co-educators know and do in order to serve students with special needs effectively?
3. What kinds of materials and assistance will be most helpful for them?
4. How might the material be presented effectively and efficiently?
5. How can follow-up and support be provided after the experiences? (This is very important.)

The collaborative consultant role is ideal for coordinating useful in-service and staff development activities about special needs. Special education personnel often inherit these responsibilities either as a part of a plan or by default. There are disadvantages as well as advantages in being a "prophet in one's own land" for conducting professional development activities, but one of the biggest advantages is knowledge of the school context, along with what participants probably already know and still need or want to know.

Characteristics of the Adult Learner

As indicated in Chapter 2, school personnel must be approached as the adult learners and professionals that they are. They are self-directed with a wide experience base on which to draw, they function within a time perspective oriented to the here and now, and they are problem-centered in their interests and needs for professional development (Knowles, 1978). They want ownership in the development process and tend to resist aspects perceived as attacks on their competence. They can and should serve as resources for their colleagues during professional development activities. This fits well with a goal of developing collaboration and co-teaching skills. Some fun and rewards are refreshing, but adult learners respond best to intrinsic motivations rather than extrinsic motivations.

The first step for professional development personnel is to acknowledge that each person's perception of the environment reflects and is filtered through his or her own stage of development (Oja, 1980). Presenters must attend to different needs of participants, including (Garmston & Wellman, 1992):

- Those looking for facts, data, and references
- Those wishing to relate the topic to themselves through interactions with colleagues
- Those wanting to reason and explore
- Those who would like to adapt, modify, or create new ideas and processes

With adult learner characteristics and individual style variations in mind, professional developers will need to arrange for participant comfort, give participants options and choices, manage their time well, deliver practical and focused help, and follow up on the effectiveness of the experience.

Busy educators value activities in which they work toward realistic, job-related, useful goals. They need to see results for their efforts as demonstrated by success when they use the material within their school context. Guskey (1985) stresses that staff development must illustrate clearly ways in which new practices can improve student performance, and how these practices can be implemented without too much disruption or extra work. This is particularly important when focusing on consultation and collaboration, because this kind of professional activity often involves more time and effort at the outset. Too often professional development is designed to focus on "attitude adjustment" before validations of successful strategies. So it begins at the wrong place, that is, telling teachers why they should do something and then expecting them to want to do it. In Guskey's (1985) well-received model of teacher change, staff development is presented to generate *change in classroom teaching practices*. This causes change in student learning outcomes, resulting in changes in teacher beliefs and attitudes.

Kelleher (2003) describes professional development as a form of adult learning that must be concerned primarily with student learning. A speaker or an activity might be interesting to participants, but the test of success is what teachers *do* with the new information they receive. He recommends allocating professional development budgets so as to encourage teachers to focus heavily on activities related to peer collaboration. A peer collaboration strand that features teachers collaborating in writing curriculum and assessments, examining student work, observing each other's classrooms, and mentoring new teachers can have significant impact on student achievement.

Determining Professional Development Needs

What do participants already know about a specified topic at this point? What do they want to learn? How can they be involved in planning, conducting, and evaluating experiences for their individual needs? This information should be solicited through needs assessment instruments. Most school personnel have had experience with completing needs assessments. Formats for needs assessments include:

- Checklists
- Questionnaires and surveys
- Open-ended surveys of areas of concern
- Interviews
- Brainstorm sessions
- More informal methods such as interviews, surveys, observations, buzz groups

Needs assessments might ask personnel to check topics of need, or to describe their concerns that can then be developed into a staff development activity.

Presenting Professional Development Activities

Garmston (1988) compares presenting in-service session or staff development with giving presents. He suggests the "present" should be something participants (presentees) want or can utilize, personalized to individual taste as much as possible, attractively wrapped, and a bit suspenseful. The presenter should:

- Know audience needs and interests
- Have something on the agenda that appeals to everyone
- Conduct the activity in an interesting, efficient, multimodal format
- Package the ISD material attractively
- Pace the session so all major points are covered within the time span
- Ensure that no one's input is overlooked
- Provide an element of surprise and intrigue
- Deliver follow-up help, support, and additional information

Formal and Informal Approaches to Professional Development

Professional development can be formal or informal in nature. Formal activities can be conducted through scheduled sessions, attendance at conferences, presentations, modules, courses, brochures, retreats, and other planned activities. Informal activities occur through conversations, observations, reports about one topic that include another aspect of education, memos, references to media productions, Internet forums and chat rooms, minipresentations by co-educators at faculty meetings, newsletters, and purposeful reading material. (See Figure 12.3)

One enterprising group of teachers organized a series of sessions called "THT—Teachers Helping Teachers" in which they took turns delivering short sessions on topics in which they had expertise. Soon the idea caught on among other teachers. A teacher who had a school-related skill to share prepared and presented, with administrator support, a half-day session for teachers in another school within the district. Other teachers followed suit at various times throughout the school year to present on topics reflecting their own particular interests and skills. As co-educators ask what they can do to help each other, they are cultivating professional development in collaborative school environments.

FIGURE 12.3   Formal and Informal In-Service and Staff Development

	Formal	Informal
Plan	Typically structured Example: Workshop	Usually casual Example: Newsletter column
Method	Designed with care Example: Speaker/discussion	Somewhat spontaneous Example: Hall chat
Evaluation	Data collection Example: Checklist	Reflection Example: Journal note

The Teachers' Workroom as a Forum for Professional Development

Very little has been written about the teachers' workroom, sometimes known as "the lounge" even though as a general rule not much lounging goes on there. This lack of attention to the place is surprising, because most teachers drop in at some time or another. Of course, some go there quite frequently, and others hardly ever do. Visits usually fall within one of three purposes—physical, social, or personal. There may be the physical benefit of refreshment, a quick "nap," or a restroom break. A few minutes of socialization with adults, squeezed between intensive hours with children and adolescents, is important to some.

Professional benefits include attending to tasks such as grading papers or reading materials, or getting one's thoughts and plans together before the next barrage of youthful energy bursts into the classroom. Oftentimes teachers just want an opportunity to interact with colleagues and share reflections about teaching practices and student needs. Good ideas for collaboration and co-teaching can spring from, or slowly unfold from, these brief moments and returned to at a later time with more focused attention. Sometimes "break room moments" are problematic because the discourse can become quite negative and cynical. When this kind of talk negatively affects one's morale, going there becomes iatrogenic and should probably be avoided. Nevertheless, the teachers' workroom has long been recognized as a useful hub of interaction, particularly by special education teachers. Here they may have the opportunity to develop rapport with general education colleagues and learn more about their classrooms and students.

It is important that collaborative consulting teachers spend enough time in the teachers' workroom ("Don't the special ed people want to be a part of our faculty?"), but not too much ("Don't those special ed people have anything to do?"). Of course, care must be taken to keep professional conversation general in nature. Confidentiality and ethical treatment of information are necessary behaviors for all teachers, and special education teachers in particular. But in this room that is provided for relaxation, reflection, and refreshment, a collaborative spirit can be nurtured and carried out the door to classrooms and offices beyond. Some special education teachers have had success with posting a "brag board" of commendations honoring any student or adult in the school.

■ ■ ■ ■ ■

APPLICATION 12.2
DESIGNING A TEACHERS' WORKROOM

In your thoughts or on sketch paper, have fun creating a "dream workroom" that would serve school personnel in their physical, social, and personal needs. What would it look like? What would it sound like? How might co-educators nurture the collaborative spirit there? What would it take to construct and outfit such a room? Could some of your suggestions be carried out right away with little cost and disruption to the school? Who would do this, and how?

More research is needed on the problems and possibilities of this important facet of school life. However, the consultant will find many opportunities in the teachers' workroom for developing rapport with consultees and initiating constructive interactions. Some may think suggestions for using teachers' lounges as professional development and collaboration forums are "off the wall," but the walls of such places contain knowledge and wisdom and can be places of rejuvenation for harried teachers. This school place must be used wisely and judiciously.

Outline for Professional Development Activity

There is no single in-service and staff development format that will be appropriate for every school context. However, the following outline is one that can be adapted to a variety of schools and staff needs.

1. Observe, query, discuss professional development with co-educators.
2. Conduct needs assessment.
3. Select the topic to be featured.
4. Determine the audience to be targeted.
5. Choose a catchy, upbeat title for the activity.
6. Determine presenters who will contribute.
7. Decide on incentives, promotion, and publicity.
8. Outline the presentation.
9. List the equipment and room arrangement needed.
10. Plan carefully the content to be covered.
11. Prepare handouts and visual materials.
12. Rehearse the presentation.
13. Determine an evaluation procedure for the activity.
14. Plan for the follow-up activity.

Finding Time for Professional Development Activities

Time is the enemy when planning whole-faculty or small-group faculty sessions where teachers can concentrate and reflect. Before-school and after-school hours might seem workable because participants are coming to school anyway, or are required to stay after school for a specific length of time. But most teachers dislike these times, finding it hard to focus on their own learning at an early hour when their thoughts are centered on beginning the school day efficiently, and feeling that by day's end their energy and emotions will be lagging and other responsibilities beckoning. Saturday sessions are no more popular as they encroach on the family time and community life so necessary for sustaining teacher vitality and support. (See Figure 12.4.)

The arrangement preferred by most teachers is released time. This means that their responsibilities with students will need to be assumed by others. Numerous suggestions have been offered by professional development experts for carving time out of schedules and responsibilities, such as occasionally hiring substitute teachers, having a permanent substitute cadre that conducts planned enrichment activities, providing roving substitute teachers, or arranging teams whereby one teacher teaches two or more classes to free up team partners for professional development activities.

The substitute cadre eliminates the necessity for detailed lesson planning by the teacher, because the enrichment activities are planned and provided by the cadre. Roving substitutes allow released teachers to have short periods of time for observing, coaching, gathering research data, or assisting in another classroom. Loucks-Horsley, Harding, Arbuckle, Murray, Dubea, and Williams (1987) counsel that the time issue is a "red herring," because the problem often lies in the constructive use of time, not its availability. Furthermore, it is not hard to envision using some of these strategies to make time for collaboration and consultation among co-educators.

Presenter and Participant Responsibilities

Colleagues who deliver in-service and staff development on their own professional turf may face some difficulty in being accepted as "prophets in their own land" (Smith-Westberry

FIGURE 12.4   "I wish professional development days were *not* on Saturdays!"

& Job, 1986). They will want to scrutinize their own capabilities and deficits first. Practice sessions can help presenters gain confidence and skill. Smith-Westberry and Job recommend videotaping practice sessions, discomforting though that may be, and critiquing the taped sessions carefully to correct deficiencies.

Participants, as presentees, have the responsibility to participate wholeheartedly in the activity, to participate in the evaluation, and to commit themselves to the follow-up activities. One of the most helpful contributions on their part is to defer negative attitudes and anticipate positive outcomes.

Follow-Up to the Professional Development Experience

Follow-up activity is the breeze that fans any fires of change which were sparked by the activity (Dettmer, 1990). Educators sometimes avoid trying new concepts and techniques because they are uncomfortable with them or uncertain about the outcomes. It is easy to revert to business as usual once the activity is over. So follow-up is vital, just as it is with the consultation process. The possibilities include peer coaching, discussion groups, observations at sites where the innovation is occurring, newsletters, and interviews. Data gathered during follow-up and follow-through can be used to plan future professional development projects. An example of one brief follow-up instrument is included in Figure 12.5. Of course, personal contact is best; therefore, the evaluator should consider conducting this follow-up as an interview.

One caution must be noted. When educators are introduced to new concepts and challenged to try new approaches, some discomfort is inevitable. The adage that training may make one worse before it makes one better is an important point to consider. It is easy and convenient to revert to former ways because learning and implementing new ways can be hard. This accents the need for follow-through efforts and perseverance on the part of the consultant.

Evaluation of Professional Development

Evaluation of a professional development activity is imperative for at least two reasons. First, professional development is conducted to implement change, so information must be gathered to assess the change (Todnem & Warner, 1994). Second, there is pressure more than ever now for accountability in education. Evaluators will want to know if participants are using the information that was presented, and whether the material has made a difference in their classrooms and the school in general.

The tool used most often for evaluation is a questionnaire that participants complete immediately following the activity. The evaluation should include both objective responses and an invitation for open-ended responses. A Likert scale of five to seven values is preferable to a Yes-No format. See Figure 12.6 on page 420 for an example of an in-service/staff development evaluation tool.

Conferences and Conventions for Professional Growth

Conventions, conferences, and workshops provide opportunities for personal and professional growth. The atmosphere at well-structured events typically is charged with energy

FIGURE 12.5 Follow-Up Information for Professional Development

Please take a few minutes to respond to these questions about the recent staff development held
___ / / ___ on the topic of _____. In doing so you will be helping staff developers and presenters plan effective staff development experiences for you and your colleagues.

1. Have you implemented any idea or strategy that was presented during the staff development?
   If so, please describe it briefly and rate the success level:

   _____

   _____

   _____

   _____ 1 = not effective _____ 2 = somewhat effective _____ 3 = very effective

2. Is there something more you would like to learn about this topic? If so, please describe your need.

   _____

   _____

   _____

3. If you did not use the staff development information, please tell why you did not.

   _____

   _____

   _____

4. This item is *very* important. Did the information or enthusiasm you received have positive ripple effects that you could identify and describe? If so, please do, and also rate the extent to which this happened.

   _____

   _____

   _____

   _____ 1 = a little _____ 2 = somewhat _____ 3 = to a great extent _____ 4 = profoundly

and enthusiasm. A smorgasbord of choices is available at the best conventions to whet adult learner appetites. Participants learn from interacting with one another, renew acquaintances, and make new connections. Networks of collaboration can be established among educators with common interests. Some gather to plan writing projects for professional journals or cross-country research projects.

Leadership skills are honed by submitting proposals to present at the event. In-district partnerships can bloom if colleagues or parents are asked to go along. One concept that is effective for some convention themes is a team model of participants in which a

FIGURE 12.6   Evaluation Form for Inservice/Staff Development

In-Service/Staff Development Evaluation

Date _____

Name (optional) _____   Teaching Area and Level(s)_____

Site of the In-Service/Staff Development_____   Topic_____

Rate the following with a value from 1 through 5:

1 = None   2 = A little   3 = Somewhat   4 = Considerably   5 = Much

1. The event increased my understanding of the topic. _____
2. The goals and objectives of the event addressed needs I had identified. _____
3. The content was well developed and organized. _____
4. The material was presented effectively. _____
5. The environment was satisfactory. _____
6. I gained ideas to use in my own situation. _____
7. I will use at least one idea from this event. _____
8. Strengths of the event: _____
9. Ways the event could be improved: _____
10. I would like to know more about: _____

classroom teacher or two, a special education teacher, and a building administrator attend the event together.

Professional events are meant to be invigorating and informative. Convention-goers can gain the most from the experience by planning their time carefully, getting to sessions early, making sure to visit exhibits areas for new ideas and materials (and sometimes publisher giveaways), taking advantage of sessions that showcase strategies that work and student products, and allowing some time and energy to go beyond the convention site for a little fun and relaxation.

Rewards of Professional Development Activities

Professional development for consultation, collaboration, and special needs of students has the potential to create positive ripple effects that have no bounds. It can encourage:

- Increased respect for individual differences, creative approaches, and educational excellence
- Teacher proficiency in innovative curriculum and teacher strategies
- Staff and parent involvement, and satisfaction with the educational system
- Collegiality and collaboration among all school personnel as well as among community and parents

In order to attain these positive outcomes, professional development experiences must be planned, conducted, evaluated, and followed up efficiently.

SYNERGY OF CONTEXT, PROCESS, AND CONTENT

Effective school consultation results from the interaction of *process* skills and *content* strategies within the immediate school *context.* Contexts of a school setting for collaborative consultation and teamwork are givens. Content strategies for consulting and collaborating and co-teaching must flow from existing school philosophies and structures. But it is the processes for collaborating and networking that are the most malleable and accessible for change. In too many school contexts and content areas, the interactive processes such as communication, problem solving, conflict resolution, and especially the valuing of adult differences tend to be either neglected or poorly carried out.

Collaboration that occurs in conjunction with consultation requires harmonious, efficient teamwork. Thus, collaborative consultation is not an oxymoron as some might suggest. It is *synergy*—"a behavior of whole systems unpredicted by the behavior of their parts taken separately" (Fuller, 1975, p. 3). When interactive teamwork is effective, there is synergy. A synergistic combination of context, process, and content is a recipe for success in the school setting.

Positive Ripple Effects of Collaborative School Consultation

Positive ripple effects, or multiplier effects as they have also been referred to from time to time, provide compelling arguments for consultation, collaboration, and co-teaching. They create benefits beyond the immediate situation involving one student and that student's teachers. When collaborating with co-educators, many skills and talents will "bubble up" to be shared and expanded. All will learn and improve their skills.

As discussed earlier, consulting teachers who might be concerned that general education teachers will be given full responsibility for special learning needs and their own positions will be eliminated, should not fret. When teachers become more proficient as collaborative colleagues, they tend to find those services more indispensable, not less, to goals of serving all students' educational needs effectively. The use of specialized intervention techniques for many more students than the ones identified, categorized, and remediated in special education programs is a positive outcome to expect from collaborative school consultation. Multiple benefits can extend well beyond the immediate classroom because consulting teachers are in a unique position to facilitate interaction among many target groups. These effects that ripple out from mutual planning and problem solving across grade levels, subject areas, and schools are powerful instruments for initiating positive changes in the educational system.

Multiplier effects provide compelling arguments for consultation, collaboration, and teaming. They augment benefits beyond the immediate situation involving one student and that student's teachers. For example, when collaborating with colleagues, school personnel are modeling this powerful tool for their students who soon will be collaborating and teaming with others in their own workplaces.

Levels of Service

Direct services for consultees are one level of positive effects (see Figure 12.7). At this level the consultation and collaboration are most likely to have been initiated for one client's need. (Note that a client can be an entity such as a student group, school, family, or community, as well as a single student.) But consultation benefits often extend beyond Level 1 of immediate need. At Level 2, consultees use information and points of view generated during the collaboration to be more effective in similar but unrelated cases. Both consultant and consultee repertoires of knowledge and skills are enhanced so that they can function more effectively in the future. When collaborative consultation outcomes extend beyond single consultant/consultee situations of Levels 1 and 2, the entire school system can be positively affected by Level 3 outcomes. Organizational change and increased family involvement are potential results of Level 3 outcomes.

Level 1 effects, for example, can result from the following types of school situations:

■ The special education teacher for learning disabilities engages in problem solving with a high school teacher to determine ways of helping a student with severe learning disabilities master minimum competencies required for graduation.

■ The audiologist helps the classroom teacher arrange the classroom environment to enable a hearing-impaired student to function comfortably in the regular classroom setting.

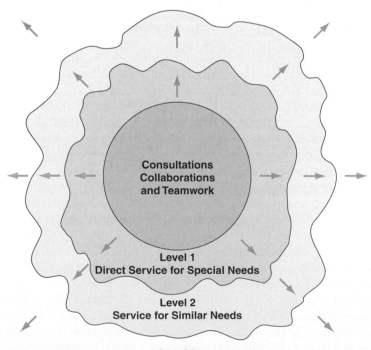

FIGURE 12.7   Positive Ripple Effects of Collaborative School Consultation

Level 2 effects include these examples:

■ The classroom teacher becomes more familiar with the concept of hyperactivity in children, subsequently regarding fewer children as having attention deficit disorder with hyperactivity, and adjusting the classroom curriculum to more appropriately address very active children's needs in that classroom setting. This reduces the incidences of hyperactivity and referrals to special education programs.

■ The classroom teacher becomes comfortable with enrichment activities provided for gifted students through collaboration with the gifted program facilitator, and makes enriching activities available to a larger group of very able children in the classroom who can handle them with no difficulty and thrive in the process.

Level 3 effects enable these kinds of outcomes:

■ The efforts toward collaboration and teamwork result in a professional development plan called "Teachers Helping Teachers," during which teachers in a school system provide training for interested colleagues in their areas of expertise.

■ The school district's emphasis on consultation, collaboration, and co-teaching pleases families who find that their children are receiving more integrated, personalized instruction for their learning needs. Families become more active and interested in the school's programs, and more positive and encouraging of their children at home.

Use of specialized intervention techniques for many more students than those identified to receive intervention and remediation services is a positive outcome of collaborative school consultation and co-teaching. All in all, the multiplier effect of these interactive processes is a powerful tool for progress in education and the effects will reach far beyond school contexts as students enter the workforce in their chosen careers.

ETHICS OF COLLABORATIVE SCHOOL CONSULTATION

Consultation, collaboration, and teamwork in school contexts require particular emphasis on ethical interaction for several reasons:

■ Special needs of students are evident that cannot be met elsewhere.

■ Confidential data must be shared among a number of individuals.

■ Collaborative consultants are out and about much more than classroom teachers, interfacing with many people in homes and schools and across the community.

■ Parent permission is not always required, but many of the issues to be dealt with approximate the sensitivity of issues that do necessitate parental consent.

■ Collaborative consultants have complex roles with many demands placed on them, but may have received little or no training in how to adapt to those roles.

■ School consultation implies power and expertise until the collaborative spirit can be cultivated.

■ Collaborative consultants may be asked on occasion to act inappropriately as a middle person, or to form alliances, or carry information, and they must respond ethically.

■ There is some risk of diminishing returns if collaborative efforts considerably reduce the amount of time available for direct service to the child (Friend & Cook, 1992).

■ Adults often have difficulty adapting to individual differences in teaching styles and preferences of colleagues, and many of them offer resistance.

■ Just as with mentorships, it is important to recognize those rare times when it is in the best interest of all concerned, but the student most of all, to withdraw from a consulting situation. Disengagement is recognized in psychological consultation as the termination of a consultative relationship. This is reality, so having a transition plan for moving into other relationships and experiences can ease feelings of loss and sadness, and dispel feelings of inadequacy or failure.

The persuasive aspects of consultation require a close, careful look at ethical practices (Ross, 1986). Ethical consultation is implemented by adhering to principles of confidentiality in acquisition and use of information about students, families, and individual school settings. It also includes a high regard for individual differences among colleagues and the constructive use of those differences to serve students' needs. It gives evidence of concern and empathy for all, onedownsmanship (downplaying status differences and communicating as partners) in the consultative role, and mutual ownership of problems and rewards in the school environment.

As expressed by Gullatt and Tollett (1997), we know that society is becoming more legally complex with many legal issues arising in school contexts. Yet few states require an educational law course as part of teacher education coursework for licensure. This is the case at the graduate level and most markedly at the undergraduate level. Issues include special education, student discipline, liability insurance, negligence, student/teacher rights, confidentiality and privacy, photographing of students, conducting research in schools, freedom of press, ever-changing laws and regulations, and much more. Gullatt and Tollett (1997) recommend that universities and legal authorities collaborate with local educational authorities to design professional development workshops for informing teachers of current educational law and new legislation as it is enacted by state and national legislative bodies. They propose that each school designate a resource teacher to be responsible for collecting and distributing information about school law. Ethical issues could be included in this assignment and kept on the front burner of co-educators' collective agenda.

Involvement of family members in the collaborative consultation process raises legal, ethical, and confidentiality issues (Kratochwill & Pittman, 2002). Consultants and collaborators should review legal requirements relating to confidentiality, such as the Family Educational Rights and Privacy Act of 1974 (Buckley Amendment), and truth-in-testing laws within states that legislate them. Requirements such as these stipulate the need for confidentiality of student data and regulate parental access to information about their children.

One concern is that privacy or confidentiality may not be an absolute right, especially when minors are involved and there is risk of serious harm (Taylor & Adelman, 1998). Sometimes professionals cannot maintain confidences legally or ethically. Such conflicted intentions can interfere with trust between consultant and client or consultee, but the concern may be outweighed by a responsibility to prevent serious harm. Taylor and Adelman point out that most ethical guidelines recognize such extenuating circumstances. They suggest that the problem might be reframed and focused on how to go about sharing the information appropriately.

Hansen, Himes, and Meier (1990) provide four general suggestions to follow in order to exercise ethical behavior in their roles:

1. Promote professional attitudes and behaviors among staff about confidentiality and informed consent.
2. Take care with the quality of information they enter in written records.
3. Take care in discussing problems of children and their families.
4. Focus on strengths of clients and share information only with those who need it to serve the student's needs.

Several well-known maxims apply to the implementation of planful, efficient, collegial, and ethical practices for consultation:

- Keep your words sweet, for you may have to eat them.
- Better to bend than to break.
- Only a fool would peel a grape with an ax.
- Eagles do not hunt flies.
- What breaks in a moment may take years to mend.

COMPETENCIES OF EFFECTIVE COLLABORATIVE SCHOOL CO-EDUCATORS

Throughout the chapters of this book, competencies for collaborating, consulting, co-teaching, and working in teams as co-educators have been woven into descriptions of processes and content for various school contexts. They include flexibility, adaptability, resilience, and tolerance for getting delayed reinforcement or none at all. Effective co-educators are knowledgeable about both special education and general education curriculum and methods. They are interested in current trends and topics, and they are innovative in generating new ideas. They recognize and value adult differences among colleagues. They understand how schools function and have a panoramic view of the educational scene. They are practical and realistic along with being innovative. This requires that they be assertive and take risks when needed, but remain diplomatic and not pushy.

Successful collaborators relate well to teacher colleagues and other staff members, administrators, parents, and of course students. They have good communication skills and a patient and understanding demeanor. They also have mature, objective viewpoints toward all aspects of education. While working to help students learn, they retain perspective on the entire school context. They link people with resources, refer people to other sources when needed, and teach when that is the most appropriate way to serve students' needs. A collaborative consultant is self-confident, but if running low on resources or ideas, does not hesitate in finding a consultant for herself or himself!

Perhaps most of all, the consultant is a change agent. As one highly experienced, long-time consulting teacher put it, "You have to be abrasive enough to create change, but pleasant enough to be asked back so you will do it some more" (Bradley, 1987). The competency checklist in Figure 12.8 summarizes the main items and can be used for self-assessment or assessment by a supervisor or colleague whose views are valued highly.

FIGURE 12.8   Competencies for Collaborators, Consultants, and Team Members as Co-Educators

Criterion Area and Competencies	Needs Work	Improving	OK	Good	Excellent
Knowledge and Awareness of Collaboration/Consultation					
Understands concepts of collaborative consultation	1	2	3	4	5
Analyzes own perspectives/preferences	1	2	3	4	5
Shows respect for others' perspectives/preferences	1	2	3	4	5
Utilizes collaborative consultation theory and research	1	2	3	4	5
Understands collaborative models and programs	1	2	3	4	5
Application of Collaborative/Co-Educator Relationships					
Values diversity and individuality	1	2	3	4	5
Practices effective listening skills	1	2	3	4	5
Practices effective nonverbal skills	1	2	3	4	5
Practices effective verbal skills	1	2	3	4	5
Establishes co-equal relationships	1	2	3	4	5
Problem-Solving Techniques					
Demonstrates skill in problem finding	1	2	3	4	5
Collects and processes pertinent data	1	2	3	4	5
Uses effective problem-solving strategies	1	2	3	4	5
Selects appropriate methods for special needs	1	2	3	4	5
Follows through with decisions, follows up on plan	1	2	3	4	5
Organization and Management					
Manages time and resources efficiently	1	2	3	4	5
Coordinates collaborative consultation effectively	1	2	3	4	5
Conducts successful observation and interviewing	1	2	3	4	5
Provides resources and personnel for special needs	1	2	3	4	5
Conducts assessment of collaborations/co-teaching	1	2	3	4	5
Partnerships with Co-Educators					
Co-plans effectively with co-educators	1	2	3	4	5
Co-teaches successfully with co-educators	1	2	3	4	5
Directs paraeducators capably	1	2	3	4	5
Works well with related services/support personnel	1	2	3	4	5
Engages in respectful, productive family interactions	1	2	3	4	5
Change Agents for Positive Ripple Effects					
Provides leadership in collaborative settings	1	2	3	4	5
Interacts effectively with school administrators	1	2	3	4	5
Makes appropriate decisions for student well-being	1	2	3	4	5
Uses technology effectively and innovatively	1	2	3	4	5
Demonstrates skills of mentoring/modeling	1	2	3	4	5

FINAL THOUGHTS

Students, our citizens and leaders of the future, will need home, workplace, and community skills (Beland, 2007; Suárez-Orozco & Sattin, 2007) including:

- Professionalism and work ethic
- Teamwork and collaboration
- Communication
- Reading comprehension and language
- Numeracy
- Critical thinking
- Technology
- Ethics and social responsibility

Their teachers in the home, school, and community are the guides to their future.

"An apple for the teacher" has been an educational tradition for many years, illustrating the caring relationship between teacher and student. The days of the little red schoolhouse with an apple lovingly placed on the lone teacher's desk by an adoring student are long gone. Different challenges await teachers today in their crowded classrooms and bustling school buildings teeming with a diversity of students—some outspoken and angry, others withdrawn and seemingly unreachable, many wishing high school would never end, and too many thinking they just might opt out of it tomorrow. So now the apple signifies important work still to be done. When individual teachers step out of their classrooms and look and listen, they know they are not alone in addressing the challenges. There are opportunities to collaborate in diverse ways with many co-educators. If each one has a symbolic apple and slices it, one outcome is a harvest of seeds. Then if those seeds are planted far and wide, who could count the apples that will grow eventually from that small collection of seeds?

Ripple effects happen in the water and they happen on the land. Most assuredly they happen as well in the hearts and minds of young people and their teachers.

TIPS FOR PUTTING IT ALL TOGETHER TO SERVE STUDENTS' SPECIAL NEEDS

1. Promote an exchange-of-roles day in which consultants teach classes and teachers observe, plan modifications, and consult with others.
2. Make a personal pledge to read at least an article a week from a professional journal.
3. Formulate a personal philosophy of collaboration, consultation, and teamwork as a co-educator.
4. Join a dynamic professional organization and become actively involved in it.
5. Observe programs in other schools and share observations with key people in your own school context.
6. Engage in research efforts for new knowledge about collaboration, consultation, teamwork, and networking with co-educators.
7. Remember that knowing how to collaborate does not guarantee one the opportunity to do it! *Create* the opportunity.

CHAPTER REVIEW

1. To acquire a visionary perspective on special education for student needs, educators are advised by authors and researchers in education to expect changes in roles, to anticipate changes in the total educational system, to accept responsibility for accountability, and to build intellectual study, reflection, and collaboration into their professional days.

2. Leadership is a key element in successful implementation of the collaborative consultation process. Listening skills and empathy enhance the likelihood of success. One important function of educational leaders is advocacy. Knowing key legislators and community leaders, and communicating needs to them in a clear, friendly, and assertive form will help ensure a receptive ear to the concerns. Students who are taught self-advocacy skills become more confident in demonstrating leadership and self-confidence. Mentorships between beginning special education teachers and experienced, effective special education teachers can produce effective growth and development through changes in both mentor and mentee, and most promisingly, reduce attrition rates among special education teachers in their early years in the profession.

3. School administrators and school board members are the decision makers for school policies and structures. Co-educators need to keep building administrators informed through brief, well-prepared fact sheets and memos. They also need to stay apprised of school board business and procedures. Attending board meetings can be informative and instructive.

4. Professional development is a major aspect of school improvement and is integral in developing a schoolwide and districtwide collaborative climate. The experiences should be planned collaboratively, and evaluated with careful attention to the follow-up components.

5. Ethical and conscientious considerations must guide consultants in every consultative and collaborative effort. The primary aim of any school interaction is the welfare of the students. Confidentiality, respect for individual differences of students and adults, careful attention to student and family members' rights, appropriate advocacy, and close monitoring of one's own professionalism are foundations for solid ethical principles. Collaborative school consultation requires skills and competencies of communication, empathy, diplomacy, organization, problem solving, change agentry, assessment, resourcefulness, and much more. These can be enhanced by well-planned and carefully executed professional development programs.

6. Positive ripple effects of collaborative school consultation and co-education include increased assistance for students, minimized labeling and stigmatizing, service in the spirit of inclusion, a more seamless curriculum, parent satisfaction with increased help for their children, enhanced skills through shared teaching, multiplier effects throughout the school context, increased interest among all teachers in helping all students succeed, and student satisfaction with having increased time and attention from teachers and resource personnel. These multiplier effects create benefits well beyond immediate learning and teaching situations.

TO DO AND THINK ABOUT

1. In a teacher's manual for a particular subject, locate references to collaboration and use of a consultant, or better still, instances in which they are encouraged. Discuss these with classroom teachers relevant to the topic and grade level(s).

2. Talk about the following quotations as they might relate to collaboration:

- "It is easier to produce ten volumes of philosophical writing than to put one principle into practice." (unknown)
- "Our goal is not to think alike, but to think together." (anonymous)
- "We're all in this boat together. If you don't care to help row, at least don't drill holes in the bottom of the boat." (contributed by some wise, anonymous person)
- "Coming together is a beginning; keeping together is progress; working together is success." (attributed to Henry Ford)
- "Teamwork divides the task and doubles the success." (unknown)
- "In a completely rational society, the best of us would be teachers, and the rest of us would just have to settle for something else." (attributed to Lee Iacocca)

3. If you were to pick up a newspaper and see a want ad for a collaborative consulting teacher to assist students with learning and behavioral problems in any of the following school contexts, what would you expect that job description to include?

- Elementary school in a suburban area
- Large consolidated middle school in a rural area
- High school in an inner-city area

4. A person's design for his or her workday provides a certain framework to the day and gives meaning to the rhythms of activity that help define the role. Using one of the settings in Activity 3 above, visualize an ideal day in a consulting teacher's life. Think of the context, role, schedule, goals, and activities for that day, and how the impact of that day's events might be appraised.

5. Create a list of school improvement research questions for the future that might be explored within the context of strong school consultation programs and competent consulting personnel.

6. Now that you have studied the content, process, and context of collaborative schools that utilize consultation services and promote team efforts, what kind of schools would you build if you could start all over in a place where no schools exist?

7. Create a motivational bumper sticker that will proclaim the importance of school, home, and community educators working together as partners for children and youth.

8. *And Finally:* Where do we, as school educators, family member educators, community citizens, and lifelong learners, go from here? If you are sharing this book in class time, or group discussion, how will the group's experience together end? Will you make a group collage to display and leave behind for the next ones who come along this path? Have you developed new friendships while studying, attending class, carpooling with someone who *was* a stranger but is no more, and you want now to stay in touch? Will you have a "group hug"? Or, on an agreed-on signal, will each simply leave quietly with confidence renewed in having the knowledge, skills, and will to help students with their special needs?

ADDITIONAL READINGS AND RESOURCES

Darling-Hammond, L. (2003). Keeping good teachers: Why it matters, what leaders can do. *Educational Leadership, 60*(8), 6–13.

Educational Leadership, 55(7).
The April 1998 issue is topical, featuring articles on reshaping school leadership that include creating effective study groups for principals, how to build leadership capacity, teacher talk about advocacy and inquiry that makes a difference, models of reform, leadership in a fishbowl with a new accreditation process, and more.

Foley, R. M., & Lewis, J. A. (1999). Self-perceived competence of secondary school principals to serve as school leaders in collaborative-based educational delivery systems. *Remedial and Special Education, 20*(4), 233–243.

Marsal, L. S. (1997). Mentoring & CEC guidelines for developing a mentorship program for beginning special education teachers. *Teaching Exceptional Children, 29*(6), 18–21.

Miller, T. N., Devin, M., Shoop, & R. J. (2007). *Closing the leadership gap: How district and university partnerships shape effective school leaders.* Thousand Oaks, CA: Corwin.

Reason, L. L., & Wellman, B. (2007). How to talk so teachers listen. *Educational Leadership, 65*(1), 30–34.
Teacher leaders encourage professional growth through conversation and a collaborative stance of co-developing ideas and co-analyzing situations and data.

Riehl, C. J. (2000). The principal's role in creating inclusive schools for diverse students: A review of normative, empirical, and critical literature on the practice of educational administration. *Review of Educational Research, 70*(1), 55–81.

Whitaker, S. D. (2000). Mentoring beginning special education teachers and the relationship to attrition. *Exceptional Children, 66*(4), 546–566.

Wong, H. K., Britton, T., & Ganser, T. (2005). What the world can teach us about new teacher induction. *Phi Delta Kappan, 86*(5), 379–384.

Also, professional periodicals, including but certainly not limited to:

Educational Leadership

Phi Delta Kappan

Teacher Education and Special Education

Journal of Educational and Psychological Consultation

And look for collaboration and team teaching articles in subject-oriented journals and periodicals, such as *Science Education* or *Teacher.*

Adler, S. (1993). *Multicultural communication skills in the classroom*. Boston: Allyn & Bacon.

"Adults and Attention Deficit Disorder." (1997, September 2). *New York Times/Manhattan Mercury*, B-10.

Allen, T. (2004). No school left unscathed. *Phi Delta Kappan, 85*(5), 396–397.

Anderson, J. D. (1997). Supporting the invisible minority. *Educational Leadership, 54*(7), 65–68.

Armas, G. C. (2004, March 18). *Topeka Capital-Journal*. Washington, DC: Associated Press.

Annunzio, S. (2001). *eLeadership*. New York: Free Press.

Aronson, E. (1978). *The jigsaw classroom*. Beverly Hills, CA: Sage.

ASCD. (2000). Finding time to collaborate. *Education Update, 42*(2), 1, 3, 8.

Ashbaker, B., & Morgan, J. (1996). Paraeducators: Critical members of the rural education team. In D. Montgomery (Ed.), *The American Council on Rural Special Education Conference-Rural Goals 2000: Building programs that work* (pp. 130–136). Stillwater: Oklahoma State University.

Ashbaker, B. Y., & Morgan, J. (2006). *Paraprofessionals in the classroom*. Boston: Pearson Education.

August, D., & Hakuta, K. (1997). *Improving schooling for language-minority children*. Washington, DC: National Academy Press.

Babcock, N. L., & Pryzwansky, W. B. (1983). Models of consultation: Preferences of educational professionals at five stages of service. *Journal of School Psychology, 21*, 359–366.

Babinski, L. M., & Rogers, D. L. (1998). Supporting new teachers through consultee-centered group consultation. *Journal of Educational and Psychological Consultation, 9*(4), 285–308.

Baca, L. M., & Cervantes, H. T. (1998). *The bilingual special education interface* (3rd ed.). Upper Saddle River, NJ: Merrill.

Bahamonde, C., & Friend, M. (1999). Teaching English language learners: A proposal for effective service delivery through collaboration and co-teaching. *Journal of Educational and Psychological Consultation, 10*(1), 1–24.

Bailey, G. D. (1981). Self-directed staff development. *Educational Considerations, 8*(1), 15–20.

Banks, J. A. (2003). *Teaching Strategies for ethnic studies* (7th ed.). Boston: Allyn & Bacon.

Banks, J. A., and Banks, C. A. M. (Eds.). (2007). *Multicultural education: Issues and perspectives* (6th ed.). Hoboken, NJ: Wiley.

Barbour, C., & Barbour, N. H. (2001). *Families, schools, and communities: Building partnerships for educating children*. Upper Saddle River, NJ: Merrill Prentice Hall.

Barbour, C., Barbour, N. H., & Scully, P. A. (2008). *Families, schools, and communities* (4th ed.). Upper Saddle River, NJ: Prentice Hall.

Barnard, W. M. (2004). Parent involvement in elementary school and educational attainment. *Children & Youth Services Review, 26*(1), 39–62.

Barnhill, G. P. (2005). Functional behavioral assessment in schools. *Intervention in School and Clinic, 40*(3), 131–143.

Bassett, D. S., Jackson, L., Ferrell, K. A., Luckner, L., Hagerty, P. J., Bunsen, T. D., & MacIsaac, D. (1996). Multiple perspectives on inclusive education: Reflections of a university faculty. *Teacher Education and Special Education, 19*(4), 355–386.

Bateman, D., & Bateman, C. F. (2001). *A principal's guide to special education*. Reston, VA: Council for Exceptional Children.

Bauer, A. M., & Shea, T. M. (2003). *Parents and schools: Creating a successful partnership for students with special needs*. Upper Saddle River, NJ: Prentice Hall.

Bauwens, J., & Hourcade, J. J. (1997). Cooperative teaching: Pictures of possibilities. *Intervention in school and clinic, 33*(2), 81–89.

Beakley, B. (1997). Inclusion: Theory, reality, survival. *The Delta Kappa Gamma Bulletin, 63*(3), 32–26.

Beckhoff, A. G., & Bender, W. N. (1989). Programming for mainstream kindergarten success in preschool: Teachers' perceptions of necessary prerequisite skills. *Journal of Early Intervention, 13*(3), 269–280.

Beland, K. (2007). Boosting social and emotional competence. *Educational Leadership, 61*(8), 68–71.

Benz, S. (1997). How I survived the paper snowstorm of special education. *CEC Today, 4*(4), 6.

Bergan, J. R. (1977). *Behavioral consultation*. Columbus, OH: Merrill.

Bergan, J. R. (1995). Evolution of a problem-solving model of consultation. *Journal of Educational and Psychological Consultation, 6*(2), 111–123.

Bergan, J. R., & Tombari, M. L. (1976). Consultant skill and efficiency and the implementation and outcome of consultation. *Journal of School Psychology, 14*(1), 3–14.

Berger, E. H. (2008). *Parents as partners in education: Families and schools working together* (7th ed.). Upper Saddle River, NJ: Prentice Hall.

Bietau, L. (1994, December). Personal correspondence.

Blank, M. J. (2004). How community schools make a difference. *Educational Leadership, 61*(8), 63–65.

Blaylock, B. K. (1983). Teamwork in a simulated production environment. *Research in Psychological Type, 6,* 58–67.

Bloom, B. S. (1976). *Human characteristics and school learning.* New York: McGraw Hill.

Bloom, B. S., Engelhart, M. D., Furst, E. J., Hill, W. H., & Krathwohl, D. R. (1956). *Taxonomy of educational objectives; Handbook I: Cognitive domain.* New York: McKay.

Bocchino, R. (March, 1991). Using mind mapping as a note-taking tool. *The Developer,* 1, 4.

Bogdan, R., & Biklen, S. (2006). *Qualitative research for education: An introduction to theory and methods* (5th ed.). Boston: Allyn & Bacon.

Bolton, R. (1986). *People skills: How to assert yourself, listen to others, and resolve conflicts.* New York: Simon & Schuster.

Boone, H. A. (1989). Preparing family specialists in early childhood special education. *Teacher Education and Special Education, 12*(3), 96–102.

Bos, C. S., Nahmias, M. L., & Urban, M. A. (1999). Targeting home-school collaboration for students with ADHD. *Teaching Exceptional Children, 31*(6), 4–11.

Boudah, D. J., Lenz, B. K., Bulgren, J. A., Schumkaer, J. B., & Deshler, D. D. (2000). Don't water down! Enhance content learning through the unit organizer routine. *Teaching Exceptional Children, 32*(3), 48–56.

Bradley, M. O. (1987). Personal communication.

Bramlett, R. K., & Murphy, J. J. (1998). School psychology perspectives on consultation: Key contributions to the field. *Journal of Educational and Psychological Consultation, 9*(1), 29–55.

Brown, A. L. (1994). The advancement of learning. *Educational Researcher, 23*(8), 4–12.

Brown, D., Wyne, M. D., Blackburn, J. E., & Powell, W. C. (1979). *Consultation: Strategy for improving education.* Boston: Allyn & Bacon.

Brown, T. E. (2007). A new approach to attention deficit disorder. *Educational Leadership, 64*(5), 22–27.

Brown-Chidsey, R. (2007). No more "waiting to fail." *Educational Leadership, 65*(2), 40–46.

Brownell, M., Adams, A., Sindelar, P., Waldron, N., & Vanhover, S. (2006). Learning from collaboration: The role of teacher qualities. *Exceptional Children, 72*(2), 169–185.

Bruner, C. (1991). *Thinking collaboratively: Ten questions and answers to help policymakers improve children's services.* Washington, DC: Education and Human Service Consortium.

Bruns, D. A., & Fowler, S. A. (1999). Designing culturally sensitive transition plans for young children and their families. *Teaching Exceptional Children, 31*(5), 26–30.

Bulgren, J. A., Schumaker, J. B., & Deshler, D. D. (1993). *The concept mastery routine.* Lawrence, KS: Edge Enterprises.

Buscaglia, L. (1986). *Loving each other: The challenges of human relationships.* Westminister, MD: Fawcett.

Bushaw, W. J. (2007). From the mouths of middle-schoolers: Important changes for high school and college. *Phi Delta Kappan, 89*(3), 189–193.

Buzan, T. (1983). *Use both sides of your brain.* New York: Dutton.

Canning, C. (1991). What teachers say about reflection. *Educational Leadership, 48*(6), 18–21.

Caplan, G. (1970). *The theory and practice of mental health consultation.* New York: Basic Books.

Caplan, G. (1995). Types of mental health consultation. *Journal of Educational and Psychological Consultation, 6*(1), 7–21.

Caplan, G., Caplan, R. B., & Erchul, W. P. (1995). A contemporary view of mental health consultation: Comments on "Types of Mental Health Consultation." *Journal of Educational and Psychological Consultation, 6*(1), 23–30.

Carlson, M. (1995). *Winning grants step by step: Support centers of America's complete workbook for planning, developing, writing successful proposals.* San Francisco: Jossey-Bass.

Carlyn, M. (1977). An assessment of the Myers-Briggs Type Indicator. *Journal of Personality Assessment, 41*(5), 461–473.

Caro, D. J., & Robbins, P. (1991, November). Talkwalking—thinking on your feet. *Developer,* 3–4.

Carver, C. L. (2004, May). A lifeline for new teachers. *Educational Leadership,* 58–61.

Caspe, M., & Lopez, M. E. (2006). *Lessons from family-strengthening interventions: Learning from evidence-based practice.* Cambridge, MA: Harvard Family Research Project. Available at www.gse .harvard.edu/hfrp.html

Caspe, M., Lopez, M. E., & Wolos, C. (2007). *Family involvement in elementary school children's education.* Cambridge, MA: Harvard Family Research Project. Available at www.gse.harvard.edu/hfrp.html

Casper, V., & Schultz, S. B. (1999). *Gay parents/straight schools: Building communication and trust.* New York: Teachers College Press.

Cawelti, G. (1997). Making the most of every minute. *ASCD Education Update, 39*(6), 1, 6, 8.

CEC Today. (1997, April/May).

CEC Today. (2000, October).

Chisholm, I. M. (1994). Preparing teachers for multicultural classrooms. *Journal of Educational Issues of Language Minority Students, 14,* 43–68.

Christie, K. (2002). States take on the training of paraprofessionals. *Phi Delta Kappan, 84*(3), 181–182.

Christie, K. (2004). AYP: The new purple pill for the slower learner. *Phi Delta Kappan, 85*(5), 341–342.

Christie, K. (2005). Changing the nature of parent involvement. *Phi Delta Kappan, 86*(9), 645+.

Cipani, E. (1985). The three phrases of behavioral consultation: Objectives, intervention, and quality assurance. *Teacher Education and Special Education, 8,* 144–152.

Clare, M. M. (2002). Diversity as a dependent variable: Considerations for research and practice in consultation. *Journal of Educational and Psychological Consultation, 13*(30), 251–263.

Clark, B. (2002). *Growing up gifted* (6th ed.). Upper Saddle River, NJ: Merrill.

Clark, S. G. (2000). The IEP process as a tool for collaboration. *Teaching Exceptional Children, 33*(2), 56–66.

Cleveland, C. B. (1981). Coming to grips with memo mania. *Penton/I.P.C., Inc. Regency,* 33–87.

Connell, J. P., Kubisch, A. C., Schorr, L. B., & Weiss, C. H. (Eds.). (1995). *New contexts.* Washington, DC: Aspen Institute.

Conoley, J. C. (1985). Personal correspondence.

Conoley, J. C. (1987). National Symposium on School Consultation. Austin: University of Texas.

Conoley, J. C. (1989). Professional communication and collaboration among educators. In M. C. Reynolds (Ed.), *Knowledge base for the beginning teacher* (pp. 245–254). Oxford, England: Pergamon.

Conoley, J. C. (1994). You say potato, I say . . . : Part I. *Journal of Educational and Psychological Consultation, 5*(1), 45–49.

Conoley, J. C., & Conoley, C. W. (1982). *School consultation: A guide to practice and training.* New York: Pergamon Press.

Conoley, J. C., & Conoley, C. W. (1988). Useful theories in school-based consultation. *Remedial and Special Education, 9*(6), 14–20.

Cosmos, C. (2001). Abuse of children with disabilities. *CEC Today, 8*(2), 1, 5, 8, 12, 14–15.

Council for Exceptional Children. (1997). Working with paraeducators. *CEC Today, 4*(3), 1, 5.

Council for Exceptional Children. (2000). Home schooling—A viable alternative for students with special needs? *CEC Today, 7*(1), 1, 5, 10, 15.

Council for Exceptional Children. (2001). A principal's guide to special education. *CEC Today, 8*(2), 10.

Countryman, L. L., & Schroeder, M. (1996). When students lead parent-teacher conferences. *Educational Leadership, 53*(7), 64–68.

Covey, S. R. (1989). *The seven habits of highly effective people.* New York: Simon & Schuster.

Coyle, N. C. (2000). Conflict resolution: It's part of the job. *Delta Kappa Gamma Bulletin, 66*(4), 41–46.

Cramer, S., Erzkus, A., Mayweather, K., Pope, K., Roeder, J., & Tone, T. (1997). Connecting with siblings. *Teaching Exceptional Children, 30*(1), 46–49.

Creswell, J. W., & Plano-Clark, V. L. (2006). *Designing and conducting mixed methods research.* Thousand Oaks, CA: Sage.

Cross, T. (1996). Developing a knowledge base to support cultural competence. *Prevention Report, 1,* 2–5.

Cross, T. L. (2003). Culture as a resource for mental health. *Cultural Diversity and Ethnic Minority Psychology, 9*(4), 354–359.

Cummings, J. A. (2001). Professional communities of the future. *The School Psychologist, 55*(2), 15.

Cummings, J. A., Harrison, P. L., Dawson, M., Short, R. J., Gorin, S., & Palomares, R. S. (2004). Follow-up to the 2002 Futures Conference: Collaborating to serve all children, families, and schools. *Journal of Educational and Psychological Consultation, 15* (3 & 4), 335–344.

Curtis, M. J., Curtis, V. A., & Graden, J. L. (1988). Prevention and early intervention assistance programs. *School Psychology International, 9,* 257–264.

Darling-Hammond, L. (2003). Keeping good teachers: Why it matters, what leaders can do. *Educational Leadership, 60*(8), 6–13.

Davies, D. (1988). Low-income parents and the schools: A research report and plan for action. *Equity and Choice, 4,* 51–59.

Davis, W. E. (1983). Competencies and skills required to be an effective resource teacher. *Journal of Learning Disabilities, 16,* 596–598.

de Valenzuela, J. S., Baca, L., & Baca, E. (2004). Family involvement in bilingual special education: Challenging the norm. In L. M. Baca & H. T Cervantes. (Eds.), *The bilingual special education interface* (4th ed., pp. 360–381). Upper Saddle River, NJ: Pearson.

de Valenzuela, J. S., Torres, R. L., & Chavez, R. L. (1998). Family involvement in bilingual special education: Challenging the norm. In L. M. Baca & H. T. Cervantes (Eds.), *The bilingual special education interface* (3rd ed., pp. 350–370). Upper Saddle River, NJ: Merrill.

Dearing, E., Krieder, H., Simpkins, S., & Weiss, H. B. (2006). Family involvement in school and low-income children's literacy: Longitudinal associations between and within families. *Journal of Educational Psychology, 89*(4), 653–664.

DeBoer, A. L. (1986). *The art of consulting.* Chicago: Arcturus.

deBono, E. (1973). *Lateral thinking: Creativity step by step.* Boston: Little, Brown.

deBono, E. (1985). *Six thinking hats.* New York: Harper & Row.

deBono, E. (1986). *CORT thinking: Teacher's notes* (Vols. 1–6, 2nd ed.). New York: Pergamon.

Demchak, M. A., & Morgan, C. R. (1998). Effective collaboration between professionals and paraprofessionals. *Rural Special Education Quarterly, 17*(2), 10–15.

Denham, A., & Lahm, E. A. (2001). Using technology to construct alternate portfolios of students with moderate and severe disabilities. *Teaching Exceptional Children, 33*(5), 10–17.

Denton, C. A., Hasbrouck, J. E., & Sekaquaptewa, S. (2003). The consulting teacher: A descriptive case study in responsive systems consultation. *Journal of Educational and Psychological Consultation, 14*(1), 41–73.

Deshler, D. D., & Schumaker, J. B. (1986). Learning strategies: An instructional alternative for low-achieving adolescents. *Exceptional Children, 52,* 583–590.

Deshler, D. D., Schumaker, J. B., Lenz, B. K., Bulgren, J. A., Hoch, M. F., Knight, J., & Ehren, B. J. (2001). Ensuring content-area learning by secondary students with learning disabilities. *Learning Disabilities Research and Practice, 16*(2), 96–108,

Dettmer, P. (1981). The effects of teacher personality type on classroom values and perceptions of gifted students. *Research in Psychological Type, 3,* 48–54.

Dettmer, P. (1989). The consulting teacher in programs for gifted and talented students. *Arkansas Gifted Education Magazine, 3*(2), 4–7.

Dettmer, P. (Ed.). (1990). *Staff development for gifted programs: Putting it together and making it work.* Washington, DC: National Association for Gifted Children.

Dettmer, P. (1994). IEPs for gifted secondary students. *The Journal of Secondary Gifted Education, 5*(4), 52–59.

Dettmer, P. (1997, September). *New blooms for established fields.* Presented at the annual conference of the Kansas Association for Gifted, Talented, and Creative, Hutchinson, KS.

Dettmer, P. (2006). New domains in established fields: Four domains of learning and doing. *Roeper Review, 28*(2), 70–78.

Dettmer, P., & Lane, J. (1989). An integrative model for educating very able students in rural school districts. *Educational Considerations, 17*(1), 36–39.

Dillman, D. A. (2007). *Mail and Internet surveys: The tailored design method* (2nd ed.). Hoboken, NJ: Wiley.

Dorris, M. (1979). Why I'm not thankful for Thanksgiving. *Midwest Race Desegregation Assistance Center Horizons, 1*(5), 1.

Dougherty, A. M., Tack, F. E., Fullam, C. B., & Hammer, L. A. (1996). Disengagement: A neglected aspect of the consultation process. *Journal of Educational and Psychological Consultation, 7*(3), 259–274.

Douglass, M. E., & Douglass, D. N. (1993). *Manage your time, manage your work, manage yourself.* New York: AMACOM.

DuFour, R. (2004). What is a professional learning community? *Educational Leadership, 61*(8), 6–11.

Dunn, R., & Dunn, K. (1978). *Teaching students through their individual learning styles.* Reston, VA: Reston Publishing.

Dunst, C. J. (2002). How can we strengthen family support research and evaluation? *The Evaluation Exchange, 8*(1), 5.

Dyck, N. (1997). *Self-advocacy form.* Lawrence, KS: Curriculum Solutions.

Dyck, N. (1999). *How to adapt text for struggling readers.* Lawrence, KS: Curriculum Solutions.

Dyck, N., & Dettmer, P. (1989). Collaborative consultation: A promising tool for serving gifted learning-disabled students. *Journal of Reading, Writing, and Learning Disabilities, 5*(3), 253–264.

Dyck, N., & Dettmer, P., & Thurston, L. P. (1985). *Special education consultation skills project.* Manhattan, KS Kansas State University, College of Education, unpublished manuscript.

Dyck, N., & Kaff, M. (1999). *Essential skills for paras.* San Antonio, TX: PCI Educational Publishing.

Dyck, N., & Pemberton, J. (1997). *A dozen tools for paras.* Lawrence, KS: Curriculum Solutions.

Dyck, N., & Pemberton, J. B. (2002). A model for making decisions about text adaptations. *Intervention in School and Clinic, 38*(1), 28–35.

Dyck, N., Pemberton, J., Woods, K., & Sundbye, N. (1996). *Creating inclusive schools: A new design for all students.* Lawrence, KS: Curriculum Solutions.

Dyck, N., & Thurston, L. P. (1998). *Getting the message across: A para's guide to communication.* San Antonio, TX: PCI Educational Publishing.

Dyck, N., Zabel, M. K., & Zabel, R. H. (1998). *Behavior management guide for paras.* Lawrence, KS: Curriculum Solutions.

Dyck, N., Zabel, M. K., & Zabel, R. H. (1998). *Behavioral management guide for paras.* San Antonio, TX: PCI Educational Publishing.

Eberle, R. (1984). *Scamper on for creative imagination development.* Buffalo, NY: DOK.

Edwards, A. T. (1997). Let's stop ignoring our gay and lesbian youth. *Educational Leadership, 54*(7), 68–70.

Edyburn, D. (2006). Text modifications. *Special Education Technology Practice, 8*(2), 16–27.

Eisner, E. W. (2003). Questionable assumptions about schooling. *Phi Delta Kappan, 84*(9), 348–357.

Epstein, J. L. (1995). School/family/community partnerships: Caring for the children we share. *Phi Delta Kappan, 76*(9), 701–712.

Erchul, W. P., & Martens, B. K. (1997). *School consultation: Conceptual and empirical bases of practice.* New York: Plenum.

Erickson, M. J., Stage, S. A., & Nelson, J. R. (2006). Naturalistic study of the behavior of students with EBD referred for functional behavioral assessment. *Journal of Emotional and Behavioral Disorders, 14,* 31–40.

Ernsperger, L. (1998). Using a paraeducator to facilitate school reentry. *Reaching Today's Youth: The Community Circle Caring Journal, 2*(4), 9–12.

Family Integration Resources. (1991). Second Family Leadership Conference. Washington, DC: U.S. Department of Education.

Federico, M. A., Herrold, Jr., W. G., & Venn, J. (1999). Helpful tips for successful inclusion: A checklist for educators. *Teaching Exceptional Children, 32*(1), 76–82.

Fennick, E. (2001). Co-teaching: An inclusive curriculum for transition. *Teaching Exceptional Children, 33*(6), 60–66.

Fiedler, C. R., Simpson, R. L., & Clark, D. M. (2007). *Parents and families of children with disabilities: Effective school-based support services.* Upper Saddle River, NJ: Prentice Hall.

Finn, J. D. (1998). Parental engagement that makes a difference. *Educational Leadership, 55*(8), 20–24.

Fisher, D. (1993). *Communication in organizations* (2nd ed.). St Paul, MN: West.

Fisher, R., & Sharp, A. (1999). *Getting it DONE: How to lead when you're not in charge.* New York: HarperCollins.

Fisher, R., & Ury, W. (1991). *Getting past no: Negotiating agreement without giving in.* New York: Bantam Books.

Fisher, R., Ury, B., & Patton, B. (1991). *Getting to YES: Negotiating agreement without giving in.* Boston: Houghton Mifflin.

Fleury, M. L. (2000). Confidentiality issues with substitutes and paraeducators. *Teaching Exceptional Children, 33*(1), 44–45.

Foley, R. M., & Lewis, J. A. (1999). Self-perceived competence of secondary school principals to serve as school leaders in collaborative-based educational delivery systems. *Remedial and Special Education, 20*(4), 233–243.

Fowler, S. A., Donegan, M., Lueke, B., Hadden, D. S., & Phillips, B. (2000). Evaluating community collaboration in writing interagency agreements on the age 3 transition. *Exceptional Children, 67*(1), 35–50.

French, N. K. (1997). Management of paraeducators. In A. L. Pickett & K. Gerlach (Eds.), *Supervising Paraeducators in School Settings.* Austin, TX: PRO-ED.

French, N. K. (1998). Working together: Resource teachers and paraeducators. *Remedial and Special Education, 19,* 357–368.

French, N. K. (1999). Paraeducators and teachers: Shifting roles. *Teaching Exceptional Children, 2*(2), 69–73.

French, N. K. (2000). Taking time to save time: Delegating to paraeducators. *Teaching Exceptional Children, 32*(3), 79–83.

French, N. K., & Pickett, A. L. (1997). Paraprofessionals in special education: Issues for teacher educators. *Teacher Education and Special Education, 20*(1), 61–73.

Frieman, B. B. (1997). Two parents—two homes. *Educational Leadership, 54*(7), 23–25.

Friend, M. (1984). Consultation skills for resource teachers. *Learning Disability Quarterly, 7,* 246–250.

Friend, M. (1988). Putting consultation into context: Historical and contemporary perspectives. *Remedial and Special Education, 9*(6), 7–13.

Friend, M. (2007). The coteaching partnership. *Educational Leadership, 64*(5), 48–52.

Friend, M., & Bursuck, W. D. (1996). *Including students with special needs: A practical guide for classroom teachers.* Boston: Allyn & Bacon.

Friend, M., & Cook, L. (1990). Collaboration as a predictor for success in school reform. *Journal of Educational and Psychological Consultation, 1*(1), 69–86.

Friend, M., & Cook, L. (1992). The ethics of collaboration. *Journal of Educational and Psychological Consultation, 3*(2), 181–184.

Fuchs, D., & Fuchs, L. S. (1994). Inclusive schools movement and the radicalization of special education reform. *Exceptional Children, 60*(4), 294–309.

Fuchs, D., Fuchs, L. S., Dulan, J., Roberts, H., & Fernston, P. (1992). Where is the research on consultation effectiveness? *Journal of Educational and Psychological Consultation, 3*(2), 151–174.

Fuller, R. B. (1975). *Explorations in the geometry of thinking synergetics.* New York: Macmillan.

Futrell, M., Gomez, J., & Bedden, D. (2003). Teaching the children of a new America. *Phi Delta Kappan, 84*(5), 381–385.

Gallessich, J. (1974). Training the school psychologist for consultation. *Journal of School Psychology, 12,* 138–149.

Gardner, H. (1993). *Multiple intelligences: The theory in practice.* New York: HarperCollins.

Garmston, R. (1988, October). Giving gifts. *The Developer, 3,* 6.

Garmston, R. J. (1994). The persuasive art of presenting: What's a Meta Phor? *Journal of Staff Development, 15*(2), 60–61.

Garmston, R. J. (1995). Techniques to increase collaboration. *Journal of Staff Development, 16*(3), 69–70.

Garmston, R. J., & Wellman, B. M. (1992). *How to make presentations that teach and transform.* Alexandria, VA: Association for Supervision and Curriculum Development.

Gazda, G. M., Asbury, F. R., Balzer, F. J., Childers, W. C., Phelps, R. E., & Walters, R. P. (1999). *Human relations development: A manual for educators* (6th ed.). Boston: Allyn & Bacon.

Geenen, S., Powers, L. E., & Lopez-Vasquez, A. (2001). Multicultural aspects of parent involvement in transition planning. *Exceptional Children, 67*(2), 265–282.

Geisler, L. (2004, December 5). Your job: School bus driver. *Topeka Capital Journal.*

Gerber, P. J., & Popp, P. A. (2000). Making collaborative teaching more effective for academically able students. *Learning Disability Quarterly, 23,* 229–236.

Gersten, R., & Baker, S. (2000). What we know about effective instructional practices for English-language learners. *Exceptional Children, 66*(4), 454–470.

Gersten, R., Darch, C., Davis, G., & George, N. (1991). Apprenticeship and intensive training of consulting teachers: A naturalistic study. *Exceptional Children, 57*(3), 226–236.

Giangreco, M. F., Dennis, R., Cloninger, C., Edelman, S., & Schattman, R. (1993). "I've counted Jon": Transformational experiences of teachers education students with disabilities. *Exceptional Children, 59*(4), 359–372.

Giangreco, M. F., Edelman, S. W., & Broer, S. M. (2001). Respect, appreciation, and acknowledgment of paraprofessionals who support students with disabilities. *Exceptional Children, 67*(4), 485–498.

Giangreco, M. F., Edelman, S. W., Broer, S. M., & Doyle, M. B. (2001). Paraprofessional support of students with disabilities: Literature from the past decade. *Exceptional Children, 68*(1), 45–63.

Giangreco, M. F., Edelman, S. W., Luiselli, T. E., & Mac-Farland, S. Z. C. (1997). Helping or hovering? Effects of instructional assistant proximity on students with disabilities. *Exceptional Children, 64*(1), 7–18.

Gill, E. K. (2007). PreK, in play: Early childhood education advocates rebound. *Education Update, 49*(8), 1–2, 5–6, 8.

Glasgow, N. A., & Hicks, C. D. (2003). *What SUCCESSFUL teachers do: 91 research-based classroom strategies for new and veteran teachers.* Thousand Oaks, CA: Corwin.

GOAL/QPC & Joiner Associates, Inc. (1995). *The team memory jogger: A pocket guide for team members.* Methune, MA: Authors.

Golombok, S., Perry, B., Burston, A., Murray, C., Mooney-Sommers, J., Stevens, M., & Golding J. (2003). Children with lesbian parents: A community study. *Developmental Psychology, 39*(1), 20–33.

Gordon, T. (1974). *T.E.T.: Teacher effectiveness training.* New York: Wyden.

Gordon, T. (1977). *Leader effectiveness training, L.E.T.: The no-lose way to release the productive potential in people.* Toronto: Bantam.

Gordon, T. (2000). *P.E.T.: Parent effectiveness training: The proven programs for raising responsible children.* New York: Three Rivers Press.

Graubard, P. S., Rosenberg, H., & Miller, M. B. (1971). Student applications of behavior modification to teachers and environments or ecological approaches to deviancy. In E. A. Ramp & B. L. Hopkins (Eds.), *A new direction for education: Behavior analysis* (pp. 80–101). Lawrence: University of Kansas.

Gravois, T. A., Knotek, S., & Babinski, L. M. (2002). Educating practitioners as consultants: Development and implementation of the instructional consultation team consortium. *Journal of Educational and Psychological Consultation, 13*(1 & 2), 113–132.

Greenburg, D. E. (1987). *A special educator's perspective on interfacing special and general education: A review for administrators.* Reston, VA: Council for Exceptional Children, Clearinghouse on Handicapped and Gifted Children.

Greer, J. V. (1989). The prime factor in education. *Exceptional Children, 56*(3), 191–193.

Gregorc, A. F., & Ward, H. B. (1977). A new definition for individual: Implications for learning and teaching. *NASSP Bulletin, 61,* 20–26.

Gresham, F. M., & Kendell, G. K. (1987). School consultation research: Methodological critique and future research directions. *School Psychology Review, 16*(3), 306–316.

Griffin, J. (1998). *How to say it at work: Putting yourself across with power words, phrases, body language, and communication secrets.* Paramus, NJ: Prentice Hall.

Gronlund, N. E. (2000). *How to write and use instructional objectives* (6th ed.). Upper Saddle River, NJ: Merrill.

Gullatt, D. E., & Tollett, J. R. (1997). Educational law: A requisite course for preservice and inservice teacher education programs. *Journal of Teacher Education, 48*(2), 120–135.

Guskey, T. R. (1985). Staff development and teacher change. *Educational Leadership, 42*(7), 57–60.

Guthrie, G. P., & Guthrie, L. F. (1991). Streamlining interagency collaboration for youth at risk. *Educational Leadership, 49*(1), 17–22.

Hall, C. S., & Lindzey, G. (1989). *Theories of personality* (3rd ed.). New York: Wiley.

Hamlin, S. (2006). *How to talk so people listen: Connecting in today's workplace.* New York: HarperCollins.

Hammond, H. (1999). Identifying best family-centered practices in early-intervention programs. *Teaching Exceptional Children, 31*(6), 42–46.

Hanna, G. S., & Dettmer, P. A. (2004). *Assessment for effective teaching: Using context-adaptive planning.* Boston: Allyn & Bacon.

Hansen, J. C., Himes, B. S., & Meier, S. (1990). *Consultation: Concepts and practices.* Englewood Cliffs, NJ: Prentice Hall.

Harris, A. J., & Sipay, E. R. (1990). *How to increase reading ability.* White Plains, NY: Longman.

Harris, K. C., & Klein, M. D. (2002). Itinerant consultation in early childhood special education: Issues and challenges. *Journal of Educational and Psychological Consultation, 13*(3), 247–257.

Harris, K. C. (2004). The relationship between educational consultation an instruction for culturally and linguistically diverse exceptional (CLDE) student: Definitions, structures, and case studies. In L. M. Baca & H. T. Cervantes, *The bilingual special education interface* (4th ed., pp. 337–359). Upper Saddle River, NJ: Pearson.

Harrow, A. J. (1972). *A taxonomy of the psychomotor domain: A guide for developing behavioral objectives.* New York: McKay.

Harry, B., Kalyanpur, M., & Day, M. (1999). *Building cultural reciprocity with families: Case studies in special education.* Baltimore, MD: Paul H. Brookes.

Haynes, M. E. (1988). *Effective meeting skills: A practical guide to more productive meetings.* Los Altos, CA: Crisp.

Hehir, T. (2007). Confronting ableism. *Educational Leadership, 64*(5), 8–14.

Henning-Stout, M. (1994). Consultation and connected knowing: What we know is determined by the questions we ask. *Journal of Educational and Psychological Consultation, 5*(1), 5–21.

Heron, T. E., & Harris, K. C. (1987). *The educational consultant: Helping professionals, parents, and mainstreamed students.* Austin, TX: PRO-ED.

Heron, T. E., & Kimball, W. H. (1988). Gaining perspective with the educational consultation research base: Ecological considerations and further recommendations. *Remedial and Special Education, 9*(6), 21–28, 47.

Hildebrand, V., Phenice, L. A., Gray, M. M., & Hines, R. P. (2000). *Knowing and serving diverse families.* Upper Saddle River, NJ: Merrill.

Hill, N. E., & Taylor, L. C. (2004). Parental school involvement and children's academic achievement: Pragmatics and issues. *Current Directions in Psychological Science, 13*(4), 161–164.

Hillerman, T. (1990). *Coyote waits.* New York: Harper & Row.

Hobbs, T., & Westling, D. L. (1998). Promoting successful inclusion through collaborative problem solving. *Teaching Exceptional Children, 31*, 12–19.

Houston, P. D. (2005). NCLB: Dreams and nightmares. *Phi Delta Kappan, 86*(6), 469–470.

Howe, K. R., & Miramontes, O. B. (1992). *The ethics of special education.* New York: Teachers College Press.

Huefner, D. S. (1988). The consulting teacher model: Risks and opportunities. *Exceptional Children, 54*(5), 403–414.

Hughes, C. E., & Murawski, W. A. (2001). Lessons from another field: Applying co-teaching strategies to gifted education. *Gifted Child Quarterly, 45*(3), 195–204.

Hughes, M., & Greenhough, P. (2006). Boxes, bags, and videotape: Enhancing home-school communication through knowledge exchange activities. *Educational Review, 58*(4), 471–487.

Hunter, M. (1985, May). Promising theories die young. *ASCD Update, 1,* 3.

Hurst, M. (2007). *Bit literacy: Productivity in the age of information and e-mail overload.* New York, NY: Good Experience Press.

Hylander, I. (2003). Toward a grounded theory of the conceptual change process in consultee-centered consultation. *Journal of Educational and Psychological Consultation, 14*(3 & 4), 263–280.

Idol, L. (1988). A rationale and guidelines for establishing special education consultation programs. *Remedial and Special Education, 9*(6), 48–58.

Idol, L., Paolucci-Whitcomb, P., & Nevin, A. (1986). *Collaborative Consultation.* Austin, TX: PRO-ED.

Idol, L., Paolucci-Whitcomb, P., & Nevin, A. (1995). The collaborative consultation model. *Journal of Educational and Psychological Consultation, 6*(4), 329–346.

Idol, L., & West, J. F. (1987). Consultation in special education (Part II): Training and practices. *Journal of Learning Disabilities, 20,* 474–497.

Idol, L., West, J. F., & Lloyd, S. R. (1988). Organizing and implementing specialized reading programs: A collaborative approach involving classroom, remedial, and special education teachers. *Remedial and Special Education, 9*(2), 54–61.

Idol-Maestas, L. (1981). A teacher training model: The resource/consulting teacher. *Behavioral Disorders, 6*(2), 108–121.

Idol-Maestas, L. (1983). *Special educator's consultation handbook.* Rockville, MD: Aspen.

Idol-Maestas, L., & Celentano, R. (1986). Teacher consultant services for advanced students. *Roeper Review, 9*(1), 34–36.

Idol-Maestes, L., Lloyd, S., & Lilly, M. S. (1981). Noncategorical approach to direct service and teachers education. *Exceptional Children, 48,* 213–220.

Idol-Maestas, L., & Ritter, S. (1985). A follow-up study of resource/consulting teachers: Factors that facilitate and inhibit teacher consultation. *Teacher Education and Special Education, 8,* 121–131.

Illsley, S. D., & Sladeczek, I. E. (2001). Conjoint behavioral consultation: Outcome measures beyond the client level. *Journal of Educational and Psychological Consultation, 12*(4), 397–404.

Inger, M. (1993, December). Teacher collaboration in secondary schools. *CenterFocus 2.* Available online at http://ncrve.berkeley.edu/CenterFocus/CF2.htm

Ingersoll, R. M. (2001). Teacher turnover and teacher shortages: An organizational analysis. *American Educational Research Journal, 38*(3), 499–534.

Ingersoll, R. M. (2002). The teacher shortage: A case of wrong diagnosis and wrong prescription. *NASSP Bulletin, 86*(631), 16–31.

Ingraham, C. L. (2003). Multicultural consultee-centered consultation when novice consultants explore cultural hypotheses with experienced teacher consultees. *Journal of Educational and Psychological Consultation, 14*(3 & 4), 329–362.

Jason, L. A., Pokorny, S. B., Ji, P., & Kunz, C. (2005). Developing community-school-university partnerships to control youth access to tobacco. *Journal of Educational and Psychological Consultation, 16*(3), 201–222.

Jenkins, J. R., & Jenkins, L. (1985). Peer tutoring in elementary and secondary programs. *Focus on Exceptional Children, 17*(6), 1–12.

Jersild, A. T. (1955). *When teachers face themselves.* New York: Teachers College Press.

Jeynes, W. H. (2007). The relationship between parental involvement an urban secondary school student academic achievement. *Urban Education, 42*(1), 82–110.

Johnson, D. W., & Johnson, R. (1991). *Teaching students to be peacemakers.* Edina, MN: Interaction Book Co.

Johnson, D. W., & Johnson, R. T. (1987). *Learning together and alone: Cooperative, competitive, & individualistic learning* (2nd ed.). Englewood Cliffs, NJ: Prentice Hall.

Johnson, D. W., and Johnson, R. T. (1995). *Reducing school violence through conflict resolution.* Alexandria, VA: ASCD.

Johnson, L. J., & Pugach, M. C. (1996). Role of collaborative dialogue in teaching conceptions of appropriate practice for students at risk. *Journal of Educational and Psychological Consultation, 7*(1), 9–24.

Johnson, S. (1992). *"Yes" or "No": A guide to better decisions.* New York: HarperCollins.

Johnson, S. M., & Donaldson, M. L. (2007). Overcoming the obstacles to leadership. *Educational Leadership, 65*(1), 8–13.

John-Steiner, V., Weber, R. J., & Minnis, M. (1998). The challenge of studying collaboration. *American Educational Research Journal, 35*(4), 773–783.

Joint Committee on Teacher Planning for Students with Disabilities. (1995). *Planning for academic diversity in America's classrooms: Windows on reality, research, change, and practice.* Lawrence: University of Kansas Center for Research on Learning.

Jones, S. L., & Morin, V. A. (2000). Training teachers to work as partners: Modeling the way in teacher preparation programs. *The Delta Kappa Bulletin, 67*(1), 51–55.

Jung, C. G. (1923). *Psychological types.* New York: Harcourt Brace.

Kaff, M., & Dyck, N. (1999). *Essential skills for paras.* Lawrence, KS: Curriculum Solutions.

Kantor, P. L. (2003). *Internet history.* Available online at http://academ.hvcc.edu/~kantopet/misc/index.php?page=net+history

Kauffman, J. (1993). Foreword. In K. R. Howe & O. B. Miramontes (Eds.), *The ethics of special education.* New York: Teachers College Press.

Kauffman, J. M. (1994). Places of Change: Special education's power and identity in an era of educational reform. *Journal of Learning Disabilities, 27*(10), 610–618.

Keirsey, D., & Bates, M. (1978). *Please understand me: Character and temperament types.* Del Mar, CA: Prometheus Nemesis.

Kelleher, J. (2003). A model for assessment-driven professional development. *Phi Delta Kappan, 84*(10), 751–756.

Keller, M. M., & Decoteau, G. T. (2000). *The military child: Mobility and education,* Fastback #63. Bloomington, IN: Phi Delta Kappa Educational Foundation.

Kellogg, W. K. (2004). *Logic model development guide.* Battle Creek, MI: W. K. Kellogg Foundation.

Kerns, G. M. (1992). Helping professionals understand families. *Teacher Education and Special Education, 15*(1), 49–55.

Keyes, R. (1991). *Timelock: How life got so hectic and what you can do about it.* New York: Academic Press.

Kirschenbaum, R. J., Armstrong, D. C., & Landrum, M. S. (1999). Resource consultation model in gifted education to support talent development in today's inclusive schools. *Gifted Child Quarterly, 43*(1), 39–47.

Kling, B. (2000). ASSERT yourself: Helping students of all ages develop self-advocacy skills. *Teaching Exceptional Children, 30*(3), 66–71.

Kluth, P., & Straut, D. (2001). Standards for diverse learners. *Educational Leadership, 59*(1), 43–46.

Knapczyk, D., Rodes, P., Chung, H., & Chapman, D. (in press). Collaborative teacher education in off-campus rural communities. *Rural Special Education Quarterly, 18*(3/4), 36–43.

Knotek, S. E., Rosenfield, S. A., Gravois, T. A., & Babinski, L. M. (2003). The process of fostering consultee development during Instructional Consultation. *Journal of Educational and Psychological Consultation, 14*(3 & 4), 303–328.

Knowles, M. (1978). *The adult learner: A neglected species.* Houston, TX: Gulf Publishing.

Knowles, W. C. (1997). *An investigation of teachers' perceptions of special education placement and inclusion: A qualitative case study of two middle schools.* Unpublished doctoral dissertation, Kansas State University, Manhattan, KS.

Kohm, B. (2002). Improving faculty conversations. *Educational Leadership, 59*(8), 31–33.

Kolb, D. A. (1976). *Learning-style inventory: Technical manual.* Boston: McBer & Co.

Koemer, M. E., & Hulsebosch, P. (1996). Preparing teachers to work with children of gay and lesbian parents. *Journal of Teacher Education, 47*(5), 347–354.

Kozoll, C. E. (1982). *Time management for educators,* Fastback #175. Bloomington, IN: Phi Delta Kappa Educational Foundation.

Krathwohl, D. R., Bloom, B. S., & Masia, B. B. (1964). *Taxonomy of educational objectives; Handbook II: Affective domain.* New York: McKay.

Kratochwill, T. R., & Pittman, P. H. (2002). Expanding problem-solving consultation training: Prospects and frameworks. *Journal of Educational and Psychological Consultation, 13*(1 & 2), 69–95.

Kreider, H., Caspe, M., Kennedy, S., & Weiss, H. (2007). *Family involvement in middle and high school students' education.* Cambridge, MA: Harvard Family Research Project. Available online at www.gse.harvard.edu/hfrp.html

Kroth, R. L. (1985). *Communication with parents of exceptional children: Improving parent-teacher relationships.* Denver: Love.

LaBonte, K., Leighty, C., Mills, S. J., & True, M. L. (1995). Whole-faculty study groups: Building the capacity for change through interagency collaboration. *Journal of Staff Development, 16*(3), 45–47.

Lakein, A. (1973). *How to get control of your time and your life.* New York: McKay.

Lamme, L. L., & Lamme, L. A. (2001–2002). Welcoming children from gay families into our schools. *Educational Leadership, 59*(4), 65–69.

Lasater, M. W., Johnson, M. M., & Fitzgerald, M. (2000). Completing the education mosaic: Paraeducator professional development options. *Teaching Exceptional Children, 33*(1), 46–51.

Laud, L. E. (1998). Changing the way we communicate. *Educational Leadership, 61*(4), 23–28.

Lawren, B. (1989, September). Seating for success. *Psychology Today, (16),* 18–19.

Lawrence, G. (1993). *People types and tiger stripes: A practical guide to learning styles* (3rd ed.). Gainesville, FL: Center for Applications of Psychological Type.

Lawrence, G., & DeNovellis, R. (1974). *Correlation of teacher personality variables (Myers-Briggs) and classroom observation data.* Paper presented at American Educational Research Association conference.

Lessen, E., & Frankiewicz, L. E. (1992). Personal attributes and characteristics of effective special education teachers: Considerations for teacher educators. *Teacher Education and Special Education, 15*(2), 124–132.

Levine, A. (2006). *Educating school teachers.* The Education School Project. September, 2006, from www.edschools.org

Lieberman, L. (1984). *Preventing special education . . . for those who don't need it.* Newtonville, MA: GloWorm.

Lilly, M. S., & Givens-Ogle, L. B. (1981). Teacher consultation: Present, past, and future. *Behavioral Disorders, 6*(2), 73–77.

Linan-Thompson, S., & Jean, R. (1997). Completing the parent participation puzzle: Accepting diversity. *Teaching Exceptional Children, 30*(2), 46–50.

Lindle, J. C. (1989). What do parents want from principals and educators? *Educational Leadership, 47*(2), 12–14.

Lippitt, G. L. (1983, March). Can conflict resolution be win-win? *The School Administrator,* 20–22.

Lipsky, D. K. (1994). National survey gives insight into inclusive movement. *Inclusive Education Programs, LRP Publications, 1,* 3, 4–7.

Lopez, E. C., Dalal, S. M., & Yoshida, R. K. (1993). An examination of professional cultures: Implications for the collaborative consultation model. *Journal of Educational and Psychological Consultation, 4*(3), 197–213.

Loucks-Horsley, S., Harding, C. K., Arbuckle, M. A., Murray, L. B., Dubea, C., & Williams, M. K. (1987). *Continuing to learn: A guidebook for teacher development.* Andover, MA: Regional Laboratory for Educational Improvement of the Northeast and Islands.

Lovett, H. (1996). *Learning to listen: Positive approaches and people with difficult behavior.* Baltimore: Paul H. Brookes.

Lovitt, T. C. (1995). *Tactics for teaching* (2nd ed.). Englewood Cliffs, NJ: Merrill Prentice Hall.

Lubetkin, B. (1997, January). Master the art of apologizing. *The Manager's Intelligence Report.*

Lugg, C. A., & Boyd, W. L. (1993). Leadership for collaboration: Reducing risk and fostering resilience. *Phi Delta Kappan, 75*(3), 253–256, 258.

Lynch, E. W., & Hanson, M. J. (1998). *Developing cross-cultural competence: A guide for working with children and their families* (2nd ed.). Baltimore: Paul H. Brookes.

MacKenzie, R. A. (1975). *The time trap.* New York: McGraw-Hill.

Maeroff, G. I. (1993). Building teams to rebuild schools. *Phi Delta Kappan, 74*(7), 512–519.

Mager, R. F. (1997). *Preparing instructional objectives* (3rd ed.). Atlanta: The Center for Effective Performance.

Maldonado, J. A. (1994). Bilingual special education: specific learning disabilities in language and reading. *Journal of Educational Issues of Language Minority Students, 4,* 127–148.

Mann, L. (2000). Finding time to collaborate. *Education Update, 42*(2), 1, 3, 8.

Margolis, H. (1986). Resolving differences with angry people. *Urban Review, 18*(2), 125–136.

Margolis, H., & Free, J. (2001). Computerized IEP programs: Guide for educational consultants. *Journal of Educational and Psychological Consultation, 12*(2), 171–178.

Margolis, H., & McGettigan, J. (1988). Managing resistance to instructional modifications in mainstream settings. *Remedial and Special Education, 9,* 15–21.

Marks, S. U., Schrader, C., & Levine, M. (1999). Paraeducator experiences in inclusive settings: Helping, hovering, or holding their own? *Exceptional Children, 65,* 315–328.

Marsal, L. S. (1997). Mentoring & CEC guidelines for developing a mentorship program for beginning special education teachers. *Teaching Exceptional Children, 29*(6), 18–21.

Martin, R. (1991). *Extraordinary children—ordinary lives.* Champaign, IL: Research Press.

Maslach, C. (1982). *Burnout: The cost of caring.* Englewood Cliffs, NJ: Prentice Hall.

Mastropieri, M. A., Scruggs, T. E., & Berkeley, S. L. (2007). Peers helping peers. *Educational Leadership, 64*(5), 54–58.

Mayer, E., Ferede, M. K., & Hou, E. D. (2006). The family involvement storybook: A new way to build connections with families. *Young Children, 61*(6), 94–97.

McCaffrey, M. E. (2000). My first year of learning: Advice from a new educator. *Teaching Exceptional Children, 33*(1), 4–8.

McCardle, P., Mele-McCarthy, J., & Leos, K. (2005). English language learners and learning disabilities: Research agenda and implications for practice. *Learning Disability Research and Practice, 20*(1), 68–78.

McCarthy, B. (1990). Using the 4MAT system to bring learning styles to schools. *Educational Leadership, 48*(2), 31–37.

McDonald, J. P. (1989). When outsiders try to change schools from the inside. *Phi Delta Kappan, 71*(3), 206–212.

McDonnell, L. M., McLaughlin, M. J., & Morrison, P. (1997). *Educating one and all: Students with disabilities and standards-based reform.* Washington, DC: National Academy Press.

McGrew-Zoubi, R. R. (1998). I can take care of it myself. *The Delta Kappa Gamma Bulletin, 65*(1), 15–20.

McKenzie, H. S., Egner, A. N., Knight, M. F., Perelman, P. F., Schneider, B. M., & Garvin, J. S. (1970). Training consulting teachers to assist elementary teachers in the management and education of handicapped children. *Exceptional Children, 37,* 137–143.

McLeskey, J., Henry, D., & Hodges, D. (1998). Inclusion: Where is it happening? *Teaching Exceptional Children, 31*(1), 4–10.

McMahon, T. J., Ward, N. L., Pruett, M. K., Davidson, L., & Griffith, E. E. H. (2000). Building full-service schools: Lessons learned in the development of interagency collaboratives. *Journal of Educational and Psychological Consultation, 11*(1), 65–92.

McNulty, R. (2003). Making leadership everyone's responsibility. *Education Update, 45*(7), 2.

Medway, F. J., & Forman, S. G. (1980). Psychologists' and teachers' reactions to mental health and behavioral school consultation. *Journal of School Psychology, 18,* 338–348.

Menlove, R. R., Hudson, P. J., & Suter, D. (2001). A field of IEP dreams: Increasing general education teacher participation in the IEP development process. *Teaching Exceptional Children, 35*(5), 28–33.

Mercer, C. D., & Mercer, A. R. (1993). *Teaching students with learning problems* (4th ed.). Columbus, OH: Merrill.

Mertens, D. M. (2005). *Research and evaluation in education and psychology: Integrating diversity with quantitative, qualitative, and mixed methods* (2nd ed.). Thousand Oaks, CA: Sage.

Meyers, J., Meyers, A. B., & Grogg, K. (2004). Prevention through consultation: A model to guide future developments in the field of school psychology. *Journal of Educational and Psychological Consultation, 15*(3 & 4), 257–276.

Michaels, K. (1988). Caution: Second-wave reform taking place. *Educational Leadership, 45*(5), 3.

Millinger, C. S. (2004). Helping new teachers cope. *Educational Leadership, 61*(8), 66–69.

Miller, T. N., Devin, M., & Shoop, R. J. (2007). *Closing the leadership gap: How district and university partnerships shape effective school leaders.* Thousand Oaks, CA: Corwin.

Monroe, L. (1997). *Nothing's impossible: Leadership lessons from inside and outside the classroom.* New York: Times Books.

Morocco, C. C., & Aguilar, C. M. (2002). Co-teaching for content understanding: A schoolwide model. *Journal for Educational and Psychological Consultation, 13*(4), 315–347.

Morris, A. (1999). *Teamwork.* New York: Lothrop, Lee, & Shepard.

Morsink, C. V., Thomas, C. C., & Correa, V. I. (1991). *Interactive teaming: Consultation and collaboration in special programs.* Columbus, OH: Merrill.

Mueller, P. H., & Murphy, F. V. (2001). Determining when a student requires para-educator support. *Teaching Exceptional Children, 33*(6), 22–27.

Munson, S. M. (1987). Regular education teacher modifications for mainstreamed mildly handicapped students. *Journal of Special Education, 20*(4), 489–502.

Murphy, C. (1995). Whole-faculty study groups: Doing the seemingly undoable. *Journal of Staff Development, 16*(3), 37–44.

Murphy, E. (1987). *I am a good teacher.* Gainesville, FL: Center for Applications of Psychological Type.

Murphy, K. D. (1987). *Effective listening: Hearing what people say and making it work for you.* New York: Bantam Books.

Murray, J. L. (1994). *Training for student leaders.* Dubuque, IA: Kendall/Hunt.

Myers, I. B. (1962). *The Myers-Briggs Type Indicator manual.* Palo Alto, CA: Consulting Psychologists Press.

Myers, I. B. (1974). *Type and teamwork.* Gainesville, FL: Center for Applications of Psychological Type,

Myers, I. B. (1980a). *Gifts differing.* Palo Alto, CA: Consulting Psychologists Press.

Myers, I. B. (1980b). *Introduction to type.* Palo Alto, CA: Consulting Psychologists Press.

National Dissemination Center for Children with Disabilities (NICHCY). (2001). Washington, DC: Research Center.

Nazzaro, J. N. (1977). *Exceptional timetables: Historic events affecting the handicapped and gifted.* Reston, VA: Council for Exceptional Children.

Neel, R. S. (1981). How to put the consultant to work in consulting teaching. *Behavioral Disorders, 6*(2), 78–81.

Nelson, G., Amio, J. L., Prilleltsky, T., & Nickels, P. (2000). Partnerships for school and community prevention programs. *Journal of Educational and Psychological Consultation, 11*(1), 121–145.

Nevin, A., Thousand, J., Paolucci-Whitcomb, P., & Villa, R. (1990). Collaborative consultation: Empowering public school personnel to provide heterogeneous schooling for all—or, who rang that bell? *Journal of Educational and Psychological Consultation, 1*(1), 41–67.

Newmann, F. M. (1991). Linking restructuring to authentic student achievement. *Phi Delta Kappan, 72,* 458–464.

Noble, L. S. (1997). The face of foster care. *Educational Leadership, 54*(7), 26–28.

Noddings, N. (1992). *The challenge to care in schools: An alternative approach to education.* New York: Teachers College Press.

Oja, S. N. (1980). Adult development is implicit in staff development. *Journal of Staff Development, 1*(1), 9–15.

Olson, D. L. (2003). Principles, impracticality, and passion. *Phi Delta Kappan, 85*(4), 307–309.

O'Neil, J. (1994–1995). Can inclusion work: A conversation with Jim Kauffman and Mara Sapon-Shevin. *Educational Leadership, 52*(4), 7–11.

Osborn, A. F. (1963). *Applied imagination: Principles and procedures of creative problem-solving.* New York: Scribner.

Page, S. E. (2007). *The difference: How the power of diversity creates better groups, firms, schools, and societies.* Princeton, NJ: Princeton University Press.

Parette, H. P., & Petch-Hogan, B. (2000). Approaching families: Facilitating culturally, linguistically diverse family involvement. *Teaching Exceptional Children, 33*(2), 4–12.

Patton, M. Q. (1997). *Utilization-focused evaluation: The new century text* (3rd ed.). Thousand Oaks, CA: Sage.

Pearce, M. (1996, September). Inclusion: Twelve secrets to making it work in your classroom. *Instructor,* 81–84.

PEATC. (1991). *Partnership series.* Alexandria, VA: Parent Educational Advocacy Training Center.

Peck, K. L., & Dorricott, D. (1994). Why use technology? *Educational Leadership, 51*(7), 11–14.

Perkins-Gough, D., Snyder, D., & Licciardi, B. (2004). The communication age: The 1990s and ASCD. *Educational Leadership,* 94.

Phillips, V., & McCullough, L. (1990). Consultation-based programming: Instituting the collaborative ethic in schools. *Exceptional Children, 56,* 291–304.

Phillips, W. L., Allred, K., Brulle, A. R., & Shank, K. S. (1990). The regular education initiative: The will and skill of regular educators. *Teacher Education and Special Education, 13*(3–4), 182–186.

Pianta, R. C., & Kraft-Sayre, M. (2003). *Successful kindergarten transition: Your guide to connecting children, families, and schools.* Baltimore, MD: Paul H. Brookes.

Pickett, A. L., & Gerlach, K. (2003). *Supervising paraeducators in schools settings: A team approach.* Austin, TX: PRO-ED.

Pisha, B., & Coyne, P. (2001). Smart from the start: The promise of universal design for learning. *Remedial and Special Education, 22*(4), 197–203.

Plucker, J. A., & Yecke, C. P. (1999). The effect of relocation on gifted students. *Gifted Child Quarterly, 43*(2), 95–106.

Plunkett, V. R. L. (1997). Parents and schools: Partnerships that count. *Journal of Education for Students Placed at Risk, 2,* 325–327.

Pollio, H. (1987, Fall). Practical poetry: Metaphoric thinking in science, art, literature, and nearly everywhere else. *Teaching-Learning Issues,* 3–17.

Polsgrove, L., & McNeil, M. (1989). The consultation process: Research and practice. *Remedial and Special Education, 10*(1), 6–13, 20.

Posavac, E. J., & Carey, R. G. (2006). *Program evaluation: Methods and case studies* (7th ed.). Englewood Cliffs, NJ: Prentice Hall.

Putnam, J. (1993). Make every minute count. *Instructor, 103*(1), 39–40.

Pryzwansky, W. B. (1974). A reconsideration of the consultation model for delivery of school-based psychological services. *American Journal of Orthopsychiatry, 44,* 579–583.

Pryzwansky, W. B. (1986). Indirect service delivery: Considerations for future research in consultation. *School Psychology Review, 15*(4), 479–488.

Pugach, M. C., & Johnson, L. J. (1989). The challenge of implementing collaboration between general and special education. *Exceptional Children, 56*(3), 232–235.

Pugach, M. C., & Johnson, L. J. (1990). Fostering the continued democratization of consultation through action research. *Teacher Education and Special Education, 13*(3–4), 240–245.

Pugach, M. C., & Johnson, L. J. (1995). *Collaborative practitioners, collaborative schools.* Denver, CO: Love.

Pugach, M. C., & Johnson, L. J. (2002). *Collaborative practitioners, collaborative schools* (2nd ed.). Denver, CO: Love.

Purcell, J. H., & Leppien, J. H. (1998). Building bridges between general practitioners and educators of the gifted: A study of collaboration. *Gifted Child Quarterly, 42*(3), 172–181.

Raschke, D., Dedrick, C., & DeVries, A. (1988). Coping with stress: The special educator's perspective. *Teaching Exceptional Children, 21*(1), 10–14.

Ray, V., & Gregory, R. (2001, Winter). School experiences of the children of lesbian and gay parents. *Family Matters,* 28–32.

Raymond, G. I., McIntosh, D. K., & Moore, Y. R. (1986). *Teacher consultation skills* (Report No. EC 182-912). Washington, DC: U.S. Department of Education. (ERIC Document Reproduction Service No. ED 170-915).

Raywid, M. A. (1993). Finding time for collaboration. *Educational Leadership, 51*(1), 30–34.

Reason, C., & Reason, L. (2007). Asking the right questions. *Educational Leadership, 65*(1), 36–40.

Reinhiller, N. (1996). Co-teaching: New variations on a not-so-new practice. *Teacher Education and Special Education, 19*(1), 34–48.

Reis, S. M., Burns, D. E., & Renzulli, J. S. (1992). *Facilitator's guide to help teachers compact curriculum.* Mansfield Center, CT: Creative Learning Press.

Renzulli, J. S., & Reis, S. M. (1985). *The schoolwide enrichment model: A comprehensive plan for educational excellence.* Mansfield Center, CT: Creative Learning Press.

Reynolds, M. C., & Birch, J. W. (1988). *Adaptive mainstreaming: A primer for teachers and principals.* White Plains, NY: Longman.

Riegel, R. H. (1981). *Making modifications in the mainstream: A consultant's guide to cooperative planning.* Unpublished manuscript. Plymouth, MI: Model Resource Room Project.

Riehl, C. J. (2000). The principal's role in creating inclusive schools for diverse students: A review of normative, empirical, and critical literature on the practice of educational administration. *Review of Educational Research, 70*(1), 55–81.

Riggs, C. G. (2001). Ask the paraprofessionals: What are your training needs? *Teaching Exceptional Children, 33*(3), 78–83.

Rinke, W. J. (1997). *Winning Management: 6 fail-safe strategies for building high-performance organizations.* Clarksville, MD: Achievement.

Robinson, A. (1990). Cooperation of exploitation? The argument against cooperative learning for talented students. *Journal for the Education of the Gifted, 14*(1), 9–27.

Rodriguez-Campos, L. (2005). *Collaborative evaluations: A step-by-step model for the evaluator.* Tamarac, FL: Lumina Press.

Rogers, J. (1993). The inclusion revolution. *The Research Bulletin, Phi Delta Kappa, 11,* 1–6.

Rosenfield, S. (1995). The practice of instructional consultation. *Journal of Educational and Psychological Consultation, 6*(4), 317–327.

Ross, R. G. (1986). *Communication consulting as persuasion: Issues and implications.* (Report No. CS506-027). Washington, DC: U.S. Department of Education. ERIC Document Reproduction Service No. ED 291-115.

Rossi, P. H., Lipsey, M. W., & Freeman, H. E. (2004). *Evaluation: A systematic approach* (7th ed.). Beverly Hills, CA: Sage.

Rothenberg, A., & Hausman, C. R. (1976). *The creativity question.* Durham, NC: Duke University Press.

Rotter, K. (2006). Creating instructional materials for all pupils: Try COLA. *Intervention in School and Clinic, 41*(5), 273–282.

Roy, P. A., & O'Brien, P. (1991). Together we can make it better in collaborative schools. *Journal of Staff Development, 12*(3), 47–51.

Rule, S., Fodor-Davis, J., Morgan, R., Salzberg, C. L., & Chen, J. (1990). An inservice training model to encourage collaborative consultation. *Teacher Education and Special Education, 13*(3–4), 225–227.

Russell, N. M. (2007). Teaching more than English: Connecting ESL students to their community through service. *Phi Delta Kappan, 88*(10), 770–771.

Ryan, A. L., Halsey, H. N., & Matthews, W. J. (2003). Using functional assessment to promote desirable student behavior in schools. *Teaching Exceptional Children, 35*(5), 8–15.

Safran, S. P. (1991). The communication process and school-based consultation: What does the research say? *Journal of Educational and Psychological Consultation, 1*(4), 343–370.

Salend, S. J. (1994). *Effective mainstreaming: Creating inclusive classrooms* (2nd ed.). New York: Macmillan.

Salend, S. J., & Duhaney, L. M. G. (1999). The impact of inclusion on students with and without disabilities and their educators. *Remedial and Special Education, 20*(2), 114–126.

Salend, S. J., & Salend, S. (1984). Consulting with the regular teacher: Guidelines for special educators. *The Pointer, 25,* 25–28.

Salisbury, C. L., & Vincent, L. J. (1990). Criterion of the next environment and best practices: Mainstreaming and integration 10 years later. *Topics in Early Childhood Education, 10*(2), 78–89.

Salisbury, G., & Evans, I. M. (1988). Comparison of parental involvement in regular and special education. *Journal of the Association for Persons with Severe Handicaps, 13,* 268–272.

Salzberg, C. L., & Morgan, J. (1995). Preparing teachers to work with paraeducators. *Teacher Education and Special Education, 18*(1), 49–55.

Sandoval, J. (1996). Constructivism, consultee-centered consultation, and conceptual change. *Journal of Educational and Psychological Consultation, 7*(1), 89–97.

Sandoval, J. (2003). Constructing conceptual change in consultee-centered consultation. *Journal of Educational and Psychological Consultation, 14*(3 & 4), 251–261.

Sapolsky, R. (1994). *Why zebras don't get ulcers: A guide to stress, stress-related diseases, and coping.* New York: W. H. Freeman.

Schein, E. H. (1969). *Process consultation: Its role in organization development.* Reading, MA: Addison-Wesley.

Schein, E. H. (1978, February). The role of the consultant: Context expert or process facilitator? *Personnel and Guidance Journal, 56*(6), 339–343.

Schindler, C., & Lapid, G. (1989). *The great turning: Personal peace, global victory.* Santa Fe, NM: Bear and Co.

Schlax, K. (1994). Eight tops for effective integration of therapists. *Inclusive Education Programs, 1*(2), 11.

Schuck, J. (1979). The parent-professional partnership: Myth or reality? *Education Unlimited, 1*(4) 26–28.

Schulte, A. C., Osborne, S. S., & Kauffman, J. M. (1993). Teacher responses to two types of consultative special education services. *Journal of Educational and Psychological Consultation, 4*(1), 1–27.

Schultz, E. W. (1980, Fall). Teaching coping skills for stress and anxiety. *Teaching Exceptional Children,* 12–15.

SEDL. (2000a). Rural student entrepreneurs: Linking commerce and community. *Benefits,* 5.

SEDL. (2000b). Collaborative strategies for revitalizing rural schools and communities. *Benefits, 5.*

Shanteau, J. (1997, October). *ISBR Newsletter,* 7. Kansas State University; Institute for Social and Behavioral Research.

Shaver, D., Golan, S., & Wagner, M. (1996) Connecting schools and communities through interagency collaboration for school-linked services. In J. G. Cibulka & W. J. Kritek (Eds.), *Coordination among schools, families, and communities: Prospects for educational reform* (pp. 349–378). Albany: State University of New York Press.

Sheridan, S. M. (1992). What do we mean when we say "collaboration"? *Journal of Educational and Psychological Consultation, 3*(1), 89–92.

Sheridan, S. M., Kratochwill, T. R., & Bergan, J. R. (1996). *Conjoint behavioral consultation: A procedural manual.* New York: Plenum.

Short, R. J., & Talley, R. C. (1999). Services integration: An introduction. *Journal of Educational and Psychological Consultation, 10*(3), 193–200.

Shroyer, G., Yahnke, S., Bennett, A., & Dunn, C., (2007). Simultaneous renewal through professional development school partnerships. *Journal of Educational Research, 100*(4), 211–224.

Sigband, N. B. (1987, February). The uses of meetings. *Nation's Business,* 28R.

Simpson, E. J. (1972). *The psychomotor domain, vol. 3.* Washington, DC: Gryphon House.

Skinner, H. (2007, November 13). Finding her true calling. *Topeka Capital Journal,* 1c.

Slavin, R. (1988). *The School Administrator, 45,* 9–13.

Slesser, R. A., Fine, M. J., & Tracy, D. B. (1990). Teacher reactions to two approaches to school-based psychological consultation. *Journal of Educational and Psychological Consultation, 1*(3), 243–258.

Smith, J. D. (1998). *Inclusion: Schools for all students.* Belmont, CA: Wadsworth.

Smith-Westberry, J., & Job, R. L. (1986). How to be a prophet in your own land: Providing gifted program inservice for the local district. *Gifted Child Quarterly, 30*(3), 135–137.

Sondel, B. (1958). *The humanity of words.* Cleveland, OH: World Publishing.

Soodak, L. C., & Erwin, E. J. (1995). Parents, professionals, and inclusive education: A call for collaboration. *Journal of Educational and Psychological Consultation, 6*(3), 257–276.

Soo-Hoo, T. (1998). Applying frame of reference and reframing techniques to improve school consultation in multicultural settings. *Journal of Educational and Psychological Consultation, 9*(4), 325–345.

St. John, E. P., Griffith, A. I., & Allen-Hayes, L. (1997). *Families in schools: A chorus of voices in restructuring.* Portsmouth, NH: Heinemann.

Stainback, S., & Stainback, W. (1985). The merger of special and regular education: Can it be done? A response to Lieberman and Mesinger. *Exceptional Children, 51*(6), 517–521.

Stanley, A. L., & Vasa, S. F. (1998). How paraeducators learn on the Web. *Teaching Exceptional Children, 30*(5), 54–59.

Starko, A. (2001). *Creativity in the classroom: School of curious delight* (2nd ed.). Mahwah, NJ: Erlbaum.

Stewart, R. A., & Brendefur, J. L. (2005). Fusing lesson study and authentic achievement: A model for teacher collaboration. *Phi Delta Kappan, 86*(9), 681–687.

Stone, D., Patton, B., & Heen, S. (1999). *Difficult conversations: How to discuss what matters most.* New York: Random House.

Strawbridge, M. (2006). *Netiquette: Internet etiquette in the age of the blog.* London: Software Reference Ltd.

Suárez-Orozco, M. M., & Sattin, C. (2007). Wanted: Global citizens. *Educational Leadership, 64*(7), 58–62.

Sue, D. W., & Sue, D. (1990). *Counseling the culturally different: Theory and practice* (2nd ed.). New York: Wiley.

Sundbye, N., & McCoy, L. (1997). *Helping the struggling reader: What to teach and how to teach it.* Lawrence, KS: Curriculum Solutions.

Talley, R. C., & Schrag, J. A. (1999). Legal and public foundations supporting service integration for students with disabilities. *Journal of Educational and Psychological Consultation, 10*(3), 229–249.

Tannen, D. (1991). *Gender and discourse.* New York: Oxford University Press.

Tannen, D. (1994). *You just don't understand: Women and men in conversation.* New York: William Morrow.

Taylor, N., & Adelman, H. S. (1998). Confidentiality: Competing principles, inevitable dilemmas. *Journal of Educational and Psychological Consultation, 9,* 267–275.

Tharp, R. (1975). The triadic model of consultation. In C. Parker (Ed.), *Psychological consultation in the schools: Helping teachers meet special needs.* Reston, VA: Council for Exceptional Children.

Tharp, R. G., & Wetzel, R. J. (1969). *Behavior modification in the natural environment.* New York: Academic Press.

Thomas, C. C., Correa, V. I., & Morsink, C. V. (2001). *Interactive teaming: Enhancing programs for students with special needs* (3rd ed.). Upper Saddle River, NJ: Prentice Hall.

Thurston, L. P. (2000). *The positive para: Helping students develop positive social skills.* Lawrence, KS: Curriculum Solutions.

Thurston, L. P., & Dover, W. (1990, October). *Rural at-risk students.* Paper presented at the twelfth annual Rural and Small Schools Conference, Manhattan, KS.

Thurston, L. P., & Kimsey, I. (1989). Rural special education teachers as consultants: Roles and responsibilities. *Educational Considerations, 17*(1), 40–43.

Thurston, L. P., & Navarrete, L. (1996). A tough row to hoe: Research on education and rural poor families. In *Proceedings of American Council on Rural Special Education (ACRES),* Baltimore.

Tiegerman-Farber, E., & Radziewicz, C. (1998). *Collaborative decision making: The pathway to inclusion.* Upper Saddle River, NJ: Prentice Hall.

Timar, T. (1989). The politics of school restructuring. *Phi Delta Kappan, 71*(4), 265–275.

Todnem, G., & Warner, M. P. (1994, September). Demonstrating the benefits of staff development: An interview with Thomas R. Guskey. *Kansas Direct Connection.* Hays: Kansas Staff Development Council.

Tomlinson, C. (1999). *The differentiated classroom: Responding to the needs of all learners.* Alexandria, VA: Association for Supervision and Curriculum Development.

Tomlinson, C. A., Coleman, M. R., Allan, S., Udall, A., & Landrum, M. (1996). Interface between gifted education and general education: Toward communication, cooperation and collaboration. *Gifted Child Quarterly, 40*(3), 165–170.

Torrance, E. P., & Safter, H. T. (1999). *Making the creative leap beyond.* Buffalo, NY: Creative Education Foundation Press.

Tovar, N. H. (1998). Addressing the needs of school-age military dependents. *Delta Delta Kappa Gamma Bulletin, 64*(4), 23–28.

Turnbull, A. P., & Turnbull, H. R. (1996). *Families, professionals, and exceptionality* (3rd ed.). Upper Saddle River, NJ: Merrill Prentice Hall.

Turnbull, A. P., & Turnbull, H. R., III. (1997). *Families, professionals, and exceptionality: A special partnership* (4th ed.). Upper Saddle River, NJ: Merrill.

Turnbull, A., Turnbull, R., Erwin, E. J., & Soodak, L. C. (2006). *Families, professionals and exceptionality: Positive outcomes through partnership and trust* (5th ed.). Upper Saddle River, NJ: Pearson.

Ury, W. (1991). *Getting past no: Negotiating with difficult people.* New York: Bantam Books.

Van Voorhis, F. L. (2003). Interactive homework in middle school: Effects on family involvement and science achievement. *Journal of Educational Research, 96,* 323–338.

VanTassel-Baska, J. (1989). Appropriate curriculum for gifted learners. *Educational Leadership, 46*(6), 13–15.

VanTassel-Baska, J. (1998). *Excellence in educating gifted and talented learners* (3rd ed.). Denver, CO: Love.

VanTassel-Baska, J., & Brown, E. F. (2007). Toward best practice: An analysis of the efficacy of curriculum models in gifted education. *Gifted Child Quarterly, 51*(4), 342–358.

Vaughn, S., Schumm, J. S., & Arguelles, M. E. (1997). The ABCDEs of co-teaching. *Teaching Exceptional Children, 30*(2), 42–45.

Voltz, D. L., Elliott, Jr., R. N., & Cobb, H. B. (1994). Collaborative teacher roles: Special and general educators. *Journal of Learning Disabilities, 27*(8), 527–535.

Vygotsky, L. S. (1978). *Mind in society: The development of higher mental processes.* Cambridge, MA: Harvard University Press.

Wallace, T., Shin, J., Bartholomay, T., & Stahl, B. J. (2001). Knowledge and skills for teachers supervising the work of paraprofessionals. *Exceptional Children, 67*(4), 520–533.

Wallings, D. R. (1990). *Meeting the needs of transient students,* Fastback #304. Bloomington, IN: Phi Delta Kappa Educational Foundation.

Walsh, J. M. (2001). Getting the "big picture" of IEP goals and state standards. *Teaching Exceptional Children, 33*(5), 18–26.

Wanat, C. L. (1997). Conceptualizing parental involvement from parents' perspectives: A case study. *Journal for a Just and Caring Education, 3*(4), 433–458.

Ward, S. B., & Landrum, M. S. (1994). Resource consultation: An alternative service delivery model for gifted education. *Roeper Review, 16,* 275–279.

Webster's new collegiate dictionary (8th ed.). (1996). Springfield, MA: Merriam-Webster.

Webster's third new international dictionary, unabridged: The great library of the English language. (1976). Springfield, MA: Merriam-Webster.

Weiss, H., Caspe, M., & Lopez, M. E. (2006). *Family involvement in early childhood education.* Cambridge, MA: Harvard Family Research Project. Available online at www.gse.harvard.edu/hfrp.html

Welch, M. (1998). The IDEA of collaboration in special education: An introspective examination of paradigms and promise. *Journal of Educational and Psychological Consultation, 9*(2), 119–142.

Welch, M., & Sheridan, S. M. (1995). *Educational partnerships: Serving students at risk.* Fort Worth, TX: Harcourt Brace.

Welch, M., Sheridan, S. M., Fuhriman, A., Hart, A. W., Connell, M. L., & Stoddart, T. (1992). Preparing professionals for educational partnerships: An interdisciplinary approach. *Journal of Educational and Psychological Consultation, 3*(1), 1–23.

Wesley, P. W., & Buysse, V. (2006). Ethics and evidence in consultation. *Topics in Early Childhood Special Education, 26*(3), 131–142.

Wesley, W. G., & Wesley, B. A. (1990). Concept-mapping: A brief introduction. *Teaching Professor, 4*(8), 3–4.

West, J. F. (1990). Educational collaboration in the restructuring of schools. *Journal of Educational and Psychological Consultation, 1,* 23–41.

West, J. F., & Brown, P. A. (1987). State departments of education policies on consultation in special education: The state of the states. *Remedial and Special Education, 8*(3), 45–51.

West, J. F., & Idol, L. (1987). School consultation (Part I): An interdisciplinary perspective on theory, models, and research. *Journal of Learning Disabilities, 20*(7), 385–408.

West, J. F., Idol, L., & Cannon, G. (1988). *Collaboration in the schools: Communicating, interacting, and problem solving.* Austin, TX: PRO-ED.

Whitaker, S. D. (2000a). Mentoring beginning special education teachers and the relationship to attrition. *Exceptional Children, 66*(4), 546–566.

Whitaker, S. D. (2000b). What do first-year special education teachers need? Implications for induction programs. *Teaching Exceptional Children, 33*(1), 28–36.

White, G. W. (2000). Nonverbal communications: Key to improved teacher effectiveness. *Delta Kappa Gamma Bulletin, 66*(4), 12–16.

Wholey, J. S., Hatry, H. P., & Newcomer, K. E. (2004). *Handbook of practical program evaluation* (2nd ed.). San Francisco: Jossey-Bass.

Wildman, T. M., & Niles, J. A. (1987). Essentials of professional growth. *Educational Leadership, 44*(5), 4–10.

Wilkinson, L. A. (2005a). Bridging the research-to-practice gap in school-based consultation: An example using case studies. *Journal of Educational and Psychological Consultation, 16*(3), 175–200.

Wilkinson, L. A. (2005b). Supporting the inclusion of a student with Asperger syndrome: A case study using conjoint behavioral consultation and self-management. *Educational Psychology in Practice, 21,* 307–326.

Will, M. (1984). Let us pause and reflect—but not too long. *Exceptional Children, 51,* 11–16.

Will, M. (1986). Educating children with learning problems: A shared responsibility. *Exceptional Children, 52*(5), 411–415.

Williams, J. M., & Martin, S. M. (2001). Implementing the Individuals with Disabilities Education Act of 1997: The consultant's role. *Journal of Educational and Psychological Consultation, 12*(1), 59–81.

Winn, J. A., & Messenheimer-Young, T. (1995). Team teaching at the university level: What we have learned. *Teacher Education and Special Education, 18*(4), 223–229.

Witt, J. C., & Elliott, S. N. (1985). Acceptability of classroom intervention strategies. In T. R. Kratochwill (Ed.), *Advances in School Psychology* (Vol. 4, pp. 251–288). Hillsdale, NJ: Erlbaum.

Wong, H. K., Britton, T., & Ganser, T. (2005). What the world can teach us about new teacher induction. *Phi Delta Kappan, 86*(5), 379–384.

Wood, M. (1998). Whose job is it anyway? Educational roles in inclusion. *Exceptional Children, 64*(2), 181–195.

Woolfolk, A. (2001). *Educational psychology* (8th ed.). Boston: Allyn & Bacon.

Woolfolk, A. (2007). *Educational psychology.* Englewood Cliffs, NJ: Prentice Hall.

Working Forum on Inclusive Schools (1994). *Creating schools for all our students: What 12 schools have to say.* Reston, VA: Council for Exceptional Children.

World Book Dictionary Volumes 1 and 2. (2003). Chicago: World Book, Inc.

Wright, J. W. (Ed.). (2002). Growth of the Web. In *The New York Times Almanac.* New York: Penguin.

Yankelovich, D. (2001). *The magic of dialogue: Transforming conflict into cooperation.* New York: Touchstone.

Yocum, D. J., & Cassairtr, A. (1996). Consultation courses offered in special education teacher training programs: A national survey. *Journal of Educational and Psychological Consultation, 7*(3), 251–258.

Zigmond, N. (1997). *What does co-teaching look like in elementary and secondary schools?* Washington, DC: Presentation at 19th International Conference on Learning Disabilities.

Zigmond, N., Levin, E., & Laurie, T. E. (1985). Managing the mainstream: An analysis of teacher attitudes and student performance in mainstream high school programs. *Journal of Learning Disabilities, 18*(9), 535–541.

Zimet, E. (1993, November). Grant-writing techniques for K–12 funding. *T.H.E.: Technological Horizons in Education,* 109–112.

ARC Sibling Support Project: www.siblingsupport.org
This site represents a national effort dedicated to the lifelong concerns of brothers and sisters of people who have special health, developmental, or mental health concerns.

Babel Fish: http://babelfish.altavista.com
Provides a quick and easy tool for translating text or web pages from one of several languages into another.

Center for Applied Technology (CAST): www.cast.org
Resources to help implement Universal Design for Learning (UDL) and make curriculum adaptations.

Center for the Prevention of School Violence: www.ncdjjdp.org
Provides information and programs for juvenile justice and delinquency prevention.

Children, Youth/Families Education and Research Network (CYFERNet): www.cyfernet.org
Facilitates networking, collaboration, and technical assistance among children, youth, and family programs and staff of the Cooperative Extension Service.

Computer-Mediated Communication: www.emailreplies.com/
Explains how to send effective e-mail replies.

Council for Exceptional Children: www.cec.sped.org/ps/perf-based-stds/knowledge_standards.html
Delineates standards for collaboration among special educators, other educators, related service providers, and community agency personnel.

Family Involvement in Early Childhood Education: www.gse.harvard.edu/hfrp/projects/fine/resources/research/earlychildhood.html
Helps philanthropists, policy makers, and practitioners develop strategies to promote educational and social success and the well-being of children, families, and their communities.

Family Involvement Storybook Corner: www.gse.harvard.edu/hfrp/projects/fine/resources/storybook/index.html
Promotes awareness and practice of family involvement through storybooks.

Keep Schools Safe: www.keepschoolssafe.org
Informative resources for schools, parents, and community members on keeping children safe in school.

National Association for Bilingual Education: www.nabe.org
Represents both English language and bilingual education professionals accounting for most of the languages spoken in the world.

National Association for the Education of Young Children: www.naeyc.org
Dedicated to improving the well-being of all young children, with particular focus on the quality of educational and developmental services for children from birth through age eight.

National Association for Multicultural Education: www.nameorg.org
Brings together individuals and groups with an interest in multicultural education from all grade levels, different academic disciplines, and diverse educational institutions and occupations.

National Dissemination Center for Children with Disabilities (NICHCY): www.nichcy.org
Serves the nation as a central source of information on disabilities in infants, toddlers, children, and youth, IDEA, No Child Left Behind, and research-based information on effective educational practices.

National Network of Partnership Schools and the Center on School, Family, and Community. Partnerships: www.csos.jhu.edu/P2000/center.htm
Committed to conducting and disseminating research, programs, and policy analyses that produce new and useful knowledge and practices that help parents, educators, and members of communities work together to improve schools, strengthen families, and enhance student learning and development.

National Resource Center for Paraeducators (NRCP): www.nrcpara.org
Provides information about conferences and upcoming events for paraeducators.

National Youth Violence Prevention Resource Center: www.safeyouth.org
Provides key leaders with dynamic resources to help support their efforts to plan, develop, implement, and evaluate effective youth violence prevention efforts.

NCATE/CEC Program standards, Programs for the Preparation of Special Education Teachers (2002): www.cec.sped.org/ps/perf_based_stds/knowledge_standards

No Child Left Behind Act of 2001 P. L. 107-110, 115 Stat. 1425 (2002): www.ed.gov/policy/elsec/leg/esea02/107-110.pdf

Northwest Regional Educational Laboratory: www.nwrel.org
Provides research-based products, technical assistance, and training to improve educational systems

and learning. Works directly with educators in the field to develop and test research-based publications and strategies that improve learners' results.

ParaEducator Learning Network: www.paraeducator.net
Helps paraeducators meet training requirements.

Parent Center funded by the U.S. Department of Education: www.taalliance.org
Discusses an innovative project that supports a unified technical assistance system for the purpose of developing, assisting, and coordinating parent training and information projects and Community Parents Resource Centers under the Individuals with Disabilities Education Act (IDEA).

Project PARA: Paraeducator Self-Study Program: http://para.unl.edu/ec
A study program for school districts that provides introductory training for their paraeducators.

Raising a Reader Program (based on the work of Judith K. Bernhard): www.ryerson.ca/~bernhard/ early.html

Represents an innovative, effective means of supporting young children's literacy.

Raising a Reader: www.pcf.org/raising_reader/research.html
Promotes engaging parents in a routine of daily "book cuddling" with their children from birth to age five to foster healthy brain development, parent-child bonding and early literacy skills critical for school success.

Response to Intervention: www.wrightslaw.com/info/rti.index.htm
Provides articles and other resources to use for new ways to identify specific learning disabilities in children.

Teaching Tolerance: www.teachingtolerance.org
A periodical available free to teachers by signing up on the Web site. A principal online destination for people interested in dismantling bigotry and creating, in hate's stead, communities that value diversity.